T0305407

Economic Modeling and Inference

Economic Modeling and Inference

Bent Jesper Christensen and
Nicholas M. Kiefer

PRINCETON UNIVERSITY PRESS

PRINCETON AND OXFORD

Published by Princeton University Press, 41 William Street,
Princeton, New Jersey 08540

In the United Kingdom: Princeton University Press,
6 Oxford Street, Woodstock, Oxfordshire 0X20 1TW

Library of Congress Cataloging-in-Publication Data
Christensen, Bent J. (Bent Jesper)
Economic modeling and inference / Bent Jesper Christensen and Nicholas M. Kiefer.
Kiefer, Nicholas M., 1951-
p. cm.
Includes bibliographical references and index.
ISBN 978-0-691-12059-1 (hardcover : alk. paper)
1. Econometric models. 2. Economics–Statistical methods. 3. Economics–Mathematical
models.
HB141 .C535 2009
330.01/5195 22

British Library Cataloging-in-Publication Data is available

This book has been composed in Times

Printed on acid-free paper. ∞

press.princeton.edu

Typeset by S R Nova Pvt Ltd, Bangalore, India

Printed in the United States of America

10 9 8 7 6 5 4 3 2 1

To Nabanita
                    BJC

To Meral
                    NMK

Contents

Preface

Economics as a discipline benefits from active and productive research in both econometrics and economic theory. We argue that these are not alternative fields of study but areas that contribute most productively when combined. Econometrics emphasizes reducing the dimension of large, unwieldy data sets while preserving information, perhaps through summarizing data in a model and a set of parameters. Economic theory provides the models, highlighting potentially important relationships among economic variables and deemphasizing others. Both enterprises provide tools with which to extract relevant information from observed economic activity. We try to convey this view in our teaching and research. There are excellent advanced textbooks on economic theory and on econometrics. The set of texts dealing with both theory and econometrics is much smaller and less satisfactory—hence this book.

The discussion is organized around the dynamic programming framework. Dynamic programming has proved to be an extremely productive approach to economic modeling. Following textbooks by Sargent (1987) and Stokey and Lucas (1989), generations of students are comfortable with dynamic programming. After early applications to macroeconomics and labor economics, dynamic programming applications now appear in almost all areas of economics. Our discussion emphasizes applications in financial economics and labor economics, reflecting our own interests, though a large number of other applications, both micro- and macroeconomic, are treated. We treat estimation and inference issues for general dynamic programming models. Although we develop the approach beginning with the simplest possible models, with discrete states and controls and finite horizons, the discussion moves swiftly and it would be difficult to argue that the treatment is elementary. A passing familiarity with dynamic programming would be useful preparation, and a deeper background in econometrics or statistics is essential.

We emphasize the theory and applications but do not provide a discussion of computational or numerical methods. This is not a judgment on the importance of these practical issues but a reluctant decision based on space and our own interests. There are excellent treatments available and the field is advancing rapidly.

We are grateful to participants in Ph.D. courses at Aarhus (University of Aarhus and GradInProWe), Gothenburg (Ekonometridagarne), Helsinki (University of Helsinki), and Ithaca (Cornell University) for useful comments, and to the Center for Analytic Economics (CAE), Centre for Analytical Finance (CAF), Centre for Research in Econometric Analysis in TimE Series (CREATES), National Science Foundation (NSF), Danish National Research Foundation, and Danish Social Science Research Council for research support. Our intellectual debt to our teachers, to our coauthors over the years, and to our colleagues and graduate students is enormous, and we thank all of them. The list of names is unmanageable. Our attempts to compile a short list without serious omissions have failed. Much of the material in chapter 7 is based on Christensen and Kiefer (1991), published in *Econometric Theory* (©1991 Cambridge University Press), that in chapter 9 on Christensen and Kiefer (1994), published in *Journal of Labor Economics* (©1994 University of Chicago), and that in chapter 19 on H. Bunzel, B.J. Christensen, P. Jensen, N. Kiefer, L. Korsholm, L. Muus, G. Neumann, and M. Rosholm (2001), published in the *Review of Economic Dynamics* (©2001 Elsevier). We are grateful to Cambridge University Press, the University of Chicago Press, and Elsevier for permission to use this material. The manuscript was substantially completed during the 2006–2007 academic year when Christensen was visiting the Department of Economics, Harvard University, and the department's generosity and hospitality are gratefully acknowledged. On the production end, we are grateful to Amy Moesch at Cornell University and Kirsten Stentoft at the University of Aarhus for secretarial support.

Chapter One

Introduction

Econometrics done as a productive enterprise deals with the interaction between economic theory and statistical analysis. Theory provides an organizing framework for looking at the world and in particular for assembling and interpreting economic data. Statistical methods provide the means of extracting interesting economic information from data. Without economic theory or statistics all that is left is an overwhelming flow of disorganized information. Thus, both theory and statistics provide methods of data reduction. The goal is to reduce the mass of disorganized information to a manageable size while retaining as much of the information relevant to the question being considered as possible. In economic theory, much of the reduction is done by reliance on models of optimizing agents. Another level of reduction can be achieved by considering equilibrium. Thus, many explanations of behavior can be ruled out and need not be analyzed explicitly if it can be shown that economic agents in the same setting can do better for themselves. In statistical analysis, the reduction is through sufficiency—if the mass of data can be decomposed so that only a portion of it is relevant, the inference problem can be reduced to analysis of only the relevant data.

Stochastic models are important in settings in which agents make choices under uncertainty or, from a completely different point of view, in models that do not try to capture all the features of agents' behavior. Stochastic models are also important for models involving measurement error or approximations. These models provide a strong link between theoretical modeling and estimation. Essentially, a stochastic model delivers a probability distribution for observables. This distribution can serve as a natural basis for inference. In static models, the assumption of optimization, in particular of expected utility maximization, has essentially become universal. Methods for studying expected utility maximization in dynamic models are more difficult, but conceptually identical, and modeling and inference methods for these models are developing rapidly.

1.1 EXPECTED UTILITY THEORY

Expected utility maximization is a widely accepted hypothesis and a widely applied tool in economic theory. A behavioral model in which the activities of an economic agent are analyzed in a setting of uncertainty would naturally be analyzed in an expected utility framework. There are two reasons for this widespread acceptance. First, the axiom systems that can be used to produce utility representations of preferences and subjective probability distributions over events are compelling. Second, pragmatically, without a universal principle to follow in constructing models, there are too many candidate ad hoc models to make for a productive research program. The optimization principle is the principle that has been widely accepted.

The key reference on expected utility theory is L.J. Savage (1954), and it is this set of axioms that we shall sketch. Pratt, Raiffa, and Schlaifer (1964) give a simple but rigorous development in the finite case. DeGroot (1970) provides an insightful textbook discussion. We stress again that our presentation is from Savage. Kiefer and Nyarko (1995) argue for the wide use of expected utility theory in dynamic economics, specifically in the study of the economics of information and learning.

A state s is a complete description of all items over which there is uncertainty. The world is the set of all states S. An event is a collection of states. The true state is the state that pertains. There is a set of consequences Q. An action f is a mapping from the set of states into the set of consequences, $f: S \rightarrow Q$. In particular, an action specifies the consequence in each state. Let A denote the set of all actions.

Agents have preferences $\preceq$ over actions. The strict preference $\prec$ is defined in the usual manner: $f \prec g$ if $f \preceq g$ but not $g \preceq f$. The axioms placed on the preferences are

P1. The preference order $\preceq$ is complete (for all f and $g \in A$, either $f \preceq g$ or $g \preceq f$) and transitive (for all $f, g, h \in A$, $f \preceq g$ and $g \preceq h$ implies $f \preceq h$). A complete transitive ordering is said to be a weak, or simple, order.

P2. $\preceq$ obeys the sure-thing principle; i.e., let f, f', g, and g' be acts and let B be a subset of S such that

(i) on B^c (the complement of B in S), $f = g$ and $f' = g'$;

(ii) on B, $f = f'$ and $g = g'$; and

(iii) $f \preceq g$.

   Then $f' \preceq g'$.

To interpret P2, suppose acts g and f agree outside of the set B and g is (weakly) preferred to f. Modify f and g outside of B, but ensure that they are still the same outside of B, and maintain their values on B. Then the modified g is (weakly) preferred to the modified f.

We say that action g is weakly preferred to action f given the event B if, when g and f are modified outside of B so that they are the same outside of B, then the modified g is weakly preferred to the modified f regardless of how the modification outside of B is done. Under the sure-thing principle the manner of modification outside of B is irrelevant. An event B is said to be a null event if for all acts f and g, $f \preceq g$ given B. As an example, suppose you are ranking two candidates for elective office. They agree on tax policy. Then your ranking does not depend on the tax policy on which they agree.

P3. Let f and g be constant actions (i.e., independent of s) and let B be an event that is not null. Then $f \preceq g$ given B if and only if $f \preceq g$.

P4. Let f, f', g, and g' be constant actions such that $f' \prec f$ and $g' \prec g$ (so that we may think of f and g as "good" constant actions and f' and g' as "bad" constant actions). Let B and C be any two events. Define the act f_B to be equal to f on B and f' outside of B and define g_B to be g on B and g' outside of B. Define f_C and g_C analogously, with C replacing B. Then $f_B \preceq f_C$ implies $g_B \preceq g_C$.

Assumption P4 breaks out probabilities from utilities by asserting essentially that the ranking of events according to their probabilities does not depend on the payoff for getting the ranking right. That is, the choice of which side one will take in a bet does not depend on the payoff. With our constant actions f and f' with $f' \prec f$, let $f_A = f$ on A and f' on A^c and let $f_B = f$ on B and f' on B^c. Then Savage defines A as not more probable than B iff $f_A \preceq f_B$.

P5. There exists a pair of consequences or constant actions f and f' such that $f' \prec f$.

Assumption P5 seems genuinely innocuous in any nontrivial application: It says that there are at least two actions that are strictly ranked.

P6. (Continuity Axiom) Let g and h be two actions with $g \prec h$ and let f be any consequence (or constant action). Then there exists a partition of S such that if g or h is modified to become g' or h' with the modification taking place on only one element of the partition and being equal to f there with the other values being unchanged, then $g' \prec h'$.

Assumption P6 essentially requires a continuous state space. Alternative assumptions deliver Theorem 1 for the discrete state space case (Pratt, Raiffa, and Schlaifer, 1964, and Gul, 1992).

P7.   Let f and g be any two actions and let B be an event. Let $g(s)$ denote
      the constant action equal to the consequence $g(s)$ regardless of the
      state. Then $f \preceq g(s)$ given B for all $s \in B$ implies $f \preceq g$ given B.

Assumption P7 allows the result to apply to actions having infinitely
many consequences (e.g., fairly general functions of a continuous state).
The result of Savage (1954) is

THEOREM 1 (*Savage*) *If $\preceq$ obeys axioms P1–P7, then there exists a (utility)
function $u : Q \to \mathbb{R}$ and a (prior) probability measure P over S such that
for all acts f and g,*

$$f \preceq g \text{ if and only if } \int u\left(f\left(s\right)\right) P\left(ds\right) \leq \int u\left(g\left(s\right)\right) P\left(ds\right).$$

The lesson of theorem 1 is that expected utility maximization need not
be a primitive assumption. The result that preference systems can be represented by expected utilities follows from axioms on preferences. These
axioms can be considered separately; each appears fairly weak, but taken
together they have very strong implications. Variations on the axioms suffice
(Fishburn, 1970). Note that there is nothing in the axiom system restricting
its applicability to the dynamic case (this assertion does require some
argument; Kreps and Porteus (1979) give details and proofs). The logic
compelling expected utility maximization modeling in static economic
models applies equally to dynamic models.

1.2 UNCERTAINTY AVERSION, ELLSBERG AND ALLAIS

The Savage axioms are individually compelling, and the implications are
strong and useful for economic modeling. Of course, the system is itself
a model of rational decision making, and therefore its axioms and hence
implications cannot be expected to hold for every individual or for every
situation. There are, however, serious objections that became apparent early,
which are also compelling and which indicate that the area, even now,
remains unsettled. The principal objection is the possibility of uncertainty
aversion, as illustrated in examples by Ellsberg (1961) and Allais (1953). We
consider two versions of Ellsberg's example. In the first, you see two urns,
urn I containing 100 red and black balls in an unknown proportion and urn
II containing 50 red and 50 black balls. You will win \$100 if your chosen
event occurs. The events being compared are red from urn I, RI, black from
urn I, BI, etc. Typical preferences are $RI = BI$, $RII = BII$ (perhaps these
make sense), $RI \prec RII$, and $BI \prec BII$. It is impossible to find probabilities
consistent with these rankings, since if RI is regarded as less likely than RII,

then *BI* must be more likely than *BII*, as the red and black probabilities must sum to 1 for each urn. This pattern of choices violates either the complete ordering assumption (P1) or the sure-thing principle (P2).

A variation on this example shows the crucial role of the sure-thing principle. Here, there is one urn containing 30 red and 60 black and yellow balls in an unknown proportion. One ball is chosen at random. Action *I* pays $100 if a red ball is drawn, $0 otherwise. Action *II* pays $100 if a black ball is drawn, $0 otherwise. Do you prefer *I* to *II* (a frequent preference)? Now consider action *III*, which pays $100 if a red or yellow ball is drawn, $0 otherwise, and action *IV*, which pays $100 if a black or yellow ball is drawn, $0 otherwise. Frequently, action *IV* is preferred to action *III*. The problem seems to be that the payoff probabilities are known in *I* and *IV*, and these are therefore preferred because of an aversion to uncertainty. However, P2, the sure-thing principle, requires that the ranking between *I* and *II* be the same as the ranking between *III* and *IV* since these comparisons differ only in the payoff in the event that a yellow ball is drawn (B^c in the notation of P2) and these payoffs are the same in *I* and *II* and the same in *III* and *IV*.

The Allais paradox is a little different, in that all the probabilities are specified. Here, suppose you have a choice between action *I*, winning $1000 with probability .33, $900 with probability .66, and $0 with probability .01, and action *II*, which is surely $900. Many will choose action *II*, in which case the chance of winning nothing is zero. Now consider action *III*, which pays $1000 with probability .33 and $0 with probability .67, and action *IV*, which pays $900 with probability .34 and $0 with probability .66. Many find it appealing to choose action *III* over action *IV*. These choices are contradictory, in that there is no expected utility rationalization supporting them. Note that there are really three events, occurring with probabilities .33, .66, and .01. Actions *I* and *II* differ from *III* and *IV* only in the payoff for the probability .66 event, and these payoffs are the same for *I* and *II* and the same for *III* and *IV*. Thus, by the sure-thing principle, *I* and *II* should have the same ranking as *III* and *IV*. The Allais paradox illustrates that, for many subjects, the change in probability from .67 to .66 is quite different from the change from .01 to .00. There appears to be a "bonus" associated with achieving certainty. This violates the sure-thing principle.

Efforts to extend the theory to accommodate uncertainty aversion are continuing. At present, the theory of rational decision making via expected utility maximization continues to provide the dominant framework for modeling individual behavior. In applications, it is typically more productive to handle apparent deviations from optimizing behavior by looking for misspecification of preferences or constraints, rather than by searching for alternative predictive theories.

1.3 STRUCTURAL VERSUS REDUCED-FORM METHODS

The distinction between stochastic and deterministic models is a distinction in modeling approaches. A distinction can also be made between the structural and reduced-form approaches. This distinction is concerned more with specification (parametrization) and estimation than with modeling. The distinction is not a sharp dichotomy. Indeed, outside of the linear simultaneous equations framework, "structural" and "reduced form" are typically undefined terms used for praise and criticism, respectively.

A notion that can be sensibly associated with the term *structural* is that of an equation that stands alone, that makes sense by itself, and that has a certain autonomy. In a market system, for example, one can consider the demand equation singly, considering the optimizing behavior of a consumer. This will lead to an equation giving quantity demanded as a function of price and income. Similarly, the supply equation has a life of its own—it can be determined by considering the behavior of a profit-maximizing producer and will give a quantity supplied as a function of price and other factors. These equations are structural in that each can be studied on its own. Adding the equilibrium condition leads to a complete system with two variables determined in the model: price and quantity. The *reduced form* consists of an equation for each of these variables. It is difficult to generate economic insight by considering either of these equations separately. This distinction between structural and reduced-form equations can be made precise in the linear simultaneous equations framework. The general notion that structural equations are autonomous equations and reduced-form equations are not is the position taken by Goldberger (*Econometric Theory* interview, 1989).

It is also common to refer to parameters, not equations, as structural. Structural parameters are the parameters of structural equations if the notion is to make any sense at all. Roughly, structural parameters are parameters that have economic interpretations on their own; reduced-form parameters are each a mishmash of several structural parameters. Unfortunately, reduced-form parameters sometimes do have economic interpretations of sorts (e.g., in the above market system, one reduced-form parameter is the equilibrium effect of income on the market price), and hence one econometrician's structural parameter is another's reduced-form parameter.

We take the view that economic theory and statistics are both guides for organizing data and reducing their dimension. From this point of view the distinction between the structural and reduced-form approaches is not sharp. Structural models rely more on theory for the reduction; reduced-form models rely more on statistics.

In one important class of models the sharp distinction can be retained. If the data distribution is in the exponential family class (see the appendix), then a fixed-dimension sufficient statistic exists and the natural parametrization in the linear exponential family form is the reduced-form model. Typically, a structural model would specify a lower-dimensional parametrization imposing restrictions on the reduced form. This curved exponential model is the structural model.

1.4 EXERCISES

1. Verify that Ellsberg's second example and Allais' example violate the sure-thing principle. *Hint:* Construct a table with columns corresponding to states of the world, rows corresponding to actions, and entries giving payoffs.

2. Merton (1973a, 1980) introduces and studies a consumption-based intertemporal capital asset pricing model. Preferences are characterized by an objective function of the form $E(\int_0^H u(c_t)dt)$, where c_t is the rate of consumption at time t, $u(\cdot)$ is a utility function, and H is the planning horizon. The particular case $u(c) = (c^{1-\gamma} - 1)/(1 - \gamma)$ implies that the rate of relative risk aversion (RRA) $-cu_{cc}/u_c$ (subscripts indicate differentiation) is constant at level γ. In the case of constant investment opportunities and constant RRA, the model implies that the excess return on the market portfolio consisting of all risky assets above the riskless interest rate is serially independent and normally distributed with mean proportional to variance, and the factor of proportionality is $\gamma/2$. In particular, if r denotes the continuously compounded riskless rate and $M(t)$ is the market capitalization of all risky assets at time t, then the market excess returns $r_t = \log M(t) - \log M(t - 1) - r$, $t = 1, \dots, T$, are independent and identically distributed (i.i.d.) $N((\gamma/2)\sigma^2, \sigma^2)$, the normal. Assume you are given data $\{r_t\}_{t=1}^T$. Derive the likelihood function for the unknown parameter $\theta = (\gamma, \sigma^2)$, the maximum likelihood estimator (MLE), and its exact and asymptotic distributions. *Hint:* For the exact distribution, note that the MLEs $\hat{\mu}$ and $\hat{\sigma}^2$ in the model $N(\mu, \sigma^2)$ are independent with known distributions involving the normal and central χ^2 distributions. Now use the change-of-variables formula.

3. Hakansson (1971) studies the growth optimal portfolio. Investors choose this portfolio if preferences are given by the Bernoulli logarithmic specification $\gamma = 1$. Derive the likelihood ratio (LR) test of the hypothesis $H_0: \gamma = 1$, and its exact and asymptotic distributions. *Hint:* For the exact distribution, note that $\Sigma_{t=1}^T r_t^2/T = \hat{\sigma}^2 + \hat{\mu}^2$. Show a formula for the density of the LR test based on the change-of-variables formula and marginalization by integration.

4. Derive the MLE of σ^2 under H_0 and its exact and asymptotic distribution. *Hint:* Note that $\Sigma_{t=1}^T r_t^2$ has a noncentral χ^2 distribution.

5. Show that the model under the alternative is a steep (indeed, regular) exponential family (see the appendix) and interpret the model under the null as a curved exponential family. Can the model under the null be rewritten as a regular exponential family with a lower-dimensional canonical statistic? Interpret your results.

1.5 REFERENCES

Utility theory is an enormous field, barely sketched here. Economists are familiar with the path-breaking work of Debreu (1959), giving conditions on preferences that lead to the existence of a utility function. Von Neumann and Morgenstern (1944) give an expected utility representation for decision making given probabilities over states. The fundamental work that establishes a foundation for decision theory is Savage (1954). It provides an axiomatic development that implies the existence of utility functions and subjective probability distributions. Pratt, Raiffa, and Schlaifer (1964) give an accessible but rigorous development for the discrete case. Knight (1921) was an early advocate of the distinction between risk and uncertainty, which many consider artificial (Arrow, 1951). The Ellsberg and Allais paradoxes have given rise to a large literature. Machina (1982) surveys the implications of changing the postulates. Gilboa and Schmeidler (1989) provide a framework for handling uncertainty aversion, essentially by considering ranges of priors. An empirical approach is taken in the work by Hansen and Sargent (2001, 2003). This remains an active research area. Halpern (2003) discusses alternative formal systems for representing uncertainty and updating beliefs. Dreze (1972), in his presidential address to the Econometric Society, reviews the connections between decision theory and econometrics. Classical econometrics textbooks (e.g., Theil (1971), Goldberger (1991)) give informal and very useful conceptual discussions of the distinction between the structural and reduced-form approaches, and Fisher (1966) and Rothenberg (1971) present technical discussions that generalize to nonlinear models.

Chapter Two

Components of a Dynamic Programming Model

The basic components of a dynamic optimization model are the objective function, the state variables, the control variables with any associated constraints, and the transition distribution giving the evolution of states as a stochastic function of the sequence of states and controls. These components are illustrated in simple examples in this chapter. The modeling decisions depend not only on the problem at hand but also on the type of data available. Possibilities are discussed following the examples. Each component of the specification is discussed in turn. Finally, we turn to two major practical problems in the application of dynamic programming models: The *curse of dimensionality* and the *curse of degeneracy*.

2.1 EXAMPLES

Example 1: A Marketing Application

Consider a firm deciding whether to invest in a marketing campaign. Suppose that there are two states of demand, high and low. The marketing decision is to run the campaign or not. Profit in any period is given by demand less costs, including marketing costs. Since there are only four configurations of states (demand) and controls (the marketing decision), the profit function is given by four numbers, $\pi(x, c)$, where $(x, c) \in \{0, 1\}^2$. Low demand is indicated by $x = 0$, and marketing by $c = 1$. A plausible profit function might be

Table 2.1 Profit.

	$c = 0$	$c = 1$
$x = 0$	7	4
$x = 1$	11	7

Here, the low-demand state with no marketing generates the same profit as the high-demand state with marketing. The objective function of the firm is to maximize the expected present discounted value of profits

$$\prod = E\sum_{t=0}^{T}\beta^t \pi(x_t, c_t),\qquad(2.1)$$

where T is a horizon, which may be infinite, and $\beta \in [0, 1)$ is a discount factor. Dynamics are incorporated in the model by letting the probability distribution of demand next period depend on the marketing decision this period. If marketing is effective, then the probability that $x_{t+1} = 1$ is greater when $c_t = 1$ than when $c_t = 0$.

A simple case has the distribution of x_{t+1} depending only on c_t and not on the current state. For example, consider the particularly simple case $p(x_{t+1} = 1 | c_t = 1) = 1$ and $p(x_{t+1} = 1 | c_t = 0) = 0$. Thus, the state of demand in period $t + 1$ is determined exactly by the marketing effort in period t. The logic of dynamic programming can be illustrated by considering the two-period problem. In the last period, clearly there is no benefit from marketing and $c = 0$ is optimal no matter what the level of demand. Now consider the first period. Here, there is a tradeoff between current period profits (maximized by $c = 0$) and future profits (maximized by $c = 1$). If the current state of demand is low ($x = 0$), then the current cost of marketing is 3 and the current period value of the gain next period as a result of marketing is 4β. Thus, for $\beta > \frac{3}{4}$ it is optimal to invest in marketing in the first period when the state of demand is low. Suppose next that the state of demand in the first period is high ($x = 1$). Then the marketing effort costs 4 in current profit and gains only 4β in current value of future profits. Since $\beta < 1$, this effort is not worthwhile. We have found the optimal policy. In particular,

$$c = \begin{cases} 1, & \text{if } x = 0, \\ 0, & \text{if } x = 1, \end{cases}\qquad(2.2)$$

is optimal if $\beta > \frac{3}{4}$. For smaller discount factors, $c = 0$ (no campaign) is always optimal. The logic of beginning in the last period in finite-horizon models and working backward in time is known as *backward recursion* and is generally the way these problems are solved. Solution methods are treated in chapter 3.

The study of optimal advertising policy in dynamic models with investment in current marketing effort affecting future demand was pioneered by Nerlove and Arrow (1962). We consider an illustrative binary state/control specification highlighting the important current and future effects of a campaign on profits. Many extensions and empirical applications exist, e.g., to the continuous state/control case (Chintagunta and Jain (1992), see also chapter 13 below) and to dynamic duopoly (Chintagunta and Vilcassim (1992), and chapter 15). A more general and plausible specification would have the distribution of the next period's demand depend on both the marketing decision and the current state of demand. As a matter of interpretation, this allows for marketing to have lasting effects (though tapering off over time). This possibility is pursued further in chapter 3, where we discuss numerical solutions of dynamic programming problems.

Example 2: The Job Search Model

The job search model was an early application of stochastic dynamic programming techniques to economic theory. The search model was among the first models to be estimated with econometric techniques exploiting the dynamic programming structure. It is a member of an important class of models known as optimal stopping models. In the simplest setup, a worker is assumed to be unemployed and searching for employment. Searching consists of sampling, once each period, a wage offer w from a known distribution of offers. Once accepted, a job is held forever. Once declined, an offer is no longer available. The state variable is the outstanding wage offer in the current period. The control is the decision to accept or reject the outstanding offer. Offers are assumed to be independently and identically distributed (i.i.d.), so the distribution of the next period's state does not depend on the current state. The state distribution does depend on the control since offers are no longer received once a job has been accepted. The worker chooses a strategy that maximizes the expected present discounted value of his income stream $E\sum_t^T \beta^t w$, where in the simplest models $T = \infty$. This model has been extended, refined and widely applied. See Devine and Kiefer (1991).

The basic logic of optimal stopping can be illustrated in the infinite-horizon model. The value for an unemployed worker is heuristically the maximized value of $E\sum_t \beta^t w$, where the maximum is taken over all possible strategies the worker might follow in his effort to maximize the present discounted value (PDV). This value V_u, whatever it is (it will be calculated in subsequent chapters), is a constant not depending either on the current wage offer (declined, since we are assuming the worker is unemployed) or on the particular period. The value does not depend on the current offer since we assume offers are i.i.d.; it does not depend on the period since we have an infinite-horizon problem and the future looks the same from any point. Now suppose the worker gets the next offer w^o. The value of accepting the offer w^o is simply $\sum_t \beta^t w^o = w^o/(1 - \beta)$. If this value is greater than the value of continued search, namely, V_u, the worker should accept the offer; if not, he should decline and continue searching. Thus, we have found the optimal strategy. The worker should decline wage offers until he receives one greater than $(1 - \beta)V_u$; then he should accept employment and stop searching. Thus,

$$c = \begin{cases} 0, & \text{if } x \leq (1 - \beta)V_u, \\ 1, & \text{if } x > (1 - \beta)V_u, \end{cases}$$

is optimal in this model regardless of the value of $\beta \in [0, 1)$, with x the state (wage) and $c = 0$ and 1 indicating the reject and accept decisions.

Note that the logic of backward recursion, as in the marketing example, does not apply here. It would if we considered a finite-horizon search, and then V_u would depend on the time left before the horizon.

Example 3: The One-sector Growth Model

This classic model forms the basis for much of modern macroeconomics. The ideas originate in Ramsey (1928) and Solow (1956), though the optimization approach and solution properties were developed in the mid-1960s and the model with uncertainty in the 1970s. Multisector models are described by Brock and Majumdar (1978) and others. The current state of the art is given in Ljungqvist and Sargent (2000). The basic stochastic model has a production function $y_t = \varepsilon_t f(k_t)$, where y is output, k is capital stock, and ε is a random shock to the production function. Output in period t is divided into consumption c_t and capital going into the next period, k_{t+1}. The state variables are k_t and ε_t; the control variable c_t is chosen given the realized values of the state variables. Allowing destruction of capital, the feasibility constraints are

$$c_t + k_{t+1} \leq \varepsilon_t f(k_t), \qquad c_t \geq 0, \ k_{t+1} \geq 0.$$

Of course, a sensible specification will imply that the first constraint binds. Thus, we can write $k_{t+1} = \varepsilon_t f(k_t) - c_t$ as the transition equation. Note that there is no uncertainty about the next period's capital stock. There is uncertainty about the next period's output, $y_{t+1} = \varepsilon_{t+1} f(k_{t+1})$, because of uncertainty about the i.i.d. state variable ε. The optimization problem is to choose the consumption function $c(k, \varepsilon)$ so as to maximize

$$V(k, \varepsilon) = E \sum_{t=0}^{\infty} \beta^t u(c_t).$$

The consumption choice then implies the savings decision

$$s(k, \varepsilon) = \varepsilon f(k) - c(k, \varepsilon).$$

It is sensible to assume that the production function $f(k)$ is increasing, is quasi-concave, and satisfies other conditions as well; the utility of consumption function $u(c)$ is bounded, is increasing, is concave, and satisfies other conditions as well; and the discount factor $\beta \in [0, 1)$. The random variable ε must also be restricted. With this setup, it is possible to characterize optimal consumption and savings behavior and to analyze steady-state economic growth in terms of utility and production parameters.

This model, because of the infinite horizon, is also not suitable for analysis by backward recursion, but it is amenable to forward recursion. Further, since both the control and the states are continuous, it is amenable to analysis by calculus, and hence Euler equation techniques. This can provide considerable simplification in continuous models.

2.2 DATA CONFIGURATIONS

Specification of each of the components of the dynamic programming model must be made with an eye toward the data available, as well as toward the focus of the economic question under consideration. Richer, more detailed data sets will support richer, more general specifications. Thus, the specification depends both on the question being asked and on the information available. Information comes in two main forms. The first is intertemporal information on a sequence of state and control variables for an agent (possibly with objective function information as well), and the second is cross-agent information on configurations of states and controls (and possibly objective functions). The first case, time series observations, forms the usual basis for macroeconomic applications of the dynamic programming model. The point of view that macro time series can be regarded as outcomes from a single agent's dynamic optimization problem has turned out to be surprisingly useful in both theory and application. There are rarer but interesting studies at the micro level of a single agent making a sequence of decisions. As an intermediate case, a firm can be modeled as a single maximizing agent (Sargent, 1978). Pure cross-section data are rarely modeled with dynamic programming methods, as there is simply too little information on dynamics. With enough structure (i.e., assumptions), one can in fact estimate dynamic parameters from cross-section data (for example, some parameters of the job search model can be fit to cross-section data on employment status and wages), but this is rarely seen and requires severe assumptions. More common in microeconomic applications is a combination of temporal and cross-individual data. Here, short sequences of states and controls are observed for a sample of individual agents. These data configurations are illustrated in figure 2.1. Both a time series and a cross-section data set are shown, and the full data set is longitudinal, consisting of a time series of cross sections.

For applied work it is often useful to restrict these components so that the model becomes a Markov decision process, i.e., a process in which the

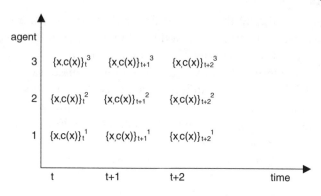

Figure 2.1 Data Configurations.

optimal decision in any period is a function only of the position at that period (and not of the path by which one arrived at that position). Both the
transition probabilities (conditional probability distributions) and the optimal policy function are assumed constant over time. This setup remains
quite general while at the same time allowing a reasonable chance for inference. The chance for inference occurs since the distributions of (x_t, c_t)
conditional on $x_{t-1} = x^0$ and (x'_t, c'_t) conditional on $x'_{t-1} = x^0$ are the
same and make up repeated observations from the same process. Thus, the
transition probabilities can be estimated by observing (x_t, x_{t+1}) pairs, and
the policy function $c(x)$ can be estimated from the contemporaneous (x_t, c_t)
pairs. The situation is illustrated in figure 2.2 for binary x and c.

In figure 2.2 there are two observations relevant for estimating the policy
function $c(x)$, two for estimating the transition probability $Q(x_t|x_{t-1} = 1)$,
and one for estimating the transition probability $Q(x_t|x_{t-1} = 0)$. Figure
2.2 also illustrates the limitations of pure cross-section data. There, only the
vertical relationships $((x, c)$ pairs) are observed. With the assumption that
the agents are the same, these can be regarded as repeated observations on a
single policy function, and the policy function can be estimated in principle.
However, there is no direct information on the model's dynamics. There is
indirect information, in the sense that the policy function depends on the
parameters of the dynamics through the optimizing assumption. The structure can be pushed, with suitable assumptions, to give some information
on dynamics. Christensen and Kiefer (1994b) give an example in which a
fundamental parameter of the search model, the ratio between an arrival
probability and a discount factor, is identified from cross-section data alone.

When a cross section of time series is available—typically fairly short
series over a number of agents—the stationarity assumptions can be relaxed
if necessary for the problem at hand. A leading example is the study of
retirement. Here, data on a sample of older workers can be regarded usefully

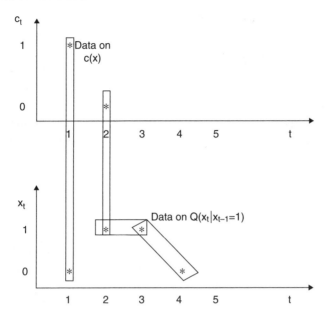

Figure 2.2 Time Series Data.

as repeated observations on the same nonstationary process. Because the observations are across individuals, information is accumulated as the same situation is observed repeatedly, though this would not be possible observing only one agent over time. Even without repeated observations, inference might be possible if the nonstationarity were suitably parametrized.

Finally, note that there is a subtle interaction between the models under consideration and the types of data required. For example, optimal stopping problems even in the simplest cases require longitudinal data. Consider the basic job search model of example 2, in which an unemployed worker samples wage offers until he sees one large enough to accept. After that point, he is employed and sees no more offers. The dynamic programming model is stationary and the transition probability is particularly simple (i.i.d.), yet the model cannot be consistently estimated by following one agent over an infinitely long time interval (the conceptual experiment behind time series asymptotics). Since employment is treated as an absorbing state, information about the state distribution is not accumulated after the decision is made to accept a job. Longitudinal data, i.e., unemployment spells and subsequent reemployment wages, are required for a sample of many unemployed workers. Indeed, in the simplest models, workers accept a job in finite time, so the number of workers must go to infinity in the conceptual experiment underlying the asymptotics.

2.3 THE OBJECTIVE FUNCTION

The objective function for a T-period problem can be as general as $u(x_0, c_0, x_1, c_1, \ldots, x_T, c_T)$, where x_t, c_t are the values of the state and control variables in period t. For an infinite-horizon problem the utility could depend in general on the entire sequence: $u(\{x_t, c_t\}_{t=0}^{\infty})$. The completely general setup is useless for applied work, as simply anything could be explained by the appropriate utility function. It is necessary to restrict the functional form of these utility functions. The usual first step is to specify temporal separability:

$$u(x_0, c_0, x_1, c_1, \ldots, x_T, c_T) = \sum_{t=0}^{T} u_t(x_t, c_t). \tag{2.3}$$

This substantially restricts the cross-period interactive effects of states and controls, though it is still too general for guiding empirical work. For example, as Rust (1994) points out, the utility function $u_t(x_t, c_t) = I[c_t^*(x_t) = c_t]$ completely explains any observed $\{x_t, c_t\}$ data. The general models of course fit the data well, but they have absolutely no predictive power. Furthermore, they do not serve to identify fundamental parameters that could have wider application. The next major simplifying step is to specify

$$u_t(x, c) = \beta^t u(x, c), \tag{2.4}$$

where $\beta \in [0, 1]$ is a discount factor and $u(x, c)$ is a function independent of the period, giving the one-period utility associated with state x and control c. The same considerations arise in the infinite-horizon case, where $T = \infty$. Here, we also assume that $\beta \in [0, 1)$, eliminating the value of 1 from consideration.[1] Even here, additional restrictions are needed for applications. At a minimum, the shape of u can be restricted (e.g., increasing in x, concave in c). In practice, a parametric form is often chosen.

The distinction between finite- and infinite-horizon specifications should not be treated as sharp. Infinite-horizon models can provide useful and accurate approximations to finite-horizon models with substantial increases in simplicity. The infinite-horizon formalization is often chosen in cases where it makes sense to consider stationary models—in which the policy at any time depends only on the state configuration at that time. In this case, situations are replicated and information is accumulated efficiently. How long must a decision horizon be before the infinite-horizon approximation

---

[1] When $\beta = 1$, many policies are typically optimal, as the discounted sum of utilities is infinite. If this is a realistic specification, one can turn to the average reward criterion, in which case these policies can be compared on a sensible basis. See Bhattacharya and Majumdar (1989a, b).

becomes sound? That depends on the complexity of the model and particularly on the discount factor. Some simple examples will be calculated below.

Identification of $u(c, x)$ is difficult. In general, as will be seen, u is not identified in models with discrete states and controls, even in the parametric case. Typically, the parameters can be bounded but not estimated without added structure in other aspects of the model. In some applications, the form of u is known (specified by the modeler). Examples include some financial models and, notably, the job search model. Here, the utility functions are typically specified as the dollar profit or wage, though it is sometimes appropriate to specify concave functions of these quantities.

Theoretical foundations for the intertemporal utility function and the restrictiveness of the time separability assumption are explored by Kreps and Porteus (1979). In practice, the problem faced in applications is usually not whether a chosen functional form is general enough. Instead, knowing that any data sequence may be explained by adopting a sufficiently general utility function, the real issue is whether even a tightly specified utility function imposes any restrictions on the data sequence.

2.4 THE STATE VARIABLES

The state variables x_t may be continuous or discrete and may be vectors. In practice, state variables are always discrete (observed data sequences, like computer calculations, are restricted in the number of digits represented), but when there are many ordered values, it is a useful simplification to model them as continuous. This point has an important implication. Namely, the discrete case is general for mathematical purposes, though the simplification afforded by considering continuous variables must be appreciated. When mathematical results rely heavily on continuous state variables, however, they are to be regarded skeptically.

Specification of the states is important at the outset in setting up a dynamic programming model, as it is useful for x_t to reflect the entire state of the system at the beginning of period t, in the sense that any action to be taken in period t depends only on the value of the state variable x_t. Thus, in an intertemporal allocation model, x_t might include net worth, or in a model with credit constraints, current assets. The state specification may also include t. State variables may be observed, completely unobserved, or observed with error. In the marketing application of example 1, the state variable is the current state of demand. This is an example of a discrete state model. Current period profits depend on the state variable. In the job search model of example 2, the state variable is the outstanding wage offer. This state variable can be continuous or discrete. The typical specification in both theoretical and applied models uses continuously distributed offers. These offers are assumed i.i.d., so the transition function for the state is known. The distribution does depend on the control: In the simplest models, once the worker accepts a job, no further offers are received. In example 3, the state is the capital stock, typically modeled as a continuous state variable.

It is trivial but worth remembering in setting up models that transition distributions or control policies that depend on any finite number of lags can be brought into the form of a single-lag model by appropriate redefinition of the state variable. For example, the transition distribution $x_t = \rho_1 x_{t-1} + \rho_2 x_{t-2} + \varepsilon_t$ can be recast as

$$z_t = R z_{t-1} + \upsilon_t, \tag{2.5}$$

with $z_t = (x_t, x_{t-1})'$,

$$R = \begin{pmatrix} \rho_1 & \rho_2 \\ 1 & 0 \end{pmatrix}, \tag{2.6}$$

and $\upsilon_t = (\varepsilon_t, 0)'$. Our emphasis on models with a single lag is therefore not restrictive in this sense.

2.5 THE CONTROL VARIABLES

The control variables c_t may similarly be continuous or discrete. The distinction really depends on the number of values considered: The continuous case is a useful approximation when controls take many ordered values. Like state variables, controls may be observed, completely unobserved, or observed with error. The marketing decision in example 1 is an example of a discrete control (though in a richer environment, a model might be constructed in which the control could be viewed as continuous, such as dollars allocated to marketing). Another example of a discrete control is the employment status in example 2. There, we have the situation of a continuous state (the outstanding wage offer) and a discrete control. This class of models turns out to be extremely important in that computationally efficient solution methods are known. These are called discrete decision processes by Rust (1994).

The growth model has a continuous control. Typically, a sensible model has the controls uniquely determined by the configuration of state variables. This somewhat restricts the menu of controls in modeling—if a single state variable is binary, for example, it is pointless to have a control variable taking more than two values: Two at most will be used in the optimal policy. An early treatment of practical considerations on states and controls in the macroeconomic policy context is Theil (1958).

2.6 THE TRANSITION DISTRIBUTION

The state variables x_t are typically modeled as evolving according to the transition distribution $Q(x_t|x_{t-1}, c_{t-1})$, depending on the last period's state and control. With this specification, the x_t process is a controlled Markov process. Some useful special cases arise frequently:

$$Q(x_t|x_{t-1}, c_{t-1}) = Q(x_t|x_{t-1}), \qquad (2.7)$$

not depending on the value of the control. In this case, x_t is a Markov process. In fact, once the model structure is imposed, implying that optimal c_{t-1} is a function of x_{t-1}, then x_t is Markov even without this restriction on Q, provided optimal controls c_{t-1} are considered. A further simplification occurs if

$$Q(x_t|x_{t-1}) = Q(x_t), \qquad (2.8)$$

not depending on the past state. In this case, the state variables follow an i.i.d. process. Finally, suppose

$$Q(x_t|x_{t-1}, c_{t-1}) = Q(x_t|c_{t-1}), \qquad (2.9)$$

depending only on the control and not on the past state. This is the case in the simplest specifications of the marketing model, example 1, and the job search model, example 2 (in the latter, the wage x_t is i.i.d. as long as c_{t-1} indicates continued searching and then is constant). All of these specifications have practical applications. Note that a purely deterministic transition equation is covered as a special case.

The transition distribution is often a good place to begin the empirical analysis of a dynamic programming model. Especially in cases where the states and controls are observed without error (in practice, this means with error negligible compared with the other approximations in effect), the transition distribution or some of its components can be estimated without the full dynamic programming likelihood computations. First, if the specification being entertained is the i.i.d. case $Q(x_t|x_{t-1}, c_{t-1}) = Q(x_t)$, then the x_t sequence can be studied for signs of dependence. There is a wide range of statistical techniques for examining a series for dependence and testing the hypothesis of independence. The hypothesis of identical distributions for each t is a little more difficult to test, but in practice simple autocorrelation tests in the continuous case (reviewed in chapter 10) or runs tests in the discrete case can serve to eliminate the i.i.d. hypothesis from consideration.

A more general and often useful specification is the Markov not depending on the control, $Q(x_t|x_{t-1}, c_{t-1}) = Q(x_t|x_{t-1})$ (see (2.7)). Here, the x_t sequence can be examined to see whether or not it is Markovian. In the continuous case, tests for high-order autocovariance can be applied. If there is second-order autocorrelation, but not higher, for example, then a respecification of the state variable of the type (2.5) and (2.6) can lead to a Markovian model. In the discrete case there are other tests that can be used. Note that a failure of the Markov property may lead to a redefinition of the state variables rather than complete rejection of the model. Also, considering the earlier comments, tests with power against departures from the structure $Q(x_t|x_{t-1})$ actually have power against any departure from the dynamic programming framework $Q(x_t|x_{t-1}, c_{t-1})$ whatsoever, since this leaves $\{x_t\}_t$ Markov when c_{t-1} is chosen optimally as a function of x_{t-1}.

When the state and control variables are observed without error, there is another quick check on the adequacy of the dynamic programming model. Namely, repeated configurations of the state variables should each be associated with the same values of the controls. In the discrete case this is easy to check (e.g., with cross-tabulations). Thus, if the single state variable is binary and the single control is also binary, of the four possible combinations of states x_t and controls c_t, only two should be seen in the data. Further, if the data and model are interesting at all, both states x should appear, and each should give rise to a different value of c. Of the four combinations $\{00, 01, 10, 11\}$, either $\{00, 11\}$ or $\{01, 10\}$ should be the combinations seen. The extension of this technique to general discrete states and controls is immediate.

Some modifications of the dynamic programming model may suggest themselves at this stage. If the states and controls do not satisfy this relationship (and they often do not), a variety of different model changes can be considered. First, perhaps the state variable under consideration is irrelevant and can be eliminated. Second, there is the theoretical possibility that the optimal control policy is "mixed"; that is, it is optimal to choose the control by a random process where the probabilities perhaps depend on the state. These policies are not optimal in "games against nature," the usual empirical setting, but they could be optimal in multiagent models. More relevant model changes allow for imperfect control, so that the best the agent can do is influence the value of the control but not determine it. Here, it is useful to avoid the purely semantic debate over whether the agent has imperfect control or whether he has perfect control over the appropriately defined controls but the controls are purely probability distributions over the support points of the observed controls. Allowing for measurement error in the state variables, the controls, or both is also relevant. An alternative approach is to assume there exist unobserved (to the econometrician) state variables (e.g., unobserved heterogeneity, random utility shocks), so that different values of the control could be optimal given the observed portion of the state. All these possibilities will be considered throughout.

When the states are continuous, the problem is a little more difficult, as an observed sample will in principle never have more than one realization of any particular value, so whether a state value is always followed by the same control is not a practical check on specification. As a practical matter, however, we expect that if the model is to be at all empirically useful, then close values of the states should imply close values of the controls, by and large. The "by-and-large" qualification occurs because a particularly useful class of models has a continuous state variable and discrete controls (optimal stopping models—e.g., the job search model). In these models, there is typically a critical value of the state at which the control changes. However, it is the case that, except for this critical value, close values of the state imply the same control.

Thus, once the specification of the states and control variables has been determined (tentatively), then an analysis of the transition distribution is the natural next step. Tentative specifications can be quickly ruled out without bothering to solve the dynamic programming equations. Sometimes the transition equation can be estimated in full without appeal to the dynamic programming setup, in particular if $Q(x_t|x_{t-1}, c_{t-1}) = Q(x_t|x_{t-1})$ or $Q(x_t|x_{t-1}, c_{t-1}) = Q(x_t)$. In this case, the estimated parameters, provided that the model survives specification checks, can sometimes be conditioned on throughout the rest of the estimation process and can in any case provide reasonable starting values for subsequent rounds of nonlinear estimation. In the general case, in which the transition distribution depends on the controls, the transition probabilities corresponding to observed state/control configurations can be estimated. Those corresponding to configurations that do not appear cannot, although these probabilities enter the value function and thus affect the choice of optimal policy. Thus, there is information about these probabilities in the observed state/control sequence once a structural model is adopted.

2.7 THE CURSE OF DIMENSIONALITY

The *curse of dimensionality* refers to the rapid proliferation of computations required to solve a dynamic programming problem as the size of the problem increases. Here, the vague notion of size refers to the number of state variables, the number of control variables, or the number of periods. While these have quite different influences, it is possible to get some intuition on the problem by considering solution of a finite-horizon, discrete state/discrete control model by backward recursion and otherwise brute force calculation.

If there are K values for the state variable and C for the control, then the final-period calculation requires C calculations of the utility function (let us refer to this as $O(C)$ operations) and retention of the maximum value for each value of the state variable, resulting in the K-vector V_T. Thus, $O(CK)$

operations are required. With this in hand, turn to the second-to-last period. For each value of the state variable, calculate the current period utility plus the discounted expected value of V_T. Here, V_T is a random variable because the final period's state is stochastic, with a distribution that typically depends on the current state and control. Calculating the expectation for each value of the current state and a single value of the control requires K multiplications (the number of future states multiplied by the appropriate transition probabilities) and summation of the K values ($O(K)$ operations). This expectation must be calculated for each value of the control (now $O(CK)$ operations) and each value of the current period state (now $O(CK^2)$). Add to that the calculations for the current utility ($O(C)$ more) and this must be done K times, and the maximum retained. Continuing, we see that a T-period problem requires approximately $O(TCK^2)$ operations. A problem in which the number of calculations increases as a polynomial in problem size is considered "tractable" in computer science terms. However, our measurement of the increase in problem size has been a little misleading—we are merely adding additional values that the state and control variables can take. Perhaps more plausible is to suppose that states and controls take values in sets S and C with cardinalities $|S|$ and $|C|$. If there are n_s states and n_c controls, then the numbers of values the states and controls can take are $|S|^{n_s}$ and $|C|^{n_c}$, respectively. Substituting shows that the number of computations increases geometrically in the number of state and control variables. From this point of view, increasing the complexity of the model specification dramatically increases the computational burden in solving the model.

As a practical matter, our calculations are at best rough and illustrative. The problem of the numerical solution of dynamic programming problems is well studied. Though it has not been satisfactorily solved, significant advances are continuing to be made, both in determining clever algorithms to break the curse of dimensionality and in increasing processor speed and consequently reducing computer costs. Often problems have special structures that can be exploited to decrease computational complexity.

Finally, note that we have considered here the classical curse of dimensionality in solving dynamic programming problems numerically. We have not even mentioned the associated computational burdens of actually estimating the parameters of the dynamic programming problem. The computational effort required in estimating these models considerably exceeds the burden of merely solving them.

2.8 THE CURSE OF DEGENERACY

Theoretical applications of dynamic programming can use the implied policy functions $c(x)$ in the stationary case or $c_t(x)$ in the nonstationary case. For applied work these functions present a problem since although the model is itself stochastic, the relationship $c(x)$ is exact. As mentioned above, this can be used as a quick check on the model: A given value of x should always lead to the same value of c. In the binary state and control case, for example, only two of the four possible pairs of contemporaneous values should be observed (and for the model to be interesting, these should be on the diagonal or contradiagonal of the two-way frequency table). In fact, this situation is unlikely to hold for data. This failure occurs for a variety of reasons—we consider various ways to model around the problem below. But primarily it occurs because the model is exactly that: a model. It is not an exact description of the world and should not be confused with the world. To be useful as a model, however, some systematic allowance must be made for the fact that the deterministic control rules resulting from solving a stochastic dynamic programming problem do not describe the data.

It is useful to put this situation in the framework of probability modeling for data. Specifically, let us adopt the Markov setup and write the data distribution as

$$p\left(\{x_t, c_t\}, t = 1, \ldots, T | x_0, c_0\right) = \prod_{t=1}^{T} p\left(x_t, c_t | x_{t-1}, c_{t-1}\right)$$

$$= \prod_{t=1}^{T} p\left(c_t | x_t\right) p\left(x_t | x_{t-1}, c_{t-1}\right). \quad (2.10)$$

Here, we have factored the joint distribution of (x, c) into the product of a marginal and a conditional and used the fact that the policy function $c(x)$ has only contemporaneous x as an argument to eliminate the conditioning variables $(x, c)_{t-1}$ from the conditional distribution of c given x.

The *curse of degeneracy* arises because the first factor, the conditional distribution of c given x, assigns point mass to the point $c(x)$. Thus, the joint distribution of x, c contemporaneously is degenerate. The model predicts an exact relationship between variables (of course, the relationship can depend on parameters). The closely related *curse of determinacy* arises because the same requirement applies to the observed data, since the likelihood function is only positive for sequences satisfying the exact relationship, and this is typically violated in practice.

An exact relationship is extremely informative about parameters. Consider the regression case $y = X\beta + \varepsilon$ in which some of the errors are known to be zero. If there are K regressors and K errors known to be zero that correspond to linearly independent rows of the regressor matrix, then the regression parameters can be determined exactly. Problems arise when we specify that $K' > K$ errors are known to be zero, and the data are inconsistent if the K'-dimensional vector y does not lie in the

K-dimensional subspace spanned by the columns of X. In that case, what we learn is that our assumption that the model is correct and the errors are zero is just wrong.

Faced with the fact that the model does not describe the data, we are led to respecification with an eye toward making $p(c|x)$ a nondegenerate distribution. There are four major approaches here. The first is to introduce measurement error in the states or the controls or both. This possibility is explored in detail. The second possibility is to assume imperfect control. In this case, the agent may affect which value of the control is realized but cannot determine it. Formally, the choice is over probability distributions of controls. Unlike the measurement error case, this changes the value function, although it does not expand the number of state variables. Third, one can simply ignore the problem, although then of course it would be necessary to move away from the likelihood framework and use other methods of estimation. Maximum likelihood (ML) is simply too efficient; it uses all of the information in the model, and this leads to nonsense results. A less efficient method such as the method of moments might require only, for example, that $c_t = c(x_t)$ in mean. Then the model can be fit, but the researcher is left with the uncomfortable certain knowledge that the model as specified is in conflict with the data. Nevertheless, these methods can be very useful tools for understanding whether there is any possibility that a particular model will work at all and for providing starting values for ML estimation in an appropriately respecified model. Finally, the researcher may introduce a completely unobserved state variable, typically with a known distribution. This both changes the value function and expands the state variable. An important special case is the random utility specification. Here, utility in each period is a random function of the state and the control. In this case, the optimum control corresponding to a given state can vary from period to period. As long as this variability is suitably restricted, the model can continue to be useful. For example, the model might have additive state- and control-dependent errors with a known distribution but a common mean function across periods.

2.9 EXERCISES

1. In example 1, suppose the transition distribution is $p(x_{t+1} = 1|c_t = 1) = .9$ and $p(x_{t+1} = 1|c_t = 0) = 0$. Find the optimal policy for the two-period problem. Then find the optimal policy for $p(x_{t+1} = 1|c_t = 0) = .5$.

2. Write down the transition distributions for examples 2 and 3.

3. Write out (2.10) for example 1. How does it depend on the discount factor?

2.10 REFERENCES

The classic dynamic programming reference is Bellman (1957), who coined the term. This was followed by Bellman and Dreyfus (1962). Ross (1983) gives an accessible and brief introduction. Harris (1987) reviews some elementary theory supplemented by economic examples using spreadsheets. A recent rigorous treatment of dynamic systems in discrete time and over an infinite horizon is Bhattacharya and Majumdar (2006). Their chapter 6 develops discrete dynamic programming systematically. The framework of Savage (1954) (see chapter 1) applies in dynamic settings just as in static. Kreps and Porteus (1978, 1979) give axioms for dynamic utility maximization. Bellman (1957) also introduced the term "curse of dimensionality." Heckman (1981) considers models and tests for dependence in discrete data series. A practical discussion of the curse of dimensionality with approaches to breaking the curse is Rust (1997).

Chapter Three

Discrete States and Controls

The discrete state/control case has many applications, can be treated with fairly elementary methods, and allows illustration of most of the important issues of identification and estimation that appear in more general settings. The simple case allows focus on issues of substance rather than on details. The latter are important but can be better handled once the substantive issues are identified. Note that the discrete case is in many ways quite general. For practical purposes, machine calculations are discrete, as are data, and indeed applications of continuous models often (but not always) require explicit discretization.

In order to apply dynamic programming (DP) models to understand data configurations or to test hypotheses, it is necessary to solve the programming problem for the optimal policies. The issue of the existence and uniqueness of solutions has been studied in wide generality. From a theoretical point of view, the best theorems are obtained with as few restrictions as possible on the preferences or transition distributions. These general theorems then indicate that the dynamic programming approach is widely applicable. From an estimation point of view the situation is different. Simply asserting that the data are generated by a dynamic programming model yields essentially no empirical implications and imposes no structure on the data. Quite specific restrictive assumptions are necessary for the approach to yield increased understanding and better predictions. Thus, it is important to study solution methods to see how restrictions on preferences generate implications for data.

It is convenient and imposes no practical restriction on the applicability of the dynamic programming model to require that the reward function be bounded, $|u(x, c)| \leq B$, for some fixed $B > 0$.

3.1 SOLVING DP PROBLEMS: FINITE HORIZON

Note at the outset that in the discrete state/control case there is no necessity to consider more than one state and one control variable. If we have, for example, two state variables x_1 and x_2 taking values in S_1 and S_2, both finite sets, we can combine them into the single state variable x_0 taking values in $S_0 = S_1 \times S_2$, also a finite set. Our specification is general, although in particular models in which it might be possible to impose restrictions on the effects of different variables, or in which hypotheses about particular variables are of interest, it can be useful to carry more complicated notation.

In the finite-horizon case it is conventional to index value functions by the number of periods left rather than by the distance from the current period (0). Thus, in a T-period optimization, the value function at the outset is

$$V_{T-1}(x) = \max_{\pi} E_{T-1,\pi} \sum_{t=0}^{T-1} \beta^t u(x_t, c_t), \qquad (3.1)$$

where $\pi = (\pi_{T-1}, \pi_{T-2}, \ldots, \pi_0)$ is a sequence of policy functions. A policy function at period t maps the current state x_t and all previous states into the current policy c_t. Thus, we are maximizing over a sequence of functions. Note that the value function itself is an $|S|$-vector with real elements. We can easily be quite general at this point. Since $|C|$, $|S|$, and T are finite, there are only finitely many possible policies π, and the maximum is clearly well defined. The expectation operator is a little more subtle—it is a conditional expectation conditioned on the current value of the state variable (hence the $(T - 1)$ subscript) and on the policy π. Since the transition distribution typically depends on controls, the expectation clearly depends on the policy.

The value function in the final period is $V_0(x)$. With $u(x, c)$ the immediate reward from using control value c with state x, the final period value function is clearly $V_0(x) = \max_{c \in C} u(x, c)$. The value function with one period left $V_1(x)$ is just the maximized value of the current reward and the discounted expected value of future rewards. But the future reward is $V_0(x)$, so the function $V_1(x)$ is given by

$$V_1(x) = \max_{c \in C} \{u(x, c) + \beta E_1 V_0(x')\}. \qquad (3.2)$$

Here, x' is the next period state—a random variable whose distribution is determined by c and x, current controls, and the state. The expectation operator E_1 here is an $|S| \times |S|$ transition matrix. Iterating, we obtain the whole sequence of value functions $V_0, \ldots, V_{T-1}$ with

$$V_i(x) = \max_{c \in C} \{u(x, c) + \beta E_i V_{i-1}(x')\}. \qquad (3.3)$$

Policies π that achieve this sequence of value functions are optimal. The backward recursion method described delivers the policy functions as well as the value functions.

Note that E_i at our current level of generality can depend on the entire history of the sequence of states up to and including the current state. In practice, this is much too general, and it is typically appropriate to specify that the state-to-state transitions are Markovian, so that the transition distribution depends only on the current state and control. In this case, the value function $V_{i-1}(x)$ is the same function whether it is the first value function in an i-period problem or the value function $(i-1)$ periods from the end in a longer-horizon problem. That is, given the current state, the future looks the same no matter how the current state was achieved. Then we can also do a forward recursion:

$$V_{T-1}(x) = \max_{\pi} E_{T-1,\pi} \sum_{i=0}^{T-1} \beta^i u(x_i, c_i)$$

$$= \max_{c \in C} \left\{ u(x, c) + E_{T-1} \left(\max_{\pi'} E_{T-2,\pi'} \sum_{i=1}^{T-1} \beta^i u(x_i, c_i) \right) \right\}$$

$$= \max_{c \in C} \left\{ u(x, c) + E_{T-1} \beta \left(\max_{\pi'} E_{T-2,\pi'} \sum_{i=0}^{T-2} \beta^i u(x_i, c_i) \right) \right\}$$

$$= \max_{c \in C} \left\{ u(x, c) + \beta E_{T-1} V_{T-2}(x') \right\}. \tag{3.4}$$

Here, $\pi' = (\pi_{T-2}, \dots, \pi_0)$ or, equivalently, $\pi = (c, \pi')$. Both recursions lead to the same relationship between the value function as a function of the current state and the problem of maximizing the sum of the current reward and the discounted expected value of the next period's value function. This equation is known as the *optimality principle* or *Bellman's equation.*

The derivation shows that optimal behavior may be decomposed through time and implemented recursively. The choice of strategy is equivalent to the choice of current policy, taking into account both the immediate reward and the expected future value, in particular how this period's action affects the next period's economic environment, and assuming optimal behavior in the future. The point is that optimal policies are forward looking; they do not take account of how the current state was achieved.

It is useful to give the optimality principle in terms of an explicit functional operator. In particular, the principle is recast as

$$V_i = T_i(V_{i-1}), \tag{3.5}$$

where T_i is the operator on the right hand side of equation (3.3). More precisely, for $t \in \{0, 1, \dots, T-1\}$ and $f : S \to R$, we define T_t by

$$T_t(f)(x) = \max_{c \in C} \{ u(x, c) + \beta E_t(f(x')|x, c) \}, \tag{3.6}$$

where the conditional expectation is over $x' \sim Q_t(\cdot|x, c)$. For a given function f, this defines a new function $T_t(f)$ by giving the value of the new

Table 3.1 Profit.

	$c = 0$	$c = 1$
$x = 0$	7	4
$x = 1$	11	7

Table 3.2 $P(x_{t+1} = 1 | x_t, c_t)$.

	$c_t = 0$	$c_t = 1$
$x_t = 0$	.1	.85
$x_t = 1$	.5	.85

function at the arbitrary point $x \in S$. In other words, T_t maps functions to functions, and we shall occasionally work explicitly with the domain and codomain, both function spaces, and accordingly write the functionality as $T_t : B_{t-1} \rightarrow B_t$. In this chapter, with discrete states, our functions can be represented as points in $R^{|S|}$; this is generalized in chapter 6. It is now clear that the equation $V_t = T_t (V_{t-1})$ is a restatement of the optimality principle. In the alternative nonrecursive form we can define the value function for the T-period problem as

$$V_{T-1}(x) = T_{T-1} \circ T_{T-2} \circ \cdots \circ T_1(V_0), \qquad (3.7)$$

where $\circ$ denotes composition of operators.

The calculations above are simple and can be done straightforwardly using, for example, a spreadsheet program. We illustrate using the marketing example from chapter 2. Here, the state variable is a level of demand $x \in \{0, 1\}$, and the control variable is a marketing decision $c \in \{0, 1\}$. The profit function is given in table 3.1.

A heuristic backward recursion argument together with a trivial transition distribution was used to obtain the solution for the two-period problem in chapter 2. Here, we make the problem a little more interesting and realistic by specifying the transition distribution in table 3.2.

Thus, when demand is low, it is unlikely that it will increase without the marketing effort; when demand is high and marketing efforts are 0, the next period's demand states are equiprobable; in either case marketing improves the probability of the next period's demand being high to .85. Discounting the future at $\beta = .75$, we calculate the value functions and optimal policies by backward recursion for the 1- through 10-period problems and report the results in table 3.3.

In the one-, two-, and three-period problems it is never optimal to run the marketing campaign. In the four-period problem, it is optimal to run the

Table 3.3 Value Functions and Optimal Policies.

t	$V_t(0)$	$V_t(1)$	$c_t(0)$	$c_t(1)$
0	7	11	0	0
1	12.55	17.75	0	0
2	16.8025	22.3625	0	0
3	20.14638	25.686875	1	0
4	22.64185	28.18746875	1	0
5	24.51672	30.06099453	1	0
6	25.92201	31.46664274	1	0
7	26.97621	32.52074664	1	0
8	27.7668	33.31135928	1	0
9	28.35976	33.90430964	1	0

marketing program in the initial period if the state of demand is low. This makes sense; it is optimal to try to shock the system into the fairly persistent high-demand state and then abandon the marketing investment. In the longer problems, it is optimal to run the marketing program if demand is low and the remaining horizon is greater than three periods. It is never optimal to run the marketing program during high-demand periods.

3.2 SOLVING DP PROBLEMS: INFINITE HORIZON

We now restrict our attention to the case of transition distributions depending only on the current state and control, i.e., to the Markov case. The infinite-horizon problem is appealing for two reasons: It is a good approximation to the finite-horizon case when the number of periods is large, and it is typically much easier to solve and estimate. The latter property is due to the existence of a stationary optimal policy, that is, a policy function $c(x)$ used at every period. Note that the finite-horizon example above has a policy function $c_t(x)$ that depends on the number of periods left.

In the infinite-horizon dynamic programming framework, backward recursion is obviously impossible. However, forward recursion remains an appealing approach. Since it no longer makes sense to index value functions backward from the terminal period, we index forward from the current period (0) in the infinite-horizon case. Define the value function $V_0(x)$ as the present discounted reward from following an optimal policy into the infinite future:

$$V_0(x) = \max_\pi E_0 \sum_{t=0}^{\infty} \beta^t u(x_t, c_t), \qquad (3.8)$$

where $\pi = (\pi_0, \pi_1, \ldots)$ is a sequence of policy functions. Breaking out the current and future gains,

$$V_0(x) = \max_{\pi} \left\{ u(x_0, c_0) + E_0 \sum_{t=1}^{\infty} \beta^t u(x_t, c_t) \right\}$$

$$= \max_{c \in C} \left\{ u(x_0, c_0) + E_0 \max_{\pi'} \sum_{t=1}^{\infty} \beta^t u(x_t, c_t) \right\}, \qquad (3.9)$$

where $\pi' = (\pi_1, \pi_2, \ldots)$ is a sequence of policy functions beginning one period in the future. But note that the term inside the expectation is just β times $V_0(x)$, suggesting that we can drop the subscript and write $V(x) = \max_{c \in C} \{u(x, c) + \beta EV(x')\}$, where x' is the next period's state. Note that the expectation operator E depends on the current state and control through the transition distribution; i.e., $EV(x')$ is shorthand for $E(V(x')|x, c)$ here. In fact, this approach works.

THEOREM 2 *The optimal value function $V(x)$ satisfies the functional equation*

$$V(x) = \max_{c \in C} \{u(x, c) + \beta EV(x')\}. \qquad (3.10)$$

Proof. Consider an arbitrary policy a that may be randomized and chooses c in the current period with probability p_c. Then

$$V_a(x) = \sum_{c \in C} p_c \left\{ u(x, c) + \beta EV_a(x') \right\}$$

$$\leq \sum_{c \in C} p_c \left\{ u(x, c) + \beta EV(x') \right\}$$

$$\leq \max_{c \in C} \left\{ u(x, c) + \beta EV(x') \right\}, \qquad (3.11)$$

and specifically $V(x) \leq \max_{c \in C} \{u(x, c) + \beta EV(x')\}$. Now consider another policy a' that chooses the optimal control ($\pi_0 = c_0(x_0)$) in the current period and then continues the policy a' into the future. Choose the future control policies a' such that $V_{a'}(x) \geq V(x) - \varepsilon$. Then $V_{a'}(x) = u(x, c(x)) + \beta EV_{a'}(x') \geq u(x, c(x)) + \beta EV(x') - \beta \varepsilon$, which implies

$$V(x) \geq \max_{c \in C} \{u(x, c) + \beta EV(x') - \beta \varepsilon\}, \qquad (3.12)$$

and the result follows.   □

The functional equation (3.10) is referred to as the *optimality equation* or *Bellman's equation*.

THEOREM 3 $V(x)$ *is the unique bounded solution to the optimality equation.*

Proof. Suppose $W(x)$ is a bounded solution to the optimality equation $W(x) = \max_{c \in C}\{u(x, c) + \beta EW(x')\}$ and that the current period policy associated with $W(x)$ is $c_w(x)$. Then

$$W(x) - V(x) = u(x, c_w(x)) + \beta E_w W(x') - \max_{c \in C}\{u(x, c) + \beta EV(x')\}$$

$$\leq \beta E_w(W(x') - V(x'))$$

$$\leq \beta \sup_{x \in S} |W(x) - V(x)|. \tag{3.13}$$

Running the argument with W and V interchanged shows that $V(x) - W(x) \leq \beta \sup_{x \in S} |V(x) - W(x)|$, so $|V(x) - W(x)| \leq \beta \sup_{x \in S} |V(x) - W(x)|$ for each value of x and hence $\sup_{x \in S} |V(x) - W(x)| \leq \beta \sup_{x \in S} |V(x) - W(x)|$, which implies that the difference is zero since $\beta < 1$. $\quad\square$

Let π be the stationary policy $\pi = (c(x), c(x), \ldots)$, where $c(x)$ is a policy that selects c to maximize $\{u(x, c) + \beta EV(x')\}$, the right hand side of the optimality equation. Then $c(x)$ is an optimal policy and $V_\pi(x) = V(x)$, the value function. To see this, note that $c(x)$ is optimal in the two-period problem, which has $V(x')$ as the final period payout, $V(x) = \max_{c \in C}\{u(x, c) + \beta EV(x')\} = u(x, c(x)) + \beta EV(x')$. But $V(x')$ is just the value in another two-period problem with initial state x' and payout $V(x'')$, and $c(x)$ is also optimal in that problem. Iterating the argument shows that

$$V(x) = E_0 \sum_{t=0}^{T} \beta^t u(x_t, c(x_t)) + \beta^{T+1} E_0 V(x_{T+1}), \tag{3.14}$$

where the policy $c(x)$ maximizes the value of the first term. Letting $T \to \infty$ and using the boundedness of V proves the result.

Define the operator $\mathcal{T}$ by

$$\mathcal{T}f(x) = \max_{c \in C}\{u(c, x) + \beta Ef(x')\} \tag{3.15}$$

by analogy with (3.6) and note that $\mathcal{T}$ need not be subscripted with t. Then the optimality equation can be written $V = \mathcal{T}V$, and we have seen that V is the unique bounded solution to this operator equation.

3.2.1 The Method of Successive Approximation

The value function solving the optimality equation can be computed as the limit of T-period finite-horizon value functions as $T \to \infty$. Let

Table 3.4 Value Function Iterations.

t	$V_t(0)$	$V_t(1)$	$c_t(0)$	$c_t(1)$
45	30.13856	35.68311	1	0
46	30.13857	35.68313	1	0
47	30.13858	35.68314	1	0
48	30.13859	35.68314	1	0
49	30.13860	35.68315	1	0

$V_0(x) = \max_{c \in C} u(x, c)$, the value in the one-period problem. Note that $V_1 = \max\{u(x, c) + \beta EV_0\} = \mathcal{T}V_0$ is the value function for the two-period problem, where $\mathcal{T}$ is the operator defined in (3.15). Then

$$V_T(x) = \max_{c \in C} \{u(x, c) + \beta EV_{T-1}(x)\}$$

$$= \mathcal{T}V_{T-1} = \mathcal{T}^T V_0 \qquad (3.16)$$

has the interpretation of the value of the $(T + 1)$-period problem with final-period state-dependent reward $V_0(x)$. We have the following theorem.

THEOREM 4 $V_T(x) - V(x) \to 0$ as $T \to \infty$.

Proof. The infinite-horizon value can be written $V(x) = V_T(x) + \beta^{T+1} EV(x_{T+1})$, where the expectation conditions on the current state. Thus, $V(x) \le V_T(x) + \beta^{T+1} B/(1 - \beta)$, where B is the least upper bound of $|u(x, c)|$. Similarly, $V(x)$ must be greater than the value associated with the policy that is optimal for T periods and thereafter arbitrary, so $V(x) \ge V_T(x) - \beta^{T+1} B/(1 - \beta)$ since $u(x, c)$ is bounded below by $-B$. Putting these together we have

$$|V_T(x) - V(x)| \le \beta^{T+1} B/(1 - \beta), \qquad (3.17)$$

yielding the desired result. □

To illustrate we consider table 3.3, giving the value function for the $T = 1, \ldots, 10$ period problems in the marketing example from chapter 2, and add the results in table 3.4 for the 46- through 50-period problems.

Here, the value function iterations are identical to six digits—the improvements in the calculations are only relative changes of order 10^{-7}. Note, however, that the policy function appears to have converged much more rapidly. This is frequently the case in discrete state/control models. It is much easier to determine a map from one finite set to another than it is to determine the exact value of a real vector (precisely, the value to a given small tolerance; exactness is not achievable on a computer). This has led to consideration of policy improvement algorithms.

3.2.2 The Method of Policy Iteration

Let a be a stationary policy with associated expected return $V_a(x)$. Typically, this would be a policy with an expected return that is easy to calculate. In general, the value function V_a can be characterized as the solution to $T_a V_a = V_a$, where the operator $T_a V_a = u(x, c_a(x)) + \beta E V_a(x')$. This operator differs from T in (3.15) in the absence of the maximization operator. Our previous results imply that V_a can be calculated by repeatedly applying the operator T_a to the final period reward $u(x, c_a(x))$. Then let b be the stationary policy that maximizes $u(x, c_b(x)) + \beta E V_a(x')$, where the expectation is taken using the transition distribution corresponding to $c_b(x)$. The resulting function is $T_b V_a$. Then, clearly $V_b(x) \geq V_a(x)$. To see this, note that $T_b V_a \geq V_a$; iterating, we have that $T_b^T V_a \geq V_a$, and taking limits, $V_b \geq V_a$. If $T V_a = V_a$, then $V_a = V$ and the policy a is optimal.

The method of policy improvement is

(a) Begin with a policy a.
(b) Calculate the associated value function by solving

$$V_a(x) = u(x, c_a(x)) + \beta E V_a(x')$$

for $V_a(x)$. Note that this is a linear system; V_a is a $|S|$-vector and E can be represented by the transition matrix P_a depending on the policy a; the solution is $V_a = (I - \beta P_a)^{-1} u_a$, where the components of the vector u_a are $u(x, c_a(x))$. Note that P_a is a Markov transition matrix and hence has a maximum eigenvalue equal to 1 and $\beta \in [0, 1)$, so the inverse exists and can indeed be represented as the infinite series $\Sigma_{t=0}^{\infty} \beta^t P_a^t$.
(c) Given the value function $V_a(x)$, calculate a new policy b so that b maximizes $u(x, c_b(x)) + \beta E V_a(x')$.
(d) Go back to (a) with b substituting for a. Stop when the value functions do not change.

Policy iteration often converges quickly in practice, especially in discrete control problems. It can be shown that policy iteration is equivalent to using Newton's method to solve $(I - T)V = 0$, and hence convergence is quadratic in the number of iterations.

To calculate the value function in our marketing example, we note that the policy function converged after four iterations (table 3.3). A little consideration shows that if $c_t(0) = 1$ for some t, then it will also equal 1 for all greater t (longer horizons). Further, $c_t(1)$ will always be 0. The real question is whether $c_t(0) = 1$ for some t or whether $c_t(0) = 0$ forever. That is, does the stationary optimal policy in the infinite-horizon policy have $c(0) = 1$ or $c(0) = 0$? Once we have seen that the $c(0) = 1$ policy is optimal, we can calculate the value function $V(x)$ directly by solving the linear

Table 3.5 Policy and Transition Information.

Policy Information			Transition Information		
	$c = 0$	$c = 1$		$x_{t+1} = 0$	$x_{t+1} = 1$
$x = 0$	0	$n(x = 0)$	$x_t = 0$	$n_x(00)$	$n_x(01)$
$x = 1$	$n(x = 1)$	0	$x_t = 1$	$n_x(10)$	$n_x(11)$

system $(I - \beta P_a)V = u_a$, where a indexes the $c(0) = 1, c(1) = 0$ policy. The result agrees with the 50-period value iteration to the number of
places reported in table 3.4 (seven digits) but can be calculated as soon as it
is clear that the policy function has been determined. To test whether this is
indeed the solution we ask whether it also satisfies the optimality equation
$V(x) = \max_{c \in C}\{u(x, c) + \beta EV(x')\}$. It does.

In the finite state/control case there are only finitely many stationary policies. Thus, once we have established that a stationary policy is optimal, there
is no issue of the existence of an optimal policy. One (at least) exists and can
be found in finite time.

Our discussion provides the background for computation of the value
function and associated policy functions. Our goal is merely to show that
these things can be computed and to sketch the basic ideas and properties
of algorithms. The computational aspects of solving dynamic programming
problems have in fact been studied in detail. Often problems have a special
structure that can be exploited. Even without the special structure, improved
methods are available.

3.3 IDENTIFICATION: A PREVIEW

A central identification issue can be easily illustrated in the context of the
marketing example. This issue will be pursued in detail in chapter 4. The
basic result is that a discrete state/control model can only determine parameters within certain ranges. More information is required in order to determine some of the economically interesting parameters. The information is
sometimes introduced in specification, and we will consider this possibility
in chapter 4.

Consider the data sequence $\{x_t, c_t\}_{t=0}^T$ generated by the optimal policy in
the marketing example. The data can be summarized in two tables reflecting the within-period information on the control rule and the intertemporal
information on the transitions (table 3.5). Here, $n(x = j)$ is the number of
time periods t the state variable x_t is observed in state j and $n_x(jk)$ is the
number of observed transitions from state j to state k.

The transition distribution can clearly be estimated at the optimal policy. Note that the components of the transition distribution at other values of the policy contribute to determination of the optimal policy. Information on these transition probabilities is available only through observation of the optimal policy and any restrictions implied by the functional equation, which depends on alternative transition probabilities and characterizes the optimal policy. This relationship is subtle, and we will set it aside for purposes of this example by simply assuming that the transition distribution is known.

Returns $u(x, c)$ may also be observed, in which case the components of the return function corresponding to the optimal policy can be estimated. The other components of the return function, corresponding to state/control configurations never observed, can be identified only through restrictions implied by the optimality equation. Again, the functional equation depends on alternative rewards and characterizes the optimal policy. We will set this aside as well, by assuming that the reward function is known.

The only remaining unknown parameter is the discount factor β. Suppose we observe the entire infinite sequence $\{x_t, c_t\}_{t=0}^{\infty}$ so that any parameter that can be estimated consistently is known. What can be said about β? Not much. We have seen (table 3.3) that the policy $c(0) = 1; c(1) = 0$ is optimal for $\beta = .75$. It is obviously optimal for any larger value of β. What about smaller values? It turns out that this policy is optimal for $\beta \geq .7143$ (approximately), and the policy of $c(0) = c(1) = 0$ is optimal for smaller values of the discount factor. Thus, the most we can expect the data to tell us is whether $\beta \geq .7143$ or not. Of course, β is a continuous parameter with parameter space $[0,1)$, but all we will be able to tell from the data is which of the sets $\{[0,.7143), [.7143,1)\}$ the parameter β is in.

This feature of finite state/control dynamic programming models, that continuous parameters are identified only up to ranges in the parameter space, is ubiquitous and not specific to our example. The situation is not completely hopeless. Of course, continuous parameters corresponding to transition probabilities at the observed policy are typically identified. Similarly, if rewards are observed, rewards corresponding to state/control combinations given by the optimal policy are typically identified. It is the parameters that must be identified through the restriction imposed by the functional equation that are typically underidentified.

Note that the above analysis applies to observations generated by a single decision maker over time or to panel data on many decision makers following the optimal policy. Panel data do not help.

Observations on the finite-horizon control policy are more informative. Here, the policy is not stationary, and information on how the horizon changes the policy is informative. However, identification is not possible— instead, we increase the number of intervals to which we can assign β. With

$\beta = .75$, we saw that the policy $c(0) = 1$ and $c(1) = 0$ is optimal if the horizon is four periods or longer (table 3.3). At $\beta = .72$ that policy is optimal if the horizon is five periods or longer. At $\beta = .715$, optimality requires seven periods or longer, at $\beta = .7145$ it requires eight periods or longer, etc. Thus, if we observe panel data on decision makers and we know their horizons, we can isolate the horizon at which the policy shifts. In this case, it is possible to use the optimality equation to narrow the range of possible β consistent with the policy. But it remains impossible to identify β more closely than an interval.

3.4 EXERCISES

1. Verify that the optimal policy for the marketing example with an infinite horizon satisfies the optimality equation.

2. Consider finding the value function for the finite state/control problem by listing the policies and testing them in order until a policy is found to satisfy the optimality equation. Does this method work? How can it be improved (consider the order in which policies are tested)?

3. Start with the policy $c(0) = c(1) = 0$ in the marketing example with an infinite horizon and complete one iteration in the policy improvement algorithm. What happens as you iterate longer?

3.5 REFERENCES

Blackwell (1962, 1965) and Maitra (1968) provide the foundations for the modern approach to dynamic programming. Bhattacharya and Majumdar (1989a,b) give a concise development, including coverage of average-reward criteria in cases of unbounded objective functions. Computation is covered by Bertsekas (1976). Puterman and Brumelle (1979) show the equivalence between policy iteration and Newton's method (see also Puterman (1994) for a survey). More recently, Rust (1994, 1997) treats computational issues. Chow and Tsitsiklis (1989) treat complexity, including dependence on the discount factor β. Judd (1998) discusses computational issues in economics generally, as well as in the context of dynamic programming. In the finite state/control case, computation is not as problematic as in the continuous state case discussed below in chapter 6. The treatment of estimation and identification is a relatively new area. Key contributions are made by Rust (1987a).

Chapter Four

Likelihood Functions for Discrete State/Control Models

We begin with the likelihood function in the simplest case: a single binary state and a single binary control variable in a stationary infinite-horizon problem. This case, while simple, illustrates properties that are general. In the case of accurate observations, the control is a deterministic function of the state, and hence the control policy can be taken as known after a small sample is realized (specifically, after both possible values of the state are realized). Of course, in many applications this would be unrealistic, in part because the model is just a model and does not purport to be an exact description of the world, but the setup is still a useful starting point for considering identification issues. In a sense, this is a situation of maximal information. If a parameter is not identified in this setting, it is hard to argue that additional data information somehow appears when the setting is generalized.

After treating the simple case, we show that the notation and techniques extend to the general discrete model. Then we consider extensions allowing measurement error and imperfect control. Identification issues are treated in detail. Parameters are split into two groups: those that relate to the transition distribution at the optimal policy and those composed of utility, discount factor, and transition probabilities for nonobserved transitions. Continuous parameters apart from the transition distribution parameters are typically unidentified. They are restricted to lie only in certain ranges in the parameter space, even asymptotically. The results from our marketing example in chapter 3 are general.

4.1 LIKELIHOOD WITH COMPLETE OBSERVABILITY

We focus on the infinite-horizon problem

$$V(x) = \max_{\pi} E \sum_{t=0}^{\infty} \beta^t u(x_t, c_t), \qquad (4.1)$$

Table 4.1 Transition Probabilities.

	$c_t = 0$		$c_t = 1$	
$x_t = 0$	$p_{00}(0)$	$p_{01}(0)$	$p_{00}(1)$	$p_{01}(1)$
$x_t = 1$	$p_{10}(0)$	$p_{11}(0)$	$p_{10}(1)$	$p_{11}(1)$

where the expectation is over a Markov transition distribution $p(x_t|x_{t-1}, c_{t-1})$ and hence the optimal policy $(c(x), c(x), \ldots)$ is stationary or, equivalently,

$$V(x) = \max_{c \in C}\{u(x, c) + \beta E V(x')\}. \tag{4.2}$$

The observables are the state sequence $\{x_r\}_{r=0}^{T}$ and the control sequence $\{c_r\}_{r=0}^{T}$, with x_r and c_r in $\{0,1\}$. We assume that the reward sequence is not observed (this will be treated later). The state transition probabilities are state- and control-dependent. Thus, we have table 4.1.

In table 4.1, $p_{ab}(c)$ is the probability of a transition from a to b when the period-t control is c. Given the adding up constraints $p_{a0}(c) + p_{a1}(c) = 1$, there are four transition probabilities in the model. The policy function $c(x)$ is a pair $(c(0), c(1)) \in \{0, 1\} \times \{0, 1\} = \{00, 01, 10, 11\}$. There are four possible policy functions, of which only two are interesting since in the other cases the policy does not depend on the states.

Given the period-0 values of the state and control, the period-1 distribution conditional on parameter vector θ is $p(x_1, c_1|x_0, c_0, \theta)$. Now, this is a singular distribution, in that c_t is a deterministic function of x_t for any t and in particular for $t = 0$ and 1. This important point has several implications. First, it suffices to condition on one of x or c; we choose to condition on x. Second, the distribution of x and c given parameters is completely described by the distribution of x alone. Nevertheless, the information given by c in addition to x in the likelihood function is enormous. In fact, the deterministic relation between c and x is learned with certainty as soon as the different values of x are seen in the data. Thus, parameters that enter only through the deterministic relation between c and x are learned rapidly if they are identified.

We proceed by conditioning. Let x, x' and c, c' refer to current and one-period-ahead values of the state and control, respectively. For the present, we suppress dependence on the parameter vector θ. Then

$$\begin{aligned} p(x', c'|x, c) &= p(x'|x, c)p(c'|x', x, c) \\ &= p(x'|x)p(c'|x', x) \\ &= p(x'|x)p(c'|x') \end{aligned} \tag{4.3}$$

Table 4.2 Sequence Indexing.

i	Sequence
0	000
1	001
2	010
3	011
4	100
5	101
6	110
7	111

since there is no point in conditioning on c as well as x and since c' is a deterministic function of x' and hence x is irrelevant for c' given x'. The second factor is just $I(c' = c(x', \theta))$, where I is the indicator function and θ has been reinserted here for emphasis: Given θ, the policy function can be calculated, and this factor of the distribution easily evaluated. The likelihood function is

$$L(\theta, x_r, c_r, r = 1, \ldots, T) = \prod_{r=1}^{T} p(x_r | x_{r-1}, \theta) p(c_r | x_r, \theta)$$

$$= \prod_{r=1}^{T} p(x_r | x_{r-1}, \theta) \prod_{r=1}^{T} p(c_r | x_r, \theta). \quad (4.4)$$

Since the second factor is zero for values of θ inconsistent with the data and the first term is positive, only values consistent with the data have positive likelihood. As a practical matter, it is useful to check early on whether there exists any parameter value consistent with the data. In many cases, using this simple specification, there will not be, and hence the model is rejected and must be modified. However, this is a good place to begin the study of identification.

Suppose we have a sample of size T, indexed by subscripts $r, s, t \in \{0, \ldots, T - 1\}$. Consider the state sequence $\{x_t\}_{t=0}^{T-1}$. There are 2^T such sequences. Arrange these sequences in lexicographic order and index them by $i, j, k \in \{0, \ldots, 2^T - 1\}$. Then the ith sequence is the binary expansion of i. This is a convenient way of thinking about the problem. Our random variable is now i, the position of the realized sequence. Table 4.2 illustrates for the case $T = 3$.

Elements of the sequences are indexed by r, s, t. Let $\xi(i, s)$ be the sth digit in the binary expansion of i. Let $\kappa(i, r) = \xi(i, r) \| \xi(i, r + 1)$ be the rth pair of digits in the binary expansion of i.

The parameters entering $p(x'|x)$ are the transition probabilities corresponding to the optimal policy. We write these p_{ab}, $a, b \in \{0, 1\}$ without an argument to select the appropriate pieces from table 4.1. Thus, there are two probabilities to be estimated. Of course, there could be restrictions relating these probabilities. Further, knowledge of the optimal policy could restrict the values of these probabilities (for example, if these were the only parameters and the optimal policy was known). However, the restricted estimators can usually be written as functions of the unrestricted, and the unrestricted maximum likelihood estimator (MLE) is easy to obtain. We will set aside consideration of these issues for the moment. The likelihood function corresponding to the first factor in (4.4) is

$$p(i|x_0) = \prod_{r=1}^{T-1} p_{\kappa(i,r)}. \tag{4.5}$$

Introducing the notation $N\kappa(i, ab) = \Sigma_{r=1}^{T-1} I(\kappa(i, r) = ab)$, the number of ab pairs in the ith sequence, we have

$$p(i|x_0) = \prod_{a,b} p_{ab}^{N\kappa(i,ab)}, \qquad a, b \in \{0, 1\}. \tag{4.6}$$

Taking logarithms and writing $p_{a1} = 1 - p_{a0}$ yields

$$l(p_{00}, p_{10}|i, x_0) = N\kappa(i, 00) \ln p_{00} + N\kappa(i, 01) \ln(1 - p_{00})$$
$$+ N\kappa(i, 10) \ln p_{10} + N\kappa(i, 11) \ln(1 - p_{10}), \tag{4.7}$$

and the maximum likelihood estimators

$$\hat{p}_{a0} = \frac{N\kappa(i, a0)}{N\kappa(i, a0) + N\kappa(i, a1)}, \qquad a \in \{0, 1\}. \tag{4.8}$$

The step of taking logarithms is justified only where the probability is positive, that is, for values of p_{a0} consistent with the control rule. This important point is illustrated below.

Consider the marketing example of chapter 3. This is a two-state, two-control problem. In chapter 3, the focus was on solving the dynamic program; here, we consider estimation. First, suppose the only unknown parameter is the transition probability p_{00}. Suppose we have a sample of length T and that in this sample each value of x is observed at least once. Then the control rule $c(x) = (c(0), c(1))$ is known. In evaluating the likelihood, only values of the parameter p_{00} consistent with the observed state/control sequence and the hypothesis of optimization are considered (the likelihood is zero for other values of the parameter). How does knowledge of the control rule constrain the value of p_{00}? With the utility function

Table 4.3 Profit; $P(x_{t+1} = 1|x_t, c_t)$.

Profit			$P(x_{t+1} = 1\|x_t, c_t)$		
	$c = 0$	$c = 1$		$c_t = 0$	$c_t = 1$
$x = 0$	7	4	$x_t = 0$	.1	.85
$x = 1$	11	7	$x_t = 1$	.5	.85

and transition distributions given in table 4.3 and with discount factor .75, we found in chapter 3 that the optimal policy in the infinite-horizon problem is $c(x) = (c(0), c(1)) = (1, 0)$. Here, the value of p_{00}, the zero-to-zero transition probability corresponding to $c = 1$, is $1 - .85 = .15$. Clearly, there are other values of this transition probability for which $c = (1, 0)$ is also optimal. For example, any smaller value would leave the optimal policy unchanged—the purpose of the marketing campaign is to shock the system into the high-demand state, so if this becomes easier, it must still be optimal. In other words, the value associated with running the campaign is increased for a higher zero-to-one transition probability (and hence a lower zero-to-zero value of our parameter). Hence, if it is optimal to run the campaign for $p_{00} = .15$, it must also be optimal for any smaller value. In fact, $c = (1, 0)$ is optimal for $p_{00} \le .20 = r$.

Thus, once the control rule is known to be $c = (1, 0)$ (i.e., after each value of the state variable has been seen), the information contained in the likelihood factor corresponding to $\Pi_t p(c_t|x_t)$ is exactly that $p_{00} \in [0, r]$. This information is in one sense extremely precise. It is accumulated quickly (this is not a $T \to \infty$ result), and it completely rules out a portion of the natural parameter space [0,1]. It is in another sense extremely imprecise. The exact value of the parameter p_{00} cannot be estimated on the basis of the information in the control rule—only bounded into an interval. There is no more information in the relevant likelihood factor even as $T \to \infty$. The situation is identical to that discussed in chapter 3 relative to estimation of the discount factor β. The difference here is that there is additional information on p_{00} available through the first factor in the likelihood function (4.4), corresponding to transition information. We turn now to this factor:

$$L(p_{00}|i, x_0) = N\kappa(i, 00) \ln p_{00} + N\kappa(i, 01) \ln(1 - p_{00}), \qquad (4.9)$$

which can be maximized subject to the constraint $p_{00} \le r$ obtained from the second factor (the control rule). The Lagrangian is

$$L(p_{00}|i, x_0) = N\kappa(i, 00) \ln p_{00} + N\kappa(i, 01) \ln(1 - p_{00}) + \lambda(r - p_{00}),$$
$$\qquad (4.10)$$

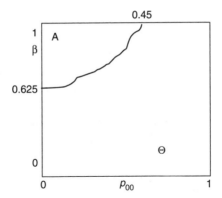

Figure 4.1 Parameters Consistent with Observed Control.

where λ is a Lagrange multiplier, the Kuhn-Tucker conditions require

$$N\kappa(i, 00)/p_{00} - N\kappa(i, 01)/(1 - p_{00}) - \lambda = 0,$$
$$r - p_{00} \geq 0,$$
$$\lambda(r - p_{00}) = 0, \tag{4.11}$$

and the solution possibilities are clearly either $\hat{\lambda} = 0$ and $\hat{p}_{cml} = \hat{p}_{ml}$ or $\hat{p}_{cml} = r$ and $\hat{\lambda} = N\kappa(i, 00)/r - N\kappa(i, 01)/(1 - r)$. A significant nonzero value for $\hat{\lambda}$ indicates that the transition information is inconsistent with the control information and that the model is therefore likely misspecified. This point is pursued later. For the present, assume that the unconstrained MLE satisfies the constraint.

In chapter 3 we saw informally that the discount factor was not identified by knowledge of the control rule, even when all other parameters including the transition probabilities were known. The parameter was bounded to an interval. In fact, the transition information is informative on the discount factor β, in that the boundary of the interval containing feasible estimates of β depends on the transition probabilities. We consider the case $\theta = (p_{00}, \beta)$: an unknown discount factor and transition probability. Here, the natural parameter space is $\Theta = [0, 1] \times [0, 1)$. As soon as the control rule is observed, this can be narrowed. Specifically, in our example with the observed control rule $c = (1, 0)$, the parameter space consistent with the observed control rule is $A \subset \Theta$, illustrated in figure 4.1.

This is all of the parameter information contained in the control rule.

Turning now to the transition information on the two parameters, the log likelihood is

$$L(p_{00}, \beta | i, x_0) = N\kappa(i, 00) \ln p_{00} + N\kappa(i, 01) \ln (1 - p_{00}), \tag{4.12}$$

to be maximized subject to the constraint from the control rule that $\theta \in A$. Note that this portion of the log likelihood does not depend on the discount factor β at all. Consequently, the constraint is once again in the form $p_{00} \leq r$ and can be imposed as above. Once again, the estimator will satisfy the constraint asymptotically if the model is well specified, and if the unconstrained estimator does not satisfy the constraint, the significance of the estimate of the Lagrange multiplier can be used as the basis of a specification test. Turning to the unconstrained estimator $\hat{p}_{00}$, we note that the transition information is informative about the discount factor β in that the interval in which β can lie and still be consistent with the known control rule depends on the value of $\hat{p}_{00}$.

Because of its particular structure, the model admits a local cut, in the sense of Christensen and Kiefer (1994a, 2000). Thus, second derivatives exist and ordinary estimation procedures for p_{00} apply in an interval for β. Marginal inference on p_{00} can be drawn from the transition distribution locally in β. Given $\hat{p}_{00}$, inference on β uses the control distribution, and the conditioning on $\hat{p}_{00}$ in the separate inference procedure is manifest as β is found to be in an interval that depends on the local cut $\hat{p}_{00}$.

Can a general result be obtained in the simple case with the control rule known? Suppose there are K state variables, the ith taking values in the discrete set $\mathbf{H}_i$ with cardinality $|\mathbf{H}_i| = H_i$, and C control variables, the jth taking values in the discrete set $\mathbf{J}_j$ with cardinality $|\mathbf{J}_j| = J_j$. The problem can be rewritten as a single discrete state/control model with the single state variable x taking $H = \Pi_i H_i$ values from the set $\mathbf{H}$ and the single control taking $J = \Pi_j J_j$ values from the set $\mathbf{J}$. The control rule is a map $c : \mathbf{H} \to \mathbf{J}$, a point in $\mathbf{L} = \mathbf{J}^H$, a finite set. Now write the control rule c as a function of the parameter θ, $c(x; \theta)$, where $\theta \in \Theta \subseteq R^k$. Regarded as a function of θ, we have $c : \Theta \to \mathbf{L}$. The identification question is whether we can map backward from knowledge of the control rule to the parameter θ, i.e., whether the map c is invertible. The general answer is no. Brouwer's theorem on the invariance of domain states that there is no homeomorphism between spaces of different dimensions. Thus, if the parameter space is even just an interval in R^1, there is no way to identify the unknown (in this case scalar) parameter from knowledge of the control rule (a point in a finite set). As we have seen, the parameter values can be bounded, but the parameter cannot be estimated without further information.

Further information comes from the transition distribution. There are H origin states and H destination states, hence H^2 transition probabilities less H from the adding-up constraint for a given value of the control rule. Since transitions are seen only under the optimal control, these are the only transition probabilities that can be estimated using transition data. Of course, the other transition probabilities enter the problem in determining the control rule. These can be estimated only from the control rule and hence can at best be bounded into an interval. The notation developed above generalizes easily. There are H^T possible sequences of states of length T. Arrange these sequences in lexicographic order and index them by $i, j, k \in \{0, \ldots, H^T - 1\}$. Then the ith sequence is the H-ary expansion of i. Let $\xi(i, s)$ be the sth digit in the H-ary expansion of i. Let $\kappa(i, r) = \xi(i, r)\|\xi(i, r + 1)$ be the rth pair of digits in the H-ary expansion of i. Finally, let $N\kappa(i, ab) = \Sigma_{r=1}^{T-1} I(\kappa(i, r) = ab)$, the number of ab pairs in the ith sequence (here a, b take on H distinct values). The log likelihood factors according to the origin state, so we have, for example, for origin state 0,

$$l(p_{0a}, a = 0, \ldots, H - 1|i, x_0) = \sum_{a=0}^{H-1} N\kappa(i, 0a) \ln p_{0a}, \qquad (4.13)$$

defined with the constraint $\Sigma_{a=0}^{H-1} p_{0a} = 1$. The model is clearly in the exponential family. The MLEs are

$$\hat{p}_{0a} = \frac{N\kappa(i, 0a)}{\sum_{a=0}^{H-1} N\kappa(i, 0a)} \qquad (4.14)$$

if these values are consistent with the observed control rule. Thus, $H(H-1)$ transition probabilities can be estimated from the transition data. Note, however, that a constraint here (e.g., some transitions are impossible, others are necessary, etc.) does not imply that there are degrees of freedom available for estimating utility function parameters. At most, these estimates can be used to refine the bounds on parameters imposed by knowledge of the control rule.

Although the model predicts that a given state should always be associated with the same control, and therefore the control rule is learned rapidly (as soon as each possible state has been observed once), the data rarely satisfy such a strong requirement. This is the curse of determinacy (chapter 2). The model, although stochastic, predicts a deterministic relationship between the state and the control. This is one of the major difficulties in applying dynamic programming models empirically. There are several approaches to modifying the model to be consistent with data not satisfying this deterministic constraint. The approaches are not equally successful.

4.2 MEASUREMENT ERROR

One natural approach to breaking the curse of determinacy is to allow for measurement error. The idea here is that the model is an accurate description

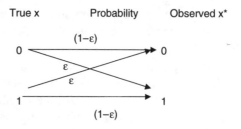

Figure 4.2 Measurement Error.

of behavior but that we are not measuring exactly the quantities entering the optimization problem. We first develop the appropriate notion of measurement for discrete models, working first with the binary situation as above. Then we consider in turn measurement error in the state and in the control. Finally, we consider the case of measurement error in both the state and the control. We find sensible specifications that do break the curse.

A simple specification for measurement error in a binary model is to allow a constant misclassification (crossover) probability ε. Letting x be the true state and x^* the observed state, the model for the measurement process is illustrated in figure 4.2.

Suppose x is a realization of a sequence from a Markov chain with transition probabilities p_{00}, $p_{01} = 1 - p_{00}$, p_{11} and $p_{10} = 1 - p_{11}$. Thus, trivially, $P(x_2 = 0 | x_1 = 0, x_0 = a) = p_{00} = P(x_2 = 0 | x_1 = 0)$. To check, note that $P(x_1 = 0 | x_0 = a) = p_{a0}$ and $P(x_2 = 0, x_1 = 0 | x_0 = a) = p_{a0} p_{00}$, and dividing gives the result. Suppose x^* is the sequence with measurement error, so that $x_t^* = x_t$ with probability $1 - \varepsilon$ and $x_t^* = 1 - x_t$ with probability ε. Let us calculate $P(x_2^* = 0 | x_1^* = 0, x_0^* = a)$. We begin by calculating $P(x_1^* = 0 | x_0^* = a)$. Note first that all $2 \times 2 = 4$ sequences of length 2 for the true state variables are consistent with observing the sequence $a0$. Thus,

$$P(x_1^* = 0 | x_0^* = a) = p_{a0}(1 - \varepsilon)^2 + p_{a1}(1 - \varepsilon)\varepsilon + p_{c0}\varepsilon(1 - \varepsilon) + p_{c1}\varepsilon^2,$$
$$(4.15)$$

where the index $c = 1 - a$. Next, calculate $P(x_2^* = 0, x_1^* = 0 | x_0^* = a)$. All 2^3 sequences are consistent with the observed pattern $a00$. The probability is thus the sum of eight terms. The term corresponding, for example, to the true sequence $a01$ is $p_{a0} p_{01}(1 - \varepsilon)^2 \varepsilon$, the probability that a process beginning in a is observed to be in a, $(1 - \varepsilon)$, times the probability of moving from a to 0, p_{a0}, multiplied by the probability of being observed correctly in the second period, $(1 - \varepsilon)$, times the probability of moving from 0 to 1 and being incorrectly observed in the final period ($p_{01}\varepsilon$). Upon adding these terms and dividing, we see that

$$P(x_2^* = 0 | x_1^* = 0, x_0^* = a) = P(x_2^* = 0, x_1^* = 0 | x_0^* = a) / P(x_1^* = 0 | x_0^* = a)$$
$$\neq P(x_2^* = 0 | x_1^* = 0). \tag{4.16}$$

Thus, the x^* process is not Markovian. This suggests a simple diagnostic before calculating estimates for a complex dynamic programming model, namely, examine the state sequence to see whether it looks Markovian. If not, either reformulate the state variable specification (sometimes the model can be made Markovian by an appropriate choice of the state variables) or consider the possibility of measurement error in the state variable.

To formulate the likelihood for the observed sequence x^*, we first calculate the probability of seeing x^* conditional on the actual underlying sequence x, then essentially marginalize with respect to x. This strategy is attractive since it is easy to calculate the probability of observing the x sequences—realizations from Markov processes. We have

$$p(x^*|i) = \prod_{t=1}^{T} \varepsilon^{|x_t^* - \xi(i,t)|} (1 - \varepsilon)^{1 - |x_t^* - \xi(i,t)|}, \tag{4.17}$$

the probability of observing the sequence x^* when the ith x sequence was actually realized (recall our convention on ordering the sequences). The probability of realizing the ith x sequence of length T is

$$p(i) = \prod_{r=1}^{T-1} p_{\kappa(i,r)}, \tag{4.18}$$

where $\kappa(i, r)$ is the rth pair of digits in the binary representation of i. Hence, the marginal probability of observing the measured sequence x^* is

$$p(x^*) = \sum_{i=0}^{2^T-1} \prod_{t=1}^{T} \varepsilon^{|x_t^* - \xi(i,t)|} (1 - \varepsilon)^{1 - |x_t^* - \xi(i,t)|} \prod_{r=1}^{T-1} p_{\kappa(i,r)}, \tag{4.19}$$

and in the absence of additional information, this would serve as the likelihood function for the unknown parameters $\theta = (p_{00}, p_{11}, \varepsilon)$.

There is, however, additional information in both the known control rule (given parameters) and the observed control sequence. Knowledge of the control rule, as we have seen, restricts the range of possible parameter estimators. Observation of the control sequence, however, is equivalent to observation of the true state sequence, given the parameters. The data series consists of the sequence c and the sequence x^*, with joint probability distribution

$$p(c, x^*) = \sum_x p(c, x, x^*)$$

$$= \sum_x p(c|x, x^*)p(x^*|x)p(x), \qquad (4.20)$$

conditioning on a value of the true sequence x and then marginalizing. This formulation is useful since $p(c|x) = p(c|x, x^*)$ is degenerate at $c = c(x)$, with $c(x)$ from the control rule (note that this function does depend on parameters). For simplicity, we treat here the 2×2 case with $c(x)$ invertible, noting that the results apply immediately to $K \times K$ models, and treat the noninvertible case below (this is the case with more state than control variables). Thus, the probability $p(c|x)$ is zero except for the ith sequence x, where the ith sequence satisfies $c_t = c(\xi(i, t))$. Hence,

$$p(c, x^*) = \prod_{t=1}^{T} \varepsilon^{|x_t^* - \xi(i,t)|}(1 - \varepsilon)^{1 - |x_t^* - \xi(i,t)|} \prod_{r=1}^{T-1} p_{\kappa(i,r)}. \qquad (4.21)$$

However, since the function $c(x)$ depends on unknown parameters through the optimization problem, so does i, by the condition $c_t = c(\xi(i, t))$. This is important: When the likelihood is evaluated at a different parameter value θ, it may require different i as well. The likelihood is thus only piecewise continuous in parameters, so some care must be taken in ensuring that the estimator $\hat{\theta}$ in fact corresponds to a global likelihood maximum. In fact, the control rule typically does not depend on the unknown parameter ε, which affects only observation of the data and does not enter the agent's optimization problem. Thus, we have an explicit solution for the maximizing value of ε given the other parameters, namely, $\hat{\varepsilon} = T^{-1} \Sigma_t |x_t^* - \xi(i(\theta), t)|$, with $i(\theta) = i(p_{00}, p_{11})$, the index of the x sequence satisfying $c = c(x; \theta)$, where the presence of parameters in this condition is now explicit for emphasis. This can be substituted back into the log likelihood

$$l(p_{00}, p_{11}, \varepsilon) = \sum_{t=1}^{T} \left\{ |x_t^* - \xi(i, t)| \ln(\hat{\varepsilon}) + (1 - |x_t^* - \xi(i, t)|) \ln(1 - \hat{\varepsilon}) \right\}$$

$$+ \sum_{r=1}^{T-1} \ln(p_{\kappa(i,r)}) \qquad (4.22)$$

to yield the profile log likelihood function

$$l(p_{00}, p_{11}|c, x^*) = \sum_{t=1}^{T} \left\{ |x_t^* - \xi(i, t)| \ln \left(T^{-1} \sum_s |x_s^* - \xi(i, s)| \right) \right.$$

$$+ (1 - |x_t^* - \xi(i, t)|) \ln \left(1 - T^{-1} \sum_s |x_s^* - \xi(i, s)| \right) \right\}$$

$$+ \sum_{r=1}^{T-1} \ln(p_{\kappa(i,r)})$$

$$= T(\hat{\varepsilon} \ln(\hat{\varepsilon}) + (1 - \hat{\varepsilon}) \ln(1 - \hat{\varepsilon})) + \sum_{r=1}^{T-1} \ln(p_{\kappa(i,r)}), \quad (4.23)$$

in which it must be emphasized that both $\hat{\varepsilon}$ and i depend on the parameters p_{00}, p_{11}. The final MLEs, $\hat{\theta} = (\hat{p}_{00}, \hat{p}_{11}, \hat{\varepsilon})$, will satisfy the implicit equation $\hat{p}_{ab} = N\kappa(i(\hat{\theta}), ab) / \Sigma_{ab} N\kappa(i(\hat{\theta}), ab)$ since in a neighborhood of $\hat{\theta}$ the first term in the profile log likelihood does not vary with (p_{00}, p_{11}).

Note that the curse of determinacy has been broken, in that the observed (c, x^*) pairs need not satisfy $c = c(x^*)$ for every observation. Thus, the data table does not have to be in the form of table 3.5. The extent to which this is not satisfied is used to estimate the crossover probability ε. Note also that ε does not enter the optimization problem and is not restricted by knowledge of the optimal control policy. The control rule is not learned quickly and with certainty as in the completely observed case.

Turning now to the case of measurement error in observation of the control, we allow misclassification with probability ε_c. With the state observed without error, the argument is analogous to the case of perfectly observed controls and states with measurement error. That is, observation of the states gives the controls deterministically as a function of parameters. The conditional distribution of the observed controls, given the state sequence is the ith, is

$$p(c^*|i) = \prod_s \varepsilon_c^{|c(\xi(i,s)) - c_s^*|} (1 - \varepsilon_c)^{1 - |c(\xi(i,s)) - c_s^*|}, \quad (4.24)$$

hence the joint distribution is

$$p(c^*, i) = \prod_s \varepsilon_c^{|c(\xi(i,s)) - c_s^*|} (1 - \varepsilon_c)^{1 - |c(\xi(i,s)) - c_s^*|} \prod_{r=1}^{T-1} p_{\kappa(i,r)}, \quad (4.25)$$

yielding the MLE $\hat{\varepsilon}_c = T^{-1} \Sigma_s |c(\xi(i, s)) - c_s^*|$. Note that the function $c(x)$ depends on the parameters (p_{00}, p_{11}) through the optimization problem, so this is the estimate of ε_c given these parameters. In this case, i does not depend on θ, so the case of measurement error in controls is simpler than that of measurement error in states. Once again, the profile log likelihood is easily obtained. It is

$$
\begin{aligned}
l(p_{00}, p_{11}|c^*, i) = \sum_s &\left\{ |c(\xi(i, s)) - c_s^*| \left(\ln(T^{-1} \sum_s |c(\xi(i, s)) - c_s^*|) \right) \right. \\
&\left. + (1 - |c(\xi(i, s)) - c_s^*|) \ln\left(1 - T^{-1} \sum_s |c(\xi(i, s)) - c_s^*|\right) \right\} \\
&+ \sum_r \ln(p_{\kappa(i,r)}) \\
= &\, T(\hat{\varepsilon}_c \ln(\hat{\varepsilon}_c) + (1 - \hat{\varepsilon}_c) \ln(1 - \hat{\varepsilon}_c)) + \sum \ln(p_{\kappa(i,r)}).
\end{aligned}
$$

$$(4.26)$$

Again, the dependence of $\hat{\varepsilon}_c$ on parameters is emphasized, although in the present case i is known. Nevertheless, $\hat{\varepsilon}_c$ and hence the profile log likelihood are discontinuous as a function of (p_{00}, p_{11}), since when probabilities are moved enough to change the control rule, this change is discrete.

The curse of determinacy is broken, in that the observed state/control sequence does not have to be degenerate. That is, the same state value can be associated with different observed controls without implying a breakdown of the statistical model. Further, it is not the case that the control rule is learned immediately after each state value has been realized—instead, information is accumulated over time.

Both specifications, measurement error in states and measurement error in controls, break the curse of determinacy. The curse of degeneracy (chapter 2) is still present, in that the model still predicts $p(c|x) \in \{0, 1\}$; imperfect observations of c or x simply make it a little more difficult to learn which. Thus, for data in which the summary statistics do not have the structure of table 3.5, i.e., for data in which the same state is associated at different time periods with different controls, one of these measurement error models might be appropriate. But they have different implications for observables, in that the observed sequence x is Markov, while x^* is not. Thus, as a practical matter, introducing measurement error in controls might be appropriate if the observed state sequence appears Markovian, and measurement error in states if it does not.

Finally, we turn to a specification with measurement error in both states and controls. Assume that the measurement errors in the states and the controls are independent, conditionally on the underlying realization of the process. Then

$$p(x^*, c^* | i) = p(x^* | i) p(c^* | i)$$

$$= \left(\prod_{t=1}^{T} \varepsilon^{|x_t^* - \xi(i,t)|} (1 - \varepsilon)^{1 - |x_t^* - \xi(i,t)|} \right)$$

$$\times \left(\prod_{s=1}^{T} \varepsilon_c^{|c(\xi(i,s)) - c_s^*|} (1 - \varepsilon_c)^{1 - |c(\xi(i,s)) - c_s^*|} \right)$$

$$= \prod_{t=1}^{T} \varepsilon^{|x_t^* - \xi(i,t)|} (1 - \varepsilon)^{1 - |x_t^* - \xi(i,t)|} \varepsilon_c^{|c(\xi(i,t)) - c_t^*|}$$

$$\times (1 - \varepsilon_c)^{1 - |c(\xi(i,t)) - c_t^*|}. \tag{4.27}$$

The marginal probability is $p(i) = \Pi_{r=1}^{T-1} p_{K(i,r)}$; multiplying and marginalizing gives

$$p(x^*, c^*) = \sum_{i=0}^{2^T - 1} \prod_{t=1}^{T} \varepsilon^{|x_t^* - \xi(i,t)|} (1 - \varepsilon)^{1 - |x_t^* - \xi(i,t)|} \varepsilon_c^{|c(\xi(i,t)) - c_t^*|}$$

$$\times (1 - \varepsilon_c)^{1 - |c(\xi(i,t)) - c_t^*|} p_{K(i,t)}, \tag{4.28}$$

leading to a likelihood function that is substantially more complicated than (4.21) and (4.25) in that it has 2^T terms and no simple closed forms for the estimators. Essentially, when either the state or the control is observed without error, then the other is known in the sense that it is a deterministic (although parameter-dependent) function of parameters. This is not the case when both are measured with error. Nevertheless, the likelihood function is not continuous in parameters. This is general since the controls make up a discrete set.

4.3 IMPERFECT CONTROL

Here we study a second approach to breaking the curse of determinacy. That is, we model a decision maker with imperfect control over the action he takes. Thus, the agent may know that $c = 0$ is optimal for $x = 0$ but may be able to achieve $c = 0$ only with high probability, not with certainty. This extension fits easily into our simple framework. The c variables, which the agent would like to control exactly but cannot, are $c \in \{0, 1\}$. Define the variables $a \in A = \{0, 1\}$ as the variables the agent actually can control; if $a = 0$ is chosen, then $c = 0$ with probability p_0; if $a = 1$, then $c = 0$ with probability p_1. Specify without loss of generality that $p_0 > p_1$, so that

Table 4.4 Profit; $P(x_{t+1} = 1|x_t, a_t)$.

	Profit			$P(x_{t+1} = 1\|x_t, a_t)$	
	$a = 0$	$a = 1$		$a_t = 0$	$a_t = 1$
$x = 0$	6.4	4.6	$x_t = 0$	.178	.700
$x = 1$	10.2	7.8	$x_t = 1$	.570	.780

$a = 0$ is the natural choice if the agent would prefer $c = 0$, etc. By choosing a, the agent chooses a probability distribution over the controls. Let p_a be the probability that $c = 0$ when action a is chosen. We can now apply the dynamic programming framework.

Define the new utility function

$$u^*(x, a) = E_a u(x, c) = p_a u(x, 0) + (1 - p_a)u(x, 1) \qquad (4.29)$$

and the new transition distribution

$$p^*(x'|x, a) = p(x'|x, c = 0)p_a + p(x'|x, c = 1)(1 - p_a). \qquad (4.30)$$

Then we can simply do dynamic programming using a as the control instead of c. The value function satisfies Bellman's equation

$$V_i(x) = \max_{a \in A}\{u^*(x, a) + \beta E_i^* V_{i-1}(x')\} \qquad (4.31)$$

in the finite-horizon case, and

$$V(x) = \max_{a \in A}\{u^*(x, a) + \beta E^* V(x')\} \qquad (4.32)$$

in the infinite-horizon case, where the conditional expectations are with respect to the new transition distribution (4.30). In our simple marketing example, the new utility function and transition distribution using $p_0 = .8$ and $p_1 = .2$ are shown in table 4.4 (compare tables 3.1 and 3.2). The first 10 value function iterations are shown in table 4.5 (compare table 3.3).

Here, we see that it is optimal to try to run the advertising policy in the low-demand period if the horizon is three or more periods (the exact control case required four or more). The policy has converged, though the value functions have not, and this is indeed the optimal policy in the infinite-horizon problem. The value function converges to (approximately) $V(0) = 29.11526$ and $V(1) = 34.21777$. Comparing the analysis of the information on β in learning the optimal policy, we see here that this policy, $(a(0), a(1)) = (1, 0)$, is optimal for $\beta > .6694$; in the perfect control case we found that $(c(0), c(1)) = (1, 0)$ was optimal for $\beta > .7143$. In contrast to the case with pure measurement error, introducing imperfect control changes the solution to the optimization problem. The lesson here is that observation error and imperfect control are quite different specifications.

Table 4.5 Value Functions and Optimal Policies: Imperfect Control.

t	$V_t(0)$	$V_t(1)$	$a_t(0)$	$a_t(1)$
0	6.4	10.2	0	0
1	11.7073	16.6245	0	0
2	15.96201	21.08258	1	0
3	19.2598	24.36055	1	0
4	21.72274	26.82542	1	0
5	23.57096	28.67345	1	0
6	24.95703	30.05954	1	0
7	25.99659	31.09909	1	0
8	26.77626	31.87876	1	0
9	27.36101	32.46351	1	0

The observables remain the $\{x, c\}_t$ sequence for $t = 0, \ldots, T$. Now, the state sequence x_t is observed without error, so we can concentrate on a single sequence (without marginalizing with respect to all possible sequences as in the case of measurement error in both states and controls). The sequence c_t is also observed without error, but it is no longer the control. The controls are the unobserved a_t. However, the observed c_t can be regarded as noisy observations on the actual controls a_t. Thus, an approach very similar to the approach in the case of measurement error can be used in developing this factor of the likelihood. Finally, note that there is more reduced-form information on the transition distribution in the case of imperfect control. That is, in the case of perfect control, even with measurement error, the only transitions observed are those corresponding to (x, c) pairs (the conditioning variables in the transition distribution) that are optimal. The other transition probabilities enter the likelihood only through their effect on the optimal policy. Without perfect control, transitions corresponding to all (x, c) pairs are observed without error and can be used to estimate the transition probabilities directly. Let us develop the likelihood:

$$p(x', c'|x, c) = p(c'|x, x', c)\,p(x'|x, c)$$
$$= p(c'|x')\,p(x'|x, c) \tag{4.33}$$

since the relation between the state and the control does not depend on lagged values, and neither does the measurement error. The first factor can be simplified to

$$p(c'|x') = \sum_{a'} p(c'|a', x')\,p(a'|x'), \tag{4.34}$$

where the sum is over all possible $\{a\}_t$ sequences. Note, however, that the term $p(a'|x')$ is degenerate, in that for given parameters there is only one a sequence corresponding to the realized states. Thus, all but one of these terms are 0 and hence

$$
\begin{aligned}
p(c'|x') &= p(c'|a', x') \\
&= p(c'|a') \tag{4.35}
\end{aligned}
$$

for that value of a' consistent with x' (and parameters). Let i be the index of the observed x sequence. Then

$$
p(c|i) = \prod_{s \in \{a(\xi(i,s))=0\}} p_0^{1-c_s}(1-p_0)^{c_s} \prod_{s \in \{a(\xi(i,s))=1\}} p_1^{c_s}(1-p_1)^{1-c_s}, \tag{4.36}
$$

and in the case where $p_0 = 1 - p_1$, as in our example, there is further simplification to

$$
p(c|i) = \prod_s p_0^{(1-|a(\xi(i,s))-c_s|)}(1-p_0)^{|a(\xi(i,s))-c_s|}, \tag{4.37}
$$

very like the first factor of the likelihood (4.25) in the measurement error case (the second factor is unaltered) but with one important difference. That is, here the function $a(\xi(i, s))$ depends on all parameters, including p_0. We can find an illustrative expression for the MLE for p_0, namely, $\hat{p}_0 = 1 - T^{-1}\Sigma_s|a(\xi(i, s)) - c_s|$, but here this is only one of many equations that must be solved simultaneously since p_0 enters the function a unlike the parameter ε in the measurement error case, where a similar expression can be used to obtain the profile log likelihood (4.26).

4.4 CONCLUSIONS

The likelihood function in a compact notation was developed for the discrete state/control setup. The curses of degeneracy (a property of the distribution of the control given the state) and of determinacy (a requirement of the data configuration) are easily illustrated here. The control rule becomes known after a few observations (i.e., there is no sampling error—as soon as all the states have been realized, the control rule is known). In general, knowledge of the control rule is not sufficient to identify underlying real parameters. Two approaches to breaking the curses were examined. The first was measurement error. Here, there are two possibilities, measurement error in the states or in the controls (or, of course, in both). Measurement error in states implies that the state-to-state transitions are not Markovian. Thus, this specification might be useful when the transitions are not Markovian. Here, the data do not have to satisfy the unlikely restrictions imposed by the perfect observation case (the curse of determinacy). However, the curse of degeneracy is not broken, essentially because the perfect observation of the controls identifies the states given the parameters. Measurement error in controls is essentially the same. Observing the states without error identifies the controls given the parameters. Here, however, the state-to-state transitions remain Markovian. Combining both types of measurement error leads to a more complicated likelihood, as it is no longer possible to recover the true states and controls given the parameters. The curse of determinacy is broken in all cases, although the curse of degeneracy remains. Real parameters are typically not identified, although their ranges may be restricted. Imperfect control is an alternative approach. The results are somewhat different from those for the measurement error case, in that the optimal policies may differ from those in the perfect control setting, although the implications are the same in that the curse of determinacy is broken but that of degeneracy is not.

Neither measurement error nor imperfect control is particularly appealing from an economic modeling point of view, and neither actually solves the problem we wish to solve. Economists have been led almost invariably to a random utility specification, which does solve the curse of degeneracy and allows identification of real parameters but which does so by introducing information in the form of highly specific assumptions. That is, the random utility specification allows the estimation of parameters that are not identified if utility is deterministic in a model that is otherwise the same. This is the topic of chapter 5.

4.5 EXERCISES

1. Write (4.6) in exponential family form.
2. For the marketing example in table 4.3, verify that $c = (1, 0)$ is optimal for $p_{00} \leq .2$.
3. Verify that (4.21) is not an exponential family distribution and conclude that there is no fixed-dimension sufficient statistic in the model with measurement error in the states.

4.6 REFERENCES

Berger and Wolpert (1984) motivate the likelihood approach in general. There has been little systematic study of the likelihood functions for dynamic programming models outside the random utility case taken up in chapter 5, in which the likelihood function can be made "regular" (Rust, 1988, 1994). Stern (1989) and Christensen and Kiefer (1994b) give applications using measurement error to break the curse of determinacy in a model with a continuous state variable. This approach to job search is treated in chapter 9. Many other studies introduce measurement error but usually in the context of a random utility model. Chow (1981) uses imperfect control to break the curse in a continuous state/control framework.

Chapter Five

Random Utility Models

5.1 INTRODUCTION

A useful and popular approach to breaking the curse of degeneracy is to introduce a random utility specification. Here, the period utility is subject to a control-specific shock. The agent sees this shock before the control choice must be made, but it is not seen in the data. Thus, the choice of the agent may depend on the realization of the shock, and hence the observed optimal control may correspond to different observed states depending on the value of the unobserved shock. Of course, the random utility shock cannot simply be "tacked on" to a dynamic programming problem; it changes the problem, the value, and the optimal policy function. The approach of specifying the random utility shock as an unobserved state variable is championed by Rust, following McFadden.

In this chapter we follow our approach of starting from the simplest possible specifications and adding complications slowly. It is useful to note once again that the simplest models are not necessarily practical for data analysis, but they serve to illustrate key issues that are present in all formulations. These issues can be obscured in complex models, so analysis of simple models is key to understanding the dynamic programming approach. To show how the problem changes with utility shocks, we give details on the value function in this case. This analysis serves to establish that, with $|C|$ controls, a formulation with $(|C| - 1)$ utility shocks is general. That is, when the problem is set up with $|C|$ utility shocks in each period, one for each value of the control, one of the shocks can be normalized to zero. This intuitive result applies because it is the comparison of utilities that determines the optimal policy, not their absolute levels.

We then turn to the likelihood factor $p(c|x)$, the choice probability. The curse of degeneracy is that this probability is zero or one—the control is a deterministic function of the current state. For simplicity, we consider the discrete-state, binary control case and focus first on the likelihood factor for one state ($x = 0$) only. This simplification allows the development of insight. Furthermore, it is appropriate for example if there is only one feasible control for the other values of the state or, equivalently, one control value that is optimal for all feasible parameter values. In this case, the statistical model is binomial,

$$p(c|x = 0) = \theta^c(1 - \theta)^{1-c}, \qquad (5.1)$$

or in exponential family form in the *mean* parametrization,

$$p(c|x = 0) = \exp\{c\ln(\theta/(1 - \theta)) + \ln(1 - \theta)\} \qquad (5.2)$$

or, alternatively with natural parameter η,

$$p(c|x = 0) = \exp\{c\eta - \ln(1 + e^\eta)\}, \qquad (5.3)$$

and the sufficient statistic is the sample fraction $t = \Sigma c_i/n$, where i indexes observations corresponding to $x = 0$, $c_i \in \{0, 1\}$ is the value of the control, and n is the size of the sample with $x = 0$. This can be re-garded as a reduced form with parameter space $\Theta = [0, 1]$ for $\theta (H = (-\infty, \infty)$ for log odds η). Because of the curse of degeneracy, the structural parameter space is $\Theta = \{0, 1\}$, so there is no hope of matching the sample fraction in practice. The MLE is 0 if $t < \frac{1}{2}$, and 1 if $t \geq \frac{1}{2}$. In practice, the data (with t not equal to zero or one) tell us that the model is too tightly specified.

To free up the specification, we consider adding utility shocks. First, we add a binary shock with a known distribution and consider identification of a preference parameter (we focus on the discount factor β). Then we allow a parameter in the distribution, noting that this improves the fit but does not aid identification of the utility parameter. We then turn to a shock distribution with continuous support. With a known distribution, the prefer-ence parameter typically becomes identified. Note that this parameter is not identified without the assumption of a known continuous distribution for the utility shock. The lesson here is that considerable care must be taken in in-terpreting results on preference parameters from discrete models. To make this point more forcefully, we characterize the relation between the assumed shock distribution and the estimated parameter.

Our next step is to consider several choice probabilities simultaneously. In this case, the dimension of the reduced-form sufficient statistic is equal to the number of states times the number of controls less the number of states, $|S| \times (|C|-1)$ (since the probabilities for a given state sum to 1 over the value of the control). This bounds the number of parameters that can potentially be estimated. Of course, in the basic case, each probability is zero or one, so we look at generalizing the model by specifying a utility shock. With a continuous, $(|C| - 1)$ variate shock distribution, at most $|S| \times (|C| - 1)$ parameters can be estimated on the basis of the function $p(c|x)$. These can include both preference parameters and parameters of the utility shock distribution. Note, however, that the lesson from the simple case still holds: Parameters unidentified without the assumed shock distribution have been identified. The random utility specification, instead of simply generalizing the simpler specification, has in fact added, purely by assumption, identifying information. That is, the $|C|$-vector of choice probabilities for each value of the state variable has ($|C| - 1$) "free" values, instead of consisting of one 1 and ($|C| - 1$) zeros, as in the structural model without utility shocks.

In this chapter, we focus on the choice probabilities. Of course, the entire likelihood is the product of the likelihoods generated by the choices and by the state-to-state transitions. These, with different reduced-form parameters, depend on the same underlying structural parameters.

5.2 THE VALUE FUNCTION

Suppose now that the utility is subject to a random shock, so that

$$u^*(x, c, \varepsilon) = \overline{u}(x, c) + \varepsilon(c), \tag{5.4}$$

where $\varepsilon(c)$ is a random shock. This formulation is not restrictive in terms of functional form in the discrete case, where the utility function $u(x, c)$ is just shorthand for a $|S| \times |C|$ table of numbers. The idea here is that at time t, when the state $x_t = k$ has been realized, a $|C|$-vector of random variables ε is added to the kth row in the utility table, then the choice of control c is made. Thus, $c = c(x, \varepsilon)$ is a deterministic function, but given only x, the control c is a random variable whose distribution depends on x. If ε has a nonzero mean, the mean can simply be absorbed into the utility specification, so it is a harmless normalization to set $E\varepsilon = 0$.

To see that a further normalization is possible in the distribution of ε, consider the binary state case. Let x', c', ε' denote one-period-ahead future values and write

$$V(x, \varepsilon) = \max_c \{\overline{u}(x, c) + \beta E_{xc} V(x', \varepsilon') + \varepsilon(c)\}$$

$$= \max\{\overline{u}(x, 0) + \beta E_{x0} V(x', \varepsilon') + \varepsilon(0), \overline{u}(x, 1)$$

$$+ \beta E_{x1} V(x', \varepsilon') + \varepsilon(1)\}$$

$$= \varepsilon(0) + \max\{\overline{u}(x, 0) + \beta E_{x0} V(x', \varepsilon'), \overline{u}(x, 1)$$

$$+ \beta E_{x1} V(x', \varepsilon') + \varepsilon(1) - \varepsilon(0)\}. \tag{5.5}$$

Here, E_{xc} denotes the expectation operator conditional on the (x, c) pair indicated. Note that the choice of c in the maximization operator in the final expression depends only on $\varepsilon(1) - \varepsilon(0)$, not on either shock individually. The next step is to argue that $E_{xc} V(x', \varepsilon')$ depends only on future

$\varepsilon'(1) - \varepsilon'(0)$. Thus,

$$E_{xc}V(x', \varepsilon') = E_{xc}\left[\varepsilon'(0) + \max\{\bar{u}(x', 0) + \beta E_{x'0}V(x'', \varepsilon''), \quad (5.6)\right.$$
$$\left.\bar{u}(x', 1) + \beta E_{x'1}V(x'', \varepsilon'') + \varepsilon'(1) - \varepsilon'(0)\}\right]$$
$$= E(\varepsilon'(0)) + E_{xc}\max\{\,,\,\}. \quad (5.7)$$

Iterating,

$$V(x, \varepsilon) = \varepsilon(0) + \beta E(\varepsilon'(0)) + \max\{\bar{u}(x, 0) + \beta E_{x0}\max\{\,,\,\}, \ldots\}$$

$$= \varepsilon(0) + E\varepsilon'(0)\sum_{i=1}^{\infty}\beta^i + \max\{\bar{u}(x, 0) + \beta E_{x0}\max\{\,,\,\}, \ldots, \}.$$

$$(5.8)$$

Let

$$W(x, \varepsilon) = V(x, \varepsilon) - \varepsilon(0). \quad (5.9)$$

Then

$$W(x', \varepsilon') = \max\{\bar{u}(x', 0) + \beta E_{x'0}V(x'', \varepsilon''), \bar{u}(x', 1)$$
$$+ \beta E_{x'1}V(x'', \varepsilon'') + \varepsilon'(1) - \varepsilon'(0)\}; \quad (5.10)$$

i.e., let

$$\tilde{\varepsilon} = \varepsilon(1) - \varepsilon(0), \quad (5.11)$$

then

$$W(x, \tilde{\varepsilon}) = \max\{\bar{u}(x, 0) + \beta E_{x0}W(x', \tilde{\varepsilon}'), \bar{u}(x, 1) + \beta E_{x1}W(x', \tilde{\varepsilon}') + \tilde{\varepsilon}\}.$$

$$(5.12)$$

Thus, the new value function $W(x, \tilde{\varepsilon})$ satisfies a modified version of the optimality principle (like the original version it is stated in terms of a contraction mapping, see chapter 6) and has only $(|C| - 1)$ arguments $\tilde{\varepsilon}$; it has exactly the same implications as $V(x, \varepsilon)$ for the sequence $\{x_t, c_t\}$. In the subsequent analysis, we will occasionally normalize one of the elements of the $|C|$-vector ε to be identically zero.

5.3 A BINARY UTILITY SHOCK

Consider the 2×2 model and suppose the utility shock is $(\varepsilon, 0)$, where ε is a scalar random variable taking the value $a \geq 0$ with probability $\frac{1}{2}$ and $-a$ with probability $\frac{1}{2}$. For simplicity, consider again the case $x = 0$ alone, so we can focus attention on the distribution $p(c|x = 0)$. Let $p_1 = p(c = 1|x = 0)$; of course, p_1 is a function of the parameter θ characterizing preferences, etc. We have, as in (5.1),

$$p(c|x = 0) = p_1^c(1 - p_1)^{1-c}, \tag{5.13}$$

and with n independent observations,

$$\prod_t p(c_t|x_t = 0) = p_1^{\Sigma c}(1 - p_1)^{n-\Sigma c}, \tag{5.14}$$

and the sample fraction $\Sigma c/n$ is a sufficient statistic for p_1. Here, n is the number of observations with $x = 0$. The natural parameter space for the reduced-form parameter p_1 is $[0, 1]$. But what values of p_1 are consistent with the dynamic programming model with random utility shocks?

In the model, the probability that $c = 1$ is chosen is given by

$$p(c = 1|x = 0) = \Pr\left(\arg\max_c\{\bar{u}(0, c) + \beta E_{0c}V(x', \varepsilon') + \varepsilon(c)\} = 1\right). \tag{5.15}$$

Recalling that $\varepsilon(0) = -a$ with probability $\frac{1}{2}$ and a with probability $\frac{1}{2}$ and $\varepsilon(1) = 0$, this probability can be written

$$p(c = 1|x = 0) = \Pr(\varepsilon < h(\theta)), \tag{5.16}$$

where $h = \bar{u}(0, 1) + \beta E_{01}V - \bar{u}(0, 0) - \beta E_{00}V$ and the generic parameter θ has been introduced as an argument in h for emphasis. Now, we have specified a binary distribution for ε, so this probability can take values in $\{0, \frac{1}{2}, 1\}$, the precise value depending on $h(\theta)$. Specifically, $c = 0$ could be optimal for both values of $\varepsilon(0)$, $c = 1$ could be optimal for $\varepsilon(0) = -a$ and $c = 0$ for $\varepsilon(0) = a$, and finally $c = 1$ could be optimal for both values of $\varepsilon(0)$. Thus, the likelihood function is flat for generic continuous parameters θ, except where the value of θ is such that the probability shifts between two of its three possible values. The most that can be obtained is that possible values of θ are restricted to intervals, corresponding to values so that the implied choice probability is as close as possible to the sample fraction. Note that this does represent some improvement over the model without shocks—if h is monotonic in the parameter θ, then without shocks, so $p(c|x) \in \{0, 1\}$, θ is restricted to one of two intervals (recall estimating β in our marketing example). With $p(c|x) \in \{0, \frac{1}{2}, 1\}$, θ is restricted to one of three intervals.

The curse of degeneracy has been broken in that $p(c|x)$ is not necessarily in $\{0, 1\}$. However, only one new point has been added to that set of possibilities, so it might be better to think of the curse as being weakened, not broken. The main point, however, is that merely adding a random utility shock with a completely known distribution appears to add information about a structural parameter but does not serve to fully identify otherwise unidentified parameters.

Let us generalize the shock distribution slightly and introduce a new parameter. Suppose the distribution of ε is $-a$ with probability $(1 - \pi)$, and a with probability π. For π not equal to $\frac{1}{2}$ and a not equal to 0, this distribution has a nonzero mean. That does not really present a problem, as the mean can be absorbed into $\bar{u}(0, 0)$, as we have seen. For a fixed value of π, we have that $\Pr(\varepsilon < h(\theta, \pi)) \in \{0, \pi, 1\}$, so again θ can at best be bounded in an interval. By varying π, however, it may be possible to match the sample fraction (it may not be possible, if the probability is zero or one for all θ, but this is not an interesting case). Here, the curse of degeneracy is unambiguously broken, in the sense that the sample fraction can be matched by choice of the parameter π. However, this amounts to no more than a reduced-form approach; no identifying information on θ is available, and it is at best restricted to an interval.

5.4 A CONTINUOUSLY DISTRIBUTED UTILITY SHOCK

Since adding a utility shock with a known two-point distribution adds one point to the model-consistent parameter space for p_1 (and hence possibly restricts the range of the generic parameter θ), it is natural to ask whether a known distribution with support on an interval might tighten things up even more. In fact, the assumption of a continuously distributed utility shock is much more common in applications for reasons that will become clear. Let us begin the analysis by supposing that, instead of a two-point distribution on $\{-a, a\}$, ε has a continuous distribution with support $[-a, a]$. Note that we are not making innocuous assumptions by changing the shock distribution—changes here, even with the mean held constant, will affect both the value of the problem and the optimal policy function. To start with, assume $f(\varepsilon) = 1/(2a)$, the uniform distribution. Then

$$p(c = 1 | x = 0) = \Pr(\varepsilon < h(\theta)) = h(\theta)/2a + \tfrac{1}{2}, \qquad (5.17)$$

for $|h| \leq a$. Recall that $h(\theta) = \bar{u}(0, 1) + \beta E_{01} V - \bar{u}(0, 0) - \beta E_{00} V$. This probability now depends on θ, continuously if h is continuous in θ, so θ can be estimated by setting $h(\theta)/2a + \tfrac{1}{2}$ equal to the sample fraction $t = \Sigma c/n$ and solving for $\hat{\theta}$, as long as this is a feasible value (again, it could be that $h(\theta)$ is such that $|h| > a$ for all values of θ, and the probability therefore always zero or one—not an interesting case).

By introducing randomness into the utility specification, we have managed to achieve identification of a parameter not identified without randomness. How can "introducing noise" serve to identify a preference parameter? What is in fact happening is that the assumption that the shock is continuously distributed with a known distribution is crucial. Our specification inserts information into the model—information on preferences. This is not necessarily inappropriate, but it is important to realize that θ is being identified completely on the basis of the assumed shock distribution. Indeed, this point can be emphasized with a little further analysis.

Let F be the distribution function for the utility shock. For simplicity, suppose F is a member of a one-parameter family of distributions indexed by γ. Then

$$p(c = 1 | x = 0) = \Pr(\varepsilon < h(\theta, \gamma)) = \int_{-a}^{h(\theta, \gamma)} dF$$

$$= H(\theta, \gamma). \tag{5.18}$$

In practice, γ is assumed known (the distribution of the utility shock is fully specified) and $H(\theta, \gamma) = t$ (the sample fraction) is solved for $\hat{\theta}(\gamma)$. Here, the dependence on the assumed distribution is indicated by the explicit dependence on γ. Assume F is continuously differentiable in γ, and h in θ and γ. This assumption rules out sudden shifts of the probability to zero or one (e.g., when h passes the value a); but rather than getting involved in details we note that we are really concerned only with properties in the neighborhood of the solution to $H(\theta, \gamma) = t$. Alternatively, we can simply set $a = \infty$, so the distribution function has full support on the real line (indeed, this is the most common practice). By the implicit function theorem,

$$d\hat{\theta}/d\gamma = -H_\gamma / H_\theta, \tag{5.19}$$

with $H_\gamma = f(h(\theta, \gamma))h_\gamma + F_\gamma(h(\theta, \gamma))$ and $H_\theta = f(h(\theta, \gamma))h_\theta$, where f is the density function $dF(x)/dx$. Writing this out gives

$$d\hat{\theta}/d\gamma = -h_\gamma / h_\theta - F_\gamma / (f h_\theta), \tag{5.20}$$

the first term giving the tradeoff between γ and θ, holding h (the utility difference between using the two controls) constant, and the second giving the effect of γ on h through the change in the probability.

This analysis indicates that the estimate of the parameter θ is a function of the assumed distribution, here indexed by γ. Further, the derivative (5.20) is typically nonzero, so the assumption matters. To push the analysis a little further, we concentrate on the parameter β, the discount factor. Then

$$h(\beta, \gamma) = ((\bar{u}(0, 1) - \bar{u}(0, 0)) + \beta(E_{01}V - E_{00}V), \tag{5.21}$$

hence $h_\beta = (E_{01}V - E_{00}V) + \beta(E_{01}V_\beta - E_{00}V_\beta))$ and $h_\gamma = \beta d(E_{01}V - E_{00}V)/d\gamma$. Let us evaluate these expressions at $\beta = 0$ in order to get a local tradeoff between the assumed distribution and the estimated discount factor at $\beta = 0$. Here,

$$h_{\beta|\beta=0} = E_{01}(\max_c \{\bar{u}(x', c) + \varepsilon'(c)\}) - E_{00}(\max_c \{\bar{u}(x', c) + \varepsilon'(c)\}), \quad (5.22)$$

a function of γ, and

$$h_{\gamma|\beta=0} = 0, \quad (5.23)$$

so there is no direct effect of the assumed distribution γ on h, the utility difference, when $\beta = 0$. Hence, all of the effect is through the change in the probability, and this is given by

$$\frac{d\hat{\beta}}{d\gamma}\bigg|_{\beta=0} = \frac{-F_\gamma/f}{E_{01}\max_c\{\bar{u}(x', c) + \varepsilon'(c)\} - E_{00}\max_c\{\bar{u}(x', c) + \varepsilon'(c)\}}; \quad (5.24)$$

all terms in this expression depend on γ, thus illustrating now in a simple case the correspondence between the specification of the utility shock distribution and the estimated discount factor. Note that (5.24) gives the effect on the estimate of β of a change in the distributional assumption, holding the data constant. The numerator is the change in the choice probability; the denominator is the density multiplied by the expected utility difference. While this expression clearly depends crucially on F (this is the point, after all), a little more may be said. In particular, if the expected utility difference between the two controls is smaller, then the role of the assumption on F is more important, in that this derivative is larger.

It is sometimes thought that by "freeing up" the random utility distribution F through the addition of unknown parameters one can mitigate the effects of directly and completely specifying an unknown distribution. Let us consider this. First, in the stylized case studied above, with only one choice probability to estimate (i.e., the probability associated with one value of the discrete state variable and a binary control), this proposition is easily rejected. Our analysis shows there is a one-to-one relationship between values of the parameter γ of the now unknown distribution and the preference parameter θ. Clearly, these are not both identified. Specifically, there is a curve in the (γ, θ) space corresponding to a given value of h and thus a set of parameter values that serve to match the fitted value h to the sample fraction. Identification of the structural parameter θ requires that the functional form of the utility shock be completely specified, not parametrized (here by γ).

Consider next analyzing multiple states simultaneously. In the most general case, in which the utility distribution is different across states, the above analysis applies. Although the preference parameters are presumably the same across states (generally some state-specific parameters might be added, but that would only make the identification more difficult), new distributions or parametrized distributions are added for each state. Suppose there are K preference parameters ($K = 1$ in the example above) and corresponding to each state there is a binary choice. Then there are $|S|$ reduced-form choice probabilities and hence a possibility of identifying at most $|S|$ parameters. If $|S| = K$, then the random utility distributions must be completely specified a priori. If $|S| > K$, then there is the possibility of fitting $(|S| - K)$ utility shock parameters and matching the reduced-form choice probabilities with the structural estimates. This is a possibility and not a certainty since the model is nonlinear and one can specify distributions so that it is impossible to match particular configurations of choice probabilities. In general, there will be many combinations of distributional assumptions for the utility shock and corresponding preference parameters that fit the structure to the reduced form equally well. As in the linear simultaneous equations case, economic judgment is crucial here. Our point is that specifying a random utility model is not freeing up or loosening the specification. It is a matter of inserting identifying information. It is important to understand exactly what is being assumed.

5.5 CHOICE PROBABILITIES

We have focused on the single-choice probability $p(c|x = 0)$ in order to simplify the calculations and to isolate critical issues. But additional information is made available by considering the choice probabilities $p(c|x = 0)$ and $p(c|x = 1)$ jointly. Of course, these probabilities are related through their dependence on the common parameters θ. Further, it is typically assumed (as above) that the shock distribution does not depend on the state, so the same shock distribution appears in both choice probabilities.

The joint likelihood function for all the choice possibilities for a given state is (generalizing (5.14))

$$\prod_{i=1}^{|C|} p(c = i|x)^{d_i}, \tag{5.25}$$

where d_i is the number of choices $c = i$. The joint likelihood on combining states is

$$\prod_{j=1}^{|S|} \prod_{i=1}^{|C|} p(c = i|x = j)^{d_{ij}}, \tag{5.26}$$

where d_{ij} is the number of observations with choice i in state j. The natural reduced-form parameters $p_{ij} = p(c = i|x = j)$ can be estimated by

$d_{ij}/\Sigma_i d_{ij}$, and the natural parameter space for each of these parameters is $[0, 1]$ subject to the adding-up constraint $\Sigma_i p_{ij} = 1$. Each of the reduced-form parameters depends on structural parameters through the solution to the dynamic program, of course. Note that the exponential family form is maintained. In the mean parametrization, we have

$$p(c|x) = \exp\left\{\sum_j \sum_i d_{ij} \ln p_{ij}\right\}, \qquad (5.27)$$

where $\Sigma_i p_{ij} = 1$ for each j. Under stationarity, the (partial) likelihood for a sequence is simply the product over time, $\ell(c|x) = \Pi_t p(c_t|x_t)$.

The full likelihood for the data on state-to-state transitions, $p(x_{t+1}|x_t, c_t)$ in the Markov case, as well as the policy choices within a period, $p(c_t|x_t)$, is formed by multiplication,

$$\ell(x, c) = \prod_{t=0}^{T-1} p(x_{t+1}|x_t, c_t) p(c_{t+1}|x_{t+1})$$

$$= \prod_{t=0}^{T-1} p(x_{t+1}, c_{t+1}|x_t), \qquad (5.28)$$

and remains in the exponential family. The full mean parametrization (or the linear parametrization) can be regarded as a reduced form. When the structural form imposes restrictions on this distribution (the interesting case), the structural model is curved exponential.

5.6 DYNAMIC CONTINUOUS RANDOM UTILITY

The general setup in a static (one-time choice) model for a given value of the state variable $x \in S$ and choices $c \in C$ in a random utility framework is

$$u^*(x, c, \varepsilon) = \bar{u}(x, c) + \varepsilon(c). \qquad (5.29)$$

Thus, we have a table consisting of $|S| \times |C|$ utility values and $|C|$ values of the random utility shock, of which one can be normalized to zero if convenient. Note that the utility shock here does not depend on the value of the state variable. The role of the shock is simply to make the map from x to the optimal c stochastic rather than deterministic; allowing the model to fit the data. Note that the actual control rule is deterministic; that is, $c(x, \varepsilon)$ chooses one element of C with probability 1 (barring ties). However, since the state variable ε is unseen by the econometrician, choices are modeled as probabilistic. The control chosen c^* is of course that for which $u^*(x, c^*, \varepsilon) > u^*(x, c, \varepsilon)$ for given x and all c.

It is convenient to choose a continuous distribution for ε and further to choose one implying that $p(c|x) > 0$ for all $c \in C$. In some applications enough theoretical structure is available so that this assumption is not tenable (see chapter 7 for an example in the continuous state space case). A specification of this sort is termed "saturated" by Rust (1994). Let f be the $|C|$-variate density of u^* and write $u_i^* = u^*(x, i, \varepsilon)$. Then

$$P(c = c_i|x) = \int_{-\infty}^{\infty} \int_{-\infty}^{u_i} \cdots \int_{-\infty}^{u_i} f \, du_1^* \dots du_{i-1}^* \, du_{i+1}^* \cdots du_{|C|}^* \, du_i^*,$$

(5.30)

where the integrals other than the first run from $-\infty$ to u_i^*, or in terms of the distributions of the ε_i directly,

$$P(c = c_i|x) = \int_{-\infty}^{\infty} \int_{-\infty}^{\bar{u}_i + \varepsilon_i - \bar{u}_1} \cdots \int_{-\infty}^{\bar{u}_i + \varepsilon_i - \bar{u}_{|C|}} g \, d\varepsilon_1$$

$$\dots d\varepsilon_{i-1} \, d\varepsilon_{i+1} \dots d\varepsilon_{|C|} \, d\varepsilon_i,$$

(5.31)

where $\bar{u}_i = \bar{u}(x, i)$ and g is the density of the shocks ε. Depending on the specification of the distribution of the utility shock, this integral can be a computational burden, although both numerical techniques and computer speeds are improving.

A particularly convenient specification, in the absence of contradictory theoretical implications, is the independent extreme value distribution with (univariate) density

$$f(\varepsilon) = \exp\{-\varepsilon + \gamma\} \exp\{-\exp\{-\varepsilon + \gamma\}\}$$

(5.32)

and distribution function $\exp\{-\exp\{-\varepsilon + \gamma\}\}$. Here, γ is Euler's constant and is added so the distribution has mean zero. With this specification, the probability that the optimal choice is $c = c_1$ is

$$P(c = c_1|x) = P\left(u_1^* > u_2^*, u_1^* > u_3^*, \dots, u_1^* > u_{|C|}^*\right)$$

$$= P(\bar{u}_1 - \bar{u}_2 + \varepsilon_1 > \varepsilon_2, \dots, \bar{u}_1 - \bar{u}_{|C|} + \varepsilon_1 > \varepsilon_{|C|}).$$

(5.33)

Using (5.31) and (5.32) and independence, this integral is

$$P(c = c_1|x) = \int f(\varepsilon_1) \left[\int \int f(\varepsilon) d\varepsilon \dots \int f(\varepsilon) d\varepsilon \right] d\varepsilon_1,$$

(5.34)

where the inner integrals are from $-\infty$ to $\bar{u}_1 + \varepsilon_1 - \bar{u}_j$ as in (5.31). Each inner integral is thus in the form $\exp\{-\exp\{-\bar{u}_1 - \varepsilon_1 + \bar{u}_j + \gamma\}\}$. Integration by parts and cancellation of the term involving γ yields

$$p(c = c_1|x) = \frac{\exp\{\bar{u}_1\}}{\sum \exp\{\bar{u}_j\}},$$

(5.35)

which is in the multinomial logit form as developed by McFadden. This is usually seen in the parameterization $\bar{u}(x, i) = z_i \beta$, where z consists of characteristics of the state and the ith control. Then $p(c = c_i|x) = \exp\{z_i\beta\}/\Sigma \exp\{z_j\beta\}$.

This model generalizes to the dynamic case, as shown by Rust (1987a). We continue to assume that the period utility has the additive form

$$u^*(x, c, \varepsilon) = \bar{u}(x, c) + \varepsilon(c) \tag{5.36}$$

and now consider the transition distribution for the state variables $(x, \varepsilon) \in S \times R^{|C|}$. Assume this factors as

$$q(x', \varepsilon'|x, \varepsilon, c) = q(x'|x, c)q(\varepsilon'|x'). \tag{5.37}$$

This assumption is called "conditional independence" by Rust. It conveniently restricts the way in which the unobserved state variable enters the dynamic programming problem. First, the transition distribution for the observed state x does not depend on ε. This implies that the (x, c) sequence continues to look like a controlled Markov process even in the random utility framework. Second, ε does not depend on lagged values given the observed state x. In fact, we typically specify $q(\varepsilon'|x') = q(\varepsilon')$, so the ε are essentially an i.i.d. process whose effects are limited to within-period effects not affecting the basic dynamic programming structure.

With this assumption, the value function becomes

$$V(x, \varepsilon) = \max_c \left\{ \bar{u}(x, c) + \beta \int \int V(x', \varepsilon')q(\varepsilon'|x')q(x'|x, c)\, dx'\, d\varepsilon' + \varepsilon(c) \right\}, \tag{5.38}$$

which depends on the unobservable ε, so it is not directly useful to the modeler. However, the sum of the first two terms in braces depends only on x and c. Write

$$v(x, c) = \bar{u}(x, c) + \beta \int \int V(x', \varepsilon')q(\varepsilon'|x')q(x'|x, c)\, dx'\, d\varepsilon' \tag{5.39}$$

and note that the maximization has the same form as in the static case, but now $v(x, c)$ replaces $\bar{u}(x, c)$. Thus, given a specification of the distribution of ε, the dynamic choice model mimics the static model upon specification of $v(x, c)$. Of course, the probabilities themselves are properly regarded as reduced-form parameters. The map to structural parameters, specifically the discount factor and preference parameters, depends on what v looks like in terms of $\bar{u}$ and β (and transition function parameters). This relation can be characterized.

Substituting (5.38) into (5.39) and applying (5.39) again gives

$$v(x, c) = \bar{u}(x, c) + \beta \int \int_{c'} \max\{v(x', c') + \varepsilon'(c')\} q(\varepsilon'|x') q(x'|x, c) \, dx' \, d\varepsilon',$$

(5.40)

which can be regarded as a map $\Lambda : R^{|S| \times |C|} \rightarrow R^{|S| \times |C|}$, i.e., mapping real-valued functions on $S \times C$ into themselves. A map $h : R^k \rightarrow R^k$ is said to be a *contraction mapping* with modulus $\delta \in (0, 1)$ if $|h(x) - h(y)| < \delta |x - y|$ for all $x, y \in R^k$. A contraction mapping in R^k has a unique fixed point, $x^* = h(x^*)$. Blackwell (1965) gives conditions under which a map can be determined to be a contraction. This topic is covered in chapter 6. It can be easily seen that Λ satisfies Blackwell's conditions of *monotonicity*, $f < g \implies \Lambda f < \Lambda g$, and *discounting*, $\Lambda(f + \alpha) \leq \Lambda f + \beta \alpha$ for $\beta \in [0, 1)$, where $(f + \alpha)(x) = f(x) + \alpha$, and Λ is therefore a contraction mapping. Consequently, there is a unique solution v to $v = \Lambda v$, and this solution can be found by iterating the contraction map Λ from any starting value. Naturally, it makes sense to choose a good starting value, such as $\bar{u}(x, c)$.

With ε distributed as independent extreme value variables, the choice probabilities are given by

$$p(c = c_i | x) = \frac{e^{v(x, c_i)}}{\sum_j e^{v(x, c_j)}}$$

(5.41)

in a natural generalization of the result (5.35) in the static case. Here, the $v(x, c)$ are given as fixed points of the map

$$\Lambda v(x, c) = \bar{u}(x, c) + \beta \int \ln \left(\sum_j \exp\{v(x', c_j)\} \right) q(x'|x, c) dx'. \quad (5.42)$$

The expressions (5.41) are substituted into the likelihood function (5.28) for estimation.

5.7 EXERCISES

1. Consider the static ($\beta = 0$) model with no state variable and with $u(1) = \theta$, $u(0) = 0$. Here, the curse of degeneracy applies, and either all observations are $c = 0$ or all are $c = 1$. Only the sign of θ is identified. Add the random utility assumption that $u(1) = \theta + \varepsilon$ with ε uniform on $[-a, a]$. Show that the curse no longer applies and that for fixed a, θ is now identified and can be estimated by solving $\Pr(\varepsilon > -\hat{\theta}) = t$, where t is the sample fraction with $c = 1$.

2. Calculate the exact dependence of $\hat{\theta}$ in exercise 1 on a.

3. Replace the uniform in exercise 1 by the normal with mean 0 and variance a, and repeat exercise 2 for this case.

5.8 REFERENCES

In a long series of papers, McFadden essentially established quantal choice models as an econometric tool. See McFadden (1973, 1981, 1984). He showed the relationship between the extreme value distribution for utility shocks and the conditional logit model. Amemiya (1985) gives an overview of estimation theory for choice models, demonstrating the concavity of the log likelihood in popular specifications. Stokey and Lucas (1989) treat contraction mappings and Blackwell's conditions. Rust (1994) discusses specification and estimation of dynamic discrete choice models—discrete Markov decision processes. Rust gives the dynamic extension of McFadden's discrete choice theories, showing the extension from the static utility function to the function $v(x, c)$ and characterizing v as a fixed point. Rust (1987a) gives a "nested fixed point" algorithm for estimating discrete (decision space) dynamic programming models. Rust (1988) further treats maximum likelihood estimation in a very general setting. Hotz and Miller (1993) note the one-to-one map between the conditional choice probabilities and the (normalized) $v(x, c)$ and suggest a focus on the former. This approach leads to a GMM estimator that does not require solutions to the fixed-point operations. It has been extended by Aguirregabiria (2002) and Aguirregabiria and Mira (2002). The role of the utility shock distribution in identification has not been adequately studied.

Chapter Six

Continuous States, Discrete Controls

6.1 INTRODUCTION

In this chapter, we give a broad outline of the dynamic programming model with continuous state variables and discrete controls. The fundamental idea is that expected utility theory still works even in multiperiod situations. The dynamic programming model is the key ingredient in this extension of the usual static model. We slightly increase the math level to allow additional generalization. Of course, the results apply in the discrete state case as well.

We consider numerous economic applications of the general dynamic programming model. Each application requires a slightly different formulation or interpretation of the general principle. For this reason, and to avoid ruling out particular models by adopting very specialized assumptions, our presentation is in general terms. This allows an easy introduction to the theoretical tools necessary for our ultimate empirical purposes, sufficiently comprehensive to cover all the central ideas useful for applications.

The dynamic programming model allows a natural and direct link between economic modeling and econometric inference. The general framework is tailored in each application to produce an inherently consistent structural model of the behavior of the economic agent, and this in turn leads to a distribution for the observables and thus forms the basis for the statistical analysis. This way, economic theory and data analysis are optimally combined in the production of information.

Consider first the environment of an agent making choices this period, taking into account both budget restrictions and the effect of current actions on the future environment. For concreteness, let x_t be the state variable describing the economic conditions in period t, when the agent is choosing the action or control c_t from a number of feasible alternatives. The new environment faced by the agent the next period is summarized by the new state variable x_{t+1}, and to allow this to depend both on the current state x_t and on the agent's choice c_t, but also possibly to involve some randomness not realized as of time t, we adopt a conditional probability distribution for x_{t+1} given x_t and c_t, indicated as

$$x_{t+1} \sim Q_t(\cdot|x_t, c_t). \tag{6.1}$$

This Markov structure will be crucial for applications. Note that the dependence of the distribution of the next period's state on any finite number of lagged values of x or c can be handled in this framework by appropriate definition of the state variable (e.g., it might include $x_{t-1}, \ldots, x_{t-k}, c_{t-1}, \ldots, c_{t-p}$). What is ruled out conceptually is the dependence on a growing number of previous realizations separately. In that case, inference would be difficult or impossible.

It will be convenient to specify that $x_t \in X_t$, $c_t \in C_t$; i.e., x_t belongs to the state space X_t, and c_t to the control space C_t. We generalize the discrete case slightly by allowing the state and control sets to vary over time. Of course, this generalization applies to the discrete case as well. To allow for continuous state variables, we consider X_t a subset of Euclidean space. We continue to consider C_t a discrete set, although the analysis in the present chapter applies even for the case of continuous controls. With $\mathcal{X}_t = \sigma(X_t)$, the Borel σ-field on X_t, the state transition equation is given by the Markov kernel, $Q_t : \mathcal{X}_{t+1} \times X_t \times C_t \rightarrow [0, 1]$.

A policy for the agent is a rule for selecting an action c_t on the basis of all of the current economic information as captured by the "partial history" h_t. Let $\bar{H}_t = \times_{i=0}^{t}(X_i \times C_i)$; $h_t \in \bar{H}_t$ is a sequence of state realizations and policies from time $i = 0$. Let H_t be the subset of $\bar{H}_t$ consistent with the transition distribution Q_t. That is, H_t does not include histories that are impossible (there is no point in defining policies for these histories). Here, we have adopted a convention that we shall make use of whenever convenient for expositional purposes, namely, that the initial time period is denoted by zero. In fact, we shall typically model the agent's behavior as of time zero, hence thinking about this as the current period. A policy is a sequence of measurable maps, $\pi = (\pi_0, \pi_1, \ldots)$, which may be finite or infinite depending on the problem being studied. Each map $\pi_t : H_{t-1} \times X_t \rightarrow P(C_t)$ gives a probability distribution on current actions as a function of history and current state. In particular, future behavior is summarized by $\pi' = (\pi_1, \pi_2, \ldots)$. The strategy $\pi = (\pi_0, \pi')$ indicates both current and future behavior and may be restricted to a certain feasible set, $\pi \in \Pi$, e.g., incorporating budget constraints. Measurability can in general be a real restriction. In applications, it is often appropriate to assume current rewards are bounded and to make additional assumptions (particularly on the continuity of the constraint sets in histories and on the transition distribution) ensuring measurability. See Stokey and Lucas (1989, ch. 9).

This setup is quite general in keeping with the static expected utility theory, and what we would like to see is a policy with each map depending only on the current state, i.e., $\pi_t : X_t \rightarrow C_t$, and choosing an action with probability 1. A policy depending only on the current state is called Markovian.

In many applications it is reasonable and convenient to specify $X_t = X, \forall t$, and $C_t = C, \forall t$; i.e., the state and action spaces do not change over time. A stationary policy is a policy π with $\pi_t(h_t)$ selecting a policy $a(x_t)$ with probability 1. Thus, the stationary policy gives the optimal action as a function of the current state. It turns out that with our Markov assumption on the state transition and a temporal separability assumption on rewards, it is possible to restrict attention to Markovian policies in the finite-horizon case and stationary policies in the infinite-horizon case.

6.2 TRANSITION DISTRIBUTIONS AND UTILITY

The study of optimal intertemporal choice requires a specification of the agent's preferences, and by analogy with expected utility theory, we adopt functional forms representing these. Let $u_t : X_t \times C_t \rightarrow \mathbb{R}$ indicate the felicity (current reward or period utility) function; i.e., if the realized state is x_t and the agent selects the control c_t, then this contributes $u_t(x_t, c_t)$ toward total utility. Note that u_t could be a result of taking expectations over a stochastic reward with distribution depending on x_t and c_t. With time additive preferences and adopting the expected utility paradigm, the total utility as of time zero is

$$U_\pi(x_0) = E\left(\sum_{t=0}^{\tau} u_t(x_t, \pi_t(x_t))|x_0, \pi_0(x_0)\right) \qquad (6.2)$$

if the initial state is x_0 and the agent adopts the strategy π. Here, τ denotes the horizon (finite or infinite, deterministic or stochastic) and $E(\cdot|x_0, \pi_0(x_0))$ indicates conditional mathematical expectation given the initial state and control and resulting from repeated application of the Markov kernels Q_t. Thus, define the multistage kernels Q_π^t recursively by $Q_\pi^0(B|x_0, \pi_0(x_0)) = Q_0(B|x_0, \pi_0(x_0))$ for $B \in \mathcal{X}_1$ and

$$Q_\pi^t(B|x_0, \pi_0(x_0)) = \int_{X_t} Q_t(B|x_t, \pi_t(x_t))Q_\pi^{t-1}(dx_t|x_0, \pi_0(x_0)) \qquad (6.3)$$

for $t \geq 1$, $B \in \mathcal{X}_{t+1}$. For arbitrary integrable functions $f_t : X_t \rightarrow \mathbb{R}$ we then have

$$E\left(\sum_{t=0}^{\tau} f_t(x_t)|x_0, \pi(x_0)\right) = \sum_{t=0}^{\tau} \int_{X_t} f_t(x_t)Q_\pi^{t-1}(dx_t|x_0, \pi_0(x_0)), \qquad (6.4)$$

where it is understood that Q_π^{-1} assigns unit mass x_0 to the conditioning event.

The probability distributions are those employed by the economic agent, but it is a useful practice to adopt a rational expectations assumption and take these subjective assessments to coincide with the true distributions of the random variables involved. This allows establishing an exact correspondence between the structural economic model and the statistical likelihood.

6.3 THE VALUE FUNCTION AND BACKWARD RECURSION

The optimizing agent's objective is to select a strategy π to maximize total intertemporal utility U_π. Consequently, if starting from the initial state $x_0 \in X_0$, the value of the optimum problem is

$$V_0(x_0) = \sup_{\pi \in \Pi} U_\pi(x_0). \tag{6.5}$$

Considered a function of the argument x_0, $V_0(x_0)$ is the value function, $V_0 : X_0 \to \mathbb{R}$. While the value function always exists, the maximizing policy may not. Usually, we will use conditions under which the optimum is attained.

Two points are worth observing at the outset. First, the leading term in $U_\pi(x_0)$ in (6.2), namely, $u_0(x_0, \pi_0(x_0))$, is completely determined by the initial state and so is unaltered by the application of the conditional expectations operator in the definition of U_π. Second, the above exposition leads by immediate extension to the definition of the value function as of time t, for any $t \in \{0, 1, \ldots, \tau\}$, say V_t. Combining these observations and switching to the max operator (i.e., assuming that the maximum is attained in all cases), we find

$$V_0(x_0) = \max_\pi \left\{ u_0(x_0, \pi_0(x_0)) + E \left(\sum_{t=1}^\tau u_t(x_t, \pi_t(x_t)) | x_0, \pi_0(x_0) \right) \right\}$$

$$= \max_{\pi_0} \left\{ u_0(x_0, \pi_0(x_0)) \right.$$

$$\left. + \max_{\pi'} E \left(E \left(\sum_{t=1}^\tau u_t(x_t, \pi_t(x_t)) | x_1, \pi_1(x_1) \right) | x_0, \pi_0(x_0) \right) \right\}$$

$$= \max_{\pi_0} \left\{ u_0(x_0, \pi_0(x_0)) \right.$$

$$\left. + E \left(\max_{\pi'} E \left(\sum_{t=1}^\tau u_t(x_t, \pi_t(x_t)) | x_1, \pi_1(x_1) \right) | x_0, \pi_0(x_0) \right) \right\}$$

$$= \max_{\pi_0} \left\{ u_0(x_0, \pi_0(x_0)) + E(V_1(x_1) | x_0, \pi_0(x_0)) \right\}, \tag{6.6}$$

where $E(\cdot | x_t, \pi_t(x_t))$ is defined by direct analogy with the case $t = 0$. The derivation shows that optimal behavior may be decomposed through time and implemented recursively. The choice of strategy is equivalent to the choice of current policy only, taking into account both the immediate reward and the expected future value, in particular how this period's action affects the next period's economic environment and assuming optimal behavior in the future. As in the discrete case, this is known as Bellman's principle of optimality, and we shall employ this principle extensively throughout this volume. The point is that optimal policies are forward looking; they do not take account of how the current state was achieved.

The first application of the optimality principle is rather straightforward. In particular, the principle is recast as

$$V_0 = T_0(V_1), \tag{6.7}$$

where T_0 is the operator on the right hand side of the equation. More precisely, for $t \in \{0, 1, \ldots, \tau - 1\}$ and $f : X_{t+1} \to R$, we define T_t by

$$T_t(f)(x) = \max_{c \in C_t}\{u_t(x, c) + E(f(x_{t+1})|x, c)\}, \tag{6.8}$$

where the conditional expectation is over $x_{t+1} \sim Q_t(\cdot|x, c)$. For a given function f, this defines a new function $T_t(f)$ by giving the value of the new function at the arbitrary point $x \in X_t$. In other words, T_t maps functions to functions, and we shall occasionally work explicitly with the domains and codomains, both function spaces, and accordingly write the functionality as $T_t : B_{t+1} \to B_t$. Of course, T_t need not be onto. It is now clear that the equation $V_0 = T_0(V_1)$ is a restatement of the optimality principle; i.e., for each $x_0 \in X_0$, we have $V_0(x_0) = T_0(V_1)(x_0)$. By the same token, $V_1 = T_1(V_2)$, and so on.

Suppose now that the economic agent faces a fixed finite planning horizon, $\tau < \infty$. This is obviously somewhat unrealistic in some cases, and the assumption will be relaxed in the sequel. For the time being, though, suppose the terminal value function V_τ is given. In this case, by induction in t and invoking the optimality principle, we may in fact construct all the remaining value functions $V_t, t = \tau - 1, \tau - 2, \ldots$, from

$$V_t = T_t(V_{t+1}). \tag{6.9}$$

Ultimately, the algorithm produces the initial value V_0. We therefore have a method of solving the optimum problem that explicitly utilizes the decomposition alluded to earlier. This method is known as *backward recursion*. It may also be stated in the alternative, albeit nonrecursive, form

$$V_0 = T_0 \circ T_1 \circ \cdots \circ T_{\tau-1}(V_\tau), \tag{6.10}$$

where $\circ$ indicates composition of maps.

6.4 EXAMPLE: EXERCISING AN AMERICAN OPTION

The finite-horizon dynamic programming backward recursion with continuous states and discrete controls can be illustrated in a simple financial application: exercising an American call option. A call option is an option to buy a specified asset or commodity (henceforth "the underlying") at a predetermined price K, the strike price. An American option can be exercised at any time before the expiration time T. A European option in contrast can be exercised only at date T. Let p_t be the price of the underlying at time t and suppose for simplicity that the price process is independent and identically distributed (i.i.d.) with finite mean. This serves as a useful first illustration and may also be an empirically relevant assumption if the underlying commodity is a perishable good, such as bananas or electricity. At T, the value of the option is

$$V_T(p_T) = \max\{p_T - K, 0\}. \tag{6.11}$$

Again for simplicity, we initially ignore discounting and assume the agent holding the option is maximizing the expected return. Continuing with the recursion,

$$V_{T-1}(p_{T-1}) = \max\{p_{T-1} - K, EV_T\} \tag{6.12}$$

since V_T is the only stochastic variable in the equation and it is greater than zero. Clearly, we have

$$V_{t-1}(p_{t-1}) = \max\{p_{t-1} - K, EV_t\}, \tag{6.13}$$

and the optimal policy is to exercise the option, if at all, in the first period for which $p_t > EV_{t+1} + K$. This problem is in the important class of problems known as optimal stopping problems. To find properties of the solution we calculate the expected values

$$
\begin{aligned}
H(x) &= E(p - K \mid p - K > x), \\
F(x) &= \Pr(p - K < x), \\
\overline{F}(x) &= 1 - F(x), \\
EV_T &= H(0)\overline{F}(0), \\
EV_{T-1} &= F(EV_T)EV_T + \overline{F}(EV_T)H(EV_T),
\end{aligned}
\tag{6.14}
$$

$$\vdots$$

$$EV_1 = F(EV_2)EV_2 + \overline{F}(EV_2)H(EV_2).$$

Clearly, $H(x) > x$, and EV_t is a convex combination of EV_{t+1} and $H(EV_{t+1}) > EV_{t+1}$. Hence, $EV_t > EV_{t+k}$ for $k > 0$—the more periods left, the more valuable the option. The sequence of minimum prices at

which the option will be exercised (the optimal exercise boundary) is therefore decreasing toward K, its value in period T.

Note that the recursion is developed not for the sequence of functions V_t
but for the sequence of scalars EV_t. This is an important simplification in
applications. Another optimal stopping model with a similar simplification
is the search model taken up later. Simplifications of this type occur outside
the class of optimal stopping models: An important example is the class of
linear-quadratic models studied in chapter 13.

Consider next the case where the underlying is a financial asset, e.g., com-
mon stock, and assume $K > 0$ and Markov asset prices, writing $f(p_{t+1}|p_t)$
for the density of p_{t+1} given p_t. This assumption is relevant for asset prices,
which must satisfy

$$p_t = \beta E(p_{t+1}|p_t), \tag{6.15}$$

where β is the discount factor. Without discounting, $\beta = 1$ and p_t is a
martingale. In general, the discounted process $p_t \beta^t$ is a martingale since
$E(p_{t+1}\beta^{t+1}|p_t\beta^t) = \beta^t \beta E(p_{t+1}|p_t) = p_t\beta^t$. This presentation assumes
risk neutrality, but in the case of risk aversion, the same condition holds,
with the expectation taken under the equivalent martingale measure or risk-
neutral distribution. We return to this point in chapter 10.

The optimal exercise strategy is analyzed by backward recursion in the
dynamic programming problem. In general,

$$V_t(p_t) = \max\{p_t - K, \beta E(V_{t+1}|p_t)\}. \tag{6.16}$$

Thus, in the ultimate period, the value of the option is

$$V_T(p_T) = \max\{p_T - K, 0\}. \tag{6.17}$$

The option is exercised at T if and only if $p_T > p_T^* = K$. Next, the value
in the penultimate time period is

$$V_{T-1}(p_{T-1}) = \max\{p_{T-1} - K, \beta E(V_T|p_{T-1})\}. \tag{6.18}$$

The option is exercised at $T - 1$ if and only if p_{T-1} exceeds $K + \beta E(V_T|p_{T-1})$. If it is not exercised, the value at $T - 1$ is $\beta E(V_T|p_{T-1})$.
In this event, the agent holding the option will receive V_T at time T, and this
will be $p_T - K$ if this is positive, and otherwise zero. This payoff structure
at time T is similar to the case where the agent holds the stock but owes the
certain amount K since the payoff at T from this position is exactly $p_T - K$.
The value at $(T - 1)$ of the stock/debt position is $\beta E(p_T - K|p_{t-1})$, or sim-
ply $p_{T-1} - \beta K$, using the martingale property. Another way to see this is
that the value of the stock at $T - 1$ obviously is p_{T-1}, and the value of the
debt is the present value of the future payment to be made. But note that

while the combined stock/debt position yields $p_T - K$ at T, this is only a lower bound of the option payoff at T (since the option value in period T is bounded below by zero). So the value of the option when not exercised at $T - 1$ must be no less than the value $p_{T-1} - \beta K$ of the stock/debt position, i.e.,

$$\beta E(V_T | p_{T-1}) \geq p_{T-1} - \beta K$$
$$> p_{T-1} - K. \tag{6.19}$$

It follows that it is optimal not to exercise the option at $T - 1$ since (6.19) identifies the maximum in (6.18) and hence

$$V_{T-1}(p_{T-1}) = \beta E(V_T | p_{T-1}). \tag{6.20}$$

Continuing the backward recursion, the same argument applies in each step. That is, we always have

$$V_t(p_t) = \max\{p_t - K, \beta E(V_{t+1} | p_t)\}, \tag{6.21}$$

but we show that it is optimal not to exercise, so we get

$$V_t(p_t) = \beta E(V_{t+1} | p_t). \tag{6.22}$$

As the result (6.22) has already been demonstrated for $t = T-1$, we proceed to establish it for all previous periods by induction. Thus, assume the result holds for $T - 1, T - 2, \ldots, t$. We first note that this also implies

$$V_t(p_t) = \beta E(\beta E(V_{t+2} | p_{t+1}) | p_t)$$
$$= \beta^{T-t} E(V_T | p_t). \tag{6.23}$$

We must now demonstrate the result for time period $t - 1$. We have

$$V_{t-1}(p_{t-1}) = \max\{p_{t-1} - K, \beta E(V_t | p_{t-1})\}$$
$$= \max\{p_{t-1} - K, \beta E(\beta^{T-t} E(V_T | p_t) | p_{t-1})\}$$
$$= \max\{p_{t-1} - K, \beta^{T-(t-1)} E(V_T | p_{t-1})\}. \tag{6.24}$$

If the option is not exercised, the value is $\beta^{T-(t-1)} E(V_T | p_{t-1})$, where V_T is as described earlier ($p_T - K$ or 0), to be received $T - (t - 1)$ periods hence. This payoff again dominates that of the position consisting of a stock and an obligation to pay K at T. Hence,

$$\beta^{T-(t-1)} E(V_T | p_{t-1}) \geq p_{t-1} - \beta^{T-(t-1)} K$$
$$> p_{t-1} - K, \tag{6.25}$$

and it is optimal not to exercise at $t-1$. We have shown that

$$V_{t-1}(p_{t-1}) = \beta^{T-(t-1)}E(V_T|p_{t-1}).\qquad(6.26)$$

By using the previous derivation of $V_{t-1}(p_{t-1})$, we see that

$$V_{t-1}(p_{t-1}) = \beta E(V_t|p_{t-1}).\qquad(6.27)$$

This completes the induction step, hence proving (6.22) for all t.

We conclude that the American option is never exercised early. The price is given by

$$V_t(p_t) = \beta E(V_{t+1}|p_t),\qquad(6.28)$$

showing that the discounted option price $\beta^t V_t$ is a martingle, like the discounted stock price $\beta^t p_t$. Equivalently, the option price is given by

$$V_t(p_t) = \beta^{T-t}E(V_T|p_t).\qquad(6.29)$$

The latter is easily represented as

$$V_t(p_t) = \beta^{T-t}E(p_T - K|p_T - K > 0)P(p_T - K > 0)$$
$$= \beta^{T-t}\int_K^\infty (p_T - K)f(p_T|p_t)\,dp_T.\qquad(6.30)$$

This coincides with the value of the corresponding European call with strike price K and expiration date T. This is as it should be since an American option that is never exercised early is equivalent to a European option.

Again, with independent prices, the exercise boundary decreases over time to K (see (6.14)), and the American call may actually be exercised early. This is because the prices in this case do not satisfy the discounted martingale property (6.15), hence showing the importance of this asset price characteristic. Note that the only martingales that are i.i.d. are constants. In both cases (martingale and nonmartingale prices), the dynamic programming backward recursions deliver the solution.

6.5 INFINITE HORIZON: CONTRACTION AND FORWARD RECURSION

With an infinite planning horizon $\tau = \infty$, there can be no terminal value, and backward recursion is impossible. Intuitively, some form of forward recursion is required. However, more structure is usually needed to make this work. A particular specification, that of stationarity, often proves especially useful in applications. Thus, assume $X_t = X$, $C_t = C$, and $Q_t = Q$; i.e., the state and control spaces as well as the transition equation are time-invariant. In addition, let utility be generated by geometric discounting of a time-invariant period utility, i.e., $u_t = \beta^t u$, where $\beta \in (0, 1)$ is the agent's subjective discount factor (equivalently, $-\log \beta$ is the continuous and $\rho = \beta^{-1} - 1$ the discrete discount rate, each positive). These time-invariant specifications could be adopted also in a model with a finite horizon, $\tau < \infty$, and if we now write V_t for the value function in this model, the calculation $\Sigma_{t=0}^{\tau} \beta^t u = u + \beta \Sigma_{t=1}^{\tau} \beta^{t-1} u = u + \beta \Sigma_{t=0}^{\tau-1} \beta^t u$ suggests redefining the operator T_t from (6.8) as

$$T(f)(x) = \max_{c \in C}\{u(x, c) + \beta E(f(y)|x, c)\}, \qquad (6.31)$$

where $y \sim Q(\cdot|x, c)$. Note that $T_t = T$ since nothing on the right hand side depends on t. It follows that

$$V^\tau = T(V^{\tau-1}), \qquad (6.32)$$

where V^t is the value function for the problem with t periods left before the last, so T maps the value function for the $(\tau - 1)$-period problem into that for the τ-period problem, and repeated application of this idea shows that

$$V^\tau = T^\tau(V^0), \qquad (6.33)$$

where by our conventions $V^0 = \max_c\{u(x, c)\}$. This suggests constructing the value function for the infinite-horizon model, say V, by forward recursion,

$$V = \lim_{\tau \to \infty} T^\tau(V^0). \qquad (6.34)$$

Under regularity conditions that we shall discuss below, this procedure in fact works, even when u is replaced by an arbitrary function in the domain of T (that is, V^0 is arbitrary; of course, the correct u must be employed in the definition (6.31) of T).

In the infinite-horizon model, the problem facing the agent looks the same whether it is started off in period 0 or in period 1; i.e., $V_0 = V_1$ (they both equal V). Substituting $V_i = V, i = 0, 1$, in the optimality principle $V_0 = T(V_1)$ (see (6.7)) produces

$$V = T(V); \qquad (6.35)$$

i.e., the infinite-horizon value is a fixed point of the operator T. This functional equation in fact under regularity conditions has exactly one solution, the function V, and it thereby uniquely characterizes the value function.

To get a better feel for these matters, it is useful to introduce a few more technical tools. The following material is treated with more detail and discussion by Stokey and Lucas (1989). First, we should be explicit about the domain of T, i.e., $B_{t+1} = B_t$, and often this will be the space of bounded continuous functions $f : X \to \mathbb{R}$, which is the space we henceforth refer to as B. Recall that in the discrete-state space case $B = \mathbb{R}^{|S|}$. We shall seek the value function V as the solution in B to the functional equation $V = T(V)$, so it becomes important to ensure that the codomain B_t is contained in B. To this end, we may specify that Q has the Feller property; i.e., if f is bounded and continuous, then so is $E(f(y)|x, c)$ (precisely, $E(f(y)|\cdot, \pi(\cdot)))$ in the definition of T. Then the theorem of the maximum implies that $T(f)$ is continuous (recall that C is discrete) and bounded (e.g., if also X is compact), and this way the functionality $T : B \to B$ is established.

It is convenient to apply some general mathematics to the function spaces we encounter. A metric space is a set M equipped with a metric or distance function $d : M \times M \to \mathbb{R}_+$ that is symmetric $(d(f, g) = d(g, f), \forall f, g \in M)$, with $d(f, g) = 0$ if and only if $f = g$, and satisfies the triangle inequality $(d(f, g) \leq d(f, h) + d(h, g), \forall f, g, h \in M)$. Then $F : M \to M$ is said to be a contraction of modulus $\delta \in (0, 1)$ if $d(F(f), F(g)) \leq \delta d(f, g), \forall f, g \in M$.

The key result on the value function V and the map T that we are after is based on the contraction mapping theorem (CMT), and to state this we need the notion of completeness. A metric space M is complete if every Cauchy sequence in M converges to a limit in M. Precisely, $\{f_n\}_{n=1}^{\infty} \subseteq M$ is Cauchy if the distance between elements sufficiently far out in the sequence becomes arbitrarily small (if $\forall \varepsilon > 0 \; \exists N \geq 0 : m, n \geq N \implies d(f_m, f_n) \leq \varepsilon)$, and M is complete if the Cauchy property implies convergence to a point in M (i.e., $\exists f \in M : \forall \varepsilon > 0 \; \exists N \geq 0 : n \geq N \implies d(f, f_n) \leq \varepsilon)$.

We are now in a position to state the contraction mapping theorem. Let M be a complete metric space and $F : M \to M$ a contraction of modulus $\delta \in (0, 1)$. Then there exists a unique fixed point f for F in M, namely, $f = F(f)$, and this may be constructed by iterating the contraction; i.e.,

$$f = \lim_{\tau \to \infty} F^{\tau}(g) \tag{6.36}$$

for $g \in M$ arbitrary.

The CMT is easily proved by invoking the definition of a contraction. First, it is shown that the sequence $f_n = F^n(g)$ is Cauchy, then that the limit f is a fixed point, and finally that no other $h \in M$ can be so.

To bring the theorem into play, we must verify that this mathematical framework applies to our particular economic setup. In fact, in this case we may often work directly with Banach spaces rather than general metric spaces. A Banach space is a complete normed vector space. Here, a norm on a vector space M is a function $||\cdot|| : M \to \mathbb{R}_+$ such that for $s \in \mathbb{R}$ and $f \in M$ we have $||sf|| = |s| \cdot ||f||$, with $||f|| = 0$ if and only if $f = 0$, and which satisfies the triangle inequality; i.e., $||f + g|| \leq ||f|| + ||g||$ for all

$f, g \in M$. We may then consider a vector space equipped with a norm as a metric space simply by defining $d(f, g) = ||f - g||$, so the definition of a Banach space as a complete normed vector space is meaningful.

The space B of bounded continuous functions is Banach with the supremum norm

$$||f|| = \sup_{x \in X} |f(x)|. \tag{6.37}$$

Thus, to invoke the CMT in the analysis of the functional equation $V = T(V)$, we have the domain and codomain of T complete and metric, and it remains to verify that T contracts. For this purpose, we appeal to Blackwell's (1965) sufficient conditions. Thus, if M is a set of bounded functions on X equipped with the supremum norm, we say that $F : M \to M$ is monotonic if $f \leq g$ (i.e., $f(x) \leq g(x), \forall x \in X$) implies $F(f) \leq F(g)$, and we say that F discounts if for some $\delta \in (0, 1)$

$$F(f + s) \leq F(f) + \delta s, \qquad \forall f \in M, s \in \mathbb{R} \tag{6.38}$$

(where $(f + s)(x) = f(x) + s, \forall x \in X, s \in \mathbb{R}$). If F is monotonic and discounts, then it is a contraction of modulus δ. To show this, note that $f \leq g + ||f - g||$, apply F to both sides, and invoke the two conditions. Interchanging f and g yields $||F(f) - F(g)|| \leq \delta ||f - g||$.

It is now clear that T is monotonic (increasing f cannot lower the maximum) and discounts since

$$
\begin{aligned}
T(f + s)(x) &= \max_{c \in C} \{u(x, c) + \beta E(f(y) + s|x, c)\} \\
&= \max_{c \in C} \{u(x, c) + \beta E(f(y)|x, c)\} + \beta s \\
&= T(f)(x) + \beta s, \tag{6.39}
\end{aligned}
$$

and it follows that T is a contraction of modulus β. The contraction mapping theorem yields existence and uniqueness of a fixed point f satisfying $f = T(f)$. We know that the value function V for the infinite-horizon dynamic programming model is one fixed point, so by the CMT, we may construct V uniquely by solving the functional equation $V = T(V)$. The second conclusion of the CMT shows that the forward induction scheme conjectured earlier renders this construction tractable.

Of course, in empirical applications, we (typically) stop the iterations after a finite number, but we can easily get an upper bound on the error thus committed in calculating V. That is, if stopping after τ recursions,

$$
\begin{aligned}
d(V, V^\tau) &\le d(V, V^{\tau+1}) + d(V^{\tau+1}, V^\tau) \\
&\le \sum_{i=\tau}^{\infty} d(V^i, V^{i+1}) \\
&\le \sum_{i=\tau}^{\infty} \beta^{i-\tau} d(V^\tau, V^{\tau+1}) \\
&= \frac{d(V^\tau, V^{\tau+1})}{1 - \beta}.
\end{aligned}
\tag{6.40}
$$

This shows that the error involved when stopping early is bounded in terms of the change in the most recent iteration.

When the maximum in the definition of T is attained (the more general supremum notation is unnecessary) and the maximizer is

$$
c(x) \in \arg \max_{c \in C(x)} \{u(x, c) + \beta E(V(y)|x, c)\},
\tag{6.41}
$$

then $\pi = (\pi_0, \pi_1, \ldots)$ defined by $\pi_t(x_t) = c(x_t)$ is an optimal stationary strategy; i.e., the agent's behavior is time-invariant. The optimal stationary policy $c(\cdot)$ is also referred to as a Markov policy, and it is clear that the controlled stochastic process $\{x_t, c_t\}_{t=0}^{\infty}$, with $c_t = c(x_t)$, is Markov. Further, it is strictly stationary if the distribution μ of x_0 is a stationary distribution for Q_π^0, i.e., if

$$
\mu(B) = \int_X Q(B|x, c(x))\mu(dx), \qquad \forall B \in X.
\tag{6.42}
$$

Otherwise the process is asymptotically stationary. The process is ergodic if and only if any such stationary μ as in (6.42) is unique, i.e., is the unique eigenmeasure of Q_π^0 corresponding to the unit eigenvalue.

6.6 EXAMPLE: OPTIMAL STOPPING IN DISCRETE TIME

We now consider an important application of the general infinite-horizon dynamic programming model with continuous states and discrete controls, namely, to optimal stopping. Here, it is useful to employ a slightly modified notation which we also return to in chapter 13 when studying smoothness. Thus, in addition to $x \in X$, the state of the system is also characterized by the variable $a \in A$; i.e., the full state vector is $\omega = (a, x)$ and the expanded state space $\Omega = A \times X$. We now restrict attention to Markov transitions for x that do not depend on the control i.e.,

$$
x_{t+1} \sim Q(\cdot|x_t),
\tag{6.43}
$$

as in (2.7), but we allow for the choice set to depend on the state; i.e., $c \in C(a, x) = C(\omega)$. The law of motion for the additional state variable a is of the simple form

$$a_{t+1} = c_t; \tag{6.44}$$

i.e., the component a of the current state $\omega = (a, x)$ is simply the lagged control or action taken by the agent in the previous period. The optimality principle now takes the form

$$V(a, x) = \max_{c \in C(a,x)} \{u(a, x, c) + \beta E(V(c, y)|x)\}, \tag{6.45}$$

where $y \sim Q(\cdot|x)$.

The essential restrictions in the case of optimal stopping are that, first, $A = \{0, 1\}$, where the current state (lagged control) $a = 1$ indicates that the decision process is still ongoing at the beginning of the current time period, whereas $a = 0$ indicates that the process has been stopped, and, second, the constraint set $C(a, x)$ is given by $C(1, x) = \{0, 1\}$, indicating that a process that has not yet been stopped may be either continued further ($c = 1$) or stopped now ($c = 0$), and $C(0, x) = \{0\}$, i.e., stopping is final. Note that the simplification $C(a, x) = C(a)$ applies to the optimal stopping model; i.e., $C(a)$ is given by $C(0) = \{0\}$ and $C(1) = A$. It follows that the functional equation is given by the system

$$V(0, x) = u(0, x, 0) + \beta E(V(0, y)|x), \tag{6.46}$$

$$V(1, x) = \max\{u(1, x, 0) + \beta E(V(0, y)|x), u(1, x, 1) + \beta E(V(1, y)|x)\}.$$

Of course, as usual, it is easy to write down a related finite-horizon version of the model.

Among the most useful instances of an optimal stopping model in economics is the job search model. Here, an initially unemployed worker receives a wage offer x each period while still unemployed ($a = 1$), and for each x decides between remaining unemployed to continue the search ($c = 1$) or accepting the offer and becoming employed ($c = 0$). Once employed, the worker receives the accepted wage x in each of the following periods, but before that only an unemployment insurance benefit (net of search costs) u (a fixed scalar) is received each period. By a slight abuse of the notation, we have $u(a, x, 0) = x$, $u(1, x, 1) = u$. We shall often adopt the assumption of no serial dependence in offers, so the transition equation for x is given by $Q(y|x, 0) = 1_x$ (indicating unit mass on the event $\{y = x\}$ after employment) and $Q(y|x, 1) = Q(y)$.

The functional equation for the infinite-horizon job search model is therefore the specialization of (6.46) to

$$V(0, x) = x + \beta E(V(0, x)|x),$$

$$V(1, x) = \max\{x + \beta E(V(0, x)|x), u + \beta E(V(1, y))\}. \tag{6.47}$$

The first equation immediately implies

$$V(0, x) = \frac{x}{1 - \beta},\tag{6.48}$$

and since $x + \beta x/(1 - \beta) = x/(1 - \beta)$, the second equation is

$$V(1, x) = \max\left\{\frac{x}{1 - \beta}, u + \beta E(V(1, y))\right\}.\tag{6.49}$$

Thus, while still searching, the value function $V(1, x)$ is of the form $\max\{V(0, x), V(1)\}$, where the value $V(0, x)$ of becoming employed increases in x and the value $V(1) = u + \beta E(V(1, y))$ of unemployment is a constant. This observation identifies the optimal stopping region; that is, the agent chooses $c = 0$ (employment) if and only if the outstanding offer x exceeds a reservation wage given by $V(0, r) = V(1)$, i.e., satisfying

$$r = (1 - \beta)(u + \beta E(V(1, y))).\tag{6.50}$$

That is, the optimum problem has the reservation wage property, and $(-\infty, r]$ is the continuation region for x. We shall study this model in detail in chapters 7–9.

6.7 EXERCISES

1. Let $x_{t+1} = \rho_0 x_t + \rho_1 x_{t-1} + \cdots + \rho_k x_{t-k} + \gamma_0 c_t + \gamma_1 c_{t-1} + \cdots + \gamma_p c_{t-p}$. Write this as a first-order vector equation.

2. Let $f : [0, 1] \to [0, 1]$ be a continuous function. Show that f has a fixed point, i.e., that there exists a point $x^* \in [0, 1]$ with $f(x^*) = x^*$. This is an instance of Brouwer's fixed-point theorem, and there are many proofs. Consider elementary methods and the function $f(x) - x$.

3. Let $g : (0, 1) \to (0, 1)$ be a continuous function. Show that g need not have a fixed point.

4. Return your attention to the f in exercise 2 and suppose in addition that $0 < |f'(x)| < 1$ for $x \in (0, 1)$. Show that f has a unique fixed point in $[0, 1]$. Prove directly and by using the CMT.

6.8 REFERENCES

Much of this chapter does not require discrete controls. Once the state space is continuous, then the value function is complicated—not merely a vector. In practice, the discrete control restriction can usually be used to simplify computation of the optimal policy by obtaining a contraction map on a vector the size of the cardinality of the control space. This is illustrated in the optimal stopping model and particularly in the job search applications sketched next. The mathematical development, however, does not simplify as a result of the discreteness of the control space. Early papers developing the mathematics of dynamic programming in quite general settings are Blackwell (1965), Strauch (1966), and Maitra (1968). Bertsekas and Shreve (1978) give a careful technical presentation. Denardo (1967) is a classic reference on contraction mappings. A quite general development is given by Bhattacharya and Majumdar (1989a,b, 2006). Bertsekas (1975) treats discretization approaches to general dynamic programming.

Optimal stopping is a classic application of dynamic programming methods, and indeed optimal stopping models provide the basis for some of the first empirical dynamic programming applications in economics (structural job search models; an earlier literature in macroeconomics applied dynamic programming methods to estimated models but did not use dynamic programming in model specification). Optimal stopping theory originated in Wald's (1945) theory of sequential analysis of statistical observations. Gittens and Jones (1974) extend the model to cover sequential experimentation. A discussion of the relation between decision theory and dynamic programming is given by Lindley (1961) with an example (sampling to decide whether a normal mean is positive or negative).

Chapter Seven

Econometric Framework for the Search Model

7.1 THE SEARCH MODEL

In this chapter we consider the exact likelihood function for the job search model. This setting is useful for several reasons. First, the search model is a simple and widely understood dynamic programming model with a continuous state space in which the optimal policy can be easily calculated and interpreted. Second, there exists a background of many empirical applications. Third, the model illustrates simply the nonlinear, nonregular statistical issues arising in more complicated dynamic programming applications. Some of these have been introduced in the discrete state context.

The particular search model we examine is simple, yet it captures features of the labor market known to be important. For this reason we refer to our basic specification as the *prototypal* search specification. Our analysis follows Christensen and Kiefer (1991a). It is worth emphasizing that we consider the full econometric implications of the assumed theoretical model. It is important to understand the full implications of a model and the specification if it is to provide a useful guide to interpreting data. The prototypal model has been widely used in data analysis. Devine and Kiefer (1991) review the empirical performance of this model and suggest areas where generalization is required. Nevertheless the model has often been fit inefficiently and occasionally has been fit and interpreted incorrectly.

Unemployed workers are assumed to know certain things about the local labor market for workers with their skills—in particular they are assumed to know the distribution of wages across firms. They do not know which firm offers which wage (alternatively, the firms offer wages at random, e.g., reflecting different subjective assessments of worker suitability). We assume that offers w are distributed with density $f(w)$, with support $[0, \infty)$ or possibly $[w_{min}, w_{max}]$. A worker who accepts a job expects to hold it forever. This assumption is easily relaxed but simplifies the presentation of the model. Further, in applications the model is typically fit to single spells of unemployment, and our specification is appropriate for this case.

A worker who is unemployed but looking for work receives a per-period income of y. One interpretation is that y is unemployment benefits net of search costs. The worker uses a per-period discount factor $\beta \in [0, 1)$.

It is empirically useful to provide a model in which the worker does not necessarily receive an offer each period. Suppose an offer is received with per-period probability p. The event of receiving an offer and the value of the offer are independent. In this simple specification the stochastic mechanism determining whether an offer is received is exogenous to the worker, while the decision to accept a job is endogenous, leading Mortensen and Neumann (1984, 1988) to distinguish between "chance" and "choice."

We are now in a position to obtain the optimal search policy for a worker who seeks to maximize the expected present discounted value of his income stream. Here our state variable x is the wage w, and we are in the optimal stopping framework. We compute the value function $V(w)$, where w is the outstanding wage offer. It is convenient to define state-dependent value functions V^e and V^u corresponding to employment and unemployment. Thus, $V(w) = \max\{V^e(w), V^u\}$ or, equivalently, $\max\{V(0, x), V(1, x)\}$, in the notation (6.47) of optimal stopping; i.e.,

$$V(w) = \max\left\{\sum_{t=0}^{\infty} \beta^t w, \, y + \beta EV\right\} = \max\left\{\frac{w}{1-\beta}, \, y + \beta EV\right\}. \quad (7.1)$$

Since V^e is monotonically increasing in w and V^u does not depend on w, a reservation wage strategy is optimal: Let w_r satisfy $V^e(w_r) = V^u$; then accept the first offer greater than w_r. To make the model interesting, we assume that there is positive probability of an offer greater than w_r (otherwise the worker does not enter the market) and that w_r is greater than 0 (otherwise the worker always accepts the first offer). We use indifference between unemployment and employment at the reservation wage to develop an implicit equation for the reservation wage,

$$w_r(y, f, p) = (1 - \beta)(y + \beta EV). \quad (7.2)$$

This is an implicit equation because EV depends on the optimal policy:

$$
\begin{aligned}
EV &= p \int_0^{\infty} V(w) f(w)\, dw + (1 - p)(y + \beta EV) \\
&= p(y + \beta EV) F(w_r(y, f, p)) \\
&\quad + p \int_{w_r(y, f, p)}^{\infty} \frac{w}{(1 - \beta)} f(w)\, dw + (1 - p)(y + \beta EV) \\
&= \frac{1}{1 - \beta} \{p[(1 - \Pi)w_r + \Pi E(w|w \geq w_r)] + (1 - p)w_r\} \\
&= \frac{1}{1 - \beta} \{(p - p\Pi + 1 - p)w_r + p\Pi E(w|w \geq w_r)\} \\
&= \frac{1}{1 - \beta} \{(1 - p\Pi)w_r + p\Pi E(w|w \geq w_r)\}. \quad (7.3)
\end{aligned}
$$

Here, Π is the acceptance probability,

$$\Pi = \Pi(y, f, p) = \int_{w_r(y,f,p)}^{\infty} f(w)dw,$$

and $\Pr(\text{employment}) = p\Pi = \lambda(y, f, p)$. The standard model is the special case $p = 1$. Mortensen (1986) gives a detailed exposition and many extensions. It is useful to note that the right hand side of (7.3) is a contraction; (7.3) implicitly defines EV as the unique fixed point of this map:

$$
\begin{aligned}
EV &= \frac{1}{1-\beta}\left\{\left(1 - p\int_{w_r}^{\infty} f\,dw\right)w_r + p\int_{w_r}^{\infty} wf\,dw\right\}\\
&= \frac{1}{1-\beta}\left\{\left(1 - p\int_{(1-\beta)(y+\beta EV)}^{\infty} f\,dw\right)(1-\beta)(y+\beta EV)\right.\\
&\qquad\left. + p\int_{(1-\beta)(y+\beta EV)}^{\infty} wf\,dw\right\}\\
&= \left(1 - p\int_{(1-\beta)(y+\beta EV)}^{\infty} f\,dw\right)(y+\beta EV) + \frac{p}{1-\beta}\int_{(1-\beta)(y+\beta EV)}^{\infty} wf\,dw\\
&= U(EV). \qquad\qquad\qquad\qquad\qquad\qquad\qquad\qquad\qquad (7.4)
\end{aligned}
$$

We verify the contraction property by calculating the derivative

$$
\begin{aligned}
U'(EV) &= p(1-\beta)\beta f(w_r)\frac{w_r}{1-\beta} + \beta(1 - p\Pi) - \frac{p}{1-\beta}(1-\beta)\beta w_r f(w_r)\\
&= \beta(1 - p\Pi), \qquad\qquad\qquad\qquad\qquad\qquad\qquad\qquad (7.5)
\end{aligned}
$$

so $0 \le U' \le \beta < 1$. Numerically, this allows solving for the expected value by iterating the contraction. By (7.2), this gives the reservation wage, too.

7.2 LIKELIHOOD: GENERAL CONSIDERATIONS

We now sketch the general framework for likelihood analysis of the search model, emphasizing geometric concepts. Many of our results, stated for the search model, apply to general optimal stopping results. Our geometric approach introduces concepts that are likely to be useful for empirical dynamic programming models generally. We illustrate the profile likelihood and the asymptotic profile likelihood. We consider maximum likelihood estimation and give some asymptotic distribution theory for the maximum likelihood estimator (MLE). Our specification implies a statistical nonregularity analogous to that arising in the well-known problem of estimating the parameter of a uniform distribution on $[\theta, 1]$. The MLE $\hat{\theta}$ is the minimum observation, and the asymptotics are nonstandard because the likelihood function is discontinuous at $\hat{\theta}$. Standard arguments via a Taylor series expansion and a central limit theorem do not apply.

Throughout, N is the number of individuals, (t_i, w_i) are the duration and accepted wage for the ith individual, N_c is the number of censored spells, $N_e = N - N_c$ is the number of uncensored spells, $T = \Sigma t_i$, $\widetilde{T} = T - N_e$ ($\widetilde{T}$ is interpreted as the total number of periods in which workers did not become reemployed), $w_m = \min\{w_i\}$, and $\overline{w} = \Sigma w_i / N_e$. Of course, wages are observed only for uncensored observations, and some of the observed t_i will be censoring times rather than completed durations.

Let the k-dimensional vector θ parametrize the offer density f and the economic model. As we have seen, a reservation wage strategy is optimal in all models, and if necessary, $w_r(\theta)$ is found via contraction. The likelihood function is of the form

$$l(\theta) = l^*(\theta)\, 1_{\{w_m \geq w_r(\theta)\}}, \qquad \theta \in \Theta,$$

where $l^*(\theta)$ is a differentiable function on $\Theta \subseteq \mathbb{R}^k$, the parameter space. We consider the graphs

$$G_l = \{(\theta, l(\theta)) | \theta \in \Theta\},$$
$$G_+ = \{(\theta, l) \in G_l | l > 0\}.$$

G_+ is a k-dimensional manifold with boundary in $\mathbb{R}^{k+1}$. The boundary, a $(k-1)$-dimensional submanifold, is denoted ∂G_+. Let $\Theta_+ = P_\Theta G_+ = \{\theta \in \Theta | w_m \geq w_r(\theta)\}$ be the projection of G_+ to Θ. We can then define the score

$$s(\theta) = \frac{d \ln l(\theta)}{d\theta}, \qquad \theta \in \text{int } \Theta_+.$$

It is often the case in optimal stopping models that (exactly or asymptotically) for some i, l is monotonic in θ_i, over int Θ_+, e.g.,

$$s_i(\theta) > 0, \qquad \theta \in \text{int } \Theta_+. \tag{7.6}$$

We illustrate this phenomenon in a specific parametrization below. Assume $i = k$ (reorder if necessary) and consider the natural decomposition $\theta = (\theta_1, \theta_2) \in \mathbb{R}^{k-1} \times \mathbb{R}$. Then the (exact or asymptotic) MLE of θ_2, given θ_1 and data, is

$$\hat{\theta}_2(\theta_1, w_m) = w_r^{-1}(\theta_1, w_m), \tag{7.7}$$

which is defined by the equation

$$w_m = w_r\left(\theta_1, w_r^{-1}(\theta_1, w_m)\right), \qquad \theta_1 \in \widetilde{\Theta},$$

where $\widetilde{\Theta} = \widetilde{P}\Theta_+$ is the projection of $\Theta_+ \subseteq \mathbb{R}^{k-1} \times \mathbb{R}$ to $\mathbb{R}^{k-1}$. When convenient, we suppress the dependence of $\hat{\theta}_2$ on w_m. In each model we study, we demonstrate that $\hat{\theta}_2(\cdot)$ is well defined and smooth. In general, this can be done by applying the implicit function theorem to the conditions (7.2) and (7.3); we are able to do this by direct inspection of explicit expressions for $\hat{\theta}_2(\cdot)$. We also note that $\hat{\theta}_2$ is not defined by setting the corresponding score equal to zero. Let

$$\tilde{l}(\theta_1) = \tilde{l}(\theta_1, \hat{\theta}_2(\theta_1)), \qquad \theta_1 \in \widetilde{\Theta}. \tag{7.8}$$

If (7.6) holds exactly, (7.8) is the *profile likelihood function*. If (7.6) holds only asymptotically, (7.8) is an *asymptotic profile likelihood function*, a particular case of a pseudo likelihood function in the sense of Barndorff-Nielsen (1988). Consider the graph

$$\widetilde{G} = \{(\theta_1, \tilde{l}(\theta_1)) | \theta_1 \in \widetilde{\Theta}\}.$$

We note that $\widetilde{G} = \widetilde{G}_+ = P_m G_+$, where $P_m = \widetilde{P} \otimes P_{k+1}$ is the projection of $\Theta \times \mathbb{R}$ to $\widetilde{\Theta} \times \mathbb{R}$. $\widetilde{G}$ is a $(k-1)$-dimensional manifold in $\mathbb{R}^k$. Indeed, $\tilde{l}$ can alternatively be defined as the function whose graph is obtained from G_+ by projection under P_m. Now, $\tilde{l}(\theta_1)$ is positive over $\widetilde{\Theta}$, so we let

$$\tilde{s}(\theta_1) = \frac{d \ln \tilde{l}(\theta_1)}{d\theta_1}, \qquad \theta_1 \in \widetilde{\Theta}.$$

In the models we study, the maximizer $\hat{\theta}_1$ of $\tilde{l}(\theta_1)$ can be found by solving the profile likelihood equation $\tilde{s}(\hat{\theta}_1) = 0$. Then, with $\hat{\theta}_2(\cdot)$ from (7.7),

$$\hat{\theta} = (\hat{\theta}_1, \hat{\theta}_2) = (\hat{\theta}_1, \hat{\theta}_2(\hat{\theta}_1))$$

is the global (exact or asymptotic) MLE of $\hat{\theta}$ even though $s(\hat{\theta}) \neq 0$. This characterizes the irregularity of the estimation problem. Under repeated sampling, $\hat{\theta}_2$ becomes an exact function (namely, $p \lim \hat{\theta}_2(\cdot)$) of $\hat{\theta}_1$ at a rate faster than $N^{1/2}$. This is *superconsistency*, i.e., $w_m - w_r$ is $O_p(N^{-1})$. Recall that the minimum of N independent and identically distributed (i.i.d.) observations from an absolutely continuous CDF G with $G' = g$ has density $N(1 - G)^{N-1}g$. For instance, in the prototypal specification in section 7.3 we have $g = f/\Pi$, so the exact distribution of $N(w_m - w_r)$ is given by f from (7.9) below. Hence, $p \lim N^a(w_m - w_r) = 0$, $a \in [0, 1)$.

Let θ_0 be the true value of θ, and $\widetilde{V}$ either the probability limit or (preferably, in practice) the observed value of

$$N\tilde{j}(\theta_1)^{-1} = -N \left(\frac{d^2 \ln \tilde{l}(\theta_1)}{d\theta_1 \, d\theta_1'} \right)^{-1}$$

or one of its asymptotic equivalents. We assume $\tilde{l}$ is well-behaved, so that the observed profile information $\tilde{j}$ is regular and satisfies $\tilde{i} = E\tilde{s}\tilde{s}'$, where $\tilde{i} = E\tilde{j}$ is the expected profile information. We let ψ denote the gradient and B the Hessian of the map $\theta_1 \rightarrow \hat{\theta}_2(\theta_1)$. In each particular model below, we demonstrate that this map is twice continuously differentiable. We now show that the MLE $\hat{\theta}$ is *consistent and asymptotically reduced rank normal* (CARRN).

THEOREM 5

$$N^{1/2}(\hat{\theta} - \theta_0) \rightarrow n_k(0, V(\theta_0)), \qquad \text{rank } V(\theta_0) = k - 1.$$

Suppressing arguments,

$$V = \begin{pmatrix} \tilde{V} & \tilde{V}\psi \\ \psi'\tilde{V} & \psi'\tilde{V}\psi \end{pmatrix} = \Psi\tilde{V}\Psi', \qquad \Psi = \begin{pmatrix} I_{k-1} \\ \psi' \end{pmatrix}.$$

Here, n_k denotes the k-dimensional (in this case singular) multivariate normal distribution.

Proof. The regularity of $\tilde{l}$ ensures that $N^{1/2}(\hat{\theta}_1 - \theta_1) \rightarrow n_{k-1}(0, \tilde{V})$ by a CLT, with $\tilde{V}$ the limiting version of $\tilde{N}\tilde{j}(\theta_1)^{-1}$. The map $\phi : \tilde{\Theta} \rightarrow \Theta$ given by $\phi(\theta_1) = (\theta_1', \hat{\theta}_2(\theta_1))'$ has Jacobian Ψ and as discussed becomes exact at a rate faster than $N^{1/2}$. Now interpret ψ as a probability limit. $\qquad \square$

For purposes of hypothesis testing, θ_0 can be replaced by $\hat{\theta}$ in V. From the theorem it is seen that the area of concentration of the approximating normal distribution is $\Theta_c = \{\theta + \Psi b | b \in \mathbb{R}^{k-1}\}$ and the direction of singularity is $\Theta_s = \{\theta + hb | b \in \mathbb{R}\}$, where h is given by $h' = (-\psi', 1)$ since, e.g., $\Psi'h = 0$. In this direction, convergence in distribution is of order N, which leads to singular order $N^{1/2}$ asymptotics. The precise way in which this convergence takes place can be further explored. In particular, it is possible to rotate coordinates in a way that separates order $N^{1/2}$ and N asymptotics. Let

$$\tau = (1 + \psi'\psi)^{1/2}, \qquad H_2 = \tau^{-1}h, \qquad H = (H_1, H_2) \in O(k),$$

where $O(\cdot)$ is the orthogonal group. Note that given H_2, H_1 is a $(k-1) \times k$ matrix that makes H orthogonal. Write

$$H'\theta = \begin{pmatrix} \theta_1^* \\ \theta_2^* \end{pmatrix} \begin{matrix} k-1 \\ 1 \end{matrix}.$$

Then $(N^{1/2}(\hat{\theta}_1^* - \theta_1^*), N(\hat{\theta}_2^* - \theta_2^*))$ has a regular (non-normal) limiting distribution. Geometrically, the rotated parameters θ_1^* and θ_2^* are the coordinates in the directions of support and singularity, respectively. Economically, these directions are those in which information is accumulated slowly

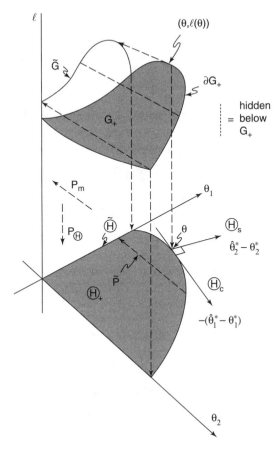

Figure 7.1 Likelihood Geometry.

and rapidly, respectively. The general situation, including the concepts already introduced, is illustrated in figure 7.1.

A similar approach was used by Phillips (1989) in a different context. In his paper, corollary 2.2(d) and corollary 3.4 study convergence at the slower of two rates and are parallels to the phenomenon that order N asymptotics results in singularity in theorem 5 above. We next follow Phillips' corollary 2.2 and theorem 3.3 and derive the asymptotic distributions of the rotated parameters, noting that one of these in our case falls outside the limiting mixed Gaussian (LMG) and limiting Gaussian functional (LGF) families discussed in Phillips (1989). This sheds further light on the nonregular nature of the present estimation problem. We define $\eta = 1/(\partial \hat{\theta}_2 / \partial w_m)$.

PROPOSITION 7.2.1

$$N^{1/2}(\hat{\theta}_1^* - \theta_1^*) \to n_{k-1}\left(0, H_1' V H_1\right), \qquad \hat{\theta}_2^* - \theta_2^* = O_p(N^{-1}).$$

Proof. The map $\tilde{\phi} : \tilde{\Theta} \times \mathbb{R}_+ \to \Theta$ given by $\tilde{\phi}(\theta_1, w_m) = (\theta_1', \hat{\theta}_2(\theta_1, w_m))'$ has Jacobian (Ψ, δ), $\delta = (0, \eta^{-1})$. The ith coordinate function has Hessian $0, i = 1, \ldots, k - 1$, and the kth coordinate function has Hessian with leading $(k - 1)' \times (k - 1)$ minor B. Then $\hat{\theta} - \theta = \Psi(\theta_1 - \theta_1) + \delta(w_m - w_r) + (0, \frac{1}{2}(\hat{\theta}_1 - \theta_1)' B(\hat{\theta}_1 - \theta_1))' + O_p(N^{-3/2})$. From theorem 5 and since $w_m - w_r = O_p(N^{-1})$ as discussed earlier, $N^{1/2}(\hat{\theta}_1^* - \theta_1^*) = H_1' \Psi N^{1/2}(\hat{\theta}_1 - \theta_1) + N^{1/2} O_p(N^{-1}) \to n_{k-1}(0, H_1' \Psi \tilde{V} \Psi' H_1)$, and since $h'\Psi = 0, h'\delta = \eta^{-1}, H_2 = \tau^{-1}h$, we have that $N(\hat{\theta}_2^* - \theta_2^*) = \tau^{-1}\eta^{-1}N(w_m - w_r) + \frac{1}{2}\tau^{-1}N(\hat{\theta}_1 - \theta_1)' B(\hat{\theta}_1 - \theta_1) + N O_p(N^{-3/2})$. Note that $(\hat{\theta}_1 - \theta_1) = O_p(N^{-1/2})$.   □

7.3 LIKELIHOOD: SPECIFICS FOR WAGE DATA

A more detailed analysis, to understand better the properties of the likelihood function, will require specification of a functional form for the offer distribution. The simplest specification is

$$f(w) = \gamma e^{-\gamma w}, \qquad w \geq 0. \tag{7.9}$$

In this case,

$$\Pi = e^{-\gamma w_r}, \qquad E(w|w \geq w_r) = w_r + 1/\gamma. \tag{7.10}$$

Substituting in (7.3),

$$EV = \frac{1}{1 - \beta} \left\{ (1 - p\Pi) w_r + p\Pi \left(w_r + \frac{1}{\gamma} \right) \right\}$$
$$= \frac{1}{1 - \beta} \left\{ w_r + \frac{p}{\gamma} e^{-\gamma w_r} \right\}. \tag{7.11}$$

Substituting (7.2) in (7.11) yields the specialization of (7.4):

$$EV = U(EV) = y + \beta EV + \frac{p}{(1 - \beta)\gamma} e^{-\gamma(1-\beta)(y+\beta EV)}. \tag{7.12}$$

Substituting instead (7.11) in (7.2) yields the alternative contraction

$$w_r = \tilde{U}(w_r) = (1 - \beta) y + \beta \left(w_r + \frac{p}{\gamma} e^{-\gamma w_r} \right), \tag{7.13}$$

again with derivative $\beta(1 - p\Pi)$. Besides being useful in computing the reservation wage for given parameters, (7.13) can be rewritten as

$$w_r = y + \frac{\beta p}{(1 - \beta)\gamma} e^{-\gamma w_r}. \tag{7.14}$$

This will prove useful for econometric identification and estimation and illustrates the point that the likelihood can sometimes be calculated without computing V by using instead a contraction on policies. Thus, the contraction in function space is reduced to a contraction on positive real numbers.

This model, with exponential offers, illustrates the important estimation issues arising in search applications and is known as the *prototypal* specification. The density of accepted wages is $f(w)/\Pi = \gamma \exp\{-\gamma(w - w_r)\}$ with support $w \geq w_r$. The likelihood for independent observations is simply the product of these densities,

$$l = \gamma^N \exp\left\{-\gamma \sum_{i=1}^{N} (w_i - w_r)\right\}, \qquad w_i \geq w_r.$$

Note that w_r depends on parameters through the optimality condition (7.14). Thus, calculation of likelihood derivatives involves this condition and the implicit function theorem. Note also that the support depends on parameters, making the inference problem nonstandard. In the prototypal model, we have the following sharpening of propostion 7.2.1.

THEOREM 6 *If f is $\exp(\gamma)$ given by (7.9), then*

$$N\left(\hat{\theta}_2^* - \theta_2^*\right) \to \xi + \mathrm{tr}\,(W), \qquad \xi \sim \exp(\gamma \tau \eta)$$

$$W \sim W_{k-1}\left(\tfrac{1}{2}\tau^{-1} B^{1/2} \widetilde{V} B^{1/2}, 1\right).$$

Here, $W_{k-1}(\Sigma, 1)$ denotes the $(k-1)$-dimensional Wishart distribution on one degree of freedom and variance matrix parameter Σ.

Proof. In the equation for $N(\hat{\theta}_2^* - \theta_2^*)$ in the previous proof, the distribution of the $(w_m - w_r)$ term has already been given. By the continuous mapping theorem, the next term converges in distribution to $q'q = \mathrm{tr}(qq')$, $q = \tau^{-1/2} B^{1/2} r / \sqrt{2}$, and $r \sim n_{k-1}(0, \widetilde{V})$ (see the proof of theorem 5).   □

In the following, we illustrate these general concepts in a series of increasingly complex versions of the prototypal job search model.

We first illustrate the nonstandard inference problem in a one-parameter specification (γ). We proceed to a two-parameter specification (y, γ) and introduce the profile likelihood function. Next, we demonstrate the identifiability of the parameter pair (γ, p) in wage data alone. Duration data contribute to efficiency but require the concept of an asymptotic profile likelihood function. With joint wage and duration data the parameter set (γ, y, p) is identified. We study the geometry of this likelihood function. The interplay between economic theory and statistics that is characteristic of the dynamic programming approach is demonstrated in the heavy reliance on theory in calculating the transformations appearing in the asymptotics.

7.3.1 Wage Data Alone—One Parameter

The case of wage data alone allows a simple demonstration of the non-standard nature of the inference problem. We now suppose that we have a sample of accepted wages and that the underlying wage offer distribution is exponential (7.9) with unknown parameter $\gamma > 0$, so the acceptance probability is Π from (7.10), with w_r given by (7.2) and $p = 1$. The density of accepted wages is $f(w)/\Pi$, so

$$l(\gamma) = \gamma^N e^{-\gamma N(\overline{w} - w_r(\gamma))} 1_{\{w_m \geq w_r(\gamma)\}}.$$

The minimal sufficient statistic is $(\overline{w}, w_m)$. It is convenient to transform this to $((\overline{w} - w_m)w_r^{-1}(w_m), w_m) = (a, w_m)$. Then a is approximately ancillary in the sense that it is an asymptotically distribution constant and in fact becomes distribution constant at a rate faster than $N^{1/2}$. It can be verified generally that the reservation wage is an increasing function of the mean offer, $w_r'(\gamma) < 0$, so $w_m \geq w_r(\gamma)$ iff $\gamma \geq w_r^{-1}(w_m)$. Hence, in $\Theta_+ = (w_r^{-1}(w_m), \infty)$,

$$\ln l(\gamma) = N \ln \gamma - \gamma N(\overline{w} - w_r(\gamma)),$$

$$s(\gamma) = \frac{N}{\gamma} - N(\overline{w} - w_r(\gamma)) + \gamma N w_r'(\gamma).$$

Now, $N/\gamma > 0, \overline{w} \geq w_m \geq w_r(\gamma)$, and $w_r'(\gamma) < 0$, so the sign of the score is ambiguous. It can be demonstrated that with positive probability the likelihood function is maximized in $\mathrm{int}\Theta_+$. However, as $N \to \infty$,

$$\frac{s(\gamma)}{N} \to \frac{1}{\gamma} - \left(w_r(\gamma_0) + \frac{1}{\gamma_0} - w_r(\gamma)\right) + \gamma w_r'(\gamma)$$

$$= \left(\frac{1}{\gamma} - \frac{1}{\gamma_0}\right) + (w_r(\gamma) - w_r(\gamma_0)) + \gamma w_r'(\gamma).$$

For $\gamma \geq \gamma_0$ this expression is nonpositive term by term. In large samples the likelihood is maximized at $\tilde{\gamma} = w_r^{-1}(w_m)$. In fact, this occurs quickly. The situation is illustrated in figure 7.2.

THEOREM 7 *Let $\tilde{\gamma} = w_r^{-1}(w_m)$ and $\hat{\gamma} = $ the MLE.*
  (a) $p\lim N^a (\tilde{\gamma} - \gamma_0) = 0$, $a \in [0, 1)$
  (b) $p\lim N^a (\hat{\gamma} - \tilde{\gamma}) = 0$, $a \in [0, 1)$
  Note that (b) implies not only that the maximum likelihood estimator is consistent, but also that it converges in distribution at a faster rate than $N^{1/2}$.

Proof. (a) This follows from the earlier discussion of w_m and the continuous mapping theorem.

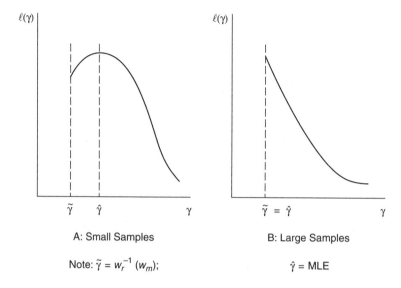

Figure 7.2 Likelihood Function.

(b) When $s(\gamma) < 0$ for all $\gamma > \tilde{\gamma}$, then $\hat{\gamma} = \tilde{\gamma}$, so it suffices to show that $\Pr(s(\gamma)N^{-a} > 0)$ goes to zero as $N \to \infty$. Note that $Es(\gamma)N^{-a} = \mu_N = -N^{1-a}c(\gamma)$, where $c(\gamma)$ is a positive function of γ and $Vs(\gamma)N^{-a} = N^{1-2a}\gamma_0^{-2}$. These expressions can be obtained by applying a CLT. Then $\Pr(s(\gamma)N^{-a} > 0) = \Pr(s(\gamma)N^{-a} - \mu_N > -\mu_N) \leq \gamma_0^{-2}/(Nc(\gamma)^2)$ by Chebyshev's inequality. Thus, $\Pr(s(\gamma)N^{-a} > 0) \to 0$ as $N \to \infty$.   □

We have illustrated that our estimation problem is nonstandard but tractable. Note that our problem is different from that of estimating a parameter whose true value is at the boundary of the parameter space.

7.3.2 Wage Data—Two Parameters

We now introduce the profile likelihood function in a setting allowing a simple geometric interpretation. We consider the parameter $\theta = (\gamma, y), \theta \in \Theta = \mathbb{R}^+ \times \mathbb{R}$ (recall that y is unemployment income net of search costs). In this case

$$l(\theta) = \gamma^N e^{-\gamma N(\overline{w} - w_r(\theta))} 1_{\{w_m \geq w_r(\theta)\}}. \tag{7.15}$$

Again the minimal sufficient statistic is $(\overline{w}, w_m)$. There is no ancillary since the minimal sufficient statistic has the same dimension as the parameter. For $\theta \in \Theta_+$ we have $\ln l(\theta) = N \ln \gamma - \gamma N(\overline{w} - w_r(\theta))$ and

$$\frac{d \ln l}{dy} = \gamma N \frac{d}{dy} w_r(\gamma, y).$$

Clearly, w_r is increasing in y, though the dependence is complicated, since EV depends on y. Hence, $\hat{y}(\gamma) = w_r^{-1}(\gamma, w_m)$ is well-defined. An explicit expression is obtained in (7.18) below. In the general terminology, $\theta_1 = \gamma, \theta_2 = y$, and $k = 2$. Upon substitution we obtain the profile likelihood $\tilde{l}(\gamma)$. Geometrically, the graph of the positive part of the likelihood function G_+ is a two-dimensional nonlinear manifold with boundary in $\mathbb{R}^3$. $\tilde{G}$, the graph of $\tilde{l}(\gamma)$, is the projection $P_m \partial G_+$ of the submanifold ∂G_+ to the (γ, l) plane. We would also look at the other profile likelihood $\tilde{l}(y)$, but note that this is not necessarily the projection of ∂G_+ to the (y, l) plane. From the geometry, the global maximum in l of G_+ occurs on ∂G_+, so the projection of ∂G_+ to (y, l) is an approximate profile likelihood function—a pseudo likelihood function in the sense of Barndorff-Nielsen (1988). However, we focus our attention on the exact profile $\tilde{l}(\gamma)$. We have

$$\ln \tilde{l}(\gamma) = N \ln \gamma - \gamma N(\overline{w} - w_m), \qquad (7.16)$$

$$\tilde{s}(\gamma) = \frac{N}{\gamma} - N(\overline{w} - w_m), \qquad (7.17)$$

and MLE $\hat{\gamma} = 1/(\overline{w} - w_m)$. Since $p \lim w_m = w_r$ and $p \lim \overline{w} = w_r + 1/\gamma_0$, $\hat{\gamma}$ is consistent. Hence, $\hat{y} = \hat{y}(\hat{\gamma}) = w_r^{-1}(1/(\overline{w} - w_m), w_m)$ is consistent by the continuous mapping theorem. In particular, the explicit expression (7.18) below shows the smoothness of the map $\hat{\theta}_2(\theta_1, w_m) = \hat{y}(\gamma, w_m)$ in the present model, hence circumventing the need to apply an implicit function theorem. In finite samples, y is identified since γ is and since, given w_m, $\hat{y}(\gamma)$ is uniquely given. The observed and expected profile informations, both measures of the curvature of $\tilde{G}$, coincide: $\tilde{j} = \tilde{i} = N/\gamma^2$. Compared with section 7.2, we have $\tilde{V} = \gamma^2, \psi = d\hat{y}/d\gamma, \Psi = (1, \psi)'$. Theorem 5 holds, with $V = \gamma^2 \Psi \Psi'$. That is, $(\hat{\theta}_1, \hat{\theta}_2) = (\hat{\gamma}, \hat{y})$ has a singular bivariate normal limiting distribution. The singularity arises because the MLE is on ∂G_+—we allow $N^{1/2}$ sampling variation along the boundary but not away from it. The direction of singularity Θ_s is given by $h = (-\psi, 1)$, and the support Θ_c of the approximating normal distribution is $\{(\hat{y} + k, \hat{y} + k\psi) | k \in \mathbb{R}\}$.

We now use the theory to develop an explicit formula for ψ, allowing calculation of asymptotic standard errors. Note that $\hat{y}(\gamma)$ is the y that solves (7.14) with $w_r = w_m$; i.e.,

$$w_r^{-1}(\gamma, w_m) = w_m - \frac{p\beta e^{-\gamma w_m}}{(1 - \beta)\gamma}, \qquad (7.18)$$

so that in the present case, where $p = 1$,

$$\psi = \left(\frac{\beta}{1 - \beta}\right)\left(\frac{e^{-\gamma w_m}}{\gamma^2}\right)(1 + \gamma w_m). \qquad (7.19)$$

By substituting $w_r - y$ from (7.14) and using (7.10), this can be interpreted economically as $\psi = (w_r - y)E(w|w \geq w_r)$.

Finally, we rotate parameters to separate orders of convergence in distribution. We get $\tau = (1 + \psi^2)^{1/2}$, $\theta_1^* = \tau^{-1}(\gamma + \psi y)$, and $\theta_2^* = \tau^{-1}(y - \psi \gamma)$. Economically, the fast parameter θ_1^* is the part of estimated unemployment income determined by w_m. From theorems 6 and 7, with $H_1' = \tau^{-1}(1, \psi)$, we then have after some algebra, $N^{1/2}(\hat\theta_1^* - \theta_1^*) \to n(0, \tau^2\gamma^2)$, $N(\hat\theta_2^* - \theta_2^*) \to \exp(\gamma\tau\eta) + W$, $\eta = 1/(1 + \gamma(w_r - y))$, and $B = -(w_r - y)(E(w|w \geq w_r)^2 + 1/\gamma^2)$.

7.3.3 Wage Data Alone—Offer Arrival Probability

Consider the parameter set $\theta = (\gamma, p) \in \Theta = \mathbb{R}_+ \times [0, 1]$, where p denotes the offer arrival probability. This section demonstrates the identification of θ and hence (Π, p) in wage data alone when y is known. It is most easily justified that y is known when search costs are ignored or not present, in which case y is interpreted as pure unemployment benefits and may be directly observable. We show later that including duration data adds to efficiency.

The analysis in the present model follows that from section 7.3.2. The likelihood function is still (7.15), keeping in mind the new θ. For $\theta \in \Theta_+ = \{(\gamma, p) | w_r(\gamma, p) \leq w_m\}$, the score in p is $\gamma N(dw_r(\gamma, p)/dp)$, which is easily seen to be positive, e.g., by differentiating (7.14). The geometry is the same as before, G_+ is a two-dimensional manifold with boundary in $\mathbb{R}^3$ and $\tilde{G}$ is the projection $P_m \partial G_+$ of the submanifold ∂G_+ to the (γ, l) plane. Given γ, the MLE for p is $\hat{p}(\gamma) = w_r^{-1}(\gamma, w_m)$. The profile likelihood and its score are again (7.16), (7.17), and $\hat\gamma = 1/(\overline{w} - w_m)$. Then $\hat p = \hat{p}(\hat\gamma) = w_r^{-1}(1/(\overline{w} - w_m), w_m)$. Theorem 5 holds for $(\hat\theta_1, \hat\theta_2) = (\hat\gamma, \hat p)$, with $\tilde V = \gamma^2 \Psi\Psi'$. In this case, $\psi = d\hat p/d\gamma$, $\tilde V = \gamma^2$, and $\Psi = (1, \psi)'$. Here, the direction of singularity Θ_s is given by $h = (-\psi, 1)$, and the area of concentration of the singular bivariate normal is $\Theta_c = \{(\hat\gamma + k, \hat p + k\psi)| k \in \mathbb{R}\}$. Given γ, $\hat{p}(\gamma)$ is found by substituting w_m for w_r in (7.14),

$$\hat{p}(\gamma) = \frac{(1 - \beta)}{\beta}(w_m - y)\gamma e^{\gamma w_m}, \qquad (7.20)$$

and hence after some algebra,

$$\psi = p\left(w_r + \frac{1}{\gamma}\right). \qquad (7.21)$$

By (7.10), this can be interpreted economically as $\psi = pE(w|w \geq w_r)$. In this model, we have $\tau = (1 + \psi^2)^{1/2}$, $\theta_1^* = \tau^{-1}(\gamma + \psi p)$, and $\theta_2^* = \tau^{-1}(p - \psi\gamma)$. From theorems 6 and 7, with $H_1' = \tau^{-1}(1, \psi)$, $N^{1/2}(\hat\theta_1^* - \theta_1^*) \to n(0, \tau^2\gamma^2)$, $N(\hat\theta_2^* - \theta_2^*) \to \exp(\gamma\tau\eta) + W$. From (7.14) and (7.10), $\eta = (w_r - y)/(p(1 + \gamma(w_r - y)))$ and $B = p(E(w|w \geq wr)^2 - 1/\gamma^2)$.

7.4 LIKELIHOOD: WAGE AND DURATION DATA

Spells of unemployment have a geometric distribution with parameter λ. Although the employment probability λ depends on underlying parameters, these cannot be separately identified from the duration data alone. Nevertheless, duration information is useful in improving efficiency and in identification. We set the stage for this discussion by reviewing the maximum likelihood estimation of λ. In practice, survey data on durations are typically censored because of the fixed length of the observation period. Suppose the maximum duration is K periods. Then, $P(t_i = k) = (1 - \lambda)^{k-1}\lambda$, $1 \leq k \leq K$, and $P(\text{censored}) = (1 - \lambda)^K$. More complicated forms of random censoring could be handled without difficulty. We use subscripts c and e on sum and product operators to indicate ranges (censored or uncensored observations). The likelihood function is

$$l(\lambda) = \prod_c (1-\lambda)^K \prod_e (1-\lambda)^{t_i-1}\lambda = (1-\lambda)^{N_c K + \sum_e t_i - N_e}\lambda^{N_e} = (1-\lambda)^{\tilde{T}}\lambda^{N_e},$$

and $\ln l(\lambda) = \tilde{T} \ln(1-\lambda) + N_e \ln \lambda$. The score is $s(\lambda) = -\tilde{T}/(1-\lambda) + N_e/\lambda$, so $\hat{\lambda} = N_e/T$. When we look at the contribution of duration data to efficiency, we will need the observed information $j(\lambda) = -s'(\lambda) = -\tilde{T}/(1-\lambda)^2 + N_e/\lambda^2$. The expected information is

$$i(\lambda) = Ej(\lambda) = N\frac{1 - (1 - \lambda)^K}{\lambda^2(1 - \lambda)}.$$

The normed MLE $N^{1/2}(\hat{\lambda} - \lambda_0)$ is asymptotically normally distributed with mean zero and variance given by $N/i(\lambda)$. The uncensored case is handled by letting K go to infinity, here as well as in the following sections.

7.4.1 Wage and Duration Data—Two Parameters

In this section we introduce a pseudo likelihood function that approximates the profile likelihood function and assess the contribution of duration data to efficiency. In the model for (γ, p) from above, suppose we are in addition given data on durations of unemployment spells. Recall that the reemployment probability in the present case can be expressed as $\lambda = p\Pi = pe^{-\gamma w_r(\gamma, p)}$. The likelihood function for $\theta = (\gamma, p)$ is the product of the likelihood functions from earlier:

$$l(\theta) = (1 - \lambda)^{\tilde{T}}\lambda^{N_e}\gamma^{N_e}e^{-\gamma N_e(\bar{w} - w_r(\theta))}1_{\{w_m \geq w_r(\theta)\}}. \tag{7.22}$$

Note that N_e replaces N in the factor corresponding to wage data since wages are observed only for uncensored spells. The score in p is

$$s_p(\gamma, p) = \left[-\frac{\widetilde{T}}{1 - \lambda} + \frac{N_e}{\lambda} \right] \lambda_p + \left[\gamma N_e \frac{d}{dp} w_r(\gamma, p) \right]$$

for $w_m \geq w_r(\gamma, p)$. Here, the first square bracket corresponds to the score from the duration model, and the second to that from the wage data model. The score s_p can be either positive or negative in finite samples. In some cases, $\hat{p}(\gamma)$ is found in the interior of the interval in which the likelihood function is positive. Hence, the exact finite-sample profile likelihood function cannot in general be graphed by projecting ∂G_+ to the (γ, l) plane. However, this projection does produce a pseudo likelihood function, identified by its graph $\widetilde{G}$, and an asymptotic argument can be given for focusing on this. It can be shown that asymptotically the score is positive where the likelihood is positive. Hence, a natural estimator is

$$\tilde{p}(\gamma) = p(\gamma, w_m) = w_r^{-1}(\gamma, w_m),$$

and for $\gamma \geq \gamma_0$, $\tilde{p}(\gamma)$ is asymptotically equivalent to the exact MLE of p, given γ. We substitute $\tilde{p}(\gamma)$ for p in (7.22) to obtain the pseudo likelihood $\tilde{l}$, an *asymptotic profile likelihood function*,

$$\tilde{l}(\gamma) = (1 - \lambda(\gamma))^{\widetilde{T}} \lambda(\gamma)^{N_e} \gamma^{N_e} e^{-\gamma N_e(\overline{w} - w_m)}, \qquad \gamma \in \widetilde{\Theta},$$

whose graph $\widetilde{G}$ is the projection $P_m \partial G_+$ of ∂G_+ to the (γ, l) plane. The domain is $\widetilde{\Theta} = \{\gamma | 0 \leq w_r^{-1}(\gamma, w_m) \leq 1\}$, $\lambda(\gamma) = \lambda(\gamma, \tilde{p}(\gamma)) = \tilde{p}(\gamma) e^{-\gamma w_m}$, and the score is

$$\tilde{s}(\gamma) = \left[-\frac{\widetilde{T}}{1 - \lambda} + \frac{N_e}{\lambda} \right] \lambda' + \left[\frac{N_e}{\lambda} - N_e(\overline{w} - w_m) \right].$$

The estimator $\tilde{\gamma}$ found by solving the asymptotic profile likelihood equation $\tilde{s} = 0$ is consistent, the brackets corresponding to the duration model and the profile score (7.17), and with $(\tilde{\gamma}, \tilde{p}) = (\tilde{\gamma}, \tilde{p}(\tilde{\gamma}))$. We have again the CARRN property,

$$N^{1/2} \begin{pmatrix} \tilde{\gamma} - \gamma \\ \tilde{p} - p \end{pmatrix} \to n_2 \left(\begin{pmatrix} 0 \\ 0 \end{pmatrix}, v(\gamma) \begin{pmatrix} 1 & \psi \\ \psi & \psi^2 \end{pmatrix} \right).$$

Both ψ and Ψ are the same as before, and again $V = \widetilde{V} \Psi \Psi'$. However, in the presence of duration data, $v(\gamma)$ replaces γ^2 in the expression for $\widetilde{V}$. Efficiency is improved by including the duration data. To see this note that

$$v(\gamma)^{-1} = \left(1 - (1 - \lambda)^K \right) \left[\frac{(\lambda')^2}{\lambda^2 (1 - \lambda)} + \frac{1}{\gamma^2} \right].$$

By using (7.14), it can be proved that $\lambda' = \lambda/\gamma$. For variance comparison, it is convenient to consider uncensored samples only. Let K go to infinity in the above expression and note that $v(\gamma)^{-1}$ equals $1/\gamma^2$ plus a term that is always positive, so the claimed efficiency gain follows.

When rotating parameters in this model, $\tau, \theta_1^*, \theta_2^*, \eta$, and H_1 are the same as before. Hence, the order N asymptotics of $\hat\theta_2^*$ is that of $\tilde\theta_2^*$ earlier. However, the efficiency gain in the present section leads to order $N^{1/2}$ asymptotics of the form $N^{1/2}(\hat\theta_1^* - \theta_1^*) \to n(0, \tau^2 v(\theta))$.

7.4.2 Wage and Duration Data—Three Parameters

Analysis of the preceding sections is easily combined for analysis in the alternative models for joint data parametrized by γ or (y, γ). Above, however, we focused on parameterization by (γ, p) to show that even though these parameters (and hence (Π, p)) are jointly identified in pure wage data, efficiency is improved by including duration data, and we considered the asymptotic profile likelihood function.

In the present section we develop the exact MLE for $\theta = (\gamma, y, p)$ in the model obtained by freeing up $y \in \mathbb{R}$. The likelihood function is (7.22), keeping in mind the new θ. G_+ is a random three-dimensional nonlinear manifold with boundary in $\mathbb{R}^4$. Since $\lambda_y = d\lambda/dy = -\gamma\lambda(dw_r/dy)$, we have that in Θ_+,

$$s_y(\theta, y, p) = \left[-\frac{\tilde T}{1-\lambda} + \frac{N_e}{\lambda}\right]\lambda_y + \left[\gamma N_e \frac{d}{dy} w_r(\theta, y, p)\right]$$

$$= \frac{\tilde T \gamma \lambda}{1-\lambda}\frac{d}{dy} w_r(\gamma, y, p) > 0$$

without invoking asymptotic arguments. Hence, $\hat y(\gamma, p) = w_r^{-1}(\gamma, w_m, p)$, given explicitly in (7.18). Geometrically, the graph G of the exact profile likelihood is obtained by projecting ∂G_+, a two-dimensional submanifold, to (γ, p, l) space. Let $\lambda(\gamma, p) = p\exp(-\gamma w_m)$. We have

$$\ln \tilde l(\gamma, p) = \tilde T \ln(1 - \lambda(\gamma, p)) + N_e \ln \lambda(\gamma, p) + N_e \ln \gamma - \gamma N_e(\overline w - w_m),$$

$$\tilde s_\gamma(\gamma, p) = \left[-\frac{\tilde T}{1-\lambda} + \frac{N_e}{\lambda}\right]\lambda_\gamma + \left[\frac{N_e}{\lambda} - N_e(\overline w - w_m)\right],$$

$$\tilde s_p(\gamma, p) = \left[-\frac{\tilde T}{1-\lambda} + \frac{N_e}{\lambda}\right]\lambda_p,$$

with $\lambda_\gamma = -w_m\lambda, \lambda_p = \Pi = \exp(-\gamma w_m)$. Note that $\hat\theta_1 = (\hat\gamma, \hat p)$ that solves the profile likelihood equation $\tilde s = 0$ is consistent, using pure duration data and pure wage data arguments on each bracket separately. However, in the present section it can be proved that the explicit solution is

$$\begin{pmatrix} \hat{\gamma} \\ \hat{p} \end{pmatrix} = \begin{pmatrix} 1/(\overline{w} - w_m) \\ N_e/\left(Te^{-w_m/(\overline{w}-w_m)}\right) \end{pmatrix}.$$

Now $\hat{y} = \hat{y}(\hat{\gamma}, \hat{p})$. The expected profile information in this case is

$$\tilde{i}(\gamma, p) = N \frac{1 - (1 - \lambda)^K}{1 - \lambda} \begin{bmatrix} (w_r)^2 + \dfrac{1 - \lambda}{\gamma^2} & -\dfrac{w_r}{p} \\[2ex] -\dfrac{w_r}{p} & \dfrac{1}{p^2}. \end{bmatrix}.$$

The matrix in this expression is regular, with determinant $(1 - \lambda)/(\gamma p)^2 \neq 0$, so we can let $\widetilde{V}(\gamma, p) = N\tilde{i}(\gamma, p)^{-1}$. Using (7.14) as in (7.19), we have

$$\psi = \begin{pmatrix} \dfrac{d\hat{y}}{d\gamma} \\[2ex] \dfrac{d\hat{y}}{dp} \end{pmatrix} = \begin{bmatrix} (w_r - y)\left(w_r + \dfrac{1}{\gamma}\right) \\[2ex] -(w_r - y)/p \end{bmatrix},$$

where the interpretation using (7.10) again is economically interesting. With $\Psi = (I_2, \psi)'$, we easily calculate $V = \Psi\widetilde{V}\Psi'$. We have arrived at the three-dimensional, rank 2 asymptotic distribution of the exact MLE, i.e., the CARRN property,

$$N^{1/2}\begin{pmatrix} \hat{\gamma} - \gamma \\ \hat{y} - y \\ \hat{p} - p \end{pmatrix} \to n_3\left(\begin{pmatrix} 0 \\ 0 \\ 0 \end{pmatrix}, V\right),$$

where $(1 - (1 - \lambda)^K)V/\gamma^2$ is given by

$$\begin{bmatrix} 1 & \dfrac{w_r - y}{\gamma} & pw_r \\[2ex] \dfrac{w_r - y}{\gamma} & \dfrac{(w_r - y)^2\left(2 - \lambda\right)}{\gamma^2} & \dfrac{p(w_r - y)}{\gamma}\left(w_r - \dfrac{1 - \lambda}{\gamma}\right) \\[2ex] pw_r & \dfrac{p(w_r - y)}{\gamma}\left(w_r - \dfrac{1 - \lambda}{\gamma}\right) & \dfrac{p^2}{\gamma}\left((w_r)^2\gamma + \dfrac{1 - \lambda}{\gamma}\right) \end{bmatrix}.$$

The direction Θ_s of singularity is given by the line $\gamma = \hat{\gamma} - k(w_m - \hat{y})(w_m + 1/\hat{\gamma})$, $y = \hat{y} + k$, $p = \hat{p} + k(w_m - \hat{y})/\hat{p}$ as k varies. The area of concentration Θ_c of the asymptotic distribution of the MLE is the hyperplane that is the orthogonal complement at $(\hat{\gamma}, \hat{y}, \hat{p})$ to this line. Replacing $(\gamma, p, w_r, \lambda)$

by $(\hat{\gamma}, \hat{p}, w_m, \hat{p}\exp(-\hat{\gamma}w_m))$ yields a variance estimate for efficient hypothesis testing. The parameters can again be rotated to separate orders of convergence in distribution. We use $\tau + (1 + \psi'\psi)^{1/2}$, $h = (-\psi, 1)$, and theorems 6 and 7 hold, with η as before and $B = \{b_{ij}\}$. Here, $b_{\gamma\gamma}$ is B from section 7.3.2, $b_{\gamma p} = \psi_1/p$, and $b_{pp} = 0$.

7.4.3 Wage and Duration Data—Gamma Distribution

In this section we illustrate the generality of the prototypal specification by considering a variation based on the gamma distribution. The parameters of the distribution are $(\gamma, \alpha) \in \mathbb{R}_+^2$, and the exponential (7.9) is the special case $\alpha = 1$. In addition, we consider the parameters $y \in \mathbb{R}$ and $p \in [0, 1]$, so $\theta = (\gamma, \alpha, y, p)$. We study the properties of the resulting four-parameter likelihood function and give a numerical estimation procedure. The density of wage offers is now

$$f(w; \gamma, \alpha) = \frac{\gamma^\alpha}{\Gamma(\alpha)} w^{\alpha-1} e^{-\gamma w}, \qquad w > 0,$$

with cumulative distribution function $F(w; \gamma, \alpha) = \int_0^w f(x; \gamma, \alpha)\,dx$, $w > 0$. The reservation wage depends on all four parameters, and the acceptance probability is $\Pi(\theta) = 1 - F(w_r(\theta); \gamma, \alpha)$. The likelihood function becomes

$$l(\gamma, \alpha, y, p) = (1 - \lambda)^{\tilde{T}} \lambda^{N_e} \prod_{i=1}^{N_e} \frac{f(w_i; \gamma, \alpha)}{\Pi} 1_{\{w_m \geq w_r\}},$$

where $\lambda = p\Pi$ is the employment probability. Let $\overline{\ln w}$ denote $\Sigma_e \ln w_i/N_e$. The minimal sufficient statistic is $(\overline{w}, w_m, \overline{\ln w}, \tilde{T}, N_e)$. For $w_m \geq w_r$,

$$\ln l(\theta) = \tilde{T} \ln(1 - \lambda) + N_e \ln \lambda$$
$$+ N_e \{\alpha \ln \gamma + (\alpha - 1)\overline{\ln w} - \gamma\overline{w} - \ln \Gamma(\alpha) - \ln \Pi\} \quad (7.23)$$

$$s_y = \frac{\tilde{T}\lambda_y}{1 - \lambda}, \qquad \lambda_y = -pf(w_r; \gamma, \alpha) \frac{d}{dy} w_r < 0,$$

so $s_y > 0$. That is, given $\theta_1 = (\gamma, \alpha, p)$, the MLE for $\theta_2 = y$ solves (7.2) with $w_r = w_m$. From (7.3), EV depends on y only through w_r, so

$$\hat{y}(\gamma, \alpha, p) = w_r^{-1}(\gamma, \alpha, w_m, p) = \frac{w_m}{1 - \beta} - \beta EV(\gamma, \alpha, w_m, p)$$

$$= \frac{1}{1 - \beta} \{(1 - \beta(1 - p\Pi))w_m$$
$$- \beta p\alpha(1 - F(w_m; \gamma, \alpha + 1))/\gamma\}, \quad (7.24)$$

where from now on Π denotes $\Pi(\gamma, \alpha) = 1 - F(w_m; \gamma, \alpha)$ and hence does not depend on p. Substituting $\hat{y}(\gamma, \alpha, p)$ in l, we obtain the profile likelihood $\tilde{l}(\gamma, \alpha, p)$. The graph G of this is the projection $P_m \partial G_+$ of

∂G_+, a three-dimensional submanifold of $G+$, to the space with coordinates (γ, α, p, l). The profile score in p is

$$\tilde{s}_p = \left[-\frac{\tilde{T}}{1-\lambda} + \frac{N_e}{\lambda} \right] \Pi, \tag{7.25}$$

where the square bracket is recognized as the score in the duration model above. Solving the profile likelihood equation $\tilde{s}_p = 0$ yields

$$\hat{p}(\gamma, \alpha) = \frac{N_e}{T\Pi(\gamma, \alpha)}. \tag{7.26}$$

Substituting this in the three-dimensional profile likelihood $\tilde{l}$, we arrive at the new two-dimensional profile likelihood $\overset{\approx}{l}$ whose graph $\overset{\approx}{G}$ is a two-dimensional submanifold of $\tilde{G}$, although it does not take the simple projection form encountered earlier.

The expression for $\overset{\approx}{l}$ is still (7.23), but λ is now fixed at N_e/T, and Π denotes $\Pi(\gamma, \alpha)$. Hence, the scores in the remaining parameters are

$$\overset{\approx}{s}_\gamma = N_e \left[\frac{\alpha}{\gamma} - \bar{w} - \frac{\Pi_\gamma}{\Pi} \right], \qquad \overset{\approx}{s}_\alpha = N_e \left[\ln \gamma + \overline{\ln w} - dg(\alpha) - \frac{\Pi_\alpha}{\Pi} \right],$$
$$\tag{7.27}$$

where $dg(\cdot)$ is the digamma function. We have the following.

LEMMA 7.4.1 $(x/\alpha) f(x; \gamma, \alpha) = F(x; \gamma, \alpha) - F(x; \gamma, \alpha + 1)$.

Proof.

$$F(x; \gamma, \alpha) = \int_0^x \left(\gamma^\alpha / \Gamma(\alpha) \right) w^{\alpha-1} e^{-\gamma w} \, dw$$

$$= \left(\gamma^\alpha / \Gamma(\alpha) \right) \left(x^\alpha / \alpha \right) e^{-\gamma x} + \int_0^x \left(\gamma^{\alpha+1} / \Gamma(\alpha) \right) \left(w^\alpha / \alpha \right) e^{-\gamma w} \, dw$$

$$= (x/\alpha) \left(\gamma^\alpha / \Gamma(\alpha) \right) x^{\alpha-1} e^{-\gamma x} + \int_0^x \left(\gamma^{\alpha+1} / \Gamma(\alpha+1) \right) w^\alpha e^{-\gamma w} \, dw$$

$$= (x/\alpha) f(x; \gamma, \alpha) + F(x; \gamma, \alpha + 1).$$

$\square$

Using the lemma, it can be shown that

$$\Pi_\gamma = -(w_m/\gamma) f(w_m; \gamma, \alpha), \tag{7.28}$$
$$\Pi_\alpha = \Pi (\ln \gamma - dg(\alpha) + E(\ln w | w > w_m)), \tag{7.29}$$

so the expression for $\overset{\approx}{s}_\alpha$ in (7.27) reduces to

$$\overset{\approx}{s}_\alpha = N_e \left(\overline{\ln w} - E(\ln w | w > w_m) \right). \tag{7.30}$$

Simultaneous solution of $\overset{\approx}{s} = 0$ in (γ, α) is necessary. This is possible for the full parameter space, whereas the untruncated case requires $\alpha > 1$; see Johnson, Kotz, and Balakrishnan (1994, p. 356). We describe an iterative procedure, analogous to a Newton-Raphson method along the nonlinear submanifold $\overset{\approx}{G}$.

The consecutive parameter estimates are $(\gamma_k, \alpha_k, (\hat{y}, \hat{p})(\gamma_k, \alpha_k))$, with $(\hat{y}, \hat{p})(\cdot)$ given in (7.24) and (7.26) above, and

$$\begin{pmatrix} \gamma_{k+1} \\ \alpha_{k+1} \end{pmatrix} = \begin{pmatrix} \gamma_k \\ \alpha_k \end{pmatrix} + t_k \overset{\approx}{V} (\gamma_k, \alpha_k) \overset{\approx}{S}_k (\gamma_k, \alpha_k). \tag{7.31}$$

In each iteration, the scalar t_k is determined by line search. $\overset{\approx}{S}_k(\gamma_k, \alpha_k)$ is $(\overset{\approx}{s}_\gamma, \overset{\approx}{s}_\alpha)'$ from (7.27) and (7.30), evaluated at (γ_k, α_k). The 2×2 matrix $\overset{\approx}{V}(\cdot)$ is the observed profile formation per observation or one of the asymptotic equivalents. Of these, we focus on

$$\overset{\approx}{V}(\gamma, \alpha) = \left(\frac{1}{N_e} \sum_e \overset{\approx}{s}_i \overset{\approx}{s}_i \right)^{-1},$$

namely, the inverse of the sample average of the outer products of profile scores per observation $\overset{\approx}{s}_i$. Note that the analysis at this stage is carried out using only uncensored observations, and from these using only the wage information, the estimation of (y, p) having exhausted all information in the duration data. $\overset{\approx}{V}$ is easily computed using

$$\overset{\approx}{s}_{i\gamma} = \frac{\alpha}{\gamma} - w_i + \frac{w_m f(w_m; \gamma, \alpha)}{\gamma \Pi}, \qquad \overset{\approx}{s}_{i\alpha} = \ln w_i - E(\ln w | w > w_m). \tag{7.32}$$

We estimate the 3×3 full-rank variance-covariance matrix of $\hat{\theta}_1 = (\hat{\gamma}, \hat{\alpha}, \hat{p})$ by

$$\tilde{V} = \left(\frac{1}{N} \sum \tilde{s}_i \tilde{s}_i' \right)^{-1}, \tag{7.33}$$

in parallel with the approach in the estimation procedure (7.31) above. The score $\tilde{s}_i$ for the ith worker is evaluated at the MLE. Note that the entire sample is now used. The entries of $\tilde{s}_i$ are, first,

$$\tilde{s}_{ip} = \left[-\frac{t_i - \delta(i)}{1 - \lambda} + \frac{\delta(i)}{\lambda} \right] \Pi, \tag{7.34}$$

the ith contribution to $\tilde{s}_p$ in (7.25) above, with $\delta(i) = 1$ if and only if the ith worker was ultimately employed, and second, $(\tilde{s}_{i\gamma}, \tilde{s}_{i\alpha})$, which can be calculated using (7.27) through (7.30), (7.32), and (7.34) as

$$\tilde{s}_{i\gamma} = \tilde{s}_{ip}\frac{p\Pi_{\gamma}}{\Pi} + \delta(i)\,\tilde{\tilde{s}}_{i\gamma}, \qquad \tilde{s}_{i\alpha} = \tilde{s}_{ip}\frac{p\Pi_{\alpha}}{\Pi} + \delta(i)\,\tilde{\tilde{s}}_{i\alpha}.$$

The gradient of the map $(\gamma, \alpha, p) \to \hat{y}\,(\gamma, \alpha, p)$ is

$$\psi = \frac{\beta\lambda}{1-\beta}\left\{ E\,(w - w_m | w > w_m) \begin{bmatrix} 1/\gamma \\ dg\,(\alpha) - \ln\gamma \\ -1/p \end{bmatrix} \right.$$
$$\left. - \begin{bmatrix} -w_m/\gamma \\ E((w - w_m)\ln w | w > w_m) \\ 0 \end{bmatrix} \right\}, \qquad (7.35)$$

and the CARRN property carries over, i.e., $N^{1/2}(\hat{y} - \gamma, \hat{\alpha} - \alpha, \hat{p} - p, \hat{y} - y)$ has the rank 3 (singular) normal asymptotic distribution of theorem 5, with variance consistently estimated by $V = \Psi \tilde{V} \Psi'$. Here, $\Psi = (I_3, \psi)'$ and $\tilde{V}$ is given by (7.33). The vector $h = (-\psi', 1)'$ gives the direction of singularity, and the support of the singular normal is the hyperplane orthogonal to this at θ. The rapid convergence of w_m still holds in the gamma case, so in the asymptotic distribution of the MLE, we can ignore the distribution of w_m at the rate $N^{1/2}$. Finally, in $\theta^* = H'\theta$, orders of convergence are separated, with the three-dimensional component $\hat{\theta}^*$ converging in distribution at rate $N^{1/2}$ and $\hat{\theta}^*_2$ at rate N.

7.5 EXERCISES

1. Verify that the distribution of the minimum observation from N i.i.d. observations from an absolutely continuous CDF G with $G' = g$ has density $N(1 - G)^{N-1}g$.

2. Consider an i.i.d. sample of N observations from the density $g(x) = 3x(2 - x)/4$ for $x \in [0, 2]$ and suppose the sample is truncated from below at the unknown value a. What is the MLE for a and its exact and asymptotic distributions? Now suppose in addition that the distribution is truncated above at the unknown value b. What are the joint MLEs for a and b and their exact and asymptotic distributions?

3. In exercise 2, suppose it is known that $b = a + 1$, so there is really only one unknown parameter. Is it possible to improve the estimators developed in exercise 2? What is the MLE for a and its exact and asymptotic distributions?

7.6 REFERENCES

The sequential job search model is due to Mortensen (1970) and McCall (1970). See also Lippman and McCall (1976a, b) and Mortensen (1986). The search model was among the first stochastic dynamic programming models to be estimated structurally. Kiefer and Neumann (1979) specify an estimable version where offered wages and reservation wages depend linearly on observed regressors, including worker and labor market characteristics, and correlated normal errors. The model is fit to survey data from the Institute for Research on Human Resources (IRHR, Penn State) and the hypothesis of constant reservation wage over time is tested. Since ability differences may cause workers to have different acceptance rates, Kiefer and Neumann (1981) introduce unobserved heterogeneity into this model, leading to a nonlinear panel model with normal random effects that is fit to the IRHR data. Flinn and Heckman (1982) discuss the imposition of the optimality equation in a model without unobserved heterogeneity and assuming either no observed regressors or exponential instead of normal errors, noting that identification in general requires a distributional assumption, and they present estimates for the homogenous case using NLSY data. Many additional empirical and policy applications are reviewed by Devine and Kiefer (1991). The statistical development in this chapter follows that of Christensen and Kiefer (1991a).

Chapter Eight

Exact Distribution Theory for the Job Search Model

8.1 INTRODUCTION

The job search model of chapter 7, one of the first empirical applications of dynamic programming in economics, has become a workhorse in labor economics. Similarly, the introduction of the option-pricing model has sparked tremendous growth in the field of financial economics, starting with the seminal papers by Black and Scholes (1973) and Merton (1973b). The search and option models are examples of optimal stopping models (see chapter 6).

Applications of optimal stopping models have now appeared in many other areas of economics, including empirical studies of European patent renewal (Pakes, 1986) and optimal replacement investment (Rust, 1987a). The models are tightly specified and nonlinear. The central implication of the dynamic programming formulation is rarely imposed though structural estimation is feasible, as shown in chapter 7. Many applications have focused on some aspects of the models, leaving others loose. Further, most estimation theory and techniques for these models have only asymptotic justification. There are method-of-moments techniques and generalizations, and these apply to models more general than those considered here, but the results are weak (consistency and some asymptotic distribution theory) and do not constitute a full solution to the estimation and inference problem. Chapter 7 provides a likelihood analysis of the job search model and establishes the appropriate nonstandard asymptotic likelihood theory.

In this chapter we follow up by considering estimation and exact inference in the job search model. We investigate how sufficiency, ancillarity, specification of likelihoods for parameters of interest, exact distribution theory, and reparametrizations of special economic relevance apply in important practical settings. The search model is the simplest optimal stopping model general enough to illustrate all the important features of the inference problem. We develop methods that preserve asymptotic results (asymptotic equivalence to the maximum likelihood estimator (MLE) and thus efficiency) but allow simple development of estimators and natural separate inference. We employ the concepts of local S-sufficiency, local

S-ancillarity, and local cuts. In many cases, exact sampling distributions of estimators can be obtained. These serve as useful complements to asymptotic distributions.

In section 8.2 we briefly review the search model. The model we use is highly stylized—we refer to it as the prototypal search model—yet general enough to illustrate the main concepts of the search approach and all the important statistical issues that arise in applications. The prototypal model, though simple, has been the basis for many applications, and many others are straightforward generalizations, making the model more adequate as a description of the data but introducing no new concepts or estimation issues. We show that in the prototypal model, the strong conditionality principle of conditioning on a local cut leads to a finite sample improvement over maximum likelihood. This provides a useful answer to the important question of how to construct likelihoods for particular parameters of interest (Reid, 1996).

In section 8.3 we consider parametrizations that are economically important, although statistically they are not the most convenient. For simplicity, we first consider the case of wage data alone in settings with two unknown parameters. These illustrate the identification of various parameters of the model, including a discount factor (often thought not estimable and not treated in the literature). Section 8.4 generalizes to the important practical case in which joint wage and duration data are available.

8.2 THE PROTOTYPAL SEARCH MODEL

We use a discrete-time framework with random offer arrivals. Since the model is presented in chapter 7, we merely record a few key equations here. In each time period an unemployed worker receives a wage offer with probability p. Offers w are distributed independently across workers and time according to $\exp(\gamma)$, the exponential distribution with parameter $\gamma > 0$. Thus, the mean offer is $1/\gamma$ and the density is

$$f(w) = \gamma e^{-\gamma w}, \qquad w \geq 0. \tag{8.1}$$

The event of receiving an offer and the value of the offer are independent. The value function is

$$V(w) = \max\left\{\frac{w}{1-\beta}, y + \beta EV\right\} = \max\left\{V^e(w), V^u\right\}, \tag{8.2}$$

where $\beta = (1+r)^{-1}$ is the discount factor ($r > 0$ is the discount rate), $0 < \beta < 1$, and EV denotes the expected value of the function $V(w)$. The reservation wage w^r equates $V^e(w)$ and V^u. In this chapter we indicate the reservation wage with a superscript, reserving subscripts to identify, at times, estimators, and at times derivatives. Thus,

$$w^r = (1 - \beta)(y + \beta EV). \tag{8.3}$$

After some calculation (see (7.13)) we find

$$w^r = T(w^r) = (1 - \beta)y + \beta \left(w^r + \frac{p}{\gamma} e^{-\gamma w^r} \right), \tag{8.4}$$

the implicit equation determining the reservation wage. Here, $T(\cdot)$ is a contraction on $\mathbb{R}$. It is useful for the calculations below that (8.4) can be rearranged as

$$w^r = y + \frac{\beta p}{(1 - \beta)\gamma} e^{-\gamma w^r} = y + \frac{p}{r\gamma} e^{-\gamma w^r}. \tag{8.5}$$

This summarizes the prototypal search model. The model is simple, yet sufficiently rich to illustrate the important statistical issues in empirical search modeling. A complete guide to the many theoretical elaborations available is given by Mortensen (1986).

Suppose the unknown parameters are $(\gamma, y) \in \mathbb{R}_+ \times \mathbb{R}$. Consider the reparametrization to $(\gamma, w^r(\gamma, y))$, which can be computed using (8.4) and the contraction mapping theorem. Clearly, for y sufficiently negative (high search costs), the unemployed worker always accepts the first offer, so $w^r = 0$. Also, there is no upper bound on w^r since $w^r \geq y$. Hence, writing θ for the parameter and Θ for the parameter space throughout, $\theta = (\gamma, w^r) \in \Theta = \mathbb{R}_+^2$. We refer to this model as M. The conditional density of the wage offer w, given it has been accepted (i.e., $w \geq w^r$), is $f/\Pi = \gamma \exp(-\gamma(w - w^r))$ based on (8.1). Here, $\Pi = \exp(-\gamma w^r)$ is the acceptance probability. Let the sample $w = (w_1, \ldots, w_N)$ of accepted wages be given. M is specified by Θ and the model function

$$p(w; \theta) = \gamma^N e^{-\gamma N(\overline{w} - w^r)} 1_{\{w_m \geq w^r\}}, \tag{8.6}$$

where $\overline{w} = \Sigma_i w_i / N$ and $w_m = \min_i \{w_i\}$.

Define $v = (v_1, \ldots, v_{N-1})$ by $(w_1 - w_m, \ldots, w_N - w_m) = (v_1, \ldots, v_i, 0, v_{i+1}, \ldots, v_{N-1})$.

LEMMA 8.2.1 $\{v_i\}$ *forms an independent and identically distributed (i.i.d.)* $\exp(\gamma)$ *sample independent of* w_m.

Proof. Conditionally on w_m, the v_i are independent, and w_i follows an exponential distribution shifted by w_m. Hence, v_i is $\exp(\gamma)$. Since the conditional distribution of v does not depend on w_m, v is independent of w_m. $\square$

Define $a = (a_1, \ldots, a_N)$ by $a_i = (w_i - \overline{w})/s$, where $s^2 = \Sigma_{j=1}^N (w_j - \overline{w})^2 / (N-1)$.

PROPOSITION 8.2.1 *M is a location-scale model, $(\overline{w}, w_m)$ is minimal sufficient, and a is maximal ancillary.*

Proof. *M* is generated as the distributions of $\{w^r + w/\gamma : w^r, \gamma > 0\}$, where $w \sim \exp(1)$, and hence the first conclusion. The result for *a* then follows (Barndorff-Nielsen, 1988). For the sufficiency result, note that (8.6) depends on *w* only through $(\overline{w}, w_m)$. □

From proposition 8.2.1, upon reparametrization from (γ, y) to (γ, w^r), the prototypal search model becomes amenable to location-scale analysis. In particular, the following proposition gives the exact distribution of the minimal sufficient statistic.

PROPOSITION 8.2.2 *The distribution of $(\overline{w}, w_m)$ is given by*

$$p(\overline{w}, w_m; \theta) = \frac{(\gamma N)^N}{(N-2)!} (\overline{w} - w_m)^{N-2} e^{-\gamma N(\overline{w} - w^r)} 1_{\{\overline{w} \geq w_m \geq w_r\}}. \quad (8.7)$$

Proof. By lemma 8.2.1, the distribution of $q = \Sigma_{i=1}^{N-1} v_i/N = \overline{w} - w_m$ is $\Gamma(N-1, \gamma N)$, independent of w_m. By a standard result on order statistics, $w_m \sim w^r + \exp(\gamma N)$. The transformation from (q, w_m) to $(\overline{w}, w_m)$ has unit Jacobian. □

We list the related distributions in a corollary.

COROLLARY 8.2.1

(*i*)

$$p(\overline{w}; \theta) = \frac{(\gamma N)^N}{(N-1)!} (\overline{w} - w^r)^{N-2} e^{-\gamma N(\overline{w} - w^r)} 1_{\{\overline{w} \geq w_r\}}.$$

(*ii*)

$$p(w_m; \theta) = \gamma N e^{-\gamma N(w_m - w^r)} 1_{\{w_m \geq w^r\}}.$$

(*iii*) $\overline{w} - w_m$ *and* w_m *are independent.*

(*iv*)

$$p(\overline{w}; \theta | w_m) = \frac{(\gamma N)^{N-1}}{(N-2)!} (\overline{w} - w_m)^{N-2} e^{-\gamma N(\overline{w} - w_m)} 1_{\{\overline{w} \geq w_m\}}.$$

(*v*)

$$p(w; \theta | w_m) = \frac{1}{(N-2)!} \gamma^{N-1} e^{-\gamma N(\overline{w} - w_m)} \prod_i 1_{\{w_i \geq w_m\}}.$$

Proof. (*i*) follows from the integration of (8.7) with respect to w_m. See the previous proof for (*ii*) and (*iii*). (*iv*) follows from (8.7) and (*ii*), and (*v*) from (8.6) and (*ii*).   □

Neither the models (*i*) for $\overline{w}$ and (*ii*) for w_m in corollary 8.2.1 nor the model (8.6) for w or (8.7) for $(\overline{w}, w_m)$ is of the exponential type. This can be seen, for example, from the dependence of the supports on θ through w^r. However, the conditional model (*iv*) for $\overline{w}$ given w_m and the conditional model (*v*) for w given w_m are exponential with sufficient statistic $N\overline{w}$. The canonical parameter is γ for both models, so it is tempting to draw inference on γ from one of these exponential models. This procedure is justified by the conditionality principle (Berger, 1985) if w_m is ancillary in some suitable sense with respect to γ. Of course, the distribution of w_m depends on γ, the parameter about which we want to draw inference in the exponential models, so w_m is not ancillary in the usual sense, but it is locally S-sufficient with respect to w^r and locally S-ancillary with respect to γ in the sense of Christensen and Kiefer (1994a); i.e., the minimum wage is a local cut in the prototypal search model.

The situation is similar to that which occurs in the orthogeodesic models of Barndorff-Nielsen and Blæsild (1993). In this class, which is defined in geometric terms, Christensen and Kiefer (2000) show that the estimator for a subparameter is a local cut and base separate inference on this. In the same manner, by treating w_m as a local cut, we may draw separate inference on γ in the exponential model (*v*) above in the prototypal search model, and on w^r in (*ii*). We establish a finite-sample improvement relative to maximum likelihood, which further motivates the specification of likelihoods for parameters of interest.

Starting with w^r, corollary 8.2.1 (*ii*) is the pseudo (marginal) likelihood for w^r, denoted $L_m(w^r)$. This function increases until $w^r = w_m$, the maximal argument for which $L_m > 0$. The estimator is $\hat{w}_m^r = w_m$ (in general, when drawing inference in the marginal and conditional models given a local cut, we indicate this by subscripts m, respectively lc).

The pseudo (conditional) likelihood for γ is corollary 8.2.1 (*v*), with logarithm and associated score

$$l_{lc}(\gamma) = (N-1)\ln\gamma - \gamma N(\overline{w} - w_m),\qquad(8.8)$$

$$s_{lc}(\gamma) = \frac{N-1}{\gamma} - N(\overline{w} - w_m).\qquad(8.9)$$

Solving the pseudo likelihood equation $s_{lc}(\gamma) = 0$ yields the estimator in the conditional model,

$$\hat{\gamma}_{lc} = \frac{N-1}{N(\overline{w} - w_m)}.\qquad(8.10)$$

For comparison, we consider the log profile likelihood $\tilde{l}(\gamma)$ as an alternative log pseudo likelihood for γ, to be compared with (8.8). $L(\gamma, w^r)$ based on (8.6) increases in w^r up to w_m, so $\hat{w}^r = w_m$. This yields the log profile likelihood and associated profile score

$$\tilde{l}(\gamma) = N \ln \gamma - \gamma N(\overline{w} - w_m), \tag{8.11}$$

$$\tilde{s}(\gamma) = \frac{N}{\gamma} - N(\overline{w} - w_m). \tag{8.12}$$

Solving the profile likelihood equation $\tilde{s}(\gamma) = 0$ yields the exact MLE

$$\hat{\gamma} = \frac{1}{\overline{w} - w_m}, \tag{8.13}$$

which clearly differs from (8.10), showing that the strong conditionality principle of conditioning on the local cut does affect estimation. However, we have the following.

PROPOSITION 8.2.3 *In the prototypal search model, the pseudo likelihood under the strong ancillarity principle based on local S-ancillarity is an asymptotic profile likelihood function.*

Proof. The asymptotic equivalence follows from comparison of l_{lc} in (8.8) and $\tilde{l}$ in (8.11), invoking no arguments on the distribution of $\overline{w} - w_m$. □

Next, we compare the exact finite sample distribution of the MLE $\hat{\theta}$ with that of the estimator under the local cut $\hat{\theta}_{lc}$.

PROPOSITION 8.2.4

(i) In the exact distribution of $\hat{\theta}$, the components $\hat{\gamma}$ and $\hat{w}^r$ are independent.

$$p(\hat{\gamma}; \theta) = \frac{(N\gamma)^{N-1}}{(N-2)!} \frac{1}{\hat{\gamma}^N} e^{-N\gamma/\hat{\gamma}}, \qquad \hat{\gamma} > 0, \tag{8.14}$$

$$p(\hat{w}^r; \theta) = \gamma N e^{-\gamma N(\hat{w}^r - w^r)}, \qquad \hat{w}^r \geq w^r. \tag{8.15}$$

(ii) In the exact distribution of $\hat{\theta}_{lc}$, the components $\hat{\gamma}_{lc}$ and $\hat{w}^r$ are independent. The marginal distributions are given by (8.15) for $\hat{w}^r$, and

$$\hat{p}(\hat{\gamma}_{lc}; \theta) = \frac{((N-1)\gamma)^{N-1}}{(N-2)!} \frac{1}{\hat{\gamma}_{lc}^N} e^{-(N-1)\gamma/\hat{\gamma}_{lc}}, \qquad \hat{\gamma}_{lc} > 0. \tag{8.16}$$

Proof. (i) follows from (8.7), and then (ii) follows from a comparison of (8.10) and (8.13). □

We further characterize the model and the estimator under the local cut.

PROPOSITION 8.2.5 *The MLE and the estimator under the local cut are both independent of the maximal ancillary a.*

Proof. Both $\hat{\theta}$ and $\hat{\theta}_{lc}$ are functions of $(\overline{w}, w_m)$, which is sufficient by proposition 8.2.1 and may be shown to be complete, so the result follows from Basu's (1958) theorem.   □

The estimator under the local cut is less biased and has lower variance than the exact MLE; while $\hat{w}_m^r = \hat{w}^r$, we have the following.

PROPOSITION 8.2.6

$$\text{bias}(\hat{\gamma}) = E_\theta \hat{\gamma} - \gamma = 2\gamma/(N-2) > \gamma/(N-2) = E_\theta \hat{\gamma}_{lc} - \gamma = \text{bias}\left(\hat{\gamma}_{lc}\right),$$
$$(8.17)$$
$$\text{var}(\hat{\gamma}) = \frac{\gamma^2 N^2}{(N-2)^2 (N-3)} > \frac{\gamma^2 (N-1)^2}{(N-2)^2 (N-3)} = \text{var}(\hat{\gamma}_{lc}).$$

Proof. Based on (8.14) and (8.16).   □

Thus, in this optimal stopping model, the strong conditionality principle of conditioning on a local cut provides a useful answer to the important question of how to construct likelihoods for particular parameters of interest. In particular, the resulting estimator is asymptotically equivalent to the MLE but dominates in small samples from this sampling theoretic point of view. The small sample improvement according to the classical mean squared error criterion is illustrated in figure 8.1, where $MSE(lc)/MSE(MLE)$ is graphed against sample size.

8.3 ALTERNATIVE ECONOMIC PARAMETRIZATIONS

In this section, we focus on the MLE for alternative economically important parametrizations of the model. These alternatives become relevant according to the economic issues under study and the data available.

The new parametrizations may not allow local cuts. However, when the MLE in the new model is a one-to-one transformation of the MLE in the original model (which is the case, e.g., if the new model is an exact reparametrization of the original), we may apply the same transformation to the estimator under the local cut in the original model. This yields an alternative to the MLE in the new model. We continue to refer to the estimator thus transformed as the estimator under the local cut. This implies that the strong inference principle of conditioning on a local cut is applicable for any model possessing a reparametrization allowing a local cut. For such models, the connection to location-scale analysis from section 8.2 can be

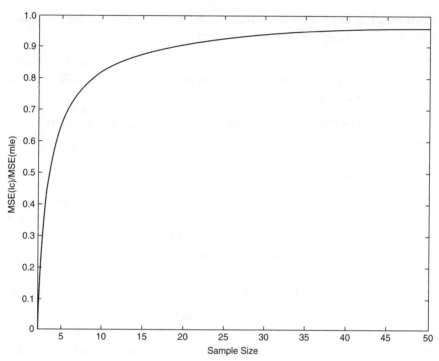

Figure 8.1 Relative Mean Squared Error.

made as well. These ideas are illustrated in numerical examples using labor
market data in this and the following section.

Consider the prototypal search model of section 8.2 with parameters
$(\gamma, y) \in \mathbb{R}_+ \times \mathbb{R}$. We studied in section 8.2 the reparametrization to
$\theta = (\gamma, w^r) \in \Theta = \mathbb{R}_+^2$ of this model. We start this section by considering the original parametrization by (γ, y). This is economically relevant
since unemployment insurance benefits net of search costs y is a fundamental primitive of the model, whereas w^r is a derived parameter that describes
the worker's decision rule for given primitives.

Let $\theta = (\gamma, y)$ and $\Theta = \mathbb{R}_+ \times \mathbb{R}$ and consider the model M_y specified by
Θ and the model function

$$p(w; \theta) = \gamma^N e^{-\gamma N(\overline{w} - w^r(\gamma, y))} 1_{\{w_m \geq w^r(\gamma, y)\}}. \qquad (8.18)$$

This is a reparametrization of the model (8.6). From parametrization invari-
ance of maximum likelihood, $\hat{\gamma} = 1/(\overline{w} - w_m)$ from (8.13), and $w^r(\hat{\gamma}, \hat{y}) =$
$\hat{w}^r = w_m$. Hence, we can without ambiguity write $\hat{y} = (w^r)_y^{-1}(\hat{\gamma}, \hat{w}^r)$,
where w^r is the function defined by (8.4) and the subscript y indicates
the argument in which the function is inverted. The Jacobian of the map

$(\hat{\gamma}, \hat{w}^r) \rightarrow (\hat{\gamma}, \hat{y})$ equals $\partial \hat{y} / \partial \hat{w}^r = 1 + \hat{\gamma}(w^r(\hat{\gamma}, \hat{y}) - \hat{y}) > 0$. The implicit function theorem applied to (8.5) is useful in obtaining this result. We have the following.

PROPOSITION 8.3.1 *The exact distribution of* $(\hat{\gamma}, \hat{y})$ *in* M_y *is given by*

$$p(\hat{\gamma}, \hat{y}; \gamma, y) = \frac{(\gamma N)^N}{(N-2)!}$$

$$\times \frac{1}{\hat{\gamma}^N(1 + \hat{\gamma}(w^r(\hat{\gamma}, \hat{y}) - \hat{y}))} e^{-\gamma N(\hat{\gamma}^{-1} + w^r(\hat{\gamma}, \hat{y}) - w^r(\gamma, y))}$$

with support $\{(\hat{\gamma}, \hat{y}) : \hat{\gamma} > 0, w^r(\hat{\gamma}, \hat{y}) \geq w^r(\gamma, y)\}$.

Proof. This follows from proposition 8.2.4 (i) and the result for the Jacobian. $\square$

In proposition 8.3.1 and the following, the function w^r can be computed using (8.4). The estimators $\hat{\gamma}$ and $\hat{y}$ in proposition 8.3.1 are not independent. Their asymptotic distribution is a singular (rank 1) normal at rate $N^{1/2}$, while a linear function of $(\hat{\gamma}, \hat{y})$ follows a nondegenerate non-normal distribution at rate N (chapter 7). In spite of these complications, we are interested in parameters such as (γ, y) since they are structural parameters in the economic model of section 8.2, whereas, e.g., the reservation wage is a derived parameter, and the theory shows that γ and y are separately identifiable and estimable. Proposition 8.3.1 provides the foundation for exact structural analysis, which is an important improvement over asymptotic analysis.

We next let $\theta = (\gamma, p)$ and $\Theta = \mathbb{R}_+ \times (0, 1]$. This parametrization is economically relevant, e.g., if data on unemployment insurance benefits are used for y, direct search costs are assumed negligible, and there is doubt about whether an offer is received every period. Consider the model M_p specified by the model function (8.18), but with $w^r(\gamma, p)$ replacing $w^r(\gamma, y)$. From (8.5) we have $\partial w^r / \partial p = (w^r - y)/\{p(1 + \gamma(w^r - y))\} > 0$. For $(\gamma, p) \in \Theta_+ = \{(\gamma, p) : w_m \geq w^r(\gamma, p)\}$, the log likelihood, the score in p and the MLE of p given γ are

$$l(\theta) = N\{\ln \gamma - \gamma(\overline{w} - w^r(\gamma, p))\}, \tag{8.19}$$

$$s_p(\theta) = \gamma N \partial w^r / \partial p > 0, \tag{8.20}$$

$$\hat{p}_\gamma = \min\{1, (w^r)_p^{-1}(\gamma, w_m)\}. \tag{8.21}$$

Let $\widetilde{\Theta} = \{\gamma : w_m \leq w^r(\gamma, 1)\}$. The log profile likelihood and profile score for γ are

$$\tilde{l}(\gamma) = N \left(\ln \gamma - \gamma \left(\overline{w} - w_m \right) \right), \qquad \gamma \in \widetilde{\Theta}, \tag{8.22}$$

$$\tilde{l}(\gamma) = N \{ \ln \gamma - \gamma (\overline{w} - w^r(\gamma, 1)) \}, \qquad \gamma \in \mathbb{R}_+ \backslash \widetilde{\Theta}. \tag{8.23}$$

$$\tilde{s}(\gamma) = N \left\{ \frac{1}{\gamma} - (\overline{w} - w_m) \right\}, \qquad \gamma \in \widetilde{\Theta}, \tag{8.24}$$

$$\tilde{s}(\gamma) = N \left\{ \frac{1}{\gamma} - (\overline{w} - w^r(\gamma, 1)) + \gamma \frac{\partial w^r(\gamma, 1)}{\partial \gamma} \right\}, \qquad \gamma \in \mathbb{R}_+ \backslash \widetilde{\Theta}. \tag{8.25}$$

By (8.5) and $E(w | w \geq w^r) = w^r + \gamma^{-1}$,

$$\frac{\partial w^r(\gamma, 1)}{\partial \gamma} = -E(w | w^r(\gamma, 1)) \frac{w^r(\gamma, 1) - y}{1 + \gamma(w^r(\gamma, 1) - y)} < 0. \tag{8.26}$$

Hence, (8.25) can be either positive or negative. From (8.26) it can also be seen that $\widetilde{\Theta} = (0, \bar{\gamma}]$, with $\bar{\gamma} = (w^r)_\gamma^{-1}(w_m, 1)$.

If the zero of (8.24) belongs to $\widetilde{\Theta}$, i.e., if $1/(\overline{w} - w_m) \leq \bar{\gamma}$, then $\hat{\gamma} = 1/(\overline{w} - w_m)$ as in M and M_y, and $\hat{p} = (w^r)_p^{-1}(1/(\overline{w} - w_m), w_m)$. If $1/(\overline{w} - w_m) > \bar{\gamma}$, we would seek a zero in (8.25) for the estimator of γ, and $\hat{p} = 1$. However, if the true offer arrival probability p is less than 1, then $1/(\overline{w} - w_m)$ belongs to $\widetilde{\Theta}$ with a probability c that converges to 1 exponentially fast. In particular, $c = P(A) = P(w^r(1/(\overline{w} - w_m), 1) > w_m)$, where corollary 8.2.1 (ii), (iii), and (iv) allow computation. Hence, we focus on the event $A = \{\hat{\gamma} = 1/(\overline{w} - w_m)\}$. Conditionally on A, M_p is a reparametrization to (γ, p) of the model of section 8.2 over

$$(\gamma, w^r) \in B = \{(\gamma, w^r) : \gamma > 0, y \leq w^r \leq w^r(\gamma, 1)\}, \tag{8.27}$$

since from (8.5) $w^r \to y$ as $p \to 0$. Note that $A = \{(\hat{\gamma}, \hat{w}^r) \in B\} = \{\hat{\gamma} \in \widetilde{\Theta}\}$.

PROPOSITION 8.3.2 *In M_p, and for $p < 1$,*

$p(\hat{\gamma}, \hat{p}; \gamma, p | A)$

$$= \frac{(\gamma N)^N}{(N-2)!} \frac{w^r(\hat{\gamma}, \hat{p}) - y}{\hat{\gamma}^N \hat{p}(1 + \hat{\gamma}(w^r(\hat{\gamma}, \hat{p}) - y))} e^{-\gamma N(\hat{\gamma}^{-1} + w^r(\hat{\gamma}, \hat{p}) - w^r(\gamma, p))}$$

with support $\widetilde{\Theta} \times (0, 1)$.

Proof. This follows from proposition 8.2.4 (i) and the Jacobian of the map $(\hat{\gamma}, \hat{w}^r) \to (\hat{\gamma}, \hat{p})$. Here, $\partial \hat{p} / \partial \hat{w}^r = (\partial \hat{w}^r / \partial \hat{p})^{-1}$, and the result for $\partial w^r / \partial p$ stated before (8.19) applies. □

Proposition 8.3.2 is easily transformed to yield the conditional distribution of $(\hat{p}, \widehat{\Pi})$ in a model $M_{p,\Pi}$ parametrized directly by (p, Π).

The transformation uses that $\gamma = -(p\Pi/r + \ln \Pi)/y$ and that the map $(\gamma, p) \to (p, \Pi)$ has Jacobian $w^r \Pi (1 + \varepsilon)$, where ε is the elasticity of w_r with respect to γ. The joint identification of the offer arrival probability p and the acceptance probability Π in the pure wage data model is a remarkable consequence of full exploitation of economic theory. These two probabilities cannot be estimated separately without functional form restrictions, and the economic theory delivers these.

Apart from $M_{p,\Pi}$, we have so far considered the models with γ together with w^r, y, or p unknown, i.e., M, M_y, and M_p. Suppose finally that the unknown parameter is $\theta = (\gamma, \beta)$. Let $\Theta = \mathbb{R}_+ \times (0, 1)$ and consider the model M_β specified by Θ and the model function (8.18), but with $w^r(\gamma, \beta)$ replacing $w^r(\gamma, y)$. The discount factor β typically causes many problems, e.g., in macroeconomic studies, and proper statistical inference on this parameter is rarely dealt with explicitly in the literature.

From $\lambda = p\Pi$ (the employment probability) and (8.5) we have

$$\frac{\partial w^r}{\partial \beta} = \frac{w^r - y + \lambda/\gamma}{1 - \beta (1 - \lambda)} > 0. \tag{8.28}$$

For $\theta \in \Theta_+ = \{(\gamma, \beta) : w_m \geq w^r(\gamma, \beta)\}$, we again have $l(\theta)$ from (8.19), with $w^r(\gamma, \beta)$ replacing $w^r(\gamma, p)$. By (8.28), $s_\beta(\theta) = \gamma N \, \partial w^r/\partial \beta > 0$, so

$$\hat{\beta}_\gamma = \min\left\{1, (w^r)^{-1}_\beta (\gamma, w_m)\right\}. \tag{8.29}$$

This corresponds to the estimator (8.21) in M_p. However, estimation of the discount factor is simpler than estimation of the offer arrival probability, as the following proposition shows.

PROPOSITION 8.3.3 *In M_β, $w^r(\gamma, \beta) \to \infty$ as $\beta \to 1$, and*

$$\hat{\beta}_\gamma = (w^r)^{-1}_\beta (\gamma, w_m). \tag{8.30}$$

Proof. By (8.29), violation of (8.30) requires $1 < (w^r)^{-1}(\gamma, w_m)$, which by (8.28) is equivalent with: $\forall \beta < 1 : w^r(\gamma, \beta) < w_m$. For any sample, this is ruled out if we can show the first claim of the proposition. Suppose on the contrary that the claim is violated. By (8.28), then $\lim_{\beta \to 1} w^r(\gamma, \beta) = K < \infty$. Consider (8.4). As $\beta \to 1$, this identity becomes $K = K + p \exp(-\gamma K)/\gamma$ or $\exp(-\gamma K) = 0$. Hence the contradiction. $\square$

In contrast with M_p we can then let $\widetilde{\Theta} = \mathbb{R}_+$ in M_β. This means that both M_β and M_y (but not M_p) are reparametrizations of the model from section 8.2. The log profile likelihood and profile score are (8.22) and (8.24), so $\hat{\gamma} = 1/(\overline{w} - w_m)$ and $\hat{\beta} = (w^r)^{-1}_\beta (\hat{\gamma}, w_m)$.

PROPOSITION 8.3.4 *In M_β,*

$$p(\hat{\gamma}, \hat{\beta}; \gamma, \beta) = \frac{(\gamma N)^N}{(N-2)!} \frac{w^r(\hat{\gamma}, \hat{\beta}) - y + pe^{-\hat{\gamma}w^r(\hat{\gamma},\hat{\beta})}/\hat{\gamma}}{1 - \hat{\beta}(1 - pe^{-\hat{\gamma}w^r(\hat{\gamma},\hat{\beta})})}$$
$$\times \frac{1}{\hat{\gamma}^N} e^{-\gamma N(\hat{\gamma}^{-1}+w^r(\hat{\gamma},\hat{\beta})-w^r(\gamma,\beta))}, \qquad (8.31)$$

with support $\{(\hat{\gamma}, \hat{\beta}) : \hat{\gamma} > 0, 0 < \hat{\beta} < 1, w^r(\hat{\gamma}, \hat{\beta}) \geq w^r(\gamma, \beta)\}$.

Proof. This follows from proposition 8.2.4 (i) and (8.28). □

We illustrate the analysis of M_β using data from the Public Use Files from the 1984 panel of the Survey on Income and Program Participation (SIPP). The SIPP is a nationwide longitudinal survey compiled by the U.S. Bureau of the Census. For our illustration we restrict attention to nonwhite males, 16–19 years old, who experienced a spell of unemployment, did not have a job in agriculture, and were neither disabled nor self-employed.

The key variables we use are hourly wages and unemployment spell lengths (see also section 8.4 below). Summary statistics for our sub-sample include $N = 44$, $\overline{w} = 3.67$, $w_m = 2.18$. In the context of our model, these are sufficient statistics. The graph of the likelihood function $L(\gamma, \beta)$ is shown from four different angles in figure 8.2. In this and the following figures, we set the unemployment insurance benefits net of search costs y equal to 0 and the per-period probability of receiving an offer as $p = .2$. Fixing p determines the time scale for the discount factor β. It is clear that the maximum lies on the nonlinear ridge shown in figure 8.2 (compare figure 7.1).

Note that for β small and γ large, w^r is low, and so the likelihood function is nonzero, but the value quickly gets so low that all the mass appears to be concentrated along the ridge in the figure. To get a better feel for the shape of the likelihood, we graph the conditional likelihoods (slices in coordinate directions) in figures 8.3 and 8.4. In our sample, the joint $MLE(\hat{\gamma}, \hat{\beta}) = (.671, .969)$, and each slice shown is for the other parameter fixed at the MLE. Here, the sharp and asymmetric drop to zero on one side of the ridge is evident.

The maxima in coordinate directions lie on the ridge, and consequently the profile likelihood for γ (shown in figure 8.5) is obtained by projection of the ridge to the (L, γ) plane (the projection P_m from chapter 7). Note the more regular appearance of the profile likelihood: The ridge is gone.

The resulting exact density of the MLE from proposition 8.3.4 is shown in figure 8.6 from four different angles, assuming true parameters $(\gamma, \beta) = (.671, .969)$ (the estimates in the sample). Note that the MLE in a given sample is on the ridge illustrated for the SIPP data in figure 8.2, but that the

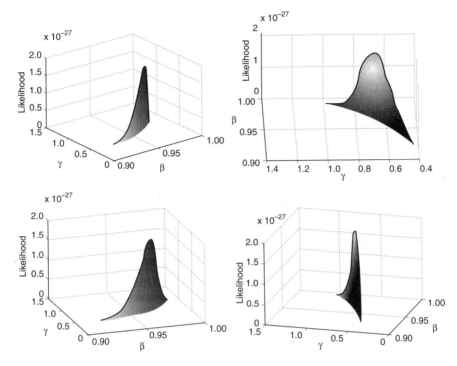

Figure 8.2 Likelihood Functions.

location of the ridge is random. For $N = 44$ this randomness is sufficiently moderate for the distribution of the MLE to take on the similar ridgelike shape evident in figure 8.6. All the mass is concentrated very close to the one-dimensional manifold $\{(\gamma, \beta) : w^r(\gamma, \beta) = w^r(.671, .969)\}$. This tradeoff between γ and β is clearly nonlinear, and the correlation between the estimates is .929 in the exact distribution, whereas they would be perfectly correlated in any approximating normal distribution concentrated on the tangent to the manifold at the MLE. The marginal densities of $\hat{\gamma}$ and $\hat{\beta}$ (determined by integration) in figures 8.7 and 8.8 are similarly far from normal and, in particular, clearly skewed. Obviously, inferences based on the exact joint and marginal distributions would be preferred over normal assessments.

For comparison, the estimators under the local cut (8.10) and (8.30) are $(\hat{\gamma}_{lc}, \hat{\beta}_{lc}) = (.656, .968)$. The equivalent subsample from the SIPP data, but for nonwhite females, has $N = 40$, $\overline{w} = 3.60$, and $w_m = 2.125$, yielding estimators under the local cut .661 and .966 and MLEs $\hat{\gamma} = .678$ and $\hat{\beta} = .968$. Thus, in particular the estimates of the subjective time preference parameter β are similar across gender in the data set. Furthermore, the

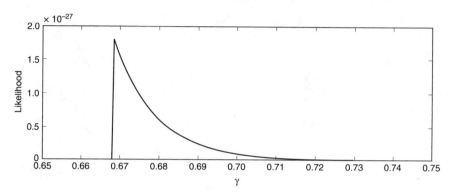

Figure 8.3 Conditional Likelihood ($\gamma|\beta = .969$).

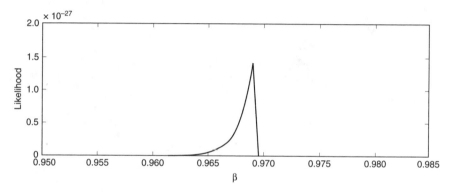

Figure 8.4 Conditional Likelihood ($\beta|\gamma = .671$).

β estimates depend less than the γ estimates on the estimation principle (local cut or MLE).

8.4 MODELS FOR JOINT WAGE AND DURATION DATA

This section extends the analysis of the previous sections to the case of joint wage and duration data. This data configuration is common in empirical applications, and more parameters can now be identified.

For N initially unemployed workers, let the sample $(t, w) = (t_1, \ldots, t_N, w_1, \ldots, w_N)$ of lengths of spells of unemployment t_i and accepted wages w_i be given and let $T = \Sigma_i t_i$. Suppose first that $(\gamma, y, p) \in \mathbb{R}_+ \times \mathbb{R} \times (0, 1)$ is unknown and consider the reparametrization to $(\gamma, w^r(\gamma, y, p), \lambda(\gamma, y, p))$, which can be computed using (8.4). Hence, $\theta = (\gamma, w^r, \lambda) \in \Theta = \{(\gamma, w^r, \lambda) : \gamma > 0, w^r > 0, 0 < \lambda < \exp(-\gamma w^r)\}$,

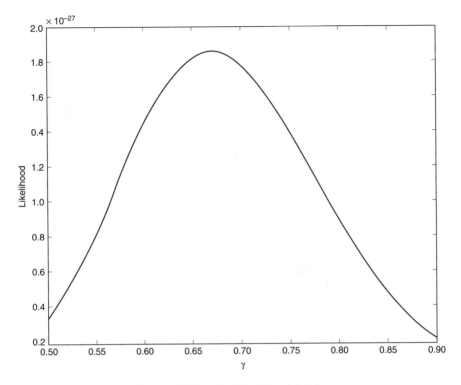

Figure 8.5 Profile Likelihood $L(\gamma)$.

and the model function is given by

$$p(t, w; \theta) = (1 - \lambda)^{T-N} \lambda^N \gamma^N e^{-\gamma N(\overline{w} - w^r)} 1_{\{w_m \geq w^r\}}. \qquad (8.32)$$

This parametrization, by (γ, w^r, λ), is the statistically most convenient, but for economic purposes, parametrization by (γ, y, p) or (γ, β, p) is more relevant, and this is an issue we explore below. Note, however, that because of the cross-restriction on λ and the other parameters in Θ, the model (8.32) does not simply factor into the original model for wage data (8.6) and an independent model for T, even in the parametrization by (γ, w^r, λ).

PROPOSITION 8.4.1 $(T, \overline{w}, w_m)$ *is minimal sufficient, T and $(\overline{w}, w_m)$ are independent, proposition 8.2.2 remains valid, and*

$$p(T; \theta) = \binom{T - 1}{T - N} (1 - \lambda)^{T-N} \lambda^N, \qquad (8.33)$$

with support $T \in \{N, N + 1, \ldots\}$, i.e., $T \sim B^-(N, \lambda)$ (negative binomial).

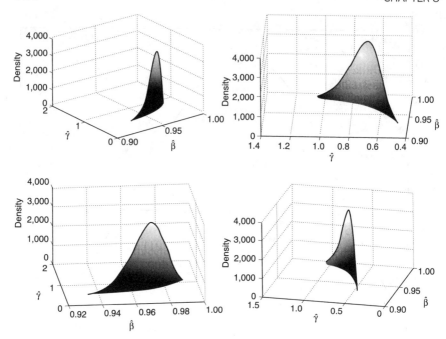

Figure 8.6 Density of the Maximum Likelihood Estimator.

Proof. Equation (8.32) depends on (t, w) only through $(T, \overline{w}, w_m)$, T and w are independent by factorization of (8.32), and $T = \Sigma_{i=1}^{N} t_i$, where $t_i \sim Ge(\lambda)$ (geometric). □

Note: The leading factor in (8.33) is a binomial coefficient.

We now consider drawing inference on λ in $p(T; \theta) = p(T; \lambda)$, on w^r in $p(w_m; \theta|T) = p(w_m; \gamma, w^r)$, and on γ in $p(\overline{w}; \theta|T, w_m) = p(\overline{w}; \gamma, w^r|w_m)$. Hence, inference on (γ, w^r) coincides with that obtained in section 8.2. The pseudo log likelihood and pseudo score for λ based on (8.33) are

$$l(\lambda) = \ln \binom{T-1}{T-N} + (T-N)\ln(1-\lambda) + N\ln\lambda, \quad (8.34)$$

$$s(\lambda) = -\frac{T-N}{1-\lambda} + \frac{N}{\lambda}. \quad (8.35)$$

Solving the pseudo likelihood equation $s(\lambda) = 0$ yields

$$\hat{\lambda}_m = \frac{N}{T}. \quad (8.36)$$

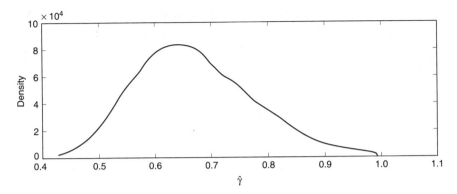

Figure 8.7 Marginal Density of $\hat{\gamma}$.

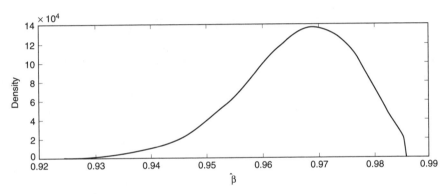

Figure 8.8 Marginal Density of $\hat{\beta}$.

PROPOSITION 8.4.2 *The estimators for γ, w^r, and λ are independent. The marginal distributions from proposition 8.2.4 remain valid, and $N\hat{\lambda}_m^{-1} \sim B^-(N, \lambda)$.*

Proof. This follows from propositions 8.2.4 and 8.4.1. $\qquad\square$

The estimator in (8.36) exceeds $\exp(-\hat{\gamma}_{lc}\hat{w}_m^r) = \exp(-(N-1)w_m/(N(\overline{w}-w_m)))$ with positive probability. In this case, $(\hat{\gamma}_{lc}, \hat{w}_m^r, \hat{\lambda}_m)$ does not belong to Θ. We would then instead consider the estimate $\exp(-\hat{\gamma}_{lc}\hat{w}_m^r)$ for λ. Note by comparing (8.32) and (8.33) that (8.36) equals the MLE for λ, and since with positive probability this exceeds $\exp(-\hat{\gamma}\hat{w}^r) = \exp(-w_m/(\overline{w}-w_m))$, the same problem arises (and even more often) under maximum likelihood. When using instead of (8.36) the suggested estimator restricted to Θ, both the independence result and the negative binomial result of proposition 8.4.2 are lost. The exact distributions of $\hat{\theta}_{lc}$ and $\hat{\theta}$ become complicated and have been left out, but we now establish that $\hat{\lambda} = \min\{\exp(-\hat{\gamma}\hat{w}^r), N/T\}$ indeed is the exact MLE for λ. We demonstrate this result in the economically important parametrization given by $(\gamma, y, p) \in \mathbb{R}_+ \times \mathbb{R} \times (0, 1)$. The log likelihood for $w_m \geq w^r(\gamma, y, p)$ by (8.32) becomes

$$l(\theta) = (T - N)\ln\left(1 - pe^{-\gamma w^r(\gamma,y,p)}\right)$$

$$+ N\left\{\ln p - \gamma w^r(\gamma, y, p) + \ln \gamma - \gamma(\overline{w} - w^r(\gamma, y, p))\right\}$$

$$= (T - N)\ln\left(1 - pe^{-\gamma w^r(\gamma,y,p)}\right) + N\{\ln p + \ln \gamma - \gamma\overline{w}\}. \quad (8.37)$$

The score in y is

$$s_y(\theta) = \frac{(T-N)\lambda\gamma(\partial w^r/\partial y)}{1 - \lambda} = \frac{(T-N)\lambda\gamma}{(1-\lambda)(1 + \gamma(w^r - y))} > 0, \quad (8.38)$$

so $\hat{y}_{(\gamma,p)} = (w^r)_y^{-1}(\gamma, w_m, p)$ in parallel with section 8.3. The log profile likelihood is

$$\tilde{l}(\gamma, p) = (T - N)\ln(1 - pe^{-\gamma w_m}) + N\{\ln p + \ln \gamma - \gamma\overline{w}\},$$

and the profile score in p is

$$\tilde{s}_p(\gamma, p) = \frac{-(T-N)e^{-\gamma w_m}}{1 - pe^{-\gamma w_m}} + \frac{N}{p}. \quad (8.39)$$

The unique solution to the partial profile likelihood equation, $\tilde{s}_p = 0$, is

$$\hat{p}_\gamma = \frac{N}{Te^{-\gamma w_m}}. \quad (8.40)$$

The function $\tilde{l}$ is evidently increasing in p up to this point, which can exceed unity, and the MLE over Θ is $\min\{1, N/(T\exp(-\gamma w_m))\}$. The previous claim on the MLE for λ has been verified since by multiplying by $\exp(-\hat{\gamma}w_m)$,

$$\hat{\lambda} = \min\left\{e^{-\hat{\gamma}w_m}, \frac{N}{T}\right\}. \quad (8.41)$$

The result (8.13) that $\hat{\gamma} = 1/(\overline{w} - w_m)$ is changed when $\hat{\lambda} = \exp(-\hat{\gamma}w_m)$. Thus, the log profile likelihood and profile score are

$$\tilde{\tilde{l}}(\gamma) = (T - N)\ln\left(1 - e^{-\gamma w_m}\right) + N\{\ln \gamma - \gamma\overline{w}\}, \quad (8.42)$$

$$\tilde{\tilde{s}}(\gamma) = \frac{(T-N)w_m}{1 - e^{-\gamma w_m}} + \frac{N}{\gamma} - N\overline{w}. \quad (8.43)$$

Clearly, for $\overset{\approx}{\gamma}$ solving the profile likelihood equation $\overset{\approx}{s} = 0$, (8.13) will be violated, even though the result (8.41) goes through.

Finally, consider the other parametrization of special economic interest, given by $\theta = (\gamma, \beta, p)$. The log likelihood is again (8.37), replacing y by β. By (8.28), $\partial w^r / \partial \beta > 0$, and by an argument similar to that in (8.38), $s_\beta(\theta) > 0$. By proposition 8.3.3, $w^r(\gamma, \beta, p) \to \infty$ as $\beta \to 1$, so we have

$$\hat{\beta}_{(\gamma, p)} = \left(w^r\right)_\beta^{-1} (\gamma, w_m, p), \qquad (8.44)$$

similar to the result (8.30) from proposition 8.3.3 in the wage data model.

All discussion and results related to (8.39)–(8.43) carry over to the model with an unknown discount factor. Again, explicit treatment of this parameter is new to the literature, and we continue the illustration using SIPP data from section 8.3. In the subsample of nonwhite males referred to in that section, the total number of weeks of unemployment is $T = 746$. Substituting $\hat{\gamma} = .671$ for γ in (8.40) yields $\hat{p} = .255$. Since $\hat{p} < 1$, the stated values are indeed the MLEs for (γ, p) in the subsample, and they in turn imply a value $\hat{\beta} = .961$, using (8.44). Note that fixing $p = .2$ in section 8.3 (where the data employed lacked a time dimension) implicitly imposed a shorter time unit (namely, a lower probability of receiving an offer) on the discount factor than the sampling interval (weeks in SIPP), and that this is reflected in heavier estimated discounting (lower β) in the joint data than in the pure wage data (section 8.3). In both cases, the relationship between the offer arrival and the discount rates is being estimated; including the duration data allows estimating in addition the relationship between these two and the actual time scale.

We compare with the estimator under the local cut by substituting instead $\hat{\gamma}_{lc} = .656$ in (8.40) and (8.44). This yields $\hat{p}_{lc} = .246$ and $\hat{\beta}_{lc} = .960$. In the equivalent subsample of nonwhite females, the total number of weeks of unemployment is $T = 625$, yielding $\hat{\gamma}_{lc} = .661$, $\hat{p}_{lc} = .261$, and $\hat{\beta}_{lc} = .956$, whereas the MLEs are $\hat{\gamma} = .678$, $\hat{p} = .270$, and $\hat{\beta} = .957$. For γ and β, the discussion from section 8.3 regarding comparison across gender and estimation method remains valid, though the point estimates of β have changed upon including the duration data. In addition, the estimated offer probabilities are less similar across gender and depend more on the estimation method (local cut or MLE) than the estimated subjective time preference parameters β.

8.5 CONCLUSION

The interaction between the theoretical specification of the model and the econometric analysis is exploited to obtain an exact distribution theory for parameter estimators for several appealing parametrizations of the job search model. In this framework, the relation between different estimators (conditional, marginal, etc.) can be illustrated. The results apply generally to optimal stopping models.

8.6 EXERCISES

1. Show that the model (8.6) for given w^r is regular exponential. Show that it is not an exponential family model when w^r is unknown.

2. Derive (8.28) from (8.5).

3. In proposition 8.2.4, determine the rate at which each coordinate of the estimator converges to a non-degenerate limiting distribution. Is any component superconsistent? Repeat the questions for proposition 8.3.1.

8.7 REFERENCES

This chapter is based on Christensen and Kiefer (1991b). Various pseudo likelihoods and different concepts of ancillarity and sufficiency exploited in this chapter are examined by Barndorff-Nielsen (1978, 1988). Log likelihood derivatives provide approximately sufficient statistics in wide generality, and block diagonality of the Fisher information matrix is a condition for independence to order proportional to squareroot of sample size of the conformable subparameter estimators and score components. The condition is satisfied within the class of orthogeodesic models, defined in geometric terms by Barndorff-Nielsen and Blæsild (1993), and the additional properties imply that the residual from quadratic regression of the score with respect to the first subparameter on the score with respect to the second subparameter is independent of the score with respect to the second subparameter to one order higher, i.e., proportional to sample size (Barndorff-Nielsen and Blæsild, 1992). Christensen and Kiefer (1994) show that the first subparameter estimator is a local cut, and separate inference is indicated. By the conditionality principle (Berger, 1985), inference should be drawn conditionally upon a suitable ancillary (weakly exogenous) statistic, and we show in the present chapter a case of a dynamic programming model where the procedure reduces both bias and sampling variance in the unconditional distribution, relative to the MLE (proposition 8.2.6).

Chapter Nine

Measurement Error in the Prototypal Job Search Model

9.1 INTRODUCTION

The simplest version of the search model that still captures the conceptual core of the search approach to labor market data analysis is described in chapter 7. This model considers the problem facing a worker who is currently unemployed and who samples job offers with probability p each period (typically a week is empirically appropriate). Data are collected across a sample of workers, and the parameters of the search model, consisting of an offer distribution parameter, a net search cost parameter, and an offer probability parameter, are estimated. The model is applied to a homogeneous sample of workers. Of course, all workers are different, but if the model is to be at all useful, we cannot have different parameters for each individual; we would like the model to apply comfortably to individuals in broad groups. Thus, we expect the model to predict and describe group behavior. This approach is equivalent to controlling heterogeneity with a complete layout of discrete regressors. The model requires data on accepted wages following spells of unemployment. Data on the durations of spells of unemployment are also useful but not essential. In the simplest case, the dependent variable is the accepted wage.

When applying the search model to a sample of accepted wages and using the assumption that wages (the state variable) are measured correctly, one parameter (more precisely, one dimension in the parameter space) is estimated based on the minimum observed accepted wage. This parameter (typically in fact a combination of several structural parameters) is thus determined at rate N, the sample size, while other parameters are determined at rate $N^{1/2}$. The statistical theory for this situation is treated in chapters 7 and 8, but some apprehension remains in applications. Intuitively, we expect that estimators based on averages (such as maximum likelihood estimators (MLEs) based on setting the score vector equal to zero) will not be terribly sensitive to measurement error, while estimators based on order statistics will be sensitive even in large samples. It is useful to recall at this point that we are considering measurement error in state variables.

Of course, whether this intuition is correct or not requires further analysis.

In this chapter we develop an approach to the prototypal search model which allows measurement error in wages. This provides an example of a continuous state/discrete control model with measurement error in the state. Our development extends the prototypal model only by assuming the econometrician does not accurately measure wages; the theoretical situation facing workers is unchanged. Thus, the interpretation of parameters is straightforward. Unfortunately, the elegant statistical theory available in the classical optimal stopping model is lost, as we no longer have fixed-dimensional sufficient statistics and are therefore operating outside of the exponential family, but the applicability of the model is demonstrated by an application to data. The specification we use is simpler than other specifications using normally distributed errors (e.g., Kiefer and Neumann (1979) and Wolpin (1987)) and allows strict separation between the economic model and the measurement error process. We find in our illustrative data from the Survey of Income and Program Participation (SIPP) that measurement error is significant for some demographic groups (we use a classification by age, race, and sex), but that for other groups the prototypal model describes the sample adequately with no modification.

9.2 THE PROTOTYPAL SEARCH MODEL

This section briefly reviews the background material on the prototypal search model of chapter 7. In each of the discrete time periods $t = 0, 1, 2, \ldots$, an unemployed worker receives a wage offer w with probability p. Jobs are distinguished here only by the value of the wage. The event of receiving an offer and the value of the offer are independent. Unemployed workers receive unemployment income y, net of search costs, until they accept a wage offer w. After this they expect to receive w every period. Workers maximize the expected present discounted value of their income stream. The value function for a worker with an outstanding offer w is

$$V(w) = \max\{V^e(w), V^u\} = \max\left\{\frac{w}{1-\beta}, y + \beta EV\right\}, \quad (9.1)$$

where β is the subjective discount factor, assumed constant, $0 < \beta < 1$, and EV denotes the expected value function. Since the value V^e of employment increases in the wage offer and the value V^u of continuing the search is constant, a reservation wage strategy is optimal. The worker accepts w if and only if it exceeds the reservation wage w_r defined by indifference between unemployment and employment,

$$w_r = (1 - \beta)(y + \beta EV). \tag{9.2}$$

If offers are distributed according to the density f, the conditional probability of acceptance given an offer has been received is

$$\Pi = \int_{w_r}^{\infty} f(w)\,dw. \tag{9.3}$$

The expected value is now given as in (7.3) by

$$EV = \frac{1}{1 - \beta}\{p\Pi E(w|w > w_r) + (1 - p\Pi)w_r\}. \tag{9.4}$$

The density of accepted offers is

$$g(w) = \frac{f(w)}{\Pi} 1_{\{w \geq w_r\}}. \tag{9.5}$$

The prototypal specification for the offer distribution is the shifted exponential

$$f(w) = \gamma e^{-\gamma(w-c)}, \qquad w \geq c, \tag{9.6}$$

with $\gamma > 0, c \geq 0$ (so that $Ew = c + \gamma^{-1}$). Note that this is a slight generalization over chapter 7, allowing a nonzero lower support point in offers. This specification is empirically relevant in that it allows clustering of accepted wages close to w_r. The resulting prototypal search model is the simplest model that allows analysis of all the important issues in applications. In this case, (9.3) specializes to

$$\Pi = e^{-\gamma(w_r-c)} \tag{9.7}$$

since clearly $w_r \geq c$ (there is no point setting the reservation wage below the lower support point of the offer distribution). This allows calculation of the density of accepted wages using (9.6) and (9.7) in (9.5); i.e.,

$$g(w) = \frac{\gamma e^{-\gamma(w-c)}}{e^{-\gamma(w_r-c)}} 1_{\{w \geq w_r\}}$$

$$= \gamma e^{-\gamma(w-w_r)} 1_{\{w \geq w_r\}}. \tag{9.8}$$

It follows that the likelihood function in the parametrization by $\theta = (\gamma, w_r)$ is given by

$$L(\theta) = \gamma^N \exp\left(-\gamma \sum_{i=1}^{N} (w_i - w_r)\right) 1_{\{w_m \geq w_r\}}. \tag{9.9}$$

From (9.7), inference on Π requires a value of c. Equilibrium theory (Burdett and Mortensen (1998), Mortensen (1990), see chapter 19) implies that $c = w_r$ is appropriate. While this restriction is not necessary for any of our results, it becomes useful in interpreting our estimates in section 9.6. The restriction further implies $\Pi = 1$, which is in line with many empirical findings (Devine and Kiefer, 1991).

9.3 THE PROTOTYPAL MODEL WITH MEASUREMENT ERRORS

In this section we extend the prototypal model to take account of errors in the measurement of wages w_i. To see why this is relevant, recall that based on (9.9) the MLE for the reservation wage is $\hat{w}_r = w_m$. This leads to asymptotics of the nonstandard form treated in chapter 7. A particular combination of parameters (in general, a nonlinear combination but under the present parametrization w_r) is $O_p(N^{-1})$, compared to $O_p(N^{-1/2})$ for the MLE in regular problems. This extremely sharp inference result depends not only on w_m being the exact wage offered to and accepted by the corresponding worker, say worker j, but also on the exactness of the measurements of w_i, $i \neq j$, so that it can be determined that w_j is in fact the smallest. However, as a practical matter, available data sets (including National Longitudinal Survey (NLS), Panel Study of Income Dynamics (PSID), Survey of Income and Program Participation (SIPP), etc.) exhibit minimum wage observations that are obviously of dubious quality (e.g., $1.00 or less when the legal minimum wage was three to four times higher), hence casting doubt also on the validity of the remaining samples. Indeed, Bound et al. (1990), in a validation study, find measurement error in earnings accounting for 15%–42% of the variance of reported earnings.

These considerations underscore the necessity of allowing for measurement errors. However, note that there is no reason to cast the underlying economic model in doubt. The problem we face is one of imperfect data. As a consequence, we continue to use the prototypal model, taking care that the only extensions are in the modeling of the process of wage measurement itself. These extensions are particularly crucial because of the dependence on order statistics in the prototypal model, while estimators based purely on sample averages would be less sensitive to measurement error.

Our approach differs substantially from earlier work using measurement errors, e.g., that by Wolpin (1987). That approach depends on the normality of both true wages (log wages) and measurement errors, and hence their sum, whereas the prototypal specification (9.6) incorporates the empirically important clustering of accepted wages in the lower region of the support.

Furthermore, Wolpin imposes a finite search horizon after which the first offer is accepted, although offers still are assumed to arrive. In the prototypal model, it is recognized that in this case it may be optimal to continue the search.

If a structural approach to inference is to be at all useful in applications, it must be based on an internally consistent model of optimizing behavior. Further, the measurement error process should not affect the structural specification. This is the idea in what follows. Thus, the underlying relationships, such as (9.1), (9.2), and (9.7), remain valid, as do the results on transformation to parameter vectors including, e.g., y, β, or p and computation of w_r via contraction from chapters 7 and 8, since these involve only the economic model.

True accepted wages (i.e., wages measured without error) are distributed according to (9.5), (9.6), and (9.8) and the accompanying discussion as

$$g(w) = \gamma e^{-\gamma(w-w_r)}, \qquad w \geq w_r. \qquad (9.10)$$

Thus, no wage will be accepted below w_r. However, given the preceding discussion, we allow that the measurement w^e available to the econometrician of an accepted wage w may be below w_r even though $w \geq w_r$. It is natural to take all measurements to be positive. This leads to problems with additive specifications such as

$$w^e = w + m, \qquad (9.11)$$

where m is the measurement error. Since $w \geq w_r$, occurrences of $w^e < w_r$ require $m < 0$, and $w^e > 0$ requires $m > -w_r$. The latter requirement is artificial and ad hoc. We therefore employ the multiplicative specification

$$w^e = wm. \qquad (9.12)$$

The factor $m > 0$ captures the measurement error. We assume m to be independent of the true accepted wage w, and it is empirically relevant to allow an interior mode as well as an expectation of 1.

Denoting the density of m by h, we use (9.12) to write

$$P(w^e \leq x) = P(wm \leq x)$$
$$= P\left(w \leq \frac{x}{m}\right)$$
$$= \int_0^\infty P\left(w \leq \frac{x}{m} \middle| m\right) h(m)\, dm. \qquad (9.13)$$

Since w and m are independent, we can ignore the conditioning and use (9.10). The cumulative distribution function for the observations is

$$P(w^e \leq x) = \int_0^{x/w_r} (1 - e^{-\gamma(x/m - w_r)}) h(m)\, dm. \qquad (9.14)$$

We wish to determine the density of observed wages by differentation of (9.14) with respect to x. A sufficient condition for Leibnitz' rule to apply is that the integrand, considered as a function of x and m, say $k(x, m)$, is differentiable in x and that $\partial k(x, m)/\partial x$ is uniformly continuous in (x, m). This derivative is given by $m^{-1}\gamma \exp(-\gamma(x/m - w_r))h(m)$, and since the exponential factor is continuous and bounded, it is sufficient that $h(m)/m$ is uniformly continuous. Taking, e.g., $h(m)/m$ to be continuous and to have an *interior mode* (a stronger condition), we may therefore differentiate (9.14) to get

$$f_e(x) = \frac{1}{w_r}(1 - e^{-\gamma(x/(x/w_r)-w_r)})h(x/w_r)$$

$$+ \int_0^{x/w_r} \frac{\gamma}{m} e^{-\gamma(x/m-w_r)} h(m)\, dm$$

$$= \gamma e^{\gamma w_r} \int_0^{x/w_r} \frac{1}{m} h(m) e^{-\gamma x/m}\, dm. \tag{9.15}$$

This expression forms the basis for all applications of the prototypal search model with measurement errors. Importantly, the model is unchanged in the worker's eye, the extension dealing solely with the consequences of imprecise wage measurement. In the following, we consider a tractable econometric model that results for a specific choice of h in (9.15).

9.4 CHARACTERIZING THE DISTRIBUTION OF MEASUREMENT ERRORS

In this section we consider a flexible family of distributions for the multiplicative error m in the measurement (9.12) available to the econometrician. The resulting distribution f_e should lead to a practically relevant but nevertheless tractable econometric model. We consider the family

$$h(m) = am^{-(b+2)}e^{-b/m}, \qquad m > 0. \tag{9.16}$$

This choice leaves the integrand in (9.15) in a convenient form. Further, this form is preserved as observations are accumulated. The specification in (9.16) is a Pearson type V distribution and is related to the "inverted-gamma" distribution discussed by Zellner (1971). It is well known that the gamma distribution and its relatives are very flexible and closely approximate a variety of alternative specifications. Below we relate h to the normal distribution. On rewriting

$$h(m) = am^{-2}e^{-b(\ln m + 1/m)}, \tag{9.17}$$

we see that $h(m)$ is an exponential family with minimal sufficient statistic $\Sigma(\ln(m)+1/m)$ and canonical parameter $-b$ (see the appendix). It is easily demonstrated by taking the logarithm of (9.17) and differentiating that

$$\text{mode}(h(m)/m) = b/(b+3) > 0, \tag{9.18}$$

thus verifying our assumption from section 9.3 of an interior mode for $h(m)/m$.

We will need the integral

$$I(b, p, y) = \int_0^y m^{-p} e^{-b/m}\, dm, \qquad b > 0,\ p > 1,\ y > 0. \tag{9.19}$$

On changing variables from m to b/m we obtain

$$I(b, p, y) = b^{-(p-1)} \Gamma(p-1, b/y), \tag{9.20}$$

where the upper incomplete gamma function is

$$\Gamma(\alpha, x) = \int_x^\infty t^{\alpha-1} e^{-t}\, dt \tag{9.21}$$

and the usual gamma function is $\Gamma(\alpha) = \Gamma(\alpha, 0)$. We will also use the upper incomplete digamma function

$$\psi(\alpha, x) = \frac{d}{d\alpha} \ln \Gamma(\alpha, x) \tag{9.22}$$

and note that the usual digamma function is $\psi(\alpha) = \psi(\alpha, 0)$.

Combining expressions (9.16), (9.19), and (9.20) yields the integrating constant

$$a = (I(b, b+2, \infty))^{-1} = b^{b+1}/\Gamma(b+1), \tag{9.23}$$

thus completing our specification of the measurement error distribution. Application of (9.16), (9.22), and (9.23) gives the integer moments

$$E(m^k) = aI(b, b+2-k, \infty)$$
$$= b^k \Big/ \prod_{i=0}^{k-1}(b-i) \tag{9.24}$$

for $k < b+1$. In particular, we have

$$E(m) = 1, \tag{9.25}$$

as desired. Further analysis shows that $E(\ln m) = \ln b - \psi(b+1)$, and

$$\text{var}(m) = \frac{1}{b-1}, \qquad b > 1, \tag{9.26}$$

$$\text{var}(\ln m) = \psi'(b+1), \tag{9.27}$$

where ψ' is the (complete) trigamma function. From (9.24), for large b, skewness and kurtosis are close to the values 0 and 3 corresponding to the normal distribution. In section 9.5 we turn to the econometric model that obtains under this measurement error distribution.

9.5 ESTIMATION IN THE PROTOTYPAL MODEL WITH MEASUREMENT ERRORS

In this section we consider the specialization of the model from section 9.3 that obtains when adopting the family of measurement error distributions introduced in section 9.4. Note that this allows maintaining the original prototypal specification from section 9.2 for the underlying economic model.

Recall that the worker receives a wage offer w, but that the econometrician has access only to an imperfect measurement w^e of this. Substituting (9.16) and (9.23) in (9.15) and using (9.20), we obtain the econometrician's observed wage distribution

$$f_e(w^e) = \gamma e^{\gamma w_r} \int_0^{w^e/w_r} am^{-(b+3)} e^{(b+\gamma w^e)/m} \, dm$$

$$= \gamma e^{\gamma w_r} a I(b + \gamma w^e, b + 3, w^e/w_r)$$

$$= \gamma e^{\gamma w_r} \frac{b^{b+1} \Gamma(b + 2, w_r(\gamma + b/w^e))}{(b + \gamma w^e)^{b+2} \Gamma(b+1)}. \tag{9.28}$$

Note that f_e has full support in $\mathbb{R}_+$, while with perfect measurement wages follow the distribution (9.8) on $[w_r, \infty)$. The nonregularity of the estimation problem with perfect measurement is eliminated by the assumption of measurement errors, and the strict interpretation of (9.28) as (9.8) with noise is retained. The importance of the original prototypal model as determinant for the shape of f_e increases as b gets large, which from (9.26) corresponds to precise wage measurement. This is easily seen by rewriting (9.28) as

$$f_e(w^e) = \gamma e^{\gamma w_r} \frac{b^{b+1}}{(b + \gamma w^e)^{b+2}} (b+1) S(w_r(\gamma + b/w^e); b+2), \tag{9.29}$$

where $S(x; a)$ denotes the survivor function for the $\Gamma(\alpha, 1)$ distribution.

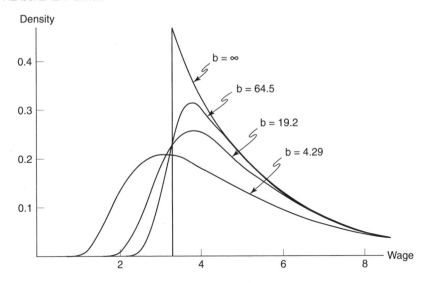

Figure 9.1 Observed Wage Densities.

Thus,

$$f_e(w^e) \sim \gamma e^{\gamma w_r} \left(1 + \frac{\gamma w^e}{b}\right)^{-b} S(bw_r/w^e; b)$$

$$\xrightarrow[b \to \infty]{} \gamma e^{-\gamma(w^e - w_r)} 1_{\{w^e \geq w_r\}}, \qquad (9.30)$$

where $\sim$ indicates asymptotic equivalence for large b and the limit coincides with (9.8).

Figure 9.1 shows the shape of f_e for different values of b. The economic parameters are fixed at $w_r = 3.184$ and $\gamma = .4691$. These values are in fact the maximum likelihood estimates based on the full data set analyzed in section 9.6. In the full sample, b is estimated to be 19.2. In various sub-samples, the MLEs of b range from 4.3 to 64.5, hence the chosen values in figure 9.1. The density (9.8) from the prototypal model with no measurement error ($b = \infty$) is shown as well. It is clear from the figure that as b is increased, the density with $b = \infty$ is approximated more closely, in accordance with the convergence result (9.30). However, only for $b = \infty$ is the support bounded by the reservation wage. Note also that the property $E(w^e) = E(w)$ implies that all four densities shown have the same mean, so that the modes do not necessarily coincide with w_r.

The distribution of observed wages f_e further satisfies

$$\text{var}(w^e) = \frac{b}{b-1}\gamma^{-2} + \frac{1}{b-1}(w_r + \gamma^{-1})^2. \qquad (9.31)$$

From (9.29), the log likelihood function for the unknown parameter $\theta = (b, \gamma, w_r) \in \mathbb{R}^3_+$, based on a random sample $w = (w_1, \ldots, w_N)$ of observed wages, is

$$l(\theta) = N\{\ln\gamma + \gamma w_r + (b+1)\ln b + \ln(b+1)\}$$

$$+ \sum_{i=1}^{N} \ln S(w_r(\gamma + b/w_i); b+2)$$

$$- (b+2)\sum_{i=1}^{N}\ln(b+\gamma w_i). \qquad (9.32)$$

In view of the noted regularity of l, the MLE satisfies the likelihood equation $s(\hat{\theta}) = 0$. Define the $\Gamma(\alpha, 1)$ hazard rate:

$$h(x;\alpha) = \frac{x^{\alpha-1}e^{-x}}{\Gamma(\alpha)S(x;\alpha)}. \qquad (9.33)$$

The score $s = (s_b, s_\gamma, s_{w_r})$ is given by

$$s_b(\theta) = N\{\ln b + (b+1)/b + 1/(b+1) - \psi(b+2)\}$$

$$+ \sum_{i=1}^{N}\{\psi(b+2, w_r(\gamma + b/w_i)) - (w_r/w_i)h(w_r(\gamma + b/w_i); b+2)\}$$

$$- \sum_{i=1}^{N}\ln(b+\gamma w_i) - (b+2)\sum_{i=1}^{N}(b+\gamma w_i)^{-1}, \qquad (9.34)$$

$$s_\gamma(\theta) = N(w_r + \gamma^{-1}) - \sum_{i=1}^{N} w_r h(w_r(\gamma + b/w_i); b+2)$$

$$- (b+2)\sum_{i=1}^{N} w_i/(b+\gamma w_i), \qquad (9.35)$$

$$s_{w_r}(\theta) = N\gamma - \sum_{i=1}^{N}(\gamma + b/w_i)h(w_r(\gamma + b/w_i); b+2). \qquad (9.36)$$

We consider estimation by Newton-Raphson iteration. The successive parameter estimates $\hat{\theta}_k$ are calculated according to

$$\hat{\theta}_{k+1} = \hat{\theta}_k - \tau_k H(\hat{\theta}_k)^{-1}s(\hat{\theta}_k). \qquad (9.37)$$

Here, $H(.)$ is the Hessian of the log likelihood function, i.e., the 3×3 matrix of the second derivatives of (9.32). In each iteration, the step length

$\tau_k > 0$ is determined by a line search. Our actual implementation uses a somewhat improved version of this approach, circumventing various difficulties often arising in practice, such as the singularity of H. Upon convergence of $\{\hat{\theta}_k\}_k$ to $\hat{\theta}$, this has a variance-covariance matrix estimated consistently by $H(\hat{\theta})^{-1}$. This allows construction of standard Wald test procedures and confidence regions.

The practical usefulness of the method is critically dependent on the ease of implementation in applications. The above specification allows maintaining the prototypal model as representing worker behavior yet reduces the necessary numerical integration to evaluations of incomplete gamma functions, which are efficiently implemented at any modern computing facility (the application below uses IMSL). This numerical procedure can be applied quite generally, allowing flexibility in the specification of functional forms.

9.6 APPLICATION TO THE SIPP DATA SET

This section applies the method of section 9.5 to the 1986 Panel of the Survey of Income and Program Participation. We consider reemployment wages for unemployed workers who became reemployed between April 1986 and November 1986. We use all four rotation groups of the panel, and three different waves are needed to cover the period in question (for a comprehensive discussion of the structure of the SIPP, see Devine (1989)). We exclude from the total sample those who did not report wages or who reported a zero wage, leaving 1,061 workers in the sample. We divide this sample into subsamples based on gender, race, and age. A further subclassification by education would be feasible and may be appropriate in larger data sets or if the cells appeared heterogeneous. This approach provides a fully nonparametric method for controlling the effects of the classification variables. While there are 906 white and 125 black workers, only 30 reported belonging to other races, and we exclude these to obtain acceptable sample sizes. We refer to the resulting sample of size 1031 as the full sample. Table 9.1 gives summary statistics.

We estimate the parameters $\theta = (b, \gamma, w_r)$ by programming the likelihood function and the derivatives in FORTRAN, accessing the necessary numerical functions in IMSL and implementing the iterations (9.37) using GQOPT. The computations were carried out to an accuracy level of 10^{-7}. Thus, in the convergence criterion, this value bounds from above the improvement in log likelihood (9.32) as well as the norms of the score (9.34)–(9.36) and the change in the parameter vector based on (9.37). If an optimum is found, the maximized likelihood value is compared to that from

Table 9.1 Summary Statistics.

Sample	N	$\bar{w}$	w_{min}	var(w)	var(ln w)
Full	1031	5.35	1.00	8.35	.180
Young white males	350	4.96	2.00	4.88	.126
Older white males	153	8.47	1.30	20.1	.279
Young black males	46	4.80	3.35	2.56	.094
Older black males	16	5.78	3.35	4.62	.111
Young white females	278	4.27	1.00	3.06	.111
Older white females	125	5.50	2.00	5.20	.136
Young black females	39	4.09	3.35	1.10	.048
Older black females	24	5.58	3.35	9.80	.165
Other	30	6.64	2.01	29.1	.521

the prototypal search model without measurement errors from chapter 7. From (9.30) the latter corresponds to $b = \infty$, or from (9.26), zero variance of m. On reparametrizing by (var(m), γ, w_r), the original prototypal model can be viewed as a nested hypothesis on the boundary of the parameter space, and the distribution of the likelihood ratio test can be determined as in Self and Liang (1987) or Andrews (1998).

In the period considered in the sample, the legal minimum wage was $3.35, and from table 9.1, this coincides with the minimum reported wage in four of the subsamples. It turns out that the prototypal model without measurement error fits well for these subsamples. In the full model, the likelihood for three of these subsamples increases in b to a point where the computations become numerically unstable. On reparametrizing by var(m), likelihood values above the maximum from the model without measurement error are obtained only for var(m) less than 10^{-12}, and again there are signs of numerical instability. It seems clear then that these samples are adequately described by the prototypal model without modification.

We conclude that the original prototypal specification is the most useful model for the three subsamples in question and use this in table 9.2, where we report parameter estimates (asymptotic standard errors are in parentheses) for all subsamples.

Figures 9.2–9.4 show slices of the log likelihood for the full sample. In each figure, two parameters are fixed at the MLEs from table 9.2, and l is shown as a function of the remaining parameter. With measurement error, the discontinuity of the likelihood function considered in chapter 7 is eliminated, but the figures are clearly not quadratic, reflecting the non-normality.

Table 9.2 Parameter Estimates.

Sample	N	b	γ	w_r	$\hat{\ell}_{full}$	$\hat{\ell}_{proto}$
Full	1031	19.16	.4691	3.184	−2142.0	−2546.8
		(2.620)	(.0239)	(.0770)		
Young white males	350	64.51	.5473	3.127	−631.83	−729.82
		(14.46)	(.0355)	(.0619)		
Older white males	153	4.289	.3136	5.516	−428.41	−454.40
		(1.925)	(.1466)	(1.496)		
Young black males	46	∞	.6897	3.350	N.A.	−63.092
		(N.A.)	(.1017)	(.0315)		
Older black males	16	35.53	.6103	4.134	−29.903	−30.206
		(39.28)	(.2824)	(.6153)		
Young white females	278	8.949	3.582	3.972	−471.01	−607.37
		(.8084)	(.3128)	(.0875)		
Older white females	125	34.74	.4559	3.315	−252.90	−281.59
		(22.14)	(.0679)	(.2534)		
Young black females	39	∞	1.370	3.350	N.A.	−26.726
		(N.A.)	(.2194)	(.0187)		
Older black females	24	∞	.4484	3.350	N.A.	−43.250
		(N.A.)	(.0915)	(.0929)		

While the full sample, as well as young white males and both white female subsamples, had minimum reported wages between \$1.00 and \$2.00, the model that allows for measurement errors in wages yields estimates of the true reservation wages in these samples between \$3.00 and \$4.00. The major advantage of the new model is the reduced importance of the minimum wage in estimation. Similarly, while older white males had a reported minimum wage of \$1.30, w_r is estimated to be in excess of \$5.00, presumably reflecting the higher stocks of human capital accumulated in this group. However, this subsample has the highest estimated measurement error (lowest b), and w_r is estimated less precisely than in the other groups. This may indicate heterogeneity among older white males.

Where the comparison applies, the full model usually fits significantly better than the original prototypal model. This is seen in the last two columns of table 9.2, where the maximized log likelihoods for the two models are given. Note that the log likelihood ratio statistic is not quite standard; drawing on the above reparametrization, the results of Self and Liang (1987) and Andrews (1998) imply that the null distribution is asymptotically a mixture of chi-squared distributions. The statistics we report would clearly be very surprising draws from this distribution. The only exception is older black males, where $-2 \log Q = .606324$. Given the nonstandard setting, this is asymptotically distributed as $\frac{1}{2}\chi_0^2 + \frac{1}{2}\chi_1^2$, so a test at level α uses the $(1 - 2\alpha)$ quantile in the χ_1^2-distribution. This subsample had

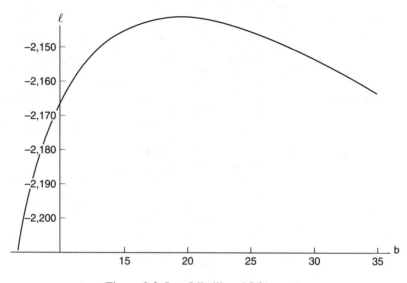

Figure 9.2 Log Likelihood $l(b|\gamma, w_r)$.

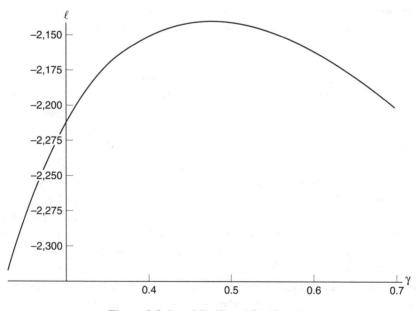

Figure 9.3 Log Likelihood $l(\gamma|b, w_r)$.

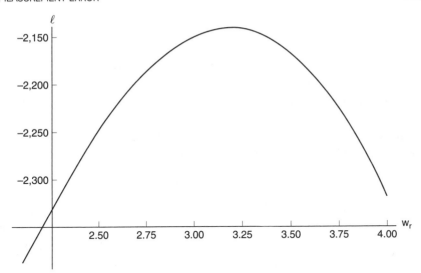

Figure 9.4 Log Likelihood $l(w_r|\gamma, b)$.

a minimum wage of \$3.35. The result that we fail to reject the hypothesis of no measurement error at all levels below $\alpha = 20\%$ (the 60% quantile in χ_1^2 exceeds the test statistic) is in line with the analysis of the other three subsamples where w_{min} was the legal minimum wage.

Our finding of significant measurement error in some groups implies that the methods of chapters 7 and 8 would lead to downward-biased estimates of the true reservation wages. This bias would typically be transmitted to the other parameters through imposition of the optimality restriction implied by the dynamic programming framework. Thus, controlling for the possibility of measurement error is important.

The maximized log likelihood for the full sample, but allowing for heterogeneity across subsamples, is found from table 9.2 to be -1947.2, assuming the original prototypal model for the three subsamples where it is appropriate. On comparing with the value -2142.0 for the restricted model from the first line of the table, we clearly reject the hypothesis of homogeneity across subsamples.

For completeness, if the starting point had been the model without measurement error, the maximized log likelihoods are found from the table to be -2236.5 with and -2546.8 without heterogeneity. Here, too, we would reject the homogeneity hypothesis.

Chapter 8 shows how to use the optimality condition from the dynamic programming framework to estimate deeper structural parameters in wage data, in addition to γ and the policy w_r. The optimality condition is the key implication of the job search model and provides the link between the observables and the economic parameters. In the present setting, using (9.7) and (9.8) in (9.4) and inserting in (9.2) yields

$$w_r = (1 - \beta)y + \beta \left(w_r + \frac{p}{\gamma} e^{-\gamma(w_r - c)} \right). \tag{9.38}$$

The right hand side, considered a function of w_r, is a contraction of modulus at most $\beta < 1$, thus identifying w_r as the unique fixed point for given values of the structural parameters β, y, p, and γ. Invoking equilibrium theory (section 9.2) allows simplifying the relationship,

$$\frac{p}{r} = \gamma(w_r - y), \tag{9.39}$$

where $r = (1 - \beta)/\beta$ is the worker's subjective discount rate. In wage data, the relationship between p and r is identified. Fixing the value of one of them allows inferring the other from (9.39). Based on table 9.2 and the invariance property of maximum likelihood, table 9.3 reports the MLE of the fundamental unitless parameter p/r. As a matter of interpretation, p/rEw is the expected present discounted value of the next period's offer. The unemployment income parameter is interpreted as net of search costs, and the first column in table 9.3 is based on a value $y = 0$. In addition, the table reports the MLE of the expected accepted wage $E(w|w > w_r)$.

The estimates of p/r and $E(w|w > w_r)$ deal with the underlying structural economic model and so are functions only of γ and w_r from table 9.2, the parameter b not entering the worker's environment. When including b from table 9.2, we can in addition compute the estimated proportion of variance of observed log wages due to measurement error, based on (9.27), as well as the ratio of predicted to observed variance of wages, based on (9.31). The results are shown in table 9.3 as well.

The estimated expected accepted wages are seen to match closely the sample statistics in table 9.1. Comparing with the last column of table 9.3, it is clear that maximum likelihood values are attained when the parameters are chosen to match means closer than variances in wages.

Denoting by P_m the proportion of variance of log wages due to measurement error, the results show that P_m ranges from .12 to .28 for the six samples where measurement error enters, except that P_m is as large as .75 for older white males and .95 for young white females. Equivalently, for these six samples, the signal-to-noise ratio $R_{s/n} = (1 - P_m)/P_m$ ranges between the reasonable values 2.5 and 7.1, with the exceptions 0.34 and 0.05 for the two above-mentioned subsamples. Particularly, young white females report wages that are best described as a cluster of little variation close to the sample average, implying an estimated reservation wage not much below the latter, and in addition a number of very different reported wages of large variation, accounting for most of the sample variance.

Table 9.3 Model Implications.

Sample	p/r	Expected Accepted Wage	Proportion of var($\ln w$) Due to Measurement Error	Ratio of Predicted to Observed var(w)
Full	1.49	5.32	.282	.760
Young white males	1.71	4.95	.123	.778
Older white males	1.73	8.70	.745	1.81
Young black males	2.31	4.80	.000	.821
Older black males	2.52	5.77	.283	.581
Young white females	14.2	4.25	.950	.771
Older white females	1.51	5.51	.208	1.13
Young black females	4.59	4.08	.000	.484
older black females	1.50	5.58	.000	.508

We have noted earlier the possibility of heterogeneity not accounted for here among older white males, and the same may apply for young white females. Still, an overall $R_{s/n} = 2.5$ for the full sample (equivalently, a .72 proportion of measured variance associated with dispersion in true accepted wages) indicates that our model explains wages across broad groups reasonably well.

In summary, the application to SIPP data of the results from earlier sections demonstrates that our model is practical and useful in the presence of measurement error and allows identification of those samples where the prototypal model with no measurement error is sufficient. Our estimated reservation wages are meaningful even in samples where minimum reported wages make no sense or where much of the sample variation is estimated to be due to measurement error. Returning again to figure 9.1, this means that the entire observed wage distribution helps identify the true w_r. The method allows interpreting outliers (e.g., very low reported wages) as outcomes of large measurement errors. Thus, the presence of such observations increases the estimated error variance without forcing an unreasonably low w_r. This is in contrast to Wolpin (1987), whose method using National Longitudinal Survey of Youth (NLSY) data yielded consistently low reservation wages and accordingly could identify only a very small fraction (about 1.2%, versus 28.2% above) of the variation in observed log wages as being due to measurement error. Stern (1989) estimates a simultaneous search model (workers apply for several jobs at once) using NLSY data and also finds a very small role for measurement error. On the other hand, in an empirical application of the Albrecht and Axell (1984) model, Eckstein and Wolpin (1990) find that almost all wage variance is due to measurement error (this is also based on NLSY data). The results reported here are consistent with the findings of Bound et al. (1990) based on direct measurement.

9.7 CONCLUSIONS

Measurement error in wage data is a widely recognized phenomenon. In the job search context, this implies measurement error in the state variable. Estimation of a job search model requires estimation of the reservation wage, either as a parameter of interest or enroute to the deeper behavioral parameters. Measurement error will affect these estimates, even asymptotically, since the MLE and related estimators for the reservation wage in the prototypal search model are based on order statistics and the reservation wage is related to all other parameters via the dynamic programming formulation. Our approach retains the classic behavioral model but adds a measurement error process to wages. An application to data from the SIPP shows that the model can be fit and interpreted straightforwardly and that the results are sensible. Reservation wages are estimated and turn out to be a priori plausible even in samples in which the minimum observed wages are clearly implausible. These are the samples for which the improvement in understanding gained by adopting the new method is the greatest. In other samples, the prototypal model without the addition of measurement error explains the data satisfactorily. Thus, the measurement error model can lead to an important increase in the applicability of dynamic programming models in practice.

9.8 EXERCISES

1. Consider a sample $\{x_i\}$ from $f(x) = 1$ on $(\theta, 1 + \theta)$. Is this an exponential family model (see the appendix)? Study the estimators $\theta_1 = \min\{x_i\}$, $\theta_2 = \max\{x_i\} - 1$, and $\theta_3 = \min\{\theta_1, \theta_2\}$.

2. Now suppose the observations are measured with error, so you see only $y_i = x_i + \epsilon_i$, where $\epsilon_i \sim N(0, \sigma^2)$ with σ^2 known. Is this an exponential family model? What are the properties of the three estimators from exercise 1? Can you improve on these estimators?

3. Now suppose the measurement error is multiplicative, so you see $z_i = x_i v_i$, where $v_i \sim \exp\{-v_i\}$. Is this an exponential family model? Consider the three estimators and offer an improvement. Note that the sign of θ is not restricted.

9.9 REFERENCES

This chapter is based on Christensen and Kiefer (1994b). There are many other applications using measurement error models, though primarily on top of a random utility specification. These include Eckstein and Wolpin (1990) and Wolpin (1987). Other studies making use of the optimality condition are Kiefer and Neumann (1979), Lancaster and Chesher (1983), Narendranathan and Nickell (1985), Ridder and Gorter (1986), Wolpin (1987), and Stern (1989). For additional discussion, see Devine and Kiefer (1991).

Chapter Ten

Asset Markets

10.1 INTRODUCTION

Asset markets are particularly interesting to economists since the good being allocated is homogeneous. This is in sharp contrast to the situation in labor market analysis. This homogeneity (a dollar is a dollar) provides an opportunity to focus on market structure without the complications of heterogeneity. We begin with a discussion of asset pricing, focusing on stocks and bonds. This leads to a development of the term structure of interest rates. We then turn to forward markets, and in the subsequent section to futures. This leads naturally to options and option pricing. We give an introduction here and a detailed development in chapter 11. The binomial model is widely used in asset pricing in practice and is a useful example of a concrete discretization of a dynamic programming problem. It is covered in section 10.7. We end the chapter with an overview of empirical applications covering time series properties, portfolio models, time-varying volatility, and term structure analysis.

10.2 GENERAL ASSET PRICING

Consider an asset trading for price p_t at time t and with future cash flows $d_{t+1}, d_{t+2}, \ldots$ It seems reasonable that for there to be no *arbitrage opportunities* (no way to make a sure future profit for zero initial investment), asset prices must be given as linear and strictly increasing functionals of their cash flows. Under wide regularity conditions, this implies that

$$p_t = E_t \left(\sum_{j \geq 1} \pi_{t+j} d_{t+j} \right), \tag{10.1}$$

where $\pi_k > 0$. This is the Riesz representation of a linear and strictly increasing functional, and the π_k are common to all assets and are also known as state-price deflators. Thus, there is no arbitrage if and only if there exists an *equivalent martingale measure* Q, i.e.,

$$p_t = E_t^Q \left(\sum_{j\geq 1} \frac{d_{t+j}}{\Pi_{i=1}^j (1 + r_{t+i})} \right). \tag{10.2}$$

Here, E_t^Q denotes conditional expectation under the transformed probability measure Q and r_k is the short interest rate pertaining to period k. The density f^Q under Q is easily obtained from that under the original (physical) measure, say P, corresponding to E_t, with density f^P, using the Radon-Nikodym derivative or likelihood ratio (LR) process

$$\frac{f_t^Q}{f_t^P} = \pi_t \prod_{j=1}^t (1 + r_j). \tag{10.3}$$

Note that this ensures that the two representations (10.1) and (10.2) of p_t are equivalent. It holds also that markets are *complete* if and only if the equivalent martingale measure is unique.

We have immediately that

$$p_t = E_t^Q \left(\sum_{j=1}^k \frac{d_{t+j}}{\Pi_{i=1}^j (1 + r_{t+i})} + \frac{p_{t+k}}{\Pi_{i=1}^k (1 + r_{t+i})} \right). \tag{10.4}$$

In particular, for $k = 1$,

$$p_t = E_t^Q \left(\frac{p_{t+1} + d_{t+1}}{1 + r_{t+1}} \right). \tag{10.5}$$

It is seen that asset prices (e.g., prices of common stocks) are expected discounted cash flows, the expectation being taken under Q. This would otherwise be true only under risk neutrality. Hence, the approach is also known as risk-neutral valuation, and Q as the risk-adjusted or risk-neutral measure. Further, if $d_{t+1} = 0$,

$$p_t = E_t^Q \left(\frac{p_{t+1}}{1 + r_{t+1}} \right); \tag{10.6}$$

i.e., discounted asset prices are martingales under the equivalent martingale measure, hence the terminology. Specifically, consider the money market account

$$b_t = \prod_{j=1}^t (1 + r_{t+j}), \tag{10.7}$$

rolling over at the short rate of interest every period. We have

$$\frac{p_t}{b_t} = E_t^Q \left(\frac{p_T}{b_T} \right), \tag{10.8}$$

so the discounted process p_t/b_t is a Q-martingale. With nonzero dividends, the discounted value w_t of a portfolio with all dividends reinvested is a martingale under Q,

$$w_{t+1} = w_t \frac{p_{t+1} + d_{t+1}}{p_t}, \tag{10.9}$$

$$E_t^Q \left(\frac{w_{t+1}}{b_{t+1}} \right) = \frac{w_t}{b_t} \frac{1}{p_t} E_t^Q \left(\frac{p_{t+1} + d_{t+1}}{1 + r_{t+1}} \right)$$

$$= \frac{w_t}{b_t}. \tag{10.10}$$

The asset price in the general case is

$$p_t = b_t E_t^Q \left(\frac{p_{t+1} + d_{t+1}}{b_{t+1}} \right)$$

$$= b_t E_t^Q \left(\sum_{j=1}^{k} \frac{d_{t+j}}{b_{t+j}} + \frac{p_{t+k}}{b_{t+k}} \right), \tag{10.11}$$

using (10.4) and (10.7).

In the special case of a constant interest rate $r_t = r$ we may write $\beta = 1/(1+r)$, and with no dividends and Markovian asset prices (10.6) reduces to (6.15).

10.3 THE TERM STRUCTURE OF INTEREST RATES

The *short rate* of interest r_{t+1} is known at time t since it is the interest rate on a short bond offering a safe unit payment at $t + 1$ and trading at t for price

$$B_{t,1} = E_t^Q \left(\frac{1}{1 + r_{t+1}} \right)$$

$$= \frac{1}{1 + r_{t+1}}, \tag{10.12}$$

using (10.5) with $p_{t+1} = 0$ and $d_{t+1} = 1$. Thus, from (10.7) and (10.12), we have the relation between short bonds and money market accounts:

$$B_{t,1} = \frac{b_t}{b_{t+1}}. \tag{10.13}$$

The price of a longer bond with unit payment at $t + k$ is given by (10.8) as

$$\frac{B_{t,k}}{b_t} = E_t^Q \left(\frac{1}{b_{t+k}} \right) \tag{10.14}$$

or

$$B_{t,k} = b_t E_t^Q \left(\frac{1}{b_{t+k}} \right)$$

$$= \frac{1}{\left(1 + r_{t,k} \right)^k}, \qquad (10.15)$$

where $r_{t,k}$ is the k-period zero-coupon rate or *yield* prevailing at t. This gives rise to a theory of the *term structure of interest rates*, namely,

$$r_{t,k} = \frac{1}{\left(b_t E_t^Q \left(\frac{1}{b_{t+k}} \right) \right)^{1/k}} - 1. \qquad (10.16)$$

The term structure is upward sloping, downward sloping, or hump-shaped at t if this expression is increasing, decreasing, or takes an interior maximum in k. If future short rates are deterministic, the expectations operator is eliminated,

$$1 + r_{t,k} = \frac{1}{(b_t/b_{t+k})^{1/k}}$$

$$= \left(\prod_{i=1}^{k} (1 + r_{t+i}) \right)^{1/k}; \qquad (10.17)$$

i.e., the long rate is given from future short rates through a geometric average. A common approximation is that

$$r_{t,k} \approx \frac{1}{k} \sum_{i=1}^{k} r_{t+i}$$

$$\approx \frac{1}{k} \sum_{i=1}^{k} E_t r_{t+i} \qquad (10.18)$$

in the stochastic case, i.e., the long rate is approximated by the expected arithmetic average of future short rates, but this is seen to be a potentially poor approximation, as the expectations operator enters differently and as $P \neq Q$ unless investors are risk-neutral. The approximation (10.18) is the *expectations hypothesis*, and if

$$r_{t,k} > \frac{1}{k} \sum_{i=1}^{k} E_t r_{t+i} \qquad (10.19)$$

the inequality is often ascribed to liquidity premia, i.e., borrowers (the government) may prefer long-term loans and investors may prefer short-term loans, thus depressing the prices of long bonds and increasing long rates, but the theory shows that there may be other reasons for the difference.

Of course, this theory for zero-coupon bonds immediately leads to a theory for *coupon bonds*. If a riskless bond pays coupons d_{t+j}, $j = 1, \ldots, k$, and face value 1 at maturity k, then the price at t is

$$B_t^c = \sum_{j=1}^{k} B_{t,j} \, d_{t+j} + B_{t,k}. \tag{10.20}$$

If the term structure at t is flat, $r_{t,k} \equiv r > 0$, and the bond pays a constant nominal yield y (constant coupon), then (10.20) reduces to

$$B_k^y = y \sum_{j=1}^{k} \frac{1}{(1+r)^j} + \frac{1}{(1+r)^k}. \tag{10.21}$$

The relation between the flat yield curve and the general case is transparent. For example, in this case $1/(1+r)^k$ is recognized as $B_{t,k}$, the *zero-coupon bond* price. The price of a perpetual coupon bond or *consol* paying y each period forever is

$$B_\infty^y = y \sum_{j=1}^{\infty} \frac{1}{(1+r)^j}. \tag{10.22}$$

Writing this as yC, where the consol factor is $C = \sum_{j=1}^{\infty} 1/(1+r)^j$, and again writing $\beta = 1/(1+r)$, we have

$$C = \sum_{j=1}^{\infty} \beta^j, \tag{10.23}$$

$$(1 - \beta)C = \sum_{j=1}^{\infty} \beta^j - \beta \sum_{j=1}^{\infty} \beta^j$$

$$= \sum_{j=1}^{\infty} \beta^j - \sum_{j=2}^{\infty} \beta^j$$

$$= \beta, \tag{10.24}$$

$$C = \frac{\beta}{1 - \beta}$$

$$= \frac{1}{r}, \tag{10.25}$$

and the consol price is $B_\infty^y = y/r$, showing the extreme interest rate sensitivity of long bond prices,

$$-\frac{\partial \log B_\infty^y}{\partial \log(1+r)} = \frac{1+r}{r}. \tag{10.26}$$

This is called the *duration* of the bond and shows that, e.g., if the interest rate r is 10%, then each percentage point change in r leads to a percentage change in bond price about 10 times as large (for an interest rate increase to 11%, the bond price drops by about 10%).

Durations are also considered for other bonds. To calculate $\Sigma_{j=1}^{k} 1/(1+r)^j$ in B_k^y in (10.21), we have in analogy with (10.23)–(10.25)

$$\sum_{j=1}^{k} \beta^j = \sum_{j=1}^{\infty} \beta^j - \sum_{j=k+1}^{\infty} \beta^j$$

$$= C - \beta^k C$$

$$= \frac{1}{r}\left(1 - \frac{1}{(1+r)^k}\right), \tag{10.27}$$

$$B_k^y = \frac{y}{r}\left(1 - \frac{1}{(1+r)^k}\right) + \frac{1}{(1+r)^k}. \tag{10.28}$$

Differentiation produces the duration or interest rate sensitivity, i.e., the weighted (by $B_{t,j}$) average waiting time until each of the future payments. Note that the waiting time (10.26) is finite even for the infinitely-lived consol.

Returning temporarily to (10.5), the *conditional expected rate of return* to a stock under Q is

$$E_t^Q\left(\frac{p_{t+1}+d_{t+1}-p_t}{p_t}\right) = \frac{(1+r_{t+1})}{p_t} E_t^Q\left(\frac{p_{t+1}+d_{t+1}}{1+r_{t+1}}\right) - 1$$

$$= r_{t+1}. \tag{10.29}$$

Thus, under the equivalent martingale measure, assets earn the riskless rate. This is true not only for stocks. Let us verify the property for another asset we have already considered, the zero-coupon or discount bond $B_{t,k}$ from (10.15). As this pays unity at $t + k$, the k-period holding period return is

$$\frac{1 - B_{t,k}}{B_{t,k}} = \frac{1}{B_{t,k}} - 1$$

$$= (1 + r_{t,k})^k - 1, \tag{10.30}$$

the *riskless* k-period rate at t. Since this is known at t, the actual return equals the expected return, whether under P or Q. This is only because the return to maturity is considered. Alternatively, we may calculate the one-period expected return under Q, using (10.14) and the fact that after one period, the riskless k-bond has turned into a riskless (i.e., *default-free*) $(k-1)$-bond,

$$E_t^Q \left(\frac{B_{t+1,k-1} - B_{t,k}}{B_{t,k}} \right) = \frac{1}{B_{t,k}} E_t^Q \left(b_{t+1} E_{t+1}^Q \left(\frac{1}{b_{(t+1)+(k-1)}} \right) \right) - 1$$

$$= \frac{b_{t+1}}{b_t B_{t,k}} b_t E_t^Q \left(\frac{1}{b_{t+k}} \right) - 1$$

$$= \frac{b_{t+1}}{b_t} - 1$$

$$= r_{t+1}, \tag{10.31}$$

the one-period riskless rate. Note the terminology: The one-period rate r_{t+1} is known at t, so this rate is certainly riskless, and so is the short bond $B_{t,1}$ paying this rate with certainty. Longer bonds $B_{t,k}$ pay a holding period return $r_{t,k}$ per period with certainty if held until maturity at $t+k$ since they are assumed default-free (government bonds), so $r_{t,k}$ is riskless in that there is a way to lock in this rate at t (*buy and hold $B_{t,k}$* until maturity). The bond $B_{t,k}$ is riskless in the looser sense that it is default-free, but investment in this involves *interest rate risk*. If it is sold after one period and $r_{t+1,k-1} > r_{t,k}$, then the realized return is less than $r_{t,k}$, so the bond is not a riskless investment vehicle for terms shorter than k. For a (government) coupon bond, there is in addition *reinvestment rate risk*. It is not known by t at which rates the coupons can be invested, so the overall return on investment is uncertain even if the bond is held to maturity.

However, that the Q-expected return is the riskless rate (or, equivalently, that prices are Q-expected discounted cash flows) is a common pricing principle for all assets, which we employ.

10.4 FORWARD CONTRACTS

A forward contract for a future claim paying X at $T > t$ has a *forward price* F_t negotiated at t. The contract pays $X - F_t$ on the *delivery date* T. For example, X may be the uncertain value of a farmer's expected production. If selling in the spot market at T, the farmer receives X. If planning ahead and selling the produce in the forward market at time t, instead, the farmer locks in the price F_t. The price risk is perfectly *hedged* since F_t is known at t. Technically, the farmer selling produce in the forward market sells a contract paying $X - F_t$ at T and receives his own produce of value X, for a position $X - (X - F_t) = F_t$ at T, hence the certainty as of t of payment at T. Selling in the forward market, the farmer is a short hedger. In the example, a company, perhaps a cereal producer, may lock in a time T payoff by buying the farmer's produce in the forward market at t, being a long hedger. Technically, the company must buy inputs worth X at T but has also bought a forward contract, for a total cash flow of $-X + (X - F_t) = -F_t$ at T, less risky as of t than if simply paying X for inputs at T (cash flow $-X$).

The forward price is negotiated so that the contract has value zero at t. Thus, by (10.8),

$$0 = b_t E_t^Q \left(\frac{X - F_t}{b_T} \right) \tag{10.32}$$

or, rearranging,

$$b_t E_t^Q \left(\frac{X}{b_T} \right) = F_t b_t E_t^Q \left(\frac{1}{b_T} \right)$$
$$= F_t B_{t,T-t}, \tag{10.33}$$

using (10.14), and it follows that the forward price is given by

$$F_t = \frac{b_t}{B_{t,T-t}} E_t^Q \left(\frac{X}{b_T} \right). \tag{10.34}$$

If short rates are deterministic and constant, $r_k \equiv r$, then from (10.7), (10.15), and (10.34),

$$b_t = (1 + r)^t, \tag{10.35}$$

$$B_{t,k} = \frac{1}{(1 + r)^k}, \tag{10.36}$$

$$F_t = E_t^Q(X). \tag{10.37}$$

The forward price is the expected future spot price under Q. The same thing happens if interest rates are random but independent (under Q) of X, since by (10.15),

$$F_t = \frac{b_t}{B_{t,T-t}} E_t^Q \left(\frac{1}{b_T} \right) E_t^Q(X)$$
$$= E_t^Q(X). \tag{10.38}$$

If the forward contract is for the stock, $X = p_T$, then in general, from (10.4) and (10.34),

$$F_t = \frac{b_t}{B_{t,T-t}} E_t^Q \left(\frac{p_T}{b_T} \right)$$

$$= \frac{1}{B_{t,T-t}} E_t^Q \left(\frac{p_T}{\Pi_{i=t+1}^T (1+r_i)} + \sum_{j=t+1}^T \frac{d_j}{\Pi_{i=t+1}^j (1+r_i)} \right.$$

$$\left. - \sum_{j=t+1}^T \frac{d_j}{\Pi_{i=t+1}^j (1+r_i)} \right)$$

$$= \frac{1}{B_{t,T-t}} \left(p_t - E_t^Q \left(\sum_{j=t+1}^T \frac{d_j}{\Pi_{i=t+1}^j (1+r_i)} \right) \right). \qquad (10.39)$$

With deterministic and constant interest rates, this is

$$F_t = (1+r)^{T-t} p_t - \sum_{j=t+1}^T (1+r)^{T-j} E_t^Q (d_j), \qquad (10.40)$$

the *cost-of-carry* formula for forward prices. Buying in the forward market may be a way to avoid *storage costs*, e.g., in the case of a commodity. This would make the forward price higher. Such costs correspond to negative dividends and are often labeled (negative) *convenience yields*. In the case of no dividends, the forward price is simply the spot price times the interest factor compounded through delivery.

Dividends (convenience yields), stochastic interest rates, and differences between Q and P are all reasons why the forward price F_t may differ from the expected future spot price $E_t(X)$. If short hedgers dominate, suppressing the forward price, or if for any of the other reasons we have

$$F_t < E_t(X), \qquad (10.41)$$

then this market condition is known as normal *backwardation*. The condition

$$F_t > E_t(X) \qquad (10.42)$$

is normal *contango* and may, e.g., prevail for commodities in the presence of significant storage costs or negative convenience yields.

10.5 FUTURES CONTRACTS

A futures contract is similar to a forward contract, but there are some important differences. Consider again the cereal producer in the example involving the farmer. The cereal producer may hedge the price risk as of t associated with the future random outlay (say, *spot price*) X at T by buying in the futures market instead. At t, a *futures price* ϕ_t for delivery of X at T prevails. Purchase in the futures market ensures delivery of X at T. Of course, if buying later, the price will change, and the contract price ϕ_{t+1} will change each period until necessarily $\phi_T = X$. Thus, the price of instant delivery of X is $\phi_T = X$, so the futures price ultimately approaches the spot price, a phenomenon labeled *convergence*.

What is described here is a long position in the futures contract. The farmer may alternatively sell produce in the futures market, i.e., take a short position.

The key feature distinguishing the futures market from the forward market is *marking to market*. Thus, if buying in the futures market, the cereal producer commits to mark the account to market, in each period effectively receiving the payment or dividend

$$d_{t+k} = \phi_{t+k} - \phi_{t+k-1}. \tag{10.43}$$

The seller of the futures contract agrees to pay this amount each period. This process of marking to market is also known as *resettlement*. It follows that the buyer, if holding the contract until maturity, receives the dividend stream

$$\sum_{j=t+1}^{T} d_j = \sum_{j=t+1}^{T} (\phi_j - \phi_{j-1})$$
$$= \phi_T - \phi_t$$
$$= X - \phi_t. \tag{10.44}$$

Of course, the calculation involving the telescoping sum ignores reinvestment and discounting. As in the case of forward contracts, since no money changes hands at t, the value of the position at t is 0, so by (10.8)

$$0 = b_t E_t^Q \left(\sum_{j=t+1}^{T} \frac{\phi_j - \phi_{j-1}}{b_j} \right). \tag{10.45}$$

This uses in addition the fact that the price of the position is zero at any point in time; i.e., we also have

$$0 = b_t E_t^Q \left(\frac{\phi_{t+1} - \phi_t}{b_{t+1}} \right)$$
$$= \frac{b_t}{b_{t+1}} E_t^Q (\phi_{t+1} - \phi_t), \tag{10.46}$$

so that the futures price ϕ_t is a Q-martingale,

$$\phi_t = E_t^Q(\phi_{t+1}). \tag{10.47}$$

This is important. The question arises why it is the futures price ϕ_t itself, not the discounted process ϕ_t/b_t, that is a Q-martingale (compare (10.8)). The reason is that in fact ϕ_t is not the price of a traded asset but simply the index used to define the dividend process $d_t = \phi_t - \phi_{t-1}$ underlying the marking-to-market or resettlement process. In particular, ϕ_t is continuously set by the market so that the true price (the value of the futures position) is zero. Properly speaking, the futures price is not the price of the futures (indeed, ϕ_t is typically not zero).

The martingale property and $\phi_T = X$ (convergence) immediately imply

$$\phi_t = E_t^Q(X). \tag{10.48}$$

Computation of the conditional expectation may be facilitated, e.g., if the spot price follows a mean-reverting process, as is typical for commodities. Note that the martingale property (10.47) applies to the derivative, since this is a traded financial contract, but not necessarily to the underlying. A related phenomenon occurred in chapter 6, where an American call might be exercised early if the underlying process is not a martingale, e.g., in the case of a commodity. A non-storable commodity (such as electricity) not only has no martingale price process representation, it is also not useful for hedging the derivative.

If interest rates are deterministic, or just independent (under Q) of X, then by (10.37), (10.38), and (10.48),

$$F_t = \phi_t; \tag{10.49}$$

i.e., forward and futures prices coincide. Obviously, the contracts also serve similar purposes; e.g., the cereal producer in the example may reason that buying in the futures market ensures an inflow X at T covering the purchase price X (e.g., of grains) for a total of $(X - \phi_t) - X = -\phi_t$, using (10.44) above; i.e., the purchase price is known already at t, and all of the price risk has been hedged, as if X had been bought in the forward market (cash flow $(X - F_t) - X = -F_t$ at T). Of course, the analogy is imperfect since this assessment of the futures position ignores reinvestment and discounting, but the equivalence $F_t = \phi_t$ when interest rates are independent of X (e.g., deterministic) is exact.

An example of a financial futures contract is a *stock index futures* offering delivery at T of the value of a broad stock market index. The owner of a share in stock i (one among many traded stocks) may wish to hedge the market risk in stock i by selling (taking a short position in or *shorting*) stock index futures. Under the *market model*

$$r_{i,t} = \alpha_i + \beta_{i,t} r_{m,t} + \varepsilon_{i,t}, \tag{10.50}$$

where $r_{i,t}$ is the return on stock i, $r_{m,t}$ is the market (index) return,

$$\beta_{i,t} = \frac{\text{cov}_t(r_{i,t}, r_{m,t})}{\text{var}_t(r_{m,t})} \qquad (10.51)$$

is the sensitivity of the stock price to market movements, α_i is the regression intercept, and $\varepsilon_{i,t}$ is the residual, it is appropriate to sell $\beta_{i,t}$ stock index futures contracts for each share of stock i owned. Often, $\beta_{i,t}$ is assumed constant and estimated as the slope in ordinary least squares (OLS) regression of $r_{i,t}$ on $r_{m,t}$ and a constant. Under the capital asset–pricing model (CAPM, see section 10.8.2), if the stock and the index returns are measured in excess above the short (riskless) rate, the intercept should vanish in equilibrium,

$$\alpha_i = 0, \qquad (10.52)$$

but this restriction is typically not imposed in hedging applications. One approach to allow for time-varying variances and covariances in (10.51), and hence *hedge ratios* $\beta_{i,t}$, is to consider multivariate autoregressive conditionally heteroskedastic (ARCH) or generalized ARCH (GARCH) models (see section 10.8.3) for stock and index returns.

The discussion assumes the index and the stock index futures are close substitutes for estimation purposes. This is valid if $r_{m,t}$ is the return over an interval ending at T or close to this, so that the terminal value of the index and the futures price coincide (or nearly so) by convergence. More generally, regression on returns on the futures price rather than the index may be warranted. In either case, the hedger benefits from the easy availability of futures contracts, and the ability to take both short and long positions in this. The hedging of market risk would be effectively ruled out for small to even moderately large investors if it required shorting all component stocks in the index (e.g., 500 stocks in Standard & Poor's 500 Index, and more in the NASDAQ).

Futures market hedging is also convenient because contracts are standardized and easy to move in and out of, especially since their running prices are zero. One disadvantage is that standardized contracts may not match the needs of the hedger exactly, e.g., with respect to the underlying asset or commodity, delivery date, contract size, or similar. Forward contracts are typically not standardized but are traded *over the counter* (OTC) and may sometimes be tailor-made to the hedger's needs. They are not easy to move in and out of since they are OTC, and because even though the initial value of the position is zero, the running value is not, being instead of the form

$$V_{t+k} = b_{t+k} E_{t+k}^Q \left(\frac{X - F_t}{b_T} \right), \qquad (10.53)$$

but typically no observable market price shows this value. Thus, a new as-sessment is required if one is trying to get out of the position through an OTC sale.

Both forward and futures markets may provide for cash settlement; i.e., physical delivery of the underlying by the seller is replaced by a cash payment at T in the amount X (more precisely, $X - F_t$ in the forward case and a final cash resettlement $X - \phi_{t-1}$ in the futures case). In both mar-kets, speculators may take the opposite side of the market if no hedger with matching but opposite needs (compare the farmer and the cereal producer) is in the market. We return to futures hedging in chapter 17.

10.6 INTRODUCTION TO OPTIONS

An *option* is a right, but not an obligation, to buy (in the case of a call option) an underlying asset at T for a price contractually fixed from the outset, i.e., the exercise or strike price K. A *put* is an option to sell rather than buy. In either case, the contract specifies the underlying asset or commodity, as well as the exercise price K and expiration date T. A European option may be exercised only at T, and an American option any time before or at T (see section 6.4). Following the forward and futures treatments above, we write X for the price of the underlying at T, unknown as of $t < T$. As the payoff at T to a European call is max $\{X - K, 0\}$, its price at t is

$$c_t = b_t E_t^Q \left(\frac{\max\{X - K, 0\}}{b_T} \right), \qquad (10.54)$$

by (10.8), and the European put value is

$$q_t = b_t E_t^Q \left(\frac{\max\{K - X, 0\}}{b_T} \right). \qquad (10.55)$$

The holder of a portfolio worth X at T may obtain *portfolio insurance* through the purchase of a *protective put*, ensuring that the portfolio value including the put at T does not drop below the fixed floor K,

$$X + \max\{K - X, 0\} = \max\{K, X\}$$
$$\geq K. \qquad (10.56)$$

Of course, this insurance comes at a premium, so $q_t > 0$, generally, and similarly $c_t > 0$. The example assumes that a put whose underlying security is the portfolio in question is traded. When this is not the case, a portfolio with a payoff structure replicating that of the put may under some conditions be constructed through a dynamic trading strategy in the underlying and riskless bonds, thus creating a *synthetic put*. We return to this in chapter 14.

A similar payoff profile to (10.56) may alternatively be secured through the purchase of a call and riskless bonds paying K at T,

$$\max\{X - K, 0\} + K = \max\{X, K\}. \tag{10.57}$$

With identical payoff profiles $\max\{X, K\}$ at T, the portfolios must have identical initial values,

$$p_t + q_t = c_t + B_{t,T-t}K,$$

writing p_t for the time t price of the underlying. This relation is known as *put-call parity*. Thus, if either the put or the call price is known, along with the current price of the underlying and the interest rate from (10.15), then the price of the other option may immediately be deduced from the put-call parity. The argument does not rely on any specific model for the underlying price process, but it does require equal strike prices and expiration dates for the options, and the parity is exact only for European options on underlying assets paying no dividends between t and T.

Suppose now that the underlying security has price process p_t. The value of the American call is

$$C_t = \max_{t \leq \tau \leq T} b_t E_t^Q \left(\frac{\max\{p_\tau - K, 0\}}{b_\tau} \right), \tag{10.58}$$

and the value of the American put is

$$P_t = \max_{t \leq \tau \leq T} b_t E_t^Q \left(\frac{\max\{K - p_\tau, 0\}}{b_\tau} \right). \tag{10.59}$$

Both values and hence prices are readily solved using dynamic programming. For example, in case of the American put, write $s_k = 1$ if the option has been exercised by time $k - 1$ or earlier, and $s_k = 0$ otherwise. The Bellman equation for the value function V_t is

$$V_t(p_t, s_t) = \max_{s_{t+1} \in S(s_t)} \left\{ U(p_t, s_{t+1}) + b_t E_t^Q \left(\frac{V_{t+1}(p_{t+1}, s_{t+1})}{b_{t+1}} \right) \right\}, \tag{10.60}$$

where feasible controls are $S(s_t) = \{0, 1\}$ if $s_t = 0$, and $S(s_t) = \{1\}$ if $s_t = 1$. Also, $U(p_t, 0) = 0$ (no exercise) and $U(p_t, 1) = \max\{K - p_t, 0\}$ (this is only received the first time t where $s_{t+1} = 1$, i.e., the put is exercised). A convenient rewrite is

$$V_t(p_t) = \max \left\{ K - p_t, \frac{1}{1 + r_{t+1}} E_t^Q (V_{t+1}(p_{t+1})) \right\}, \tag{10.61}$$

using $b_t/b_{t+1} = 1/(1 + r_{t+1})$ and with the understanding that the process is stopped if the first alternative is selected. In either case, $P_t = V_t$. The terminal condition is $V_T = \max\{K - p_T, 0\}$ if there has been no exercise earlier. Solution by backward recursion is possible even in the absence of the usual discount factor $\beta \in (0, 1)$ due to the finite time horizon. Of course, the parallel American call calculation is $C_t = V_t^c$, with

$$V_t^c (p_t) = \max\left\{ p_t - K, \frac{1}{1 + r_{t+1}} E_t^Q \left(V_{t+1}^c (p_{t+1}) \right) \right\}, \qquad (10.62)$$

and $V_T^c = \max\{p_T - K, 0\}$. This is the extension of (6.16) allowing for stochastic interest rates and risk aversion (through Q). With no dividends prior to T, the proof from chapter 6 that the American call is never exercised early carries over to the present case. The American put may sometimes be exercised early, as may the American call in case of dividends.

10.7 THE BINOMIAL METHOD

A common numerical approach especially in finance, and often in option-pricing contexts, is to use the binomial method of Cox and Ross (1976). The idea is to allow the relevant underlying process (e.g., the stock price) to take only two possible values (i.e., a binomial distribution) the next period, given its current value. This may be used either as a model of the true process or as a particular discretization of this. A full discretization of the state space for a Markov stock price process with N states would require an $N \times N$ transition matrix, and the binomial method is an approximation to this. The approximation works best if most of the weight in the Markov matrix is near the diagonal, i.e., if the process has continuous sample paths or at most small, infrequent jumps. In either case, the parameters of the binomial model are set so that the conditional expected return under Q is r_{t+1}, to satisfy (10.29), and the variance to a sufficient degree matches that under P. The latter condition is used to ensure that the binomial model converges to the true model in a suitable sense in the case where it is used as a discretization tool. The binomial tool is very flexible and can be used as a numerical technique in general dynamic programming models. We illustrate it in the option case, and many extensions are immediate.

The stock price process in the binomial approach is modeled as

$$p_{t+1} = p_t m_{t+1}, \qquad (10.63)$$

where m_t is an independent and identically distributed (i.i.d.) binomial sequence taking values u and d with risk-neutral probability q and $1 - q$, respectively. It is ensured that the stock price increases in the up state and decreases in the down state by taking $u > 1$ and $d < 1$ (e.g., a monotonically increasing stock price process is then avoided). In fact, we may simply set $d = 1/u$. It is not relevant to specify the physical probabilities of these up and down moves, and they do not enter the option-pricing formulas. Assume the short rate is deterministic and constant, $r_t \equiv r$. Since q is the risk-neutral probability under which the conditional expected stock return is the interest rate, we require

$$
\begin{aligned}
r &= E_t^Q \left(\frac{p_{t+1} - p_t}{p_t} \right) \\
&= E_t^Q (m_{t+1} - 1) \\
&= qu + (1 - q)\frac{1}{u} - 1.
\end{aligned}
\tag{10.64}
$$

Solving for q,

$$
q = \frac{(1 + r)u - 1}{u^2 - 1}.
\tag{10.65}
$$

As $u > 1$, q is ensured to be a probability in $(0, 1)$ by taking $u > 1 + r$; i.e., the stock earns more than the short bond in the up state and less in the down state (anything else would lead to arbitrage).

It remains to specify u. For empirical purposes, it is important that prices (e.g., of options) calculated under the risk-neutral approach satisfy the requirement that the measure Q applied is consistent with the observation measure P. As in applications the binomial model is typically thought of as an approximation to (a discretization of) a true continuous-time model or, more precisely, as a numerical tool for obtaining prices in the latter, it is important to set u consistently with the underlying true P-model. In particular, the requirement that P and Q be equivalent (corresponding to the terminology, "equivalent martingale measure," i.e., the events of zero probability are the same under P and Q) leads to a condition that the conditional variance be equal under P and Q if the true model is a continuous-time one. The conditional variance is

$$
\begin{aligned}
E_t^Q \left(\frac{p_{t+1} - p_t}{p_t} - r \right)^2 &= E_t^Q (m_{t+1} - (1 + r))^2 \\
&= E_t^Q (m_{t+1}^2) - (1 + r)^2 \\
&= qu^2 + (1 - q)\frac{1}{u^2} - (1 + r)^2.
\end{aligned}
\tag{10.66}
$$

Using the expression (10.65) for q, we get

$$E_t^Q\left(\frac{p_{t+1}-p_t}{p_t}-r\right)^2 = \frac{(1+r)u^3 - u^2 + 1 - (1+r)(1/u)}{u^2-1} - (1+r)^2,$$

(10.67)

which may be equated to the P-variance of the stock return, say σ^2, to finally set u, and hence both d and q. Note that the physical measure does enter this way, through the variance, to tie down Q, whereas expected returns under P remain irrelevant. In short, σ^2 and r determine Q and hence option prices.

With the parameters for the stock price process under the equivalent martingale measure, i.e., u, $d = 1/u$ and q set, it is clear that the stock price at T, when started at p_t at t, takes the value $p_t u^j/u^{T-t-j}$ if there are j up moves and $(T-t-j)$ down moves between t and T, which under Q happens with probability

$$Q(j|T-t) = \frac{(T-t)!}{j!(T-t-j)!}q^j(1-q)^{T-t-j},$$

(10.68)

$j = 0, 1, \ldots, T-t$, the binomial probability of j up moves out of $T-t$, each with probability q. It follows that the expected stock price at T is

$$E_t^Q(p_T) = p_t \sum_{j=0}^{T-t} Q(j|T-t)u^{2j-(T-t)}.$$

(10.69)

With this model for the stock price under Q, there are $(T-t+1)$ possible values for p_T. The probability of each value depends only on the number of up and down moves required to reach it, not on the order in which they occur.

Of course, q has been set so that the expected return per period is r, and although it is not obvious from the formula (10.69), it follows that in fact $E_t^Q(p_T) = p_t(1+r)^{T-t}$. What is more interesting is that we now have a simple numerical technique for calculating the appropriate price of any derivative security. For example, the European call price from (10.54) is

$$c_t = \frac{b_t}{b_T}E_t^Q(\max\{X-K,0\})$$

$$= \frac{1}{(1+r)^{T-t}}\sum_{j=0}^{T-t} Q(j|T-t)\max\{p_t u^{2j-(T-t)} - K, 0\},$$

(10.70)

using the constant interest rate assumption. Obviously, this expression is completely explicit and can be quickly computed in practice. Similarly, the

European put price (10.55) is

$$q_t = \frac{1}{(1+r)^{T-t}} \sum_{j=0}^{T-t} Q(j|T-t) \max\{K - p_t u^{2j-(T-t)}, 0\}. \quad (10.71)$$

For the corresponding American call from (10.62), we use dynamic programming, in particular, backward recursion. Here, it is useful to calculate in advance the lattice of possible stock price values at each point in time; i.e., $p_t u^{2j-k}$, $j = 0, 1, \ldots, k$, for time $t + k$, $k = 1, \ldots, T - t$. The terminal condition is then

$$C_T^j = \max\{p_t u^{2j-(T-t)} - K, 0\}, \quad (10.72)$$

$j = 0, 1, \ldots, T - t$, and from the dynamic programming setup, the Bellman equation for backward recursion is

$$C_{t+k}^j = \max\left\{ p_t u^{2j-k} - K, \frac{1}{1+r} \left(q C_{t+k+1}^{j+1} + (1 - q) C_{t+k+1}^j \right) \right\}, \quad (10.73)$$

$j = 0, 1, \ldots, k$. The American call price is $C_t = C_t^0$.

In fact, if the stock pays no dividends prior to T, the American call should not be exercised early, and $C_t = c_t$. See section 6.4 for a proof. However, it may be optimal to exercise the American put early, even if the stock pays no dividends. Here, the terminal condition is

$$P_T^j = \max\{K - p_t u^{2j-(T-t)}, 0\}, \quad (10.74)$$

$j = 0, 1, \ldots, T$, and from the dynamic programming setup, the Bellman equation (10.61) for backward recursion is now

$$P_{t+k}^j = \max\left\{ K - p_t u^{2j-k}, \frac{1}{1+r} \left(q P_{t+k+1}^{j+1} + (1 - q) P_{t+k+1}^j \right) \right\}, \quad (10.75)$$

$j = 0, 1, \ldots, k$. The American put price is $P_t = P_t^0$. Note that all option prices depend on the risk-neutral distribution Q, i.e., on σ^2 and r, but only on the physical distribution P through the variance σ^2 used to tie down q, not through expected returns under P.

If the stock pays dividends before T, the American call (and, of course, the American put) should sometimes be exercised early, i.e., prior to expiration at T. For example, consider the simple case of a constant dividend yield y. This implies that the effective risk-neutral expected return is $(1+r)(1-y) - 1 = g$, so q and u from (10.65) and (10.67) are redefined using g in place of r, but discounting is still at rate r, so the same formulas

(10.73) and (10.75) for C_{t+k}^{j} and P_{t+k}^{j} apply ($k = 0, 1, \ldots, T - t$) with the revised q and u. Of course, the binomial formulas (10.70) and (10.71) for the European options also apply in the dividend-paying stock case, with q and u (but again not r) revised in the same manner.

By setting up the numerical procedure carefully, it is possible to get the binomial model to converge weakly to desired continuous-time processes. Thus, the time interval from t to expiration is split into an increasing number of subintervals, and the parameters r, q, u, and d adjusted accordingly. As the number of subintervals is increased, the basic binomial process (10.63) with parameters set as described above converges to the risk-neutralized geometric Brownian motion

$$\frac{dp_t}{p_t} = r\,dt + \sigma\,dW_t,$$

with W_t standard (arithmetic) Brownian motion, and so the call price (10.70) converges to the Black and Scholes (1973) formula (11.22) and (14.58). Similarly, if (10.67) is equated to other volatility (variance) functions, other weak limits are reached; e.g., replacing σ^2 by $(\sigma p_t^{\gamma-1})^2$ generates the Cox and Ross (1976) constant elasticity of variance (CEV) process

$$dp_t = rp_t\,dt + \sigma p_t^{\gamma}\,dW_t,$$

with the Black-Scholes model the special case $\gamma = 1$ and the square-root process the special case $\gamma = \frac{1}{2}$. We return to continuous-time models in chapter 14.

The analysis of option prices, including inference, is continued in chapter 11. As noted there, option price data as of time t can be used in empirical work. Hence, even though the spacing between option price observation is of fixed length, the length of the subintervals discretizing the interval from t through expiration in the binomial method may shrink, as this is simply a device for computing fair prices.

10.8 EMPIRICAL APPLICATIONS

Consider first the general asset-pricing formula (10.1). The return $\tilde{r}_{t+1}$ at time $t + 1$ is

$$\tilde{r}_{t+1} = \frac{p_{t+1} + d_{t+1}}{p_t} - 1. \tag{10.76}$$

By (10.5), we have $E_t^Q(p_{t+1} + d_{t+1}) = p_t(1 + r_{t+1})$. Inserting this above yields

$$E_t^Q(\tilde{r}_{t+1}) = r_{t+1}, \tag{10.77}$$

as in (10.29). This says that the conditional expected return of any asset under the equivalent martingale measure Q is given by the (short) riskless interest rate r_{t+1}. Equivalently, conditional expected *excess returns* above the riskless rate are all zero, $E_t^Q(\tilde{r}_{t+1} - r_{t+1}) = 0$, showing in particular that the excess returns $\tilde{r}_{t+1} - r_{t+1}$ are serially uncorrelated under Q. If the market does not require risk compensation and if the short rate is deterministic and constant, this implies that the returns $\tilde{r}_{t+1}$ themselves are serially uncorrelated under the actual (physical) measure P. Serially uncorrelated returns are traditionally viewed as a sign of market efficiency. Thus, if returns are uncorrelated, then future price changes cannot be forecast, and asset prices are random walks. Typically, *weak form efficiency* is the term used to refer to this situation, where the conditional expected return is zero, given past returns. If the same holds when the conditioning information set is expanded to all publicly available information, then this is called *semi-strong form efficiency*. Finally, *strong form efficiency* is the term used when the conditioning may be on all public and private information. This follows Roberts (1967).

10.8.1 Time Series Properties

To test market efficiency, it is therefore natural to test whether returns are serially uncorrelated. The traditional test for this hypothesis is the Box and Pierce (1970) statistic

$$Q_k = T \sum_{i=1}^{k} \hat{\rho}(i)^2, \tag{10.78}$$

where T is the length of the time series of observed returns $\{\tilde{r}_t\}_{t=1}^T$ and $\hat{\rho}(i)$ is the sample analog of the ith-order autocorrelation coefficient,

$$\rho(i) = \frac{\text{cov}(\tilde{r}_{t+k}, \tilde{r}_t)}{\text{var}(\tilde{r}_t)}. \tag{10.79}$$

As $T \to \infty$, Q_k is asymptotically χ_k^2 under the null. In applications, k is set at about the lag length for which autocorrelation is suspected. From the above, it makes good sense from a financial economics viewpoint to carry out the test with excess returns $\tilde{r}_t - r_t$ replacing raw returns $\tilde{r}_t$ everywhere. Also, improved small sample properties are obtained by the Ljung and Box (1978) test,

$$\tilde{Q}_k = T(T+2) \sum_{i=1}^{k} \frac{\hat{\rho}(i)^2}{T-i}, \tag{10.80}$$

which is also asymptotically χ_k^2.

An alternative approach to testing for zero autocorrelation is to consider the variance ratios of long- and short-term returns. Thus, with $\tilde{r}_t$ the one-period return from $t - 1$ to t, we may consider $\tilde{r}_t + \tilde{r}_{t+1}$ as the two-period return from $t - 1$ to $t + 1$. This would literally be true for the case of no dividends and continuously compounding returns, in which case $\tilde{r}_t = \log(p_t) - \log(p_{t-1})$, so that the effective return is $p_t/p_{t-1} - 1 = \exp(\tilde{r}_t) - 1$, while the two-period return is $\log(p_{t+1}) - \log(p_{t-1}) = \tilde{r}_{t+1} + \tilde{r}_t$. The *variance ratio* of long and short returns, $\text{var}(\tilde{r}_{t+1} + \tilde{r}_t)/(2\,\text{var}(\tilde{r}_t))$, is then unity under zero autocorrelation and an additional assumption of constant variance. More generally, the k-period variance ratio is

$$VR(k) = \frac{\text{var}(\tilde{r}_t + \cdots + \tilde{r}_{t-k+1})}{k\,\text{var}(\tilde{r}_t)}$$

$$= \sum_{i=0}^{k-1}\sum_{j=0}^{k-1} \frac{\text{cov}(\tilde{r}_{t-i}, \tilde{r}_{t-j})}{k\,\text{var}(\tilde{r}_t)}$$

$$= \frac{k\,\text{var}(\tilde{r}_t) + 2(k-1)\,\text{cov}(\tilde{r}_t, \tilde{r}_{t-1}) + \cdots + 2\,\text{cov}(\tilde{r}_t, \tilde{r}_{t-k+1})}{k\,\text{var}(\tilde{r}_t)}$$

$$= 1 + 2\sum_{i=1}^{k-1}\left(1 - \frac{i}{k}\right)\rho(i) \qquad (10.81)$$

under weak (second-order) stationarity, i.e., constant autocovariances. Again, if $\rho(i) = 0$ for $i > 0$ by market efficiency, we expect $VR(k)$ near unity, and this is the basis for the test. Thus, $\widehat{VR}(k)$ is calculated by replacing $\text{var}(\Sigma_i \tilde{r}_{t-i})$ and $\text{var}(\tilde{r}_t)$ in the expression for $VR(k)$ by their sample analogs, and this is typically compared to the asymptotic distribution given by

$$\sqrt{T}(\widehat{VR}(k) - 1) \sim N(0, 2(k-1)), \qquad (10.82)$$

which applies to i.i.d. returns. Lo and MacKinlay (1988) show how to adjust the asymptotic variance in the test in the case of serially uncorrelated but possibly heteroskedastic returns, assuming a constant conditional mean return and uncorrelated sample autocorrelations $\hat{\rho}(i)$ (across lag lengths i).

A *unit root* process for log prices is actually implied by the constant-mean specification for the returns (log price differences) $\tilde{r}_{t+1} = \log(p_{t+1}) - \log(p_t)$. Specifically, $E(\tilde{r}_{t+1}) = \mu$ leads to

$$\log(p_{t+1}) = \mu + \gamma \log(p_t) + \varepsilon_{t+1}, \qquad (10.83)$$

with $\gamma = 1$, the unit root. Unit root tests are typically designed to test the null $\gamma = 1$ against $|\gamma| < 1$ (stationary, mean-reverting log prices), assuming stationary ε_{t+1}, whereas market efficiency tests correspond to testing the null of no autocorrelation in ε_{t+1}. Thus, even with a unit root, future price changes are forecastable if ε_{t+1} is. At the same time, even with ε_{t+1} serially uncorrelated, future price changes are forecastable if $\gamma < 1$.

The test for $\gamma = 1$ in (10.83) is nonstandard since $\log(p_t)$ is nonstationary under the null. If $\mu = 0$ and ε_t is i.i.d., then $\sqrt{T}(\hat{\gamma} - \gamma)$ converges to $N(0, 1 - \gamma^2)$ under the stationary, first-order autoregressive or AR(1) alternative $|\gamma| < 1$, with $\hat{\gamma}$ the OLS estimator. Under the unit root null, $\gamma = 1$, $\sqrt{T}(\hat{\gamma} - 1) \to 0$; i.e., OLS is *superconsistent*. In fact, it converges at rate T as opposed to $\sqrt{T}$, and $T(\hat{\gamma} - 1)$ converges to the Dickey and Fuller (1979) distribution,

$$T(\hat{\gamma} - 1) \to \frac{\frac{1}{2}(W_1^2 - 1)}{\int_0^1 W_t^2 \, dt}, \tag{10.84}$$

where W_t is a standard Wiener process or Brownian motion, e.g., $W_t \sim N(0, t)$. Note that the OLS estimate $\hat{\gamma}$ imposes $\mu = 0$ in (10.83), i.e.,

$$\hat{\gamma} = \frac{\sum_{t=2}^{T} \log(p_t) \log(p_{t-1})}{\sum_{t=2}^{T} \log(p_{t-1})^2}. \tag{10.85}$$

Fuller (1976) tabulated the distribution by Monte Carlo; e.g., the 5% critical value in a one-sided test of $\gamma = 1$ against $\gamma < 1$ with T large is -8.1. The one-sided case is relevant since we are investigating whether log prices are stationary ($\gamma < 1$) or have a linear *stochastic trend* ($\gamma = 1$). The explosive case ($\gamma > 1$) was considered by Anderson (1959). Note that superconsistency of $\hat{\gamma}$ in the unit root model does not stem from the properties of extreme order statistics as in the job search model of chapter 7, and the distribution (10.84) differs from the trace-Wishart distribution in theorem 6 for the prototypal model.

The standard OLS estimate of $\text{var}(\hat{\gamma})$ of the type $\sigma^2(X'X)^{-1}$ in the present case with zero intercept is $\hat{\sigma}_\gamma^2 = T^{-1}\Sigma_t \hat{\varepsilon}_t^2 / \Sigma_t \log(p_t)^2$, and the conventional t-statistic for testing $\gamma = 1$ is $t_\gamma = (\hat{\gamma} - 1)/\hat{\sigma}_\gamma$. Under the unit root null, this is not asymptotically normal, but

$$t_\gamma \to \frac{\frac{1}{2}(W_1^2 - 1)}{\left(\int_0^1 W_t^2 \, dt\right)^{1/2}}, \tag{10.86}$$

so the t-statistic is still informative. When the correct asymptotic distribution is used, this is referred to as a Dickey-Fuller (DF) test and is an alternative to the test based on $T(\hat{\gamma} - 1)$ in (10.84). The 5% critical value for the DF test is -1.95, and again insignificant values of t_γ are consistent with a unit root, whereas significant values reject this in favor of a stationary AR(1). Note that the critical value -1.95 should not be confused with the usual cutoff -1.96 from the $N(0, 1)$ asymptotic distribution of the t-test in stationary regression; e.g., this arises in a two-sided test (it is the 2.5% point) and the distributions are clearly different, the DF distribution being asymmetric and with a heavier left tail.

Thus, the DF machinery does allow handling of the nonstandard distribution issues that arise because of the unit root under the null. A related approach is developed by Phillips (1987) and Phillips and Perron (1988). However, care must be taken when applying all these tests, as distributions depend on specifics in the implementation and assumptions because of the nonstandard features of the problem. Details are as follows, staying here in the DF framework. First, practical implementation would often include the intercept μ in (10.83) in OLS regression, and in this case the distribution of $T(\hat{\gamma} - 1)$ is shifted to the left, with a 5% cutoff now at -14.1 instead of the -8.1 for (10.84) above, even though the true $\mu = 0$. Similarly, the critical value of the DF t_γ-test is now -2.86 as opposed to the -1.95 from (10.86) above.

All of these critical values are for the case of a zero intercept, interpreted as no deterministic trend in the data. But from the outset, μ represents the mean return $E(\tilde{r}_{t+1})$ in the asset-pricing application, and $\mu \neq 0$ should generally be allowed in this case. Under the revised null $\gamma = 1$, $\mu \neq 0$, the DF regression (10.83) with two parameters produces a standard OLS t_γ-statistic that is in fact asymptotically $N(0, 1)$ as $T \to \infty$, just as in ordinary stationary regression, so testing for a unit root in asset prices is straightforward and avoids referral to DF tables, etc.

Again, the presence of a unit root is only one aspect of interest, whereas treatment of market efficiency requires addressing residual serial behavior. In fact, to control for serial correlation in residuals, the DF regression (10.83) is usually replaced by the augmented DF (ADF) specification

$$\log(p_{t+1}) = \mu + \gamma \log(p_t) + \delta_1 \Delta \log(p_t) + \cdots + \delta_k \Delta \log(p_{t-k+1}) + \varepsilon_{t+1},$$
$$(10.87)$$

with k large enough to leave ε_{t+1} i.i.d. As $\Delta \log(p_t) = \log(p_t) - \log(p_{t-1}) = \tilde{r}_t$, the return, the ADF regression may be recast as

$$\tilde{r}_{t+1} = \mu + \eta \log(p_t) + \delta_1 \tilde{r}_t + \cdots + \delta_k \tilde{r}_{t-k+1} + \varepsilon_{t+1}, \qquad (10.88)$$

in which $\eta = \gamma - 1$ and the unit root hypothesis is $\eta = 0$ (returns do not depend on past prices). Another equivalent representation is

$$\log(p_{t+1}) = \mu + \gamma_1 \log(p_t) + \cdots + \gamma_{k+1} \log(p_{t-k}) + \varepsilon_{t+1}, \qquad (10.89)$$

with $\gamma = \gamma_1 + \cdots + \gamma_{k+1}$ and $\delta_j = -(\gamma_{j+1} + \cdots + \gamma_{k+1})$ for $j = 1, \ldots, k$. If $\mu = 0$ and this is imposed in the ADF regression, then the asymptotic distribution under the unit root null $\gamma = 1$ (equivalently, $\eta = 0$) of the OLS t-statistic for testing $\gamma = 1$ (or $\eta = 0$) is given by (10.86), as without the augmentation; i.e., the 5% critical value is again -1.95. If the ADF regression is run with intercept but the true $\mu = 0$, then again the cutoff is -2.86. Finally, as before, asset pricing suggests $\mu \neq 0$, and in this case, all t-tests and F-tests on the coefficients $\gamma, \eta, \delta_1, \ldots, \delta_k$ may be referred to standard $N(0, 1)$ and χ^2 tables with no need to bring in the special DF distributions.

The discussion has assumed no dividends, calculating returns as log price differences, but dividends can be accommodated, too, and Campbell and Shiller (1988a, b) have introduced a log linear approximate asset-pricing framework in which unit root analysis and the related concept of *cointegration* can be used to study the relation among prices, dividends, and returns. Starting from (10.76), the approximation is

$$\tilde{r}_{t+1} = \frac{p_{t+1} + d_{t+1}}{p_t} - 1$$

$$\approx \log(1 + \tilde{r}_{t+1})$$

$$\approx k + \rho \log(p_{t+1}) + (1 - \rho) \log(d_{t+1}) - \log(p_t), \quad (10.90)$$

a first-order Taylor expansion, with $\rho = 1/(1 + \exp(\overline{\log(d)} - \overline{\log(p)}))$ and $k = -\log(\rho) - (1 - \rho) \log(1/\rho - 1)$, where $\overline{\log(d)} - \overline{\log(p)}$ is the average log *dividend-price ratio*. Thus, the log linearization of returns involves a weighted average of log prices and log dividends, with ρ the weight on log prices, $0 < \rho < 1$. For asset pricing, we may rearrange to solve for the current price and iterate on the resulting forward difference equation in $\log(p_t)$ under the *transversality* condition $\rho^i \log(p_{t+i}) \to 0$, producing

$$\log(p_t) = \frac{k}{1 - \rho} + \sum_{i=0}^{\infty} \rho^i ((1 - \rho) \log(d_{t+i+1}) - \tilde{r}_{t+i+1}). \quad (10.91)$$

Thus, fundamentals enter explicitly. If asset prices are up, it must be due to higher future dividends or lower future returns. This is a present value relation. In particular, by taking conditional expectation as of time t, by which operation the left hand side is unaltered, it is seen that the current log price is (approximately) the conditional expectation of the discounted stream of log dividends less returns, up to a constant. This may be rewritten in terms of the log dividend-price ratio,

$$\log(d_t) - \log(p_t) = -\frac{k}{1 - \rho} + E_t \left(\sum_{i=1}^{\infty} \rho^i (-\Delta \log(d_{t+i+1}) + \tilde{r}_{t+i+1} \right).$$

$$(10.92)$$

Assume dividends are nonstationary and follow a log linear unit root process. This may be tested using the previous unit root tests, in particular ADF regression (10.87), replacing $\log(p_t)$ by $\log(d_t)$. If a unit root is not rejected, then $\log(p_t)$ is also nonstationary, by (10.91), whereas $\Delta \log(d_t)$ is stationary, and if $\tilde{r}_t$ is also stationary, then log prices and log dividends are cointegrated by (10.92). That is, $\log(d_t)$ and $\log(p_t)$ each has a unit root, but there exists a linear combination of the two that is stationary, in this case given by the difference between the two series. This makes good sense; i.e., both prices and dividends can move a lot in the long run, without any tendency to return to previous levels, but the two would tend to move together, in the sense that the price-dividend ratio tends to stay within a reasonably narrow range.

To establish statistically that the two series are cointegrated, based on data $\{(p_t, d_t)\}_{t=1}^T$, the ADF test or a similar test may first be applied to each series separately to confirm that both $\log(p_t)$ and $\log(d_t)$ are well described by unit root processes. In this case, $\Delta \log(p_t)$ and $\Delta \log(d_t)$ are stationary. This is sometimes emphasized by saying that the differenced series are integrated of order zero, or they are $I(0)$, whereas the raw log series are integrated of order one, $I(1)$, simply meaning that first differencing them makes them $I(0)$. The cointegrating regression is

$$\log(p_t) = \alpha + \beta \log(d_t) + u_t. \tag{10.93}$$

If there exists a β such that the resulting residual series u_t is $I(0)$, then $\log(p_t)$ and $\log(d_t)$ are cointegrated. In particular, this is $(I(0) - I(1))$ cointegration. This is tested simply by examining whether u_t is stationary or, specifically, $I(0)$, and this can be done by testing whether in fact u_t has a unit root. If this test rejects, then the indication is that u_t is stationary, and this is evidence in favor of cointegration. If the unit root test on u_t fails to reject, then cointegration of the original two series is rejected.

The concept of cointegration, that two nonstationary series move together in the long run, was introduced by Granger (1983) and analyzed further in Engle and Granger (1987), including the idea of applying unit root tests to the original series and the residuals from the cointegrating regression (10.93) in turn.

In the log dividend-price ratio case, $\beta = 1$ in (10.93) by (10.92), and the unit root test is readily applied to the series $u_t = \log(p_t) - \log(d_t)$ as the potential presence of α does not alter the unit root or stationary behaviour of u_t.

In general, if β is unknown, it must be estimated, e.g., by OLS. Because of the nonstationarity of the variables entering the regression (10.93), the properties of the OLS estimator are nonstandard, and Stock (1987) shows that the OLS estimator $\hat{\beta}$ is *superconsistent*; i.e., $\sqrt{T}(\hat{\beta} - \beta) \to 0$, and

$T(\hat{\beta} - \beta)$ has a nonstandard limiting distribution that differs from both the DF distribution (10.84) and the trace-Wishart distribution of the superconsistent parameter in the job search model in theorem 6, chapter 7.

Upon estimation of $\hat{\beta}$ in (10.93), unit root tests may be applied to the estimated OLS residuals $\hat{u}_t$, but the asymptotic distribution of the tests is now different since they are applied to estimated residuals rather than data. Phillips and Ouliaris (1990) show how to handle this situation, and we outline their results briefly. For alternative approaches to cointegration testing, see Stock and Watson (1988) and Johansen (1991).

The ADF regression for the residuals $\hat{u}_t$ from (10.93) is similar to (10.87),

$$\hat{u}_{t+1} = \gamma \hat{u}_t + \delta_1 \Delta \hat{u}_t + \cdots + \delta_k \Delta \hat{u}_{t-k+1} + v_{t+1}. \qquad (10.94)$$

No intercept μ is included since the test is applied to residuals. Although this point is clearest when $\hat{u}_t$ are obtained from the cointegrating regression (10.93) with estimated intercept α, we first consider the case where $\alpha = 0$ is imposed in this. Assume $(\Delta \log(p_t), \Delta \log(d_t))$ has no deterministic component. Thus, let the *Wold decomposition* be of the form

$$\begin{pmatrix} \Delta \log(p_t) \\ \Delta \log(d_t) \end{pmatrix} = \begin{pmatrix} \alpha_1 \\ \alpha_2 \end{pmatrix} + \sum_{i=0}^{\infty} \Psi_i w_{t-i}, \qquad (10.95)$$

with w_t a vector-valued i.i.d. process with zero mean, finite fourth moments, and the condition $\sum_{i=0}^{\infty} |i\Psi_i| < \infty$ on the *impulse response function* Ψ_i. Then the assumption of no deterministic component amounts to $\alpha_1 = \alpha_2 = 0$. In this case, the OLS t-test for $\gamma = 1$ in the ADF regression (10.94) for $\hat{u}_t$ has 5% critical value in large samples in a one-sided test against $\gamma < 1$ equal to -2.76. This may be compared to the critical values -1.95 and -2.86 for the tests without and with intercept μ in the ADF regression (10.87) applied to data, not residuals. Note that the null is $\gamma = 1$, i.e., a unit root in the residuals. This is the case referred to as *spurious regression* by Granger and Newbold (1974). In particular, if u_t is nonstationary, then $\log(p_t)$ and $\log(d_t)$ do not move together in (10.93), and the relation between the two is spurious. This is the case of no cointegration. An ADF t-statistic from (10.94) less than -2.76 is then required for cointegration; i.e., the null is alternatively described as $\gamma = 1$ (unit root in residuals) or no cointegration.

In other applications, there could be more right-hand-side variables in the cointegrating regression (10.93); i.e., $\log(d_t)$ is replaced by a vector x_t of data series, of dimension m, say, and β by an m-vector of coefficients, and the test is for whether the $(m + 1)$ data series are cointegrated. The ADF regression (10.94) for $\hat{u}_t$ looks the same, but the 5% critical value for the t-test of $\gamma = 1$ (no cointegration) depends on m. Again, for $m = 1$ it is -2.76, and it is -3.27 for $m = 2$, -3.74 for $m = 3$, -4.38 for $m = 4$, -4.67 for $m = 5$, etc.

Often α is estimated in the cointegrating regression (10.93), rather than being forced to equal 0. In the dividend-price ratio application, by (10.92) this accommodates that the parameter $-k/(1 - \rho)$ is nonzero even if $\Delta \log(d_t)$ and $\tilde{r}_t$ are zero mean processes. In this case, the resulting distribution of the ADF t-test of $\gamma = 1$ for $\hat{u}_t$ in (10.94) is more spread out than with $\alpha = 0$ imposed. Thus, the 5% critical values for no cointegration are -3.37 for $m = 1$ (as compared to -2.76 with $\alpha = 0$), -3.77 for $m = 2$, -4.11 for $m = 3$, -4.45 for $m = 4$, -4.71 for $m = 5$, etc.

If the differenced series do contain a deterministic component, i.e., $(\alpha_1, \alpha_2) \neq 0$ in the Wold decomposition (10.95), then the distribution of the ADF t-test from (10.94) is yet more spread out. This case has been studied by Hansen (1992) and is relevant in the asset-pricing application, where again a nonzero mean of $\Delta \log(p_t)$ should be admitted; i.e., $\alpha_1 = \mu = E(\tilde{r}_t)$, the expected return. Now the 5% critical value for no cointegration is -3.42 (compared to -3.37 with $\alpha_1 = 0$ and -2.76 when in addition $\alpha = 0$). With more regressors, we get -3.80 for $m = 2$, -4.16 for $m = 3$, -4.49 for $m = 4$, -4.74 for $m = 5$, etc.

If the log dividend-price ratio is indeed stationary, i.e., $\log(p_t)$ and $\log(d_t)$ cointegrate, with the cointegrating vector in (10.93) given by $\beta = 1$, then it may be used as an ordinary stationary variable in regressions. The present value formula (10.92) suggests that $\log(d_t) - \log(p_t)$ should forecast future returns, particularly if future dividend growth is not too variable. This may be examined in the type of long-horizon return regression

$$\tilde{r}_{t+1} + \cdots + \tilde{r}_{t+K} = \alpha_K + \beta_K (\log(d_t) - \log(p_t)) + v_{t+K,K}, \quad (10.96)$$

which has been considered, e.g., by Fama and French (1988). From the present value relation (10.92), the forecasting power should actually increase with the length of return horizon K, and this is confirmed empirically.

We started this section testing for market efficiency by testing that returns cannot be forecast. We end the section by concluding they can be. This is not necessarily due to a violation of market efficiency, but rather to a generalization of the model in which market efficiency is tested.

10.8.2 Portfolio Models

In a market with N stocks and data over T periods, the return on stock i in period t is of the same form as (10.76),

$$r_{i,t} = \frac{p_{i,t} + d_{i,t}}{p_{i,t-1}} - 1, \quad (10.97)$$

where $p_{i,t}$ is the stock price at the end of period t and $d_{i,t}$ is the dividend paid over the period. The market (index) return $r_{m,t}$ is defined similarly, with

$p_{m,t}$ the index level appropriately aggregating individual stock prices and $d_{m,t}$ aggregate dividends. The market risk of stock i is typically measured by beta, the coefficient on the market return in the market model (10.50), taken to be constant over time, $\beta_{i,t} = \beta_i$, and estimated by OLS in the excess return market model regression over time,

$$r_{i,t} - r_t = \alpha_i + \beta_i(r_{m,t} - r_t) + \varepsilon_{i,t}, \qquad t = 1, \ldots, T, \qquad (10.98)$$

where again r_t is the riskless interest (say, T-bill) rate over period t. The market portfolio has $\beta_m = 1$, and stocks are considered safe or risky according to whether β is below or above unity. The estimated variance matrix of $(\hat{\alpha}_i, \hat{\beta}_i)$ is $\sigma_i^2 (X'X)^{-1}$, where $\sigma_i^2 = \text{var}(\varepsilon_{i,t})$ is the residual variance and X is the $T \times 2$ design matrix with typical row $(1, r_{m,t} - r_t)$. By working out the upper left corner of $(X'X)^{-1}$, it is seen that the t-statistic for the capital asset pricing model (CAPM) zero intercept restriction $\alpha_i = 0$ from (10.52) is

$$t_{\alpha_i} = \sqrt{T} \frac{\hat{\alpha}_i}{\sigma_i \sqrt{1 + (\mu_m/\sigma_m)^2}}. \qquad (10.99)$$

Here, μ_m/σ_m is the aggregate return-risk tradeoff or the Sharpe ratio, the ratio of the mean to the standard deviation of the market excess return $r_{m,t} - r_t$. From (10.98), departures from CAPM are harder to detect if the equity risk premium in the economy is high. In practice, μ_m is estimated by the sample mean of $r_{m,t} - r_t$. The sample variances of this and of $\hat{\varepsilon}_{i,t}$ are used to estimate σ_m^2 and σ_i^2, respectively, and (10.99) is treated as approximately $N(0, 1)$.

Even if $\alpha_i = 0$ is rejected, β_i is often used as a measure of market risk, and raw rather than excess returns are sometimes used in (10.98) in this case. If $\alpha_i = 0$ is not rejected, a more efficient β_i estimate may be obtained by imposing a zero intercept in (10.98).

While the market model (10.50) is an attempt at a useful statistical description of returns, the CAPM is an equilibrium theory. The implication of the CAPM for expected returns is that

$$E(r_{i,t} - r_t) = \beta_i E(r_{m,t} - r_t). \qquad (10.100)$$

Clearly, imposing the CAPM theory restriction (10.100) on the statistical market model (10.98) leads to the hypothesis $\alpha_i = 0$ tested in (10.99). The well-known risk measure is β_i, and the test is on α_i.

It is instructive to see how (10.100) comes about. Essentially, β_i measures the contribution of stock i to the risk of the overall portfolio demanded, which in equilibrium (assuming common beliefs across investors) must be the market portfolio consisting of all assets in the relative proportions in which they are supplied. Hence, it is β_i that is priced for stock i, as reflected in the expected excess return (10.100). A low value of β_i (low market risk) tends to lower the portfolio risk and is associated with a stock in high demand, i.e., a high initial stock price $p_{i,t-1}$ or, equivalently (see (10.97)), a low expected (required) return. More explicitly, let $R_t = (r_{1,t}, \ldots, r_{N,t})$ be the vector of contemporaneous stock returns and write $\mu = E(R_t)$ for the N-vector of mean returns, $V = \text{var}(R_t)$ for the $N \times N$ variance matrix, and c for the N-vector of portfolio weights (fractions of the investor's wealth) placed in the stocks. Thus, c is the choice or control variable, and any remaining wealth is invested in the riskless asset; i.e., this gets weight $1 - e'c$, where e is an N-vector of ones. If this is negative, the investor borrows to enter a leveraged stock market position.

The stock portfolio return is now $c'R_t$, with mean $c'\mu$ and variance $c'Vc$, whereas the riskless portion of the overall portfolio contributes with a return $(1 - e'c)r_t$. The Markowitz (1959) mean-variance portfolio selection problem is therefore

$$c^* = \arg\min_{c}\{c'Vc : c'\mu + (1 - e'c)r_t \geq \mu_p\}, \qquad (10.101)$$

i.e., minimization of the portfolio variance subject to a threshold expected portfolio return μ_p. This is a quadratic programming problem and may be motivated in a two-period model with quadratic utility of terminal wealth function, or if μ and V fully characterize the joint return distribution (e.g., R_t is multivariate normal or elliptically distributed) and investors are risk-averse. With the Lagrangian $c'Vc + \lambda(\mu_p - c'\mu - (1 - e'c)r_t)$, where λ is a Lagrange multiplier, the first-order conditions are

$$2Vc - \lambda(\mu - r_t e) = 0. \qquad (10.102)$$

The constraint will be binding, so $\lambda \neq 0$, and hence $\mu - r_t e = 2Vc/\lambda$. Premultiplication by c' yields $c'\mu - e'cr_t = 2c'Vc/\lambda$. From the constraint, it also holds that $c'\mu - e'cr_t = \mu_p - r_t$. Combining, we get the multiplier at the optimum, $\lambda = 2c'Vc/(\mu_p - r_t)$. Inserting this in $\mu - r_t e = 2Vc/\lambda$ from above yields

$$\mu - r_t e = \frac{Vc}{c'Vc}(\mu_p - r_t). \qquad (10.103)$$

Note that Vc is the vector of covariances between the individual stocks and the portfolio, $\text{cov}(R_t, c'R_t) = Vc$. Hence, the first-order condition (10.102) from the mean-variance analysis implies (10.103), that mean excess returns are proportional to the β's or regression coefficients (ratios of covariance to variance) of assets on the portfolio held, the factor of proportionality being the portfolio excess return. The equilibrium argument of Sharpe (1964) and Lintner (1965) is that the portfolio demanded must be that supplied, the market portfolio, and writing out (10.103) for the individual capital assets produces the CAPM (10.100). The beta of the individual stock, β_i, comes out as the relevant priced risk measure from economic theory, i.e., the ith coordinate of $Vc/c'Vc$ in (10.103), and may be measured as the regression coefficient in (10.98). The CAPM is a case of a close relation between economic modeling and inference.

Recalling that the model is one of portfolio selection, it is not in general reasonable to assess the usefulness of the CAPM restriction in a given market based on only one asset, as in (10.99). The t-test can be repeated for each of the N stocks, but the N tests are not independent. Indeed, the stocks are generally contemporaneously correlated, i.e., V is not diagonal, and hence the importance of portfolio analysis and beta pricing. Nevertheless, it is unnecessary to estimate the N regressions (10.98) for the N stocks simultaneously as a seemingly unrelated regressions (SUR) system. The reason is that the regressors X (intercept and market excess return) are common across regressions, one of Zellner's (1962) sufficient conditions for OLS and GLS (SUR) to be identical. Still, a joint test of H_0: $\alpha_1 = \cdots = \alpha_N = 0$ is required for the CAPM (10.100) for the whole market. To this end, the contemporaneous variance matrix $\Sigma = \text{var}(\varepsilon_t)$ of the error terms $\varepsilon_t = (\varepsilon_{1,t}, \ldots, \varepsilon_{N,t})'$ is estimated as $\widehat{\Sigma} = \Sigma_{t=1}^{T}\hat{\varepsilon}_t\hat{\varepsilon}_t'/T$. With $\alpha = (\alpha_1, \ldots, \alpha_N)'$, the Wald test $\hat{\alpha}'\text{var}(\hat{\alpha})^{-1}\hat{\alpha}$ takes the form

$$W = T\frac{\hat{\alpha}'\widehat{\Sigma}^{-1}\hat{\alpha}}{1 + \left(\hat{\mu}_m/\hat{\sigma}_m\right)^2} \qquad (10.104)$$

and is asymptotically χ_N^2 as $T \to \infty$ under the null. If $\varepsilon_t = (\varepsilon_{1,t}, \ldots, \varepsilon_{N,t})'$ is serially independent (we have implicitly assumed uncorrelated) and multivariate normal, $\varepsilon_t \sim N(0, \Sigma)$, then an exact finite sample test is $J = (T - N - 1)W/(TN) \sim F_{N,T-N-1}$. Under this distributional assumption, we may calculate how much W is off in finite samples. Say a is the nominal size of the asymptotic test, $a = 1 - F_W(q)$, where F_W is the c.d.f. of χ_N^2 and q is the cutoff (critical value) of the Wald test. Then the true size is

$$1 - F_J\left(q\frac{T - N - 1}{TN}\right) = 1 - F_J\left(F_W^{-1}(1 - a)\frac{T - N - 1}{TN}\right), \quad (10.105)$$

where F_J is the cumulative distribution function (CDF) of the $F_{N,T-N-1}$ distribution. Further, when the CAPM is violated ($\alpha \neq 0$), $J \sim F_{N,T-N-1}(\delta)$, the noncentral F with noncentrality $\delta = T\alpha'\Sigma^{-1}\alpha/(1 + (\mu_m/\sigma_m)^2)$ and CDF F_δ. As the exact test has critical value $F_J^{-1}(1 - a)$, it has exact power (rejection probability when the CAPM is false, i.e., hopefully high) given by $1 - F_\delta(F_J^{-1}(1 - a))$. The true power of the Wald test is $1 - F_\delta(F_W^{-1}(1 - a)(T - N - 1)/(TN))$. Without normality of ε_t, the exact results are no longer valid, but W from (10.104) is still asymptotically χ^2_N under $\alpha = 0$, the CAPM null. Tests of the CAPM have been considered by Black, Jensen, and Scholes (1972), Jobson and Korkie (1985), and Gibbons, Ross, and Shanken (1989), among many others.

If the CAPM test rejects, it may not mean that the theory should be abandoned but just that the chosen proxy for the market portfolio is poor. This is Roll's (1977) critique of the asset-pricing theory's tests. Thus, a joint hypothesis of the theory and validity of the proxy is being tested. In principle, the market portfolio should contain all the assets in the world, but in practice the upshot is that the mean-variance efficiency of the chosen proxy relative to the N stocks in the data set is tested. A related problem is that tests of any model must be viewed as joint tests of the theory in question and the additional assumptions imposed in order to implement the empirical model.

The idea in the CAPM is that it is the contribution to market risk that matters for pricing of the individual asset, and hence the market portfolio and no other explanatory variables enter (10.98). Sometimes a good statistical model of returns may be obtained by including other, perhaps multiple, factors. A general linear factor model (LFM) is

$$R_t - r_t e = \alpha + Bf_t + \varepsilon_t, \tag{10.106}$$

where B is an $N \times K$ matrix of loadings on the K-vector of common return-generating factors f_t, $K < N$. The market model (10.98) is the special case $K = 1$, $f_t = r_{m,t} - r_t$. As an alternative to the equilibrium CAPM, the arbitrage pricing theory (APT) implies

$$E(R_t - r_t e) = B\eta, \tag{10.107}$$

where η is a K-vector of risk prices associated with the K factors. Thus, mean excess returns are spanned by the factor loadings. To see why this is necessary for the absence of arbitrage opportunities, consider first the simple case $\varepsilon_t = 0$ (all uncertainty is factor-related). Choose a portfolio c so that $c'B = 0$ (this is possible since $N > K$). From (10.106) the portfolio excess return is $c'(R_t - r_t e) = c'\alpha$ and hence riskless (deterministic). To avoid arbitrage opportunities, the portfolio excess return $c'\alpha$ must equal the excess return on r_t, the other riskless asset, which is clearly 0. It follows that $c'(R_t - r_t e) = 0$, and on taking expectation, $c'E(R_t - r_t e) = 0$. What happened in this argument was that $c'B = 0$ implied that also $c'E(R_t - r_t e) = 0$. By Farkas' lemma, (10.107) must then hold for some K-vector η. Intuitively, expected excess returns must be related to (spanned by) the columns of B if $c'E(R_t - r_t e) = 0$ is an implication of $c'B = 0$. For $\varepsilon_t \neq 0$, Ross (1976) derives an approximate version of (10.107) for $N \to \infty$. Since equilibrium implies the absence of arbitrage opportunities, the APT is in a sense more general than the CAPM, but it does require some amount of factor structure.

Consider the case where the factors in f_t are excess portfolio returns. An example is the CAPM, $f_t = r_{m,t} - r_t$. Without loss of generality, such a factor may be viewed as one of the entries in $R_t - r_t e$ in (10.106), and it must have unit loading on itself and zero on other factors. By (10.107), the η-coordinate corresponding to this factor is therefore the factor mean (the mean excess factor portfolio return). Again, the CAPM is the special case where the price of risk is the mean excess market return (the quantity of risk is β_i, and the risk premium is their product (10.100)). From (10.106), $E(R_t - r_t e) = \alpha + B E(f_t)$, and since now $\eta = E(f_t)$, the APT (10.107) implies $\alpha = 0$ in (10.106). As in the CAPM, zero intercepts are the key model implication. To test this in excess return data, consider the system (10.106) across time periods $t = 1, \ldots, T$. Again, regressors (now f_t) are common across the N equations, and N separate time series OLS regressions may be applied. This is a simple extension of the CAPM case; e.g., the Wald test of the APT null $H_0 : \alpha = 0$ given by

$$W = T \frac{\hat{\alpha}' \widehat{\textstyle\sum}^{-1} \hat{\alpha}}{1 + \hat{\eta}' \widehat{\textstyle\sum}_f^{-1} \hat{\eta}} \tag{10.108}$$

is asymptotically χ_N^2 as $T \to \infty$, with $\hat{\eta}$ and $\widehat{\Sigma}_f$ the sample mean and $K \times K$ variance matrix of the factors; i.e., $\eta' \Sigma_f^{-1} \eta$ is a generalized Sharpe ratio (return-risk trade-off). Since Ross' argument relied on $N \to \infty$ and showed that deviations from (10.107) were bounded in a suitable sense, but not necessarily zero, rejection using (10.108) does not imply rejection of the APT in general, only of the tightened version with equality in (10.107).

If the factors f_t are not asset (excess) returns but, e.g., macroeconomic factors thought to matter for returns, then the prices η of the factor risks need not equal the factor means. In this case, the linear factor model (LFM) (10.106) with the APT mean return restriction (10.107) imposed is

$$R_t - r_t e = B\theta + B f_t + \varepsilon_t, \qquad t = 1, \ldots, T, \tag{10.109}$$

where $\theta = \eta - E(f_t)$. The APT null is no longer of the form $\alpha = 0$, but $\alpha = B\theta$ for some K-vector θ. A natural way to test this is to estimate the unrestricted and restricted models (10.106), respectively (10.109), and perform a likelihood ratio test. This requires a distributional assumption, e.g., again $\varepsilon_t \sim N(0, \Sigma)$. In (10.109), the term $B\theta$ imposes cross-equation restrictions, so it cannot be estimated by equation-by-equation OLS. The cross-equation covariance through nondiagonal Σ will matter for the estimates of B and θ. But again, standard SUR is not the appropriate system approach, this time because of nonlinearity in parameters. Specifically, because of the product $B\theta$, the restricted model is in the quadratic-in-parameters class. A natural estimation method is maximization of the log likelihood for the $N \times T$ system once the distributional assumption has been adopted. The unrestricted LFM (10.106) can again be estimated using N separate OLS regressions, which is maximum likelihood (ML) for this system. The likelihood ratio (LR) test is asymptotically χ^2_{N-K} as $T \to \infty$ (there are N parameters in α and K parameters in θ). If the test fails to reject, the risk prices may be estimated as

$$\hat{\eta} = \hat{\theta} + \bar{f}, \tag{10.110}$$

with $\hat{\theta}$ the MLE from the restricted APT model and $\bar{f} = \Sigma^T_{t=1} f_t / T$ the factor sample means. Note that a factor may happen not to be priced (η-coordinate 0), even if it is covariance-generating (the associated column in B is nonzero).

From (10.110), judging the significance of the risk prices is based on standard errors that involve the variance matrices of both $\hat{\theta}$ and the factor means, and possibly the covariance between these two vectors. Shanken (1992) in related models studies situations where this covariance is zero, so the standard errors of the factor averages provide lower bounds on the standard errors of the risk prices. He also presents conditions under which equally efficient estimates of risk prices are obtained by a two-step method, first regressing excess returns on factors to estimate loadings (this is the unrestricted model above), then as motivated by (10.107) regressing average excess returns on estimated loadings to get at the risk prices. Two-step procedures of this kind were originally introduced by Fama and MacBeth (1973).

Chen, Roll, and Ross (1986) use observed macroeconomic factors as suggested above, whereas Roll and Ross (1980) instead estimate loadings using the classical factor analysis with unobserved factors. In this case, risk prices may again be estimated based on (10.107) by regressing average excess returns on the estimated factor loadings that are now exclusively extracted from the variance-covariance matrix of excess returns. However, under the APT null (10.107) average excess returns are informative about the loadings B, too, and Christensen (1994) shows that Shanken's result on the efficiency of the two-step approach does not carry over to this case with unobservable factors. Christensen (1994) shows that the estimated factor loadings and risk prices are strictly more efficient in a one-step procedure imposing the APT restriction from the outset and that, indeed, the efficiently estimated factor loadings depend on a certain weighted average of the variance-covariance matrix and the outer product of the vector of sample averages of excess returns, with strictly more weight on the sample mean returns than the variance-covariance matrix used in the classical factor analysis. This illustrates the interplay between the economic theory and statistical inference, here revolving around cross-restrictions on first and second moments under the null.

10.8.3 Time-Varying Volatility

The portfolio models (the CAPM and the APT) are aimed at explaining the cross section of expected stock returns, but the above methods do not account for the common finding that conditional return variances (and covariances) are time-varying and tend to cluster in time. To capture the observed serial correlation in second moments, Engle (1982) introduced the autoregressive conditionally heteroskedastic (ARCH) model,

$$\sigma_t^2 = w + \alpha(L)u_t^2, \tag{10.111}$$

where u_t is a suitably demeaned return, σ_t^2 is the conditional variance of u_{t+1}, given information through t, and $\alpha(L) = \Sigma_{i=0}^{q-1}\alpha_i L^i$ is a polynomial in the lag operator L (defined by $Lu_t^2 = u_{t-1}^2$). The parameters w and α_i must be non-negative to ensure $\sigma_t^2 \geq 0$. Since

$$u_{t+1}^2 = \sigma_t^2 + u_{t+1}^2 - \sigma_t^2$$

$$= w + \sum_{i=0}^{q-1}\alpha_i u_{t-i}^2 + (u_{t+1}^2 - \sigma_t^2), \tag{10.112}$$

where $E_t(u_{t+1}^2 - \sigma_t^2) = 0$, it is seen that u_t^2 follows a qth-order autoregressive or $\mathrm{AR}(q)$ model, and the $\mathrm{ARCH}(q)$ model may be estimated by regressing the squared return on its first q lags. Improvements on this can be made, accounting for the fact that the error term $u_{t+1}^2 - \sigma_t^2$ is conditionally heteroskedastic (like the returns u_{t+1}).

Bollerslev (1986) introduced the generalized ARCH (GARCH) model,

$$\sigma_t^2 = w + \beta(L)\sigma_{t-1}^2 + \alpha(L)u_t^2, \tag{10.113}$$

where $\mathrm{GARCH}(p,q)$ has $\beta(L) = \Sigma_{i=0}^{p-1}\beta_i L^i$. This may be parsimonious relative to a high-order $\mathrm{ARCH}(q)$. Again, w, α_i, and β_i non-negative guarantee $\sigma_t^2 \geq 0$. Similarly to before,

$$u_{t+1}^2 = \sigma_t^2 + u_{t+1}^2 - \sigma_t^2$$
$$= w + \beta(L)\sigma_{t-1}^2 + \alpha(L)u_t^2 + (u_{t+1}^2 - \sigma_t^2)$$
$$= w + (\alpha(L) + \beta(L))u_t^2 + (u_{t+1}^2 - \sigma_t^2) - \beta(L)(u_t^2 - \sigma_{t-1}^2),$$
$$\tag{10.114}$$

so u_t^2 follows an autoregressive moving average (ARMA) process of order $(m, p+1)$, $m = \max\{p, q\}$, with autoregressive polynomial $\alpha + \beta$, error terms $u_t^2 - \sigma_{t-1}^2$, and a moving average polynomial with coefficients $1, -\beta_0, \ldots, -\beta_{p-1}$. We may also rewrite (10.113) as

$$\sigma_t^2 = w + (\alpha(L) + \beta(L))\sigma_{t-1}^2 + \alpha(L)(u_t^2 - \sigma_{t-1}^2), \tag{10.115}$$

showing that α governs the way squared return shocks enter conditional variances, whereas $\alpha + \beta$ measures the degree of persistence in volatility.

A common estimation procedure for both ARCH and GARCH is maximum likelihood, adopting a distributional assumption for normalized returns u_{t+1}/σ_t, e.g., $N(0, 1)$ or a t-distribution with low degrees of freedom. In the normal case, the log likelihood is (see (17.44) for the multivariate case)

$$\ell(w, \alpha, \beta) = -\frac{1}{2} \sum_{t=q}^{T-1} \left(\log(2\pi) + \log \sigma_t^2 + \frac{u_{t+1}^2}{\sigma_t^2} \right), \tag{10.116}$$

where the first $(q-1)$ squared returns are set aside to start the recursion on (10.111) or (10.113), and suitable values for the initial σ_t^2-terms are adopted, as well, e.g., a raw sample variance.

The portfolio models, the CAPM and the APT, suggest that expected returns may be related to second moments (covariances) in the cross section. With the models for time-varying volatility (ARCH, GARCH) in hand, it is natural to look for a risk-return relation in the time series dimension as well. One approach to this is the GARCH-in-mean (GARCH-M) model of Engle, Lilien, and Robins (1987), specifying

$$r_{t+1} = \gamma_0 + \gamma_1 \sigma_t^2 + u_{t+1}, \tag{10.117}$$

where still $\sigma_t^2 = \text{var}_t(u_{t+1})$ follows (10.111) or (10.113) and r_{t+1} is the return or interest rate subject to analysis. Thus, γ_1 measures the extent to which conditional variance matters for conditional expected return.

The original application of the GARCH-M model by Engle, Lilien, and Robins (1987) was to interest rate data, but applications to other markets are of financial interest, too, particularly the stock market, since the parameter γ_1 has an interpretation as the market price of risk. Empirical experience with GARCH models in general suggests that they fit better at a daily frequency than at longer, say, monthly or quarterly frequencies, particularly in the case of the stock market. Nevertheless, since the modeling of mean returns and the risk-return tradeoff (such as given by γ_1 in (10.117)) is of interest for longer-horizon returns, several GARCH-M applications have been to monthly data; e.g., Campbell and Hentschel (1992) introduce an asymmetric version geared to the monthly frequency.

Another possibility is to compute returns and volatilities using different frequencies; e.g., Merton (1980) studied the risk-return relation by running regressions of the form (10.117), with $(\ldots, r_t, r_{t+1}, \ldots)$ monthly returns and σ_t^2 the *realized volatility* over the course of month $t+1$, computed as the sample variance of daily returns,

$$\sigma_t^2 = \frac{1}{m-1}\sum_{i=1}^{m}(r_{t,i} - \bar{r}_t)^2, \tag{10.118}$$

with m the number of daily returns $r_{t,i}$ during the month and $\bar{r}_t$ their average. For continuously compounding returns (log price differences), $r_{t+1} = \log(p_{t+1}) - \log(p_t)$ at the monthly frequency, and $r_{t,i} = \log(p_{t+i/m}) - \log(p_{t+(i-1)/m})$ are the equidistant intramonthly returns, with an obvious adjustment, e.g., in the case of daily price observations on weekdays but none over weekends and holidays. We have $r_{t+1} = \Sigma_i r_{t,i}$ and, in particular, $\bar{r}_t = r_{t+1}/m$. Merton (1980) investigated whether σ_t or some other transformation should replace σ_t^2 in the regression (10.117) and was able to relate γ_1 to the average rate of relative risk aversion of individual investors (see exercise 2 in chapter 1)

This realized volatility approach has continued to develop. French, Schwert, and Stambaugh (1987) and Schwert (1989) explicitly consider the monthly time series $\{\sigma_t^2\}$, with each element calculated from intramonthly returns as in (10.118). Poterba and Summers (1986) model monthly realized volatility as an AR(1) process,

$$\sigma_t^2 = \rho_0 + \rho_1 \sigma_{t-1}^2 + v_t, \tag{10.119}$$

the same process which by (10.112) squared monthly returns should follow to be consistent with an ARCH(1) model for monthly returns, and they derive the elasticity of changes in the level of the stock market with respect to changes in volatility stemming from this specification. Christensen and Nielsen (2007) consider the bivariate system arising from the combination of (10.117) and (10.119),

$$r_{t+1} = \gamma_0 + \gamma_1 \sigma_t^2 + u_{t+1}, \tag{10.120}$$

$$\sigma_t^2 = \rho_0 + \rho_1 \sigma_{t-1}^2 + v_t. \tag{10.121}$$

Writing $x_{t+1} = (r_{t+1}, \sigma_t^2)'$ and $w_{t+1} = (u_{t+1}, v_t)'$, the system is

$$x_{t+1} = \mu + Ax_t + w_{t+1}, \tag{10.122}$$

with six parameters in (μ, A) and three in $\Omega_{t+1} = \text{var}_t(w_{t+1})$ in the unrestricted reduced form. By inserting (10.121) in (10.120), it is seen that

$$\mu = \begin{pmatrix} \gamma_0 + \gamma_1 \rho_0 \\ \rho_0 \end{pmatrix}, \tag{10.123}$$

$$A = \begin{pmatrix} 0 & \gamma_1 \rho_1 \\ 0 & \rho_1 \end{pmatrix}, \qquad (10.124)$$

so the structure imposes two testable restrictions on the system. Also, even if treating $\Omega_{t+1} = \Omega$ as a constant and taking $\text{cov}(u_{t+1}, v_t) = 0$, uncorrelated errors in returns and volatilities, we have

$$\Omega = \begin{pmatrix} \sigma_u^2 + \gamma_1^2 \sigma_v^2 & \gamma_1^2 \sigma_v^2 \\ \gamma_1^2 \sigma_v^2 & \sigma_v^2 \end{pmatrix}, \qquad (10.125)$$

with two additional free parameters, so the structure places one more restriction on Ω (for a total of three on the model), and the system errors are correlated ($\gamma_1^2 \sigma_v^2 \neq 0$) even if the errors in (10.120) and (10.121) are not, i.e., if $\text{cov}(u_{t+1}, v_t) = 0$. Christensen and Nielsen (2007) use estimated realized volatilities σ_t^2 from higher than daily frequency (namely, 5-minute intradaily) returns, as well as implied volatilities backed out from option prices, and consider also specifications with $\text{cov}(u_{t+1}, v_t) \neq 0$. Since σ_t^2 should provide an estimate of $\text{var}_t(u_{t+1})$, $\mathcal{F}_t$-measurable in particular if implied volatilities from options sampled at t are used to estimate σ_t^2, this could be entered into Ω_{t+1}. Taking instead Ω as constant allows treatment of the model (10.122) as a bivariate vector ARMA (VARMA) system and testing the theory restrictions in a straightforward manner, at the loss of some statistical efficiency. Further properties and uses of implied volatility and realized volatility are covered in a continuous-time framework in chapter 14.

Christensen and Nielsen (2007) generalize the model (10.122) to allow for long-memory (fractional integration) in volatility, which was shown to be emprically relevant by Andersen et al. (2003), and for the financial *leverage effect* of Black (1976), i.e., drops in stock price (increases in the debt-equity ratio) are followed by increases in expected risk, and they derive the implications of these generalizations for the relation between volatility and the level of the stock market.

10.8.4 Term Structure Analysis

Consider next the expectations hypothesis (10.18) on the term structure of interest rates, now for empirical testing sharpened to

$$r_{t,k} = \frac{1}{k} \sum_{i=1}^{k} E_t r_{t+i}, \qquad (10.126)$$

with $r_{t,k}$ the yield of maturity k prevailing at t, i.e., the yield on a k-period zero-coupon (discount) bond at t, and r_{t+i} the short rate realized at $t + i$. After one period, at $t + 1$, the k-period discount bond has turned into a

$(k-1)$-period discount bond with yield $r_{t+1,k-1}$. We calculate

$$E_t((k-1)r_{t+1,k-1}-kr_{t,k}) = E_t\left(\sum_{i=2}^{k}r_{t+i} - \sum_{i=1}^{k}r_{t+i}\right) = -r_{t+1}, \quad (10.127)$$

as the short rate is riskless. Hence,

$$(k-1)E_t(r_{t+1,k-1} - r_{t,k}) = r_{t,k} - r_{t+1}, \quad (10.128)$$

which is the maturity k yield spread at t. This is now seen to give the best forecast of $r_{t+1,k-1} - r_{t,k}$, the change in the long (k-period) rate, under the expectations hypothesis. To test this implication, form the long-rate change yield spread regression

$$r_{t+1,k-1} - r_{t,k} = \alpha_k + \beta_k\frac{r_{t,k} - r_{t+1}}{k-1} + v_{t+1}, \quad (10.129)$$

$t = 1, \ldots, T-1$, a time series OLS regression. The null to be tested is H_0: $\beta_k = 1$. This may be repeated for each maturity k.

For further implications of (10.18), note that $r_{t+k} + r_{t+k-1} + \cdots + r_{t+1}$ may be rewritten as $(r_{t+k}-r_{t+k-1})+2(r_{t+k-1}-r_{t+k-2})+\cdots+(k-1)(r_{t+2}-r_{t+1}) + kr_{t+1}$, so (10.18) is

$$r_{t,k} = E_t\frac{1}{k}\sum_{i=1}^{k}(k-i)(r_{t+i+1} - r_{t+i}) + r_{t+1}. \quad (10.130)$$

Let $\Delta r_t = r_{t+1} - r_t$ denote the short-rate change and define

$$y_{t+1,k} = \sum_{i=1}^{k-1}\left(1 - \frac{i}{k}\right)\Delta r_{t+i}, \quad (10.131)$$

a certain measure of weighted average future short-rate changes from $t+1$ through $t+k$, with more weight on earlier changes. Then by (10.130) the k-period spread is the best forecast of this, too, under the expectations hypothesis. To test, regress future short-rate changes on the spread,

$$y_{t+1,k} = \gamma_k + \delta_k(r_{t,k} - r_{t+1}) + w_{t+1}, \quad (10.132)$$

again a time series regression, $t = 1, \ldots, T-k$. In this case, though, there is $MA(k-1)$ structure in w_{t+1}, because of the overlap in intervals covered by $y_{t+1,k}$, and this should be corrected for. The null is again unit slope, H_0: $\delta_k = 1$, which may be inspected for each maturity k.

Thus, what is being tested is the predictive power of the term structure of interest rates. For example, an upward-sloping yield curve should predict both a shift up in long rates over the short term by (10.129) and increases in short rates over a longer term by (10.132).

The need for $MA(k-1)$ correction in the short-rate change regression may be circumvented using a system analysis due to Campbell and Shiller (1987, 1991). Thus, let

$$z_t = \begin{pmatrix} \Delta r_t \\ r_{t,k} - r_{t+1} \end{pmatrix} \qquad (10.133)$$

and assume z_t is measured in deviations from time series averages. Assume a vector autoregressive (VAR) system of order 1,

$$z_t = A z_{t-1} + \varepsilon_t, \qquad (10.134)$$

with ε_t serially uncorrelated, if necessary by including lags,

$$z_t = (\Delta r_t, \ldots, \Delta r_{t-p}, r_{t,k} - r_{t+1}, \ldots, r_{t-p,k} - r_{t-p+1})'. \qquad (10.135)$$

In the VAR(1) system,

$$E_t(z_{t+i}) = A^i z_t. \qquad (10.136)$$

Let $e_1 = (1, 0)'$ and $e_2 = (0, 1)'$ denote the unit vectors (focusing for presentation purposes on the simple case $p = 0$). The yield spread–short rate change relation (10.130)–(10.131) is then

$$
\begin{aligned}
e_2' z_t &= \sum_{i=1}^{k-1} \left(1 - \frac{i}{k} \right) e_1' A^i z_t \\
&= e_1' A \left(I_2 - \frac{1}{k} (I_2 - A^k)(I_2 - A)^{-1} \right) (I_2 - A)^{-1} z_t,
\end{aligned}
\qquad (10.137)
$$

with I_2 the identity on $\mathbb{R}^2$. Since this holds for all z_t, it implies the two testable restrictions

$$e_2' - e_1' A \left(I_2 - \frac{1}{k} (I_2 - A^k)(I_2 - A)^{-1} \right) (I_2 - A)^{-1} = 0 \qquad (10.138)$$

on the VAR(1) system. These may be tested using LR or nonlinear Wald tests.

The discussion has assumed that a zero-coupon term structure or yield curve is available in each time period. That is, for each t, the zero-coupon yields $r_{t,k}$, $k = 1, 2, \ldots$, are in the data set. Equivalently, from $(1 + r_{t,k})^k = 1/B_{t,k}$ (see (10.15)), a complete set of zero-coupon bond prices $B_{t,k}$, $k = 1, 2, \ldots$, is available for each t. In practice, these prices, also known as the *discount function*, must be estimated from available data at t, which typically consist of prices of a number of traded coupon bonds. Assume that the ith coupon bond observed at time t pays a constant coupon $d(i) > 0$ each period until maturity at $t + k(i)$, when in addition the face value of 1 is paid.

The bond trades for $B_t^c(i)$ at t. Viewing the coupon bond as a portfolio of zero-coupon bonds, it should hold by no arbitrage (see (10.20)) that

$$B_t^c(i) = d(i) \sum_{j=1}^{k(i)} B_{t,j} + B_{t,k(i)}. \qquad (10.139)$$

In principle, this should be for all coupon bonds $i = 1, \ldots, N_t$, say. The data set at t is then of the type $\{(B_t^c(i), d(i), k(i))\}_{i=1}^{N_t}$, where $B_t^c(i)$ is the market price of bond i prevailing at t and $(d(i), k(i))$ are associated contractual characteristics. The estimation problem is to determine $\{B_{t,j}\}_{j=1}^{k_{max}}$, the discount function at t or, by implication, $\{r_{t,j}\}_{j=1}^{k_{max}}$, the term structure of interest rates. Here, $k_{max} = \max_i\{k(i)\}$, the maximum maturity across bonds actually traded at t.

Consider first the simplest possible case where the indices $i = 1, \ldots, N_t$ may be rearranged so that $k(i) = i, i = 1, \ldots, N_t$. In this case, $k_{max} = N_t$. There is exactly one bond of each maturity of interest. Clearly then, $B_t^c(1) = (d(1) + 1)B_{t,1}$, from which the first discount bond price is determined,

$$B_{t,1} = \frac{B_t^c(1)}{d(1) + 1}. \qquad (10.140)$$

Working through the system (10.139) recursively, we find

$$B_{t,i} = \frac{B_t^c(i) - d(i) \sum_{j=1}^{i-1} B_{t,j}}{d(i) + 1} \qquad (10.141)$$

for $i = 2, \ldots, N_t$. The term structure of interest rates at t has been estimated from available data.

The simplest case does not cover all situations arising in practice. Suppose $N_t > k_{max}$; i.e., there are more bonds than terms to maturity in data, so some bonds necessarily have the same maturity date although different coupons. In general, no term structure $\{B_{t,j}\}_{j=1}^{k_{max}}$ will match all observed bond prices exactly. This suggests the cross-sectional regression approach

$$B_t^c(i) = d(i) \sum_{j=1}^{k(i)} B_{t,j} + B_{t,k(i)} + \varepsilon_t(i) \qquad (10.142)$$

for $i = 1, \ldots, N_t$. This may be rearranged as

$$B_t^c(i) = x(i)\beta_t + \varepsilon_t(i) \qquad (10.143)$$

for $i = 1, \ldots, N_t$. Here, β_t is a vector of regression coefficients to be estimated, of dimension k_{max}, the jth component giving the hypothetical discount bond price $B_{t,j}$. The regression errors are $\varepsilon_t(1), \ldots, \varepsilon_t(N_t)$.

The vector of regressors $x(i) = \{x(i, j)\}_{j=1}^{k_{\max}}$ is defined from contractual terms as $x(i, j) = d(i)$ if $j < k(i)$ (bond i is still on the run at $t + j$), $x(i, k(i)) = d(i) + 1$ (cash flow at maturity), and $x(i, j) = 0$ if $j > k(i)$ (the bond will mature before $t + j$). It is natural to estimate the term structure of interest rates β_t by OLS in (10.143). If it is thought that some bond prices $B_t^c(i)$ are much more precisely determined in the marketplace than others (e.g., trading volume is much higher and hence the variance of $\varepsilon_t(i)$ is lower), a weighted (e.g., by trading volume) regression may be preferred.

In practical applications, what usually happens is in fact the opposite: $N_t < k_{\max}$. That is, there are fewer bonds in the data set at time t than number of points (terms to maturity j) for which the discount function $B_{t,j}$ is sought. In this case, it is natural to parametrize the discount function, say, as $B_{t,j} = D(\theta_t, j)$, where θ_t is a parameter to be estimated, of dimension $k_\theta < N_t$. The cross-sectional regression equation is now

$$B_t^c(i) = \sum_{j=1}^{k_{\max}} x(i, j) D(\theta_t, j) + \varepsilon_t(i) \qquad (10.144)$$

for $i = 1, \ldots, N_t$. Thus, in each period t, a parameter $\hat{\theta}_t$ is estimated, and the term structure of interest rates at t is upon estimation given by $\hat{B}_{t,j} = D(\hat{\theta}_t, j)$ and $\hat{r}_{t,j} = 1/\hat{B}_{t,j}^{1/j} - 1$. The cross-sectional regression across coupon bonds traded at t may be linear or nonlinear, depending on the assumed functional form of $D(\theta_t, j)$. If $D(\theta_t, j) = 1 + \Sigma_{k=1}^{k_\theta} \theta_{t,k} s_k(j)$, where the $s_k(\cdot)$ are known functions, then the regression is linear,

$$B_t^c(i) = \sum_{j=1}^{k_{\max}} x(i, j) \left(1 + \sum_{k=1}^{k_\theta} \theta_{t,k} s_k(j) \right) + \varepsilon_t(i)$$

$$= x(i) 1_{k_{\max}} + \sum_{k=1}^{k_\theta} \theta_{t,k} \sum_{j=1}^{k_{\max}} x(i, j) s_k(j) + \varepsilon_t(i) \qquad (10.145)$$

for $i = 1, \ldots, N_t$, where $1_{k_{\max}}$ is a vector of ones, of dimension $k_{\max}$, the number of points where the yield curve is to be assessed. The equation may be rewritten, defining $y_t(i) = B_t^c(i) - x(i) 1_{k_{\max}}$ and $z(i, k) = \Sigma_{j=1}^{k_{\max}} x(i, j) s_k(j)$, as

$$y_t(i) = \sum_{k=1}^{k_\theta} \theta_{t,k} z(i, k) + \varepsilon_t(i) \qquad (10.146)$$

for $i = 1, \ldots, N_t$, which is estimated by OLS or weighted linear regression.

The reason for making the parametrized discount function $D(\theta_t, j)$ affine rather than linear in θ_t is that if $s_k(0) = 0$ then the specification ensures $D(\theta_t, 0) = 1$; i.e., the discount function starts at 1 for maturity 0 (cash currently in hand is not discounted). A simple example of suitable functions $s_k(\cdot)$ is polynomials, $s_k(j) = j^k$. McCulloch (1971, 1975) instead uses spline functions. In the case of a cubic spline, the $s_k(\cdot)$ functions determine a separate third-order polynomial over each of a number of intervals for j, typically about five intervals, and the coefficients $\theta_{t,k}$ are restricted to ensure that the discount function $D(\theta_t, j)$ is continuous and once differentiable in maturity j where the intervals meet.

It is natural to require that the discount function be downward sloping in j, corresponding to positive interest rates. This may be more easily imposed by parametrizing the yield curve directly instead of the discount function, i.e., $r_{t,j} = r(\theta_t, j)$, for a suitable non-negative function $r(\cdot, \cdot)$. In this case, the regression

$$B_t^c(i) = \sum_{j=1}^{k_{\max}} \frac{x(i, j)}{(1 + r(\theta_t, j))^j} + \varepsilon_t(i) \tag{10.147}$$

for $i = 1, \ldots, N_t$, is nonlinear. Again, upon estimation of $\hat{\theta}_t$, a full yield curve $\{\hat{r}_{t,j}\}_j$ is available in period t, with $\hat{r}_{t,j} = r(\hat{\theta}_t, j)$. When the regression has been implemented for each t, a full panel of interest rates results of the type used to study the forecasting power of interest rates in the foregoing.

A classical example of specification of a flexible functional form for the yield curve $r(\theta_t, j)$ is that of Nelson and Siegel (1987). Expressing this in terms of the continuously compounding yields $y(\theta_t, j)$ defined by $B_{t,j} = \exp(-jy(\theta_t, j))$ rather than the effective yields $r(\theta_t, j)$, the Nelson-Siegel yield curve is

$$y(\theta_t, j) = \theta_{t,1} + \theta_{t,2} \frac{1 - e^{-j\theta_{t,4}}}{j\theta_{t,4}} + \theta_{t,3} \frac{1 - (1 + j\theta_{t,4})e^{-j\theta_{t,4}}}{j\theta_{t,4}^2}, \tag{10.148}$$

viewed as a function of term to maturity j. By the convexity of the exponential function, $\exp(x) \geq 1 + x$, the yields are clearly non-negative for $\theta_t \geq 0$, although this condition is not necessary. Note that $k_\theta = 4$ in this case. The regression at time t is now

$$B_t^c(i) = \sum_{j=1}^{k_{\max}} x(i, j) e^{-jy(\theta_t, j)} + \varepsilon_t(i), \tag{10.149}$$

i.e., a nonlinear regression for determining $\hat{\theta}_t$. The Nelson-Siegel curve has the level, slope, and curvature features found by Litterman and Scheinkman (1991) to be characteristic for observed yield curves. In particular, $\theta_{t,1}$ is a level parameter. The factor multiplying $\theta_{t,2}$ in (10.148) is downward sloping, so a negative value for the slope parameter $\theta_{t,2}$ helps generate the common upward-sloping yield curve shape, and the other parameters (including the level parameter $\theta_{t,1}$) can adjust to guarantee positive yields in the relevant domain. The factor multiplying $\theta_{t,3}$ is hump-shaped, reaching an interior maximum and with a positive slope for small j and a negative slope for large j. Thus, $\theta_{t,3}$ is a curvature parameter, and $\theta_{t,4}$ an additional shape parameter. The Nelson-Siegel curve is heavily used, e.g., by many central banks.

One problem that arises with the Nelson-Siegel curve is that it is not consistent with arbitrage-free term structure movements across calendar time t. Thus, if interest rates are of the form $y(\theta_t, j)$ for each t, then no matter how the sequence θ_t is chosen, there exist arbitrage opportunities. This is shown by Björk and Christensen (1999). They consider yield curves moving over time in a completely general fashion, as in Heath, Jarrow, and Morton (1992). The latter paper shows that in the absence of arbitrage opportunities, the stochastic process of yield curves is characterized by the volatilities of yields and risk premia. Björk and Christensen (1999) derive necessary and sufficient conditions for a yield curve shape (a parameterized functional form) to be consistent with a given volatility function and risk premium specification, in the sense that the yield curve is of the specified shape on each date t (for some parameter value θ_t) and the dynamics are those given by the volatility function and risk premium. The conditions imply that if at any point in time t the yield curve is of the Nelson-Siegel shape $y(\theta_t, j)$ then it is not possible to specify a dynamic structure (yield volatilities and risk premia) such that the resulting future yield curves take the Nelson-Siegel form $y(\theta_s, j)$ no matter how the θ_s are allowed to vary for $s > t$. As modern term structure models are characterized by the volatility function—e.g., the Vasicek (1977) model is the one where the short rate has constant volatility, and the Cox, Ingersoll, and Ross (1985b) model is the one where volatility is proportional to the square root of the short rate—the result is bad news for the Nelson-Siegel curve shape. It is inconsistent with all term structure models.

Björk and Christensen (1999) also show that a slight augmentation of (10.148),

$$y(\theta_t, j) = \theta_{t,1} + \theta_{t,2} \frac{1 - e^{-j\theta_{t,4}}}{j\theta_{t,4}} + \theta_{t,3} \frac{1 - (1 + j\theta_{t,4})e^{-j\theta_{t,4}}}{j\theta_{t,4}^2}$$

$$+ \theta_{t,5} \frac{1 - e^{-2j\theta_{t,4}}}{2j\theta_{t,4}}, \tag{10.150}$$

is sufficient to make the resulting curve shape consistent with an arbitrage-free term structure model, namely, the extended Vasicek or Hull and White (1990) model. Note that now $k_\theta = 5$, and the new parameter $\theta_{t,5}$ is an additional slope parameter (i.e., there are two slope factors with different steepness and possibly different sign). The augmented Nelson-Siegel model (10.150) is again fit by the nonlinear regression (10.149). This approach avoids the problem with arbitrage opportunities in the Nelson-Siegel curve.

10.9 EXERCISES

1. Farkas' lemma asserts that either there exists an $x \geq 0$ such that $Ax = b$ or there exists a y such that $y'A \leq 0$ and $y'b > 0$. Interpret A as a matrix whose columns are assets, rows are states of the world, and elements are net returns relative to the risk-free rate. Use Farkas' lemma to show that the absence of arbitrage opportunities implies that there exists a distribution such that all assets have an expected net return (i.e., a return in excess of the risk-free rate) of zero. Further, if markets are complete (the rank of A is equal to the number of states), then the distribution is unique. *Hint:* note that long and short positions are included by considering the matrix $[A, -A]$.

2. From the first order condition (10.102), derive the N-dimensional control c (the optimal stock portfolio holdings). How much is held in the riskless asset?

3. Use (10.110) to show that a lower variance bound on the estimated price of risk is given by the factor variance divided by the number of time periods in the sample.

10.10 REFERENCES

Harrison and Kreps (1979) and Harrison and Pliska (1981) are standard references on the equivalences between the absence of arbitrage opportunities and the existence of an equivalent martingale measure and between the uniqueness of this measure and market completeness. Market efficiency was studied by Fama (1970). An early theoretical and empirical investigation of stocks, bonds, and interest rates was that by Macaulay (1938), who defined the duration of a bond. Meiselman (1962) used these ideas to study the term structure of interest rates (the yield curve) and the expectations hypothesis. Keynes (1930) used negative hedging pressure from producers to explain backwardation in forward markets, and Kaldor (1939) studied convenience yields in a theory of storage. Cox, Ingersoll, and Ross (1981) analyzed the relation between forward prices and futures prices, including conditions for equivalence. Schwartz (1997) considers mean reversion in commodity prices and the implications for associated forward and futures prices. Options are considered further in chapter 11, and continuous-time models in chapter 14. Throughout this chapter we have listed some, but far from all, of the relevant references for this rapidly growing literature.

Chapter Eleven

Financial Options

11.1 INTRODUCTION

In this chapter, we continue financial options begun in section 10.6. Along with job search models, option models are among the most important applications of optimal stopping in economics. An option of the American call type is a contract that in each time period gives the owner the right (although not the obligation) to buy a share of a specified asset or commodity (henceforth "the underlying") for a specified price, namely, the exercise price x, say, regardless of the going market price. Needless to say, the holder will not exercise the option (i.e., buy the underlying) if x exceeds the market price, since in this case it would be cheaper simply to purchase the asset or commodity in question without invoking the option contract. Also, if the option has been exercised once, it may not be exercised again in future time periods, so the timing of exercise is an optimal stopping problem.

We establish a close link (indeed, equivalence under regularity conditions) between the job search (chapters 7–9) and option models. The equivalence concerns the respective economic models, but we go further and demonstrate an important efficiency advantage in the option case. The efficiency gain results from the use of price data, which are typically available in the options application. An analogous (although not equivalent) data structure in the job search case would allow observation of declined wage offers.

11.2 FINANCIAL OPTION EXERCISE AND JOB SEARCH

The value of the option to buy the underlying good for x is

$$W(s) = \max\{s - x, \beta EW\}, \qquad (11.1)$$

where s is the current market price of the underlying good. We first consider the case of a nondurable commodity and then return to the case of a storable underlying asset below. Assume s is distributed independently over time according to the exponential distribution, with density $f(s) = \gamma e^{-\gamma s}$, $s > 0$. We may now compare the option-pricing model with the job search model of chapter 7. In particular, if we set the exercise or strike price x of the option equal to the unemployment insurance benefits net of search costs y from chapter 7, then the value functions are related as in

$$W = (1 - \beta) V - x. \tag{11.2}$$

From (11.1), the option should be exercised if and only if s exceeds the optimal *exercise boundary* or reservation price

$$s^r = x + \beta E W, \tag{11.3}$$

and if (11.2) is inserted in (11.3), then s^r coincides with the reservation wage (7.2). That is, options are exercised at the same level at which wage offers are accepted in the search model. This is a remarkable fact. Hence, we state it as a theorem.

THEOREM 8 *Consider the search model with unemployment insurance benefits net of search costs y and offer probability $p = 1$ each period, and consider also the option-pricing model with exercise price x. Suppose the discount factor β is common to both models and that $x = y$. Then we have the following:*

(i) The optimal policies (continuation regions) in the two models coincide; i.e., $w_r = s^r$.

(ii) The value functions are related as in (11.2).

(iii) With the prototypal specification (7.9), the reservation prices may be computed by iterating the contraction (7.13).

Proof. See the derivation related to (11.1)–(11.3).   □

The reason for the difference in value functions is that s measures a stock and w a flow. Also, since the option can be exercised any time, $p = 1$ in the present case. Of course, the particular distributional assumption is not needed for the theorem, except for (iii).

Turning to the inference issue, the exercise price x is contractually specified and part of the data in the option case. The unknown parameters to be estimated are γ and β; i.e., the above contraction determines a function $s^r(\gamma, \beta)$. With data $s = (s_1, \ldots, s_N)$ on the prices at which options on N independent commodities were exercised, the results from (7.15), (7.16), and (7.17) carry over, replacing wages by the prices of the underlying. In particular, the exact distribution of the maximum likelihood estimator (MLE) in the option case is given by proposition 8.3.1, with $p = 1$, $y = x$, and w_r replaced by s^r.

It is reasonable to assume that the N underlying distributions differ. Unobserved heterogeneity may be entered by letting $\gamma \sim \exp(\alpha)$ for $\alpha > 0$.

In this case, $\theta = (\alpha, \beta)$, and (8.18) is replaced by the option model likelihood function

$$p(s; \theta) = \prod_{i=1}^{N} \int_{(s^r)_\gamma^{-1}(s_i,\beta)}^{\infty} \alpha\gamma e^{-\gamma(\alpha+s_i-s^r(\gamma,\beta))} \, d\gamma, \qquad (11.4)$$

where evidently sufficient statistics are lost. Even so, (11.4) does not allow dependence across commodities, and this may be important in applications. It is more useful in practice to move to a time series of options on the same underlying. In fact, infinitely lived options as above are not common. Typically, a new option is introduced at the beginning of each of a series of regularly spaced time intervals, say months, expires at the end of the month, and may be exercised any time during the month. This is an important difference between the types of data available in search applications (typically one unemployment spell per individual) and option applications. The second important difference is that declined wage offers are typically not observed in the search model, while the underlying price sequence is typically observed whether or not the option is exercised.

11.3 MULTIPLE FINITE-HORIZON OPTIONS

To analyze this situation, let W_k and s_k^r denote the value function and reservation price with k periods left to expiration. This is a finite-horizon, discrete control, continuous-state dynamic programming model (see chapter 6) that can be solved by backward recursion. At expiration, there is no expected future value, such as EW in (11.1), so

$$W_0(s) = \max \{s - x, 0\}, \qquad (11.5)$$

$$s_0^r = x, \qquad (11.6)$$

$$EW_0 = \int_x^\infty (s - x) f(s) ds = \frac{1}{\gamma} e^{-\gamma x}. \qquad (11.7)$$

Starting at $k = 0$, it is now possible to find the values and reservation prices of options with longer times to expiration ($k > 0$) iteratively, namely,

$$W_k(s) = \max \{s - x, \beta EW_{k-1}\}, \qquad (11.8)$$

$$s_k^r = x + \beta EW_{k-1}, \qquad (11.9)$$

$$EW_k = \int_{s_k^r}^{\infty} (s - x) f(s)ds + \beta EW_{k-1} P(s \le s_k^r)$$

$$= \frac{1}{\gamma} e^{-\gamma s_k^r} + \beta EW_{k-1} \left(1 - e^{-\gamma s_k^r}\right). \tag{11.10}$$

Note that the specific functional forms in (11.7) and (11.10) are based on the exponential distribution for prices, but that the expressions involving integrals and expectations are general.

Suppose that in each month $t, t = 1, \ldots, T$, we collect data on the day τ_t on which the option for that month was exercised, as well as the underlying price S_{t,τ_t} at which this occurred. The parameter is $\theta = (\gamma, \beta)$, and $\Theta = \mathbb{R}_+ \times (0, 1)$. If there are m_t trading days in month t, the likelihood or model function is

$$p(\tau, s; \theta) = \prod_{t=1}^{T} \gamma e^{-\gamma S_{t,\tau_t}} 1_{\{S_{t,\tau_t} \ge s_{m_t-\tau_t}^r (\gamma, \beta)\}} \prod_{u=1}^{\tau_t-1} \left(1 - e^{-\gamma s_{m_t-u}^r} (\gamma, \beta)\right)$$

$$\tag{11.11}$$

in analogy with (8.6). Note that in the numerical implementation, the value function $W_k(\cdot)$ in (11.8) need not be given a representation on the computer, since only the (scalar) reservation prices s_k^r are needed in (11.11), and they may be obtained for given parameter values by iterating on (11.9) and (11.10) only, not (11.8), and with initial conditions (11.6) and (11.7). As in (8.28), the dependence of the reservation prices on the discount factor is positive, but in the present nonstationary case, (11.9) and (11.10) are used to verify

$$\frac{\partial s_k^r}{\partial \beta} > 0 \tag{11.12}$$

for all $k > 0$. Instead of (8.29), the estimator of β is based on the first s_{t,τ_t} that fails to exceed $s_{m_t-\tau_t}^r (\gamma, \beta)$ as β is increased. If this happens in month u, say, then

$$\hat{\beta}_\gamma = \left(s_{m_{u(\gamma)}-\tau_{u(\gamma)}}^r\right)_\beta^{-1} \left(\gamma, s_{u(\gamma),\tau_{u(\gamma)}}\right). \tag{11.13}$$

The point here is that while the minimum order statistic w_m is entered in the stationary job search case (8.29), the nonstationarity in the option case makes the month u where the "relative minimum" underlying price (relative to the going exercise boundary) occurs vary with γ. Substitution of (11.13) in (11.11) produces an asymptotic profile likelihood function, and γ may be estimated, e.g., by line search, which is numerically straightforward.

The computational burden is in calculating the reservation prices from (11.9) and (11.10) and determining the relative minimum underlying prices for varying γ.

11.4 MARKOV STOCK PRICES

In practice, it is more realistic to assume a Markov process for the sequence of underlying prices. In particular, this is relevant when the underlying is a stock (or storable commodity) rather than a perishable commodity. With the above analysis in hand, it is seen immediately that (11.8)–(11.10) generalize to

$$W_k(s) = \max\{s - x, \beta E(W_{k-1}|s)\}, \tag{11.14}$$

$$s_k^r = x + \beta E(W_{k-1}|s_k^r), \tag{11.15}$$

$$E\left(W_k|s_{k+1}^r\right) = \int_{s_k^r}^{\infty} (s-x) f\left(s|s_{k+1}^r\right) ds + \beta \int_0^{s_k^r} E\left(W_{k-1}|s\right) f\left(s|s_{k+1}^r\right) ds, \tag{11.16}$$

where $f(\cdot|\cdot)$ is the Markov transition density. Here, (11.14) corresponds to (10.61), whereas (11.16) is more explicit and allows other numerical approaches than the binomial (10.73), e.g., direct integration or Monte Carlo methods. Again, the option-pricing problem is solved by iterating on (11.15) and (11.16), only, while the function in (11.14) need not be calculated. Specifically, starting at $k = 0$, (11.15) first implies $s_0^r = x$. Next, (11.16) gives $E(W_0|s_1^r)$ as a function of s_1^r. Iterating, for arbitrary $k \geq 0$, (11.15) uses the function $E(W_{k-1}|\cdot)$ produced in the previous step in the iterations and determines s_k^r as the fixed point of (11.15). Thus, s_k^r is a constant depending only on the parameters θ to be estimated. This way, a definite exercise boundary $\{s_k^r : k = 0, 1, \ldots\}$ is determined. In addition, in step k, (11.16) delivers the function $E(W_k|\cdot)$, using the value s_k^r already determined in (11.15) and the function $E(W_{k-1}|\cdot)$ from the previous step in the iteration.

The specification of f may be motivated by the continuous-time geometric Brownian motion

$$ds_t = \mu s_t \, dt + \sigma s_t \, dW_t, \tag{11.17}$$

an Itô stochastic differential equation driven by the standard Wiener process W_t. Here, μ is the drift parameter and σ is the volatility or diffusion parameter. The price process (11.17) is commonly used for share prices in the case of common stocks, stock indices, and so forth. In this case, ds_t/s_t is interpreted as the instantaneous stock return and μ as the mean return.

By Itô's lemma, the Euler approximation to the log price process corresponding to (11.17) is given by

$$p\left(\log s_{t+1} \mid \log s_t\right) = N(\log s_t + \gamma, \sigma^2),$$ (11.18)

where $\gamma = \mu - \frac{1}{2}\sigma^2$, so that in (11.16),

$$f(s \mid s') = \frac{1}{\sqrt{2\pi}\, s\sigma} e^{-\frac{1}{2\sigma^2}(\log(s/s') - \gamma)^2}.$$ (11.19)

This allows evaluating the first integral in (11.16) analytically; i.e.,

$$\int_{s_k^r}^{\infty} (s - x)\, f\left(s \mid s_{k+1}^r\right) ds = s_{k+1}^r e^{\mu} \Phi\left(d_k\right) - x \Phi\left(d_k - \sigma\right),$$ (11.20)

where Φ is the standard normal cumulative distribution function and

$$d_k = \frac{\log\left(s_{k+1}^r / s_k^r\right) + \gamma}{\sigma}.$$ (11.21)

   As an important special case, consider the situation when $k = 0$. As in (11.6), $s_0^r = x$. If the option cannot be exercised one period earlier, then by (11.14), $W_1(s) = \beta E(W_0 \mid s)$, which may be calculated from (11.20) and (11.21) with $s_k^r = x$ and $s_{k+1}^r = s$. If we assume $\beta e^{\mu} = 1$, i.e., the stock earns the discount rate $r = -\log(\beta)$ on average, then this amounts to

$$W_1(s) = s \Phi(d) - x e^{-r} \Phi(d - \sigma),$$ (11.22)

$$d = \frac{\log(s/x) + r + \frac{1}{2}\sigma^2}{\sigma},$$ (11.23)

which is the famous Black and Scholes (1973) and Merton (1973b) option-pricing formula originally derived in continuous time (see (14.58)). This applies to European call options, corresponding to the restriction that the option cannot be exercised before expiration. For general k and for American call options on commodities, which may indeed be exercised prior to expiration, we do not impose this restriction, but it is still useful to insert (11.20) and (11.21) into the iterations (11.14)–(11.16) to aid in computation. Furthermore, for American calls on non-dividend-paying stocks, the restriction of no early exercise may in fact be imposed without loss of generality (see chapter 6 for proof), so that (11.22) and (11.23) may be applied even to American claims in this case. The same does not hold when the underlying assets are commodities since a convenience yield (positive or negative) is associated with their storage, in effect corresponding to a dividend, and because their discounted price processes need not be martingales (chapters 6 and 10). The application of (11.22) and (11.23) to longer-term American calls on non-dividend-paying stocks may be accomplished by redefining the period length or multiplying r and σ^2 in the formula by k, provided it is known with certainty in advance that the stock will pay no dividends for the k periods until expiration.

A put option is a right to sell (rather than buy) the underlying for x. It may be optimal to exercise an American-style put even if the underlying pays no dividends before expiration of the put. The analog of (11.14) in the put case is hence

$$W_k^P(s) = \max\left\{x - s, \beta E\left(W_{k-1}^P|s\right)\right\},$$

and the put is exercised if and only if the share price drops below an appropriate exercise boundary, say $s_k^{r,P}$, when there are k periods left to expiration. The obvious analogs of (11.15) and (11.16) of course apply. Again, compared to (10.62), they utilize the Markovian structure and allow alternatives to the binomial approach (10.75), e.g., numerical integration or simulation. We may also adopt the additional distributional assumption (11.18) in the put case, and combination of the analogs of (11.15) and (11.16) and (11.20) and (11.21) now yields

$$s_k^{r,P} = x - \beta E\left(W_{k-1}^P|s_k^{r,P}\right),$$

$$E\left(W_k^P|s_{k+1}^{r,P}\right) = x\Phi\left(\sigma - d_k\right) - s_{k+1}^{r,P}e^r\Phi\left(-d_k\right)$$
$$+ \beta \int_{s_k^{r,P}}^{\infty} E\left(W_{k-1}^P|s\right) f\left(s|s_{k+1}^{r,P}\right) ds,$$

with d_k from (11.21), and $\gamma = r + \frac{1}{2}\sigma^2$. Thus, iteration on these two equations from $k = 0$ (initial condition $s_0^{r,P} = x$) until the relevant time to expiration produces the American put price under the Black-Scholes model (11.18), and under alternative distributional assumptions using the analogs of (11.15) and (11.16) for the put case instead. Letting the period length Δ shrink toward 0 and $k \to \infty$ such that $k\Delta$ equals the relevant term to expiration yields the Black-Scholes American put price as the limit

$$W_\infty^P(s) = \lim_{k\to\infty, \Delta\to 0} W_k^P(s), \qquad (11.24)$$

the closed-form expression for which has eluded the profession. However, the above recursion is quite explicit and readily implemented for trial parameter values θ.

We now take $\theta = (\gamma, \sigma, \beta) \in \Theta = \mathbb{R} \times \mathbb{R}_+ \times (0, 1)$ and label the resulting specification the prototypal option-pricing model. Instead of (11.11), the model function with complete underlying price data $s_{t,u}, u = 1, \ldots, m_t$

and exercise dates τ_t (namely, first hitting times for the stopping regions) for each month t in the present Markovian case is

$$
p(\tau, s; \theta) = \prod_{t=1}^{T} \left\{ \prod_{u=1}^{\tau_t - 1} f\left(s_{t,u}; \theta \mid s_{t,u-1}; s_{t,u} \leq s^r_{m_t - u}(\gamma, \sigma, \beta)\right) \right.
$$

$$
\times P\left(s_{t,u} \leq s^r_{m_t - u}(\gamma, \sigma, \beta); \theta \mid s_{t,u-1}\right) \Bigg\}
$$

$$
\times f\left(s_{t,\tau_t}; \theta \mid s_{t,\tau_t - 1}; s_{t,\tau_t} \geq s^r_{m_t - \tau_t}(\gamma, \sigma, \beta)\right)
$$

$$
\times P\left(s_{t,\tau_t} \geq s^r_{m_t - \tau_t}(\gamma, \sigma, \beta); \theta \mid s_{t,\tau_t - 1}\right) \prod_{v=t+1}^{m_t} f\left(s_{t,v}; \theta \mid s_{t,v-1}\right)
$$

$$
= \prod_{t=1}^{T} \left\{ \prod_{u=1}^{\tau_t - 1} f\left(s_{t,u}; \theta \times \mid s_{t,u-1}\right) 1_{\left\{ s_{t,u} \leq s^r_{m_t - u}(\gamma, \sigma, \beta) \right\}} \right\}
$$

$$
\times f(s_{t,\tau_t}; \theta \mid s_{t,\tau_t - 1}) 1_{\left\{ s_{t,\tau_t} \geq s^r_{m_t - \tau_t}(\gamma, \sigma, \beta) \right\}} \prod_{v=\tau_t+1}^{m_t} f(s_{t,v}; \theta \mid s_{t,v-1}),
$$

$$(11.25)$$

with f from (11.19), and the identification $s_{t,0} = s_{t-1,m_{t-1}}$. The model function for maximum likelihood estimation and inference has been stated for the case of call options, but the corresponding model function for put options is obtained by reversing all weak inequalities and replacing s^r by $s^{r,p}$ throughout. In either case, since s^r_k (respectively, $s^{r,p}_k$) varies with k, there are so many separate data-dependent constraints on the parameters that we get superconsistent estimation of all three subparameters in the prototypal option-pricing model, namely, $T^{1/2}(\hat{\theta} - \theta) \to 0$, almost surely, instead of a single superconsistent direction in the parameter space as in the stationary case (the prototypal job search model of chapter 7). This shows that the detailed optimal stopping modeling, including calculation of the reservation prices for given dates and parameters, is a powerful tool for extracting information from the data.

11.5 VALUE FUNCTIONS FOR AMERICAN OPTIONS

We now consider some theoretical and numerical properties of value functions for American options, in particular dimension reduction, characterization as Snell envelope, and computation by the simplex method. The result given in chapter 6 that the American call is never exercised early does not carry over to situations where the underlying asset is a dividend-paying stock, or a commodity whose storage is associated with a (positive or negative) convenience yield, and whose discounted price process need not be a martingale (chapters 6 and 10). Thus, we do not restrict attention to the case where early exercise is necessarily suboptimal. We saw that we achieved a simplification in the recursion (11.9)–(11.10) in the independent and identically distributed (i.i.d.) price case. The model with Markov prices does not admit a corresponding simplification in (11.15)–(11.16). Here, using the notation from sections 6.4 and 10.6, with p for the underlying and K for the exercise or strike price, we first illustrate the simple case where underlying prices follow a random walk:

$$p_t = p_{t-1} + \varepsilon_t, \tag{11.26}$$

where $\{\varepsilon_t\}$ is an i.i.d. sequence with density f. We suppress discounting, but, e.g., $E\varepsilon_t \neq 0$ may still imply that early exercise is optimal. Ultimately, we will have the price of the American call in the initial time period, say $t = 0$, represented as $V_0 = V_0(p_0)$, the value function for the dynamic program. This will be determined by backward recursion. Along the way we find the optimal policy of the agent holding the option. The value functions are again indexed by calendar date, as opposed to periods remaining, and T denotes the expiration date of the option.

In the ultimate time period T, the value is given as in (11.5) by

$$V_T(p_T) = \max\{p_T - K, 0\}. \tag{11.27}$$

Thus, the optimal policy is to exercise if $p_T > p_T^* = K$. In the penultimate period we similarly have

$$V_{T-1}(p_{T-1}) = \max\{p_{T-1} - K, E\left(V_T | p_{T-1}\right)\}, \tag{11.28}$$

and the optimal policy at $T - 1$ is to exercise the option if and only if

$$p_{T-1} > K + E\left(V_T | p_{T-1}\right). \tag{11.29}$$

This is now an implicit relation, in contrast to the case of i.i.d. prices (6.12) where there was no conditioning on the right hand side, so that the reservation price (the optimal exercise boundary) was given by $K + EV_T$. In the serially dependent case, we seek conditions ensuring the existence of a reservation price policy, so that optimal exercise occurs beyond a threshold level p_{T-1}^* satisfying the implicit equation

$$p_{T-1}^* = K + E\left(V_T | p_{T-1}^*\right). \tag{11.30}$$

The condition is that the graph of the map $p \to K + E(V_T | p)$ cuts the $45°$ line at a unique point—and from above. For this analysis, it is convenient to write out the implicit equation in more detail as

$$p_{T-1}^* = K + \int V_T(p_T) f(p_T - p_{T-1}^*) dp_T. \tag{11.31}$$

Combining with the optimal exercise policy at time T, we get

$$p^*_{T-1} = K + \int_K^\infty (p_T - K)f(p_T - p^*_{T-1})dp_T. \tag{11.32}$$

Continuing the recursion, we have

$$V_{T-2}(p_{T-2}) = \max\{p_{T-2} - K, E(V_{T-1}|p_{T-2})\}, \tag{11.33}$$

and the condition for optimal exercise is

$$p_{T-2} > K + E(V_{T-1}|p_{T-2}). \tag{11.34}$$

The associated implicit equation for the reservation price, if it exists, is

$$p^*_{T-2} = K + E(V_{T-1}|p^*_{T-2})$$
$$= K + \int_{p^*_{T-1}}^\infty (p_{T-1} - K)f(p_{T-1} - p^*_{T-2})dp_{T-1}$$
$$+ \int_{-\infty}^{p^*_{T-1}} E(V_T|p_{T-1})f(p_{T-1} - p^*_{T-2})dp_{T-1}. \tag{11.35}$$

This shows that to calculate p^*_{T-2} we need p^*_{T-1} from the previous iteration, as well as the map

$$p \to E(V_T|p) \tag{11.36}$$

on the domain $(-\infty, p^*_{T-1}]$. The general equation is

$$p^*_t = K + \int_{p^*_{t+1}}^\infty (p - K)f(p - p^*_t)dp + \int_{-\infty}^{p^*_{t+1}} E(V_{t+2}|p)f(p - p^*_t)\,dp,$$
$$\tag{11.37}$$

where both p^*_{t+1} and $E(V_{t+2}|\cdot)$ are known from the previous iteration (compare (11.15)–(11.16)). Thus, in the American option-pricing problem with serially dependent prices, we do not get a dimension reduction in the backward recursion of the type we get in the case of i.i.d. prices, where we only need to do a recursion on reservation prices. We do get a dimension reduction in the job search model (chapter 7), where we only need to do a recursion on reservation wages, and in the linear-quadratic model (chapter 12), where we do a recursion on matrices but not on the entire value function, as well as in the random utility model (chapter 5), where the recursion is also not on the entire value function but on its conditional expectation given only the observables one period earlier, again an object of lower dimension than the full value function. What we do get in the American option problem with dependent prices is the simplification that instead of tracking the entire value function $V_t(\cdot)$ through the iterations, we only need to carry along p_t^* and $\{E(V_{t+1}|p) : p \in (-\infty, p_t^*]\}$. In particular, the function involved has a truncated domain, whereas carrying $V_t(\cdot)$ along would require storing its values on the full, untruncated domain.

The equations for the American call are of course given for a simple case here, but it is straightforward to introduce additional issues, such as dividends, discounting, changes in the contract, etc. For example, the corresponding American put option should be exercised at prices below p_t^* satisfying

$$p_t^* = K + \int_{-\infty}^{p_{t+1}^*} (p - K) f(p - p_t^*) dp + \int_{p_{t+1}^*}^{\infty} E(V_{t+2}|p) f(p - p_t^*) dp,$$

$$(11.38)$$

with the iterations started at $V_T(p_T) = \max\{K - p_T, 0\}$.

In the following, we further characterize the value function of the American option-pricing problem using the general optimal stopping framework. Thus, the option value is generally of the form

$$V_0 = \max_{0 \leq \tau \leq T} E(Z_\tau) \qquad (11.39)$$

for an appropriately defined process $\{Z_t\}$ and with τ the candidate stopping time. The problem is solved via dynamic programming by introducing the value functions

$$V_t = \max_{t \leq \tau \leq T} E_t(Z_t) \qquad (11.40)$$

for $t = 0, 1, \ldots, T$, where T is the expiration date. For an American call,

$$Z_t = \beta^t \max\{p_t - K, 0\}, \qquad (11.41)$$

where β is the discount factor, and for an American put,

$$Z_t = \beta^t \max\{K - p_t, 0\}, \qquad (11.42)$$

but the following analysis is general and applies to any contingent claim. The condition on the stopping time is that $\{\tau = t\} \in \mathcal{F}_t$, the information set at time t; i.e., the investor knows whether to stop now or continue. Thus, the Bellman equation is

$$V_t = \max\{Z_t, E_t(V_{t+1})\}. \qquad (11.43)$$

The terminal condition is $V_T = Z_T$, and for any earlier period, it is optimal to stop at t if and only if $V_t = Z_t$. At this level of generality, there is no condition that p_t or Z_t be i.i.d., Markov or martingales; i.e., we allow for general stochastic processes. We note immediately that

$$V_t \geq E_t(V_{t+1}), \qquad (11.44)$$

$$V_t \geq Z_t. \qquad (11.45)$$

Recall that V_t would be a martingale if beside a finite mean condition it satisfied

$$V_t = E_t \left(V_{t+1} \right), \tag{11.46}$$

whereas (11.44) shows that V_t in fact is a supermartingale (similarly, a submartingale would be obtained if $V_t \leq E_t \left(V_{t+1} \right)$). Combining with (11.45), V_t is a supermartingale greater than or equal to Z_t. Sometimes this is stated by saying that V_t is a supermartingale that dominates or majorizes Z_t. This is natural; i.e., some opportunities may be lost over time, and the value function declines in this sense, toward $V_T = Z_T$. In fact, we have the following.

THEOREM 9 V_t is the smallest supermartingale majorizing Z_t.

Proof. We have already that V_t is a supermartingale majorizing Z_t. Let S_t be any other supermartingale majorizing Z_t. We show by induction that $S_t \geq V_t$. At T,

$$
\begin{aligned}
S_T &\geq Z_T \qquad (S \text{ majorizes } Z) \\
&= V_T \qquad \text{(terminal condition)},
\end{aligned} \tag{11.47}
$$

so $S_t \geq V_t$ is satisfied at $t = T$. For the induction step, assume $S_{t+1} \geq V_{t+1}$. We have

$$S_t \geq Z_t, \tag{11.48}$$

since by assumption S_t majorizes Z_t, and

$$
\begin{aligned}
S_t &\geq E_t \left(S_{t+1} \right) \qquad (S \text{ supermartingale}) \\
&\geq E_t \left(V_{t+1} \right),
\end{aligned} \tag{11.49}
$$

where the last inequality follows from the induction assumption. Combining (11.48), (11.49) and (11.43),

$$
\begin{aligned}
S_t &\geq \max\{Z_t, E_t(V_{t+1})\} \\
&= V_t.
\end{aligned} \tag{11.50}
$$

$\square$

The smallest supermartingale majorizing Z_t is called the Snell envelope of Z_t (Karatzas and Shreve (1998, p. 56)). Thus, the theorem shows that the value of the contingent claim is given by the Snell envelope. In particular, the option price in the initial time period is the value of the Snell envelope of Z at $t = 0$.

The Snell envelope property can actually be used to solve the American option-pricing problem. To see how this works in a simple case, assume now that p_t is Markov and further restrict attention to a discrete state space

$P = \{0, 1, \ldots, \overline{p}\}$; i.e., p_t is a Markov chain on P. This may, e.g., be the result of a discretization of the original problem. Let $Q = \{q_{ij}\}$ be the Markov transition probability matrix for p_t; i.e.,

$$q_{ij} = P\left(p_{t+1} = j | p_t = i\right), \quad i, j = 0, 1, \ldots, \overline{p}. \quad (11.51)$$

We again have Z_t given as a known function of underlying prices, e.g., for the American put $Z_t(p) = \beta^t \max\{K - p, 0\}$. The Bellman equation is

$$V_t(p) = \max\left\{ Z_t(p), \sum_{j=0}^{\overline{p}} q_{pj} V_{t+1}(j) \right\}, \quad p = 0, 1, \ldots, \overline{p}, \quad (11.52)$$

for $t = 0, 1, \ldots, T$, with $V_{T+1} = 0$.

We may also write this out, saying again that V_t is a supermartingale,

$$V_t(p) \geq \sum_{j=0}^{\overline{p}} q_{pj} V_{t+1}(j) \quad (11.53)$$

for all p and t, and it majorizes Z_t,

$$V_t(p) \geq Z_t(p). \quad (11.54)$$

By theorem 9, V_t is the Snell envelope of Z_t, i.e., the smallest process with the properties (11.53)–(11.54). Since the inequalities are linear, we can now simply solve for the value function by linear programming (LP). Thus, we solve

$$\min_{\{V_t(p)\}} \sum_{t=0}^{T} \sum_{p=0}^{\overline{p}} V_t(p) \quad (11.55)$$

subject to

$$V_t(p) - \sum_{j=0}^{\overline{p}} q_{pj} V_{t+1}(j) \geq 0, \quad t = 0, 1, \ldots, T-1; \quad p = 0, 1, \ldots, \overline{p},$$

$$V_t(p) \geq Z_t(p), \quad t = 0, 1, \ldots, T; \quad p = 0, 1, \ldots, \overline{p}. \quad (11.56)$$

Note that the Snell envelope, which is less than or equal to other candidate value functions $V_t(p)$ at each t and p separately, obviously also solves the above LP problem. Although the LP problem may be large, with $(T+1)(\overline{p}+1)$ variables and $(2T + 1)(\overline{p} + 1)$ constraints, it is easily and efficiently solved, e.g., using the simplex algorithm, and the solution V_t is the optimal value function. In particular, the option price at $t = 0$ is $V_0(p_0)$, where p_0 is the initial price of the underlying.

As a useful by-product of solving for the option price, the method in addition delivers the optimal exercise strategy explicitly. In particular, if the solution V_t satisfies

$$V_t(p) = Z_t(p) \qquad (11.57)$$

for a given (t, p), then it is optimal to exercise in period t if the price of the underlying is p. Otherwise, it is optimal to keep the option alive. In the latter case, by (11.43),

$$V_t = E_t(V_{t+1}), \qquad (11.58)$$

showing that the value function (option price) is a martingale throughout the continuation region (whereas globally it is a supermartingale). This (super-) martingale property of the value function holds even if the underlying is not a martingale under any (equivalent) measure, which could happen, e.g., in the i.i.d. case, or more generally for an option on a perishable commodity.

11.6 OPTION PRICE DATA

In some cases, in particular if there is a risk of error in measurement, the heavy reliance on the particular model structure that produces superconsistent estimators (section 11.4) may not be warranted. An explicit model for measurement error in the search application is developed in chapter 9. In option markets, there is typically access to market data on option prices. Suppose that in month t, the initial price W_{t,m_t} of the option (which then has m_t days to expiration) is observed, but that the exact timing of exercise τ_t is unobserved. This allows another way of drawing inference on the optimal stopping model, which (upon suitable modification—see below) leads to a regular estimation problem, with estimators converging to a limiting distribution at rate $T^{1/2}$.

The availability of option price data offers an opportunity of inference that is unique in the class of dynamic programming models. In effect, we have data on the value function itself, evaluated at the relevant state variables, and this is a dramatic change in the statistical problem that we now explore.

In principle, the model function is

$$p(W, s; \theta) = \prod_{t=1}^{T} 1_{\{W_{t,m_t} = W_{m_t}(s_{t,1};\theta)\}} \prod_{u=1}^{m_t} f(s_{t,u}; \theta | s_{t,u-1}), \qquad (11.59)$$

with $s_{t,u}$ the price of the underlying on day u in month t (compare (11.25)) and $W_{m_t}(s_{t,1}; \theta)$ the theoretical option price, which for given parameters is computed by iterating (11.15) and (11.16) until $k = m_{t-1}$ and then inserting the resulting $EW_{m_{t-1}}$ and the data point $s = s_{t,1}$ in (11.14). Note that (11.59) is degenerate: No parameter vector $\theta = (\gamma, \sigma, \beta)$ will in practice be consistent with $W_{t,m_t} = W_{m_t}(s_{t,1}; \theta)$ for all t, so the model function vanishes identically. This curse of determinacy (see chapters 2 and 4) is a more extreme outcome of the detailed modeling than the previous super-consistency without option price data (section 11.4). A modified model function that allows useful inference is obtained by explicitly introducing measurement error to capture the necessarily nonsynchronous measurement of option and stock prices W_{t,m_t} and $s_{t,1}$. Assume that

$$W_{t,m_t} = W_{m_t}(s_{t,1}; \theta)\varepsilon_t, \tag{11.60}$$

where ε_t is a positive, unit mean proportional measurement error term independent of $s_{t,1}$, consistent with non-negative option prices, and imposing the condition $E(W_{t,m_t}|s_{t,1}) = W_{m_t}(s_{t,1}; \theta)$. An empirically useful specification that was shown by Christensen and Kiefer (1994b) (see chapter 9) to capture measurement errors well in the closely related job search model is given by

$$f_\varepsilon(\varepsilon; \psi) = \frac{(1 + \psi^{-2})^{2+\psi^{-2}}}{\Gamma(2 + \psi^{-2})\varepsilon^{3+\psi^{-2}}} e^{-\frac{1+\psi^{-2}}{\varepsilon}}, \tag{11.61}$$

that is, the Pearson type V of variance ψ^2 (Johnson, Kotz, and Balakrishnan, 1994, p. 21). We now have $\theta = (\gamma, \sigma, \beta, \psi) \in \Theta = \mathbb{R} \times \mathbb{R}_+ \times (0, 1) \times \mathbb{R}_+$. The resulting nondegenerate model function, replacing (11.59), is

$$p(W, s; \theta) = \prod_{t=1}^{T} \frac{1}{W_{m_t}(s_{t,1}; \theta)} f_\varepsilon\left(\frac{W_{t,m_t}}{W_{m_t}(s_{t,1}; \theta)}; \psi\right) \prod_{u=1}^{m_t} f(s_{t,u}; \theta | s_{t,u-1}). \tag{11.62}$$

It is evident that the detailed way in which the parameters enter in (11.62) reflects the fine structure of the optimal stopping model at hand. Of course, the variance ψ^2 of the measurement error does not enter into the basic economic model but must still be estimated along with the other parameters in (11.62), and it is worth asking whether this leads to an efficiency loss. Suppose the parameters of main interest are those governing the underlying stock price movements, i.e., $\phi = (\gamma, \sigma^2)$ from (11.18). The question is whether these should be estimated from the marginal likelihood for the stock prices,

$$p(s; \phi) = \prod_{t=1}^{T} \prod_{u=1}^{m_t} f(s_{t,u}; \phi | s_{t,u-1}),$$ (11.63)

with f from (11.9), instead of using (11.62), this way avoiding both the error-ridden information (option prices) and the nuisance parameters $\chi = (\beta, \psi)$. The following proposition gives the answer to this question.

PROPOSITION 11.6.1 *Let* $v_\varepsilon(\phi)$ *and* $v(\phi)$ *be the asymptotic variance matrices for the estimates of* ϕ *obtained by maximizing (11.62), respectively (11.63). Then*

$$v_\varepsilon(\phi) \le v(\phi).$$ (11.64)

Proof. Write

$$p(W; \theta | s) = \prod_{t=1}^{T} \frac{1}{W_{m_t}(s_{t,1}; \theta)} f_\varepsilon \left(\frac{W_{t,m_t}}{W_{m_t}(s_{t,1}; \theta)}; \psi \right)$$ (11.65)

for the conditional likelihood for W given s. Let i, i^ε, and i^c be the information matrices obtained by differentiating the negative of the logarithms of (11.63), (11.62) and (11.65), respectively. Then

$$i^\varepsilon = \begin{pmatrix} i_{\phi\phi} + i^c_{\phi\phi} & i^c_{\phi\chi} \\ i^c_{\chi\phi} & i^c_{\chi\chi} \end{pmatrix},$$ (11.66)

with subscripts indicating the relevant blocks in the matrices. Hence,

$$v_\varepsilon(\phi) = (i^{\varepsilon-1})_{\phi\phi} = \left(i_{\phi\phi} + i^c_{\phi\phi} - i^c_{\phi\chi} \left(i^c_{\chi\chi} \right)^{-1} i^c_{\chi\phi} \right)^{-1},$$ (11.67)

whereas

$$v(\phi) = i^{-1}_{\phi\phi}.$$

The result (11.64) is equivalent to

$$i^c_{\phi\phi} - i^c_{\phi\chi} \left(i^c_{\chi\chi} \right)^{-1} i^c_{\chi\phi} \ge 0,$$

or equivalently, $(i^c)^{-1}_{\phi\phi} \ge 0$, which follows because (11.65) is a (conditional) likelihood, so that $i^c \ge 0$ and hence $(i^c)^{-1} \ge 0$. □

From the proposition, adding data on option prices leads to an efficiency gain, even though additional parameters are introduced. This would have been impossible in the job search case and in any other dynamic programming model where data on the value function itself are unavailable.

It is straightforward to modify our approach to accommodate other situations relevant in practice. We have already seen in connection with the Black-Scholes formula (11.22) how to handle European-style options, which unlike American-style options may not be exercised prior to expiration. If the stock pays dividends, it is frequently optimal to exercise the American call early, and our framework accommodates this case.

11.7 TESTING OPTION MARKET EFFICIENCY

The condition (11.64) allows testing option market efficiency. Thus, suppose (11.63) is the correct model for the stock price process. A test of option market efficiency can now be formed as a test for whether (11.65) is the correct model for the option prices conditioned on the stock prices. If this is the case, then the estimates of ϕ from (11.62) and (11.63) are both consistent, so they should be close in sample, but only the first is efficient by proposition 11.6.1, so their difference has asymptotic variance $v(\phi) - v_\varepsilon(\phi)$. If (11.63) is correct but (11.65) and hence (11.62) are wrong, i.e., options are not priced according to the optimal stopping model, then the estimates of ϕ will diverge. The test statistic

$$(\hat{\phi} - \hat{\phi}_\varepsilon)' (v(\phi) - v_\varepsilon(\phi))^{-1} (\hat{\phi} - \hat{\phi}_\varepsilon), \qquad (11.68)$$

with $\hat{\phi}_\varepsilon$ and $\hat{\phi}$ from (11.62) and (11.63), may then be treated as a χ^2 variate on R degrees of freedom, where $R = \mathrm{rank}(v(\phi) - v_\varepsilon(\phi))$. If $R = 1$, the inversion in (11.68) is understood in the Moore-Penrose generalized sense. Thus, (11.68) is a test of structure, i.e., a test of correct option pricing, given correct specification for the stock price process.

Another approach to efficiency testing relies on the relation between implied and realized volatility. Thus, a common practice is to invert the option-pricing formula, which in our approach would amount to calculating

$$\sigma_{IV,t} = (W_{m_t})_\sigma^{-1}(s_{t,1}; \gamma, W_{t,m_t}, \beta), \qquad (11.69)$$

the so-called *implied volatility* that exactly aligns the observed and theoretical option prices at a given time. If option market participants are rational and markets are efficient, then option prices should reflect expectations about the distribution of future returns to the underlying, in particular future volatility. Thus, implied volatility backed out from option prices should forecast the subsequently realized volatility. Using the Black-Scholes model and data on one-month, at-the-money ($s = x$) call options on the S&P 100 index (the OEX options), Christensen and Prabhala (1998) find empirically that implied volatility (11.69) is an unbiased and efficient forecast of realized volatility, i.e., the sample standard deviation of subsequent log price (i.e., index) differences, at least after the October 1987 stock market crash. This lends support to the theory and is consistent with (11.22).

The relevant regression format is

$$\sigma_t^2 = \alpha_0 + \alpha_1 \sigma_{t-1}^2 + \alpha_2 \sigma_{IV,t}^2 + v_t,$$

where σ_t^2 is the *realized volatility* (10.118) over the course of month t, calculated as in French, Schwert, and Stambaugh (1987) and Schwert (1989) from daily returns during the month, and $\sigma_{IV,t}^2$ is implied volatility (here in squared or variance form) at the beginning of month t. If option markets are efficient, then $\sigma_{IV,t}^2$ should subsume the information content of past return information before t, such as that in σ_{t-1}^2, so α_1, should be 0 and α_2 positive. Unbiasedness of the implied volatility forecast amounts to the additional hypotheses $\alpha_2 = 1$ and $\alpha_0 = 0$. Christensen and Prabhala (1998) consider the square root and logarithmic transformations of the variables σ^2 and σ_{IV}^2 in the regressions, in which case negative intercepts α_0 are expected under the null, by Jensen's inequality and since realized volatility should exhibit greater time-series variation than its conditional expectation given by implied volatility. Nonsynchronicity of stock and option prices, model misspecification, etc., may give rise to measurement error in implied volatility, and an instrumental variables approach is used to address the resulting errors-in-variables (EIV) problem through the specification

$$\sigma_{IV,t}^2 = \beta_0 + \beta_1 \sigma_{t-1}^2 + \beta_2 \sigma_{IV,t-1}^2 + w_t, \qquad (11.70)$$

the first stage of a two-stage least squares estimation, leaving α_2 insignificantly different from unity and α_1 statistically equal to zero. The specification allows testing whether option market participants use available past information in setting option prices, and both β_1 and β_2 are found to be significant at about .45.

The unbiasedness result $\alpha_2 = 1$ shows that beginning-of-the-month implied volatility from option prices moves closely together with realized volatility measured from returns over the remainder of the month; i.e., implied volatility forecasts realized volatility, consistent with market efficiency. If both implied and realized volatility exhibit sufficiently strong serial dependence, the relation is rather of the cointegration type (chapter 10), i.e., two strongly serially dependent series moving together in the long run, and in this case, the hypothesis $\alpha_2 = 1$ is one of long-run unbiasedness.

Andersen et al. (2001) show that realized volatility σ_t^2 exhibits strong serial dependence, but not of the unit root kind. In particular, σ_t^2 is stationary but exhibits *long memory*; i.e., it is *fractionally integrated* of order $d \in (0, 1/2)$ or $\sigma_t^2 \in I(d)$, with a point estimate of d in the vicinity of .4. Here, the fractional integration $\sigma_t^2 \in I(d)$ means that

$$(1 - L)^d \sigma_t^2 = \varepsilon_t,$$

where $\varepsilon_t \in I(0)$, i.e., ε_t is covariance stationary and has positive finite spectral density at the origin, L is the lag operator ($L\sigma_t^2 = \sigma_{t-1}^2$), and $(1 - L)^d$ is defined by its binomial expansion,

$$(1 - L)^d = \sum_{j=0}^{\infty} \frac{\Gamma(j - d)}{\Gamma(-d)\Gamma(j + 1)} L^j,$$

where Γ is the gamma function,

$$\Gamma(\alpha) = \int_0^{\infty} x^{\alpha - 1} e^{-x} dx.$$

For $d \in (0, \frac{1}{2})$, σ_t^2 is stationary but exhibits long memory, with autocorrelations decaying at a slow hyperbolic rate asymptotically, as opposed to the exponential decay applicable, e.g., to finite-order stationary autoregressive moving average (ARMA) processes (which are $I(0)$). An order $d > \frac{1}{2}$ would leave σ_t^2 nonstationary; e.g., $d = 1$ is the unit root case (chapter 10).

Christensen and Nielsen (2006) show that implied volatility $\sigma_{IV,t}^2$ exhibits long memory too, $\sigma_{IV,t}^2 \in I(d)$, and also in the stationary range, with d near .4, as for realized volatility σ_t^2. They futhermore show that these two stationary fractionally integrated processes move together in the long run, i.e., they are *stationary fractionally cointegrated*, and, finally, that the long-run unbiasedness hypothesis $\alpha_2 = 1$ cannot be rejected, and neither can the additional forecasting efficiency hypothesis that the cointegration residuals are $I(0)$, i.e., $d_e = 0$, where d_e is the fractional integration order of the residuals. These results are consistent with option market efficiency, i.e., implied volatility forecasts realized volatility, and they are important since ordinary least squares (OLS) does not yield consistent parameter estimates in the case of stationary long memory processes. Instead, α_2 is estimated by a semiparametric narrow-band frequency domain least squares (NBFDLS) method introduced by Robinson (1994), who proved the consistency of this method. Robinson and Marinucci (2003) prove some asymptotic distribution results for the NBFDLS method but only in the case $d + d_e > \frac{1}{2}$, and this for $d_e = 0$ ($I(0)$ residuals) implies nonstationary volatility series, $d > \frac{1}{2}$, which is not empirically warranted. Christensen and Nielsen (2006) contribute with the missing asymptotic distribution theory for the coin-tegration vector (in particular, α_2) for the case $d + d_e < \frac{1}{2}$, along with $d > d_e \geq 0$, relevant to realized and implied volatility. It is this distribu-tion theory that allows hypothesis testing on the cointegrating vector, in particular, of the relevant long-run unbiasedness hypothesis $\alpha_2 = 1$.

To see the cointegration, consider the demeaned series and write

$$\sigma_t^2 = \alpha_2 \sigma_{IV,t}^2 + e_t,$$

with implied volatility measured from option prices at the beginning of period t and realized volatility measured from returns over the course of period t. Christensen and Nielsen (2006) consider weekly data using high-frequency (5-minute) returns in the computation of realized volatility σ_t^2. The NBFDLS estimator of α_2 is

$$\hat{\alpha}_2 = \frac{\sum_{j=1}^m \text{Re}\left(\sum_{s=1}^T \sigma_{IV,s}^2 e^{is\lambda_j} \sum_{t=1}^T \sigma_t^2 e^{-it\lambda_j}\right)}{\sum_{j=1}^m \text{Re}\left(\sum_{s=1}^T \sigma_{IV,s}^2 e^{is\lambda_j} \sum_{t=1}^T \sigma_{IV,t}^2 e^{-it\lambda_j}\right)},$$

where $\lambda_j = 2\pi j/T$ are the Fourier frequencies, $\text{Re}(\cdot)$ is the real part, and $1/m + m/T \to 0$ for the narrow-band property (a shrinking portion of the spectrum near the long-run end is used). Under the tightened criterion $1/m + m^{1+2\alpha}/T^{2\alpha} \to 0$ for some $\alpha \in (0, 2]$ and related regularity conditions, Christensen and Nielsen (2006) show the asymptotic normality result

$$\sqrt{m}\lambda_m^{d_e-d}(\hat{\alpha}_2 - \alpha_2) \to N\left(0, \frac{g_e(1 - 2d)^2}{2g(1 - 2d - 2d_e)}\right),$$

where g_e and g are the long-run variances of $(1 - L)^{d_e} e_t$ and $(1 - L)^d \sigma_{IV,t}^2$. The result does not require that the cointegration residuals e_t be uncorre-lated with the regressor $\sigma_{IV,t}^2$ as in ordinary regression but just that the cross-spectral density between the two tends to 0 as the frequency tends to the long-run end ($\lambda = 0$), i.e., the cointegration hypothesis. Conver-gence is slower than rate $\sqrt{T}$ but faster if the strength of cointegration $d - d_e$ is higher. The inference procedure is thus quite different from the usual $I(0) - I(1)$ cointegration analysis for unit root processes (chapter 10). By asymptotic normality, long-run unbiasedness is tested off the t-ratio for $\hat{\alpha}_2 - 1$, and the additional efficiency hypothesis $d_e = 0$ off the estimated in-tegration order d_e of the cointegration errors e_t. The semiparametric nature of the approach stems from the fact that assumptions are made only on the long-run properties (the spectrum near zero frequency), and the empirical results are consistent with option market efficiency.

11.8 EXERCISES

1. Verify the details of theorem 8.
2. Consider the data density $\exp\{(\theta, \varphi)x + \kappa(\theta, \varphi)\}h(x, \varphi)$ where the measure h depends on φ, which determines its support. Show that this is not an exponential family model. Show that the conditional model given the parameter φ is an exponential family model. Show that there exists a local cut such that inference on φ can be done marginally based on $h(x, \varphi)$ and on θ conditionally on the local cut.
3. Interpret (11.68) as a Hausman (1978) test. Give an equivalent score test.

11.9 REFERENCES

Dixit and Pindyck (1994) consider investment models not necessarily in the optimal stopping framework, with applications to real options. Longstaff and Schwartz (2001) suggest a least-squares Monte Carlo approach to calculation of the continuation value in the American option recursions, by regression across simulated paths of next period values on flexible functional forms (say, Laguerre polynomials) in current state variables (underlying prices). Stentoft (2004) provides the mathematical foundation for this approach. Rubinstein (1994) finds that option implied volatilities exhibit a smile (precisely, a smirk) after the crash on Black Monday, October 19, 1987, when the stock market dropped more than 20%. Out-of-the-money (low strike) put implied volatility is high relative to at-the-money implied volatility after the crash, but not before. Potentially, investors pay increased attention to possibilities of portfolio insurance through protective puts (chapter 10) after the 1987 event. A related regime shift around the time of the crash is documented by Christensen and Prabhala (1998), who show that at-the-money implied volatility is an unbiased and efficient forecast of future realized volatility and subsumes the information content of past realized volatility in the period after the crash, but not before, again consistent with increased focus on the option market following the event. Program trading activities implementing dynamic strategies to create synthetic puts by selling off stock as prices fall may have been related to the crash itself, and we return to dynamic option replication in chapter 14 below.

Chapter Twelve

Retirement

12.1 INTRODUCTION

Retirement from the labor market is an important area of application where the dynamic approach has been used extensively. We consider the retirement model in the framework of chapter 6. Specifically, assuming that retirement is an absorbing state, the relevant model is of the optimal stopping type. Our starting point is the simple discrete-time optimal stopping model of section 6.6. It was applied in that section to the problem of optimal job search. We build a related model of optimal retirement along similar lines and discuss the implications for inference. In the following sections, we extend the model and consider a number of popular alternatives.

12.2 A SIMPLE RETIREMENT MODEL

Assume that an initially employed worker receives a wage x each period while working (state $a = 1$) and given x decides between remaining employed (control $c = 1$) or retiring from the labor market ($c = 0$). Once retired, the worker receives retirement benefits, yielding utility of leisure b in each of the following periods. This model fits into the discrete-time optimal stopping framework from section 6.6. In particular, the state variable (lagged control) a belongs to the state space $A = \{0, 1\}$, with $a = 1$ indicating work and $a = 0$ indicating retirement. The control space $C(a, x)$ takes the form $C(a)$, with $C(1) = A$ and $C(0) = \{0\}$, since retirement is an absorbing state. Writing $u(a, x, c)$ for the utility function as usual, the general functional equation for the value function $V(a, x)$ from section 6.6 is

$$V(0, x) = u(0, x, 0) + \beta E(V(0, y)|x), \qquad (12.1)$$

$$V(1, x) = \max \{u(1, x, 0) + \beta E(V(0, y)|x),$$
$$u(1, x, 1) + \beta E(V(1, y)|x)\}. \qquad (12.2)$$

In the retirement case, $u(a, x, 1) = x$ and $u(a, x, 0) = b$. The first relation in the functional equation (12.1) implies

$$V(0, x) = \frac{b}{1 - \beta}, \qquad (12.3)$$

and the second relation (12.2) therefore is

$$V(1, x) = \max \left\{ \frac{b}{1 - \beta}, x + \beta E\left(V(1, y)\,|x\right) \right\}. \qquad (12.4)$$

The structure of the retirement model thus resembles that of the job search model. The models are different, though, and this is most easily highlighted by assuming initially that wages are serially independent, $Q(y|x, a) = Q(y)$. Then evidently, retirement occurs whenever the current wage drops below the reservation level

$$r = \frac{b}{1 - \beta} - \beta E\left(V(1, y)\right). \qquad (12.5)$$

To interpret this equation, recall that $b/(1 - \beta) = b + \beta b/(1 - \beta)$, and hence

$$r - b = \beta \left\{ \frac{b}{1 - \beta} - E\left(V(1, y)\right) \right\}. \qquad (12.6)$$

The right hand side is the opportunity cost of not retiring, i.e., the discounted present value of the future benefit stream less the value of remaining employed. Work is continued only if current wages exceed benefits by an amount at least covering the opportunity cost.

To illustrate, consider the prototypal case with exponentially distributed wages, with mean $1/\gamma$ and density given as in (7.9) by

$$f(x) = \gamma e^{-\gamma x}, \qquad x > 0. \qquad (12.7)$$

The probability of continuing work is

$$\pi = P(x > r)$$
$$= e^{-\gamma r}. \qquad (12.8)$$

The conditional mean wage given continued work is

$$E(x|x > r) = r + \frac{1}{\gamma}. \qquad (12.9)$$

The expected value function $EV = E(V(1, x))$ is

$$EV = \pi \left(r + \frac{1}{\gamma} + \beta EV \right) + (1 - \pi) \frac{b}{1 - \beta}. \qquad (12.10)$$

Using $r = b/(1 - \beta) - \beta EV$ from (12.5) and simplifying yields

$$EV = \frac{b}{1 - \beta} + \frac{\pi}{\gamma}. \qquad (12.11)$$

Inserting expression (12.8) for π produces

$$EV = \frac{b}{1-\beta} + \frac{1}{\gamma} \exp\left\{-\frac{\gamma b}{1-\beta} + \gamma\beta EV\right\}. \qquad (12.12)$$

Considering the right hand side of this equation a function of EV, say $\mathcal{T}(EV)$, and differentiating yields $\mathcal{T}'(EV) = \beta\pi$, which is clearly in the interval $(0, 1)$. This shows that $\mathcal{T}$ is a contraction. Hence, the expected value EV is given as the unique fixed point of $\mathcal{T}$. Furthermore, for fixed values of the parameters $\theta = (b, \beta, \gamma)$, the contraction may be iterated to calculate $EV = \lim_{n\to\infty} \mathcal{T}^n(0)$ and hence r. In addition, the same equation identifies EV as a function of θ as the parameters vary.

Other distributions may be considered along the same lines as the exponential. At this level, the retirement model is as simple as the job search model. More complications arise when wages are not serially independent, but follow some Markov process, with transition distribution $Q(y|x)$. Here, we write $f(y|x)$ for the conditional density,

$$Q(y|x) = \int_0^y f(z|x)\,dz, \qquad y > 0. \qquad (12.13)$$

In this case, we still have $V(0, x) = b/(1 - \beta)$, as in (12.3), and the reservation property holds, but the reservation wage is now implicitly given by

$$\frac{b}{1-\beta} = r + \beta E(V(1, y)|r). \qquad (12.14)$$

The probability of continuing the work next period, given it is continued in the current period, is

$$\pi(x) = P(y > r|x)$$
$$= \int_r^\infty f(y|x)dy. \qquad (12.15)$$

Unlike in the case of independent wages, where $\pi = \exp(-\gamma r)$ (see (12.8)), this probability now depends explicitly on the current wage x.

The next period's conditional mean wage given continued work and current wage x is

$$E(y|y > r, x) = \frac{\int_r^\infty yf(y|x)\,dy}{\pi(x)}. \qquad (12.16)$$

The expected next period value function is

$$E(V(1, y)|x) = \pi(x)E(y|y > r, x)$$
$$+ \beta \int_r^\infty E(V(1, z)|y)f(y|x)dy$$
$$+ (1 - \pi(x))\frac{b}{1-\beta}. \qquad (12.17)$$

The functional equations (12.14), (12.15), and (12.17) must be solved simultaneously for $E\,(V\,(1,\,y)\,|\cdot)$ and r. Again, for $f\,(\cdot|\cdot)$ parametrized, say, by γ, the functional equations determine the mapping from the parameters $\theta = (b, \beta, \gamma)$ to the conditional expected value function and r.

12.3 THE LIKELIHOOD FUNCTION

For exposition, consider first the independent wage case. Assume data are drawn from a population of individuals who have not retired prior to the sampling date. Consider a representative individual drawn at random from this population. On the sampling date, this individual either continues work or retires. The probability of continuing work is π. Assume that the wage x is observed in this case and write f for the density of x. The probability of retirement is $1-\pi$. In this event, the worker has in effect turned down a wage x in favor of retirement. We assume that this wage is unobserved by the econometrician. Hence, the contribution to the likelihood of an individual who continues work is $\pi f\,(x|x > r)$, and the contribution of an individual who retires is $1 - \pi$.

Let $\{(x_i, c_i)\}_{i=1}^{N}$ be data for a random sample of size N from this population. Here, $c_i = 1$ indicates that the ith individual continues work on the sampling date, and $c_i = 0$ indicates that the ith individual retires on the sampling date. By a slight abuse of notation, x_i is the wage of the ith individual if $c_i = 1$ (work), and $x_i \equiv 0$ (the rejected wage is unobserved) if $c_i = 0$ (retirement). Note that in the general notation, $a_i = 1$ for all i since we condition on working status in the previous period. The likelihood function is

$$L = \prod_{\{i:c_i=1\}} \pi f\,(x_i|x_i > r) \prod_{\{i:c_i=0\}} (1 - \pi)$$
$$= \pi^{N_w}(1 - \pi)^{N_r} \prod_{\{i:c_i=1\}} f(x_i|x_i > r), \qquad (12.18)$$

where N_w is the number of individuals who continue work and N_r is the number who retire. Of course, we have

$$f\,(x|x > r) = \frac{f\,(x)}{\pi}, \qquad x > r, \qquad (12.19)$$

so the likelihood function simplifies to

$$L = (1 - \pi)^{N_r} \prod_{\{i:c_i=1\}} f(x_i)1_{\{x_i>r\}}, \qquad (12.20)$$

where $1_{\{x_i>r\}}$ is the indicator function for the event $\{x_i > r\}$. Also, $\pi = P\,(x > r) = \int_r^{\infty} f\,(x)\,dx$.

The unknown parameters to be estimated are some or all components of $\theta = (b, \beta, \gamma)$, where γ parametrizes f. For given parameters, EV and hence r are determined by iterating the contraction, and the result is used to calculate L. This allows a maximum likelihood estimation and hence efficient inference.

To illustrate, consider the exponential wage case (12.7). Here, the likelihood function is

$$L = (1 - e^{-\gamma r})^{N_r} \gamma^{N_w} e^{-\gamma N_w \bar{x}} 1_{\{x_{min} > r\}}, \qquad (12.21)$$

where $\bar{x}$ and x_{min} are the average and minimum observed wages and $r = \lim_{n \to \infty} \mathcal{T}^n(0)$, with

$$\mathcal{T}(r) = b - \frac{\beta}{\gamma} e^{-\gamma r}. \qquad (12.22)$$

Note that $\mathcal{T}'(r) = \beta \pi$, and $\mathcal{T}$ is a contraction with fixed point r. In the prototypal retirement model, not only the value and expected value function, but also the policy function, as determined by the reservation wage r, are fixed points of contraction maps. For trial parameters, r is solved by iterating the contraction, and the result is inserted in the expression for L.

Note that $r = \mathcal{T}(r) < b$. The individual will accept work for a wage below the benefit (utility of leisure) level b on the chance that future periods will bring higher wages.

Suppose the only unknown parameter is b. This is relevant because b captures the utility of leisure, which typically depends on actual benefits, but may have other arguments. Treating b as a utility of leisure parameter to be estimated leaves the precise relation to observed and unobserved arguments free.

We may introduce

$$F(r, \theta) = r - b + \frac{\beta}{\gamma} e^{-\gamma r}. \qquad (12.23)$$

Then $F \equiv 0$ identifies the reservation wage r as an implicit function of $\theta = (b, \beta, \gamma)$. For the parameter of interest b, we are looking for the comparative statics with respect to this parameter. The implicit function theorem yields

$$\frac{dr}{db} = -\frac{\partial F/\partial b}{\partial F/\partial r} = \frac{1}{1 - \beta \pi} > 1. \qquad (12.24)$$

Thus, as b increases, r increases even more. When the utility of leisure is high, the individual is not willing to work for much less than b.

For sufficiently low b, such that $r < x_{min}$, the log likelihood function is

$$\ell = N_r \log(1 - e^{-\gamma r}) + N_w \log \gamma - \gamma N_w \bar{x}. \qquad (12.25)$$

The score in b is

$$s_b = N_r \frac{\gamma \pi}{(1 - \beta \pi)(1 - \pi)} > 0. \qquad (12.26)$$

Thus, b should be set as high as possible while still satisfying $r \leq x_{\min}$. Hence,

$$\hat{b} = r_b^{-1}(x_{\min}) \qquad (12.27)$$

is the maximum likelihood estimator (MLE), with $r_b(\cdot)$ the strictly increasing map from b to r. Note that this map is given by the theory and does not depend on the sample. The MLE of b depends on the observed wages only through the minimum. Hence, the nonstandard properties of the inference problem are evident. In particular, the estimator is not asymptotically normal. Because of the order statistic property, it is superconsistent; i.e.,

$$N(\hat{b} - b) = O_p(1). \qquad (12.28)$$

If instead β is the only parameter to be estimated (say, if in fact actual benefits are known and may reasonably be used for b), the results are similar. The comparative statics are

$$\frac{dr}{d\beta} = -\frac{\partial F / \partial \beta}{\partial F / \partial r} = \frac{-\pi / \gamma}{1 - \beta \gamma} < 0, \qquad (12.29)$$

so that heavier discounting (lower β) implies a higher reservation wage. For β high enough that $r < x_{\min}$, we have ℓ from (12.25) above, and the score in β,

$$s_\beta = -N_r \frac{\pi^2}{(1 - \beta \pi)(1 - \pi)} < 0. \qquad (12.30)$$

Hence, in this case, β should be set as low as possible consistent with $r \leq x_{\min}$; i.e., the MLE is

$$\hat{\beta} = r_\beta^{-1}(x_{\min}), \qquad (12.31)$$

with $r_\beta(\cdot)$ the strictly decreasing map from β to r. Again, $\hat{\beta}$ is non-normal and superconsistent for β.

If both b and β are known, but γ must be estimated, the relevant comparative statics are

$$\frac{dr}{d\gamma} = -\frac{\partial F / \partial \gamma}{\partial F / \partial r} = \frac{\beta \pi (r + 1/\gamma)}{\gamma (1 - \beta \pi)} > 0. \qquad (12.32)$$

Thus, a lower mean wage implies a higher reservation wage. To understand this result, note that a lower mean wage implies that there are fewer gains to waiting for higher wages, and hence retirement may occur earlier. For γ low enough that $r < x_{\min}$, we have the score

$$s_\gamma = N_r \frac{\pi \left(r + \beta\pi \left(r + 1/\gamma\right) / \left(1 - \beta\pi\right)\right)}{1 - \pi}$$

$$+ N_w \left(\frac{1}{\gamma} - \bar{x}\right). \tag{12.33}$$

A random sample of size N_w from f would have a score given by the second term above, and hence MLE $\hat{\gamma} = 1/\bar{x}$. The first term in s_γ is positive, hence showing that $\hat{\gamma}$ in the structural retirement model is higher than $1/\bar{x}$. The reason is that the N_w observed wages are a selected sample from the high end.

Suppose next that two of the parameters in $\theta = (b, \beta, \gamma)$ must be estimated. Then one of these must be b or β. Maximizing with respect to this first allows setting $r = x_{\min}$, as is evident from (12.27) and (12.31) above, and this yields the log profile (partially maximized or concentrated) likelihood

$$\tilde{\ell}(\gamma) = N_r \log(1 - e^{-\gamma x_{\min}}) + N_w \left(\log \gamma - \gamma\bar{x}\right). \tag{12.34}$$

Clearly, whether this was achieved by maximizing out b or β, there is no information on the other of these two parameters left in $\tilde{\ell}(\gamma)$. Thus, at most two parameters may be estimated in the simple retirement model, and one of them must be γ. The researcher has a choice between treating b or β as known. Furthermore, regardless of which is chosen, the inference on γ is the same. Thus, the profile score is

$$\tilde{s}_\gamma = N_r \frac{x_{\min} e^{-\gamma x_{\min}}}{1 - e^{-\gamma x_{\min}}} + N_w \left(\frac{1}{\gamma} - \bar{x}\right). \tag{12.35}$$

The nature of the estimation problem for γ is preserved from the one-parameter case. In particular, $\hat{\gamma} > \bar{x}^{-1}$ again. The profile Hessian is

$$\tilde{h}_{\gamma\gamma}(\gamma) = -N_r \left(\frac{x_{\min}^2 e^{-\gamma x_{\min}}}{1 - e^{-\gamma x_{\min}}} + \frac{x_{\min}^2 e^{-2\gamma x_{\min}}}{(1 - e^{-\gamma x_{\min}})^2}\right) - \frac{N_w}{\gamma^2}. \tag{12.36}$$

Since the first parameter estimator (whether $\hat{b}$ or $\hat{\beta}$) is used to guarantee the condition $x_{\min} = r$, this may be inserted in the estimating equation $\tilde{s}_\gamma = 0$, and since the estimated reservation wage is hence superconsistent, $\tilde{s}_\gamma$ may be treated as a regular score function. In particular, the Fisher information on γ is $i_\gamma(\theta) = -E\tilde{h}_{\gamma\gamma}/N$;

$$i_\gamma(\theta) = \pi \left(\frac{1}{\gamma^2} + \frac{r^2}{1 - \pi}\right), \tag{12.37}$$

to be compared to $1/\gamma^2$ for a random sample from f. Iterative estimation of γ is carried out as

$$\gamma_{k+1} = \gamma_k + a_k \tilde{s}_\gamma (\gamma_k), \tag{12.38}$$

with $a_k = i^{-1}/N$ evaluated at $\gamma = \gamma_k$ for the method of scoring and $a_k = -\tilde{h}_{\gamma\gamma}(\gamma_k)^{-1}$ for Newton-Raphson iteration. The resulting estimator $\hat{\gamma} = \lim_{k\to\infty} \gamma_k$ is asymptotically normal,

$$N^{1/2}(\hat{\gamma} - \gamma) \to N(0, i_\gamma(\theta)^{-1}). \tag{12.39}$$

Of course, the maps r_b and r_β to the reservation wage from b, respectively β, involve γ. Consequently, the final estimate of the first parameter (whether b or β) depends on $\hat{\gamma}$, and unlike in the one-parameter case is therefore not superconsistent. The required distribution theory is developed as follows. The fact that the condition $r = x_{\min}$ is met implies that $F(r, \theta) \equiv 0$, with F from (12.23) and r fixed at $x_{\min}$. This introduces a functional dependence between the parameters in θ. If b is to be estimated, we get

$$b = r + \frac{\beta}{\gamma} e^{-\gamma r}, \tag{12.40}$$

with β known and r fixed at $x_{\min}$. Note that it is not necessary to construct the implicitly determined function r_b by iterating the contraction and then inverting it to get $\hat{b} = r_b^{-1}(x_{\min})$. Instead, the inverse function is given analytically in (12.40). Thus, b may be treated as a function of γ. In particular, suppressing the circumflex,

$$\frac{db}{d\gamma} = -\frac{\beta\pi}{\gamma}\left(r + \frac{1}{\gamma}\right) < 0, \tag{12.41}$$

showing a negative tradeoff along the curve given by the constraint $r = x_{\min}$. Note that $r + 1/\gamma$ is recognized as $E(x|x > r)$ from (12.9). By the δ-rule,

$$N^{1/2}\begin{pmatrix} \hat{b} - b \\ \hat{\gamma} - \gamma \end{pmatrix} \to N\left(0, i_\gamma(\theta)^{-1}\Psi\Psi'\right), \tag{12.42}$$

where Ψ is the relevant gradient,

$$\Psi = \begin{pmatrix} -\frac{\beta\pi}{\gamma} E(x|x > r) \\ 1 \end{pmatrix}. \tag{12.43}$$

Hence, we have found that $\hat{\gamma}$ should first be estimated iteratively, and then

$$\hat{b} = x_{\min} + \frac{\beta}{\hat{\gamma}} e^{-\hat{\gamma} x_{\min}} \tag{12.44}$$

and $(\hat{b}, \hat{\gamma})$ are consistent and asymptotically reduced rank normally distributed (CARRN). Similarly, if instead β is to be estimated along with γ, we have from (12.23),

$$\beta = \gamma e^{\gamma r} (b - r). \tag{12.45}$$

Again, r_β^{-1} is analytic, and

$$\frac{d\beta}{d\gamma} = (1 + \gamma r) \frac{b - r}{\pi} > 0, \tag{12.46}$$

showing a positive tradeoff along $r = x_{\min}$. We get

$$N^{1/2} \begin{pmatrix} \hat{\beta} - \beta \\ \hat{\gamma} - \gamma \end{pmatrix} \rightarrow N \left(0, i_\gamma (\theta)^{-1} \Lambda\Lambda'\right), \tag{12.47}$$

with

$$\Lambda = \begin{pmatrix} (1 + \gamma r) \frac{b-r}{\pi} \\ 1 \end{pmatrix}. \tag{12.48}$$

Note that $\hat{\gamma}$ is numerically the same whether b or β is chosen for estimation. If b is known and β is chosen for estimation, then

$$\hat{\beta} = \hat{\gamma} e^{\hat{\gamma} x_{\min}} (b - x_{\min}) \tag{12.49}$$

and $(\hat{\beta}, \hat{\gamma})$ are jointly CARRN. Note that in none of the two-parameter cases does inference require running the contraction.

12.4 LONGITUDINAL DATA

So far, we have considered cross-section data of the form $\{(x_i, c_i)\}_{i=1}^{N}$. Time series or longitudinal data present a relevant and practically important alternative. Of course, since retirement is treated as an absorbing state, no further information is accumulated by following individual i after $c_i = 0$ (retirement) is observed. Suppose, for the sake of the argument, that each originally sampled individual is followed until retirement. In each period before retirement the wage is recorded. Suppose the duration until retirement is d_i for the ith individual, with $d_i = 0$ indicating retirement on the original sampling date. Let the recorded wages before retirement be $x_{i,0}, \ldots, x_{i,d_i-1}$. The contribution to likelihood of the ith individual is

$$L_i = \prod_{t=0}^{d_i-1} \pi f \left(x_{i,t} | x_{i,t} > r\right) (1 - \pi)$$

$$= (1 - \pi) \prod_{t=0}^{d_i-1} f(x_{i,t}) 1_{\{x_{i,t} > r\}}; \tag{12.50}$$

with the convention $\Pi_{t=0}^{-1} = 1$. Pure time series data are obtained in the case where only one individual, say the ith, is followed over time. Since d_i is finite with probability 1 and L_i does not change any further after d_i periods, information accumulation is finite, and there is no possibility of consistent estimation of any component of θ.

The simplest case of panel data arises if individuals are sampled as in the cross-section case and each individual is followed through time as in the time series case. Modifications to handle censoring at the survey end are easily introduced. For simplicity, we consider the uncensored case. The panel likelihood is

$$L = \prod_{i=1}^{N} L_i$$

$$= (1 - \pi)^N \prod_{i=1}^{N} \prod_{t_i=0}^{d_i-1} f(x_{i,t_i}) 1_{\{x_{i,t_i}>r\}}. \tag{12.51}$$

For illustration, consider again the exponential wage case (12.7). We have

$$L = (1 - e^{-\gamma r})^N \gamma^{N_d} e^{-\gamma N_d \bar{x}_d} 1_{\{x_{\min}>r\}}, \tag{12.52}$$

with $N_d = \sum_{i=1}^{N} d_i$ the total duration observed and $\bar{x}_d = \sum_{i=1}^{N} \sum_{t_i=0}^{d_i-1} x_{i,t_i}/N_d$ the average wage across all periods under observation. Evidently, the panel likelihood (12.52) resembles the cross-section likelihood (12.21) closely, and the main results carry over. In the one-parameter cases, $\hat{b} = r_b^{-1}(x_{\min})$ and $\hat{\beta} = r_\beta^{-1}(x_{\min})$, these estimators being superconsistent, as $N \to \infty$, the minimum now being taken over N_d wages, and $\hat{\gamma}$ is found by solving the profile score equation $\tilde{s}_\gamma = 0$, now with N, N_d, and $\bar{x}_d$ replacing N_r, N_w, and $\bar{x}$ in the expression (12.35) for $\tilde{s}_\gamma$.

Again, at most two parameters are identified, and one of them must be γ. The theory of inference on two parameters carries over, with the same change of data variables in the profile Hessian. Efficiency is increased by the use of panel data. In particular, expression (12.37) for the Fisher information on γ should be divided by $1 - \pi$. Thus, efficiency in the panel case is $(1 - \pi)^{-1}$ times that in the cross-section case when measured by the variance ratios. This reflects an expected duration until retirement of $\pi/(1-\pi)$, whereas the cross-sectional probability of not retiring is only π. The effective sample becomes $(1 - \pi)^{-1}$ times larger in the panel case. The optimal estimators are again CARRN.

Finally, in the panel case, it is natural to consider the generalization to Markovian wages. The conditional likelihood function given initial period observations on retirement decisions and wages for those not retiring is

$$L_c = \prod_{\{i:\, d_i > 0\}} \prod_{t_i=1}^{d_i-1} \pi(x_{i,t_i}-1) f(x_{i,t_i}|x_{i,t_i} > r, x_{i,t_i}-1)(1 - \pi(x_{i,d_i}-1))$$

$$= \prod_{\{i:\, d_i > 0\}} (1 - \pi(x_{i,d_i}-1)) \prod_{t_i=1}^{d_i-1} f(x_{i,t_i}|x_{i,t_i}-1) 1_{\{x_{i,t_i} > r\}}. \qquad (12.53)$$

It holds again that b or β should be fixed. The other of these two parameters may then be estimated superconsistently by $\hat{b} = r_b^{-1}(x_{\min})$, respectively $\hat{\beta} = r_\beta^{-1}(x_{\min})$, if the parameters γ of f are also fixed. Note that $r(\cdot)$ is calculated differently in the Markov case and is more complicated, requiring a simultaneous solution for r and $E(V(1, y)|\cdot)$ from (12.14), (12.15), and (12.17). If γ is to be estimated along with b or β, this is done by inserting $x_{\min}$ for r in L_c from (12.53) and then treating the resulting profile likelihood as an ordinary likelihood. In particular, γ is estimated by setting the profile score vector equal to zero and solving. Minus the inverse profile Hessian estimates the information matrix and inverse asymptotic variance consistently, in spite of the conditioning on initial observations, and Newton-Raphson iteration or its analogs may be used for the estimation of γ. The final estimate of the remaining parameter (whether b or β) is a function of $\hat{\gamma}$ given by inserting this for γ and $x_{\min}$ for r in the optimality condition. The δ-rule may be applied, with $(\hat{b}, \hat{\gamma})$, respectively $(\hat{\beta}, \hat{\gamma})$, again jointly CARRN of dimension $k + 1$ and rank k in wide generality, where $k = \dim(\gamma)$.

The treatment of the Markov case so far is conditional on the initial observations. This is typically a satisfactory approach, yielding a sampling distribution reasonably close to that of the efficient estimator, provided the initial observations are drawn from the stationary distribution of the controlled Markov process. Still, of course, it may be desirable to calculate the efficient estimator. This is the unconditional maximum likelihood estimator. The relevant likelihood function L is obtained by multiplying L_c from (12.53) by the stationary distribution for the initial observations. Thus,

$$L = \prod_{\{i:d_i=0\}} (1 - \pi) \prod_{\{i:d_i>0\}} \pi f(x_{i,0}|x_{i,0} > r) L_c$$

$$= (1 - \pi)^{N_r} \prod_{\{i:d_i>0\}} f(x_{i,0}) 1_{\{x_{i,0} > r\}} L_c, \qquad (12.54)$$

where, as before, N_r is the number of individuals retiring in the initial period. The quantities f and $1 - \pi$ are the stationary distribution and unconditional retirement probability, respectively, and should be distinguished from the related quantities in the independent wage case. In particular, given $f(\cdot|\cdot)$, the transition density of the Markov process, the stationary distribution f satisfies

$$f(y) = \int f(y|x) f(x) dx. \qquad (12.55)$$

For example, if a discretization of the state space is employed, then $f(y|x)$ is represented by a Markov probability transition matrix and f corresponds to the vector of probabilities given by the unique eigenvector of unit eigenvalue. Given this f, we have $\pi = \int_r^\infty f(x) dx$ as usual. This allows computing L. Note that including the stationary distribution adds information not only on the parameters γ of the wage process but also on the reservation wage r, and hence the structural parameters.

12.5 REGULARIZING THE LIKELIHOOD

The analysis so far shows that the nonstandard properties of the likelihood function typical of dynamic programming models also occur in the retirement model. Some of the estimators are superconsistent, and in the vector case asymptotic distributions are reduced rank normal. This is so for cross-section as well as panel data.

Superconsistency is evidence of rapid information accumulation, and reduced rank normality indicates a strong empirical link between parameters. Both properties reveal important aspects of the structure of the inference problem and show that data are highly informative about the parameters. This is good news from the point of view of the econometrician interested in sharp inferences.

Nevertheless, a more regular likelihood function with more standard properties is sometimes desired. This will be less informative about parameters of interest, but the hope is typically that it is more robust to minor model deficiencies, while still allowing insights on the most important model features. The question of whether this combined purpose is in fact fulfilled is rarely asked and seldom easy to answer. Common ways to regularize the likelihood are based on measurement errors or random utility, as discussed in previous chapters, and we have already seen that inferences on structural parameters may depend critically on the precise way in which such additional random terms are introduced. Still, it is useful to consider these extensions explicitly in the context of the retirement model.

Suppose first that wages are observed with error,

$$x = w \cdot m, \qquad (12.56)$$

where x is the observed wage, w the true wage, and $m > 0$ a measurement error. This follows the treatment of measurement error in the prototypal search model (chapter 9). The multiplicative specification is convenient for preserving positivity. We take w and m to be independent. The unit mean condition $Em = 1$ ensures that the mean observed and mean true wages are equal. Assume that the true wages are independent across time and drawn from f as in the previous subsection. Nothing in the underlying structural retirement model is changed by the introduction of measurement errors m. Of course, the condition that the true wage exceeds the reservation wage, $w > r$, translates into the constraint

$$m < \frac{x}{r} \tag{12.57}$$

on permissible measurement errors. With g the density of m, the observed wages have density given as in (9.15) by

$$h(x) = \int_0^{x/r} \frac{1}{m} f(x/m) g(m) \, dm. \tag{12.58}$$

The likelihood function in the panel case is

$$L = (1 - \pi)^N \prod_{i=1}^{N} \prod_{t_i=0}^{d_i-1} \int_0^{x_{i,t_i}/r} \frac{1}{m_{i,t_i}} f(x_{i,t_i}/m_{i,t_i}) g(m_{i,t_i}) dm_{i,t_i}. \tag{12.59}$$

The support restriction $\{x_{i,t_i} > r\}$ is gone, at the expense of introducing the unknown parameters σ of g, typically at the minimum a spread measure. The full parameter vector is now $\theta = (b, \beta, \gamma, \sigma)$, with γ and σ parametrizing f, respectively g. Still, either b or β must be known since both enter only through r. If one of these is included among the parameters to be estimated, it is no longer the case that this is estimated by setting $r = x_{\min}$ given the remaining parameters (γ, σ). The likelihood has been regularized. All parameters are now estimated by setting the score equal to zero and solving, and standard errors are estimated in the usual fashion from the square roots of the diagonal elements of minus the inverse of the Hessian of L at the optimum. The estimators are consistent and asymptotically normal (CAN) (full rank) in wide generality, and superconsistency is lost.

The independent wage case is tractable for the measurement error analysis because the integration with respect to the individual measurement errors factorizes. This is not so for the Markovian wage case. Here, the conditional likelihood function, even when assuming measurement errors that are independent across time and of all wages, is

$$
L_c = \prod_{\{i:\, d_i > 0\}} \int_0^{x_{i,d_i-1}/r} (1 - \pi(x_{i,d_i-1}/m_{i,d_i-1}))
$$

$$
\times \int_0^{x_{i,d_i-2}/r} \cdots \int_0^{x_{i,1}/r} \prod_{t_i=1}^{d_i-1} f(x_{i,t_i}/m_{i,t_i}|x_{i,t_i-1}/m_{i,t_i-1})
$$

$$
\times \frac{1}{m_{i,t_i}} g(m_{i,t_i}) dm_{i,t_i}, \tag{12.60}
$$

where the rule $m_{i,0} = 1$ may be invoked, given conditioning on initial observations and an assumption that these are precisely measured. The latter assumption may be relaxed by adding a further integration over $m_{i,0}$ with density g. Note that the panel likelihood does not factorize, despite the independence assumption on the measurement errors.

The inferential properties carry over from the independent wage case. Thus, the parameters γ and σ in f and g may be estimated along with b or β in an ordinary fashion, yielding full rank CAN results, without superconsistency. Similar conclusions hold if measurement errors are introduced in the full unconditional likelihood, using the stationary distribution for initial observations.

The above discussion has focused on regularizing the likelihood function by introducing measurement errors in the wage, which is the relevant state variable. Of course, measurement errors could be introduced in the control, too, namely, in the retirement decision. Here, it is probably reasonable to assume that if a wage is observed, then retirement has not yet occurred. On the other hand, some individuals who are registered as retired could perhaps be working. This would call for an additional probability in the likelihood function, capturing the possibility of incorrectly measured retirement. We have already discussed such mismeasurement of discrete controls in chapter 4 and shall not go into further detail here. One point is that measurement errors in wages suffice for regularizing the likelihood. As noted earlier, no discrete measurement error probability (say, on the controls) will do the same since the parameters take values in a continuum and are bounded only by discrete observations. In fact, the measurement error in the wage works out nicely in this respect because the wage (and the associated error) is continuous.

Of course, it is even more important to consider the actual quality of measurement in the application at hand. Regularizing the likelihood through mismeasured wages makes sense only if it is indeed plausible that this mechanism is at work and that wages are not really recorded correctly.

Otherwise, the approach may not give reasonable estimates of the structural parameters. However, it could be that wages as such are measured correctly, but that these are only imprecise measures of the relevant state variables, which include other unobservable factors such as job conditions, quality of leisure, etc. In this case, the measurement error approach could indeed be useful even with precisely measured raw wages. In addition, there are empirical studies suggesting that the measurement error approach and alternative methods for regularizing the likelihood function yield similar inferences on the structural parameters of interest. Hence, it is not absolutely necessary to believe that all wages are literally measured with an error as large as suggested by the estimated distribution for m. Still, it is only prudent to compare with results from other approaches to regularizing the likelihood.

As usual, an alternative approach is to introduce an additional random and unobservable term in the utility function. Thus, suppose

$$u(a, x, 0) = b + \varepsilon_0, \tag{12.61}$$

$$u(a, x, 1) = x + \varepsilon_1, \tag{12.62}$$

where ε_0 and ε_1 are independent of each other and across time and of all wages x. Here, ε_0 is the random utility shock if retirement is selected and ε_1 is the corresponding shock in case of continued work. Assuming $E\varepsilon_i = 0$, we get from (12.1)

$$EV(0, x) = \frac{b}{1 - \beta}, \tag{12.63}$$

and hence from (12.2)

$$V(1, x, \varepsilon_0, \varepsilon_1) = \max\left\{ \frac{b}{1 - \beta} + \varepsilon_0, x + \varepsilon_1 + \beta E(V(1, y)|x) \right\}. \tag{12.64}$$

With serially independent wages we get a reservation wage

$$r(\varepsilon_0, \varepsilon_1) = \frac{b}{1 - \beta} - \beta E(V(1, y)) + \varepsilon_0 - \varepsilon_1. \tag{12.65}$$

Evidently, the reservation wage can be either higher or lower than in the deterministic utility case (12.5). Note carefully, though, that unlike in the measurement error case $E(V(1, y))$ is different now, reflecting the change in economic environment, but this does not change the conclusion on the reservation wage. Thus, if ε_0 and ε_1 (specifically, $\varepsilon_0 - \varepsilon_1$) follow a continuous distribution with unbounded support, there is no bound on parameters implied by the condition $x > r$, and this is the key to regularization of the likelihood in the random utility case.

To set up the likelihood function for the random utility case, we need to calculate the value function. Suppose for simplicity that wages and utility shocks are mutually independent of each other and across time, with f the density of the wage x, as usual, and h_i the density of the independent shocks ε_i, $i = 0, 1$. We write $EV = E(V(1, y))$ and get

$$
\begin{aligned}
EV &= \int_0^\infty \int_{-\infty}^\infty \Biggl\{ \int_{-\infty}^{b/(1-\beta)+\varepsilon_0-x-\beta EV} \left(\frac{b}{1-\beta} + \varepsilon_0 \right) h_1(\varepsilon_1)\, d\varepsilon_1 \\
&\quad + \int_{b/(1-\beta)+\varepsilon_0-x-\beta EV}^\infty (x + \varepsilon_1 + \beta EV) h_1(\varepsilon_1)\, d\varepsilon_1 \Biggr\} h_0(\varepsilon_0)\, d\varepsilon_0\, f(x)\, dx \\
&= \int_0^\infty \int_{-\infty}^\infty \Biggl\{ \left(\frac{b}{1-\beta} + \varepsilon_0 \right) H_1 \left(\frac{b}{1-\beta} + \varepsilon_0 - x - \beta EV \right) \\
&\quad + \left(1 - H_1 \left(\frac{b}{1-\beta} + \varepsilon_0 - x - \beta EV \right) \right) \left(x + \beta EV \right) \\
&\quad + E\left(\varepsilon_1 \middle| \varepsilon_1 > \frac{b}{1-\beta} + \varepsilon_0 - x - \beta EV \right) \Biggr\} h_0(\varepsilon_0)\, d\varepsilon_0\, f(x)\, dx.
\end{aligned}
\tag{12.66}
$$

Here, H_1 is the cumulative distribution function (cdf) corresponding to h_1. Writing the equation as $EV = T(EV)$, we have that T is a contraction, so EV may be computed at any given value of the parameter vector as $T^n(EV_0)$, for large n and arbitrary EV_0.

To derive the likelihood function for the panel case, note that the reservation wage changes every period, with the utility shocks ε_0 and ε_1. Whether or not this is realistic is an important issue to consider if relying on the random utility approach to break the curses of determinacy and degeneracy (chapters 2 and 4) in empirical analysis of retirement behavior. In any case, within the present framework, we may write

$$
r(\varepsilon_0, \varepsilon_1) = \frac{b}{1-\beta} - \beta EV + \varepsilon_0 - \varepsilon_1
\tag{12.67}
$$

for the reservation wage, given utility shocks ε_0 and ε_1, and

$$
\pi(\varepsilon_0, \varepsilon_1) = P(x > r(\varepsilon_0, \varepsilon_1))
\tag{12.68}
$$

for the conditional probability of continuing work, given these shocks. Thus, the contribution to the likelihood of a single individual with observed wages

$x_{i,t}$ and duration until retirement d_i is

$$
\begin{aligned}
L_i = \prod_{t=0}^{d_i-1} & \int_{-\infty}^{\infty} \int_{r(\varepsilon_{0,t}, x_{i,t})}^{\infty} \pi(\varepsilon_{0,t}, \varepsilon_{1,t}) f(x_{i,t} | x_{i,t} > r(\varepsilon_{0,t}, \varepsilon_{1,t})) \\
& \times h_1(\varepsilon_{1,t}) d\varepsilon_{1,t} h(\varepsilon_{0,t}) d\varepsilon_{0,t} \\
& \times \int_{-\infty}^{\infty} \int_{-\infty}^{\infty} (1 - \pi(\varepsilon_{0,d_i}, \varepsilon_{1,d_i})) h_1(\varepsilon_{1,d_i}) d\varepsilon_{1,d_i} h(\varepsilon_{0,d_i}) d\varepsilon_{0,d_i}.
\end{aligned}
$$
(12.69)

To understand this likelihood, note that for the last period d_i, where retirement occurs, it corresponds to the earlier form $(1 - \pi)$, giving the probability that the unobserved wage offer falls short of the reservation requirement, but the utility shocks are integrated out. For the earlier time periods, the form $\pi f(x|x > r)$ is recognized from (12.50), where π is the probability of continuing work and $f(x|x > r)$ is the conditional density of the observed wage x given that this exceeds the reservation wage, and again, the utility shocks are integrated out. In particular, for x to be acceptable, it must be that $x > r(\varepsilon_0, \varepsilon_1)$, and given the form of the reservation wage mapping $r(\cdot, \cdot)$ in (12.67), this produces the lower limit $\varepsilon_1 > r(\varepsilon_0, x)$ in the integral with respect to ε_1. Once this limit is observed, the observed wages $x_{i,t}$ are such that they are consistent with the reservation wages, and no bounds on the parameters are implied. The likelihood function has been regularized. Since $f(x|x > r) = f(x)/\pi$ within these limits, we have the simplification

$$
\begin{aligned}
L_i = \prod_{t=0}^{d_i-1} & \int_{-\infty}^{\infty} \int_{r(\varepsilon_{0,t}, x_{i,t})}^{\infty} f(x_{i,t}) h_1(\varepsilon_{1,t}) d\varepsilon_{1,t} h_0(\varepsilon_{0,t}) d\varepsilon_{0,t} \\
& \times \int_{-\infty}^{\infty} \int_{-\infty}^{\infty} (1 - \pi(\varepsilon_{0,d_i}, \varepsilon_{1,d_i})) h_1(\varepsilon_{1,d_i}) d\varepsilon_{1,d_i} h_0(\varepsilon_{0,d_i}) d\varepsilon_{0,d_i} \\
= \prod_{t=0}^{d_i-1} & f(x_{i,t}) \int_{-\infty}^{\infty} (1 - H_1(r(\varepsilon_{0,t}, x_{i,t}))) h_0(\varepsilon_{0,t}) d\varepsilon_{0,t} \\
& \times \int_{-\infty}^{\infty} \int_{-\infty}^{\infty} (1 - \pi(\varepsilon_{0,d_i}, \varepsilon_{1,d_i})) h_1(\varepsilon_{1,d_i}) d\varepsilon_{1,d_i} h_0(\varepsilon_{0,d_i}) d\varepsilon_{0,d_i}.
\end{aligned}
$$
(12.70)

As an example, consider again the exponential wage case (12.7) and assume that ε_0 and ε_1 are exponential with standard deviations σ_0 and σ_1, respectively. We have

$$L_i = \frac{\gamma^{d_i}}{\sigma_0^{d_i+1}\sigma_1} \prod_{t=0}^{d_i-1} e^{-\gamma x_{i,t}} \int_0^\infty e^{-(b/(1-\beta)-\beta EV+\varepsilon_{0,t}-x_{i,t})/\sigma_1 - \varepsilon_{0,t}/\sigma_0} \, d\varepsilon_{0,t}$$

$$\times \int_0^\infty \int_0^\infty \left(1 - e^{-\gamma(b/(1-\beta)-\beta EV+\varepsilon_{0,d_i}-\varepsilon_{1,d_i})}\right)$$

$$\times e^{-\varepsilon_{1,d_i}/\sigma_1} \, d\varepsilon_{1,d_i} e^{-\varepsilon_{0,d_i}/\sigma_0} \, d\varepsilon_{0,d_i}$$

$$= \frac{\gamma^{d_i}}{\sigma_0^{d_i+1}\sigma_1} e^{-r(0,0)d_i} \prod_{t=0}^{d_i-1} e^{-(\gamma-(1/\sigma_1))x_{i,t}} \int_0^\infty e^{-\left(\frac{1}{\sigma_0}+\frac{1}{\sigma_1}\right)\varepsilon_{0,t}} \, d\varepsilon_{0,t}$$

$$\times \int_0^\infty \left(\sigma_1 - \int_0^\infty e^{-\gamma(b/(1-\beta)-\beta EV+\varepsilon_{0,d_i})-((1/\sigma_1)-\gamma)\varepsilon_{1,d_i}} \, d\varepsilon_{1,d_i}\right)$$

$$\times e^{-\varepsilon_{0,d_i}/\sigma_0} \, d\varepsilon_{0,d_i}$$

$$= \frac{\gamma^{d_i}}{\sigma_0^{d_i+1}\sigma_1} e^{-r(0,0)d_i} \left\{ \prod_{t=0}^{d_i-1} e^{-(\gamma-(1/\sigma_1))x_{i,t}} \right\} \frac{1}{\left(\frac{1}{\sigma_0}+\frac{1}{\sigma_1}\right)^{d_i}}$$

$$\times \left(\sigma_0\sigma_1 - \int_0^\infty e^{-\gamma(b/(1-\beta)-\beta EV+\varepsilon_{0,d_i})} \frac{e^{-\varepsilon_{0,d_i}/\sigma_0}}{\frac{1}{\sigma_1}-\gamma} \, d\varepsilon_{0,d_i}\right)$$

$$= \frac{\gamma^{d_i}}{\sigma_0^{d_i+1}\sigma_1} e^{-r(0,0)d_i} \left\{ \prod_{t=0}^{d_i-1} e^{-(\gamma-(1/\sigma_1))x_{i,t}} \right\} \frac{1}{\left(\frac{1}{\sigma_0}+\frac{1}{\sigma_1}\right)^{d_i}}$$

$$\times \left(\sigma_0\sigma_1 - e^{-r(0,0)} \frac{1}{\left(\frac{1}{\sigma_0}+\gamma\right)\left(\frac{1}{\sigma_1}-\gamma\right)}\right). \tag{12.71}$$

Writing $\bar{x}_i = \Sigma_{t=0}^{d_i-1} x_{i,t}/d_i$ for the average wage paid to the ith worker and combining terms, we get

$$L_i = \left(\frac{\gamma}{1+\frac{\sigma_0}{\sigma_1}}\right)^{d_i} e^{-(b/(1-\beta)-\beta EV)d_i-(\gamma-(1/\sigma_1))d_i\bar{x}_i} \left(1 - \frac{e^{-(b/(1-\beta)-\beta EV)}}{(1+\gamma\sigma_0)(1-\gamma\sigma_1)}\right). \tag{12.72}$$

This is a complicated likelihood, in spite of the fact that a simple exponential distribution is used for the utility shocks. However, it is in exponential family form, with sufficient statistic $(d_i, d_i\bar{x}_i)$. For the full sample, the sufficient statistic is $(N_d, N_d\bar{x}_d)$, in the notation from (12.52).

The results are interesting. In the present case, adding exponential random utility shocks brings the model into the exponential family. The dimension

of the minimal sufficient statistic is two, thus ensuring that as many parameters (namely, two) as in the specification (12.52) without random utility
shocks (where the sufficient statistic was $(N_d, \overline{x}_d, x_{\min})$) are identified, and
in this case without relying on the minimum order statistic $x_{\min}$.

As an alternative approach to the random utility model, consider again
the expression (12.70) for L_i before going to the exponential case. This
is the product of d_i factors consisting of the density of the observed wage
$x_{i,t}$ multiplied by the probability that retirement is postponed, given such
a wage, i.e., the probability of $\varepsilon_{0,t}$ and $\varepsilon_{1,t}$ consistent with no retirement.
Finally, there is one factor simply giving the unconditional probability of
retirement (which occurs in period d_i). Recall that the first d_i of these probabilities are calculated from $V(1, x)$, given the distribution of the utility
shocks. If instead of the exponential distribution we adopt the extreme value
distribution and impose equal variances on $\varepsilon_{0,t}$ and $\varepsilon_{1,t}$, then the d_i first
probabilities take the conditional logit form from chapter 5 given $x_{i,t}$. This
is not the case for the last probability in the present formulation since x_{i,d_i}
is unobserved. However, by changing the order of integration we can obtain
an integral of conditional logit probabilities in the special case of extreme
value shocks with equal variances. Thus, let the conditional probability of
work given wage x based on (5.41) be

$$\pi(x) = \frac{e^{(x+\beta EV)/\sigma}}{e^{(x+\beta EV)/\sigma} + e^{b/((1-\beta)\sigma)}}, \tag{12.73}$$

where σ is now the common scale parameter for both $\varepsilon_{0,t}$ and $\varepsilon_{1,t}$. Then the
contribution to likelihood in the identical extreme value shock case
simplifies to

$$L_i = \left\{ \prod_{t=0}^{d_i-1} f(x_{i,t})\pi(x_{i,t}) \right\} \int_0^\infty (1 - \pi(x))f(x)dx. \tag{12.74}$$

As the earlier derivations using the exponential distribution show,
deviations from the assumptions of independently and identically distributed extreme value shocks to utility may change the likelihood considerably.
In the identical extreme value shock case, the sufficient statistics obtained in
the exponential utility shock case (12.72) are lost. Since there is no a priori
reason that the utility shocks should have equal variances in the work
and retirement states, or that they should be extreme value–distributed, the
exponential distribution is more attractive from the point of view of offering
sufficient statistics and allowing different variances. On the other hand, the
restrictive assumptions on the utility shocks do allow for a tractable
extension to the case of Markov wages. Here, the conditional likelihood

contribution for a single individual is

$$L_{c,i} = \left\{ \prod_{t=1}^{d_i-1} f(x_{i,t}|x_{i,t-1})\pi(x_{i,t}) \right\} \int_0^\infty (1 - \pi(x)) f(x|x_{i,d_i-1})dx \quad (12.75)$$

if $d_i > 0$. If a full likelihood is desired, the ith contribution may be calculated as the product of $L_{c,i}$ and

$$L_{0,i} = f(x_{i,0})\pi(x_{i,0}) \quad (12.76)$$

if $d_i > 0$, and simply as $L_{0,i} = \int_0^\infty (1 - \pi(x)) f(x)dx$ if $d_i = 0$. All the Markovian developments are under the conditional independence assumption (5.37) that the distribution of $x_{i,t}$ depends on the past only through $x_{i,t-1}$, not through the utility shocks, and the distribution of the latter is independent of all past information. Rust (1987b) has exploited this extreme-value random utility approach in dynamic programming modeling of the retirement decision.

12.6 GENERALIZATIONS

So far, we have used the specifications $u(a, x, 1) = x$ for the utility of work (x is the current wage) and $u(a, x, 0) = b$ for the utility of retirement, along with a constant discount factor β. A number of generalizations are natural in the retirement case and important in applications. First of all, survival probabilities can be entered, particularly since older workers are the ones typically facing the retirement problem. Survival probabilities are age-dependent, and so the stationary nature of the model is lost. Similarly, the utility of retirement can vary over time, again introducing a nonstationarity. Benefits can depend on the age of retirement, e.g., Social Security benefits in the United States are available only from age 62 (Social Security early retirement benefits) and are higher from ages 65–67 (Social Security normal benefits). In addition, health is likely to vary over time and may on average deteriorate, hence introducing a nonstationarity in the utility of work as well as leisure. Also, we have used a linear specification for the utility of wage income, implying risk neutrality, and risk aversion may well be required in applications. Writing δ_{t+1} for the probability of surviving through period $t + 1$ given survival through t, b_t for the time-varying utility of retirement, and $u_t(\cdot)$ for the time-varying and possibly nonlinear utility of wages, the dynamic programming model is generalized to

$$V_t(0, x) = b_t + \beta \delta_{t+1} V_{t+1}(0, x), \quad (12.77)$$

$$V_t(1, x) = \max\{b_t + \beta \delta_{t+1} V_{t+1}(0, x), u_t(x) + \beta \delta_{t+1} E(V_{t+1}(1, y)|x)\}. \quad (12.78)$$

Without stationarity, the model must be solved by backward recursion. This produces all the value functions $V_t(0, \cdot)$, $V_t(1, \cdot)$. Only $V_t(1, \cdot)$ depends on its second argument, and by a slight abuse of notation we write $V_t(0)$ for $V_t(0, \cdot)$. The reservation wage is now time-varying and given implicitly by

$$r_t = u_t^{-1}(b_t + \beta\delta_{t+1}(V_{t+1}(0) - E(V_{t+1}(1, y)|r_t))), \qquad (12.79)$$

which is explicit for serially independent wages. This implies time-varying work probabilities

$$\pi_t(x_{t-1}) = P(x_t > r_t|x_{t-1}). \qquad (12.80)$$

The conditional likelihood for the panel case is now

$$L_c = \prod_{\{i:d_i>0\}} (1 - \pi_{d_i}(x_{i,d_i-1})) \prod_{t_i=1}^{d_i-1} f(x_{i,t_i}|x_{i,t_i-1})1_{\{x_{i,t_i}>r_{t_i}\}}. \qquad (12.81)$$

This is easily recognized as a variation over the earlier L_c from (12.53) in the stationary model. By the same token, also the generalized likelihood can be regularized, e.g., by introducing measurement error, or random utility shocks from exponential, extreme value, or other distributions. In each case, a specific parametrization must be adopted, e.g., u_t and b_t would be set functions of the parameters to be estimated. One problem is initialization of the backward recursions to calculate the value functions. Typically, these are set, e.g., at 0 for some distant future date. However, a more satisfactory approach is often to adopt the previous stationary model beyond such a future horizon, iterate the contraction to calculate the stationary value function, and then initiate the backward recursions from this stationary value function at the horizon date.

There are other extensions that are relevant or even necessary in some applications. Part-time employment is one possibility that might be included as an additional option by expanding the state space. Similarly, it may sometimes be relevant to model the phenomenon that some retired workers may reenter the labor force at a later stage, thus relaxing the assumption that retirement is an absorbing state. We illustrate these generalizations briefly. Thus, let 0, 1, and 2 indicate the retirement, full-time, and part-time work states, respectively, and let x_1 and x_2 be the full-time, respectively part-time, wage. The model is now

$$V_t(k, x_1, x_2) = \max_{j=0,1,2} \left\{ u_t^j(x_j) + \beta\delta_{t+1}E(V_{t+1}(j, y_1, y_2)|x_1, x_2) \right\}, \qquad (12.82)$$

where $u_t^0(\cdot) \equiv b_t$, and $u_t^1(\cdot)$ and $u_t^2(\cdot)$ may differ since part-time work (state 2) offers more leisure time than full-time work and hence potentially higher utility for the same wage. Note that in retirement (state $k = 0$), returning to work is now an option. This in fact implies that the lagged state variable a_t may be redundant; i.e., we may in the simplest case write $V_t(x_1, x_2)$ for $V_t(k, x_1, x_2)$ above. Past retirement choices are no longer binding. However, the assumed processes for incomes, health, etc., in the various states could incorporate dependence on past states, which would typically be realistic (e.g., future wages in a full-time job are higher if this job has been held steadily over a period, a tenure effect). Other elaborations are possible and may be introduced similarly, e.g., the survival probability δ_{t+1} may be set as a function of the state, to capture the effect of work on health.

The likelihood function for the model with a return to work and partial retirement (part-time work) is slightly different from those considered earlier. First, there is no reason to stop observation at the time of retirement since the worker still faces a decision problem when a return to work is possible. Second, even though it is assumed above that the worker in each period can compare the potential incomes in the various states, the researcher can typically observe income only in the state chosen. With the state-dependent value functions above, this requires integration over unobserved incomes in the likelihood function. Details depend on the precise approach adopted, i.e., using the original or a somehow regularized likelihood, whether through an allowance for measurement error or the introduction of random utility shocks, but in general follow the above discussion.

So far, we have considered known or parametrized benefit or utility of retirement streams b_t. This corresponds to the case of defined benefit pension plans where benefits are specified, although the savings requirement (e.g., tax payments) may vary. We may also consider defined contribution plans where the worker chooses whether to save and where benefits (payoffs to savings) may vary, depending on returns on saving vehicles (e.g., stocks and bonds). To see how this complicates the model, consider the simplest specification (12.1)–(12.2) and generalize to

$$V(0, W) = \max_c \left\{ c + \beta E(V(0, \widetilde{W})|W, c) \right\}, \qquad (12.83)$$

$$V(1, x, W) = \max\{\max_c\{c + \beta E(V(0, \widetilde{W})|W, c)\},$$
$$\max_c\{c + \beta E(V(1, y, \widetilde{W})|W, c, x)\}\}, \qquad (12.84)$$

$$\widetilde{W} = (W + x - c)R, \qquad (12.85)$$

where c is consumption, R is the return on retirement savings and W and $\widetilde{W}$ are the current and the next period's wealth. In fact, the wage x is replaced by benefits b in the equation (12.85) for future wealth $\widetilde{W}$ in the retirement case. Of course, the other generalizations from above can be incorporated here, too, such as risk aversion, survival probabilities, etc., but are left out here for simplicity.

The likelihood function may incorporate stochastic returns R_t, which in this case are additional state variables (beyond wages) with a transition density that enters the likelihood function. A simplification to serially independent returns is often better justified empirically than independent wages, and in this case R is not required as part of the state vector of the dynamic program. However, it may be relevant to impose equal or strongly correlated returns across individuals within each time period as they invest in the same market, and this is a complication not present in the treatment of the wage variable. In any case, the value function now has an additional argument (wealth), so a solution, by forward or backward recursion, is computationally more demanding.

Finally, an important generalization is to allow the various parameters already considered to depend on regressors. To illustrate this, consider again the prototypal model, using (12.7), with parameters (b, β, γ), and assume that $b = b_i$ for the ith individual is given by

$$b_i = z_i'\theta, \tag{12.86}$$

where z_i is a vector of individual specific characteristics, e.g., age, gender, education, occupation, and health, and θ is a vector of associated regression coefficients. Before, the single parameter b was estimated from the minimum observed wage $x_{\min}$ (see (12.27)). Clearly, it is still possible to pick one of the coordinates in θ, say θ_1, and increase it (assuming $z_{i1} > 0, \forall i$) until the reservation wage r_i, given implicitly from (12.22) by

$$r_i = b_i - \frac{\beta}{\gamma}e^{-\gamma r_i}, \tag{12.87}$$

exactly equals x_i, for one of the individuals i, whereas $r_j \leq x_j$ for $j \neq i$. This determines the maximizing level for θ_1 given the other parameters. However, θ_2 may now be increased (again if $z_{i2} > 0, \forall i$) until $r_j = x_j$, for some $j \neq i$, and so on. It is seen that all regression parameters in $b_i = z_i'\theta$ are superconsistent if β and γ are known. Similar regression parameters introduced in β are superconsistent, by the same token, if b and γ are known. If the other parameters are not known, then regression parameters can be estimated in both b and γ or in both β and γ, and the estimated parameter vectors in both cases are CARRN (the development follows the simplest model closely). If the likelihood is regularized by allowing measurement error or introducing random utility shocks, regression parameters may then be estimated in all of (b, β, γ) as well as in parametrized portions of $b_t, u_t(\cdot)$, etc., in the generalized models above. Note that parameters in both

b and β can be estimated jointly when regressors are available, whereas without regressors only one of the two is analyzed at a time.

12.7 ALTERNATIVE MODELS

In the empirical analysis of retirement, a number of alternatives to the full dynamic programming approach have been considered. We briefly review duration models, methods using prediction equations, one-shot decision approaches, and option value models.

The form of the individual contribution to likelihood in the panel case L_i reflects the fact that the wage process is modeled as part of the likelihood function. The factor $f(x_{i,t})1_{\{x_{i,t}>r\}}$ in (12.50) results from $\pi f(x_{i,t}|x_{i,t}>r)$, where π is the work probability and r is the reservation wage. A *duration model* results from the simplifying assumption that wages are exogenous, in which case $f(\cdot|\cdot)$ may be dropped from the likelihood, and there remains

$$L_i = (1 - \pi_{d_i}) \prod_{t=0}^{d_i-1} \pi_t. \tag{12.88}$$

Here, the work probability π_t is typically modeled using regressors in an ad hoc fashion without attempting to solve the dynamic programming problem. Regressors could include wages (now considered exogenous), health, age, gender, marital status, occupation, local unemployment rate, etc.

A variation is to write π_t as the work probability in a formulation of the dynamic programming approach where π_t is not either 0 or 1, e.g., with measurement error or random utility introduced. In particular, if r is the solution for the reservation wage from the dynamic programming model and g is the density of measurement errors, as in (12.58) above, then

$$\pi = P(w > r)$$
$$= P\left(\frac{x}{m} > r\right)$$
$$= P\left(m < \frac{x}{r}\right)$$
$$= G\left(\frac{x}{r}\right), \tag{12.89}$$

where G is the CDF corresponding to g. We could now consider

$$L_i = \left(1 - G\left(\frac{x_{d_i}}{r}\right)\right) \prod_{t=0}^{d_i-1} G\left(\frac{x_t}{r}\right) \tag{12.90}$$

as our duration model likelihood, attempting to build in aspects of the dynamic programming framework. However, note that if g involves a scale parameter (as, e.g., in the exponential and normal distributions), then r is not separately identified from this, and solution of the dynamic programming model to determine r for given parameters is left redundant. In this case, the analysis has no structural aspect after all, since the only parameters identified are those in the measurement error distribution.

Another possibility is to introduce random utility and use $\pi(x)$ from (12.73) in

$$L_i = (1 - \pi(x_{d_i})) \prod_{t=0}^{d_i-1} \pi(x_t). \qquad (12.91)$$

Compared to the earlier approach, this leaves out much of the information available for estimation of the wage process by dropping f from the likelihood (12.74) as a separate factor and estimating it only indirectly via its contribution to π via EV. Furthermore, both of the above likelihoods (12.90) and (12.91) take the wage x_{d_i} that was turned down by the agent in favor of retirement as being observable to the researcher. If x_{d_i} is unobservable, as we have otherwise assumed, it must be integrated out of the likelihood function, thus necessitating specifying its distribution, even though wages are now taken as exogenous. These considerations illustrate the shortcomings of the duration approach if inference on the underlying dynamic programming model is the ultimate goal.

There is one case in which the latter likelihood function (12.91) does apply, at least as an approximation, for the full dynamic programming model. This is the simplifying case where future wages are assumed known. Under this assumption, it is no further restriction that the final wage x_{d_i} above is treated as observable. In this case, all uncertainty in the random utility form of the dynamic programming model enters through the utility shocks. In practice, to calculate EV, which enters $\pi(\cdot)$, it is necessary for the researcher to obtain values of future wages x_{it} up to some distant future date, say T, and use backward recursion on $V_t\,(1, x_t, \varepsilon_{0t}, \varepsilon_{1t})$, which is now (with known x_t) in the form $V_t\,(1, \varepsilon_{0t}, \varepsilon_{1t})$, i.e.,

$$V_t\,(1, \varepsilon_{0t}, \varepsilon_{1t}) = \max\left\{\frac{b}{1-\beta} + \varepsilon_{0t},\, x_t + \varepsilon_{1t} + \beta EV_{t+1}\,(1, \varepsilon_{0t+1}, \varepsilon_{1t+1})\right\}.$$
$$(12.92)$$

In fact, since only expected value functions are needed in $\pi_t(\cdot)$, the iterations may be directly on

$$EV_t\,(1) = \log\left(e^{b/(\sigma(1-\beta))} + e^{(x_t+\beta EV_{t+1}(1))/\sigma}\right) \qquad (12.93)$$

under the assumption that ε_{0t} and ε_{1t} are independent and identically extreme value distributed with dispersion parameter σ. In this case, the work probability is

$$\pi(x_t) = \frac{e^{(x_t + \beta EV_{t+1}(1))/\sigma}}{e^{b/(\sigma(1-\beta))} + e^{(x_t + \beta EV_{t+1}(1))/\sigma}}, \tag{12.94}$$

and the likelihood function for individual i is

$$L_i = (1 - \pi(x_{i,d_i})) \prod_{t=0}^{d_i-1} \pi(x_{i,t}), \tag{12.95}$$

considering that wages are taken as exogenous.

Typically, future wages are predicted from a *wage regression* on variables such as gender, education, and possibly individual specific fixed effects that are assumed constant through time, as well as variables such as age, Social Security eligibility, etc., that may be unambiguously predicted for future time periods as functions of age. Still, the regression model is fit only across periods where wage observations are available, i.e., prior to retirement, which therefore poses a sample selection problem when applying the estimated model to forecasting into the period where the individual is actually observed to be retired. In essence, observed wages would tend to be from the upper end of the distribution relevant for forecasting. This problem is avoided in the full dynamic programming approach, where the wage process is estimated as part of the structural model, and so is not subject to selection bias.

One-shot decision models are related to the wage prediction equation approach in that current observables are used as regressors for predicting a future realization, but in this case the actual retirement date is predicted rather than just the future wage. This implies that a single random shock is employed in modeling the choice between multiple possible retirement dates. This is obviously a simplification relative to the dynamic programming model, which allows reoptimization every period, depending on new realizations of shocks. Gustman and Steinmeier (1986) is an early example of a structural one-shot model. The model is explicitly dynamic and uses a constant elasticity of substitution period utility function of consumption and leisure. The likelihood function is formed by assuming that each individual gets a single draw from a bivariate distribution of a vector representing the elasticity of substitution and the relative weight on leisure in the utility function. Given this, the agent solves a deterministic dynamic problem.

Finally, so-called *option value models* have been applied frequently in retirement modeling. Here, the idea is to simplify calculations by taking the expectation of future random variables before choosing the maximum. The dynamic programming approach, on the other hand, allows the agent to look for positive realizations of future shocks before deciding on a policy. This way, the option value model in general predicts earlier retirement than the dynamic programming model since it ignores the potential benefits that could be obtained by deferring the retirement decision and sampling more information. Lumsdaine, Stock and Wise (1992) compare probit, option value, and dynamic programming models of retirement.

To illustrate, suppose the decision as to whether to retire or not must be made in the current time period t and that the potential current and future wages and benefits are $x_t, x_{t+1}, \ldots, x_T$ and $b_t, b_{t+1}, \ldots, b_T$. Thus, the option value approach is among those based on prediction equations for future incomes. The value of retiring now is assessed as

$$V_t^r = b_t + \varepsilon_{0t} + \sum_{i=t+1}^{T} \beta^{i-t} b_i$$

$$= b_t + \varepsilon_{0t} + V^b(t+1, T). \qquad (12.96)$$

Here, ε_{0t} is a random utility shock. Such shocks are associated with future time periods, too, but are assumed to be of expectation zero, and the sum represents the expected value as of t of the future stream. The value of retiring in any later period, say j, $j \geq t + 1$, is

$$V_j^0 = x_t + \varepsilon_{1t} + \sum_{i=t+1}^{j-1} \beta^{i-t} x_i + \sum_{i=j}^{T} \beta^{i-t} b_i$$

$$= x_t + \varepsilon_{1t} + V^x(t+1, j-1) + V^b(j, T), \qquad (12.97)$$

where ε_{1t} is the random utility shock associated with employment, also assumed to be of expectation zero and thus vanishing in the expected value of the future stream. In the option value model, retirement at t is assumed to take place if

$$V_t^r > V_{t+}^0, \qquad (12.98)$$

where V_{t+}^0 is the maximum over later possible retirement dates,

$$V_{t+}^0 = \max_j \left\{ V_j^0 \right\}. \qquad (12.99)$$

Thus, the optimization problem at t is of the form

$$V_t^0 = \max\{b_t + \varepsilon_{0t} + V^b(t+1, T), x_t + \varepsilon_{1t} + V^m(t+1, T)\}, \qquad (12.100)$$

with the definition

$$V^m(t+1, T) = \max_j \left\{ V^x(t+1, j-1) + V^b(j, T) \right\}. \qquad (12.101)$$

Assuming ε_{0t} and ε_{1t} are independent and identically extreme values distributed with parameter σ, this produces the work probability

$$\pi_t = \frac{e^{(x_t + V^m(t+1,T))/\sigma}}{e^{(b_t + V^b(t+1,T))/\sigma} + e^{(x_t + V^m(t+1,T)/\sigma)}} \qquad (12.102)$$

and the likelihood function for individual i

$$L_i = (1 - \pi_{d_i}) \prod_{t=1}^{d_i-1} \pi_t. \tag{12.103}$$

Even in this case, where future wages and benefits are presumed known with certainty, the dynamic programming approach differs distinctly from the option value model. The dynamic programming approach is to calculate the value of retirement now as V_t^r, exactly as in the option value model from (12.96), and calculate the value of continued work not as V_{t+}^0 from (12.99) but as

$$V_t^w = x_t + \varepsilon_{1t} + \beta E \left(\max \left\{ V_{t+1}^r, V_{t+1}^w \right\} \right). \tag{12.104}$$

The essential difference is that the expectation operator and the maximum operator have been interchanged. As these operators commute only if the random variables of the problem are degenerate, the difference is nontrivial. To appreciate the difference, note that only the dynamic programming model accounts for the agent's comparison of the random realizations of the next period's values of retirement and work, V_{t+1}^r, respectively V_{t+1}^w. Writing out V_t^w in more detail,

$$V_t^w = x_t + \varepsilon_{1t} + \beta E \left(\max \left\{ b_{t+1} + \varepsilon_{0,t+1} + V^b \left(t+2, T \right), \right. \right.$$
$$\left. \left. x_{t+1} + \varepsilon_{1,t+1} + \beta E \left(\max \left\{ V_{t+2}^r, V_{t+2}^w \right\} \right) \right\} \right). \tag{12.105}$$

This makes it clear that the next period's maximization, taking into account the realizations of $\varepsilon_{0,t+1}$ and $\varepsilon_{1,t+1}$, are incorporated into the expected next period's value assessment in the dynamic programming approach. Thus, the solution to the overall period t problem,

$$V_t = \max \left\{ V_t^r, V_t^w \right\}, \tag{12.106}$$

clearly differs from the solution to the option value problem V_t^0.

12.8 APPLICATION: THE JOINT RETIREMENT OF MARRIED COUPLES

In this section we consider an application to a panel of married couples. Both spouses are initially working. The unit of observation is the couple, and two durations are observed for each: the duration until the husband's retirement and the duration until the wife's retirement. It is of interest to study the dependence pattern between the two durations. Thus, a multivariate model is required. An, Christensen, and Datta Gupta (2004) introduce a *bivariate mixed proportional hazard* (BMPH) model that allows two different sources of dependence between the husband's and the wife's durations, as well as estimation of the own effects and cross-effects of income, health, pension eligibility, etc. The husband and wife may coordinate retirement dates due to complementarities in leisure times. Alternatively, the durations until retirement may be correlated even conditionally on regressors due to assortative mating/matching on unobservables. The BMPH model allows identifying both sources of dependence and separating them empirically.

Let d_h and d_w denote the observed durations until retirement for the husband and the wife, respectively, starting from a certain base year specified for each couple. Assume there are three latent random duration variables, namely, D_h and D_w for the husband and wife, and an additional couple-specific variable D_c. In the BMPH model, the observed durations are modelled as

$$d_h = \min\{D_h, D_c\} \tag{12.107}$$

for the husband and

$$d_w = \min\{D_w, D_c\} \tag{12.108}$$

for the wife. The interpretation is that the husband and wife will retire together if the couple variable D_c is the smallest of the three latent variables. This is used to capture active retirement coordination, corresponding to complementarities in leisure times. On the other hand, assortative mating/matching is captured by allowing D_h and D_w to depend on unobserved heterogeneity terms (fixed effects or frailty terms) that may correlate across spouses without necessarily forcing simulatenous retirement. The specification for the hazards of the three latent durations is of the proportional type,

$$h(D|z, v) = \lambda(D)e^{z\beta}v, \tag{12.109}$$

where λ is the baseline hazard that may be taken to be exponential or otherwise to reflect duration dependence, z is a vector of observed regressors, and v is unobserved heterogeneity. The BMPH model allows different λ, z, β, and v for the three latent durations.

The model is estimated by maximum likelihood applied to a sample of older married couples from Denmark, with the results reported in table 12.1. The detailed results show that both sources of dependence are empirically important. From the table, baseline duration dependence is positive for husbands and insignificant for wives (asymptotic t-statistics in parentheses), whereas it is negative for the couple's hazard. The latter

Table 12.1 Hazard Functions.

	Husband's Hazard	Wife's Hazard	Couple's Hazard
Income, husband	−6.1	−.10	−3.45
	(−6.54)	(−1.83)	(−2.36)
Income, wife	−.01	−.55	−3.08
	(−0.4)	(−4.29)	(−2.77)
Wealth	0.1	−.08	.61
	(.16)	(−1.56)	(2.12)
Health, husband	2.91	−1.54	
	(3.80)	(−2.10)	
Health, wife	−.62	2.89	
	(−1.15)	(3.73)	
Eligibility, husband	.90	2.64	
	(.80)	(2.38)	
Eligibility, wife	1.35	3.91	
	(2.39)	(3.62)	
Duration dependence	.93	.27	−2.59
	(5.07)	(1.04)	(−2.14)

result suggests that couples that actively coordinate their retirement planning are couples that choose to retire relatively early and then do so jointly (simultaneously for husband and wife). From the own effects, both husband and wife retire earlier if their own income is low or they receive a health shock. The cross-effects of health show that wives retire later if husbands receive health shocks. Both increase their retirement hazard if the spouse becomes eligible for pensions. Interestingly, wealth is significant only in the third (couple's) hazard that is specific to the BMPH model. Thus, increases in wealth increase the rate of joint retirement.

12.9 EXERCISES

1. Show that in the limiting reduced rank distribution of the CARRN estimator in (12.47), the direction of support is given by (Λ_1, Λ_2) with $\Lambda_1 = \beta E(x|x > r)$, the discounted conditional expected wage given continued work. Interpret the result.

2. Derive the measurement error likelihood (12.59) using the Pearson type V error distribution (9.16) for g. Are the resulting estimators CARRN?

3. Let the unobserved heterogeneity in (12.109) be degenerate, $v = 1$. Show that the observed durations d_h and d_w are nevertheless dependent. Now drop the third (couple) hazard (set $D_c = \infty$), allow general common frailty v, and show that the observed durations are again dependent. Interpret the difference between the two sources of dependence.

12.10 REFERENCES

Das (1992) discusses the utilization and retirement of capital in a dynamic framework. Rust (1987b, 1992) and Berkovec and Stern (1991) apply dynamic programming to retirement behavior in the labor market with an eye toward policy analysis. Stock and Wise (1990) model the effect of pension schemes on retirement. Clark et al. (1980) and Henretta and O'Rand (1983) are early studies on the joint retirement of married couples.

Chapter Thirteen

Continuous States and Controls

13.1 INTRODUCTION

With continuous states and controls, much of the framework from chapter 6 (continuous states, discrete controls) may still be used. Note that none of the functional analysis (contraction mapping theorem, etc.) in that chapter required discrete controls.

Computation of the optimal policy and value function is typically more difficult in the continuous state/control case. We saw in the job search model that the iteration on the value function mapping wage offers into reals can be replaced by an iteration on the reservation wage, the critical value of the state variable determining which control (employment or continued search) is chosen. This is typically the case when discrete controls are used. The state space can be divided up into partitions implying different controls, and if the boundaries of these regions can be simply described by a few coefficients, the iteration can proceed on these coefficients rather than on the value function itself. Generally, this is not possible with continuous controls. In important cases, however, the value function iteration can be reduced to iteration on finitely many numbers, a valuable simplification. Most notably, the linear-quadratic (LQ) model admits a recursion on matrices.

Throughout we note the omnipresence of the curse of degeneracy. That is, the distribution of controls given the state is degenerate. Controls are generally deterministic functions of the state. Of course, this demands data configurations that simply do not occur (analogous to the zero requirements on the data tables in the discrete case)—this is the curse of determinacy. The curse of determinacy can be broken through assumptions on measurement error, as in the discrete control case, but the curse of degeneracy remains. That is, there is simply no data information on transition probabilities corresponding to nonoptimal choices of the controls. It is sometimes possible to identify these probabilities using the restrictions imposed by the dynamic programming specification. An approach via imperfect control breaks the curse. A potentially more attractive modeling approach, however, as in the discrete case, is a random utility specification.

In section 13.2 we take up the illuminating framework of finite-horizon linear-quadratic dynamic programming. In section 13.3, we extend to the infinite-horizon case. These models provide a useful setting for discussion of the econometric implications of the rational expectations approach—implications that are still being worked out and that raise questions about the feasibility of providing useful macroeconomic policy prescriptions based on econometric models. In section 13.4, we turn to a discussion of error specification, identification, and estimation of LQ models. At a conceptual level, these remarks carry over to generally specified models. Section 13.5 treats general properties of dynamic programming solutions to continuous state/control models. Sections 13.6 through 13.8 discuss smoothness, various examples, and random utility in the general case.

13.2 THE LINEAR-QUADRATIC MODEL: FINITE HORIZON

Suppose the utility function in any period is quadratic,

$$u(x, c) = x' Rx + c' Qc, \tag{13.1}$$

with $x \in R^K$ the state variable and $c \in R^c$ the control and $R(K \times K)$ and $Q(c \times c)$ negative definite. Anticipating further developments, suppose the objective is to maximize an expected discounted sum of utilities over T periods, i.e.,

$$\max_{c_0,\dots,c_T} E \sum_{t=0}^{T} \beta^t u(x_t, c_t), \tag{13.2}$$

and suppose the transition equation is linear,

$$x_{t+1} = Ax_t + Bc_t + \varepsilon_t, \tag{13.3}$$

with A a $K \times K$ matrix, $Ba K \times c$ matrix, and ε_t an error term with $E\varepsilon_t = 0$, $E\varepsilon_t \varepsilon_t' = \Sigma$, and $E\varepsilon_t \varepsilon_{t'}' = 0$ for $t' \neq t$.

The final-period problem is easy; the transition equation is irrelevant, and the control enters only through the term $c_T' Qc_T$; its optimal value is zero, obtained at $c_T = 0$. The final-period value is thus

$$V_T(x_t) = x_T' Rx_T = x_T P_T x_T, \tag{13.4}$$

defining P_T and we have

$$V_{T-1}(x_{T-1}) = \max_{c_{T-1}} \{ x_{T-1}' Rx_{T-1} + c_{T-1}' Qc_{T-1}$$
$$+ \beta E((Ax_{T-1} + Bc_{T-1} + \varepsilon_{T-1})'$$
$$\times P_T(Ax_{T-1} + Bc_{T-1} + \varepsilon_{T-1})) \}. \tag{13.5}$$

Taking expectations,

$$V_{T-1}(x_{T-1}) = \max_{c_{T-1}} \left\{ x'_{T-1} R x_{T-1} + c'_{T-1} Q c_{T-1} + \beta(Ax_{T-1} + Bc_{T-1})' P_T \right.$$
$$\left. \times (Ax_{T-1} + Bc_{T-1}) + \beta tr\, (P_T \Sigma) \right\}. \tag{13.6}$$

Solving the first-order condition gives the control rule

$$c_{T-1} = -\beta(Q + \beta B' P_T B)^{-1} B' P_T A x_{T-1}, \tag{13.7}$$

and substituting gives $V_{T-1}(x)$ explicitly as

$$V_{T-1}(x) = x' P_{T-1} x + \beta tr\, P_T \Sigma, \tag{13.8}$$

with

$$P_{T-1} = R + \beta^2 A' P_T B H^{-1} Q H^{-1} B' P_T A$$
$$+ \beta(A' - \beta A' P_T B H^{-1} B') P_T (A - \beta B H^{-1} B' P_T A), \tag{13.9}$$

where $H = Q + \beta B' P_T B$ and the first term gives the uncontrollable (negative) utility associated with the current value of the state variable x_{T-1}, the second gives the utility associated with the current control, and the third gives the utility associated with the expected effect of the current control on the future state. Upon simplification we find

$$P_{T-1} = R + \beta A' P_T A - \beta^2 A' P_T B(Q + \beta B' P_T B)^{-1} B' P_T A. \tag{13.10}$$

A little additional effort makes it clear that this form is preserved, so that the entire sequence of value functions is given by

$$V_t(x) = x' P_t x + \sum_{i=1}^{T-t} \beta^i \operatorname{tr} P_{t+i} \Sigma, \tag{13.11}$$

with the P_t satisfying the backward recursion

$$P_{t-1} = R + \beta A' P_t A - \beta^2 A' P_t B(Q + \beta B' P_t B)^{-1} B' P_t A \tag{13.12}$$

and with $P_T = R$. The controls are given by

$$c_t = -\beta(Q + \beta B' P_{t+1} B)^{-1} B' P_{t+1} A x_t. \tag{13.13}$$

The linear-quadratic setup exhibits several interesting properties. First, the backward recursion has become a recursion not on general functions but on a $K \times K$ matrix. This is an important simplification of the general problem. As we have seen, there are other cases when the general functional recursion can be reduced to a simpler problem. Second, the uncertainty really doesn't matter here—the control rule is the same as that which would be obtained if the error term were known to be zero in every period (of course, the value itself is reduced by the presence of uncertainty). This is essentially the only case in which this "certainty equivalence" holds. Third, each value function in the sequence $V_T, \ldots, V_0$ is concave—that is, the general shape is preserved by the backward recursion. This can be easily established by induction: P_T is negative definite; assume P_t is negative semidefinite, then $V_{t-1}(x)$ is the maximum in c_{t-1} of a nonpositive function, nonpositivity is preserved under maximization, so $V_{t-1}(x) \leq 0$ for any x, so P_{t-1} is negative semidefinite.

Our formulation attempts to keep the state variables and controls near zero; this is merely a normalization. An interaction between states and controls, e.g., $x_t' S c_t$, can be introduced but involves no essential increase in generality (transform to new controls $c + Q^{-1} S x$). The matrices R, Q, A, and B can all depend on t, and an almost identical derivation of the optimal policy applies. These matrices can be stochastic—then certainty equivalence is lost as the control rule depends on variance and covariances. As discussed below, adding the right kind of randomness in the objective function can serve to break the curse of degeneracy. Finally, the state itself can be unobserved and an observation equation $z_t = D x_t + v_t$ introduced (D is $L \times K$). With a normality assumption this leads to the Kalman filter.

13.2.1 An Application: Macroeconomic Control

The finite-horizon linear-quadratic model had early applications in economics. Theil (1964) applied the LQ model to problems of the firm— production and employment decisions—as well as to macroeconomics. This insightful book sports the modern notation $x_1(\mathcal{F}_0), \ldots, x_T(\mathcal{F}_{T-1})$, where $\mathcal{F}_t$ are information sets consisting of information available at the end of the tth period. Many other early applications were to the analysis of policy using macroeconomic models. This ambitious search for optimal activist government policies led to the rational expectations revolution in macroeconomics. Chow (1975) developed control rules and computational techniques and applied them to the control of macroeconomic models. As an example, one of many applications, Chow (1978) proposed to use the LQ framework together with a macroeconometric model to analyze the effects of government policy. The model chosen was the Michigan Quarterly Econometric Model as of 1977. As a warning to the eager reader, this model, with its 77 endogenous variables (related by 30 identities) and 35 exogenous variables, would no longer be used in economic research. It was, however, a state-of-the-art model in its prime. The objective function was

$$ E \sum_{t=1}^{8} (0.75(u - 4.0)^2 + 0.75(GNPgap)^2 + TB^2 + (p - 2)^2), \quad (13.14) $$

where u is the unemployment rate, $GNPgap$ is the deviation of gross national product (GNP) from its potential as a percentage of potential, TB is the trade balance as a percentage of GNP, and p is the annual inflation rate. This objective function measures instability. The control variables are the Treasury bill rate and federal nondefense purchases of goods and services.

In order to measure policy effectiveness, three control regimes were considered: (1) smooth trends, in which the control variables follow first-order autoregressions with estimated parameters; (2) empirical reaction functions, in which the control variables are modeled with more lags and with exogenous variables (this fits better than the smooth trend model and captures what the government was actually doing); and (3) the optimal control rule. The findings were that government policy did serve to reduce instability relative to the regime of smooth trends for the controls. This was interpreted as evidence against the hypothesis that government policies intensify instability. However, the improvement of the actual policy over the smooth trend is small relative to what could be achieved by the optimal control policy. Of course, the result is qualified by feasibility considerations and the fact that the government has other simultaneous objectives.

13.2.2 Rational Expectations

The missing qualification in the literature at the time was provided by Lucas (1976). Lucas argued convincingly that an agent's decision rules could not be taken as fixed with respect to government policy and that changes in policy would lead therefore to changes in the structure of the economy. Thus, equations estimated in a precontrol period and then used to recommend policy would no longer be relevant when the policy changes were instituted. This point was made even more strongly by Kydland and Prescott (1977), who argue that taking the best discretionary decisions at every point in time, given the current state, will not lead to maximization of a social objective function. This paradox arises because the decisions of agents in the economy depend on expectations of future policy decisions. Policy makers do not properly take into account the effect of the policy rule on the actions of the agents, and time-consistent policy rules are suboptimal. Essentially, the policy in $t + s$ specified in period t may have been chosen to influence allocation decisions in periods t through $t + s - 1$. However, when $t + s$ rolls around, these decisions have already been made and so are irrelevant for $(t + s)$ policy given the state variables in $t + s$. Chow (1981), Taylor (1979), Hansen and Sargent (1980), and many others instituted an econometric program that incorporated rational expectations into econometric models. This approach and its subsequent development answer the objection made by Lucas, in that the estimated equations are consistent with rational expectations assumptions. It does not directly address the objections raised by Kydland and Prescott.

13.3 THE LINEAR-QUADRATIC MODEL: INFINITE HORIZON

The objective function for the time-homogeneous LQ model with discounting is

$$E \sum_{t=0}^{\infty} \beta^t \left(x_t' R x_t + c_t' Q c_t \right), \tag{13.15}$$

with transition equation

$$x_{t+1} = A x_t + B c_t + \varepsilon_t, \tag{13.16}$$

with $E\varepsilon_t = 0$, $E\varepsilon_t \varepsilon_t' = \Sigma$, and $E\varepsilon_t \varepsilon_{t'}' = 0$ when $t \neq t'$. This is an example of a model with the utility unbounded below. There is no terminal state, so backward recursion from a final-period optimum is ruled out. However, we can do forward recursion from an arbitrary function $V_0(x)$. In view of our analysis in the finite-horizon case, it makes sense to start with a quadratic function

$$V^0(x) = x' P^0 x + m^0, \tag{13.17}$$

and in fact $P^0 = R$ and $m^0 = 0$ correspond to our convention of taking $V^0 = \max_c u(x, c)$.

Having started with a quadratic, each V^t in the iterative sequence is quadratic and the sequence $T^t(V^0)$ is characterized by the sequences $P^0 = R, m^0 = 0$, and

$$\begin{aligned}
P^t &= R + \beta A' P^{t-1} A \\
&\quad - \beta^2 A' P^{t-1} B (Q + \beta B' P^{t-1} B)^{-1} B' P^{t-1} A \\
&= T_P(P^{t-1}),
\end{aligned} \tag{13.18}$$

$$\begin{aligned}
m^t &= \beta m^{t-1} + \beta \operatorname{tr} P^{t-1} \Sigma \\
&= \sum_{i=1}^{t} \beta^i \operatorname{tr} P^{t-i} \Sigma \\
&= \operatorname{tr} \left(\sum_{i=1}^{t} \beta^i P^{t-i} \Sigma \right).
\end{aligned} \tag{13.19}$$

Conditions under which these sequences converge to fixed points P, m are well studied. Sufficient conditions are given by Anderson et al. (1996). Note that the value functions satisfy $V^t(x) \leq V^{t-1}(x)$ since they differ only in a nonpositive term. Thus, the sequence P^t either converges to a constant matrix or diverges to minus infinity. As a practical matter, it soon becomes apparent on iteration which case will occur.

This setup is convenient since the value function and control rules are easily computed—the stationary control rule is

$$c_t = -\beta (Q + \beta B' P B)^{-1} B' P A x_t. \tag{13.20}$$

The linear structure, stationarity, and explicit solutions lend themselves to applied work. An alternative derivation of the value function is simply to guess that the solution is quadratic, plug into the Bellman equation, verify that a quadratic satisfies the equation, and calculate the appropriate updating rule. While perhaps the simplest derivation, this method does require an initial guess. In fact, the linear-quadratic model is the only model for which a polynomial value function is a good guess. Anderson et al. (1996) discuss in detail the computation of solutions to the LQ model. Efficient algorithms and programs are available. Direct iteration on (13.18) and (13.19) is not an efficient computational method, although the recursive representation is intuitively appealing.

13.3.1 Application: Macro Policy with Rational Expectations

Taylor (1979) applied infinite-horizon linear-quadratic control to obtain optimal monetary policy rules consistent with rational expectations. He specified a model in which an agent's actions depend on expected inflation and expected output and constrained these expectations to be those predicted by the model. The dependent variables are real aggregate expenditures in logarithms measured as deviations from a trend and the inflation rate. Real expenditures depend on their lagged values, the price level, real money balances, expected inflation, and a time trend. Inflation depends on its lagged value and expected real expenditures. The constraint that the expectations are in fact the expected values predicted by the model is imposed, and the model is fit by nonlinear least squares to U.S. quarterly data over 1953:1–1975:4. The fitted model is then used as the transition equation for the dynamic programming problem with the objective of maximizing

$$-E[\lambda(y - y^*)^2 - (1 - \lambda)(\pi - \pi^*)^2] \tag{13.21}$$

for steady-state values of y and π, where the starred values are the targets, with respect to m, real money balances. Taylor obtains a feedback control rule for money balances and concludes that the optimal policy would have given more stability than the actual policy and that a constant growth policy would also have done well. Faced with the Kydland-Prescott argument that policy makers would want to change their previously announced policies after seeing the actions of the agents in the economy, Taylor is forced to argue that policy makers are somehow constrained not to do so, perhaps by law. This seems to be about the best one could hope to do.

13.4 ESTIMATION OF LINEAR-QUADRATIC MODELS

Note that the work described above applied dynamic programming techniques using estimated models as transition equations for the state variables. The problem of analyzing a sequence of state/control variables with the intention of recovering not only the transition equations but also the objective function was not addressed.

13.4.1 The Curse of Degeneracy

Although the states and the controls are both continuous, the problem of degeneracy remains. That is, the optimal control rule gives the control c_t as a deterministic function of the state x_t. Thus, we have the density for the observed variables at time t,

$$
\begin{aligned}
p(c_t, x_t | x_{t-1}, \theta) &= p(c_t | x_t, x_{t-1}, \theta) p(x_t | x_{t-1}, \theta) \\
&= p(c_t | x_t, \theta) p(x_t | x_{t-1}, \theta),
\end{aligned}
\tag{13.22}
$$

where lagged c does not enter since it is a function of lagged x and in the factor $p(c|x)$ lagged x does not enter since c is a deterministic function of the state x_t. Thus, the first factor is a degenerate distribution. It gives point mass at the value of c that is optimal for the state configuration x_t (given parameters θ). As we accumulate (x, c) pairs, we learn θ exactly and rapidly. In practice, of course, the curse of determinacy obtains, and we will see almost immediately that the data do not correspond to the model for any parameter.

13.4.2 Sources of Noise

In order to make the model practically useful, the observed control c must be made to have a distribution around its implied value given the state. Otherwise, the curse of determinacy arises since the model requires the control observations to be exactly determined by the state observations, and this simply does not hold in practice. One approach is to assume that c comes with additive error uncorrelated with the error in the transition equation.

This approach has become so usual that it is often unmentioned and taken to be part of the specification of the LQ model. If we make this assumption, then we have the system of equations

$$x_{t+1} = Ax_t + Bc_t + \varepsilon_t, \tag{13.23}$$

$$c_t = Dx_t + v_t, \tag{13.24}$$

where the matrix D is obtained from the solution to the LQ problem

$$\max E \sum \beta^t (x_t' Rx_t + c_t' Qc_t) \tag{13.25}$$

subject to the transition equation $x_{t+1} = Ax_t + Bc_t + \varepsilon_t$. Here, $E\varepsilon = Ev = 0$, $E\varepsilon\varepsilon' = \Omega$, $Evv' = \Lambda$, and $Ev\varepsilon' = 0$. In forming the likelihood function, these are assumed to be normally distributed and thus characterized by these moments. Chow (1981) interprets the errors in the control equation as reflecting imperfect control, errors in carrying out the optimal policy. As in chapter 4, there is a substantial difference between the interpretation of noise in c as measurement error and the interpretation as optimization error.

It is useful to make a simple count of parameters as a first attack on the possibility of identification. The matrices have the following dimensions: A $(K \times K)$, B $(K \times c)$, D $(c \times K)$, R $(K \times K)$, and $Q(c \times c)$. The matrices R and Q can without loss of generality be taken to be symmetric. The discount factor β is a scalar parameter. The fundamental (structural) parameters are A, B, R, Q, and β. In total, taking into account symmetry, these number $K^2 + Kc + (K(K+1) + c(c+1))/2 + 1$. Of these, $K^2 + Kc$ are parameters of the transition distribution, and the remaining $(K(K+1) + c(c+1))/2 + 1$ are preference parameters.

Now consider the data information. With our setup, including the assumption that ε and v are uncorrelated, the data on x and c can deliver at most estimates of A, B, and D. These are the reduced-form parameters. There are $K^2 + 2Kc$ parameters here. A simple count shows that the structural parameters are not identified unless $Kc - (K(K+1) + c(c+1))/2 - 1 > 0$ (this is an order condition, therefore not a sufficient condition). Thus, some restrictions are typically required. These can occur anywhere, though it is often reasonable to assume that some elements of R and Q are known (frequently known to be zero).

The assumption that the controls have errors is not innocuous. Suppose there were no errors. Then we might as well take D known. However, it is impossible to estimate both A and B from the transition equation since c is a deterministic (and linear) function of x. We can obtain only K^2 coefficients from the transition equation, giving a total of $(K^2 + Kc)$ pieces of information. Although Kc parameters are known with certainty after a few observations, because of the curse of degeneracy, there are simply not as many independent pieces of information as the $(K^2 + 2Kc)$ in the case with error (compare chapters 4 and 5). Thus, adding error in the control equation provides identifying information, a somewhat unsettling situation.

13.4.3 Measurement Error

Note further that the "pure" measurement error interpretation does not provide identifying information. If the only source of error in the control equation is measurement error, then the c that enters the transition is not the observed control but its unseen error-free version. Then, the matrix D can certainly be estimated from data on states and controls. Going back to the transition equation and regressing x_{t+1} on x_t and c_t gives coefficients $A + BD$ on x_t and zero on c_t. That is, as in chapters 2–4, there is no information on the transition distribution for nonoptimal values of the control. Note that the assumption of measurement error does not affect the optimization problem, its value, or the optimal policy. Here, we again have $(K^2 + cK)$ pieces of information, though at least the curse of determinacy is broken. That is, with pure measurement error in the controls, we no longer insist on data configurations that simply do not happen (perfect alignment between states and controls), but we do not generate any identifying information.

In recent work it is often assumed that measurement error occurs in both the states and the controls, avoiding an embarrassing asymmetry in assumptions. The pure measurement error case, in which the noise in c is not driving the transition equation, is often written in state-space form, accommodating noise in the state observations as well. Then the likelihood function can be effectively calculated with the aid of the Kalman filter. This approach has been extensively studied.

13.4.4 Imperfect Control

Chow (1981) offers an interpretation of errors in the control equation as the effects of imperfect control. Here, there are two further interpretations, optimization error and genuine lack of complete control over the values of c_t. The former interpretation, while realistic, is not so appealing as it seems to open the door to essentially any behavior. The second is more appealing. Here, the mean values of c_t are taken as the controls; realized values then affect the transition equation and the value. In contrast to the case of pure measurement error, the realized controls affect the transitions, and so the matrices A and B in (13.23) can be separately identified. Further, the curse of degeneracy is eliminated. The matrix D in (13.24) can be estimated in the usual way (e.g., as a reduced-form parameter by least squares) or as a function of the underlying preference and transition parameters by maximum likelihood. Since the errors in the controls are additive, the optimization problem is unchanged except for the addition of a constant term depending on Q and the variance of the control errors. The optimal policy remains the same, with the mean of c given as a linear function of x.

Specifically, write $c_t = \bar{c}_t + v_t$, where $\bar{c}_t$ is under the control of the agent. Then the period utility function is

$$u(x_t, c_t) = x_t' R x_t + \bar{c}_t' Q \bar{c}_t + 2v_t' Q \bar{c}_t + v_t' Q v_t, \tag{13.26}$$

with expectation

$$E_t u(x_t, c_t) = x_t' R x_t + \bar{c}_t' Q \bar{c}_t + \operatorname{tr} Q \Lambda, \tag{13.27}$$

and the maximization problem is to choose $\bar{c}_t$ in period t to maximize

$$E_t \sum_{j=t}^{T} \beta^{j-t} u(x_j, c_j) = x_t' R x_t + \bar{c}_t' Q \bar{c}_t + \operatorname{tr} Q \Lambda$$

$$+ E_t \sum_{j=t+1}^{T} \beta^{j-t} u(x_j, c_j), \tag{13.28}$$

so as in (13.13) the optimal control is $\bar{c}_t = -\beta(Q + \beta B' P_{t+1} B)^{-1} B' P_{t+1} A x_t$ in the finite-horizon case. Remove the subscripts for the optimal stationary policy in the infinite-horizon case. Here, the sequence of events is that $\bar{c}_t$ is chosen on the basis of the state variables x_t, then v_t and hence c_t are realized, and then c_t is used to generate the next state via the transition equation $x_{t+1} = A x_t + B c_t + \varepsilon_t$. Thus, imperfect control is a potentially attractive assumption that breaks the curse of degeneracy in the LQ model. This works because the error is additive and does not depend on the value of the control. Note the contrast with the discrete case analyzed in chapter 4.

13.4.5 Random Utility

In the discrete case the random utility specification offers the most attractive specification in terms of realistic modeling in an optimizing framework (chapter 5). The same is true in the case of continuous states/controls. Consider adding a linear stochastic term in the control in the quadratic objective function so that

$$u(c, x) = x' R x' + c' Q c + a' c, \tag{13.29}$$

where the random vector a has mean zero and variance Λ (and, when we specify the likelihood function, is normally distributed). This random vector is assumed to be seen by the optimizing agent but not available in the data. Following the development above, we find that the optimal control is

$$c_{t-1} = -\beta(Q + \beta B' P_t B)^{-1} B' P_t A x_{t-1} - (Q + \beta B' P_t B)^{-1} a_{t-1} \qquad (13.30)$$

in the finite-horizon case and

$$c_t = -\beta(Q + \beta B' P B)^{-1} B' P A x_t - (Q + \beta B' P B)^{-1} a_t \qquad (13.31)$$

in the infinite-horizon case, where the matrix P is defined as the fixed point of (13.18) above. Thus, the optimal control is random from the point of view of the econometrician. Further, it varies enough to identify the B matrix in the transition equation (13.3) separately from the A matrix. The value function takes an additional term reflecting the discounted present value of the sequence $\text{tr}(Q + \beta B' P_t B)^{-1} \Lambda$.

The difference between this case and the case of imperfect control is in the timing. Here, the optimizing agent sees a_t before carrying out the optimization, but the econometrician does not see a_t, ever. Note that the cases of imperfect control and of the random utility specification are typically observationally equivalent. The only way to distinguish these cases appears to be through a priori restrictions on the variance matrix Λ. The variance of c is Λ in the case of imperfect control; it is $\beta^2(Q + \beta B' P_{t+1} B)^{-1} \Lambda (Q + \beta B' P_{t+1} B)^{-1}$ in the case of random utility. If Λ is restricted, for example, to diagonality, then these models can be distinguished. However, restrictions of this sort seem highly implausible a priori.

The analogy with the discrete case is complete. Allowing sufficient randomness in the objective function breaks the curse of degeneracy within the optimizing framework. It allows the full set of transition parameters to be estimated from the model's reduced form, permitting an attractive inferential separation.

Hansen and Sargent (1980) adopt this specification strategy, with the additional complication of autocorrelation in the $\{a_t\}$ and $\{\varepsilon_t\}$ processes. Autocorrelation introduces a new source of dynamics into the model, as optimal controls depend on anticipated future values of a and ε. In the uncorrelated case, these are all zero, but with autocorrelation there is a gain to be had from forecasting future values. With the linear specification, only expectations of future values enter. Thus, the model provides a natural and simple setting for modeling rational expectations. The anticipated values of a_t and ε_t entering the decision rules are those implied by the parameters of the model.

13.5 THE GENERAL (NON-LQ) CASE

Results that make the general continuous state/control model useful in applications often require special assumptions. If the model is differentiable, then first-order conditions can be used to generate implications and sometimes estimating equations. In the dynamic case, these first-order conditions are known as Euler equations. Essentially, Euler equations guarantee that the value along a path cannot be improved by reallocating resources along the path. Of course, this property can hold for many suboptimal paths as well as along the optimal path. To see this, consider the analogy of a consumer maximizing utility subject to a budget constraint in a single period. The optimal allocation has price ratios equal to ratios of marginal utilities. Many allocations satisfy this condition. Of these, the best also meets the budget constraint with equality. The analog of this last condition in the infinite-horizon dynamic case is the transversality condition. The transversality condition is necessary for a path to be optimal.

It is useful to review (briefly) the results available in the deterministic setting. Here, issues can be isolated by avoiding considerations of measurability and of required properties of the transition distribution. The problem is set up in canonical form,

$$\max \sum_{t=0}^{\infty} f(x_t, x_{t+1}, t),$$
(13.32)

with respect to the $\{x_t\}$ sequence,

$$\text{subject to } x_{t+1} \in \Gamma(x_t), \ x_0 \text{ given,}$$
(13.33)

and the value function is $V(x_0) = \Sigma_{t=0}^{\infty} f(x_t^*, x_{t+1}^*, t)$, where x_t^* indicates an optimal path. Our problem, maximizing $\Sigma \beta^t u(c_t, x_t)$ subject to $x_{t+1} = h(x_t, c_t)$, can be brought into this form by identifying x in (13.32) with our c and hiding the constraints given by the transition equations and the effects of the state variables in the sequence of sets $\Gamma(x_t)$ and the time dependence of the period objective functions. The transversality condition is $\lim_{t\to\infty} f_2(x_t, x_{t+1}, t) x_{t+1} = 0$ or, using the Euler equation $f_2(x_t, x_{t+1}, t) + f_1(x_{t+1}, x_{t+2}, t+1) = 0$, the transversality condition is sometimes usefully written $\lim_{t\to\infty} f_1(x_t, x_{t+1}, t) x_t = 0$. The basic results are that if $f(\cdot, x_{t+1}, t)$ is strictly increasing for all t and if the sets $\Gamma(x_t)$ are monotone $(x < x' \implies \Gamma(x) \subset \Gamma(x'))$ and convex, then the value function V is strictly increasing. Monotonicity implies that V is differentiable almost everywhere. If $f(\cdot, \cdot, t)$ is strictly concave, then V is strictly concave, which also implies differentiability almost everywhere. Under the assumption that $f(\cdot, x_{t+1}, t)$ is differentiable and x_{t+1} is interior to $\Gamma(x_t)$, this result can be strengthened to differentiability of V.

In many cases the differentiability of the policy function itself is of interest. Adding the assumption that $f(\cdot, \cdot, t)$ is twice continuously differentiable (write C^2) and concave (plus a little more—Santos, (1991)) implies that the policy function is differentiable (C^1) and the value function V is C^2. It is tempting to hope that adding more differentiability assumptions on f will lead to further differentiability of the policy function. Araujo (1991) shows that this is not so. If $f(\cdot, \cdot, t)$ is C^3, the policy function is certainly C^1 but need not be C^2.

Returning to the stochastic case, we seek to find

$$V(x) = \max_{\{c_t\}} E \sum \beta^t u(c_t, x_t) \qquad (13.34)$$

subject to the transition distribution $x_{t+1} \sim Q(\cdot | x_t, c_t)$. The forward recursion arguments together with the regularity conditions and boundedness assumptions of chapter 6 imply that the solution satisfies

$$V(x) = \max_{c \in C(x)} \{u(c, x) + \beta EV\}. \qquad (13.35)$$

The equivalence of these two definitions of the value is more subtle than is first apparent, as discussed in some detail in Stokey and Lucas (1989). Considerable progress can be made by studying the function $\mathcal{T}$ defined in chapter 6 by $\mathcal{T}f = \max_c\{u(x, c) + \beta Ef\}$ and noting that the value function V is the fixed point $\mathcal{T}V = V$. When $\mathcal{T}$ is a contraction mapping, the fixed point is unique. It is useful to try to restrict the functionality of $\mathcal{T}$. In chapter 6, we considered $\mathcal{T} : B \rightarrow B$, mapping bounded continuous functions into bounded continuous functions. Of course, this implies that the fixed point, the value function, is bounded and continuous. If $u(c, x)$ is increasing and Q is *monotone*, i.e., f increasing implies that Ef is also increasing, then it can be shown that $\mathcal{T}$ maps nondecreasing continuous bounded functions into nondecreasing continuous bounded functions. This space is compact, so the fixed point, obtainable by iterating the map $\mathcal{T}$, is nondecreasing, continuous, and bounded. A corresponding result can be obtained for the (weakly) concave case. It is not feasible to use this line of argument to obtain differentiability results, as the limit of a sequence of differentiable functions need not be differentiable.

To proceed further, it is useful to drop or weaken the assumption of the monotonicity of Q by restricting the distribution of the state variable. To do this, as well as to set up for the discussion of concavity, smoothness, and the like, it is useful to rewrite the dynamic programming framework so that the transition density does not formally involve the controls. This is achieved by an expansion of the state vector that was first introduced in connection with optimal stopping in chapter 6. Thus, in addition to $x \in X$, the state of the system is characterized also by the variable $a \in A$; i.e., the full state vector is $\omega = (a, x)$ and the expanded state space $\Omega = A \times X$. The restriction on the Markov transitions for x imply that

$$x_{t+1} \sim Q(\cdot|x_t), \tag{13.36}$$

and we allow the choice set to depend on the full state, $c \in C(a, x) = C(\omega)$. The law of motion L for a is of the form

$$a_{t+1} = L(a_t, c_t, x_{t+1}), \tag{13.37}$$

so Q generates all the next period's uncertainty, but the current control c_t affects the next period's state ω_{t+1} only through a_{t+1}, not x_{t+1}. When convenient, we may write ω_t and ω_{t+1} as (a, x) and (b, y), e.g., $b = L(a, c, y)$. This rephrased dynamic programming setup is under some conditions equivalent to the previous general one (see below). We largely focus on two instances of the setup. The first is

$$L(a, c, y) = c, \tag{13.38}$$

in which case the component a of the current state ω is simply the lagged control or action chosen by the agent in the previous period. In the optimal stopping case, this was motivated as the state variable indicating whether the process had already been stopped in the previous period. Another example would be an investment problem, where the current output available for consumption and investment is a function of the last period's investment.

With these specifications, let us now reconsider the issue of monotonicity of the value function V. The earlier result required that Q be monotone, and this is the condition we want to relax. We now focus on the case $L = c$. The optimality principle takes the form

$$V(a, x) = \max_{c \in C(a,x)} \{u(a, x, c) + \beta E(V(c, y)|x)\}, \tag{13.39}$$

where $y \sim Q(\cdot|x)$. We maintain the assumptions from before, except that we no longer require Q to be monotone, and we take u and C to be increasing in a instead of in x. This allows us to conclude that V is strictly increasing in a. This complements the monotonicity in x discussed earlier (the latter is retained even with the extended state space if all the original assumptions are in place).

Another key property of V to look for is concavity. Here, the central result is that if u is strictly concave in (a, c) and if the set of (a, c) such that $c \in C(a, x)$ is convex for each $x \in X$, then the value function V is strictly concave in a, and the maximizer $c(a, x)$ unique. In fact, if the contraction is iterated in the construction of V, with c_t the maximizer in iteration t, then $c_t \to c$ as $t \to \infty$; i.e., the unique optimal stationary policy is constructed along the way, too.

The concavity of V implies continuity, as well as differentiability almost everywhere. Since a does not enter the conditional expectation in the optimality principle, it is straightforward to strengthen this general result to differentiability of V in a everywhere. Precisely, if a and $c(a, x)$ are interior to the budget (constraint) set, then $V(a, x)$ is differentiable in a with

$$\frac{\partial V}{\partial a}(a, x) = \frac{\partial u}{\partial a}(a, x, c(a, x)). \tag{13.40}$$

This is often referred to as the *envelope condition*.

The second instance we pay particular attention to is

$$Q(y|x) = Q(y), \qquad C(a, x) = C(a), \tag{13.41}$$

in which case $\omega = a$ (i.e., we do have a new realization $x_{t+1} = y$ in the next period, but it is unnecessary to include x_t in ω_t since it does not condition Q).

Smoothness (to any order) may instead be studied under this alternative paradigm where Q and C are restricted instead of L. Here, the optimality principle takes the form

$$V(a) = \max_{c \in C(a)} \{u(a, c) + \beta E(V(L(a, c, y)))\}, \tag{13.42}$$

where $y \sim Q(\cdot)$. The expectation is not explicitly conditional, but the current state and control, a and c, affect the next period's expected value through the law of motion L. This is in fact equivalent to our original formulation, namely,

$$V(x) = \max_{c \in C(x)} \{u(x, c) + \beta E(V(y)|x, c)\}, \tag{13.43}$$

where $y \sim Q(\cdot|x, c)$. To see this, note first that if to avoid confusion we now write ε for the variable distributed according to $Q(\cdot)$ in (13.42), then $y = L(a, c, \varepsilon)$ clearly has a conditional distribution given (a, c) that we may label $Q(\cdot|a, c)$, and the original formulation obtains when identifying a with x. In the reverse direction, if $y \sim Q(\cdot|x, c)$, take the case $X = \mathbb{R}$ and define

$$K(x, y, c) = \int_{-\infty}^{y} Q(ds|x, c). \tag{13.44}$$

Then $\varepsilon = K(x, y, c)$ has a uniform distribution, conditionally on (x, c), and hence also unconditionally. Now let L be the inverse of K defined such that $L(x, c, K(x, y, c)) = y$. This is the desired function $L(a, c, \varepsilon)$, $\varepsilon \sim Q = U(0, 1)$.

13.6 SMOOTHNESS: EULER EQUATIONS

With smoothness, we may of course use first-order conditions. In the study of $V(a, x)$ from (13.39) we find, proceeding formally,

$$0 = \frac{\partial u}{\partial c} + \beta E \left(\frac{\partial V}{\partial a} \right), \tag{13.45}$$

and for $V(a)$ from (13.42), we find

$$0 = \frac{\partial u}{\partial c} + \beta E \left(\frac{\partial V}{\partial a} \cdot \frac{\partial L}{\partial c} \right). \tag{13.46}$$

In both cases, the control gradient of the reward (often marginal utility) is expressed in terms of an expectation. In the first case, for $V(a, x)$, we may carry the analysis a little further. Thus, we have

$$0 = \frac{\partial u}{\partial c} + \beta E \left(\frac{\partial u}{\partial a} \right), \tag{13.47}$$

which is easily obtained by substituting the envelope condition $\partial V / \partial a = \partial u / \partial a$ from (13.40) into the first-order condition (13.45). The result is a relationship between derivatives of u over time, not involving V, and it is referred to as the stochastic Euler equations.

The Euler equations are extremely useful for empirical work. Although they do not completely characterize the optimal policy (recall the discussion above), they are satisfied by the optimal policy. Thus, it is possible to examine the implications of the Euler equations associated with a particular specification for observed data, and to reject specifications inconsistent with the data. These equations are the essential implications for observables, as transversality conditions are difficult or impossible to check in data. A classic application is Hall's (1978) model of life-cycle consumption, noted below and treated in more detail in chapter 16. A simple version considers the optimization problem max $U_\pi(w_0) = E_0 \Sigma_{t=0}^{T} \beta^t u(c_t)$ subject to the intertemporal budget constraint $\Sigma_{t=0}^{T} \beta^t (c_t - w_t) = A_0$, where c is consumption, w is income, and $(1 - \beta)/\beta$ is both the rate of time preference for the consumer and the risk-free rate of return in the asset market. The Euler equations imply that marginal utility is a martingale: $E_t u'(c_{t+1}) = u'(c_t)$. With the added assumption of quadratic utility, consumption itself is a martingale. This implication can be checked using consumption data. The insufficiency of the Euler equations can be seen by noting that we can add a constant to each point in the consumption sequence and still satisfy the martingale property.

13.7 DISCUSSION AND EXAMPLES

The theme in all of the above has been that once we impose sufficient structure, the value function for the dynamic programming model can be determined. In the discrete-time finite-horizon model this is done by backward recursion. In the infinite-horizon stationary model it is done by forward recursion. In the diffusion case (chapter 14 below), there is no contraction map, but Bellman's equation is still used to characterize the value function, and we shall see how it sometimes permits explicit construction.

In applications of the general theme, it is often convenient to transform the problem slightly, depending on the situation at hand, so that sometimes it is not necessarily the value function itself that is calculated numerically but some other related and empirically relevant quantity. An example appeared in our study of the LQ model, where it was possible to iterate a matrix equation. In the job search model, the contraction map identifying the value function is easily turned into a companion contraction that instead determines the reservation wage and thereby the optimal strategy, without having to calculate V, and this is exactly what is needed in order to compute the likelihood function. Similarly, in chapter 18, we consider intertemporal asset-pricing models where the contraction characterizing V is transformed into an associated contraction which is used to calculate the asset price directly (in fact, the asset price times the agent's marginal utility), and again the likelihood function may be obtained without going via the value function for the dynamic program. In all cases, though, the general framework based on the CMT is exactly that already described. In continuous-time option-pricing models, we similarly turn the Bellman equation into a partial differential equation that uniquely identifies the option value, and again, tractable computational algorithms for solving the equation and calculating the likelihood function exist.

In other cases, the framework of this chapter works without modification, and we briefly mention a few examples of this. Consider first the simple optimal stochastic growth model. Here, each period the agent decides on how much to consume and how much to leave for the next time period. The quantity invested then becomes the next period's capital stock. If starting with capital k_t in the current period, this is first applied as input in production before making the consumption-investment decision. Thus, the total amount available in period t is the initial stock k_t plus the output of the production function f, say, minus depreciation, which we take to occur at rate δ. The production output is not known with certainty at the time of investment; i.e., f has also a stochastic aspect generated by the random production shock x_t. It follows that the quantity available for consumption and investment is $f(k_t, x_t) + (1 - \delta)k_t$. It is convenient to include k_t in the current state variable, and since k_{t+1} is controlled by the agent, we specify $a_t = k_t$ and $a_{t+1} = L(a_t, c_t, x_{t+1}) = c_t$ as in (13.38); i.e., the current control c_t is the next period's capital stock. The reward function $u(a, x, c)$ is now simply a utility of current consumption function, so Bellman's principle of optimality posits

$$V(a, x) = \max_{c \in C(a,x)} \{u(f(a, x) + (1-\delta)x - c) + \beta E(V(c, y)|x)\}, \qquad (13.48)$$

where $y \sim Q(\cdot|x)$ and $C(a, x) = [0, f(a, x) + (1-\delta)x]$. Thus, if the utility function u is strictly increasing, strictly concave, and differentiable, and if the production function f is so in a, then V is, too. Strict monotonicity in x obtains if u is strictly increasing, f is strictly increasing in x, $\delta \le 1$, and Q is monotone. A unique optimal stationary investment policy $c : A \times X \to \mathbb{R}_+$ exists ($A = X = \mathbb{R}_+$) and may be computed by iterating the contraction. The shadow price of capital is

$$\frac{\partial V}{\partial a} = u' \cdot \frac{\partial f}{\partial a}, \qquad (13.49)$$

and the first-order condition is

$$u' = \beta E \left(\frac{\partial V}{\partial a} | x \right). \qquad (13.50)$$

Combining the two equations and including explicit time subscripts, we have the stochastic Euler equation

$$u'_t = \beta E_t \left(u'_{t+1} \cdot f'_{t+1} \right), \qquad (13.51)$$

where u' is the marginal utility, f' is the marginal product (i.e., with respect to capital), and $E_t(\cdot)$ indicates conditional expectation as of time t.

The closely related model of optimal consumption and saving may be derived along similar lines. This time, let the control c_t indicate current consumption and simply take a_t to be the agent's current assets. Thus, total savings equal $a_t - c_t$ and earn a random return x_{t+1}, say, so that the next period's wealth is $a_{t+1} = x_{t+1}(a_t - c_t)$. Here, we may specify the law of motion as $L(a, c, y) = y(a - c)$. With u as in the growth model, the optimality principle takes the form

$$V(a, x) = \max_{c \in C(a)} \{u(c) + \beta E(V(y(a - c), y)|x)\}, \qquad (13.52)$$

where $y \sim Q(\cdot|x)$ and $C(a) = [0, a]$. Since $C(a, x) = C(a)$ already, we are close to the specification considered earlier. Indeed, with serially independent returns we have $Q(y|x) = Q(y)$ and

$$V(a) = \{u(c) + \beta E(V(y(a - c)))\}. \qquad (13.53)$$

An optimal consumption plan exists, and V may be obtained by forward recursion. This time, the smoothness of V follows along the alternative route in the general treatment, and we find that the shadow price of assets is

$$V'(a) = \beta E(yV'(y(a - c(a)))). \tag{13.54}$$

The first-order condition is

$$u'(c(a)) = \beta E(yV'(y(a - c(a)))). \tag{13.55}$$

The right hand side of the two equations are the same, and equating the left hand sides produces the particular instance $V'(a) = u'(c(a))$ of the general envelope condition (13.40) encountered earlier. Further, substituting u' for V' in the first-order condition yields a stochastic Euler equation which, by analogy with the growth model, we write as

$$u'_t = \beta E_t \left(x_{t+1} u'_{t+1} \right). \tag{13.56}$$

In the particular case where Q is degenerate at $x_{t+1} = 1 + r_f$ and this risk-free interest rate r_f equals the subjective discount rate $\rho = \beta^{-1} - 1$, Hall's famous random walk model of consumption

$$u'_t = E_t \left(u'_{t+1} \right) \tag{13.57}$$

follows, i.e., marginal utility follows a martingale. The further specialization $u(c_t) = -\frac{1}{2}c_t^2$ (quadratic utility) yields the familiar form

$$c_t = E_t c_{t+1} \tag{13.58}$$

of this theory.

The consumption and growth models show that the general framework sometimes applies without modification. We have considered the stationary versions of the models and so have appealed to the contraction mapping theorem (CMT), etc. It is worth noting that the dynamic programming setup often may also be applied to nonstationary infinite-horizon models. A concrete example is the case where stationarity sets in beyond a certain future date, however distant, whereas the problem exhibits time-varying characteristics before that. It is then possible to use the contraction mapping approach to construct the value function V for the stationary (far-end) portion of the program. With $\tau < \infty$ the first date at which time invariance sets in, $V_\tau = V$ is then a fully theoretically justified starting point for the backward recursions studied earlier in the context of finite-horizon models. In this case,

$$V_0 = \mathcal{T}_0 \ldots \mathcal{T}_{\tau-1} \left(\lim_{t \to \infty} \mathcal{T}^t(0) \right) \tag{13.59}$$

is the correct value function for an infinite-horizon dynamic program that includes both stationary and nonstationary features.

13.8 RANDOM UTILITY IN THE GENERAL CASE

The models lead to policy functions of the form $c_t = c_t(x_t)$, so the curse of degeneracy applies. In the discrete case and in the LQ model it is convenient and natural to break this degeneracy with a random utility specification. The same applies in the general setting. We introduce the unobserved state variable a_t (following the notation in the LQ case). To ensure that $p(c_t|x_t)$ is nondegenerate, a_t and c_t must interact. A particularly simple but effective case is to write $u^*(c_t, x_t, a_t) = u(c_t, x_t) + a_t'c_t$, where $u(c_t, x_t)$ is the original (nonrandom) utility function and a_t is a stochastic shock. More generally, we specify $u^*(c_t, x_t, a_t)$ directly. Under the assumption that $\{a_t\}$ is an independent and identically distributed (i.i.d.) sequence, the transition distribution takes the form $(x_t, a_t) \sim Q(\cdot|x_{t-1}, c_{t-1})$. This leads to convenient calculations in the the dynamic programming problem and preserves the essence of the original nonrandom utility specification, while breaking the curse of degeneracy (as long as there is sufficient interative between c_t and a_t in the utility function). In the nonrandom utility specification where there is no a_t, the transition distribution can be simplified to depend only on x_{t-1} since c_{t-1} is a deterministic function of x_{t-1} through the optimal policy. Here, in the random utility case, c_{t-1} depends on x_{t-1} and a_{t-1}, so this simplification cannot be made. As in the LQ case, this additional source of variation in the control serves to identify parameters of the transition distribution directly. Without the random specification, these parameters are identified only through the implications of the optimality equation. In this sense, adding noise to the original model in the form of a utility shock provides identifying information. This situation is not uncommon, though perhaps unsettling.

If the shocks themselves are Markovian, then the transition distribution is $(|x_t, a_t) \sim Q(\cdot|x_{t-1}, c_{t-1}, a_{t-1}) = Q^*(\cdot|x_{t-1}, a_{t-1})$ since c_{t-1} is a deterministic function of x_{t-1} and the unobserved a_{t-1}. In this case, the optimizing agent is typically interested in forecasting future shocks as part of determining the optimal policy. Hansen and Sargent (1980) provide an early application in the LQ case.

13.9 EXERCISES

1. Let the matrices M and N be of dimension $m \times n$ and $n \times m$, respectively. Show that $\mathrm{tr}MN = \mathrm{tr}NM$, where tr denotes the matrix trace.

2. Let ϵ be a random k-vector with $E(\epsilon) = \mu$, $\mathrm{var}(\epsilon) = \Omega$, and let P be a $k \times k$ matrix. Show that $E(\epsilon'P\epsilon) = \mu'P\mu + \mathrm{tr}P\Omega$.

3. Consider the random utility model from section 13.8 expanded to $u^*(c, x, a) = u(c, x) + a'c + c' \Gamma c$ where Γ is a random matrix. Discuss how this specification changes the solution and the possibility for inference.

13.10 REFERENCES

The LQ model is a classic. It is a workhorse of applied optimal control and is in wide use in electrical engineering and in economics. Simon (1956) is an early economic reference. Chow (1975) develops algorithms and applications of the LQ model in finite-horizon control of macroeconomic models. Chow (1981) suggests using sequential LQ approximations to control nonlinear macro models and gives a variety of applications. Ljungqvist and Sargent (2000) present several derivations of the solution to the infinite-horizon LQ problem. Anderson et al. (1996) give a comprehensive discussion of the computation of solutions to the LQ problem and of estimation using the Kalman filter to calculate the likelihood functions. Chow (1981) and Zadrozny (1988) provide derivative calculations useful for estimating LQ models. Benveniste and Scheinkman (1979) give a simple proof of differentiability of the value function and an expression for the derivative. Transversality conditions are studied by Ekeland and Scheinkman (1986). Araujo (1991), Araujo and Scheinkman (1984), and Santos (1991) provide smoothness results in the deterministic case. Kamihigashi (2001, 2002) presents a proof of the necessity of the transversality condition that does not depend on dynamic programming arguments. Blume, Easley, and O'Hara (1982) give differentiability results, to any desired order, for the value and policy functions in stochastic models. The contrast with Araujo (1991) shows how different the deterministic and stochastic specifications are. It is often useful to ask whether a policy or value function is continuous or differentiable in a parameter (which is a separate question from smoothness in the main argument, the state variable). Results are provided by Dutta, Majumdar, and Sundaram (1994). The estimation of models imposing rational expectations assumptions in the form of typically nonlinear coefficient restrictions was treated in an explosion of papers following the appearance of Lucas (1976). In addition to Taylor (1979), important papers include Hansen and Sargent (1980, 1982), Kennan (1979), and Chow (1980). The stochastic growth model is routinely used to apply dynamic programming to economic questions. For a small selection from many papers, see Brock and Mirman (1972), Cass and Shell (1976), Foley, Shell, and Sidravski (1969), and Mirman and Zilcha (1975). The growth model is used by Tauchen (1991) and Taylor and Uhlig (1990) to illustrate numerical solution methods.

Chapter Fourteen

Continuous-Time Models

14.1 INTRODUCTION

Continuous-time models are useful complements to the preceding analysis because the choice of period in the discrete-time framework often is arbitrary. In addition, continuous modeling sometimes leads to closed-form solutions. In financial economics, continuous time can have the substantive impact of completing the markets. Bellman's principle of optimality, which we have used so extensively already, is also sometimes referred to as the *Bellman equation*. While the two are the same in discrete-time scenarios, there is a slight distinction between them when we move to continuous time. In the following, we use the optimality principle considered so far to derive Bellman's equation in continuous time.

We let $t \in [0, \tau]$ but otherwise proceed by analogy with the earlier analysis. Total intertemporal utility is taken to be

$$U_{\pi,0}(x_0) = E \left(\int_0^\tau u_t(x_t, \pi_t(x_t)) \, dt + H(x_\tau) | x_0, \pi_0(x_0) \right), \qquad (14.1)$$

where H is a terminal value (e.g., a bequest) function. The integral replaces the summation employed earlier. We shall again consider geometric discounting, $u_t = \beta^t u$, and we now write $\beta = e^{-\rho}$, with ρ the rate of continuous subjective discounting. Similarly, we have specified that the policy function is of the form $\pi_t = \pi_t(x_t)$ from the outset, where x_t is the state variable. The optimal value function is $V_t(x_t) = \sup_\pi U_{\pi,t}(x_t)$. The optimality principle (6.6) therefore indicates that

$$V_0(x_0) = \max_{\pi \in \Pi} E \left(\int_0^t e^{-\rho s} u(x_s, \pi_s(x_s)) \, ds + e^{-\rho t} V_t(x_t) | x_0, \pi_0(x_0) \right).$$
$$(14.2)$$

We now multiply through by $\beta^{-t} = e^{\rho t}$, then subtract $V_0(x_0)$ from both sides and divide by t, producing

$$\frac{e^{\rho t} - 1}{t} V_0(x_0) = \max_{\pi \in \Pi} \left\{ E \left(\frac{1}{t} \int_0^t e^{(t-s)\rho} u(x_s, \pi_s(x_s)) \, ds \right) \right.$$

$$\left. + E \left(\frac{V_t(x_t) - V_0(x_0)}{t} \right) \right\}, \qquad (14.3)$$

where the conditioning is suppressed in the expectation to avoid clutter. Next, we let $t \to 0$, using l'Hopital's rule on the left hand side, and obtain

$$\rho V_t(x_t) = \max_{\pi_t} \left\{ u(x_t, \pi_t) + E \left(\frac{dV_t(x_t)}{dt} | x_t \right) \right\}, \qquad (14.4)$$

where we have stated the limit for arbitrary t rather than for the particular value $t = 0$. This is the Bellman equation in continuous time. It says that the equivalent flow value at time t equals the maximum attainable value of the sum of the current reward and the expected rate of change of the total future (stock) value. Thus, (14.4) is the infinitesimal restatement of the optimality principle.

For concreteness, we shall apply the Bellman equation (14.4) mainly in the context of rather particular stochastic state variable processes. Thus, chapter 19 presents an equilibrium search application of a Poisson process specification. Here, we study an alternative Itô process specification, which is the foundation of many continuous-time finance applications. Thus, consider the controlled stochastic differential equation

$$dx_t = a_t(x_t, c_t)\, dt + \sigma_t(x_t, c_t)\, dW_t, \qquad (14.5)$$

where $\{W_t\}_t$ is distributed according to the Wiener measure. That is, $W_0 = 0$, and the increments $W_t - W_s$ over nonoverlapping intervals (s, t) are distributed independently and normally with mean zero and variance $t - s > 0$; i.e., W_t is standard Brownian motion. In the multivariate case, W_t is a vector comprising, say, n independent standard Brownian motions. If $X = \mathbb{R}^m$, then the drift a_t is an m-vector; i.e., $a_t : X \times C \to \mathbb{R}^m$, and the volatility σ_t is an $m \times n$ matrix. The controlled stochastic differential equation is understood to mean

$$x_t = x_0 + \int_0^t a_s(x_s, c_s)\, ds + \int_0^t \sigma_s(x_s, c_s)\, dW_s, \qquad (14.6)$$

where $\int \cdot ds$ is an ordinary integral in the sense of Lebesgue and $\int \cdot dW_s$ is a stochastic integral in the sense of Itô. Protter (1986) offers a gentle introduction to stochastic integration. Under wide regularity conditions, the feature that a_t and σ_t depend only on the history through the current state x_t implies that the restriction to Markov policies $c_t = \pi_t(x_t)$ is without loss of generality. This leaves the coefficients $a_t(x_t, \pi_t(x_t))$ and $\sigma_t(x_t, \pi_t(x_t))$ functions of x_t, and hence the controlled stochastic process x_t follows a (Markov or Itô) diffusion.

We shall employ the diffusion property to assess the expected rate of change of the value V_t of the dynamic program that appears in the Bellman equation. To this end, we note that since x_t is a diffusion, and if $F :$

$X \times \mathbb{R} \to \mathbb{R}$ is twice continuously differentiable, then the stochastic differential dy_t of the process $y_t = F(x_t, t)$ may be calculated easily in terms of the drift and volatility of x_t and the derivatives of F. The ordinary calculus would suggest that $dy_t = (\partial F/\partial x)' dx_t + (\partial F/\partial t) dt$, and substituting for dx_t, we would have $dy_t = \{(\partial F/\partial x)' a_t + (\partial F/\partial t)\} dt + (\partial F/\partial x)' \sigma_t dW_t$. However, the stochastic calculus is different since a term $E((dW_t)^2) = dt$ is picked up in the application of Taylor's theorem. The reason this term is not negligible is that Brownian motion is not of bounded variation. Hence, *Itô's lemma* adds the second-order term $\frac{1}{2}\sigma_t^2(\partial^2 F/\partial x^2)$ to the drift in the univariate case ($m = n = 1$), and in general

$$
dy_t = \left\{ a_t(x_t, \pi_t)' \frac{\partial F}{\partial x}(x_t, t) + \frac{\partial F}{\partial t}(x_t, t) \right.
$$

$$
\left. + \frac{1}{2} \sum_{i=1}^{n} \sigma_t(x_t, \pi_t)_i' \frac{\partial^2 F}{\partial x^2}(x_t, t) \sigma_t(x_t, \pi_t)_i \right\} dt
$$

$$
+ \frac{\partial F}{\partial x'}(x_t, t) \sigma_t(x_t, \pi_t) \, dW_t, \tag{14.7}
$$

where the gradient $\partial F/\partial x$ and the Hessian $\partial^2 F/\partial x^2$ of F in x are of dimension $m \times 1$ and $m \times m$, respectively, and $\sigma_t(\cdot)_i$ indicates the ith column of σ_t. The alternative statement of Itô's lemma as $dy_t = L^{\pi_t} F \, dt + (\partial F/\partial x)' \sigma_t \, dW_t$ implicitly defines the *infinitesimal generator* L^{π_t}.

Recall now that the value function $V_t(x_t)$ from (14.4) for the continuous-time stochastic dynamic programming model precisely is a function of the two variables x_t and t, like F above. Subject to suitable smoothness conditions, we may calculate the stochastic differential $dV_t(x_t)$ using Itô's lemma. In fact, in the Bellman equation (14.4), we need only the drift $E(dV_t(x_t)) = L^{\pi_t} V_t(x_t) dt$ since $z_t = \int_0^t (\partial V_s/\partial x_s)' \sigma_s \, dW_s$ is a martingale starting at $z_0 = 0$ and so has zero mean; i.e., $E_s(z_t) = z_s$ for $t > s$ (this together with $E|z_t| < \infty$ is the martingale property) and in particular $E(z_t) = E(E_0 z_t) = 0$, and we find

$$
\rho V_t(x_t) = \max_{\pi_t} \left\{ u(x_t, \pi_t) + L^{\pi_t} V_t(x_t) \right\}. \tag{14.8}
$$

Writing out and reorganizing terms yields

$$
0 = \max_{\pi_t} \left\{ \frac{1}{2} \sum_{i=1}^{n} \sigma_t(x_t, \pi_t)_i' \frac{\partial^2 V_t(x_t)}{\partial x^2} \sigma_t(x_t, \pi_t)_i + a_t(x_t, \pi_t)' \frac{\partial V_t(x_t)}{\partial x} \right.
$$

$$
\left. + \frac{\partial V_t(x_t)}{\partial t} - \rho V_t(x_t) + u(x_t, \pi_t) \right\} \tag{14.9}
$$

for the Bellman equation in the case of diffusion uncertainty. Because of the maximization operator, this is not a standard partial differential equation (PDE) in V. This complicates numerical solution. Optimal stopping, however, is one instance where simplification occurs.

14.2 OPTIMAL STOPPING IN CONTINUOUS TIME

We now consider the simplifications that obtain in the case of optimal stopping of a diffusion in continuous time. Here, we write the value function as $V_t(1, x_t) = V_t(x_t)$ in the continuation region, whereas a terminal value $V_t(0, x_t) = H_t(x_t)$ is received if the process is stopped at t. Thus, as of $t = 0$, the problem is $V_0(x_0) = \max_\tau U_\tau(x_0)$, where by analogy with (14.1) we have

$$U_\tau(x_0) = E\left(\int_0^\tau u_t(x_t)dt + H_\tau(x_\tau)|x_0\right). \tag{14.10}$$

Similarly, in the continuation region we have

$$dx_t = a_t(x_t)\,dt + \sigma_t(x_t)\,dW_t, \tag{14.11}$$

where again we focus on a diffusion rather than a jump process. It follows from the Bellman equation (14.9) that, in the continuation region,

$$0 = \frac{1}{2}\sum_{i=1}^n \sigma_t(x_t)'_i \frac{\partial^2 V_t(x_t)}{\partial x^2} \sigma_t(x_t)_i + a_t(x_t)' \frac{\partial V_t(x_t)}{\partial x}$$

$$+ \frac{\partial V_t(x_t)}{\partial t} - \rho V_t(x_t) + u(x_t), \tag{14.12}$$

where there is no maximization since the only control is the horizon τ. In each instant, though, the agent must choose between the value of continuing $V_t(x_t)$ and the value of stopping $H_t(x_t)$. Let us take a closer look at the case $m = 1$. By analogy with the job search model, under wide conditions (including that $u(x) - \rho H_t(x)$ is decreasing in x for all t), the optimal strategy indicates continuation ($c = 1$) unless x_t exceeds a critical boundary r_t satisfying

$$V_t(r_t) = H_t(r_t), \tag{14.13}$$

the *value-matching* condition (compare the reservation wage condition (6.50)). Since r_t is chosen optimally, rather than being prespecified, it is referred to as a free boundary, and the problem of solving for r_t and V_t is a *free-boundary problem*. In continuous time, the free boundary indicates the continuation region, and hence the optimal strategy in addition satisfies

$$\frac{\partial V_t}{\partial x}(r_t) = \frac{\partial H_t}{\partial x}(r_t), \tag{14.14}$$

the *high-order contact* or *smooth pasting* condition. Thus, instead of the general nonstandard PDE (14.9) involving an additional maximization operator, Bellman's equation in the continuous-time optimal stopping case is the standard PDE (14.12) in V, with value-matching and high-order contact (smooth pasting) conditions (14.13) and (14.14). The classic American put option problem (see chapter 10) is the case where the expectation is under an equivalent martingale measure, $u = 0$, and H_t gives the discounted payoff $\exp(-\rho t) \max\{K - x_t, 0\}$ received if the put is exercised (K is the strike price). Here, since $u - \rho H$ is increasing in x, the process is stopped (i.e., the option is exercised) if the underlying price x drops below the free boundary.

In the present framework, time dependence may obtain because of the dependence of the diffusion parameters a_t and σ_t on t, because of the dependence of H_t on t, or because a finite horizon is imposed, e.g., $t \in [0, t_0]$, for some $t_0 < \infty$. When H, a and σ do not depend on t and $t_0 = \infty$, time invariance again obtains, and the value function V satisfies the Bellman equation (where $\partial V / \partial t$ has dropped out)

$$0 = \frac{1}{2} \sum_{i=1}^{n} \sigma(x)_i' \frac{\partial^2 V(x)}{\partial x^2} \sigma(x)_i + a(x)' \frac{\partial V(x)}{\partial x}$$
$$- \rho V(x) + u(x) \qquad\qquad (14.15)$$

in the continuation region $(-\infty, r]$, which in turn is given by $V(r) = H(r)$, $\partial V(r)/\partial x = \partial H(r)/\partial x$. Thus, the partial differential equation has been reduced to an ordinary differential equation (ODE). This is an important further simplification in applications.

14.3 A JUMP PROCESS APPLICATION: ALLOCATION OF TIME OVER TIME

Although we derived the Bellman equation in the diffusion case, with continuous sample paths x_t and uncertainty generated by Brownian motion, it is possible to work by analogy in the case of jumps in the state process. We illustrate this using the application to time allocation due to Burdett et al. (1984). The model is a continuous-time Markov chain for individual movement among labor market states. Given the current state, the problem is again of the optimal stopping type, the decision being when to end the sojourn in the current state and venture into another.

An individual at each instant is employed at wage w, unemployed and looking for work, or not participating in the labor force. At random intervals, an individual experiences a utility shock consisting of a wage shock and a utility of unemployment shock. The utility of nonparticipation is normalized to zero, as only relative shocks are identified (only movements among states are observed, not utilities). The shocks arrive at intervals governed by Poisson processes, which are different among labor market states. Thus, the decision at each time has long-run consequences, as it affects the arrival of future shocks. With this assumption, the duration in each state is exponential. Further, the state-to-state transition process is Markovian. Thus, there is information in the state durations and in the transition ratios in the "embedded chain," the process of state-to-state transitions, regardless of the time between transitions.

The labor market states $i = 1, 2, 3$ refer to employment, unemployment, and nonparticipation, with associated instantaneous utilities $u_1 = z + e$, $u_2 = u$, and $u_3 = 0$. Here, z represents an expected earnings level, a parameter of the model. The state variable of the dynamic program is $x = (i, z + e, u)$. The variables e and u are independent and identically distributed (i.i.d.) across time, with distribution function $F(e, u)$. The arrival rates of shocks are given by μ_1, μ_2, and μ_3. It is reasonable to assume that μ_2 is the largest of these; that is, unemployed and searching workers are most likely to get offers. With the Poisson assumption, the probability that a shock arrives to an individual in state i in an interval of small length h is $\mu_i h$. When the outstanding shock is (e, u), the state-dependent value function over the interval h, with discount rate ρ, is

$$V_i(z + e, u) = \frac{1}{(1 + \rho h)} \left\{ u_i h + \mu_i h E \max_{k=1,2,3} V_k(z + \tilde{e}, \tilde{u}) \right.$$

$$\left. + (1 - \mu_i h) V_i(z + e, u) \right\} + o(h^2), \qquad (14.16)$$

where $o(h^2)$ is proportional to the probability of two events occurring in the interval h and $o(h^2)/h \to 0$ as $h \to 0$. The first term in braces is the utility flow rate times the interval length, the second is the probability that a shock arrives times the value of following the optimal policy given the shock, and the third is the probability that no shock arrives in the interval times the value of continuing in state i with the current values of the shocks. Rearranging and taking limits as $h \to 0$ gives

$$V_i(z + e, u) = \frac{u_i + \mu_i T(z)}{\mu_i + \rho}, \qquad i = 1, 2, 3, \qquad (14.17)$$

where

$$T(z) = E \max_{k=1,2,3} V_k(z + \tilde{e}, \tilde{u}). \qquad (14.18)$$

This is the jump process analog of Bellman's equation in continuous time. The variable z is carried along since it will be convenient to analyze and subsequently estimate the different dynamics associated with different expected earnings flows. When a shock occurs, the worker must make a decision based on the new values of the shocks. The optimal strategy is easily characterized by looking at the effect of shocks on the state-dependent values V_i:

$$\frac{\partial V_i(z+e,u)}{\partial e} = \begin{cases} 0, & \text{if } i \neq 1, \\ \dfrac{1}{\rho + \mu_1}, & \text{if } i = 1, \end{cases} \qquad (14.19)$$

$$\frac{\partial V_i(z+e,u)}{\partial u} = \begin{cases} 0, & \text{if } i \neq 2, \\ \dfrac{1}{\rho + \mu_2}, & \text{if } i = 2. \end{cases} \qquad (14.20)$$

These results imply that the optimal strategy is a generalized reservation wage strategy characterized by three critical values which depend on the expected earnings parameter z : $e(z), u(z)$, and $a(u, z)$. These are defined by equalizing the values in each pair of states with respect to the shocks. The definitions are:

$$V_1(z+e,u) \lessgtr V_3(z+e,u) \quad \text{as } e \lessgtr e(z),$$
$$V_2(z+e,u) \lessgtr V_3(z+e,u) \quad \text{as } u \lessgtr u(z),$$
$$V_1(z+e,u) \lessgtr V_2(z+e,u) \quad \text{as } e \lessgtr a(u, z).$$

The interpretations are that employment is preferred to nonparticipation if the utility flow from employment is at least $z + e(z)$, unemployment is preferred to nonparticipation if the utility flow while unemployed is at least $u(z)$, and employment is preferred to unemployment if the utility flow from employment is at least $z + a(u, z)$. Thus, the (e, u) plane is partitioned into three regions, A_1, A_2, and A_3, corresponding to the optimal states. Burdett et al. (1984) show that $A_1(z) \subset A_1(z')$ and $A_3(z') \subset A_3(z)$ for $z < z'$, and therefore employment is more likely to be preferred to nonparticipation by workers with higher expected earnings. The effect on employment/unemployment is ambiguous without further restrictions.

Let γ_i be the probability that state i is chosen, given that a shock has occurred,

$$\gamma_i(z) = \int_{A_i(z)} dF(\tilde{e}, \tilde{u}). \qquad (14.21)$$

Of course, γ_i depends on z, but this dependence will be suppressed when convenient. Then, the flow rate from state i to state j is given by $\lambda_{ij} = \mu_i \gamma_j$, the product of the shock arrival rate in state i, and the probability that state j is chosen given that an offer arrives. The hazard rate while in state i, that is, the rate at which individuals leave the state, is

$$\lambda_i(z) = \sum_{j=1, j\neq i}^{3} \lambda_{ij}(z), \qquad i = 1, 2, 3. \tag{14.22}$$

Since this hazard rate does not depend on the elapsed duration in the state, the implied distribution of state durations is exponential with parameter $1/\lambda_i$.

The transition rates and hazard functions imply that state-to-state transitions occur according to a continuous-time Markov chain. Specifically, let M be the 3×3 matrix with ij elements λ_{ij} for i not equal to j and with jth diagonal element $1 - \lambda_j$. Let $p(t) = (p_1(t), p_2(t), p_3(t))$ be the vector of probabilities associated with being in any particular state at time t. Under mild conditions, $p(t) \to p^*$, a steady state. The steady state in the Markov framework can be interpreted on the individual level as giving the long-run fraction of time spent in each state. On an aggregate level, averaging over many individuals, it gives the fraction of individuals in each state at any time. With this interpretation, the steady state may be interpreted as giving natural rates, for example, the natural rate of unemployment is $p_2^*/(p_2^*+p_1^*)$. These steady states can be easily calculated by simply equating flows into each state to flows out and solving for the equilibrium. Reintroducing z, to emphasize that these results are for fixed human capital and not aggregated over heterogeneous individuals,

$$p_1^*(z) = \mu_2\mu_3\gamma_1(z)/R(z),$$
$$p_2^*(z) = \mu_1\mu_3\gamma_2(z)/R(z),$$
$$p_3^*(z) = \mu_1\mu_2\gamma_3(z)/R(z),$$

where $R(z) = \mu_2\mu_3\gamma_1(z) + \mu_1\mu_3\gamma_2(z) + \mu_1\mu_2\gamma_3(z)$. These formulas together with the results above imply that $p_1^*(z)$ is increasing in z and $p_3^*(z)$ is decreasing in z.

The model is highly suited for empirical application. It is straightforward to move between the hazards and the distribution functions F_i for durations using the relation

$$F_i(t|z) = 1 - \exp(-t\lambda_i(z)). \tag{14.23}$$

Further, the conditional probability of moving to state j given that the current state is i is λ_{ij}/λ_i. Hence, the likelihood contribution of a spell of length t in state i ending in a transition to state j is

$$f_{ij}(t|z) = \frac{\lambda_{ij}(z)}{\lambda_i(z)} f_i(t|z) = \lambda_{ij}(z)(1 - F_i(t|z)), \tag{14.24}$$

where $f_i(t|z) = dF_i(t|z)/dt$ is the density. Since $\ln(1 - F_i(t|z)) = -t\lambda_i(z)$, the sample log likelihood is

$$\ln L = \sum_{k=1}^{K} \left\{ d_k \ln \lambda_{i_k j_k}(z_k) - T_k \lambda_{i_k}(z_k) \right\}. \qquad (14.25)$$

where K is the sample size, $d_k = 1$ if the kth spell is complete, and T_k is the duration of the kth spell. Using the proportional hazard specification

$$\lambda_{ij}(z_k) = \exp(x_k \beta_{ij}), \qquad (14.26)$$

with x_k a set of regressors controlling for heterogeneity in general and thought to matter for expected earnings z_k in particular, the log likelihood becomes

$$\ln L = \sum_{k=1}^{K} \left\{ d_k x_k \beta_{i_k j_k} - T_k \sum_{n=1,n\neq i_k}^{3} \exp\left(x_k \beta_{i_k n}\right) \right\}. \qquad (14.27)$$

Burdett et al. (1984) fit this model to data from the Denver Income Maintenance Experiment (DIME). The regressors x_k include the usual suspects: age, education, race, assets, and number of children, as well as an estimate of the expected wage. The Markov specification turns out to be fairly good in describing the transitions and even the spell lengths. The regressors substantially improve the fit. That is, employment spells in particular and perhaps even unemployment spells do not look exponential in the aggregate. However, controlling for heterogeneity improves the fit of the exponential distribution dramatically, indicating the importance of worker heterogeneity in determining the aggregate distribution of durations. The theory is substantially supported. Higher expected wages lead to longer employment spells and more frequent transitions to employment. Higher expected wages also imply shorter nonparticipation spells and fewer transitions out of the labor force. The elasticity of the equilibrium unemployment rate with respect to the expected wage, an effect that cannot be estimated from the reduced form but requires the structural model, is negative and large in absolute value.

14.4 DYNAMIC CONSUMPTION AND PORTFOLIO CHOICE

We consider the problem of an investor who continuously decides on how much of current wealth to consume and to save and how to split the savings between investments in safe and risky assets. Merton (1969, 1971) initiated research in this direction. Our formulation, with constant coefficients, is relatively simple but suffices for highlighting the important concepts involved.

Assume there are k stocks and that the price process for each is a geometric Brownian motion with drift,

$$dp_{i,t} = \mu_i \, p_{i,t} \, dt + p_{i,t} \sigma_i' \, dW_t, \tag{14.28}$$

$i = 1, \ldots, k$. Here, μ_i is the expected return to stock i and σ_i is the n-vector of volatility coefficients. Writing $p_t = (p_{1,t}, \ldots, p_{k,t})'$ and $\mathrm{diag}(p_t)$ for the $k \times k$ diagonal matrix with p_t along the diagonal, the stock price process is hence

$$dp_t = \mathrm{diag}(p_t)(\mu \, dt + \sigma \, dW_t), \tag{14.29}$$

where μ is the k-vector of expected returns and σ is the $k \times n$ volatility matrix. Let x_t be the total assets (wealth) of the investor at time t and let w_t be the k-vector of portfolio weights on the stocks. The portion of x_t not invested in stocks is held in the riskless asset, earning a constant interest rate r, and as the portfolio weights add to 1, the weight on the safe asset is $1 - w_t' 1_k$, with 1_k the k-vector of 1s. Running consumption c_t is extracted from the returns to investment, so the evolution of wealth is given by

$$\begin{aligned} dx_t &= \left(x_t \left(w_t' \mu + \left(1 - w_t' 1_k \right) r \right) - c_t \right) dt + x_t w_t' \sigma \, dW_t \\ &= \left(x_t \left(w_t' \lambda + r \right) - c_t \right) dt + x_t w_t' \sigma \, dW_t, \end{aligned} \tag{14.30}$$

where $\lambda = \mu - r 1_k$ is the k-vector of mean excess returns to the stocks above the riskless rate. Note that consumption reduces the drift, and hence future wealth, which follows a controlled diffusion process (see (14.5)). The policy or control variables are $\pi_t = (w_t, c_t)$, giving the investment and consumption strategy, and the state variable is wealth x_t, so that $m = 1$, in terms of the general notation. The objective is

$$U_\pi(x_t) = E \left(\int_t^\tau e^{-\rho s} u(c_s) \, ds + H(x_\tau) | x_t, \pi_t \right), \tag{14.31}$$

in line with the general problem discussed earlier. The value function is

$$V_t(x_t) = \sup_\pi U_\pi(x_t), \tag{14.32}$$

and the Bellman equation (14.9) in this case takes the form

$$\begin{aligned} 0 = \max_{\pi_t} &\left\{ \frac{1}{2} x_t^2 \frac{\partial^2 V_t(x_t)}{\partial x^2} w_t' \sigma \sigma' w_t + \left(x_t \left(w_t' \lambda + r \right) - c_t \right) \frac{\partial V_t(x_t)}{\partial x} \right. \\ &\left. + \frac{\partial V_t(x_t)}{\partial t} - \rho V_t(x_t) + u(c_t) \right\} \end{aligned} \tag{14.33}$$

since, in particular, the wealth (i.e., state) process involves the controlled drift and diffusion coefficients

$$a_t(x_t, \pi_t) = x_t \left(w_t' \lambda + r \right) - c_t, \tag{14.34}$$

$$\sigma_t(x_t, \pi_t) = x_t w_t' \sigma, \tag{14.35}$$

with $\pi_t = (w_t, c_t)$, the control. The maximization in the Bellman equation with respect to the stock portfolio weights w_t makes use of the fact that these do not enter the term $\partial V_t/\partial t - \rho V_t + u(c_t)$. Hence, the first-order condition for w_t is

$$x_t^2 \frac{\partial^2 V_t(x_t)}{\partial x^2} \sigma\sigma' w_t + x_t \frac{\partial V_t(x_t)}{\partial x} \lambda = 0, \tag{14.36}$$

with solution

$$w_t = -\frac{\dfrac{\partial V_t(x_t)}{\partial x}}{x_t \dfrac{\partial^2 V_t(x_t)}{\partial x^2}} \left(\sigma\sigma'\right)^{-1} \lambda$$

$$= \frac{1}{RRA(V_t)} \left(\sigma\sigma'\right)^{-1} \lambda, \tag{14.37}$$

where $RRA(V_t)$ denotes the Arrow-Pratt relative risk aversion with respect to V_t.

Thus, the relative proportions of wealth held in the various stocks are constant and given by the vector $(\sigma\sigma')^{-1}\lambda$. For example, the ratio of investments in stocks i and j is fixed at the ratio between entries i and j in $(\sigma\sigma')^{-1}\lambda$. The actual portfolio weights vary through time if risk aversion does, and so does the (residual determined) weight on the riskless asset, $1 - 1_k'(\sigma\sigma')^{-1}\lambda/RRA(V_t)$. This two-fund separation result is interesting. It is also known as the *mutual fund theorem*. At all times, the investor holds only two mutual funds: the riskless asset and the stock fund with relative weights indicated by $(\sigma\sigma')^{-1}\lambda$. The only controls applied over time are the rate c_t of consumption and the asset allocation control (between the two funds) given by the relative risk aversion coefficient. Thus, the dynamic consumption and portfolio choice problem with $(k + 1)$-dimensional control $\pi_t = (w_t, c_t)$ has been reduced to an asset allocation problem (market timing between risky and riskless assets) with two-dimensional control.

Of course, full solution requires determining optimal consumption, too. Let us first consider the case $u = 0$, so that $c_t = 0$, i.e., no intermediate consumption. All utility is derived from the ultimate wealth x_τ. To illustrate, assume further the utility of terminal wealth (or bequest) function $H(x) = x^{1-\gamma}$, with constant RRA (CRRA) given by γ. In this case, it is reasonable to guess a value function of similar shape,

$$V_t(x) = v(t) x^{1-\gamma}, \tag{14.38}$$

with terminal condition

$$v(\tau) = 1, \tag{14.39}$$

so that $V_\tau = H$. With this guess, we have $\partial V_t/\partial x = v(t)(1-\gamma)x^{-\gamma}$, $\partial^2 V_t/\partial x^2 = -v(t)\gamma(1-\gamma)x^{-\gamma-1}$, and $\partial V_t/\partial t = v'(t)x^{1-\gamma}$. It is clear that we have $RRA(V_t) = \gamma$, and hence $w_t = (\sigma\sigma')^{-1}\lambda/\gamma$. Inserting in the Bellman equation yields

$$0 = x_t^{1-\gamma}\left\{\left((1-\gamma)\left(\frac{\lambda'(\sigma\sigma')^{-1}\lambda}{2\gamma}+r\right)-\rho\right)v(t)+v'(t)\right\}$$

$$= x_t^{1-\gamma}\left\{\eta v(t)+v'(t)\right\}, \tag{14.40}$$

defining here the constant parameter $\eta = (1-\gamma)(\lambda'(\sigma\sigma')^{-1}\lambda/(2\gamma)+r)-\rho$. Thus, $v(t)$ satisfies the ODE $v'(t) = -\eta v(t)$ with terminal condition $v(\tau) = 1$. The solution is $v(t) = e^{\eta(\tau-t)}$. It follows that

$$V_t(x) = e^{\eta(\tau-t)}x^{1-\gamma} \tag{14.41}$$

solves the Bellman equation. In the present case, this is both a necessary and sufficient condition for an optimal solution, and the optimal investment strategy is indeed that given by the time-invariant stock portfolio weights $w_t = (\sigma\sigma')^{-1}\lambda/\gamma$.

Let us next consider the case with intermediate consumption, $u(x) = c^{1-\gamma}$, $H(x) = 0$. Thus, the CRRA assumption is shifted from the bequest function to the current reward. We may guess a solution of the same form, $V_t(x) = v(t)x^{1-\gamma}$, but now with terminal condition $v(\tau) = 0$, such that again $V_\tau = H$. We have once more $RRA(V_t) = \gamma$, and hence $w_t = (\sigma\sigma')^{-1}\lambda/\gamma$. The Bellman equation now becomes

$$0 = \max_{c_t}\left\{x_t^{1-\gamma}\left(\eta v(t)+v'(t)\right)-c_t v(t)(1-\gamma)x_t^{-\gamma}+c_t^{1-\gamma}\right\}, \tag{14.42}$$

and the first-order condition for c_t is

$$v(t)(1-\gamma)x_t^{-\gamma} = (1-\gamma)c_t^{-\gamma}. \tag{14.43}$$

The solution is

$$c_t = x_t v(t)^{-1/\gamma}. \tag{14.44}$$

That is, optimal consumption is linear in wealth. Inserting in the Bellman equation,

$$0 = x_t^{1-\gamma}\left\{\eta v(t)+v'(t)-v(t)^{1-(1/\gamma)}(1-\gamma)+v(t)^{-(1-\gamma)/\gamma}\right\}$$

$$= x_t^{1-\gamma}\left\{v'(t)+\eta v(t)+\gamma v(t)^{(\gamma-1)/\gamma}\right\}.$$

It follows that $v(t)$ should be determined from the ODE

$$v'(t)+\eta v(t)+\gamma v(t)^{1-(1/\gamma)} = 0, \tag{14.45}$$

with terminal condition $v(\tau) = 0$. Again, two-fund separation applies, and the relative stock portfolio weights are as before. The optimal consumption policy follows from solution of the indicated ODE. In fact, this has a solution, and the asset allocation and consumption-saving problems are solved completely.

14.5 APPLICATION: CHANGING INVESTMENT OPPORTUNITIES

The solutions to the asset allocation problems with and without intermediate consumption share the property that constant relative portfolio weights are invested in the assets. As the weights do not respond to changes in state variables, the solutions are sometimes described as myopic. This property disappears when investment opportunities are changing, e.g., when returns are not i.i.d. but instead expected excess returns λ, volatilities σ, or the interest rate r varies through time with state variables. For recent contributions on the resulting strategic asset allocation problems, see Campbell and Viceira (2002) and the references therein.

Brandt (1999) introduces a novel method for taking these models to the data. Here, the idea is to establish a normative approach, using data on returns and state variables to derive the optimal consumption and investment rules for investors with given preference structures, without estimating the preference structure of a representative agent describing the aggregate market. The latter would be a descriptive or positive approach, and Hansen and Singleton (1982) have used the generalized method of moments (GMM) to this end, estimating parameters such as γ and ρ above from data on returns and aggregate consumption. The estimating equations are based on the first-order conditions (stochastic Euler equations, chapter 13) of the representative investor's problem. The alternative normative approach is to consider the similar equations but instead to take preference parameters such as γ and ρ as given, supplied by the user (individual investor), and apply the equations to solve for the optimal policy. For example, instead of letting the consumption variable be given by aggregate observation, it is solved for as the individual investor's preference-dependent choice given observed returns.

To sketch briefly the normative approach, note that Brandt (1999) actually works in discrete time, so the details differ, but the idea is still apparent from the following simple two-period example. Thus, c_t and w_t are chosen to maximize the expected discounted stream of utilities $u(c_t) + \beta E_t(u(c_{t+1}))$ in this simple case, writing $H = u$ and $\beta = e^{-\rho}$. From the budget constraint (compare (14.30)), since $c_{t+1} = x_{t+1}$ in the last period,

$$c_{t+1} = x_t(1 + r_{t+1} + w_t' R_{t+1}) - c_t,$$

with r_{t+1} the risk-free rate known at t and R_{t+1} the vector of excess returns on the risky assets, $R_{t+1} = (R_{1,t+1}, \ldots, R_{k,t+1})$, where $R_{i,t+1} = (p_{i,t+1} - p_{i,t})/p_{i,t} - r_{t+1}$. The first-order conditions are

$$u'(c_t) = \beta E_t(u'(c_{t+1}))$$

for consumption c_t and

$$E_t(u'(c_{t+1})R_{t+1}) = 0$$

for the portfolio weights w_t. Form the vector function

$$m_{t+1}(c_t, w_t) = \begin{pmatrix} \beta \dfrac{u'(x_t(1 + r_{t+1} + w_t' R_{t+1}) - c_t)}{u'(c_t)} - 1 \\ u'(x_t(1 + r_{t+1} + w_t' R_{t+1}) - c_t)R_{t+1} \end{pmatrix}$$

and write $c_t = \tilde{c}_t x_t$. With $u(c) = (c^{1-\gamma} - 1)/(1 - \gamma)$ so that $u'(c) = c^{-\gamma}$, the Euler equation $E_t m_{t+1}(c_t, w_t) = 0$ does not depend on x_t; i.e.,

$$m_{t+1}(\tilde{c}_t, w_t) = \begin{pmatrix} \beta \left(\dfrac{1 + r_{t+1} + w_t' R_{t+1} - \tilde{c}_t}{\tilde{c}_t} \right)^{-\gamma} - 1 \\ (1 + r_{t+1} + w_t' R_{t+1} - \tilde{c}_t)^{-\gamma} R_{t+1} \end{pmatrix}$$

may replace $m_{t+1}(c_t, w_t)$. The point is to consider $m_{t+1}(\tilde{c}_t, w_t)$ as a function of unknowns $\tilde{c}_t$ and w_t to be solved for, given marketwide data on r_{t+1} and R_{t+1} and user-specified β and γ. Thus, consider

$$\frac{1}{T-1} \sum_{t=1}^{T-1} m_{t+1}(\tilde{c}, w) = 0,$$

and with data $\{(r_{t+1}, R_{t+1})\}_{t=1}^{T-1}$, solve for $(\tilde{c}, w)$. This is the normative approach, allowing application by an investor with arbitrary preferences (β, γ), whereas the positive approach is to insert aggregate consumption levels in $u'(c_{t+1})$ and $u'(c_t)$ from the outset and solve $\Sigma_t m_{t+1}/(T-1) = 0$ for (β, γ), following Hansen and Singleton (1982).

Both the normative and the positive approaches may be extended to allow for instrumental variables z_t in the information set at t; e.g., $E_t m_{t+1} = 0$ implies $E_t(z_t \otimes m_{t+1}) = z_t \otimes E_t(m_{t+1}) = 0$, so with $h_{t+1} = z_t \otimes m_{t+1}$, the equations $H_T \equiv \Sigma_t h_{t+1}/(T-1) = 0$ may be solved with respect to $(\tilde{c}, w)$ using the normative approach and (β, γ) using the positive approach. With $\dim H_T$ exceeding $k + 1$, respectively 2, meaning more equations than unknowns (overidentifying restrictions), the approach of solving $H_T = 0$ may be replaced by minimizing $H_T' \text{var}(H_T)^{-1} H_T$.

The method can actually be improved upon whether $H_T = 0$ is solved or the quadratic in H_T is minimized. Thus, in both cases, the optimal procedure is to solve

$$\frac{1}{T-1} \sum_{t=1}^{T-1} E_t \left(\frac{\partial m'_{t+1}}{\partial \theta} \right) (\text{var}_t (m_{t+1}))^{-1} m_{t+1} = 0$$

with respect to θ, given as $(\tilde{c}, w)$ in the normative and (β, γ) in the positive case, provided the conditional mean and variance in the equation, which may depend on z_t, can be calculated, e.g., by simulation, kernel smoothing, or a similar method.

Note the step where return data across all time periods $t = 1, \ldots, T$ are used to solve for a single control vector $(\tilde{c}, w)$ of dimension $k + 1$. Conceptually, $(T-1)$ similar two-period problems are solved, and averaging across time allows a consistent estimate of $(\tilde{c}, w)$ to be found. The variance of $\sqrt{T}(\hat{c} - \tilde{c}, \hat{w} - w)$ tends to $(E(\partial m'_{t+1}/\partial \theta) \text{var}(m_{t+1})^{-1} E(\partial m_{t+1}/\partial \theta'))^{-1}$ if $H'_T \text{var}(H_T)^{-1} H_T$ is minimized, and in the efficient case to

$$\left(E \left(E_t \left(\frac{\partial m'_{t+1}}{\partial \theta} \right) (\text{var}_t (m_{t+1}))^{-1} E_t \left(\frac{\partial m_{t+1}}{\partial \theta^1} \right) \right) \right)^{-1},$$

which is less.

The reason the conditional means and variances improve efficiency, and the reason for bringing in conditioning variables z_t in the first place, is that in fact that $(T-1)$ investment problems are not identical. Rather, investment opportunities, such as conditional distributions of returns, vary through time. After all, this is the main reason for leaving the explicit continuous-time solutions and taking the problem to the data. If the changing investment opportunities are at least to some extent characterized by changes in z_t, this suggests looking for the optimal policy as a function of this, $(\tilde{c}(z_t), w(z_t))$. This is the idea of Brandt (1999). Since averaging across time as above does not give a function $(\tilde{c}(\cdot), w(\cdot))$ but a constant control, a kernel-smoothing approach is introduced. Instead of minimizing $H'_T \text{var}(H_T)^{-1} H_T$ or solving $\Sigma_t m_{t+1}/(T-1) = 0$, the system

$$M_T(z) = \frac{1}{T-1} \sum_{t=1}^{T-1} \omega \left(\frac{z - z_t}{b_T} \right) m_{t+1}$$

is introduced. For each z of interest, $M_T(z) = 0$ is solved with respect to the policy $(\tilde{c}(z), w(z))$. This is a conditional (on hypothetical z) moments approach. As the procedure is repeated for different z, the policy function $(\tilde{c}(\cdot), w(\cdot))$ is traced out. This solves the asset allocation problem with investment opportunities varying with z.

In $M_T(z)$, the kernel function is $\omega(\cdot)$ and b_T is a bandwidth. The idea is that to find the policy corresponding to a specific value z, most weight in the estimating equation should be placed on m_{t+1} from time periods where observed z_t is relatively close to the hypothetical value z of interest. Brandt (1999) considers the simple case $k = 1$, with R_{t+1} the aggregate stock market excess return, and includes four stationary variables in z_t known to characterize investment opportunities, namely, the dividend yield, the default premium (the interest differential between safe and risky (high- and low-grade) bonds), the term premium (the yield spread between long and short government bonds), and the lagged excess return R_t. Thus, the dimension of z_t is $K = 4$ in this specification. The kernel is Gaussian, $\omega(u) = \Sigma_{i=1}^K \phi(u_i)$, with ϕ the standard normal density. For each z, the resulting policy estimate $(\hat{c}(z), \hat{w}(z))$ is consistent and asymptotically normal. The variance of $(Tb_T^K)^{1/2}(\hat{c}(z) - c(z), \hat{w}(z) - w(z))$ tends to

$$\left(E_t\left(\frac{\partial m_{t+1}}{\partial \theta'}\right)\right)^{-1} \text{var}_t(m_{t+1})\left(E_t\left(\frac{\partial m'_{t+1}}{\partial \theta}\right)\right)^{-1}\frac{\Phi^K}{f(z)}$$

as $T \to \infty$, where the conditional means and variances may depend on z (these are the changing investment opportunities), $\Phi = \int_{-\infty}^{\infty} \phi(u)^2\, du$, and $f(z)$ is the density of z. Note that $\theta = (\tilde{c}(z), w(z))$, and in this case the dimensions of θ and m_{t+1} are equal, at $k + 1$. The conditions on the bandwidth are that $b_T \to 0$, $Tb_T^{K+4} \to 0$, and $Tb_T^K \to \infty$ as $T \to \infty$.

The τ-period asset allocation problem may be solved similarly, working backward from the solution to the two-period problem. The first-order conditions $E_t m_{t+1} = 0$ for the τ-period problem at t take into account that a $(\tau - 1)$-period problem is faced at $t + 1$, with the solution already estimated. Thus, the data $\{(r_{t+1}, R_{t+1}, z_t)\}_{t=1}^{T-1}$ are used heavily: For each $\tau = 2, 3, \ldots$, an entire policy function $(\tilde{c}(\cdot), w(\cdot))_\tau$ is estimated. In this normative approach, the investor specifying the preferences (β, γ), taken as fixed through the calculations, may now apply the policy $(\tilde{c}(\cdot), w(\cdot))_\tau$ in practice for the relevant τ. Again, this is not the policy of the representative investor, who may have entirely different (β, γ) or may not even exist in the given economy, and no aggregate consumption (or portfolio choice) data are used.

14.6 DERIVATIVES, HEDGING, AND ARBITRAGE PRICING

The analysis of optimal consumption and savings and the proper asset allocation across stocks and bonds requires full specification of intertemporal preferences and solution of the associated dynamic programming problem. Much of continuous-time finance deals with the slightly different problem of setting fair prices and hedging strategies for redundant securities. For example, by showing that a derivative security (e.g., an option) may be spanned through trading in basis securities (e.g., stocks and bonds), it is possible to express the price of the derivative as a combination of the basis security prices. This is an arbitrage argument. The resulting derivative price does not depend on specific assumptions about preferences or about which equilibrium prevails. If the derivative price differed from the cost of setting up a *replicating portfolio* with an identical payoff, an obvious arbitrage opportunity would present itself (buy the cheapest of the two and finance the purchase through a short position in the other), and this would be inconsistent with any economic equilibrium. In the following, we consider this arbitrage approach in more detail.

Consider first the Black and Scholes (1973) model. The stock price is again governed by geometric Brownian motion, and we focus on the univariate case, $k = 1$,

$$dp_t = \mu p_t \, dt + \sigma p_t \, dW_t, \tag{14.46}$$

where also W_t is taken to be univariate standard Brownian motion, $n = 1$. The interest rate is deterministic and constant, $r > 0$. This implies that the safe investment, the money market account, evolves according to

$$db_t = rb_t \, dt, \tag{14.47}$$

i.e., with no uncertainty, so we have

$$b_t = e^{rt} \tag{14.48}$$

if the account is started at $t = 0$ in the amount $b_0 = 1$.

Consider now a derivative security or contingent claim c, whose payoff at expiration T is some function g of the stock price at that time, p_T. For example, for a European call option, the payoff at expiration is

$$g(p_T) = \max\{p_T - K, 0\}, \tag{14.49}$$

where K is the exercise or strike price. It is reasonable to assume that the derivative price at earlier times, $t < T$, will be a function of the stock price and time, $c(p_t, t)$. In particular, the stock price process is Markovian. We are now in a position to apply Itô's lemma, which yields

$$dc(p_t, t) = \left\{ \mu p_t \frac{\partial c}{\partial p}(p_t, t) + \frac{\partial c}{\partial t} + \frac{1}{2}\sigma^2 p_t^2 \frac{\partial^2 c}{\partial p^2}(p_t, t) \right\} dt$$
$$+ \frac{\partial c}{\partial p}(p_t, t)\sigma p_t \, dW_t. \tag{14.50}$$

Next, we turn to the task of building a replicating portfolio strategy, providing a perfect hedge of the derivative security. Thus, let s_t denote the number of shares of stock and m_t the number of bonds (units in the money market account) in the portfolio. Let x_t denote the portfolio value at time t,

$$x_t = s_t p_t + m_t b_t. \tag{14.51}$$

The portfolio value evolves according to

$$\begin{aligned} dx_t &= s_t \, dp_t + m_t \, db_t \\ &= \{s_t \mu p_t + m_t r b_t\} \, dt + s_t \sigma p_t \, dW_t. \end{aligned} \tag{14.52}$$

The goal is to set the *dynamic trading strategy* (s_t, m_t) so that the portfolio x_t replicates the derivative security $c(p_t, t)$. To make dx_t and $dc(p_t, t)$ agree, we first match the diffusion coefficients in (14.50) and (14.52), setting $s_t \sigma p_t = (\partial c / \partial p) \sigma p_t$, which is achieved by holding at all times t a number of shares

$$s_t = \frac{\partial c}{\partial p}(p_t, t). \tag{14.53}$$

To determine the other component in the trading strategy, we solve (14.51) for the bond holdings m_t, inserting $s_t = \partial c / \partial p$ and $x_t = c$, which produces

$$m_t = \frac{1}{b_t}\left(c(p_t, t) - \frac{\partial c}{\partial p}(p_t, t)p_t\right). \tag{14.54}$$

We should also match the drift coefficients in dx_t and $dc(p_t, t)$, see (14.50) and (14.52). Here, $s_t \mu p_t$ from dx_t matches $\mu p_t \partial c / \partial p$ from $dc(p_t, t)$ since $s_t = \partial c / \partial p$. Inserting m_t from (14.54) in dx_t and equating the remaining terms in the drifts of dx_t and dc produces

$$\frac{1}{2}\sigma^2 p_t^2 \frac{\partial^2 c}{\partial p^2}(p_t, t) + rp_t \frac{\partial c}{\partial p}(p_t, t) + \frac{\partial c}{\partial t}(p_t, t) - rc(p_t, t) = 0. \tag{14.55}$$

This is a second-order partial differential equation (PDE) for the derivative security price $c(\cdot, \cdot)$. This point may be clarified by dropping the time subscripts on p_t, writing

$$\frac{1}{2}\sigma^2 p^2 \frac{\partial^2 c}{\partial p^2}(p, t) + rp \frac{\partial c}{\partial p}(p, t) + \frac{\partial c}{\partial t}(p, t) - rc(p, t) = 0. \tag{14.56}$$

This is known as the fundamental PDE of asset pricing. The terminal condition is

$$c(p, t) = g(p). \tag{14.57}$$

The derivation shows that if there is a function c satisfying the PDE with the given terminal condition, then the portfolio (s_t, m_t) has the value $x_t = c(p_t, t)$, including at expiration, where $x_T = g(p_T)$. Since the derivative security also has payoff $g(p_T)$ at T, absence of arbitrage opportunities requires that the portfolio x_t and the derivative must also agree in price initially. As the initial $t = 0$ price of the portfolio is $x_0 = c(p_0, 0)$, hence this must be the initial derivative price. In short, if the PDE can be solved, then the solution gives the derivative pricing formula, showing how to set the derivative security price as a function of the underlying security price, $p \rightarrow c(p, 0)$, i.e., the pricing rule is given by the function $c(\cdot, 0)$. Different derivative securities are characterized by different terminal payoff functions $g(\cdot)$, and hence yield different pricing rules $c(\cdot, 0)$.

In the particular case of a European call option, it may be verified by direct differentiation that the solution to the fundamental PDE is the call option price of the Black and Scholes (1973) and Merton (1973b) formula (see also (11.22)–(11.23)),

$$c(p, t) = p\Phi(d) - e^{-r(T-t)} K \Phi(d - \sigma\sqrt{T - t}),$$

$$d = \frac{\log\left(\frac{p}{K}\right) + \left(r + \frac{\sigma^2}{2}\right)(T - t)}{\sigma\sqrt{T - t}}, \qquad (14.58)$$

where $\Phi(\cdot)$ is the standard normal cumulative distribution function (CDF). The European put price $q(p, t)$ corresponding to the terminal payoff $g(p_T) = \max\{K - p_T, 0\}$ is immediately obtained from put-call parity (section 10.6),

$$q(p, t) = c(p, t) + e^{-r(T-t)} K - p. \qquad (14.59)$$

The Black-Scholes formula highlights the striking feature that the mean return μ to the stock does not enter the option price. As it does not enter the PDE (14.56), all derivative prices determined by this (i.e., corresponding to various different terminal conditions) are in fact free of μ. Since the market allows building a riskless hedge, risk compensation (such as an equilibrium model would imply through a risk premium in μ) is unnecessary for the pricing of the redundant security. The market for stocks and bonds is *dynamically complete* in this model. For related discrete-time approaches, see (10.70) and (11.22).

The analysis gives not only the fair price of the derivative security but also the proper trading strategy, in particular, the way to hedge the derivative. Thus, the writer (seller) of the derivative should cover the short position by going long $s_t = \partial c/\partial p$ shares of stock per derivative contract written. In the call option case, this is

$$\frac{\partial c}{\partial p}(p, t) = \Phi(d) \qquad (14.60)$$

from the Black-Scholes formula (14.58), commonly known as the *hedge ratio* or the *delta* of the option. A hedge ratio or delta of one unit less (corresponding to the minus in (14.59)) generates a synthetic put, e.g., for portfolio insurance purposes, cf. section 10.6.

The practice of trading as indicated is referred to as *delta hedging*. In the model, this generates a perfect hedge, i.e., future cash flows net out to zero. Hence, any writer who manages to sell the derivative for more than $c(p_0, 0)$ has locked in an arbitrage profit. Alternatively, if selling at $c(p_0, 0)$, the position is safe.

In general, for different derivatives (different terminal payoffs g), it is typically not possible to guess and verify a solution to the fundamental PDE in each case. Fortunately, the *Feynman-Kac formula* provides a general solution for arbitrary terminal payoffs g, given by

$$c(p, t) = e^{-r(T-t)} E\left(g\left(y_T^{p,t}\right)\right). \tag{14.61}$$

Here, the expectation is taken with respect to the artificial random variable $y_T^{p,t}$, whose distribution is specified through the stochastic process

$$dy_s^{p,t} = r y_s^{p,t}\, ds + \sigma y_s^{p,t}\, dW_s, \tag{14.62}$$

started at $s = t$ at the level $y_t^{p,t} = p$. Thus, $y_T^{p,t}$ is the value of the artificial process at $s = T$. To interpret the Feynman-Kac result, note that if started at $p = p_t$ at time t, the artificial process $y_s^{p,t}$ and the true stock price process p_s are governed by the same geometric Brownian motion, except that the mean return parameter μ from the process (14.46) for p_t has been replaced by the riskless rate of interest r in the case of $y_s^{p,t}$. Again, this reflects the lack of need for risk compensation. The Feynman-Kac representation of the derivative price shows that this may be considered the expected discounted future payoff, calculated as if investors were risk-neutral (replacing μ by r when calculating the expectation and discounting at rate r outside the expectation (14.61)).

Not surprisingly, given the analysis so far, the condition that the coefficients μ and σ must be constant is not important. The exact same derivations show that with dependence on stock price and time, $\mu(p, t)$ and $\sigma(p, t)$, the fundamental PDE of asset pricing still obtains,

$$\frac{1}{2}\sigma(p, t)^2 p^2 \frac{\partial^2 c}{\partial p^2}(p, t) + rp\frac{\partial c}{\partial p}(p, t) + \frac{\partial c}{\partial t}(p, t) - rc(p, t) = 0, \tag{14.63}$$

again not depending on $\mu = \mu(p, t)$, and the Feynman-Kac result (14.61) applies, now with $\sigma = \sigma(y, s)$ in the process for $y_s^{p,t}$. Of course, the specific Black-Scholes formula (14.58) no longer applies in the case of time-varying coefficients.

As a complement, it is useful to consider the option-pricing problem from a slightly different angle. Thus, write the solution as

$$c(p, t) = e^{-r(T-t)} E_t^Q(g(p_T)), \qquad (14.64)$$

where Q is an equivalent martingale measure, i.e., under Q,

$$dp_t = rp_t\, dt + \sigma p_t\, dW_t^Q, \qquad (14.65)$$

where W_t^Q is a standard Brownian motion. This therefore specifies the distribution under Q of p_T in the formula (14.64). Also, an equivalent martingale measure is defined to be one under which discounted prices $p_t/b_t = p_t/e^{rt}$ are martingales (compare (10.8)), but this is equivalent to p_t earning the expected return r instead of μ under Q. Since W_t and W_t^Q are distributed identically, it is clear that running $y_s^{p,t}$ and p_s through $s = T$, starting both at p_t at $s = t$, will produce equal option prices. To appreciate the difference between the Feynman-Kac solution and the equivalent martingale measure approach, note that the Feynmann-Kac solution came about as a tool from analysis, providing the solution to a given PDE and using the artificially introduced process $y_s^{p,t}$. In contrast, the equivalent martingale measure result does not require that a PDE characterization has been established. It simply asserts that derivative prices are expected discounted payoffs calculated as in a risk-neutral world, i.e., using the riskless rate of interest both for discounting and for the expected stock return. Here, dp_t is not to be viewed as an artificial process but rather as the actual stock process, albeit that different probabilities are used in completing the formula (of course, the distinction is only conceptual since only the distribution is important for the expected-value calculation).

The equivalent martingale measure approach also allows general drift and diffusion coefficients $\mu(p_t, t)$ and $\sigma(p_t, t)$; i.e., $\sigma(p_t, t)$ may replace σ in (14.65). In general, two important steps must be taken before proceeding to the final formula (14.64). First, the existence of an equivalent martingale measure for the stock and bond price processes must be established. This is equivalent to establishing that the market for stocks and bonds is arbitrage-free. One possible approach in this step is to appeal to *Girsanov's theorem*. In the second step, it should be determined whether any equivalent martingale measure from the first step is unique. This is equivalent to asking whether markets are complete. If they are, then derivative securities are indeed redundant, and the formula may be applied. If not, then it must be verified that the candidate martingale measure from the first step is also a martingale measure for the derivative security, and Girsanov's theorem can typically be used again to this end.

We now consider these issues, including Girsanov's theorem, in a little more detail. Girsanov's theorem for a general k-dimensional Itô process,

$$dx_t = \mu_t \, dt + \sigma_t \, dW_t, \qquad (14.66)$$

where μ_t is $k \times 1$, σ_t is $k \times n$, and W_t is n-dimensional standard Brownian motion, provides conditions under which the drift μ_t may be shifted to another k-dimensional drift η_t, say, by going to a different probability measure. The first requirement is that there must exist an n-dimensional process λ_t such that

$$\eta_t = \mu_t + \sigma_t \lambda_t. \qquad (14.67)$$

Thus, the desired change in drift must belong to the image space or column span of the volatility matrix. Second, λ_t must satisfy *Novikov's condition*,

$$E\left(\exp \frac{1}{2} \int_0^T \lambda_t' \lambda_t \, dt \right) < \infty. \qquad (14.68)$$

Third, the random variable

$$\xi_T = \exp \int_0^T \lambda_t' dW_t - \frac{1}{2} \int_0^T \lambda_t' \lambda_t dt \qquad (14.69)$$

must have finite variance, $\text{var}(\xi_T) < \infty$. Under these conditions, there exists a probability measure Q, which is equivalent to the original or physical measure P (i.e., the two share the same null sets), such that under Q,

$$dx_t = \eta_t \, dt + \sigma_t \, dW_t^Q, \qquad (14.70)$$

where W_t^Q is standard n-dimensional Brownian motion under Q. Thus, the drift of x_t has been shifted from μ_t to η_t of the form (14.67), as desired. Furthermore, the new Brownian motion is given in terms of the original as

$$dW_t^Q = dW_t - \lambda_t \, dt. \qquad (14.71)$$

Note that the representation works out; i.e.,

$$\begin{aligned}
dx_t &= \eta_t \, dt + \sigma_t \, dW_t^Q \\
&= (\mu_t + \sigma_t \lambda_t) \, dt + \sigma_t \, (dW_t - \lambda_t \, dt) \\
&= \mu_t \, dt + \sigma_t \, dW_t,
\end{aligned}$$

so the process is unchanged, but the distribution is different under Q and P.

The *likelihood ratio process* or Radon-Nikodym derivative dQ/dP is given by

$$\xi_t = \exp \int_0^t \lambda_s' \, dW_s - \frac{1}{2} \int_0^t \lambda_s' \lambda_s \, ds,$$

so that, in particular, if $E^Q(|z|) < \infty$ for a random variable z, then $E^Q(z) = E(z\xi_T)$.

Let us apply Girsanov's theorem to the derivative-pricing problem above. Consider first the market for the stock and the bond (a money market account), with price processes p_t and b_t. In the notation of the theorem, write $x_t = (b_t, p_t)'$. We have $k = 2$ (two assets) and $n = 1$ (one driving Brownian motion). The drifts are

$$\mu_t = \begin{pmatrix} rb_t \\ \mu(p_t, t)p_t \end{pmatrix}, \tag{14.72}$$

and the volatilities are

$$\sigma_t = \begin{pmatrix} 0 \\ \sigma(p_t, t)p_t \end{pmatrix}. \tag{14.73}$$

The absence of arbitrage opportunities is equivalent to the existence of an equivalent martingale measure, making the relevant price processes martingales. Certainly, if some measure Q could make the (undiscounted) price processes $x_t = (b_t, p_t)$ martingales, then there would be no arbitrage opportunities. Since a martingale has drift zero, this would require $\eta_t = 0$, and so the condition is

$$\begin{pmatrix} 0 \\ 0 \end{pmatrix} = \begin{pmatrix} rb_t \\ \mu(p_t, t)p_t \end{pmatrix} + \begin{pmatrix} 0 \\ \sigma(p_t, t)p_t \end{pmatrix} \lambda_t. \tag{14.74}$$

Since the first equation has no solution if the interest rate is positive, the approach is not fruitful. Instead, we utilize the notion that absence of arbitrage opportunities also is equivalent to the existence of an equivalent martingale measure Q making the relevant discounted price processes martingales. Which discounting process δ_t is chosen is irrelevant, as long as $\delta_t > 0$, and x_t/δ_t is a martingale under Q. Our attempt, based on the idea from chapter 10, is to use $\delta_t = b_t$, the money market account. Then $x_t/\delta_t = (1, p_t/b_t)$. Of course, the constant process 1 (the first coordinate of x_t/δ_t) is a martingale under any measure. We apply Girsanov's theorem to the second coordinate p_t/b_t. Writing $p_t/b_t = F(b_t, p_t)$ and using Itô's lemma, we have

$$d\left(\frac{p_t}{b_t}\right) = \left(-\frac{p_t}{b_t^2}, \frac{1}{b_t}\right)\begin{pmatrix} rb_t \\ \mu(p_t, t)p_t \end{pmatrix} dt$$

$$+ \frac{1}{2}(0, \sigma(p_t, t)p_t)\begin{pmatrix} 2\dfrac{p_t}{b_t^3} & -\dfrac{1}{b_t^2} \\ -\dfrac{1}{b_t^2} & 0 \end{pmatrix}\begin{pmatrix} 0 \\ \sigma(p_t, t)p_t \end{pmatrix} dt$$

$$+ \left(-\frac{p_t}{b_t^2}, \frac{1}{b_t}\right)\begin{pmatrix} 0 \\ \sigma(p_t, t)p_t \end{pmatrix} dW_t$$

$$= \left(-r\frac{p_t}{b_t} + \mu(p_t, t)\frac{p_t}{b_t}\right) dt + \sigma(p_t, t)\frac{p_t}{b_t} dW_t. \tag{14.75}$$

Thus, in the notation of Girsanov's theorem, the drift is $\mu_t = (\mu(p_t, t) - r)p_t/b_t$ and the volatility $\sigma_t = \sigma(p_t, t)p_t/b_t$. The desired drift is $\eta_t = 0$ for p_t/b_t to be a martingale. From (14.67), this yields the condition

$$0 = (\mu(p_t, t) - r)\frac{p_t}{b_t} + \sigma(p_t, t)\frac{p_t}{b_t}\lambda_t \qquad (14.76)$$

or

$$\lambda_t = -\frac{\mu(p_t, t) - r}{\sigma(p_t, t)}. \qquad (14.77)$$

This is recognized as the negative of the *Sharpe ratio*, i.e., the ratio of the mean excess return above the riskless rate and the volatility. This may well satisfy the conditions (14.68) and (14.69) of Girsanov's theorem. For example, if λ_t is bounded, then the conditions are clearly satisfied. This occurs, e.g., when the mean and the volatility of the stock return are constant at μ and σ, as in the original Black-Scholes model, where $\lambda_t = -(\mu - r)/\sigma$. Whenever these conditions are satisfied, Girsanov's theorem ensures the existence of an equivalent martingale measure and hence no arbitrage opportunities. This completes the first step from above.

For the second step, markets are complete if and only if the rank of the volatility matrix is n. In the application, $n = 1$, and clearly the volatility matrix x_t/b_t given by $(0, \sigma(p_t, t)p_t/b_t)$ has rank 1. With complete markets in stocks and bonds, options are redundant and so are priced according to $c(p, t) = e^{-r(T-t)}E_t^Q(g(p_T))$ as in (14.64). This provides the mathematical foundation for what if often labelled risk-neutral valuation (although clearly it does not require risk-neutrality on the part of investors, this is the point behind the change of measure).

14.7 STOCHASTIC VOLATILITY AND JUMPS

Markets are typically no longer complete if volatility is driven by a process involving a separate source of uncertainty or if prices may jump randomly. The simple stochastic volatility extension

$$\begin{aligned} dp_t &= \mu p_t \, dt + \sigma_t p_t \, dW_t, \\ d\sigma_t^2 &= \alpha\sigma_t^2 \, dt + \xi\sigma_t^2 \, dW_t^\sigma \end{aligned} \qquad (14.78)$$

of the Black-Scholes model (14.46) was considered by Hull and White (1987). Thus, volatility changes randomly through time, with σ_t^2 (instantaneous variance) governed by a process of the same geometric Brownian motion type as the stock price p_t but driven by a separate Brownian motion W_t^σ. A perfect hedge of an option on the stock can no longer be established through dynamic trading in the stock and the bond only; i.e., markets are incomplete. Trading can hedge moves in W_t, but not in both W_t and W_t^σ simultaneously.

Without a replicating portfolio strategy, an equilibrium pricing approach might be attempted,

$$c(p_t, \sigma_t, t) = \beta^{T-t} E_t \left(\frac{u_T'}{u_t'} g(p_T) \right), \tag{14.79}$$

noting that conditioning is now on both p_t and the additional state variable σ_t, volatility. As usual, u_t' is the marginal utility and β is the subjective discount factor, which may be close to e^{-r}, although this is not necessary. The equilibrium approach is complicated since it would typically require taking consumption as an argument in marginal utility, specifying its joint distribution with (p_t, σ_t), and adding necessary state variables conditioning the distribution of consumption at T. With constant relative risk aversion γ, the marginal utility ratio is $u_T'/u_t' = (c_T/c_t)^{-\gamma}$, and if consumption growth is independently distributed across time, e.g., if c_t follows geometric Brownian motion just like p_t in the Black-Scholes model (so that $\log c_t$ is arithmetic Brownian motion with drift, as follows from Itô's lemma), then no additional state variable is needed to compute the conditional expectation, but specification of the covariance structure of the joint process for (p_t, σ_t, c_t) is nonetheless required.

Although geometric Brownian motion is not necessarily an unrealistic model for consumption, a more common approach is to use again an equivalent martingale measure Q as in (14.64), so that

$$c(p_t, \sigma_t, t) = e^{-r(T-t)} E_t^Q (g(p_T)). \tag{14.80}$$

The absence of arbitrage opportunities still implies (indeed, is equivalent to) the existence of an equivalent martingale measure, even with incomplete markets, although it will not be unique. Under Q, the mean return μ is again replaced by r, for p_t/b_t to be a martingale, and equivalence requires that the volatility-of-volatility coefficient ξ be unaltered, whereas the drift of σ_t^2 could change under Q, reflecting the price of volatility risk. Writing λ for the latter, the drift $\alpha\sigma_t^2$ in (14.78) would shift to $(\alpha + \xi\lambda)\sigma_t^2$, using Girsanov's theorem. These specifications suffice for calculating $c(p_t, \sigma_t, t)$. Whereas the Black-Scholes formula $c(p_t, t)$, besides the stock price p_t and time t, involves only the interest rate r, the contractual terms (K, T), and volatility, the stochastic volatility option-pricing formula depends in addition on the volatility process parameters under Q, namely, ξ and $\alpha^Q = \alpha + \xi\lambda$, as well as the correlation between W_t and W_t^σ, say ρ.

Hull and White (1987) show that if $\rho = 0$, i.e., changes in prices and volatilities are uncorrelated, then the stochastic volatility option-pricing formula is an expected Black-Scholes formula,

$$c(p_t, \sigma_t, t) = E_t(c(p_t, t)), \qquad (14.81)$$

where $c(p_t, t)$ is the Black-Scholes price (14.58) using

$$\sigma^2 = \frac{1}{T - t} \int_t^T \sigma_s^2 \, ds. \qquad (14.82)$$

In particular, the expectation is over the conditional distribution of this *integrated volatility* given σ_t^2 and using the stochastic volatility process assumption (14.78).

The geometric Brownian motion specification for volatility implies in particular that σ_t^2 is nonstationary, and neither this nor a zero correlation between price and volatility changes is empirically warranted. Heston (1993) instead specifies that σ_t^2 is stationary,

$$d\sigma_t^2 = \kappa(\alpha - \sigma_t^2) \, dt + \xi \sigma_t \, dW_t^\sigma; \qquad (14.83)$$

i.e., σ_t^2 mean-reverts toward the level $\alpha > 0$ at rate $\kappa > 0$, and the volatility-of-volatility function is proportional to σ_t rather than σ_t^2 (instantaneous variance follows a square root process). By assuming a price of volatility risk proportional to volatility, $\lambda_t = \lambda \sigma_t^2$, the risk-neutral drift of σ_t^2 (i.e., under Q) is $\kappa(\alpha - \sigma_t^2) + \lambda \sigma_t^2 = (\kappa - \lambda)(\alpha^Q - \sigma_t^2)$, i.e., of the same form as under P, with $\alpha^Q = \kappa\alpha/(\kappa - \lambda)$. Under these assumptions, Heston (1993) derives an (almost) analytical option-pricing formula. Subsequent work along these lines has even allowed Poisson-driven jumps of random size in prices, e.g., Bakshi, Cao, and Chen (1997) and Pan (2002).

One of the reasons for considering stochastic volatility in the first place is that deterministic volatility specifications such as in the Black-Scholes case do not seem to explain observed asset return distributions and option prices well. In the Black-Scholes model, returns $\Delta \log p_t$ are normally distributed, but observed return distributions are more heavy-tailed (excess kurtosis). Time-varying variance such as in a generalized autoregressive conditionally heteroskedastic (GARCH) or stochastic volatility model is consistent with excess unconditional kurtosis. Also, squared returns are i.i.d. in the Black-Scholes model but are observed to be serially correlated, which is consistent with these more general models. If observed option prices are matched to the Black-Scholes formula and the only unknown in the relation, volatility, is backed out, then this is the variable usually referred to as *implied volatility*, cf. (11.69). Such implied volatilities backed out from options with different strike prices K but a common expiration date T typically exhibit a U-shaped or sloping pattern (a smile or a smirk, or skew) as a function of K, so not all of these implied volatilities could equal current volatility of the underlying asset. This suggests that the pricing formula is wrong. If in fact returns are generated by a distribution with heavy tails, and option prices account for this, then naively backing out Black-Scholes implied volatilities would lead to a smile pattern.

Dumas, Fleming, and Whaley (1998) examine empirically whether a more flexible volatility specification $\sigma(p_t, t)$ instead of σp_t (the Black-Scholes specification) can explain option prices without introducing stochastic volatility involving a separate source of uncertainty such as W_t^σ. They note that U.S. data exhibit a smile before the stock market crash of October 1987 and a smirk/skew/sneer afterward (see chapter 11). An out-of-the-money (low-K) put is relatively expensive, leading to high implied σ (Black-Scholes put and call prices are increasing in σ). This may suggest portfolio insurance motives outside the arbitrage framework, but the alternative is different stochastic processes. With a given specification $\sigma(\cdot, \cdot)$, option prices can be determined by solving the PDE (14.63) or by simulation based on the Feynman-Kac representation (14.61). Dumas, Fleming, and Whaley (1998) fit a cross-sectional nonlinear regression each day and find in-sample improvements over the Black-Scholes model. In out-of-sample prediction, using the last week's parameters, improvements over the Black-Scholes model are less, and in a delta-hedging experiment (see (14.60)), Black-Scholes is the best performing model. These results point to the potential relevance of genuine stochastic volatility, involving an additional source of uncertainty.

Bakshi, Cao, and Chen (1997) introduce stochastic volatility, stochastic interest rates, and jumps. The model under Q is

$$
\begin{aligned}
dp_t &= (r_t - \lambda\mu_J)p_t\, dt + \sigma_t p_t\, dW_t + p_t J_t\, dq_t, \\
d\sigma_t^2 &= \kappa_\sigma(\alpha_\sigma - \sigma_t^2)\, dt + \xi_\sigma \alpha_t\, dW_t^\sigma, \\
dr_t &= \kappa_r(\alpha_r - r_t)\, dt + \xi_r\sqrt{r_t}\, dW_t^r,
\end{aligned}
\tag{14.84}
$$

with r_t the interest rate. Here, q_t is a Poisson process with arrival rate λ driving the jump component, $P(dq_t = 1) = \lambda\, dt$, and J_t is the random size of the jump,

$$
\log(1 + J_t) \sim N\left(\log(1 + \mu_J) - \frac{1}{2}\sigma_J^2, \sigma_J^2\right).
\tag{14.85}
$$

The expected jump $\lambda\mu_J$ is subtracted in the expected return to guarantee the martingale property under Q. Again, a nearly analytical option-pricing formula is obtained, with state variables (p_t, σ_t, r_t). In daily cross-sectional regressions, σ_t is treated as an additional parameter. The model is an improvement over the Black-Scholes model, including for out-of-sample prediction and hedging. The time series of estimated $\hat{\sigma}_t^2$ is too volatile and exhibits too little correlation with returns compared to the average daily parameters (ξ_σ, ρ). Recent studies even allow for jumps in the σ_t^2 process (e.g., Eraker, Johannes and Polson (2003)).

Chernov and Ghysels (2000) consider the Heston (1993) specification, i.e., constant r_t and no jumps J_t, and draw time series inference instead of running a new cross-sectional (across options) regression each day. The data series are p_t or Black-Scholes implied volatilities (thus reflecting option prices) or both jointly. The efficient method of moments (EMM) of Gallant and Tauchen (1996) is used to fit the model. To see how this works, let the data be y_t and define a quasi likelihood function $\Sigma_t \log f(y_t|Y_t, \eta)$ from a flexible conditional density f parametrized by η, where Y_t contains lags of y_t; i.e., f includes vector autoregression (VAR) and GARCH features as necessary to describe data. Let $\hat{\eta}$ be the estimate, i.e.,

$$\sum_t \frac{\partial \log f(y_t|Y_t, \hat{\eta})}{\partial \eta} = 0. \tag{14.86}$$

Let θ be the parameters of the structural (Heston) model, the drift and volatility parameters of the volatility process (14.83), in particular, and assume dim $\eta \geq$ dim θ. With

$$M(\theta) = E_\theta \left(\frac{\partial \log f(y_t|Y_t, \hat{\eta})}{\partial \eta} \right), \tag{14.87}$$

in general $M(\theta) = 0$ identifies the true θ. Now, θ is estimated by minimizing $M(\theta)'W^{-1}M(\theta)$, with $W = \Sigma_t(\partial \log f(y_t|Y_t, \hat{\eta})/\partial \eta)(\partial \log f(y_t|Y_t, \hat{\eta})/\partial \eta)'$. The estimator $\hat{\theta}$ is consistent and asymptotically normal, and the approximate variance of $\sqrt{T}(\hat{\theta} - \theta)$ is $((\partial M/\partial \theta)'W^{-1}(\partial M/\partial \theta))^{-1}$. If the expectation in M cannot be calculated analytically, then the structural model allows simulating it for each trial θ. In contrast to the cross-sectional regressions, EMM does not produce volatility estimates $\hat{\sigma}_t^2$ directly. However, after the estimation of $\hat{\theta}$, a long series $y_t = (p_t, \sigma_t^2, c(p_t, \sigma_t^2, t))$ can be simulated, allowing calculation, e.g., by kernel methods of the density of σ_t^2 given past information $\mathcal{F}_{t-1}$, and $\hat{\sigma}_t^2 = E(\sigma_t^2|\mathcal{F}_{t-1})$ can be calculated with actual observations in the conditioning set for a volatility estimate. Chernov and Ghysels (2000) label this procedure "reprojection".

With the increasing availability of high-frequency return data, e.g., tick-by-tick data with many trades each minute, allowing the computation of very precise returns, for example, at a 5-minute frequency in many major markets, it is actually possible to calculate volatility over reasonably short intervals, say, daily, without much error. This *realized volatility* approach is a useful alternative to treating volatility as a second, unobserved process in the (p_t, σ_t^2) system (14.78). With a measured series σ_t^2 in hand, based on many high-frequency return observations within each interval $(t - 1, t)$, ordinary time series methods designed for observed series may be applied to σ_t^2 directly. Thus, the realized volatility approach complements both the discrete-time GARCH approach, which works well for time-varying volatilities if returns are observed, e.g., at a daily frequency, and the related continuous-time stochastic volatility approach designed among others to go well with the arbitrage pricing framework.

It is useful to define the high-frequency returns (log-price differences) in continuous time by

$$r_{t,\Delta} = \log p_t - \log p_{t-\Delta}, \qquad (14.88)$$

with Δ, e.g., at 5 minutes if precise daily frequency volatilities are desired. Let the realized volatility over the course of day $t + 1$ be

$$RV_{t,t+1}(\Delta) = \sum_{j=1}^{1/\Delta} r_{t+j\Delta,\Delta}^2. \qquad (14.89)$$

Because of the miniscule (and in the sequel shrinking) return horizon Δ, it is unnecessary to adjust for the mean return over the day. Note that $t, t+1, \ldots$, in this discussion is the daily time index and that $1/\Delta > 1$ is the number of high-frequency intradaily returns recorded from $t - 1$ to t. Such precisely measured daily realized volatilities have been the object of empirical study in markets with sufficient liquidity, e.g., Andersen et al. (2001a) show that realized volatility is approximately log-normally distributed in the foreign exchange market, and Andersen et al. (2001b) is a related application to the U.S. stock market.

The relevant asymptotics in this high-frequency data case is $\Delta \to 0$, i.e., increasing observation frequency or equivalently shrinking the interval between observations, while the number of returns per day $1/\Delta \to \infty$. Assume now a general process of the form

$$d \log p_t = \mu_t \, dt + \sigma_t \, dW_t + J_t \, dq_t \qquad (14.90)$$

for the asset price dynamics under P. This corresponds to the price portion, e.g., of the Bakshi et al. (1997) model from (14.84), but without parametrizing the drift, volatility, (interest rate), and jump components. From the theory of quadratic variation (QV) of stochastic processes, see, e.g., Protter (2004), QV is exactly the limit of realized volatility; i.e.,

$$RV_{t,t+1}(\Delta) \to QV_{t+1} - QV_t = \int_t^{t+1} \sigma_s^2 \, ds + \sum_{q_t < i \le q_{t+1}} J_{t_i}^2, \qquad (14.91)$$

where again q_t from (14.90) is the Poisson process counting the number of jumps through t, with possibly time-varying intensity or arrival rate λ_t,

$P(dq_t = 1) = \lambda_t \, dt$, and t_i are the jump times during the day, $i = q_t + 1$, $\ldots, q_{t+1}$, with J_{t_i} the random jump sizes. Thus, realized volatility from high-frequency returns consistently estimates quadratic variation, as given by integrated volatility corresponding to continuous sample path movements driven by W_t, plus the sum of squared jumps, during the course of the day.

Since jumps (including rare events like market crashes, with $J_t \ll 0$) may be hard to forecast and behave quite differently from smooth volatility $\int \sigma_s^2 \, ds$ across time, it is of interest to separate the continuous sample path and jump components of realized volatility. This may be done using a robust, nonparametric approach due to Barndorff-Nielsen and Shephard (2006). Thus, define realized bipower variation

$$BV_{t,t+1}(\Delta) = \frac{\pi}{2} \sum_{j=2}^{1/\Delta} |r_{t+j\Delta,\Delta}| \cdot |r_{t+(j-1)\Delta,\Delta}|. \tag{14.92}$$

Here, if there is a jump between two return measurements, i.e., $t + (j - 1)\Delta < t_i < t + j\Delta$ for some i, $q_t < i \le q_{t+1}$, then it will not matter much for bipower variation $B_{t,t+1}(\Delta)$ since the adjacent returns are likely small, for small Δ. On the other hand, realized volatility (14.89) should react strongly since it includes the squared jump $J_{t_i}^2$. The factor $\pi/2$ in realized bipower variation is an adjustment to get the right asymptotic mean. Thus, as $\Delta \to 0$, the continuous sample path movements matter for both realized volatility and bipower variation, but jumps only for the former, and

$$BV_{t,t+1}(\Delta) \to \int_t^{t+1} \sigma_s^2 \, ds. \tag{14.93}$$

Bipower variation is a consistent estimate of integrated continuous sample path volatility, which is the relevant volatility concept, e.g., in the Hull-White option-pricing formula (14.81)–(14.82). Thus, the option price is the expected value of the Black-Scholes price, the latter evaluated at σ^2 given by integrated volatility and the expectation taken over the distribution of this. In particular, if future volatility follows a predictable, deterministic process σ_s^2, then the Black-Scholes formula applies without modification, except that σ^2 should be calculated as integrated volatility through expiration of the option.

In contrast, as jumps do matter for realized volatility, a consistent estimate of the sum of squared jumps during the course of the day is readily calculated; i.e.,

$$RV_{t,t+1}(\Delta) - BV_{t,t+1}(\Delta) \to \sum_{q_t < i \le q_{t+1}} J_{t_i}^2 \tag{14.94}$$

as $\Delta \to 0$. Since the sum of squared jumps is nonnegative, whereas this property may fail for the left-hand-side variable, a natural estimate of the sum of squared jumps is

$$J_{t,t+1}(\Delta) = \max\{RV_{t,t+1}(\Delta) - BV_{t,t+1}(\Delta), 0\}. \tag{14.95}$$

Corsi (2004) considers simple time series models for realized volatility. In fact, it is useful to extend the above definitions to intervals covering arbitrary numbers of days $(t, t + h)$, $h \geq 1$. Then the heterogeneous autoregressive realized volatility (HAR-RV) model is

$$RV_{t,t+h} = \beta_0 + \beta_1 RV_{t-1,t} + \beta_2 RV_{t-5,5} + \beta_3 RV_{t-22,t} + \varepsilon_{t,t+h}. \tag{14.96}$$

Thus, the volatility over the next h-day period (say, a month, a week, or a day) is forecast by the volatility over the last day, the last week ($h = 5$ trading days), and the last month (22 trading days). This accommodates the possibility that recent squared returns are most relevant in a dynamic setting, whereas volatilities calculated over longer intervals may be more precise and hence more informative. Also, a distributed lag structure may be captured by the specification, picking up both short- and long-run components of the volatility process. Note that Δ has been dropped from the notation, as this is fixed in the application.

Since the time series behavior of jumps may, as argued, differ from that of continuous sample path volatility components, it makes sense to account separately for the jump component (14.95) in the model, as in

$$R_{t,t+h} = \beta_0 + \sum_{i=1}^{3} \beta_i RV_{t-h_i,t} + \sum_{i=1}^{3} \gamma_i J_{t-h_i,t} + \varepsilon_{t,t+h}, \tag{14.97}$$

with $h_1 = 1$, $h_2 = 5$, $h_3 = 22$. This follows Andersen, Bollerslev, and Diebold (2007). As a further refinement, it is possible to check first whether each jump component is statistically significant. Following Barndorff-Nielsen and Shephard (2006) and Huang and Tauchen (2005), the relevant test statistic is

$$Z_{t,t+1}(\Delta) = \frac{1 - \dfrac{BV_{t,t+1}(\Delta)}{RV_{t,t+1}(\Delta)}}{(\Delta(\mu_1^{-4} + 2\mu_1^{-2} - 5)\max\{1, TQ_{t,t+1}(\Delta)BV_{t,t+1}(\Delta)^{-2}\})^{1/2}},$$

where $TQ_{t,t+1}(\Delta)$ is tripower quarticity,

$$TQ_{t,t+1}(\Delta) = \frac{1}{\Delta\mu_{4/3}^3} \sum_{j=3}^{1/\Delta} \left|r_{t+j\Delta,\Delta}\right|^{4/3} \left|r_{t+(j-1)\Delta,\Delta}\right|^{4/3} \left|r_{t+(j-2)\Delta,\Delta}\right|^{4/3},$$

which converges to $\int_t^{t+1} \sigma_s^4 ds$ as $\Delta \to 0$. Also, $\mu_p = E|x|^p$ with $x \sim N(0, 1)$, so $\mu_p = 2^{p/2}\Gamma((p+1)/2)/\Gamma(\frac{1}{2})$, e.g., $\mu_1 = (2/\pi)^{1/2}$. The test is based on the asymptotic distribution $Z_{t,t+1}(\Delta) \to N(0, 1)$ as $\Delta \to 0$ under the null of no jumps. Large values of the statistic indicate that realized volatility greatly exceeds bipower variation, so the difference may be attributed to (squared) jumps (see (14.94)). Including only significant jumps in the jump component of volatility,

$$J_{t,t+1,\alpha}(\Delta) = \begin{cases} RV_{t,t+1}(\Delta) - BV_{t,t+1}(\Delta), & \text{if } Z_{t,t+1}(\Delta) > \Phi_\alpha, \\ 0, & \text{otherwise,} \end{cases}$$

where Φ_α is the $(100-\alpha)\%$ point in the $N(0, 1)$ distribution. The continuous component of realized volatility is then

$$C_{t,t+1,\alpha}(\Delta) = RV_{t,t+1}(\Delta) - J_{t,t+1,\alpha}(\Delta). \tag{14.98}$$

As before, the definitions and theory immediately extend to arbitrary intervals $(t, t + h)$. Andersen, Bollerslev, and Diebold (2007) use $\alpha = 0.1\%$ and replace the jump components and RV on the right hand side of (14.97) by the significant jump components and the continuous components from (14.98). Busch, Christensen, and Nielsen (2008) add implied volatility $IV_{t,t+h}$ from an option on the same underlying asset used to calculate RV and with life span $(t, t + h)$ (IV is calculated at t, and $t + h$ is the option's expiration date) and consider separate forecasting of the continuous and jump components. Thus, the continuous-component (of volatility) forecasting model is now

$$C_{t,t+h,\alpha} = \beta_0 + \delta IV_{t,t+h} + \sum_{i=1}^{3} \beta_i C_{t-h_i,t,\alpha} + \sum_{i=1}^{3} \gamma_i J_{t-h_i,t,\alpha} + \varepsilon_{t,t+h},$$

with a similar specification for the case with $J_{t,t+h,\alpha}$ (or the sum $RV_{t,t+h} = C_{t,t+h,\alpha} + J_{t,t+h,\alpha}$) on the left hand side.

The findings are that C is more forecastable than J, as expected, and that the IV from option prices is the most powerful volatility forecast, even in the presence of high-frequency-based nonparametrically separated continuous and jump components of realized volatility in the forecasting relation. Thus, IV has incremental forecasting power for both C and J, and lagged J also helps forecast future jumps. In the foreign exchange market, option-implied IV subsumes all the explanatory power of the RV components in forecasting the future RV or its continuous component. In the stock market, IV is also the most important volatility forecast, although recent (one day back) squared returns improve the forecast slightly in-sample (out-of-sample forecasting experiments favor using IV as the sole forecasting variable). The situation is similar in the bond market (30-year U.S. treasuries), with the IV from bond options the best volatility predictor, but in this case it is the long (one month back, $C_{t-22,t,\alpha}$ and $J_{t-22,t,\alpha}$) volatility components that retain marginal significance (again, in-sample only) along with the strongly significant implied forecast IV.

14.8 THE TERM STRUCTURE OF INTEREST RATES IN CONTINUOUS TIME

Let us write the no-arbitrage condition that the asset price p_t discounted by the money market account b_t rolled over at the interest rate r_t be a martingale under the equivalent martingale measure Q as in (10.8),

$$\frac{p_t}{b_t} = E_t^Q \left(\frac{p_T}{b_T} \right). \tag{14.99}$$

In bond-pricing applications, the short rate r_t can no longer reasonably be taken to be fixed and deterministic as in the Black-Scholes model. With r_t a stochastic process, the dynamics $db_t = r_t \, dt$ now produce

$$b_t = e^{\int_0^t r_s ds} \tag{14.100}$$

instead of (14.48) for the money market account started at $b_0 = 1$. If the asset pays out nothing between t and T, then

$$p_t = E_t^Q \left(e^{-\int_t^T r_s ds} p_T \right). \tag{14.101}$$

For a zero-coupon bond maturing at $T = t + k$, let us write $B_{t,k}$ as in the discrete-time case. Since this has price 1 at T, we have

$$B_{t,k} = E_t^Q \left(e^{-\int_t^{t+k} r_s ds} \right) \tag{14.102}$$

or $B_{t,k} = E_t^Q (b_t / b_{t+k})$, again as in (10.14) discrete time. Now, a stochastic process specification for the short rate r_t delivers a model for the entire term structure (i.e., for $B_{t,k}$ across calendar time t and term to maturity k).

Duffie and Kan (1996) consider state variables x_t satisfying

$$dx_t = \mu(x_t) \, dt + \sigma(x_t) \, dW_t, \tag{14.103}$$

with $\dim x_t = \dim W_t = n$ and $r_t = r(x_t)$. Then also $B_{t,k} = f(x_t, k)$ for some f to be determined. One condition is clearly (since the short rate is the yield of an arbitrarily short term to maturity) given by

$$r(x) = \lim_{k \to 0} \frac{-\log f(x, k)}{k}. \tag{14.104}$$

For fixed T, let $F(x, t) = f(x, T - t)$. From the representation of $F(x, t) = B_{t, T-t}$ in terms of an expectation or, more precisely,

$$F(x, t) = E_t^Q \left(e^{-\int_t^T r(x_s) ds} \right), \tag{14.105}$$

with $x_t = x$, we have from the Feynman-Kac result (14.61) the fundamental term structure equation

$$\frac{1}{2}\sum_{i=1}^{n}\sigma(x)_i'\frac{\partial^2 F(x,t)}{\partial x\,\partial x'}\sigma(x)_i+\mu(x)'\frac{\partial F(x,t)}{\partial x}+\frac{\partial F(x,t)}{\partial t}-r(x)F(x,t)=0,$$

where $\sigma(x)_i$ is the ith column of $\sigma(x)$. This is a second-order partial differential equation (PDE) in F. The equation allows the seeking of conditions for log-affine (in state variables x) bond prices

$$f(x,k)=e^{A(k)+B(k)x}. \tag{14.106}$$

Inserting this desired form in the fundamental term structure equation yields the affine term structure condition

$$\frac{1}{2}\sum_{i=1}^{n}\sum_{j=1}^{n}B_i(k)B_j(k)\sigma(x)_i'\sigma(x)_j+B(k)\mu(x)=r(x)+A'(k)+B'(k)x.$$

If f is log-affine then $r(\cdot)$ is affine, and hence so is the right hand side. From the condition, f is log-affine if and only if μ, $\sigma\sigma'$, and r are all affine (constant plus linear) in x. This yields the state variable process

$$dx_t=(ax_t+b)\,dt+\sum v(x_t)^{1/2}\,dW_t, \tag{14.107}$$

where a is $n\times n$, b is $n\times 1$, Σ is $n\times n$, and both

$$v(x)=\text{diag}\{\alpha_i+\beta_i x\} \tag{14.108}$$

and the drift ax_t+b are affine in x. Thus, $\mu(x)=ax+b$ and $\sigma(x)=\Sigma\,\text{diag}\{\alpha_i+\beta_i x\}^{1/2}$. Inserting these for μ and σ in the affine term structure condition actually allows solving of the model, i.e., solving for $A(\cdot)$ and $B(\cdot)$, and hence bond prices. This is the affine term structure theory. To see this, collect the terms in x in the resulting condition, since this must hold for all x, to find a condition of the form

$$B'(k)=\mathcal{B}(B(k)), \tag{14.109}$$

with $B(0)=0$, where $\mathcal{B}(\cdot)$ is linear-quadratic in B. This is a Ricatti-type ordinary differential equation (ODE; note that the fundamental term structure equation from the outset was a second-order PDE), and efficient numerical methods may be used to solve for $B(\cdot)$. Terms without x in the affine term structure condition require

$$A'(k)=\mathcal{A}(B(k)), \tag{14.110}$$

with $A(0)=0$, where again $\mathcal{A}(\cdot)$ is linear-quadratic, i.e.,

$$A(k)=\int_0^k \mathcal{A}(B(s))\,ds \tag{14.111}$$

is given immediately since B has already been determined. The case $n = 1$ is the Cox, Ingersoll, and Ross (1985b) or CIR model, and the case $\beta_i = 0$ is the Vasicek (1977) model.

The CIR short-rate process is

$$dr_t = \kappa(\theta - r_t)\, dt + \sigma\sqrt{r_t}\, dW_t \tag{14.112}$$

under P, and the fundamental term structure equation is

$$\frac{1}{2}\sigma^2 r \frac{\partial^2 F}{\partial r^2} + \mu \frac{\partial F}{\partial r} + \frac{\partial F}{\partial t} - rF = 0. \tag{14.113}$$

Here, μ should be the drift under Q of r_t,

$$\mu_t = \kappa(\theta - r_t) - \lambda_t \sigma \sqrt{r_t}. \tag{14.114}$$

The parameter λ_t is the market price of risk, determined from $dB/B = \eta_t\, dt + v_t\, dW_t$ using $\eta_t = r_t + \lambda_t v_t$. Assuming $\lambda_t = \lambda\sqrt{r_t}/\sigma$ yields

$$\begin{aligned}
\mu_t &= \kappa(\theta - r_t) - \lambda r_t \\
&= (\kappa + \lambda)(\theta^Q - r_t),
\end{aligned} \tag{14.115}$$

with $\theta^Q = \theta\kappa/(\kappa + \lambda)$. It follows that the parameters in the bond price are $\phi = (\kappa + \lambda, \theta^Q, \sigma^2)$. The functions A and B in the affine term structure framework may be solved analytically in terms of these three parameters. Brown and Dybvig (1986) fit this model to cross-sectional data on coupon bond prices. Writing $B_{t,k}(r_t, \phi)$ for the theoretical discount function $\exp(A(k) + B(k)r_t)$ at time t, the cross-sectional nonlinear regression takes the form

$$B_t^c(i) = \sum_{k=1}^{n_i} c_i\, B_{t,k}(r_t, \phi) + B_{t,n_i}(r_t, \phi) + \varepsilon_t(i) \tag{14.116}$$

for $i = 1, \ldots, N_t$, with N_t the number of coupon bonds observed at t, with $B_t^c(i)$ the observed market price of a coupon bond paying (observed contractual terms) c_i each period through $t + n_i$, and with $\varepsilon_t(i)$ the regression error. The parameters estimated are (r_t, ϕ). This is the case of a parameterized term structure, e.g., upon estimation the yield curve may be computed as $y_{t,k} = -\log(B_{t,k}(\hat{r}_t, \hat{\phi}))/k$ for arbitrary k. This CIR curve is an alternative to the Nelson-Siegel curve (10.148), for example. An advantage of the CIR curve (or any other curve from a more general affine term structure model) is that it is derived from an arbitrage-free model, whereas the Nelson-Siegel curve has already been seen to admit arbitrage opportunities (chapter 10). On the other hand, a CIR or general affine term structure model curve cannot fit any arbitrary term structure. Instead, functional forms and the limited number of parameters place restrictions on the set of attainable shapes. This is a disadvantage when trying to price contingent claims in a manner compatible with the current observed structure.

Brown and Dybvig (1986) repeat the cross-sectional regressions each period t and obtain a time series of estimates $(\hat{r}_t, \hat{\phi}_t)$. The sequence $\hat{r}_t$ may be compared to observed short (say, 3-month) interest rates, computing, e.g., a t-test for the difference. Without comparing with outside observations r_t, average variance estimates may be computed from estimated rates,

$$\hat{s}^2 = \frac{1}{T}\sum_t (\hat{r}_t - \bar{r}_t)^2, \tag{14.117}$$

and from model variance estimates,

$$\bar{s}^2 = \frac{1}{T}\sum_t \hat{\sigma}_t^2 \hat{r}_t, \tag{14.118}$$

over subintervals i (say, months or years), and the relation assessed, e.g., by regression,

$$\hat{s}_i = a + b\bar{s}_i + u_i. \tag{14.119}$$

Significant differences from $b = 1$ are evidence against the model. With data on r_t, $\hat{s}_i$ could be based on this also, and a new $\hat{b}$ computed. Similarly, the rate of mean reversion may be computed as the first-order autocorrelation coefficient of $\hat{r}_t$ (or data r_t) and compared to the (average) estimate from the model, $\hat{\kappa} + \hat{\lambda}$. Here, care must be taken; i.e., $\kappa + \lambda$ is the rate of mean reversion under Q, but for nonzero risk price λ an estimate of this is required to back out κ, the mean reversion under P, to be compared to empirical autocorrelations. This is not possible using cross-sectional regressions alone but requires instead a time series approach to the estimation of the model. All these issues are general and are not specific to the one-factor CIR model.

Chen and Scott (1993) present a maximum-likelihood-based panel (combined time series and cross-sectional) procedure for a (multifactor) CIR model. A related analysis appears in Pearson and Sun (1994). The multi-factor model is

$$dx_{i,t} = \kappa_i(\theta_i - x_{i,t})\,dt + \sigma_i\sqrt{x_{i,t}}\,dW_{i,t} \tag{14.120}$$

for the K state variables $x_{i,t}$, $i = 1, \ldots, K$. From the affine approach,

$$B_{t,k} = \sum_{i=1}^{K} e^{A_i(k) + B_i(k)x_{i,t}} \tag{14.121}$$

for known (as functions of parameters) A_i and B_i. In the CIR model, the transition density $f_i(x_{i,t+1}|x_{i,t})$ is known (a noncentral χ^2). With a panel $\{B_{t,k}: t = 1, \ldots, T, k = 1, \ldots, m\}$ of width $m \geq K$, the empirical model is

$$\log B_{t,k} = \sum_{i=1}^{K} (A_i(k) + B_i(k)x_{i,t}) + u_{t,k}, \qquad (14.122)$$

with $k = 1, \ldots, m$ and $t = 1, \ldots, T$. Note that data $B_{t,k}$ are for zero-coupon or discount bonds or, equivalently, their yields $-\log B_{t,k}/k$, so some preceding yield curve estimation at each t may be necessary to build the sample. The approach is now to select K of the bonds, say, the first K, and solve for the state variables $x_{i,t}$ from these, for given parameters. Specifically, impose

$$u_{t,1} = \cdots = u_{t,K} = 0, \qquad (14.123)$$

solve for $\hat{x}_{1,t}, \ldots, \hat{x}_{K,t}$ from the resulting K equations, and repeat this for each $t = 1, \ldots, T$. This way, the predicted state variables depend on the parameters in A_i and B_i, which from the CIR model we recall are $\phi^Q = \{\phi_i\}_{i=1}^{K}$, with $\phi_i = (\kappa_i + \lambda_i, \theta_i^Q, \sigma_i^2)$. With real data on the state variables, the log likelihood for these would be constructed from $\log L_i(\phi_i^P) = \log f_i(x_{i,1}) + \Sigma_{t=2}^{T} \log f_i(x_{i,t}|x_{i,t-1})$ as $\log L^P(\phi^P, \{x_{i,t}: i = 1, \ldots, K, t = 1, \ldots, T\}) = \Sigma_{i=1}^{K} \log L_i(\phi_i^P)$. Again, the transition density $f_i(\cdot|\cdot)$ is known from the CIR framework as a noncentral χ^2. Since this is for the time series transitions, it depends on the parameters ϕ_i^P under the physical measure P, not on the martingale or pricing measure Q; i.e., $\phi_i^P = (\kappa_i, \theta_i, \sigma_i^2)$ and $\phi^P = \{\phi_i^P\}_{i=1}^{K}$. The stationary distribution $f_i(x_{i,1})$ corresponding to the transition distribution is a gamma also depending on ϕ_i^P, although for $T \to \infty$ inference does not depend on including it. Note that risk prices λ_i do not enter the time series model parameters ϕ_i^P.

Combining time series and cross-section data in the panel allows the separation of risk prices and the estimation of both P and Q parameters. First, consider

$$\log \hat{L}(\phi) = \log L^P(\phi^P, \{\hat{x}_{i,t}: i = 1, \ldots, K, t = 1, \ldots, T\}) \quad (14.124)$$

obtained by substituting predicted state variables $\hat{x}_{i,t}$ for the (missing, true) $x_{i,t}$ in $\log L^P$. Since $\log L^P$ depends on ϕ^P and the predicted state variables on ϕ^Q, the parameter in $\log \hat{L}$ is the full set $\phi = \{\kappa_i, \lambda_i, \theta_i, \sigma_i^2\}_{i=1}^{K}$. Thus, risk prices λ_i are estimated by the panel approach, along with the time series parameters $(\kappa_i, \theta_i, \sigma_i^2)$, whereas they were buried in the shifted mean reversion rate $\kappa_i + \lambda_i$ in the pure cross-sectional approach.

To get the log likelihood, two more steps must be taken. First, the Jacobian of the transform from $(x_{1,t}, \ldots, x_{K,t})$ to $(\log B_{t,1}, \ldots, \log B_{t,K})$ is seen from (14.122) to be given by $B = \{B_i(k)\}_{i,k=1}^{K}$ and should be included, as it depends on ϕ^Q. Second, to get the log likelihood for the full panel $\{\log B_{t,k}: k = 1, \ldots, m, t = 1, \ldots, T\}$ in the case where $m > K$, the measurement error $u_{t,k}$ is introduced for the remaining bonds $k = K + 1, \ldots, m$ not used to identify the state variables. Chen and Scott (1993) consider $m = 4$ bonds and try out $K = 1, 2,$ or 3 state variables. A distributional assumption is made on the measurement error; i.e., $u_{t,k}$ is taken as an autoregression (AR(1)) process $u_{t,k} = \rho_k u_{t-1,k} + \varepsilon_{t,k}$, with $\varepsilon_t = (\varepsilon_{t,K+1}, \ldots, \varepsilon_{t,m})$ i.i.d. normal and potentially contemporaneously correlated, $\varepsilon_t \sim N(0, \Omega)$. Thus, the full parameter vector is $\Phi = (\phi, \Omega, \rho_{K+1}, \ldots, \rho_m)$. Writing $M = m - K$ for the number of measurement errors each period, the full panel log likelihood is therefore

$$\log L(\Phi) = \log \hat{L}(\phi) - T \log |B| - \frac{MT}{2} \log(2\pi)$$

$$- \frac{T}{2} \log |\Omega| - \frac{1}{2} \sum_{t=2}^{T} \varepsilon_t' \Omega^{-1} \varepsilon_t, \qquad (14.125)$$

where parameters of course also enter $\varepsilon_{t,k} = u_{t,k} - \rho_k u_{t-1,k}$ with $u_{t,k} = \log B_{t,k} - \Sigma_i(A_i(k) + B_i(k)x_{i,t})$. Maximization of $\log L$ allows the estimation of all P and Q parameters (plus those in the measurement error distribution) simultaneously.

For ease of exposition we have written the above as though it is the K shortest bond (yields) that are used to identify the state variables. It could of course be any K of the m bonds. Perhaps an idea is to take the K most heavily traded bonds. However, the choice is somewhat arbitrary, and in fact it may not be reasonable to insist that exactly K bonds are observed without any error while there is noise in the remaining.

Pennacchi (1991) gets around this by allowing measurement error in all bonds. This leads to a filtering problem; i.e., even for fixed parameters the best bet on any state variable given data through t depends on all current and past observations, not just K contemporaneous bonds. By shifting from the CIR to a linear Gaussian process (a Vasicek (1977) model) for the state variables, the linear Kalman filter may be applied. Thus, with $x_t = (x_{1,t}, \ldots, x_{K,t})'$, the transition equation is

$$x_t = C + D x_{t-1} + v_t, \qquad (14.126)$$

with v_t i.i.d. $N(0, \Sigma_v)$. Then state variable predictions are obtained recursively as

$$E_t(x_{t+1}) = C + D E_t(x_t), \qquad (14.127)$$

with prediction error variance $\Sigma_{t+1|t} = \text{var}(x_{t+1} - E_t(x_{t+1}))$ given by

$$\Sigma_{t+1|t} = D \Sigma_{t|t} D' + \Sigma_v. \qquad (14.128)$$

The updating step is

$$E_{t+1}(x_{t+1}) = E_t(x_{t+1}) + \Sigma_{t+1|t} B' \Sigma_{w,t+1}^{-1} w_{t+1}, \qquad (14.129)$$

with prediction error variance $\Sigma_{t+1|t+1} = \text{var}(x_{t+1} - E_{t+1}(x_{t+1}))$ given by

$$\Sigma_{t+1|t+1} = \left(\Sigma_{t+1|t}^{-1} + B'\Omega B \right)^{-1}. \qquad (14.130)$$

The additional terms in the recursion are from the model, written as

$$y_t = A + Bx_t + u_t, \qquad (14.131)$$

where $y_t = \{\log B_{t,k}\}_{k=1}^m$ and A and B again depend on the model parameters (in this case C, D, and Σ_v) through the affine term structure framework. It is assumed that the measurement errors u_t are i.i.d. $N(0, \Omega)$, this time with full rank m (no restriction $u_{t,k} = 0$ is imposed). The innovations in the bond price data are

$$w_{t+1} = y_{t+1} - (A + BE_t(x_{t+1})), \qquad (14.132)$$

with variance

$$\Sigma_{w,t+1} = B\Sigma_{t+1|t} B' + \Omega. \qquad (14.133)$$

For given parameters from the structural model (C, D, Σ_v) and the measurement error distribution Ω, collected in $\theta = (C, D, \Sigma_v, \Omega)$, the recursions allow calculation of the sequence of innovations w_t and their variances $\Sigma_{w,t}$, both depending on θ, and hence the log likelihood function

$$\log L(\theta) = -\frac{mT}{2} \log(2\pi) - \frac{1}{2} \sum_{t=1}^{T} \left(\log |\Sigma_{w,t}| + w_t' \Sigma_{w,t}^{-1} w_t \right). \qquad (14.134)$$

Parameter estimates are obtained by maximizing this with respect to θ. This entails running the Kalman filter again at each trial θ. As before, C and D are amended with risk prices Λ as they enter the pricing formulas for A and B, whereas the time-series dimension allows estimation of the P-values; i.e., the panel approach allows the expansion of θ with Λ to get a separate estimate of this, too.

Dai and Singleton (2000) estimate more general affine term structural models by EMM, using the ability to simulate from the structural model. The data set is again a panel $\{y_t\}_{t=1}^T$, where y_t is a vector of yields at different maturities. The auxiliary (quasi-likelihood) model is given by a density,

$$f(y_t|Y_{t-1}, \gamma) = c(Y_{t-1}, \gamma)\{\varepsilon_0 + (h(z_t|Y_{t-1}))^2\}\phi(z_t), \qquad (14.135)$$

with $z_t = R_{t-1}^{-1}(y_t - (\psi_0 + \psi_1 y_{t-1}))$, where R_{t-1}^2 is an autoregressive conditionally heteroskedastic (ARCH) variance-covariance matrix, i.e., the auxiliary model accounts for VAR and ARCH effects. In f, Y_{t-1} is lagged observations, c is a normalization, h is a Hermite polynomial shifting the shape of the density, and $\phi(\cdot)$ is the standard normal. This is a non-Gaussian VAR-ARCH semi-nonparametric (SNP) score generator. The auxiliary parameter γ includes the VAR parameters ψ_0, ψ_1, as well as the parameters in the ARCH and density shift components. First, an estimate $\hat{\gamma}$ is obtained from the data by solving the quasi-score equation $\Sigma_{t=1}^{T} \partial \log f(y_t|Y_{t-1}, \gamma)/\partial \gamma = 0$ with respect to γ. Given parameters θ of the affine term structure model, $m(\theta) = \tau^{-1}\Sigma_{s=1}^{\tau} \partial \log f(y_s^{\theta}|Y_s^{\theta}, \hat{\gamma})/\delta \gamma$ is calculated for a large (size τ) sample $\{y_s^{\theta}\}$ simulated from the affine term structure model. If θ is close to the true value, then it should describe the actual data y_t well, and so it should give rise to a simulated y_t^{θ} similar to y_t; in particular, $m(\theta)$ should be close to 0, the value of the quasi score at $\hat{\gamma}$ when using the observed y_t. Thus, θ is estimated by minimizing the (GMM) norm of $m(\theta)$. At each trial θ, a new sample $\{y_s^{\theta}\}_{s=1}^{\tau}$ is simulated. Specifically, the state variables x_s^{θ} are simulated first, and the Ricatti equations (14.109) are solved for the functions $A_i(\cdot)$ and $B_i(\cdot)$ associated with the given θ so that yields y_s^{θ} may be constructed from state variables and the bond-pricing formula (14.106). This approach allows a very general analysis of the class of affine term structure models.

Nonaffine alternatives may also be analyzed. Chan et al. (1992) consider the short-rate process

$$dr_t = (\alpha + \beta r_t)\, dt + \sigma r_t^{\gamma}\, dW_t. \qquad (14.136)$$

This is a constant elasticity of variance (CEV) specification; i.e., $\partial \log(\sigma r_t^{\gamma})^2/\partial \log r_t = 2\gamma$. For $\gamma = \frac{1}{2}$, the CIR model (14.112) is returned, and for $\gamma = 0$, the Vasicek model. For other γ, the model is outside the affine class. Chan et al. consider the time series analysis of short-rate data $\{r_t\}_{t=1}^{T}$, in contrast to the cross-sectional and panel approaches involving yields of different maturities. Thus, P-parameters, but not Q-parameters (risk premia) are estimated. The Euler discretization is

$$r_{t+1} - r_t = \alpha + \beta r_t + \varepsilon_{t+1}. \qquad (14.137)$$

A GMM approach is established based on

$$E_t(\varepsilon_{t+1}) = 0,$$
$$E_t(\varepsilon_{t+1}^2) = \sigma^2 r_t^{2\gamma}. \qquad (14.138)$$

The parameter vector is $\theta = (\alpha, \beta, \gamma, \sigma^2)$. The moment conditions considered are $m_{t+1} = (\varepsilon_{t+1}, \varepsilon_{t+1}^2 - \sigma^2 r_t^{2\gamma})$ with instruments $z_t = (1, r_t)$, so $H_T = 0$ is solved for θ, where $H_T = \Sigma_t h_t/T$ and $h_{t+1} = m_{t+1} \otimes z_t$. Since $\dim \theta = \dim H_T = 4$, there are no overidentifying restrictions.

Chan et al. find γ near 1.5 in U.S. data, thus casting doubt on affine models, which have a much lower γ.

Since the Euler discretization is not exact, and in fact $E_t m_{t+1} \neq 0$, the GMM estimator $\hat{\theta}_{\text{GMM}}$ is inconsistent. Christensen and Poulsen (2001) use EMM to correct this problem. The auxiliary model is taken as the Chan et al. GMM framework. After obtaining $\hat{\theta}_{\text{GMM}}$, simulated samples are used to implement EMM. The final estimator $\hat{\theta}_{\text{EMM}}$ is only about half the value of that obtained by Chan et al. using the same data. This suggests that an inconsistency of GMM led to the high γ estimate by Chan et al. A conceptually important point here is that the inconsistency of the auxiliary model estimator (here, $\hat{\theta}_{GMM}$) is critical for EMM. Had the auxiliary estimator been consistent, then no asymptotic improvement would have been obtained by EMM. In fact, $\hat{\theta}_{\text{EMM}}$ is asymptotically equivalent to the auxiliary estimate when this is consistent. The importance of starting with an inconsistent auxiliary estimator for the nonredundancy of the (simulation-based) correction step is perhaps awkward. Of course, the issue is less clear if an auxiliary model completely different from the structural model is set up, in particular with different parameters so that the requirement of inconsistency with respect to structural parameters cannot be or is not easily imposed on the auxiliary model.

To see the inconsistency, consider the first moment equation $E_t(\varepsilon_{t+1}) = 0$. In fact, the exact first moment is

$$E_t(r_{t+\Delta}) = (1 - e^{\beta\Delta})\left(-\frac{\alpha}{\beta}\right) + e^{\beta\Delta} r_t \qquad (14.139)$$

for $\Delta > 0$. Thus, let the intercept and slope parameters with $\Delta = 1$ be a and b satisfying

$$E_t(r_{t+1}) = a + br_t. \qquad (14.140)$$

The GMM or any consistent method such as ordinary least squares (OLS) can be used to estimate these reduced form parameters a and b consistently. Clearly, upon estimation, α and β in the continuous-time model must be solved from $\hat{a} = (1 - e^{\beta})(-\alpha/\beta)$, and $\hat{b} = e^{\beta}$ in order to get consistent estimates; i.e.,

$$\hat{\alpha} = \frac{\hat{a} \log \hat{b}}{\hat{b} - 1}, \qquad (14.141)$$

$$\hat{\beta} = \log \hat{b} \qquad (14.142)$$

are consistent for the structural parameters. On the other hand, the α-estimate from GMM based on the Euler discretization (14.137)–(14.138) converges to $(1 - e^{\beta})(-\alpha/\beta)$, and the β-estimate to $e^{\beta} - 1$. It is this inconsistency that EMM can be used to correct.

As usual, it is attractive to consider alternative likelihood procedures. For a general short-rate diffusion

$$dr_t = \mu(r_t)\,dt + \sigma(r_t)\,dW_t, \qquad (14.143)$$

the transition density $f(\Delta, r_{t+\Delta}|r_t)$ satisfies the Kolmogorov forward equation (KFE), also known as the Fokker–Planck equation,

$$\frac{\partial f(\Delta, r_{t+\Delta}|r_t)}{\partial \Delta} = -\frac{\partial}{\partial r_{t+\Delta}}(\mu(r_{t+\Delta})f(\Delta, r_{t+\Delta}|r_t))$$

$$+ \frac{1}{2}\frac{\partial^2}{\partial r_{t+\Delta}^2}(\sigma^2(r_{t+\Delta})f(\Delta, r_{t+\Delta}|r_t)). \qquad (14.144)$$

Lo (1988) suggests selecting parametric forms for μ and σ (e.g., as in the Chan et al. case), and for each trial parameter solving the KFE with the initial condition for $\Delta = 0$ given by $f(0, y|x) = \delta_x(y)$, the Dirac delta function, since if not going forward the density is concentrated at the current observation. Here, $\int_A \delta_x(y)\,dy = 1$ if $x \in A$, and 0 otherwise. In practice, $\delta_x(y)$ may be replaced by a normal density with $Ey = x$ and a very small variance. Starting at $\Delta = 0$, the KFE allows solving for the transition density for larger and larger Δ. With $f(\Delta, r_{t+\Delta}|r_t)$ calculated up to the Δ relevant for the data, the maximum likelihood can be performed. The generalized residuals

$$u_{t+\Delta} = F(\Delta, r_{t+\Delta}|r_t) = \int_0^{r_{t+\Delta}} f(\Delta, u|r_t)\,du \qquad (14.145)$$

should be i.i.d. uniform $U(0, 1)$ as a check on the distributional assumption.

Ait-Sahalia (1996) parametrizes only $\mu(r) = a + br$ but estimates $\sigma(\cdot)$ nonparametrically. The stationarity of r_t implies

$$\int f(\Delta, r_{t+\Delta}|r_t)\pi(r_t)\,dr_t = \pi(r_{t+\Delta}), \qquad (14.146)$$

with $\pi(\cdot)$ the stationary distribution. Note that π, unlike f, has derivative 0 with respect to Δ. Multiply the KFE by $\pi(r_t)$ and integrate out r_t,

$$0 = -\frac{d}{dr}(\mu(r)\pi(r)) + \frac{1}{2}\frac{d^2}{dr^2}(\sigma^2(r)\pi(r)). \qquad (14.147)$$

Integrate twice (use $\pi(0) = 0$) to get

$$\sigma^2(r) = \frac{2}{\pi(r)}\int_0^r \mu(u)\pi(u)\,du. \qquad (14.148)$$

A nonparametric estimate of $\pi(\cdot)$ and a parametric (like the above) of $\mu(\cdot)$ yield a (semiparametric) estimate of $\sigma^2(\cdot)$. Here, a kernel estimate is

$$\hat{\pi}(r) = \frac{1}{Tb_t}\sum_{t=1}^{T}\omega\left(\frac{r - r_t}{b_T}\right), \qquad (14.149)$$

with kernel $\omega(\cdot)$ and bandwidth b_T. Insert this and $\hat{\mu}(\cdot)$ in $\sigma^2(\cdot)$ from (14.148) to get $\hat{\sigma}^2(\cdot)$. Then $\hat{\sigma}^2(\cdot)$ is pointwise consistent and asymptotically normal,

$$\sqrt{Tb_T}(\hat{\sigma}^2(r) - \sigma^2(r)) \to N(0, v(r)), \tag{14.150}$$

where $v(r) = \sigma^4(r) \int_{-\infty}^{\infty} \omega(u)^2 \, du / \pi(r)$. Clearly, inspection can show whether $\hat{\sigma}^2(\cdot)$ seems to be of a shape similar to $r^{2\gamma}$, the CEV case, perhaps with γ near 0 or $\frac{1}{2}$ (the affine case). Other studies have similarly tried flexible functional forms for the drift $\mu(\cdot)$, finding, e.g., that it is flat and near 0 at typical interest rate levels, but $\mu(r) \to \infty$ as $r \to 0$ and $\mu(r) \to -\infty$ for $r \to \infty$.

Instead of focusing on the short rate, whether for time series analysis or to find bond prices by assuming a process for the short rate and using the arbitrage conditions, the Heath, Jarrow, and Morton (1992) approach is to take the initial (e.g., the current) yield curve shape as given, not necessarily derived from a given assumption on the short-rate process, and then study the process of subsequent yield curves for a given function specifying the volatilities of different yields. Then no arbitrage implies that the drift of the process is characterized by the volatilities and risk prices.

The analysis was originally carried out on instantaneous forward rates, i.e., writing

$$B_{t,k} = e^{-\int_t^{t+k} f_{t,s} ds}; \tag{14.151}$$

then $f_{t,s}$ is the forward rate at t for maturity date $s > t$. Since alternatively $B_{t,k} = e^{-ky_{t,k}}$, the relation between yields and forward rates is clear; i.e., $f_{t,t+k} = y_{t,k} + k \, dy_{t,k}/dk$. The short rate is $r_t = f_{t,t}$. The model is

$$df_{t,T} = \alpha_{t,T}^f \, dt + \sigma_{t,T}^f \, dW_t, \tag{14.152}$$

where α^f and σ^f are general adapted processes. Considering the entire term structure at t as given by the forward curve $T \to f_{t,T}$, (14.152) is (for T continuous) an infinite-dimensional equation for the dynamics of interest rates. The dimension of W_t is finite, say n. Brace and Musiela (1994) reparametrized slightly, writing $r_{t,k} = f_{t,t+k}$, with k the term to maturity. In this notation,

$$dr_{t,k} = \beta_{t,k} \, dt + \sigma_{t,k} \, dW_t, \tag{14.153}$$

with $\sigma_{t,k} = \sigma_{t,t+k}^f$ and $\beta_{t,k} = \partial r_{t,k}/\partial k + \alpha_{t,t+k}^f$. The Heath, Jarrow, and Morton no-arbitrage drift condition is

$$\beta_{t,k} = \frac{\partial r_{t,k}}{\partial k} + \sigma_{t,k} \left(\lambda_t + \int_0^k \sigma_{t,s}' \, ds \right) \tag{14.154}$$

under P, and is the same with $\lambda_t = 0$ under Q, where λ_t is the market price of risk (dimension n). The drift is a function of the volatility, the risk premium, and the slope of the term structure (the first term in (14.154)).

The question arises again of how to measure the term structure $k \to r_{t,k}$ at time t. Suppose a flexible functional form G is adopted, parametrized by θ, so that $r_{t,k} = G(\theta_t, k)$. Here, θ_t can be estimated by cross-sectional regression

$$B_t^c(i) = \sum_{k=1}^{n_i} c_{i,k} e^{-\int_0^k G(\theta,u)du} + e^{-\int_0^{n_i} G(\theta,u)du} + \varepsilon_t(i), \qquad (14.155)$$

$i = 1, \dots, N_t$, where $B_t^c(i)$ are the prices of the N_t coupon bonds observed at t, the ith bond paying coupons $c_{i,k}$ at future dates $k = 1, \dots, n_i$ periods hence, and face value 1 at maturity $t + n_i$. Upon estimation of $\hat{\theta}_t$, the fitted forward curve is $\hat{r}_{t,k} = G(\hat{\theta}_t, k)$ or, more precisely, the function $G(\hat{\theta}_t, \cdot)$ (hence the yield curve $\hat{y}_{t,k}$ is also given, and the discount function $\hat{B}_{t,k}$). Typical examples of the specification of G include the Nelson-Siegel curve and McCulloch (1971, 1975) cubic splines.

Björk and Christensen (1999) study the question of whether a given fitted term structure, i.e., a flexible functional form G, is consistent with the dynamic model characterized by the volatility function $\sigma_{t,k}$ and the risk price λ_t. Thus, if the initial term structure (say, at $t = 0$, maybe current time) is of the given shape G; i.e., there is some θ_0 such that $r_{0,k} = G(\theta_0, k)$ for all $k \geq 0$, and subsequent term structures are driven by the dynamic model (14.153)–(14.154), does there for each $t > 0$ also exist θ_t such that $r_{t,k} = G(\theta_t, k)$, across all terms to maturity $k \geq 0$? If so, the dynamic model (σ, λ) and the curve shape G are consistent. If not, it is not meaningful to keep fitting the nonlinear regression using G each day to get the term structure. A different functional form $\tilde{G}$ should be chosen, one that is consistent with the model (σ, λ).

The main result in Björk and Christensen (1999) is that the term structure shape G and the dynamic model (σ, λ) are consistent if and only if there exist coefficients $\gamma(\theta)$, $\delta(\theta)$ such that

$$\frac{\partial G(\theta, k)}{\partial k} + \sigma(r, k) \int_0^k \sigma(r, s)' \, ds - \frac{1}{2} \frac{\partial \sigma(r, k)}{\partial r} \sigma(r, k) = \gamma(\theta)' \frac{\partial G(\theta, k)}{\partial \theta},$$

the *consistent drift condition*, and

$$\sigma(r, k) = \delta(\theta)' \frac{\partial G(\theta, k)}{\partial \theta},$$

the *consistent volatility condition*, for all θ, where r denotes the curve $k \to r_k$ given by $r_k = G(\theta, k)$. Here, it is assumed that $\sigma_{t,k}$ depends on t only

through the current term structure $k \to r_{t,k}$. The conditions do not involve
the risk prices λ_t, i.e., consistency is a property of the pair (G, σ), the curve
shape and the volatility function. For example, the conditions imply that
the popular Nelson-Siegel curve shape (10.148) is not consistent with any
term structure model, i.e., with any volatility function σ. On the other hand,
it can be augmented simply to be consistent, e.g., with the Hull and White
(1990) extended Vasicek model. The nonlinear regressions (14.155) should
at a minimum use this augmentation, and even this suffices only if the Hull
and White model drives interest rates (e.g., not the CIR model). Björk and
Christensen (1999) also show the corresponding necessary and sufficient
conditions for consistency between curve shape and dynamics for the case
of jumps in interest rates.

14.9 EXERCISES

1. Solve the optimal stopping problem (14.15) in the case $m = n = \sigma = 1$,
$a = u = 0$, $H_t(x) = \max\{1 - x, 0\}$. Interpret your result.
2. In the model of allocation of time over time, the hazard rate in state i
is the sum of the flow rates to states j and k (see (14.22)). Verify this result.
Hint: Consider two independent durations and prove that the hazard rate of
the minimum of the two is given by the sum of the two individual hazards.
3. You are given a cross-sectional data set on prices of call options for different strikes on the same underlying and with the same time to expiration.
The current price of the underlying is known, as is the interest rate.
Consider the nonlinear regression of option prices on the Black-Scholes
formula (14.58). The unknown parameter to be estimated is the volatility.
Interpret the estimate as an implied volatility. Derive the asymptotic
standard error of the estimator. Relate this to the vega of the option.

14.10 REFERENCES

Kushner (1990) discusses numerical methods for continuous-time problems.
Hazard function modeling is treated by Kiefer (1988), Lancaster (1990),
and Lawless (1982). Stochastic integration is discussed by Protter (1986,
2004). Brock (1976) is an unpublished but early and influential introduction
to stochastic calculus. Krylov (1980) is an insightful treatment of controlled
diffusions.The Bellman equation in continuous time is sometimes referred
to as the Hamilton-Jacobi-Bellman equation due to a connection to earlier
work in physics. Frequently, a classical (smooth) solution does not exist, and
Crandall and Lions (1983) introduce the notion of a generalized or viscosity
solution that in wide generality exists and uniquely determines the value

function. Samuelson (1965) studied the American put on an underlying geometric Brownian motion from an optimal stopping point of view, including the high-order contact or smooth pasting condition, and McKean (1965) in a paper actually published as an appendix to Samuelson's derived equations characterizing the free boundary. The equations have a unique solution, so the put pricing and optimal early exercise strategy problem is in principle solved, but the solution is not in explicit closed form such as the Black and Scholes (1973) formula for the European case (see also (11.24)). The alternative characterization as the Snell envelope (see chapter 11) carries over to the continuous-time case. Merton (1973a) in his intertemporal capital asset pricing model derives the equilibrium implication that expected excess returns depend on covariances (betas) not only with the market portfolio but also with hedge portfolios tracking changes in investment opportunities. Harrison and Kreps (1979) and Harrison and Pliska (1981) study existence and uniqueness of an equivalent martingale measure and the equivalence to the absence of arbitrage opportunities respectively market completeness. The Feynman and Kac relation between analysis (PDE solution) and probability (representation as expectation) is another connection to earlier work in physics.

Chapter Fifteen

Microeconomic Applications

15.1 INTRODUCTION

The earliest empirical structural dynamic programming models were discrete-control, continuous-state optimal stopping models, specifically the job search model. Since then, technology and computing capacity have improved dramatically. With that, and with the increasing realization that the structural approach delivers useful, practical results, the number of applications has exploded. This chapter surveys a selection of empirical discrete-control models to illustrate the range of applications of the model. Details are omitted. Detailed analyses of the search model and the retirement model are the topics of separate chapters. It seems that the bulk of microeconomic applications study the discrete decisions of individuals or firms. Here, we consider Rust (1987) on bus engine replacement, a paper that breaks new ground not only in its application of dynamic programming to the sequential decisions of a single individual but more importantly in proposing the nested fixed-point algorithm for estimating the model. This has had wide influence. We then turn to an application to aircraft engine maintenance. This paper, Kennet (1994), follows Rust in its specification and estimation of the model but shows that the approach works in studying the decisions of multiple decision makers with common objectives. Then, we cover a study of the dynamic demand for medical treatment and absentee behavior of acutely ill workers. These results by Gilleskie (1998) are important for policy decisions on health insurance and sick leave coverage. Rust and Rothwell (1995) model the operators of nuclear power plants. The periodic decisions are to close, shutdown for refueling or maintenance, or continue operation at some level conditional on the state of the reactor. These applications all use the random utility specification with extreme value distributed shocks (see chapter 5). They all demonstrate that the specification can lead to useful results.

The next paper concerns fertility. Wolpin (1984) studies the childbearing decisions of a sample of Malaysian married women over time in a dynamic programming framework. The specification is a random utility model with normal shocks. Then we consider price adjustment when price changes are costly. The study by Slade (1998) uses micro data on grocery store pricing. Next, we consider the simultaneous determination of schooling, labor force participation, and occupation. Keane and Wolpin (1997) use a specification that is a dynamic generalization of a multivariate probit model. The dynamic programming framework is used to identify structural parameters, for example, a return to schooling estimate that takes into account the endogenous schooling and occupation decisions. Following this, we consider the Pakes (1986) study of patent renewal. The model is in the optimal stopping class, and we compare and contrast it to option models from previous chapters. Aggregate data are used to estimate the structural parameters of this firm level model.

Finally, we turn to three papers that use equilibrium considerations to restrict their specification. The first is a marketing example (Gonul and Shi, 1998). This paper studies the decision of a direct mailer to mail a catalog to a particular consumer. The consumer is assumed to order from the catalog in accordance with a policy set by dynamic optimization. The consumer's and mailer's problems interact. The second is a paper on automobile replacement (Adda and Cooper, 2000). It describes the dynamic decision to replace a car and the effects of various subsidy policies. The last treats dynamic on-the-job search and the implications for the cross-sectional wage distribution (Christensen, Lentz, Mortensen, Neumann, and Werwatz, 2005).

15.2 BUS ENGINE REPLACEMENT

In a classic paper in empirical microeconomics, Rust (1987a) studies the behavior of a single decision maker (Harold Zurcher) over time. The data concern the bus fleet in Madison, Wisconsin. Bus engines are inspected periodically and replaced as needed. The problem of aggregation across possibly heterogeneous decision makers is avoided (though the assumption of homogeneity over time for the individual decision maker is maintained). Data are analyzed for four groups of bus types. The single state variable is mileage since the last engine replacement on the bus. Operating costs are an increasing function of mileage, estimated not observed. It turns out that mileage at replacement varies from 82,400 to 387,300, so a fixed optimal stopping rule will not explain the data. Rust therefore assumes the existence of unobserved state variables explaining the variation in replacement. Of course, this assumption is vastly preferable to the alternative that either decision makers are making repeated large errors or the bulk of sample variation is based on measurement error. The unobserved state variables are introduced as choice-dependent utility shocks, leading to a random utility model. Rust makes the conditional independence assumption (5.37), based on which the state-to-state transitions of the observable state variable (mileage) do not depend on the unobserved shocks, and the shock process is temporally independent given the observed state process. With this assumption the likelihood function factors naturally into the policy choice distribution given the state and the state-to-state transition distribution.

The state space, mileage, is discretized into 90 groups. The transition distribution is multinomial over three possible steps (thus the transition matrix is filled largely, and reasonably, with zeros). The cost function is specified as various nonlinear functions of mileage. The unobserved utility shocks are assumed to follow an extreme value distribution, leading to a tractable functional form. In estimation, the transition distribution is estimated first, then the structural parameters in the choice probabilities are estimated conditional on the transition probabilities. In this second stage, the conditional expected value function (5.40) is calculated by forward recursion for each trial parameter value in the iterative estimation procedure. This is Rust's *nested fixed-point algorithm*. Finally, a third stage is used to estimate parameters imposing all structural restrictions on parameters of the choice probabilities and transition distributions, thus producing efficient estimators and appropriate standard errors. The discount factor β appears not to be identified, a common occurrence, and is set at 0.0 and .9999 (data are monthly). The results show that Zurcher is not a myopic maximizer; the fit is much better with discount factor .9999 than 0.0. The four types of buses are significantly different. When attempts are made to estimate the discount factor, it approaches 1.0. As the cost function specification is generalized, for example, with more polynomial terms, it becomes increasingly difficult to estimate the discount factor, suggesting that one of these must be restricted in order to identify the other. Various specification diagnostics, such as changing the grid for the state variable or changing the parametric form of the cost function, do not change the results much.

The application shows that a dynamic optimization model can usefully be fit and interpreted in a practical application. Further, the data are roughly consistent with the model. There are significant and interpretable differences among the four bus types. To illustrate the usefulness of the structural parameters, Rust calculates a demand function for bus engines as a function of their cost.

15.3 AIRCRAFT ENGINE MAINTENANCE

This study by Kennet (1994) extends Rust's model of bus engine replacement to aircraft engine overhaul decisions. It is unlikely that many applications as "clean" as Rust's, in that they apply to a sequence of decisions made by a single decision maker, will arise in practice. Hence, it is useful to see whether the modeling techniques work in a setting with multiple decision makers and an assumption of homogeneity. Aircraft safety is an important issue in its own right, and engine maintenance is clearly relevant. Further, Kennet is interested in possible changes in engine overhaul decisions after deregulation.

The sample consists of 42 Pratt and Whitney jet engine histories from as early as 1964 and through 1988. Deregulation occurred in 1978. There were two types of engines, and the model is estimated separately for four groups: two engine types before and after deregulation. The groups are clearly significantly different. Inspections occur on a regular basis—exogenously; the time of inspection is not a choice variable. Upon inspection, an engine can be continued in service with minor maintenance or sent to the shop for an overhaul. The latter is costly. Thus, the control variable is binary. The state variable consists of the time in service since the last overhaul and whether or not the engine has experienced a shutdown since the last overhaul. In addition, a random utility specification is adopted, in which an additional unobserved state variable is added to the utility associated with each state at each time. The transition distribution is Markovian, with conditional independence (5.37) between the observed and unobserved state variables. Hours are discretized into 44 groups. Hence, there are 88 values of the observed state variable (the shutdown indicator is binary). To estimate the model, the transition distribution is first estimated from the observed transitions, then the conditional choice probabilities are estimated. These are solved for structural parameters (service costs associated with overhaul and the costs of continued service as a function of hours and shutdown history) using the nested fixed-point algorithm. Finally, the likelihood function is maximized directly using these two-step estimators as starting values. This is useful since there are structural restrictions between the parameters of the transition distributions and the parameters of the choice probabilities.

The results show that deregulation made a difference. In the regulated period, there was no significant difference in behavior across airlines. Further, there was no discernible improvement in fit from the dynamic model (discount factor $\beta > 0$) relative to the myopic model (the case $\beta = 0$). In the deregulated period, firm heterogeneity became important, as firms developed their own maintenance policies. Engine overhauls became less frequent overall after deregulation, although the shutdown probabilities did not change. This is interpreted as an improvement in cost efficiency in the maintenance procedures attributable to deregulation. In the deregulated period, there was clear evidence for the dynamic optimization specification.

15.4 MEDICAL TREATMENT AND ABSENTEEISM

Control of health care costs while ensuring adequate health care is a major policy issue. There has been a large increase in medical care consumption over time, accompanied by a substantial decrease in the fraction of medical costs paid by the consumer. Further, scheduled work time lost to absenteeism due to illness stands at 2%. Gilleskie (1998) addresses the behavior underlying medical care consumption and absenteeism with an eye toward policy analysis using a structural dynamic model.

Gilleskie is concerned with choices made by workers with acute illnesses (flu, colds, viruses, etc.). At any period, a worker can work, seek medical treatment, skip work, or skip work and seek medical treatment. This is the control set in each period. The state variables are the type of illness (unobserved unless the worker is well), the number of physician visits since the last well period, the number of absences from work since the last well period, and the length of the current illness. State transitions are deterministic. Let $\pi^s(k)$ be the probability that a well person gets illness k and let $\pi^w(x)$ be the probability that a person becomes well, conditional on the state variable that includes the illness type. The period utility of a well person u^w depends on consumption. The period utility of an ill person $u^s(x, d)$ depends on the state, consumption, and the control. The period utilities of an ill person have additive errors specific to the control, time period, illness type, and individual. These are conveniently assumed to have an extreme value distribution, substantially reducing the computational burden of estimation. Policy parameters, such as the extent of health insurance coverage and sick leave provisions, enter through the budget constraint. A finite horizon is specified.

The choice-dependent values are

$$V_j^s(x_t) = u^s(x_t) + \beta \left[\pi^w(x_{t+1}) V^w + \left(1 - \pi^w(x_{t+1})\right) V^s(x_{t+1}) \right] + \varepsilon_{jt}(k),$$

(15.1)

and the value of being ill is $V^s(x) = E \max\{V_j^s(x)\}$. The value of being well is

$$V^w = u^w + \beta \left[\left(1 - \sum_k \pi^s(k)\right) V^w + \sum_k \pi^s(k) V^s(x_{t+1}) \right].$$

(15.2)

The data are from the 1987 National Medical Expenditure Survey (NMES). Respondents fill in a daily log on their health and health care history and are periodically interviewed. The data set analyzed consisted of men 25–64 years old. The sample was 3797 individuals, of whom 726 experienced an acute illness at least once. Individuals were assigned to one of three income classes, four insurance coverage classes, two sick leave classes, two health status classes, and two age classes. The discount factor was fixed in advance. The model was solved by backward recursion on the choice-specific values and the choice probabilities. There were two unobserved illness types.

The results are reasonable and the estimates are put to use in policy evaluation experiments. This application emphasizes the advantages of using a structural form. Some implications are that consumption when ill is less valued than consumption when well, insurance parameters clearly affect treatment choice, and staying home and resting is clearly better than continuing to work and seeking treatment in terms of recovery. The policy experiments include moving to universal health insurance, under which everyone is covered with no deductible or copayment. In this experiment, physician visits increased by 12%. Absenteeism was reduced. The latter result occurs since some individuals do not have paid sick leave and absenteeism and treatment seem to be substitutes. A second experiment combined universal coverage as above with paid sick leave. Here, physician visits increased by 5.6%, while absenteeism increased by 10.6%. Moving insurance coverage to 0% coverage reduced physician visits by 20%.

This paper clearly shows the importance and feasibility of dynamic modeling in a key policy area. Although it is clear that the model can be extended in several dimensions, the point that health policy discussions should involve sick leave issues and medical insurance coverage simultaneously is made emphatically.

15.5 NUCLEAR POWER PLANT OPERATION

Concern with global oil prices, energy shortages, and the pollution associated with fossil fuels is generating new interest in the nuclear power generation option. There have been no new nuclear power plant orders in the United States since 1978. This is attributed to the increase in regulatory costs and the change in the public perception of safety in the industry following the Three Mile Island accident. How well are reactors operated, and what are the effects of regulatory pressures? Rust and Rothwell (1995) seek to model the operation of nuclear power plants in a dynamic programming framework.

Operating these enormous plants is extremely complex. Rust and Rothwell abstract from day-to-day operating decisions to model major decisions on a monthly basis. In particular, they consider the decision to operate the plant, to shut it down for preventive maintenance or refueling, or to close it. If operation is continued, the scale of operation (the percentage of capacity) is modeled. Six classes of operation are considered, so the control variable has eight possibilities. The data are from the Nuclear Regulatory Commission Licensed Operating Reactors—Status Survey Report and various updates, leading to a monthly series from 1975 to 1993 for each operating reactor. The data identify the reactor, the date of the last outage, the length of the last outage, the type of outage (forced or scheduled), the reason for the outage (eight possibilities), and the method of shutdown. The utilization rates do vary over time for each reactor, mostly because of shutdowns.

Firms are assumed to maximize the expected discounted value of the profit stream subject to technology and regulatory constraints. The period profit associated with control c is $\pi(c, x, \varepsilon) = u(c, x) + \varepsilon(c)$. Thus, the specification is in the random utility framework and the problem is to maximize $E \Sigma_{t=0}^{T} \beta^t \pi_t$. The finite horizon is given by the 40-year operating license. Although renewal is a theoretical possibility, no license has been renewed. The state variables are the type of spell last month (problem, refueling, operating), the current "signal" (none, one or more forced outages, major problem), and durations (operating duration, refueling duration, major problem duration). The state transition distribution factors into $Q(x_{t+1}|x_t) p(\varepsilon_{t+1})$, where x is the observable part of the state vector, and the control and time-specific shocks are i.i.d. extreme value distributed. With this specification, the choice probabilities are in the generalized logit form (5.41).

The transition distribution can be estimated separately. Only the signal is stochastic—the other observed state variables are updated deterministically. The choice probabilities are then estimated. The control-specific values can be computed by backward recursion. These enter the logits for the choice probabilities. The parameters are estimated by maximum likelihood on the choices given the transition distributions.

The results are reasonable. Somewhat surprisingly, the number of forced outages decreases with the age of the reactor. This is consistent with the reduced-form evidence and is attributed to technological improvement or learning by doing on the part of the reactor operating staff. Utilities are clearly not myopic and indeed place a high value on the future. The costs of availability increase linearly in duration. The costs of forced outages are high, although the costs of running after a high-outage signal are higher (much higher than the value of electricity generation). The predictions of the model are also reasonable. The conditional choice probabilities are close to the nonparametric reduced form. The model tracks well the decrease in availability over time since the last refueling. The operators show a strong aversion to start/stop operations, which are costly. The regulatory change in 1979 lead to refueling downtime being increased from 8 to 14 weeks on average. The resulting behavior by operators extended the mean time between refueling from 12 months to 18 months.

This paper again demonstrates the feasibility of modeling optimizing behavior and using the results for policy analysis. A number of potentially useful extensions are mentioned, including moving to a finer time scale, incorporating outside data on the costs of operation (these are currently estimated), and incorporating the price of electricity.

15.6 FERTILITY AND CHILD MORTALITY

Understanding the choices underlying the number, timing, and spacing of children is crucial to population policy as well as to understanding and predicting population trends. An early attempt to model these decisions in a dynamic programming framework is Wolpin (1984). Here, the choice variable in each period is whether or not to have a child. The state variable is the stock of children. Observed exogenous processes include income and schooling. Utility in each period is a function of the stock of live children and consumption. The period of fertility for each woman is fixed and known. The problem facing each household is to maximize at time t

$$E_t \sum_{k=0}^{\tau-t} \beta^k u_{t+k}(m_{t+k}, x_{t+k}), \tag{15.3}$$

where m is the number of children and x is consumption. Maximization is over the sequence of births in the current and subsequent periods. A birth in period t is indicated by $n_t = 1$, otherwise $n_t = 0$. Here, τ is the life span, the horizon over which utility is maximized. The state updating equations are

$$m_t = m_{t-1} + n_t - d_t, \quad \text{for } t = 1, \dots, T,$$
$$= m_{t-1} \quad \text{for } t = T + 1, \dots, \tau. \tag{15.4}$$

Here, T is the last period of fertility and $d_t = 1$ if there is a death in period t of a child born in that period. Children surviving one period subsequently outlive their parents. This turns out to be realistic; most child mortality in the sample is very early. Deaths are stochastic and occur according to a probit model in each period (possibly different variable values and common coefficients). The budget constraint is given by

$$y_t = x_t + b(n_t - d_t) + cn_t, \tag{15.5}$$

where y is income, b is the cost of maintenance of a child in the first period, and c is the cost of childbirth. Income is generated each period according to an i.i.d. process depending on observable regressors. Distributions are assumed normal.

Data consist of Malaysian household survey data on 188 women older than 30, married once and still married (this is a subsample from a survey of 1262 households). The period was set at 18 months. The survival probabilities were estimated in a first stage, and then a conditional likelihood was formed based on the choice probabilities. The utility function was specified as quadratic, with the linear term in m subject to a random shock. Thus, the model is in the random utility framework. This assumption is particularly convenient in the continuous state/control specification of the linear-quadratic (LQ) model, as we have seen (chapter 13). In the current setting, there is no real simplification, but no restriction either, and many plausible specifications are equivalent. Heterogeneity in the mean of the random linear term in the utility function is considered by allowing two different values and estimating a mixture model; the heterogeneous specification is not a significant improvement over the homogeneous one.

The results indicate that the variables are jointly significant, so the specification has explanatory power. The estimated costs of births are overly high but exhibit a reasonable pattern, decreasing and then increasing over the course of the period of fertility. The discount factor was estimated at .92 (recall that periods are 18 months). Increasing infant mortality does not imply additional births. The survival probability effects are important. Decreasing the survival probability leads to having more children earlier, though to a reduction in the total number of children. A mother's increased schooling reduces the expected number of children.

Keeping in mind that this was a very early and innovative application, there are some troubling aspects. First, no standard errors were reported because the second derivative matrix of the log likelihood function at the maximum likelihood estimator (MLE) was not negative definite. This clearly indicates a problem, either with identification or with the computation of the derivatives. Second, a difference in implication between the reduced-form probit model and the structural predictions is noted. In fact, the advantage of structural modeling is that new questions can be addressed. When the same question can be addressed in the reduced form, the answers should agree.

This paper was important in establishing that empirical dynamic programming models were feasible and indeed useful outside the existing applications in macroeconomics and job search models. The paper inspired an ongoing and productive literature on structural models of fertility.

15.7 COSTS OF PRICE ADJUSTMENT

"Menu costs," that is, the costs associated with price adjustment, are sometimes argued to be a source of stickiness in prices. When should prices be changed when demand is stochastic but price adjustment is costly? This problem is addressed by Slade (1998), who studies grocery store pricing for saltine crackers at the micro level. The specification assumes a linear demand function,

$$q_t = a + X_t\beta - bp_t + dG_t + \varepsilon_t, \tag{15.6}$$

where q and p are the quantity and price, X is a vector of characteristics including prices at competing stores, and G is goodwill on the part of consumers. Cost is linear with marginal cost c_t. Price adjustment costs are specified by $A_t = f + g|p_{t+1} - p_t|$. The fixed cost f is incurred only if the price is changed. The state variables k are taken to be the current price p, the stock of goodwill G, the quantity q, and the cost c. Assemble these in the vector k_t. The control variable is the price change Δp. The store's net profit in period t is $\pi_t = p_t q_t - c_t q_t - A_t$. The store's problem is

$$\max\left\{ E \sum_{t=0}^{T} \beta^t \pi_t \right\}, \tag{15.7}$$

with respect to the sequence of controls $\{\Delta p_t\}_{t=1}^{T}$ subject to the transition equation

$$k_{t+1} = \alpha + Bk_t + \gamma \, \Delta p_t + v_t, \tag{15.8}$$

where the vectors α and γ and the matrix B are restricted for parsimony (many known zeros) and the shocks are serially uncorrelated. The Bellman equation is, as usual,

$$V^T(k_0) = \max\left\{ \pi(k_0, \Delta p_0) + \beta E_0 V^{T-1} \right\}. \tag{15.9}$$

The optimal policy turns out to have the form $\Delta p_t = S_t^L - p_t$ if $p_t < s_t^L$, $\Delta p_t = S_t^U - p_t$ if $p_t > s_t^U$, and $\Delta p_t = 0$ otherwise. This form essentially arises because of the fixed cost. Optimal prices are in a band. The thresholds are functions of the state variables.

The goodwill variable G is constructed from the regression of quantities q on a distributed lag in prices. The control space is discretized with two values, and the state space with 24. The reduced-form choice probabilities for each state are calculated, following Hotz and Miller (1993). The reduced-form state-to-state transition probabilities are also calculated by their relative frequencies. Then generalized method of moments (GMM) is used to match the structural specification to these sufficient statistics. Note that the model, given the discretization of the state and control space, is in the exponential family, with the reduced-form statistics reflecting the mean parametrization. The structural model is curved exponential (see the appendix).

The model was fit to data on sales of saltine crackers in Williamsport, PA, collected by Information Resources, a Chicago based marketing firm. There were four brands in the sample, three national brands and a generic house brand. Data were compiled weekly. Fixed costs of adjustment f did turn out to be important and were estimated fairly accurately. Variable costs g were insignificant. Surprisingly, fixed costs of price changes seemed to vary across cracker brands.

15.8 SCHOOLING, WORK, AND OCCUPATIONAL CHOICE

Potential new entrants into the labor market make choices about when to leave school and what occupation to choose. These decisions must depend on the life cycle implications of the choices. This is a natural setting for a dynamic programming model. Keane and Wolpin (1997) specify and estimate a model using data from the youth cohort of the National Longitudinal Survey of Labor Market Experience (NLSY).

The decision problem allows individuals to choose among three types of work, white collar, blue collar, and military; schooling; and "home production" (i.e., other). The state space consists of age, accumulated schooling, and accumulating experience, specific to occupation. The period in which decisions are made is a year. Within-period utility is given by $R(s) = \sum_{i=1}^{5} R_i(s) d_i(s)$, where s is the state variable, R_i is the choice-specific reward, and d is an indicator variable indicating the choice. For the employment choices, the reward is earnings, given by an occupation-specific earnings function whose parameters are estimated. For schooling and home production, the reward functions are estimated. Each of these choice-specific rewards has an error term, assumed correlated across choices and independent over time. A terminal age of 65 is assumed. The problem at age a is therefore

$$\max E \sum_{t=a}^{65} \beta^{t-a} R(s_t). \tag{15.10}$$

The sample consists of approximately 1,400 white males with initial age 16–21. These are assumed heterogeneous; specifically, there are four types, and the type for each individual is unknown. The state transition distribution is deterministic, so the likelihood function is based entirely on the choice probabilities. The overall likelihood is a mixture of the likelihoods for each of the four types. Substantial numerical integrations and approximations are necessary to solve the model.

The results of the estimation of the basic model, 50 parameters, gave estimates of the return to schooling at 9.4% for white collar occupations, 1.9%

for blue collar, and 4.4% for military. The return to experience was 11.7% for white collar occupations and 14.3% for blue collar. These estimates are theoretically more appealing than those from conventional earnings regressions since they take into account the endogeneity of schooling choice and occupational choice. The discount factor β was .79. The fit was better than that of the static probit model, indicating clearly the importance of the dynamic specification, but still not good. Specifically, the model badly overpredicted wage growth. An extended model with 83 parameters was next specified, allowing more general age effects, etc. Here, the return to schooling was estimated at 7% for white collar, 2.4% for blue collar, and 5.8% for military. The experience effects were higher for the first year than in the basic model but decreased faster. The extended model fitted substantially better than the basic one, though there was still a problem explaining persistence. Possibly, temporal correlation in wage equation errors could generate the persistence, though the computational difficulties would be substantial.

The application shows the feasibility of dynamic modeling in a serious empirical setting. The model allows a simultaneous analysis of schooling, participation, and occupational choice. The specification permits clean estimates of reward function parameters corresponding to preference parameters.

15.9 RENEWAL OF PATENTS

By taking out patents, a firm can obtain proprietary rights to its innovations and thus protect the initial rewards to its investment in research and development activities. Ideally, then, patent laws can be designed to further technical progress. The issue arises that after a certain point, an innovation is more useful if made publicly available, and excessive patent protection may allow a narrow group to reap disproportionate benefits. Thus, patent laws are at the heart of industrial policy, and important determinants of market structures. It complicates the analysis that returns to patent holdings generally are not observable. Pakes (1986) establishes a method for estimation of the unobserved distribution of returns to patents from aggregate data on renewal rates by patent age and cohort. Individual patents are modeled very much like financial options (chapter 11) held by the firms, and the model is in the optimal stopping class. Starting with this paper, the structural estimation approach has seen strong development in the industrial organization (IO) area. Recent studies involve analysis of firm level data using a host of models of competition, market power, regulation, etc.

In the original paper by Pakes, the firm faces the choice between renewing a patent for a fee K_t to continue protection of the return R_t, or letting the patent lapse. Thus, the Bellman equation is

$$V_t = \max\{R_t - K_t + \beta E_t(V_{t+1}), 0\},$$

where V_t is the value of holding the patent in period t, $t = 1, \ldots, T$, with T the statutory limit to patent lives. This is similar to a call option with strike price K_t (see (11.28)). In both cases, continuation is associated with an expected discounted future value. The difference between the patent and option problems is that in the former, continuation (renewal) in addition generates the running payoff $R_t - K_t$, and stopping (the patent lapses) generates zero, whereas continuation in the call case generates zero running payoff, and it is stopping (option exercise) that generates $R_t - K_t$. The structure implies that patents may be renewed even if current payoff is negative, $R_t < K_t$, on the chance of improved future returns.

Pakes assumes that the transition distribution $Q_t(R_{t+1}|R_t)$ is stochastically increasing in R_t and decreasing in t, and that the renewal fee schedule K_t is nondecreasing over time. Then $E_t V_{t+1}$ is increasing in R_t and decreasing in t. Furthermore, a reservation policy is optimal, i.e., there is a reservation or renewal boundary B_t such that the patent is renewed if and only if $R_t > B_t$. The renewal boundary is increasing over time (age of the patent).

Given specific assumptions on Q_t and the unconditional distribution Q of R_0, the model allows calculating the unconditional probability that the patent is renewed k times, $k = 1, \ldots, T$. Thus, these T probabilities are functions of the structural parameters θ, namely, β along with the parameters in Q and Q_t. For given θ, the model is solved by backward recursion, and the T probabilities calculated by simulation. Provided there are $T - 1$ or fewer parameters in θ, the multinomial likelihood is now computed from the probabilities and the counts of patents renewed k times, $k = 1, \ldots, T$. A likelihood is constructed for each of a number of cohorts identified by year of patent application, and the overall log likelihood is the sum of the cohort log likelihoods. The model is fit to cohorts from the 1950s through the 1970s from France, Germany, and the U.K., where T during the period was 20, 16, and 18 years, respectively.

The paper illustrates that it is possible to take a model of the individual decision maker (the firm) to aggregate data, and feasible to estimate the conditional return distributions Q_t even in the absence of return data.

15.10 MARKETING—DIRECT MAILING OF CATALOGS

Firms that specialize in catalog sales must decide whether and when to mail catalogs to particular target consumers. Consumers who order from catalogs decide whether to order in any period, whether they get a catalog that period or not. Consumers know that the receipt of future catalogs depends on their ordering behavior. In equilibrium, firms know how consumers make decisions, and consumers know how firms make decisions. This is the context of the analysis by Gonul and Shi (1998).

This model has consumers who use dynamic optimization in making their ordering decisions and direct mailers who also dynamically optimize. The objective of the consumer is to maximize lifetime utility. The firm maximizes the expected lifetime discounted value of profits from each customer. Decisions are made monthly; since there are many months, the horizon is taken to be infinite, vastly simplifying the analysis since then decision rules are stationary. The consumer maximizes

$$E \sum_{t=1}^{\infty} \beta^t u_t \, d_t, \qquad (15.11)$$

where d_t is the control, a buy indicator, and utility is given by

$$u_t = \alpha + \beta_1 m_t + \beta_2 r_t + \beta_3 r_t^2 + \beta_4 f_t + \beta_5 f_t^2 + \varepsilon_t. \qquad (15.12)$$

Here, r is the recency, the elapsed time since the last order, and f is the frequency, the total number of times a purchase is made. These are the state variables, $x = (r, f)$. Their transitions are deterministic. The variable m is an indicator for whether or not the individual received a mailed catalog that month. The error term is assumed normally distributed, with zero mean and unit variance. The value function for the consumer is

$$V_t(x_t) = \max\{u_t + \beta EV_{t+1}(x_{t+1}), \beta EV_{t+1}(x_{t+1})\}, \qquad (15.13)$$

where the branches correspond to the two choices, buy or not buy.

The firm has period profit

$$\pi_t(x_t, m_t) = R \cdot P(d_t = 1 | m_t, x_t) - c \cdot m_t, \qquad (15.14)$$

where R is the net revenue from a sale and c is the cost of mailing. The control is m. The discounted profit stream is

$$P(x_t) = \sum_{j=t}^{\infty} \beta^{j-t} \pi_j. \qquad (15.15)$$

It is not necessary that consumers and firms use the same discount factor. The dynamic programs are solved simultaneously by successive approximation on P and V. Specifically, these are started at zero (the one-period maxima might give better starting values), P is computed, then V given P is computed, and so on. Gonul and Shi note that convergence is slow.

The data consist of the purchase histories of 530 households. These households receive five or six catalogs a year on average, at an average cost of \$2.53. The net revenue on a sale is \$27.00. The item sold lasts 1.5–2 years. The likelihood function is made up of the response and the nonresponse probabilities. For comparison, a myopic model for the consumer is also fit (the $\beta = 0$ case).

The results show that the effect of the mailing is small but significant in terms of its effect on the order rate. The effects of both recency and frequency are U-shaped. Generally, the purchase probability since a recent purchase declines for about 2 years and then increases. The optimal policy for mailing to a consumer depends on both recency and frequency. If recency is low, do not mail. If frequency is low to medium, mail. The effects are significantly different from those based on the static problem for the consumer. In that model, mailing is insignificant.

15.11 SCRAPPING SUBSIDIES AND AUTOMOBILE PURCHASES

Older cars generally pollute more than newer ones. A case can be made that newer cars are safer as well. The French government instituted two programs to encourage auto owners to upgrade to new cars by subsidizing the replacement of old cars with new cars. The goal, in addition to the potential social benefits listed above, was to subsidize employment, output, and income in the automobile sector. There is no doubt that the subsidies increased auto replacement during the period of the subsidy. A careful assessment of the overall effect and cost of these programs requires a dynamic view, taken by Adda and Cooper (2000).

Adda and Cooper consider a model in which, at each period, the consumer can trade a car, scrap it and buy a new one, or keep it another period. Transactions occur at the end of a period. Consumers are assumed homogeneous, so interconsumer trade is irrelevant. It will not occur in equilibrium, and anyway it does not affect the objects of interest, namely, the vintage distribution of autos or the profitability of the auto industry. Let y be income, s_i the service flow from a car of age i, p_i the price of a car of age i, π the scrap value of a car (crucially not depending on age), and β the discount factor. The value of owning a car of age i is given by the Bellman equation,

$$V_i = \max\{s_i + y + \beta V_{i+1}, s_1 + y + \pi - p_1 + \beta V_2\}, \qquad (15.16)$$

where the age of a new car is $i = 1$. In equilibrium,

$$p_i = s_i + \beta(V_{i+1} - V_0) - z, \qquad (15.17)$$

where V_0 is the value of having no car, and z is the surplus utility from car ownership. It can be shown that $V_i > V_{i+1}$, etc. In this case, the optimal policy is an optimal stopping policy. There is a vintage J such that when a car reaches age J, it is scrapped and replaced with a new car.

With this model of consumer behavior, aggregate car sales are a simple function of the cross-section distribution of car vintages. To make the model useful for describing the data accurately, it is expanded with aggregate shocks to income and to the price of a new car, an exogenous car destruction mechanism, and utility shocks.

The data are from several sources. Aggregate data are from monthly new car sales in France, 1984–1997. There is also annual information on the cross-section distribution of cars by age. Micro data are from a survey of 6,000 households. This survey collects auto age and purchase data, as well as household income. In aggregate, roughly 20% of owners replace a car in any given year. Of these, 45% buy new cars. The model is estimated in two steps. First, the aggregate income and price transition distribution is estimated as a vector autoregression (VAR). In the second step, these are incorporated into the dynamic programming model, and the additional parameters are fit by matching certain moments—the fraction of cars in age intervals of about 5, 10, and 15 years—and by matching sales. This estimator cannot be expected to be efficient, but it is consistent, and standard errors can be correctly calculated.

Results imply hazard functions that are flat until age 3 and then upward sloping. Hazards are at approximately 10% at age 5, 17% at age 10, and 40% at age 20. At age 10, a 10% increase in income implies a 6% increase in the replacement probability. A 10% price increase implies a decrease in the replacement probability of 13%. The subsidy clearly reduces the scrapping age. The effect on the cross-section distribution reduces the long-run effect on the industry. Using the structural estimates, the effect on government revenues can be calculated. The subsidies imply additional sales of new cars, which implies more revenue from value-added tax (VAT). But subsidies are expensive, and the total effect is a net loss to the government.

15.12 ON-THE-JOB SEARCH AND THE WAGE DISTRIBUTION

In many countries, workers have experienced considerable wage growth over the last several decades. In the U.S. Census data from the University of Michigan's Integrated Public Use Microdata Series (IPUMS) project, earnings of males aged 31–35 in 2000 were 109% higher than earnings of males aged 21–25 in 1990. In 1970 and 1980, the difference was 87%. Nevertheless, the estimated effect of tenure on wages is small, probably less than

10% per decade, so firm-specific human capital models only explain a small portion of wage growth. An alternative explanation, based on labor market frictions, is that wages are dispersed across firms and employed workers move up the job ladder, from lower- to higher-paying jobs. This is the viewpoint adopted by Christensen, Lentz, Mortensen, Neumann, and Werwatz (2005).

The model is one of on-the-job search, i.e., a job search model closely related to the prototypal model of chapter 7. Workers maximize the expected discounted value of the future income stream over an infinite horizon. The difference compared to the prototypal model is that workers no longer expect to keep the same job for ever upon becoming employed. Instead, the search for better job offers is continued. While employed, the reservation wage (for moving to a better job) is not determined by an implicit equation as in the prototypal model, but is simply given by the wage in the current job. Search effort is assumed costly, so as the current wage is increased, optimal search effort is decreased. The function $s(w)$ giving optimal search effort as a function of the wage w is determined by a functional equation derived from the Bellman equation. The state is $x = (w, a)$, where a is employment status (employed or unemployed). The control is $c = (s, b)$, where b is the decision whether or not to accept a new offer (an employed worker accepts if and only if the new offer exceeds the current wage w). This is an example of a continuous-time dynamic programming model with mixed discrete and continuous states, and mixed discrete and continuous controls (w and s are the continuous state and control, a and b are the discrete).

A job ends if an offer is received (this occurs with Poisson arrival rate s, given by on-the-job search effort) and accepted. Given an offer is received, the probability that it is accepted is $1 - F(w)$, where F is the wage offer distribution (this follows as in (9.3), recalling that the reservation wage is now the current wage). A job may also end for exogenous reasons, which occurs at the job destruction rate δ. The job separation hazard is constant at

$$h(w) = \delta + s(w)(1 - F(w)),   \tag{15.18}$$

so job durations are exponential, with parameter depending on the wage in the job. Note that unemployed workers do not have a current wage (they may receive unemployment insurance benefits that are constant or less dispersed than w), so the arrival rate determined by p in the prototypal model (chapter 7) instead of the function $s(w)$ in (5.18) makes sense in this case.

The model is fit to register data on the 1,514,022 employees in the 113,325 private sector firms in Denmark in 1994. In addition to the full sample, four occupational subsamples of managers as well as salaried, skilled, and unskilled workers are analyzed. The parameters estimated are the job destruction rate δ, a cost of search effort parameter, and the arrival rate at the lowest wage. Again, the offer arrival rate at higher wages is given endogenously by $s(w)$, which represents a generalization relative to the original treatment of on-the-job search by Burdett (1978). The estimates imply that the search cost function is close to quadratic both for salaried workers and the full sample. On-the-job search is more costly for managers and unskilled workers, and less costly for skilled workers. The offer arrival rate at the lowest wage is lower for managers than for the other occupational groups. The job destruction rate is highest for unskilled workers, and then follow skilled workers, salaried workers, and managers, in that order. Thus, δ falls with occupational level as ranked by the skill-education hierarchy.

Equilibrium conditions are invoked on the flows of workers in and out of unemployment, as well as in and out of employment categories defined by wage levels. As workers tend to move up the job ladder, the cross-section earned wage distribution stochastically dominates the offer distribution F, and converges to a steady state distribution G that may be calculated from F and the estimated structural parameters. Nonparametric estimates of F and G confirm that the quantiles of G exceed those of F for the full sample and all subgroups. Furthermore, the model predicted $\hat{G}$, calculated from the nonparametric F and the estimated structural parameters, is very close to the actual nonparametric G. Thus, define the employment effect at the α-quantile as the difference between the α-quantiles of G and F, and let the explained portion of this be the difference between the α-quantiles of $\hat{G}$ and F. Then the model explains 95% of the employment effect at the median in the full sample. It explains 113% at the first quartile and 111% at the third quartile. Finally, it explains 84% of the employment effect at the median for managers, and it explains 99% for salaried, 77% for skilled, and 105% for unskilled workers.

Thus, in contrast to tenure effects, the notion that labor market frictions exist, with wages dispersed and workers flowing from lower- to higher-paying jobs, does explain the observed wage growth.

15.13 EXERCISES

1. In the marketing model, can the recursions on (15.13) and (15.15) be run separately, or is simultaneous solution necessary?

2. In the automobile market model, is it possible to solve first for the values (15.16), then insert these in (15.17) to get the prices, or must the two systems be solved simultaneously?

3. In the search model, suppose data on job separations and wages are used to estimate $h(w)$ nonparametrically, and data on wage offers is used to

estimate $F(w)$ nonparametrically. These are inserted in (15.18) to generate an estimate of the function $s(w)$. Which property of this estimated function should one look for to test the model? *Hint*: Does the worker search more or less as the wage is increased?

15.14 REFERENCES

There are many other studies, particularly in labor economics, where not only the search model but also other models of schooling and occupational choice have been estimated. Gotz and McCall (1984) apply dynamic programming to a model of retention of Air Force officers. Retirement is also a growing area in which in particular the finite-horizon specification is important; it is the subject of chapter 12. See, for example, Eckstein and Wolpin (1990) and Eckstein (1989) on dynamic labor force participation, Miller (1984) on occupational choice, and many others. Dynamic programming models can also form the basis for econometric evaluation of the effects of social programs. The subtle identification issues involved are treated by Abbring and Heckman (2007). Altonji and Williams (1997) study tenure effects (see section 15.12) and place the consensus estimate of the portion of wage growth explained by tenure between 6.6% and 11%. Griliches (1984) considers the role of patents in research and development and productivity growth.

Chapter Sixteen

Macroeconomic Applications

Applications of dynamic programming, particularly Euler equation methods and the linear-quadratic model, have been extremely fruitful in macroeconomics. In this chapter we review a few applications: Hall's consumption model, Hansen-Singleton's model of consumption and asset returns, and Sargent's labor demand application (the linear-quadratic model). We then turn to the Kydland-Prescott result on time inconsistency of optimal plans mentioned briefly in chapter 13. This is followed by a discussion of Kydland and Prescott's paper, "Time to Build," which led to an ongoing literature explaining macro time series with structural models. A crucial specification choice in Kydland and Prescott (1982) is nonseparable utility. This subject is taken up empirically by Eichenbaum, Hansen, and Singleton (1988), which is treated in section 16.6. Section 16.7 discusses monetary policy in a framework that allows estimation of the preference parameters of the monetary authority (Broadbent and Barro, 1997). We follow with a labor economics application that focuses on microeconometric evidence on a key macro parameter: the Heckman-MaCurdy model of intertemporal labor supply. Finally, we discuss an application (Fisher and de Gorter, 1992) that uses dynamic programming to assess the effects of U.S. farm policy.

16.1 CONSUMPTION AS A RANDOM WALK

The life cycle permanent income hypothesis is that consumers forecast their income over the life cycle, then set their consumption accordingly. Thus, the links between consumption and short-term fluctuations in income over the life cycle are weak. Testing and measurement in this model are difficult because of the simultaneous determination of income and consumption. Thus, regressions of consumption on current income (or distributed lags of income) do not satisfy the usual statistical assumptions and are typically inappropriate. This problem is classic in econometrics and has been realized since the 1940s. Hall (1978) considers the intertemporal utility maximization problem

$$\max U_\pi(w_0) = E_0 \sum_{t=0}^{T} \beta^t u(c_t), \tag{16.1}$$

where w_t is earnings in period t, the policy function π gives c_t as a function $c_t(w_0, \ldots, w_t)$, and the consumption choices satisfy the intertemporal budget constraint

$$\sum_{t=0}^{T} \delta^t (c_t - w_t) = A_0, \tag{16.2}$$

with A_0 the asset stock at time 0 and $\delta = (1+r)^{-1}$, where r is the interest rate. The optimality equation in this case takes the form

$$V^t(w_t, A_t) = \max \left\{ u(c_t) + \beta E_t V^{t-1}(w_{t-1}, A_{t-1}) \right\}, \tag{16.3}$$

and the transition equation is

$$A_{t-1} = (1+r)(A_t - c_t + w_t), \tag{16.4}$$

$$w_{t-1} \sim Q(w'|w_t). \tag{16.5}$$

The Euler equation (see also (13.56)) is

$$E_t u'(c_{t+1}) = (\delta/\beta) u'(c_t). \tag{16.6}$$

Note that δ/β is likely to be nearly 1. If the utility is quadratic, then the consumption at time $t+1$ will be a linear function of the consumption at time t, with a constant term nearly zero and the slope coefficient nearly 1. If utility is nearly quadratic over the year-to-year variation, the same will hold. Most importantly, lagged income or assets, given lagged consumption, should not influence consumption.

This model is fit to quarterly U.S. data on per-capita consumption of nondurables and services from 1948:1 through 1977:1. Adding income does not significantly improve the fit. Adding additional lags of consumption does not significantly improve the fit. Adding lagged corporate stock returns does change the results and marginally improves the fit. Hall argues that this is not inconsistent with the life cycle model.

This approach has the statistically disquieting property that one's hypothesis is confirmed by a failure to reject. That is, the model is supported by the finding that extra variables do not significantly affect the relationship between consumption and its lagged value. The absence of evidence becomes evidence.

Hall (1988) revisits this model, allowing for stochastic interest rates. Note that the coefficient on lagged consumption, expected to be nearly unity, depends on the interest rate. Hall uses variation in the interest rate to measure intertemporal substitution in consumption and finds that the substitution parameter is empirically nearly zero.

16.2 CONSUMPTION AND ASSET RETURNS

In simple general equilibrium models of asset returns with risk-neutral consumers, asset prices are determined so that the expected return on each asset is the same. This implies, as noted by Hansen and Singleton (1983), that asset returns will be serially uncorrelated and independent of lagged consumption. The risk-neutrality assumption is strong and is rejected in a number of studies. This suggests studying consumption and asset prices together. Suppose the consumer maximizes the intertemporal utility function

$$E_0 \sum_{t=0}^{\infty} \beta^t \frac{c_t^{1-\gamma} - 1}{1 - \gamma}, \tag{16.7}$$

where β is the discount factor and γ is the coefficient of relative risk aversion. Thus, $\gamma = 0$ for risk-neutral consumers and $\gamma > 0$ for risk-averse consumers. The maximization is of course subject to a budget constraint. The consumer holds positions in each of N assets (zero holdings are allowed). These positions are given by the vector w_t in period t. The vector of asset prices is p_t. Maximization is over both the consumption stream c and the asset holdings w. In each period, the budget constraint is

$$c_t + p_t' w_{t+1} = p_t' w_t + y_t, \tag{16.8}$$

where y_t is period-t income. The Euler equation is

$$c_t^{-\gamma} = \beta E_t c_{t+1}^{-\gamma} r_{it+1}, \tag{16.9}$$

where the return on asset i is $r_{it+1} = (p_{it+1} - p_{it})/p_{it} + 1$ (see also (13.56)). The expectation of the product of the marginal utility of consumption and the return is the same across assets. This is a strong, testable restriction imposed by the optimization and equilibrium hypothesis. If $\gamma = 0$, so there is no risk aversion, then the expected rates of return are equalized across assets.

Writing Y_t as the vector of observables $(\ln(c_t/c_{t-1}), \ln r_{1t}, \ldots, \ln r_{Nt}) = (X, R_1, \ldots, R_N)_t$ and assuming that Y is a Gaussian vector autoregression, Hansen and Singleton characterize the autoregressive properties of consumption and asset returns in terms of the risk-aversion parameter γ. Specifically, γ determines some of the coefficients in the VAR model for Y. The model is fitted to monthly data from February 1959 through December 1978 on consumption, excluding durables and a variety of assets. The parameter γ is not precisely determined: Its estimated value depends on the number of lags allowed in the vector autoregression and on the particular asset series used. Although there appears to be evidence of risk aversion, other restrictions are rejected.

Hall (1988) used a similar specification with a different interpretation of γ. He argued that γ, which also turns out to be an intertemporal substitution parameter, could be interpreted independently of its role as a utility function parameter. That is, the empirical specification consistent with the model could arise from other models in which the empirical counterpart of γ in the relation between consumption changes and asset returns measured intertemporal substitution without being a risk-aversion parameter. Hall's work, finding little evidence of intertemporal substitution, would, strictly speaking, imply extreme risk aversion in the Hansen-Singleton model. It is shown in chapter 18 that in this model, the elasticity of intertemporal substitution is exactly $1/\gamma$. Perhaps the Hansen-Singleton results are best interpreted as additional evidence against large intertemporal substitution effects in consumption.

16.3 DYNAMIC LABOR DEMAND

The paper by Sargent (1978) emphasizes the role of rational expectations and the restrictions imposed by rational expectations as well as by the optimization hypothesis. The focus is on the relation between real wages and employment. There is a complicated dynamic interaction between real wages and employment, with the causality appearing to flow from wages to employment. Sargent employs a dynamic programming framework to understand these complicated dynamics. The assumed production function depends on two kinds of labor—straight-time workers and overtime workers. The key idea is that straight-time work is cheaper for the firm on an hourly wage basis but is costly to adjust. Overtime work is more costly on an hourly basis but is cheaper to adjust. The workers are equally productive, except for exogenous random shocks. Production is given by

$$f(n_1, n_2) = (f_0 + a_1)n_1 - \left(\frac{f_1}{2}\right) n_1^2 + (f_0 + a_2)n_2 - \left(\frac{f_1}{2}\right) n_2^2, \qquad (16.10)$$

where n_1 is straight-time employment, n_2 is overtime employment, a_1 and a_2 are shocks, and all of these variables are also subscripted by t. The shocks are exogenous, and the coefficients f_0 and f_1 are positive. The capital stock is assumed fixed, so the focus is on labor adjustment and substitution between the two kinds of employment. Adjustment costs per period are

$$\frac{d}{2}(n_{1t} - n_{1t-1})^2 \qquad (16.11)$$

and

$$\frac{e}{2}(n_{2t} - n_{2t-1})^2 \qquad (16.12)$$

for the two kinds of labor. Here, $d > e$; it is more costly to adjust straight-time labor. On the other hand, straight-time labor is paid the rate w, while overtime is pw, where $p > 1$. The wage process is exogenous and stochastic. Sargent offers evidence on the exogeneity of the wage process. The firm's problem is therefore to maximize at each t,

$$
E_t \sum_{j=0}^{\infty} \beta^j \left[\left(f_0 + a_{1t+j} - w_{t+j} \right) n_{t+j} - (f_1/2) n_{1t+j}^2 \right.
$$
$$
- (d/2) \left(n_{1t+j} - n_{1t+j-1} \right)^2 + \left(f_0 + a_{2t+j} - pw_{t+j} \right) n_{2t+j}
$$
$$
\left. - (f_1/2) n_{2t+j}^2 - (e/2) \left(n_{2t+j} - n_{2t+j-1} \right)^2 \right]. \tag{16.13}
$$

This is a random utility specification; cf. chapter 13.

The productivity shocks are assumed to follow a first-order Markov process,

$$
\begin{pmatrix} a_{1t} \\ a_{2t} \end{pmatrix} = \begin{pmatrix} \rho_1 & 0 \\ 0 & \rho_2 \end{pmatrix} \begin{pmatrix} a_{1t-1} \\ a_{2t-1} \end{pmatrix} + \begin{pmatrix} \zeta_{1t} \\ \zeta_{2t} \end{pmatrix}, \tag{16.14}
$$

where $(\zeta_1, \zeta_2)_t$ are serially uncorrelated, and w is assumed to follow an nth-order autoregression. This is a linear-quadratic model, and the optimal decision rules for n_1 and n_2 are linear functions of their own lagged (once) values and current and $(n - 1)$ lagged values of the wage. The coefficients are nonlinear functions of the basic parameters of the production function, adjustment cost function, discount factor, etc. The model is overidentified if the order of the autoregression for wages is greater than 1. Sargent fits the model to quarterly data from 1947:1 to 1972:4. The structural model exhibits multiple local likelihood maxima. Generally, the model is consistent with the data, though there is some potential interaction between n_1 and n_2 not captured by the model (this could be incorporated into the Markov specification for the two productivity shocks by allowing off-diagonal elements). Sargent speculates that longer lags in the Markov specification of the productivity shocks might also be useful.

The model shows that the dynamic programming specification, combined with the rational expectations hypothesis, imposes restrictions on a vector autoregression (VAR) specification for the observables (the reduced form) and allows identification and estimation of structural parameters. It is generally true that the linear-quadratic (LQ) dynamic programming setup with rational expectations imposes restrictions in the VAR representations of economic time series. This allows deep interpretation of the VAR parameters. In this sense, the VAR approach advocated by Sims (1980) is not inconsistent with economic theory; rather, it is typically not interpreted in theoretical terms.

16.4 TIME INCONSISTENCY OF OPTIMAL PLANS

Kydland and Prescott (1977) showed in an influential paper that optimal plans in economies in which agents have rational expectations are typically inconsistent, in that the plan that is optimal at the initial period 0 will not be followed because the period-k policy selected at period 0 will no longer be optimal at period k and will be revised. Rational agents will anticipate this and react accordingly. This feature arises because future policies affect current variables and are chosen with this effect in mind. Of course, after the current variables are realized, future policies can be recalculated without bothering about this effect. This argument, following up on the Lucas critique, is especially damaging to the idea of policy choice through dynamic programming. While other authors developed techniques to incorporate rational expectations into econometric models, by making the expectations of future policies correct expectations, Kydland and Prescott argued forcefully that the whole exercise was futile. Indeed, policy papers recommending rules now typically include a discussion of commitment—how the policy maker can commit now to rules that in the future will no longer appear optimal. Perhaps this can be achieved by law or by infrequently scheduled policy reviews.

The point can be made in the context of a simple model. Consider the quadratic utility function

$$u(x, c) = -x^2 - c^2 \tag{16.15}$$

and the objective

$$V^T(x_1) = \max \sum_{t=1}^{r} u(x_t, c_t), \tag{16.16}$$

with the transition equation

$$x_{t+1} = a + \beta_1 c_t + \beta_2 c_{t+1} + \cdots + \beta_{T-t+1} c_T + \gamma x_t + \varepsilon_{t+1}. \tag{16.17}$$

The feature that is new here is that the transition distribution depends not only on the current policy but also on the future policies as well. Of course, these are not really known at the time x_{t+1} is generated, so it is natural (and rational) to suppose that they are replaced with their expectations. Let us fix ideas by considering a three-period model with a somewhat restricted transition distribution. Further, since uncertainty really doesn't matter in this model, we will drop it. Thus,

$$V^3(x_1) = \max_{c_1, c_2, c_3} \left\{ -x_1^2 - c_1^2 - x_2^2 - c_2^2 - x_3^2 - c_3^2 \right\} \tag{16.18}$$

subject to

$$x_2 = \alpha + \beta_1 c_1 + \beta_2 c_2, \tag{16.19}$$

$$x_3 = \gamma + \delta c_2. \tag{16.20}$$

The model is simplified in that the transition equations do not depend on controls lagged more than once and do not depend on the lagged state variables. The point is that c_2 affects x_2. Solving by direct maximization, we find the global optimum at the controls

$$c_1^* = -(\alpha\beta_1 + \beta_1\delta^2\alpha - \beta_1\beta_2\delta\gamma)/\phi, \tag{16.21}$$

$$c_2^* = -(\alpha\beta_2 + \delta\gamma + \beta_1^2\delta\gamma)/\phi, \tag{16.22}$$

$$c_3^* = 0, \tag{16.23}$$

where $\phi = 1 + \beta_1^2 + \beta_2^2 + \delta^2 + \beta_1^2\delta^2$.

Now reconsider the policy after one period. Here, we have run c_1^* and have realized a value for x_2. From this moment, the problem is

$$V^2(x_2) = \max_{c_2, c_3} \left\{ -x_2^2 - c_2^2 - x_3^2 - c_3^2 \right\} \tag{16.24}$$

subject to

$$x_3 = \gamma + \delta c_2. \tag{16.25}$$

Direct maximization gives

$$c_2^{**} = -\delta\gamma/(1 + \delta^2), \tag{16.26}$$

$$c_3^{**} = 0, \tag{16.27}$$

not the same value for c_2 as (16.22) in the original problem. The difference is that the first calculation took account of the effect of c_2 on x_2 due to the inclusion of the future control in the transition equation to x_2. After x_2 is realized, this effect is gone.

This inconsistency raises the question of which value of c_2 to use in the transition equations. Kydland and Prescott argue that rational agents will ignore the announced plan c_2^*, will recognize that c_2^{**} will be used, and will therefore use c_2^{**} in the determination of x_2.

Backward recursion can be applied to determine a time-consistent plan. Clearly, c_3^{***}, the optimum determined by backward recursion, is zero. Further, $c_2^{***} = c_2^{**}$. Substituting and solving the initial period problem gives

$$c_1^{***} = -\beta_1 \left(\alpha + \delta^2\alpha - \beta_2\delta\gamma\right) / \left((1 + \beta_1^2)(1 + \delta^2)\right), \tag{16.28}$$

which is not the same as the first-period control (16.21) in the unconstrained problem. Backward recursion leads to the optimal policy subject to the time consistency constraint. Of course, imposing the constraint leads to a loss in value. Thus, for example, with $(\alpha, \beta_1, \beta_2, \gamma, \delta) = (1, 1, 1, 1, 1)$ and starting with $x_1 = 0$, the value in the unconstrained problem is -0.6, and in the consistency constrained problem it is -0.625. The former is infeasible unless the policy maker can make a convincing binding commitment to the future policy. The latter is probably more robust and plausible.

Kydland and Prescott apply this general principle in an analysis of attempts to manage the inflation-unemployment tradeoff. In their setup, the discretionary policy leads to higher inflation and the same unemployment compared to a nondiscretionary price stabilization rule (which may, however, be infeasible since policymakers do not like to yield discretionary power).

16.5 TIME TO BUILD

Kydland and Prescott (1982) used a dynamic programming framework to model fluctuations or correlations in output, investment, consumption, productivity, inventories, hours, and capital stock. This research project did not concentrate on parameter estimation but rather on the capability of the model with reasonable parameter guesses to mimic second moments of actual data series. The basic finding is that the model could do so reasonably well, which is somewhat surprising because the model is quite simple and highly stylized. The results led to a boom in research activity.

The classical growth model (chapter 13) is modified in two respects. First, time is required to build new capital, specifically four quarters. Second, preferences of the representative individual have the form of the discounted infinite sum of period utilities, where period utility is a function of period consumption and a distributed lag on leisure. In this way, there is more room for intertemporal substitution than in the purely time-separable case. The agent in each period decides on labor supply, consumption, next-period inventory, and investment given the history, a noisy indicator of current productivity and the capital stock. The specification rests on the result that the competitive equilibrium is a Pareto optimum. Thus, it suffices to examine the utility maximization problem of the consumer subject to the budget and technology constraints. With parametric form assumptions, the steady state is calculated. Then, the problem is approximated by an linear-quadratic model around the steady state. The quadratic approximation is different from a Taylor expansion; for details see Kydland and Prescott (1982). The resulting laws of motion, essentially a highly restricted VAR, are then fit using a priori parameter estimates for some parameters; for example, the assumption that the required time to build is four quarters with equal contributions each quarter. Other parameters are fit using aggregate information. Still others are constrained or set using estimates of related parameters from studies in the literature. A few are estimated using the time series data at hand.

In fact, the model fits surprisingly well. Of course, it would fit better if it were actually estimated on the basis of the data available. There is, however, some evidence that the full parameter set is not well determined by these data. The authors report that the results were surprisingly insensitive to some of the parameter values they had selected. This means that the data set is not particularly informative about those parameters; if they were estimated, the estimates would not be precise. Substantively, the permanent component of the technology shock had to be large in order to explain some of the persistence properties of the data. This may not be surprising. The dependence of utility on the distributed lag of leisure turns out to be quite important. It allows employment to fluctuate more than productivity. The time-to-build assumption is also important, though not well determined in the data in the sense that the fit is also good with three or five quarters specified as the time required to achieve productivity.

This paper spurred a large and ongoing literature examining aggregate time series data as solutions to a dynamic programming problem. As might be expected, various combinations of constraints, production, and utility specifications yield reasonable fits to the data characteristics considered. This is not surprising since identification here relies heavily on theory; many preference and technology assumptions can provide a structural description of the same data series. Nevertheless, although identifying the "best" structural specification on the basis of data alone may be out of reach, ruling out bad specifications is feasible and productive.

16.6 NONSEPARABLE UTILITY

One of the features of the Kydland-Prescott (KP) model is utility that is not time-separable in leisure. This issue is taken up further by Eichenbaum, Hansen, and Singleton (1988). They specify a model with nonseparability in both consumption and leisure, using the functional form of the KP model. The model is fit to time series data, allowing some checking of the parametric assumptions made by Kydland and Prescott.

The motivating macroeconomic issue is that wages are generally smooth relative to hours worked and hours are procyclical. These features of the data can be explained by temporal nonseparabilities. Eichenbaum, Hansen, and Singleton (1988) do not fit a complete equilibrium model but concentrate on analysis of the consumption and leisure decisions of the representative consumer. Consumption service at time t, c_t^*, is given by a distributed lag of consumption $A(L)c_t$. Similarly, leisure services l_t^* are $B(L)l_t$. A is linear. Two specifications of B are considered, one linear and one corresponding to the assumed form in the KP model (an infinite distributed lag). The utility function is specified as

$$u(c^*, l^*) = \left(\left(c^{*\gamma} l^{*(1-\gamma)} \right)^\theta - 1 \right) \Big/ \theta, \qquad (16.29)$$

and the consumer chooses a consumption and leisure path that maximizes $E\Sigma_{t=0}^{\infty}\beta^t u(c_t^*, l_t^*)$. The utility parameter θ is estimated, and the model with $\theta = 0$ is interpreted as the log linear case, separable in consumption and leisure services. Intertemporal substitution is possible with the assumption that there is a one-period asset with price unity and random payoff r in the subsequent period. Utility maximization implies the marginal conditions

$$w_t MC_t = ML_t, \qquad (16.30)$$

$$E\left[r_{t+1} MC_{t+1}\right] = MC_t, \qquad (16.31)$$

where MC is the marginal utility of consumption and ML is the marginal utility of leisure (w is the wage). Note that these are not the same as MC^* and ML^*, the marginal utilities associated with the consumption and leisure services that enter the period utility function. These are related by, for example, $MC = E[A(L)^{-1}MC^*]$. These relations give two estimating equations. The data consist of monthly time series from January 1959 through December 1978 on consumption per capita, asset returns (1-month T bills), wages and hours worked.

There are two estimating equations with either five or six parameters, depending on which specification of the distributed lag on leisure is chosen. There are 16 orthogonality conditions, so a test of the overidentifying restrictions is available. With the KP model specification of leisure services (the infinite distributed lag), θ is clearly different from zero, indicating non-separable utility between leisure and consumption services within a period. The parameter γ is much less than $\frac{1}{3}$, the value assumed by Kydland and Prescott. The parameter α, reflecting the lagged effect of consumption on consumption services, is positive (about .35), indicating that consumption goods this month yield utility this month and next month. The coefficient on lagged leisure in leisure services is negative, contradicting the assumption of Kydland and Prescott, though it is not precisely estimated. When the linear specification of the leisure services function is used, θ is close to zero, indicating separability within periods of consumption and leisure services. The lagged effect of consumption remains positive, and that of leisure remains negative. The estimates are sensitive to changes in the definition of the wage series. Testing the overidentifying restrictions rejects the model. The latter finding cannot be taken too seriously, as tightly specified structural models (micro as well as macro—consider the search model) are normally outfit by reduced forms. This does not mean they are not useful. Indeed, Kydland and Prescott argue that they do not bother to compare their fit with that of the reduced-form VAR, essentially since the answer is obvious.

Generally, this project found convincing evidence that preferences are non-time-separable both in consumption and in leisure. Leisure today reduces the value of leisure in the subsequent period. The first-order conditions from a dynamic maximization problem, the Euler equations, provide a convenient and sensible route to interpretable estimating equations.

16.7 PREFERENCES OF MONETARY AUTHORITIES

Suppose monetary authorities have preferences over price surprises, inflation rates, and nominal interest rates. In principle, one should be able to recover these preferences from movements in prices, inflation, and interest rates, given the relevant transition distribution. The transition distribution here is generated by a structural economic model. Broadbent and Barro (1997) undertook this project.

Broadbent and Barro studied price, interest rate, output, and money quarterly data from 1954 to 1995 to study the monetary authority's preferences for the tradeoff between price surprises and inflation. They first propose a simple model of the private sector, with three stochastic equations giving supply as a function of price surprises, demand as a function of the real interest rate, and money demand as a function of the price level, the output, and the nominal interest rate. Two additional equations are equilibrium conditions for the output and money markets. The sixth equation is an identity defining the real rate. Contemporaneous prices and output are not observed. The money supply is the policy variable of the monetary authority. Suppose first that the monetary authority chooses money supply to minimize the expected discounted sum of price-forecasting errors,

$$E \sum \beta^t (p_t - E_{t-1} p_t)^2. \tag{16.32}$$

Then it is shown that the optimal innovation in the money supply is a function of current and lagged nominal interest rates, lagged output, lagged real rate, and the predictable part of a composite error term. If current prices were observable, then the objective function could be made zero, so the information structure matters (and is reasonable). With this objective function, optimization leaves the rate of inflation and the nominal interest rate undetermined, reflecting a general result in this type of model. Basically, expected inflation is fully accommodated by monetary policy. These can be tied down by adding an interest rate target or an inflation target.

A nominal interest rate target can be hit exactly without affecting the price-forecasting objective function. Suppose, however, that the target is inflation. The authority wants inflation π to hit a target value π^*. The target process π_t^* is exogenous. The new objective function is given by

$$E \sum \beta^t (p_t - E_{t-1} p_t)^2 + \chi E \sum \beta^t \left(\pi_t - \pi_t^*\right)^2. \qquad (16.33)$$

Here, the expectation $E_{t-1}\pi_t^*$ can be fully controlled, but if there are surprises $\pi_t^* - E_{t-1}\pi_t^*$, then there is a genuine tradeoff between the two parts of the objective function.

Before fitting the model, Broadbent and Barro note that the rules-versus-discretion issue has not really arisen so far since the monetary authorities have the same preferences as everyone else in the economy. This can be changed by supposing that the authorities have a positive target for the price surprise, leading to increased output. In this case, with discretion, the inflation rate is too high, reflecting the Kydland and Prescott (1977) result. With commitment, the inflation rate is lower, but still higher than optimal when the objective functions agree. The nominal interest rate is lower with commitment.

Broadbent and Barro develop four estimating equations for the four data series. These equations are in the form of a highly restricted autoregressive integrated moving average (ARIMA) system, with the restrictions resulting from the structural specification. The key parameter is χ, the weight given to the inflation target. The estimate is about 3.0, with a standard error of about 1.6. In keeping with the conventions in this literature, a comparison of the specification to the unrestricted ARIMA is not reported. Broadbent and Barro clearly illustrate the possibility of identifying preference parameters from macro data using an optimization structure. They note that extensions allowing structural breaks associated with changes in the policy regime improve the fit and precision of the estimated parameters.

16.8 DYNAMIC LABOR SUPPLY

The response of hours of work to wage changes is a crucial ingredient in areas of economics from policy analysis—What are the potential effects of a productivity-enhancing training program?—to macroeconomics—How and why do hours vary over the cycle? Measurement of this quantity is difficult. A coefficient on wages in a cross-section regression of hours of work on wages is difficult to interpret. Does it measure the effect of wages as wages change over the life cycle for a given worker? Does it measure the potential effect of a one-period contemporaneous wage shock? Does it measure the effects of a change in the life cycle pattern of wages? Heckman and MaCurdy (1980) and MaCurdy (1981) address this question in a life cycle model of consumption and labor supply. This model takes into account that labor supply decisions in any period depend on the entire lifetime pattern of wages, as well as on assets. The model is cleverly formulated, so that it is amenable to estimation using panel data, without requiring data on the lifetime pattern of wages for each individual or on the individual's asset stock.

The consumer maximizes the intertemporal utility function

$$\sum_{t=0}^{T} \beta^t u(c_t, n_t), \tag{16.34}$$

where c_t and n_t are consumption and labor supplied in period t, u is increasing and concave in c and decreasing in n, and β is a subjective discount factor, subject to the budget constraint

$$A_0 = \sum_{t=0}^{T} \delta^t (c_t - w_t n_t), \tag{16.35}$$

where δ is $1/(1+r)$ and r is the interest rate. A_0 and the real wage sequence $\{w_t\}$ are exogenous and known. We can write

$$V^0(A_0) = \max \sum_{t=0}^{T} \beta^t u(c_t, n_t), \tag{16.36}$$

where the maximization is over the sequences $\{c_t\}$ and $\{n_t\}$, subject to the budget constraint. The Bellman equation is

$$V^t(A_t) = \max_{c,n} \{u(c_t, n_t) + \beta V^{t+1}(A_{t+1})\}, \tag{16.37}$$

with transition equation

$$A_{t+1} = \delta^{-1} A_t - \delta^{-1}(c_t - w_t n_t). \tag{16.38}$$

The first-order conditions are

$$u_1^t - (\beta/\delta)V_1^{t+1} = 0, \tag{16.39}$$

$$u_2^t + (\beta/\delta)w_t V_1^{t+1} = 0. \tag{16.40}$$

The derivative V_1^t is the marginal value of an additional unit of the asset received in period t. Since assets are completely fungible in this model, we have

$$V_1^{t+1} = (\beta/\delta)^{-1} V_1^t \tag{16.41}$$

or

$$V_1^t = (\beta/\delta)^{-t} V_1^0 \tag{16.42}$$

along the optimal path. Note that β/δ is likely to be nearly unity. The term $V_1^0(A_0)$ codes the effect of the entire wage path as well as the asset value for the individual.

The key here is that V_1^0 is an individual specific number capturing the life cycle planning data for the individual. With an appropriate choice of utility function, for example,

$$u(c, n) = c^\alpha - n^\theta, \tag{16.43}$$

the labor supply function in period t is

$$\log(n_t) = (\theta - 1)^{-1} \left(-\log \theta - t \log (\beta/\delta) + \log \left(V_{1i}^0 \right) + \log(w_{it}) \right). \tag{16.44}$$

As a practical matter, a multiplicative factor $h(x_{it}, \gamma)$ could be added in the utility function, $u(c, n) = c^\alpha + h(x_{it}, \gamma)n^\theta$, reflecting the effects of observable individual characteristics. The result is to add a term in $\log(h(x_{it}, \gamma))$ in the labor supply function. A time- and individual-specific additive error term is assumed. The term involving V_1 is an individual-specific, time-constant fixed effect. As pointed out by Heckman and MaCurdy, the term cannot be modeled as a random effect orthogonal to regressors (specifically, to the wage) since it is a function of the wage sequence, etc. However, with panel data, a fixed-effect specification can be used. The coefficient on the log of wages is interpreted as an intertemporal substitution parameter, giving the response of labor supply to wage changes (foreseen) over an individual's life cycle.

Heckman and MaCurdy maximize (16.34) directly, imposing the constraint (16.35), using a Lagrangian with multiplier λ. The resulting estimating equations are then referred to as "λ-constant" consumption and labor supply functions. Of course, λ is $V_1^0(A_0)$.

MaCurdy (1981) estimates this model using data from the Michigan Panel Study of Income Dynamics (PSID). He focuses on married white men 25–46 years old in 1967 and uses data from 1967–1977. This sample selection allows avoidance of the issue of labor force participation. Estimated intertemporal substitution parameters are small. By turning to estimates of the fixed effects and attempting to explain these on the basis of observables, MaCurdy is able to estimate asset elasticities (very small) and other elasticities. Heckman and MaCurdy (1980) focus on married women and include an analysis of the labor force participation decision. They find a very small response to transitory income shocks, a finding consistent with the permanent-income hypothesis.

16.9 EFFECTS OF U.S. FARM SUBSIDIES

Farming in the United States, like farming in many countries, is heavily
subsidized. These subsidies directly affect exports. Much trade negotiation
is geared toward the reduction of farm subsidies and the opening of agricultural markets. At present, countries often apply protective measures as
bargaining chips in order to achieve favorable multilateral agreements. The
system of subsidies changes over time according to international negotia-
tions and political expediency. Evaluating the effect of agricultural policies
can be difficult, as dynamics depend on expectations. Dynamics also enter
the farmers' planning problems since subsidies for reduced production depend to some extent on *base acreage*, which is an average of acreage planted
in previous years. Thus, increasing planting now can lead to future subsidies
if the program is expected to continue or expand.

Fisher and de Gorter (1992) use dynamic programming to analyze the
effect of farm policies on corn, cotton, rice, and wheat, the principal
export crops of the United States. The supply behavior of farmers is analyzed. Farmers incur costs of $Fx + vu$, where x is base acreage, F is a fixed
cost, u is acreage planted, and v is variable cost if the acreage planted is
less than the base acreage. If the acreage planted is greater than the base
acreage (note that base acreage is not the same as capacity), the cost is
$Fu + vu + \alpha(u - x)^2$. Two types of subsidies are analyzed, one paying
according to the difference between the world price of the crop and the target price, in proportion to acreage planted. The other subsidy, a "diversion"
payment, is paid according to the amount by which acreage planted falls
below base acreage. At the time of planting, the yield and the world price
are unknown. Farmers have the option to participate in the programs or not.
Current planting affects future base acreage according to a deterministic
formula. This problem is set up as a dynamic programming problem with
state variable x, base acreage, and control u, acreage planted. The state
space, control space, and transition distribution are discretized. The cost
function was estimated using historical averages. The only estimated parameter was the adjustment cost parameter α. The discount factor was fixed
at $(1.05)^{-1}$. Farms were allocated to two groups, highly productive and less
productive. These problems were solved separately and, for policy simulations, output was aggregated. External estimates of the demand side were
combined with the rather elaborate supply model in the simulations.

The results show that farming in the United States would generally be
unprofitable without subsidies. Most of the policies that reduce subsidies
would make low-yield farms unprofitable. Subsidy programs do reduce
output. Diversion payments do not restrict production in the short run. None
of the policies has a large effect on prices since demand is highly

elastic. Freezing base acreage, a policy considered but not implemented, raises prices. Policies emphasizing supply controls, increasing diversion payments and requirements, are problematic. Farmers with large bases might participate; smaller farmers will opt out and build up base acreage for future years. Increasing the amount of acreage a farmer must leave unplanted makes high-yield farms with high base acreages opt out of the programs.

This study illustrates that dynamic programming can be used to study quantitatively programs that have been proposed but never implemented. Thus, experience with proposed policies is not required to estimate their effects, given a structural model.

16.10 EXERCISES

1. Show that the value (16.28) of the control from backward recursion is greater in magnitude than when time consistency of the plan is imposed. Discuss the implications for the value of the objective function.

2. Consider the Euler equation (16.9) for the case of a riskless asset. Derive a condition on γ that makes consumption follow a martingale process. Interpret the resulting value of γ in terms of the criterion (16.7).

3. Show that the Arrow-Pratt coefficient of relative risk aversion with respect to consumption in the nonseparable utility model (16.29) is given by $1 - \gamma\theta$.

16.11 REFERENCES

The literature is huge. For life cycle consumption, see the early formulation by Friedman (1956) and the review by Deaton (1987). Heckman (1974) discusses joint consumption and labor supply models. For monetary policy, see Taylor (1999), Clarida, Gali, and Gertler (1999), Woodford (2003), and the included references. For real business cycles, see Eichenbaum (1991), King and Rebelo (1999), and the included references. Additional evidence on the "time-to-build" model is given by Altug (1989). Hansen and Jagannathan (1991) discuss further use of asset price data in dynamic models. A further application of the λ-constant dynamic labor supply model in studying the effects of tax reform is Ziliak and Kniesner (1999).

Chapter Seventeen

Finance Application: Futures Hedging

17.1 HEDGING STRATEGIES

Consider hedging a future claim through trading in safe and risky assets. Specifically, let the future claim to be hedged be represented by a random variable taking the value X in the future time period T. The goal is to set up a dynamic trading strategy in, say, stocks and cash, that replicates X as closely as possible at T. If the market is dynamically complete (see chapter 14), then any contingent claim can be replicated exactly, i.e., there is a portfolio-trading strategy using stocks and cash whose portfolio value at T is X. Thus, hedging is perfect in this case. The initial cost of setting up the portfolio is then the initial fair value of an asset paying X at T.

If markets are incomplete, hedging is imperfect. We study possible hedging strategies in this case. Let s_t be the number of shares of stock in the portfolio at time t and let b_t be the dollar amount held in safe assets (cash) at t. The stock price is denoted by p_t, and total portfolio wealth by w_t. The budget constraint at t requires w_t to be no greater than the payoffs to stock and cash investments at $t - 1$ plus any additional investments (cash infusions) i_t made at t. Depending on portfolio performance, such additional investments may be called for in order to keep the portfolio on track toward X at T. Thus, we have

$$w_t = s_t\, p_t + b_t$$
$$\leq s_{t-1} p_t + b_{t-1} + i_t. \tag{17.1}$$

With all funds invested, the budget constraint is satisfied with equality. Also, adding and subtracting last period's stock investment value $s_{t-1} p_{t-1}$ yields

$$w_t = s_{t-1}(p_t - p_{t-1}) + s_{t-1} p_{t-1} + b_{t-1} + i_t$$
$$= s_{t-1}(p_t - p_{t-1}) + w_{t-1} + i_t. \tag{17.2}$$

Let the initial time period where the trading strategy is set up be $t = 0$. A *self-financing trading strategy* is one where $i_t = 0, t = 1, \ldots, T - 1$; i.e., the only cash infusions are in the first and last periods. Specifically, without loss of generality, a final cash payment i_T is used to obtain the hedge

$$w_T = X. \tag{17.3}$$

In addition, there is always the initial setup cost $w_0 = s_0 p_0 + b_0$ (the infusions, $i_1, i_2, \ldots$, are additional). Note that for a self-financing trading strategy,

$$w_T = w_0 + \sum_{t=0}^{T-1} s_t (p_{t+1} - p_t) + i_T. \tag{17.4}$$

For a non-self-financing strategy,

$$w_T = w_0 + \sum_{t=0}^{T-1} (s_t (p_{t+1} - p_t) + i_{t+1}). \tag{17.5}$$

The difference between the two lies in whether only the terminal infusion i_T or a sequence of supplementary investments i_t must be made to maintain the strategy. In either case, the investor would ideally prefer a perfect hedge with $w_T = X$ and no additional investments. We assume that the objective is to minimize the risk of these; i.e., the objective is

$$V_0(p_0) = \min_{w_0, \{i_t\}_{t=1}^{T}, \{s_t\}_{t=0}^{T-1}} \left\{ E_0 \sum_{t=1}^{T} \beta^t i_t^2 : w_T = X \right\}. \tag{17.6}$$

We have from (17.2) that

$$i_t = w_t - w_{t-1} - s_{t-1}(p_t - p_{t-1}), \tag{17.7}$$

so we equivalently have

$$V_0(p_0) = \min_{\{w_t, s_t\}_{t=0}^{T-1}} E_0 \sum_{t=0}^{T-1} \beta^t (w_{t+1} - w_t - s_t (p_{t+1} - p_t))^2, \tag{17.8}$$

with the terminal condition $w_T = X$ (actually, this objective has been divided by an inconsequential β). We consider first the case of non-self-financing strategies; i.e., running inflows i_t into the strategy are allowed. Bellman's equation is

$$V_t(p_t) = \min_{w_t, s_t} E_t \{ (w_{t+1} - w_t - s_t (p_{t+1} - p_t))^2 + \beta V_{t+1}(p_{t+1}) \}. \tag{17.9}$$

As $V_{t+1}(p_{t+1})$ does not depend on current controls w_t, s_t, the problem is simply to minimize current conditional mean squared error in reaching w_{t+1} using $w_t + s_t (p_{t+1} - p_t)$, given p_t, by choice of w_t and s_t, and treating w_{t+1} as a given random variable. Of course, this is the conditional mean squared value of the (error or) investment i_{t+1} required to fill this gap. The problem is one of regression of w_{t+1} on $p_{t+1} - p_t$ and a constant, and the solution is

$$s_t = \frac{\text{cov}_t(w_{t+1}, p_{t+1})}{\text{var}_t(p_{t+1})}, \tag{17.10}$$

$$w_t = E_t(w_{t+1}) - s_t E_t(p_{t+1} - p_t). \tag{17.11}$$

The first quantity (17.10) is the optimal hedge ratio (compare (14.60) in the dynamically complete market case). The minimized conditional mean squared error is

$$
\begin{aligned}
E_t i_{t+1}^2 &= \text{var}_t(w_{t+1}) - s_t^2 \, \text{var}_t(p_{t+1}) \\
&= \text{var}_t(w_{t+1})(1 - R_t^2),
\end{aligned} \tag{17.12}
$$

with R_t^2 the conditional coefficient of determination in the regression, which would be unity in a complete market. This uses the presence of a constant in the regression, so that the mean squared error is a variance,

$$
E_t i_{t+1}^2 = \text{var}_t(i_{t+1}), \tag{17.13}
$$

$$
E_t i_{t+1} = 0. \tag{17.14}
$$

The latter condition (17.14) shows that while not self-financing, the trading strategy is mean-self-financing (and market completeness would allow taking it self-financing).

The determination of the regressand (next period portfolio wealth) w_{t+1} follows from backward recursion in the dynamic programming problem. Recall that $w_T = X$, the hedging requirement. At $T - 1$, from (17.11),

$$
w_{T-1} = E_{T-1}(X) - s_{T-1} E_{T-1}(p_T - p_{T-1}). \tag{17.15}
$$

Iteration produces

$$
w_t = E_t\left(X - \sum_{j=t}^{T-1} s_j E_j(p_{j+1} - p_j)\right). \tag{17.16}
$$

In particular, the required initial investment is

$$
w_0 = E_0\left(X - \sum_{j=0}^{T-1} s_j E_j(p_{j+1} - p_j)\right). \tag{17.17}
$$

This is the cost of setting up the hedge. As the hedge is in fact perfect, $w_T = X$ (obtained through the infusion of funds), this is related to the fair value or price of X, but it is not the same. The fair value or price would involve risk premia in this incomplete market setting, and the particular minimum mean squared hedging error objective function need not be related to actual pricing. Instead, it serves as a tool for generating subjectively preferred hedging rules.

The supplementary hedging investments are

$$i_t = w_t - w_{t-1} - s_{t-1}(p_t - p_{t-1})$$

$$= E_t\left(X - \sum_{j=t-1}^{T-1} s_j E_j(p_{j+1} - p_j)\right)$$

$$-E_{t-1}\left(X - \sum_{j=t-1}^{T-1} s_j E_j(p_{j+1} - p_j)\right)$$

$$- s_{t-1}(p_t - E_{t-1}(p_t)); \qquad (17.18)$$

i.e., the expectations revisions with respect to two terms—the stock price p_t and the extent to which the stock market gains from $t-1$ forward will cover X.

It is worth inspecting what happens when the stock price process is in fact a martingale,

$$p_t = E_t(p_{t+1}), \qquad (17.19)$$

i.e., the random walk model for stock prices. In this case, from (17.11) and (17.18),

$$w_t = E_t(X), \qquad (17.20)$$

$$i_t = E_t(X) - E_{t-1}(X), \qquad (17.21)$$

$$s_t = \frac{\text{cov}_t(E_{t+1}(X), p_{t+1})}{\text{var}_t(p_{t+1})}. \qquad (17.22)$$

Thus, portfolio wealth (17.20) takes a simple form and is now a martingale,

$$w_t = E_t(E_{t+1}(X))$$
$$= E_t(w_{t+1}). \qquad (17.23)$$

Hedging investments (17.21) are again expectations revisions like in (17.18), but now just with respect to X. The optimal hedge ratio (17.22) is more explicitly expressed in terms of X and the stock price than in (17.10) and is readily interpreted.

17.2 SELF-FINANCING TRADING STRATEGIES

Next, relax again the martingale condition (17.19) on p_t but consider the problem of hedging using a self-financing trading strategy. The objective is still the same, but the restrictions $i_t = 0, t = 1, \ldots, T-1$, are added.

This implies that i_t cannot be used to set current portfolio wealth w_t at the desired level. Instead, from (17.2),

$$w_t = s_{t-1}(p_t - p_{t-1}) + w_{t-1} \tag{17.24}$$

becomes an additional state variable. We have

$$V_t^s(p_t, w_t) = \min_{s_t} \beta E_t V_{t+1}^s(p_{t+1}, s_t(p_{t+1} - p_t) + w_t) \tag{17.25}$$

for $t \leq T - 2$ since, here, $i_{t+1} = 0$. The superscript s on V indicates self-financing. The first-order condition for s_t is

$$E_t \left\{ \frac{\partial V_{t+1}^s}{\partial w_{t+1}} (p_{t+1}, s_t(p_{t+1} - p_t) + w_t) (p_{t+1} - p_t) \right\} = 0. \tag{17.26}$$

At $t = T - 1$, the situation is different since i_{t+1} may be nonzero, i.e., $w_T = X$ requires $i_T = X - w_{T-1} - s_{T-1}(p_T - p_{T-1})$, and

$$V_{T-1}^s(p_{T-1}, w_{T-1}) = \min_{s_{T-1}} \beta E_{T-1}(X - w_{T-1} - s_{T-1}(p_T - p_{T-1}))^2. \tag{17.27}$$

The first-order condition is

$$E_{T-1}\{(X - w_{T-1} - s_{T-1}(p_T - p_{T-1}))(p_T - p_{T-1})\} = 0. \tag{17.28}$$

This is recognized as a regression through the origin, the optimal hedge ratio being

$$s_{T-1} = \frac{E_{t-1}\{(X - w_{T-1})(p_T - p_{T-1})\}}{E_{T-1}\{(p_T - p_{T-1})^2\}}. \tag{17.29}$$

This differs somewhat from the ordinary (through the means) regression coefficient (17.10) for the optimal hedge ratio in the non-self-financing trading strategy.

Inserting the optimal hedge ratio, say s_{T-1}^* from (17.29) in (17.27), we have

$$V_{T-1}^s(p_{T-1}, w_{T-1}) = \beta E_{T-1}(X - w_{T-1} - s_{T-1}^*(p_T - p_{T-1}))^2. \tag{17.30}$$

By the envelope theorem (see (13.40)),

$$\frac{\partial V_{T-1}^s}{\partial w_{T-1}}(p_{T-1}, w_{T-1}) = -2\beta E_{T-1}(X - w_{T-1} - s_{T-1}^*(p_T - p_{T-1}))$$

$$= 2\beta(w_{T-1} + s_{T-1}^* E_{T-1}(p_T - p_{T-1}) - E_{T-1}(X)). \tag{17.31}$$

Thus, combining (17.24), (17.26), and (17.31), the first-order condition for s_{T-2} is

$$E_{T-2}\{(s_{T-2}(p_{T-1} - p_{T-2}) + w_{T-2} + s_{T-1}^* E_{T-1}(p_T - p_{T-1})$$
$$- E_{T-1}(X))(p_{T-1} - p_{T-2})\} = 0. \qquad (17.32)$$

It follows that

$$s_{T-2} = \frac{E_{T-2}\{(E_{T-1}(X) - w_{T-2} - s_{T-1}^* E_{T-1}(p_T - p_{T-1}))(p_{T-1} - p_{T-2})\}}{E_{T-2}\{(p_{T-1} - p_{T-2})^2\}}. \qquad (17.33)$$

Thus, we are able to derive the important optimal revisions in hedge ratios. Continuing the recursions, for the first-order condition for s_{T-3}, $\partial V_{T-2}^s / \partial w_{T-2}$ is needed. We have

$$V_{T-2}^s(p_{T-2}, w_{T-2}) = \min_{s_{T-2}} \beta E_{T-2} V_{T-1}^s(p_{T-1}, s_{T-2}(p_{T-1} - p_{T-2}) + w_{T-2}), \qquad (17.34)$$

and by the envelope theorem,

$$\frac{\partial V^s}{\partial w_{T-2}}(p_{T-2}, w_{T-2}) = \beta E_{T-2} \frac{\partial V_{T-1}^s}{\partial w_{T-1}}$$
$$\times (p_{T-1}, s_{T-2}(p_{T-1} - p_{T-2}) + w_{T-2})$$
$$= 2\beta^2 E_{T-2}(w_{T-2} + s_{T-2}(p_{T-1} - p_{T-2})$$
$$+ s_{T-1} E_{T-1}(p_T - p_{T-1}) - E_{T-1}(X)). \qquad (17.35)$$

The first-order condition for s_{T-3} is then

$$E_{T-3}\{E_{T-2}(w_{T-3} + s_{T-3}(p_{T-2} - p_{T-3}) + s_{T-2}(p_{T-1} - p_{T-2}))$$
$$+ s_{T-1} E_{T-1}(p_T - p_{T-1}) - E_{T-1}(X))(p_{T-2} - p_{T-3})\} = 0. \qquad (17.36)$$

It follows that

$$s_{T-3} = \frac{E_{T-3}\{E_{T-2}(X - w_{T-3} - s_{T-2}(p_{T-1} - p_{T-2}) - s_{T-1}(p_T - p_{T-1}))(p_{T-2} - p_{T-3})\}}{E_{T-3}\{(p_{T-2} - p_{T-3})^2\}}. \qquad (17.37)$$

We get the general solution for the optimal self-financing incomplete market hedge ratios,

$$s_t = \frac{E_t\left\{\left(X - w_t - \sum_{j=t+1}^{T-1} s_j(p_{j+1} - p_j)\right)(p_{t+1} - p_t)\right\}}{E_t\{(p_{t+1} - p_t)^2\}}, \qquad (17.38)$$

the coefficient of regression (through the origin) of the portion of the final hedging error not covered by i_T or current stock investments on $p_{t+1} - p_t$.

At $t = 0$,

$$V_0^s(p_0) = E_0 \left(X - w_0 - \sum_{j=0}^{T-1} s_j(p_{j+1} - p_j) \right)^2. \tag{17.39}$$

There are now two possibilities. Either w_0 is taken as given, i.e., it determines the initial budget for hedging purposes. In this case, the previous formula (17.38) for s_t, $t = 0, 1, \ldots, T-1$, determines the hedging strategy, and dependence on w_0 comes in through $w_t = w_0 + \Sigma_{j=0}^{t-1} s_j(p_{j+1} - p_j)$. Thus, s_t is calculated using both w_0 and $s_0, \ldots, s_{t-1}$ from the hedge ratio formula. Alternatively, $V_0^s(p_0)$ in (17.39) is minimized with respect to w_0. This can be done since w_0 enters quite explicitly, both directly and through s_t. Here, s_t depends explicitly on $s_{t+1}, \ldots, s_{T-1}$ and on $s_0, \ldots, s_{T-1}$ through w_t, which also involves w_0. Therefore, there are T equations involving the T unknowns $\partial s_t / \partial w_0$, $t = 0, \ldots, T-1$. This allows solving for these unknowns and using them in the first-order condition $\partial V_0^s / \partial w_0 = 0$ for w_0. We shall not pursue this further since w_0 plays the role of a cash infusion into the investment problem, and in any case more flexible cash infusion and hence lower total hedging error have already been solved for optimally in the non-self-financing case (see (17.10)).

The martingale stock price case is of interest for the self-financing trading strategy problem, too. In this case,

$$s_t = \frac{\text{cov}_t(X, p_{t+1})}{\text{var}_t(p_{t+1})}, \tag{17.40}$$

the ordinary (through the means) regression coefficient, and portfolio wealth w_t follows a martingale. In this case, since s_t does not depend on w_0, this formula gives the optimum for given w_0 directly. In addition, it is easy to minimize V_0 with respect to w_0. In particular, $w_0 = E_0(X)$ is optimal.

Most of the hedging literature for incomplete markets considers either a one-period problem or locally risk-minimizing strategies, with a separate objective function for each period (see Schweizer (1995) and the references therein), but by weighing together the contributions from different time periods in the objective, our approach allows using dynamic programming and recovering the classical regression-type hedge ratios, showing when generalizations of these apply.

17.3 ESTIMATION

Haigh and Holt (2002) provide an empirical comparison of the relative merits of static and dynamic hedge ratios. Specifically, time-varying hedge

ratios are estimated by fitting a bivariate generalized autoregressive conditional heteroskedasticity (GARCH) model to spot and futures prices and
using the estimated time-varying variances and covariances from the model
to calculate hedge ratios. Let $y_t = (x_t, \phi_t)'$, where x_t denotes the spot price
and ϕ_t the futures price. The first differences are modelled as

$$\Delta y_t = \mu + e_t, \tag{17.41}$$

$$e_t \sim N(0, H_t), \tag{17.42}$$

$$H_t = W'W + A'e_{t-1}e'_{t-1}A + B'H_{t-1}B, \tag{17.43}$$

with μ the 2×1 mean parameter and W, A, and B the 2×2 matrices
of variance-covariance parameters. Only 3 parameters are identified in W,
which may be taken upper triangular without loss of generality. This leaves
13 parameters to be estimated by maximum likelihood. This is an application of the Engle and Kroner (1995) version of multivariate GARCH (here,
a bivariate GARCH(1,1) specification), known as BEKK from an earlier
working paper by Baba, Engle, Kraft, and Kroner (1990), which ensures
positive semidefiniteness of the consecutive conditional variance-covariance
matrices $H_t = \{h_{ij,t}\}_{i,j=1,2}$. For comparison, note that in the univariate
autoregressive conditional heteroskedasticity (ARCH) model introduced by
Engle (1982), y_t and hence H_t are scalars, and $B = 0$, but p lags $A_j e_{t-j}^2$
are allowed in the ARCH(p) version. The GARCH was introduced by
Bollerslev (1986), adding q terms $B_j H_{t-j}$ in GARCH(p, q). Many variations exist, including different ways to build multivariate versions. Other
applications to futures hedging include Myers (1991), Baillie and Myers
(1991), and Kroner and Sultan (1993). The underlying may be a commodity
(soybeans, sugar, copper, etc.), foreign exchange, a stock index, or similar.

Given data y_t, $t = 1, \ldots, N$, the conditional GARCH log likelihood
function is (see (10.116) for the univariate case)

$$\log L(\theta) = \sum_{t=3}^{N} \log L_t(\theta), \tag{17.44}$$

where θ is the vector of parameters (in the application, parameters of
μ, W, A, and B) to be estimated, and

$$\log L_t(\theta) = -2\log(\sqrt{2\pi}) - \tfrac{1}{2}\log|H_t|$$
$$-\tfrac{1}{2}(\Delta y_t - \mu)' H_t^{-1}(\Delta y_t - \mu). \tag{17.45}$$

This requires setting H_3 at a suitable value. Of course, $e_2 = y_2 - y_1 - \mu$ is
available, given μ, but an initial condition for H_2 is required. As $N \to \infty$,

consistency of the maximum likelihood estimator $\hat{\theta}$ obtains regardless of the choice of H_2, even if the true distribution of e_t is non-normal (but with mean zero and variance H_t). A reasonable initial choice for H_2 is the unconditional sample variance-covariance matrix $\widehat{\Sigma}_{\Delta y}$ of Δy_t. After finding $\hat{\theta}$, a sequence $H_t (t \geq 3)$ is obtained. One possibility is to use $\Sigma_{t=3}^{N} H_t / (N-2)$ as a revised initial value for H_2 and reestimate. The asymptotic properties of the resulting estimator are unchanged under correct model specification, but any change is a sign of warning. Of course, the procedure may be iterated. In any case, $\hat{\theta}$ (whether after one or more iterations) is usually treated as asymptotically normal for inference purposes. In fact, the asymptotic distribution of GARCH estimators is a delicate issue. For robustness against non-normality of e_t, Bollerslev and Wooldridge (1992) use a similar likelihood function but calculate standard errors not from the square roots of the diagonal of minus the inverse of the Hessian $\mathcal{H}_N$ but from the *sandwich formula*,

$$\text{var}(\hat{\theta}_N) = \mathcal{H}_n^{-1} O_N \mathcal{H}_N^{-1}, \tag{17.46}$$

with O_N the outer-product matrix of the score, i.e., N times the sample variance of the score contributions $\partial \log L_t(\hat{\theta}) / \partial \theta$ (see White (1982) on quasi-maximum likelihood (QML) inference). General GARCH(p, q) models require using similar initial estimates (e.g., $\widehat{\Sigma}_{\Delta y}$) for $H_2, \ldots, H_{q+1}$. Bollerslev (1987) suggests using other parametrized distributions (in particular, the t-distribution) for e_t to avoid misspecification with respect to normality and uses the resulting inverse Hessian for standard errors. Of course, generalized method of moments (GMM) could be used, thus avoiding the need for a specific distributional assumption.

Upon estimation, the relevant time-varying conditional hedge ratio is obtained as

$$\begin{aligned} s_t &= \frac{\text{cov}_{t-1}(x_t, \phi_t)}{\text{var}_{t-1}(\phi_t)} \\ &= \frac{h_{12,t}}{h_{22,t}}. \end{aligned} \tag{17.47}$$

This should be compared to a simple (unconditional) ordinary least squares (OLS) regression coefficient of Δx_t on $\Delta \phi_t$ for the hedge ratio. Of course, (17.47) is well motivated only for a position entered at $t-1$. For longer hedges, our dynamic programming analysis suggests using

$$s_{t-k,k} = \frac{\text{cov}_{t-k}(x_t, \phi_{t-k+1})}{\text{var}_{t-k}(\phi_{t-k+1})} \tag{17.48}$$

if ϕ_t is a martingale (see (17.12)). Here, the notation $s_{t-k,k}$ indicates a k-period ahead hedge, applicable at $t-k$.

Haigh and Holt (2002) do not explicitly use dynamic programming, but they do impose the martingale assumption on ϕ_t and minimize the total variance of hedging error between $t-k$ and t to obtain the similar expression divided by a discount rate. It is not addressed how to calculate these hedge ratios for $k > 1$ (Haigh and Holt consider $k = 1, \ldots, 4$) from the estimated GARCH model. In fact, we may now show that because a GARCH model is used, the longer-term hedge ratios equal the short-term hedge ratios:

$$s_{t-k,k} = s_{t-k,1}. \qquad (17.49)$$

To see this, recall the following identity for conditional covariances,

$$\text{cov}_{t-2}(Y, Z) = E_{t-2}(\text{cov}_{t-1}(Y, Z)) + \text{cov}_{t-2}(E_{t-1}(Y), E_{t-1}(Z)), \qquad (17.50)$$

which is easily verified for arbitrary random variables Y, Z with second moments using the definition of conditional covariance,

$$\text{cov}_{t-1}(Y, Z) = E_{t-1}(YZ) - E_{t-1}(Y)E_{t-1}(Z). \qquad (17.51)$$

Calculation of $s_{t-k,k}$ is illustrated for $k = 2$; i.e.,

$$
\begin{aligned}
\text{cov}_{t-1}(x_t, \phi_{t-1}) &= \text{cov}_{t-2}(\Delta x_t + \Delta x_{t-1}, \Delta \phi_{t-1}) \\
&= \text{cov}_{t-2}(\Delta x_t, \Delta \phi_{t-1}) + \text{cov}_{t-2}(\Delta x_{t-1}, \Delta \phi_{t-1}) \\
&= \text{cov}_{t-2}(\Delta x_t, \Delta \phi_{t-1}) + h_{12,t-2}. \qquad (17.52)
\end{aligned}
$$

Using the identity (17.50), we have

$$
\begin{aligned}
\text{cov}_{t-2}(\Delta x_t, \Delta \phi_{t-1}) &= E_{t-2}(\text{cov}_{t-1}(\Delta x_t, \Delta \phi_{t-1})) \\
&\quad + \text{cov}_{t-2}(E_{t-1}(\Delta x_t), E_{t-1}(\Delta \phi_{t-1})). \qquad (17.53)
\end{aligned}
$$

Obviously, since $\Delta \phi_{t-1}$ is known at $t - 1$, the first term on the right is zero. Since in the GARCH model

$$
\begin{aligned}
E_{t-1}(\Delta x_t) &= E_{t-1}(\mu_1 + e_{1,t}) \\
&= \mu_1, \qquad (17.54)
\end{aligned}
$$

a constant, the second term on the right vanishes, too, and $\text{cov}_{t-2}(\Delta x_t, \Delta \phi_{t-1}) = 0$. Thus, from (17.52), $\text{cov}_{t-2}(x_t, \phi_{t-1}) = h_{12,t-2}$ (which is also $\text{cov}_{t-2}(x_{t-1}, \phi_{t-1})$), so

$$
\begin{aligned}
s_{t-2,2} &= \frac{\text{cov}_{t-2}(x_{t-1}, \phi_{t-1})}{\text{var}_{t-2}(\phi_{t-1})} \\
&= s_{t-2,1}. \qquad (17.55)
\end{aligned}
$$

An immediate extension to more periods shows $s_{t-k,k} = s_{t-k,1}$. The upshot is that when hedging a claim paying off at t, the consecutive hedge ratios applied at $t-k, t-k+1, \ldots$, may all be set as if a claim paying off one period ahead were hedged in each period. Of course, as conditional variances and covariances from the GARCH model change, this one-period-head hedge ratio $s_{t-k,1}$ is updated, too, and this time-varying property is important. Note also that it is precisely the fact that μ_1 from the mean structure is constant that delivers the results. In particular, this coefficient need not be zero and typically it will not be; i.e., the martingale property would more often apply to the futures price, $\mu_2 = 0$, than to the underlying.

The OLS case is a different matter. It is not quite fair to compare the performance of GARCH-based hedge ratios $s_{t,1} = h_{12,t+1}/h_{22,t+1}$ to an overall constant OLS regression coefficient $\text{cov}(\Delta x_t, \Delta \phi_t)/\text{var}(\Delta \phi_t)$. In fact, the analysis shows that for the k-periods-ahead hedge,

$$s_k^{\text{OLS}} = \frac{\text{cov}(x_t - x_{t-k}, \phi_{t-k+1} - \phi_{t-k})}{\text{var}(\phi_{t-k+1} - \phi_{t-k})} \tag{17.56}$$

should be considered. This is easily obtained from the regression

$$x_t - x_{t-k} = c_k + s_k(\phi_{t-k+1} - \phi_{t-k}) + \varepsilon_t \tag{17.57}$$

separately for each k. In particular, s_k^{OLS} may vary with k empirically even though the earlier analysis assuming the GARCH model shows that $s_{t-k,k} = s_{t-k,1}$ under these assumptions. Still, Haigh, and Holt's analysis of s_1^{OLS} (in this notation) gives a lower bound on how well hedging strategies based on s_k^{OLS} would do.

A few comments are in order. First, we have established the theoretical martingale property for futures prices only under the equivalent martingale measure Q (see (10.47)). Whether it holds under the observation measure P is an empirical matter. The condition is $\mu_2 = 0$ in the model, and this is not rejected by Haigh and Holt. Second, even if ϕ_t is also a P-martingale, this helps only if the conditional variances and covariances in the hedge ratios are calculated under P, too. They are, of course, if empirical estimates are used. Still, this shows that the entire analysis hinges on an assumption that the hedger's objective function is a variance (or, as in our dynamic programming formulation, a sum of mean squared error terms) taken under P, not Q. This assumption may be relevant, but it does reinforce that the hedger is not a pricer.

Empirical hedge ratios are less than unity on average. Sources of this effect may include possibly negative convenience yields, as appearing in the cost-of-carry formula (10.40). Later purchase (namely, through the futures market) avoids costly storage.

In their empirical work, Haigh and Holt (2002) use weekly spot and futures prices for cocoa and sugar for the period 1985–2001. The estimated OLS hedge ratio is 0.9 for cocoa (an anticipated spot (cash) purchase of one unit is hedged through the purchase of 0.9 unit in the futures market) and 0.7 for sugar. The time-varying (conditional) hedge ratios vary considerably around these values, with standard deviations of the order 0.1 for cocoa and 0.2 for sugar and sometimes changing sign in the latter case. Of course, it is expected that the use of time-varying conditional hedge ratios contributes more to overall hedging performance in markets where variances, covariances and, in particular, hedge ratios, are highly volatile since here there is a greater difference between conditional and constant strategies. In the application, a better relative performance of the conditional approach vis-a-vis the OLS constant strategy would hence be expected in the sugar market compared to the less volatile cocoa market. Haigh and Holt confirm this empirically, showing a 9% reduction in hedging error variance in the conditional case relative to OLS for the more volatile sugar market compared to a 2% reduction in variance for the cocoa market. In an out-of-sample experiment, the improvement is 2% in the sugar market compared to a 2% loss relative to OLS in the cocoa market. The greater relevance of the conditional (time-varying) hedge ratios thus holds up out of sample. However, an empirically lower volatility in the cocoa market in the out-of-sample period (August 11, 2000–September 9, 2001) than in the in-sample period may also explain the relative deterioration in performance of the conditional approach in this market.

Much additional work can be done on time-varying optimal hedge ratios. Different multivariate GARCH models can be used. Several models exist, but not all have been used in the hedging context. For example, Bollerslev, Engle, and Wooldridge (1988) introduce the model

$$h_{ij,t} = W_{ij} + A_{ij}e_{i,t-1}e_{j,t-1} + B_{ij}h_{ij,t-1}, \qquad (17.58)$$

in which H_t is positive semidefinite if each of the matrices W, A, and B is. There are $3L(L+1)/2$ parameters, where $L = \dim(y_t)$, plus those in μ. For example, for $L = 2$ as in the hedging application, there are 9 parameters in (17.58) compared to 11 in the BEKK case (17.43). Another example is the constant-correlation model of Bollerslev (1990),

$$h_{ii,t} = W_i + A_i e_{i,t-1}^2 + B_i h_{ii,t-1}, \qquad (17.59)$$

$$h_{ij,t} = \rho_{ij}\sqrt{h_{ii,t}h_{jj,t}}; \qquad (17.60)$$

i.e., each component of the multivariate time series follows a univariate GARCH model, and components i and j have constant correlation ρ_{ij}. Here, H_t is positive semidefinite if W_i, A_i, and B_i are non-negative, and the ρ_{ij} form a positive semi-definite correlation matrix. There are $3L + L(L-1)/2$ parameters in the H_t-process, or 7 in the case $L = 2$.

Other work on hedge ratios could modify our dynamic programming formulation, e.g., by considering a mean-variance criterion instead of period-by-period mean squared supplementary investment or hedging error.

17.4 EXERCISES

1. Derive the expectations revision representation (17.18) of the investment series. *Hint*: Use (17.16).

2. Derive an alternative to (17.48) in the case where the futures price is not a martingale under P.

3. Carefully derive an alternative to (17.10) in the case where the risk minimization criterion (17.6) is replaced by a suitable utility maximization criterion.

17.5 REFERENCES

We have listed selected empirical references in the text. The theory of risk-minimizing hedging was studied by Föllmer and Sondermann (1986) and Schweizer (1991). The related notion of quadratic or mean-variance hedging was pursued by Schäl (1994) and Schweizer (1995).

Chapter Eighteen

Intertemporal Asset Pricing

18.1 INTRODUCTION

We have already considered the stochastic Euler equations for the simple one-sector optimal stochastic growth model (13.51) and for the consumption model (13.56), (16.6). A close relative is the corresponding equation for the intertemporal asset pricing model (16.9). Here, we derive the latter, following Lucas (1978), since it is useful to see how it accommodates multiple financial assets and because it allows easy derivation of some of the important empirical models we consider.

Let there be n assets with prices at time t given by the n-vector p_t and let the n-vector a_t indicate the agent's asset holdings as of time t. Each asset pays a random dividend in period t, and x_t denotes the n-vector of dividends. The agent thus has a budget of $a_t'(p_t + x_t)$, which is allocated to consumption and investment in the n assets. Since consumption is determined by the residual for any increasing utility of consumption function u, we can simply specify the current control c_t as the n-vector of next period's asset holdings, purchased at time t at a total cost of $c_t' p_t$; i.e., in the general notation (13.38) we have $L(a, c, y) = c$ for the law of motion. Bellman's principle of optimality has it that

$$V(a, x) = \max_c \{u(a'(p + x) - c'p) + \beta E(V(c, y)|x)\}, \qquad (18.1)$$

where we have moved directly to the time-invariant formulation and with $y \sim Q(\cdot|x)$, i.e., the distribution of future dividends depends on current dividends but not on the agent's actions. As usual, we find immediately the envelope condition from (13.40)

$$\frac{\partial V}{\partial a} = (p + x)u', \qquad (18.2)$$

the shadow value of shares, whereas the first-order condition is

$$pu' = \beta E\left(\frac{\partial V}{\partial a}(c, y)|x\right), \qquad (18.3)$$

and on combining the two,

$$p_t u_t' = \beta E_t((p_{t+1} + x_{t+1})u_{t+1}') \qquad (18.4)$$

is the n-dimensional multivariate stochastic Euler equation (recall that p and x are vectors). The condition makes good economic sense: Assets paying off in future states where marginal utility is high (consumption is low in the decreasing marginal utility case) are valued highly. This is the consumption-based intertemporal capital asset pricing model (ICAPM).

18.2 PRICES AND RETURNS

A couple of important observations are in order. First, we wish to study equilibrium asset pricing and to this end either take all agents in the economy to be identical or the markets to be complete so that the above agent may be interpreted as a representative agent for the economy (in which the competitive equilibrium in this case is Pareto optimal and so may be supported by a planning problem). In either case, we may study the single agent in isolation, and equilibrium requires that exactly the current dividend is consumed every period, i.e., $u'_t = u'_t(x_t)$ above, where by a slight abuse of notation x_t is understood as the sum of its coordinates when entered as an argument in the (marginal) utility function. Second, we wish to solve endogenously for the equilibrium prices as functions of state variables; in particular, we seek a mapping $p{:}X \to \mathbb{R}^n$ such that in equilibrium $p_t = p(x_t)$, and for this reason p_t was not included among the state variables above. Indeed, p_t is known once x_t is.

The problem is to solve for $p(\cdot)$, and the Euler equation implies that

$$p(x)u'(x) = \beta E((p(y) + y)u'(y)|x). \qquad (18.5)$$

This is the functional equation of main interest in the intertemporal asset-pricing model. That is, the general dynamic programming framework of chapters 3 and 13 is modified slightly to suit the present purposes, but the underlying theme is the same. Thus, defining $f(x) = p(x)u'(x)$, we consider the map T given by

$$T(f)(x) = \beta E(f(y)|x) + \beta E(yu'(y)|x), \qquad (18.6)$$

and we seek a fixed point of the functional equation

$$f = T(f). \qquad (18.7)$$

It is easy to see that T is monotonic and discounts; i.e., $T(f+s) = T(f) + \beta s$ for s constant, and in this case T is in fact linear. It maps $B = \{f : X \to \mathbb{R}^n \text{ continuous and bounded}\}$ to B if the function on $X \subseteq \mathbb{R}^n$ given by $x \to xu'(x)$ belongs to B and Q has the Feller property. In this case Blackwell's sufficient conditions are satisfied, so T is a contraction, and we conclude that there exists a unique fixed point $f \in B$ from which we may compute the equilibrium asset pricing function as

$$p(x) = \frac{f(x)}{u'(x)}. \qquad (18.8)$$

The general framework of chapter 13 may be used to obtain monotonicity, smoothness, and the like, for p.

The total return on the ith asset over the period is $r_{t+1}^i = (p_{t+1}^i + x_{t+1}^i)/p_t^i$, where coordinates are indicated by superscript, and dividing the ith Euler equation by p_t^i yields

$$u_{t+1}' = \beta E_t(r_{t+1} u_{t+1}'), \qquad (18.9)$$

where $r_t = (r_t^1, \ldots, r_t^n)$ is the return vector. For $n = 1$ this is the Hall consumption model. Similarly, we may define the intertemporal marginal rate of substitution as $s_{t+1} = \beta u_{t+1}'/u_t'$ and get

$$E_t(r_{t+1} s_{t+1}) = 1, \qquad (18.10)$$

a form of the ICAPM that really suffices for most asset pricing applications. Another compact version is obtained by considering the excess returns above the first asset, $R_t^i = r_t^i - r_t^1$, so that

$$E_t(R_{t+1} u_{t+1}') = 0, \qquad (18.11)$$

where $R_t = (R_t^2, \ldots, R_t^n)$. Often the first asset is taken to be risk-free as of t, say a one-period T-bill.

18.3 CAPITAL ASSET PRICING MODEL

Let us now write $d_t = \Sigma_{i=1}^n x_t^i$ for consumption and suppose for the moment that (d_t, R_t) follows a multivariate normal distribution, conditionally on information through $t-1$. Recall that if (d, R) is bivariate normal and f is differentiable with $E(|f'(d)|) < \infty$, then $\operatorname{cov}(f(d), R) = E(f'(d))\operatorname{cov}(d, R)$. With $f = u'$ it follows from (18.11) that

$$0 = E(u'(d)R^i)$$
$$= \operatorname{cov}(u'(d), R^i) + E(u'(d))E(R^i)$$
$$= E(u''(d))\operatorname{cov}(d, R^i) + E(u'(d))E(R^i),$$

so we have

$$E_t(R_{t+1}) = -\frac{E_t(u_{t+1}'')}{E_t(u_{t+1}')}\operatorname{cov}_t(d_{t+1}, R_{t+1}); \qquad (18.12)$$

i.e., the expected excess return is a linear function of the covariance with future consumption. This is the consumption-based capital asset pricing model (C-CAPM).

In a two-period model, if $i = 2$ is the market portfolio consisting of all risky assets in proportion to outstanding values, then the next period's consumption will be proportional to the market return, $d_1 = w_0 R_1^2$, where w_0 indicates initial wealth. Hence, $\text{cov}_0(d_1, R_1^2) = w_0 \text{var}_0(R_1^2)$ and $E_0(R_1^2) = -(E_0 u_1''/E_0 u_1')w_0 \text{var}_0(R_1^2)$, so the excess return on the market portfolio, say $\mu_m = E_0(R_1^2)$, is proportional to $\sigma_m^2 = \text{var}_0(R_1^2)$, the market variance (compare exercise 2 in chapter 1), and we may write $-(E_0 u_1''/E_0 u_1')w_0 = \mu_m/\sigma_m^2$. Similarly, $\text{cov}_0(d_1, R_1^i) = w_0 \text{cov}_0(R_1^2, R_1^i)$, so $E_0(R_1^i) = (\mu_m/\sigma_m^2)\text{cov}_0(R_1^2, R_1^i)$. We may define $\beta^i = \text{cov}_0(R_1^2, R_1^i)/\sigma_m^2$ and $\beta = (\beta^2, \ldots, \beta^n)$ so that

$$E_0(R_1) = \mu_m \beta, \tag{18.13}$$

which is the standard CAPM from (10.100). Expected excess returns are a linear function of β, the slope being the market excess return. The standard arbitrage pricing theory (APT) may be derived similarly, and all these models may be derived without necessarily assuming normality.

18.4 ESTIMATION

Sometimes models of the type considered here are estimated and tested using only the zero-mean condition implied by the dynamic programming framework. Equations such as $E_t(r_{t+1}s_{t+1}) = 1$ and $E_t(R_{t+1}u_{t+1}') = 0$ (cf. (18.10)–(18.11)) imply that a certain function m_{t+1} satisfies $E_t(m_{t+1}) = 0$ (in the examples, $m_t = r_t s_t - 1$ and $R_t u_t'$, respectively). This is an orthogonality condition stating that m_{t+1} is orthogonal to all information through t. In particular, if instruments z_t known as of t are available, then $M_{t+1} = m_{t+1} \otimes z_t$ (here, $\otimes$ is the Kronecker product) satisfies $E_t(M_{t+1}) = 0$. This has a number of implications. First, M_t has an unconditional mean of zero by iterated expectations; i.e., $E(M_t) = E(E_{t-1}(M_t)) = E(0) = 0$. Second, all serial correlations vanish as well; e.g., $E(M_t M_{t+1}') = E(E_t(M_t M_{t+1}')) = E(M_t E_t(M_{t+1}')) = E(M_t 0') = 0$. Note also that for a given value θ of the unknown parameter of the model (in particular, the utility function), M_t may be calculated from data on the instruments z_t along with returns, consumption, etc., as required by the model. The generalized method of moments (GMM) of Hansen (1982) estimates θ by making the sample average $M = \Sigma_{t=1}^T M_t/T = M(\theta)$ as close to the theoretical mean of zero as possible,

$$\hat{\theta} = \arg\min_\theta M(\theta)' \text{var}(M)^{-1} M(\theta). \tag{18.14}$$

Typically, $\dim M = p$ exceeds $\dim \theta = k$, so the quadratic form does not vanish at the optimum, but by the usual generalized least squares (GLS) analogy, the norm $\text{var}(M)^{-1}$ results in the minimum (over a choice of norms) variance estimator. The resulting estimator is consistent and asymptotically normal under wide conditions,

$$\sqrt{T}(\hat{\theta} - \theta) \rightarrow N\left(0, \left(E\left(\frac{\partial M'}{\partial \theta}\right) \text{var}(M)^{-1} E\left(\frac{\partial M}{\partial \theta'}\right)\right)^{-1}\right), \quad (18.15)$$

and the minimized objective is asymptotically χ^2_{p-k} under the null and serves as a test of the overidentifying (orthogonality) restrictions implied by the dynamic programming framework.

It remains to estimate $\text{var}(M)$ consistently, and typically an initial estimator $\hat{\theta}_0$ is obtained by setting $\text{var}(M) = I_p$ in the objective (18.14). Then residuals $\widehat{M}_t = M_t(\hat{\theta}_0)$ are computed and $\text{var}(M)$ is estimated by

$$\widehat{\text{var}}(M) = \frac{1}{T^2} \sum_{t=1}^{T} \widehat{M}_t \widehat{M}'_t, \quad (18.16)$$

which is then substituted for $\text{var}(M)$ in the objective for calculation of the final estimator $\hat{\theta}$. GMM accounts for the possibility that M_t may be serially correlated (although, as noted above, in the particular asset pricing application considered here, theory shows it is not). Accordingly, $\text{var}(M)$ may be estimated by

$$\widehat{\text{var}}(M) = \frac{1}{T^2(2L+1)} \sum_{s=L}^{T-L} \sum_{t=s-L}^{s+L} w(s-t) M_s M'_t, \quad (18.17)$$

where L is a suitable lag length. To ensure positive definiteness, various weighting schemes may be considered, a common choice due to Newey and West (1987) being $w(i) = 1 - |i|/(L+1)$.

The approach of minimizing the norm of $M(\theta) = \Sigma_{t=1}^{T} M_t(\theta)/T$ can actually be improved upon if the conditional mean $E_t(\partial M_{t+1}/\partial \theta')$ and the conditional variance $\text{var}_t(M_t)$ can be calculated, e.g., by simulation, kernel smoothing, or a similar method. In this case, the estimator obtained by solving the k equations

$$\frac{1}{T} \sum_{t=0}^{T-1} E_t\left(\frac{\partial M'_{t+1}}{\partial \theta}\right) \text{var}_t(M_{t+1})^{-1} M_{t+1} = 0,$$

is more efficient than GMM. It has asymptotic variance

$$\left(E\left(E_t\left(\frac{\partial M'_{t+1}}{\partial \theta}\right) \text{var}_t(M_{t+1})^{-1} E_t\left(\frac{\partial M_{t+1}}{\partial \theta'}\right)\right)\right)^{-1},$$

which indeed is smaller than that in (18.15).

The approach to empirical asset pricing just outlined is useful in that it applies under weak assumptions on the involved stochastic processes, but it does not utilize the full structure of the dynamic programming setup. As we have seen, the general model naturally leads to a likelihood function, and we now turn to an application of this. A type of reduced-form likelihood analysis can be attempted, where the distribution of observables is assumed at the outset and the model implications then tested as parametric restrictions. However, we introduce a full, structural likelihood approach along the lines outlined in the general setting of chapters 4 and 13. Our particular application furthermore illustrates the generalization to the case of serially correlated unobservables that do not satisfy the conditional independence assumption (5.37).

18.5 A STRUCTURAL MODEL

We consider a real exchange economy that still most closely resembles that of Lucas (1978). Related continuous-trading models (see chapter 14) are considered by Merton (1973a), Breeden (1979), and Cox, Ingersoll, and Ross (1985a). We model the price p of a single infinitely lived asset in terms of a perishable numeraire consumption good, and as in Hansen and Singleton (1983) we allow a random utility shock y to enter the period utility function $u(c, y)$, where c indicates consumption. The asset pays off a random dividend d each period. We write a for the number of shares held at the beginning of a given period. We impose in the sequel sufficient conditions for the planning problem to be representable as a stationary Markov stochastic dynamic program with state vector (a, d, y). Indicating the next period's quantities by a tilde, the control variables are $(c, \tilde{a})$, current consumption and the next period's asset holdings, and the optimal value function V satisfies

$$V(a, d, y) = \max_{c, \tilde{a}}(u(c, y) + \beta E(V(\tilde{a}, \tilde{d}, \tilde{y},)|d, y)) \qquad (18.18)$$

subject to

$$c + p\tilde{a} \leq a(p + d).$$

The first-order conditions, along with the market-clearing conditions $c = d$ and $a = 1$, imply the stochastic Euler equation

$$p = \beta E\left(\frac{\tilde{u}_c}{u_c}(\tilde{p} + \tilde{c})|c, y\right), \qquad (18.19)$$

where $u_c = \partial u / \partial c$ is the marginal utility of consumption.

Our implementation is based on the particular random utility specification

$$u(c, y) = y \log c. \qquad (18.20)$$

With a subscript t indicating leading t times, e.g., $p_1 = \tilde{p}$, the transversality condition $\beta^t cE(y_t p_t/c_t|c, y)/y \to 0$ almost surely for $t \to \infty$ in combination with (18.19) produces the equilibrium asset-pricing function

$$p(\omega) = \frac{d}{y} \sum_{t=1}^{\infty} \beta^t E(y_t|\omega), \qquad (18.21)$$

where ω captures the current state (d, y).

To close the model, a Markovian stochastic process is adopted for the state variables. Specifying ω in (18.21) as $(x, y)'$, where $x = \log d$, we assume

$$\tilde{\omega} = A\omega + \tilde{\varepsilon}, \qquad (18.22)$$

where the driving terms $\tilde{\varepsilon}$ are strictly stationary and independent of past information, and

$$A = \begin{pmatrix} a_{xx} & a_{xy} \\ a_{yx} & a_{yy} \end{pmatrix} \qquad (18.23)$$

is the transition matrix. Asset pricing per se requires only the eigenvalues of A to be less than $1/\beta$ in magnitude, but for our empirical purposes we shall ultimately require the ω-process to be stationary and so take the eigenvalues of A to be less than unity in magnitude.

We are now in a position to state the first main result of this section.

PROPOSITION 18.5.1 *If $a_{yx} \neq 0$, then the equilibrium asset-pricing function is invertible in the state variable y. The inverse function $y : \mathbb{R}^2 \to \mathbb{R}$ is given by*

$$y(p, x) =$$
$$\frac{\beta a_{yx} e^x x}{\left[(1 - \beta a_{xx})(1 - \beta a_{yy}) - \beta^2 a_{xy} a_{yx}\right] p - \beta\left[a_{yy}(1 - \beta a_{xx}) + \beta a_{xy} a_{yx}\right] e^x}.$$
$$(18.24)$$

Proof. From (18.21) and (18.22) we have

$$p(\omega) = \frac{d}{y} \sum_{t=1}^{\infty} \beta^t (0, 1) A^t \omega$$

$$= \frac{d}{y} (0, 1) \left\{ \sum_{t=1}^{\infty} (\beta A)^t \right\} \omega$$

$$= \frac{d}{y} (0, 1) \beta A (I - \beta A)^{-1} \omega, \qquad (18.25)$$

where I denotes the identity on $\mathbb{R}^2$. Using (18.23), and since $x = \log d$, we get

$$p(x, y) = \frac{\beta a_{yx} e^x x/y + \left[a_{yy}(1 - \beta a_{xx}) + \beta a_{xy} a_{yx} \right] e^x}{(1 - \beta a_{xx})(1 - \beta a_{yy}) - \beta^2 a_{xy} a_{yx}}, \tag{18.26}$$

from which the result easily follows. ☐

The proposition says that if x causes y in the sense that a_{yx} does not vanish, then a knowledge of prices and dividends (consumption) is sufficient to solve for the state variables y. Of course, if $a_{yx} = 0$ (x does not cause y), expression (18.26) reduces to $p = [a_{yy}/(1 - \beta a_{yy})]d$, independent of y, and with $a_{yy} = 1$ this yields the well-known result $p = [(1 + r)/r]d$, where r is the discount rate. This is less useful for empirical purposes than our general specification with x causing y.

The model naturally permits a full structural likelihood analysis. Thus, the distributional assumptions may be imposed directly on the fundamentals, and the distribution of the observables may then be derived endogenously rather than being imposed at the outset. The structure allows both the observable and the unobservable components of the fundamentals to be serially correlated.

In terms of the variables introduced above, we take prices p and (log) dividends x to be observed by the econometrician. The utility shock y is an unobservable (to the econometrician) state variable. We consider a data set $\{(p_t, x_t)\}_{t=0}^{T}$, and statistical inference on an unknown parameter vector $\theta \in \Theta$ is desired. The latter may include part or all of the Markov transition matrix A from (18.23), as well as the subjective discount factor β and parameters in the bivariate distribution determining the forcing process ε. We take this to be the bivariate normal $N(0, \Sigma)$, where

$$\Sigma = \begin{pmatrix} \sigma_{xx} & \sigma_{xy} \\ \sigma_{xy} & \sigma_{yy} \end{pmatrix} \tag{18.27}$$

is positive definite. Of course, σ_{yy} is not identified. By noting that u in (18.18) is a von Neumann-Morgenstern expected utility function and so is unique only up to affine transformations, we may without loss of generality take $\sigma_{yy} = 1$. The full parameter space is therefore given by

$$\Theta = \Big\{ (A, \beta, \Sigma) : a_{yx} \neq 0, |\lambda_i(A)| < 1, \quad i = 1, 2 \quad \beta \in (0, 1),$$

$$\sigma_{yy} = 1, \sigma_{xx} > \sigma_{xy}^2 \Big\}, \tag{18.28}$$

where $\lambda_i(A)$ denotes the ith eigenvalue of A. The conditions on A are the stationarity and invertibility conditions, whereas $\beta \in (0, 1)$ says that the future matters, but is discounted, and the last condition is positive definiteness of Σ.

The analysis is based on the conditional log likelihood function for $\{(p_t, x_t)\}_{t=1}^T$, given (p_0, x_0), which is of the form

$$L(\theta) = \sum_{t=1}^T l(\theta; p_t, x_t | p_{t-1}, x_{t-1}). \qquad (18.29)$$

We are now ready to state the second main result of this section.

PROPOSITION 18.5.2 *The individual log likelihood contributions l are given by*

$$l(\theta; \tilde{p}, \tilde{x} | p, x) = \log \beta + \log a_{yx} - \log((1 - \beta a_{xx})(1 - \beta a_{yy}) - \beta^2 a_{xy} a_{yx})$$

$$-2 \log \left(\tilde{p} - \frac{\beta(a_{yy}(1 - \beta a_{xx}) + \beta a_{xy} a_{yx})}{(1 - \beta a_{xx})(1 - \beta a_{yy}) - \beta^2 a_{xy} a_{yx}} e^{\tilde{x}} \right)$$

$$-\frac{1}{2} \log(\sigma_{xx} - \sigma_{xy}^2)$$

$$-\frac{1}{2(\sigma_{xx} - \sigma_{xy}^2)} \left\{ (\tilde{x} - a_{xx}x - a_{xy}y(p, x, \theta))^2 \right.$$

$$-2\sigma_{xy}(\tilde{x} - a_{xx}x - a_{xy}y(p, x, \theta))(y(\tilde{p}, \tilde{x}, \theta$$

$$-a_{yx}x - a_{yy}y(p, x, \theta))$$

$$\left. +\sigma_{xx}(y(\tilde{p}, \tilde{x}, \theta) - a_{yx}x - a_{yy}y(p, x, \theta))^2 \right\}.$$

Here, the dependence of the function $y(\cdot)$ from Proposition 18.5.1 on the parameters in θ has been made explicit.

Proof. By assumption, the density of $\tilde{\varepsilon} = (\tilde{\varepsilon}_x, \tilde{\varepsilon}_y)'$ in (18.22) is

$$f\left(\tilde{\varepsilon}_x, \tilde{\varepsilon}_y; \theta\right) = \frac{1}{2\pi |\Sigma|^{1/2}} e^{(-1/2)(\tilde{\varepsilon}_x, \tilde{\varepsilon}_y)\Sigma^{-1}(\tilde{\varepsilon}_x, \tilde{\varepsilon}_y)'}.$$

The Jacobian of the transformation from $\tilde{\varepsilon}$ to $\tilde{\omega} = (\tilde{x}, \tilde{y})'$ is unity, so the conditional density of $\tilde{\omega}$ given ω is

$$f\left(\tilde{x}, \tilde{y}; \theta | x, y\right) = \frac{1}{2\pi |\Sigma|^{1/2}} e^{(-1/2)(\tilde{x}-\hat{x}, \tilde{y}-\hat{y})\Sigma^{-1}(\tilde{x}-\hat{x}, \tilde{y}-\hat{y})'},$$

where $\hat{x} = a_{xx}x + a_{xy}y$ and $\hat{y} = a_{yx}x + a_{yy}y$ are the conditional means. The Jacobian of the transformation from $(\tilde{x}, \tilde{y})$ to $(\tilde{p}, \tilde{x})$ is $|y_p(\tilde{p}, \tilde{x})|$, where the derivative $y_p = \partial y/\partial p$ of the map in Proposition 18.5.1 is given by

$$y_p(p, x) =$$

$$-\frac{\beta a_{yx} e^x x \left[(1 - \beta a_{xx})(1 - \beta a_{yy}) - \beta^2 a_{xy} a_{yx}\right]}{\left(p - \beta[a_{yy}(1 - \beta a_{xx}) + \beta a_{xy} a_{yx}]/[(1 - \beta a_{xx})(1 - \beta a_{yy}) - \beta^2 a_{xy} a_{yx}]\right)^2}.$$

The conditional density of $(\tilde{p}, \tilde{x})$ given (p, x) is now obtained as $f((\tilde{p}, \tilde{x}; \theta) | p, x) = |y_p(\tilde{p}, \tilde{x})| f((\tilde{x}, y(\tilde{p}, \tilde{x}; \theta)) | x, y(p, x)))$. The term $x + \log x$ resulting from taking the logarithm of y_0 and the term $-\log 2\pi$ stemming from $\log f$ do not depend on θ and so need not be included in l. The results follow by combing all the above expressions. $\qquad\square$

We have seen in earlier chapters how random utility specifications can be used to break the curse of degeneracy and lead to useful empirical models. The above asset pricing application of the random utility concept shows similarly how a likelihood procedure is established. The approach is useful in addressing many issues arising in intertemporal asset pricing. We discuss some classical examples in the following.

18.6 ASSET PRICING PUZZLES

Iteration on the forward difference equation (18.4) yields the representation of the asset pricing function

$$p_t = E_t \left(\sum_{i=1}^{\infty} \beta^i \frac{u'_{t+i}}{u'_t} x_{t+i} \right) \qquad (18.30)$$

under the transversality condition $E_t \beta^i u'_{t+i} p_{t+i} \to 0$ as $i \to \infty$. Here, we have switched back to the general notation where x_t is the state vector, in this case the n-vector of dividends. If a perfect foresight price $p_t^* = \sum_{i=1}^{\infty} \beta^i (u'_{t+i}/u'_t) x_{t+i}$ is defined, then the relation $p_t = E_t(p_t^*)$ leads to the condition

$$\text{var}(p_t) \leq \text{var}(p_t^*) \qquad (18.31)$$

if the variances exist. Taking this to the data, truncating at a finite i when calculating p_t^*, Shiller (1981) and Grossman and Shiller (1981) find that the inequality is violated empirically. This is the *excess stock market volatility puzzle*. Stock prices fluctuate too much (var(p_t) is too high) to be justified by subsequent changes in dividends x_{t+i}. LeRoy and Porter (1981) show that the puzzle remains if earnings are substituted for dividends. Actually, asset prices may be expected to be nonstationary, so that the variances do not exist, as argued by Kleidon (1986), but the fact remains that dividends seem to move too smoothly to justify observed stock market fluctuations. If a standard utility function is adopted, e.g., the constant relative risk aversion specification $u_t = u(c_t) = (c_t^{1-\gamma} - 1)/(1 - \gamma)$, so that $u'_{t+i}/u'_t = (c_{t+i}/c_t)^{-\gamma}$, then this does not seem to add enough variability to explain the observations. In this case, the random utility generalization of section 18.5 is useful, bringing in an additional source of variation through $u'_{t+i}/u'_t = (y_{t+i}/y_t)/(c_{t+i}/c_t)$.

Variance-bound tests is the term used to refer to this type of analysis, inspecting whether a sample variance exceeds a lower bound requirement derived from asset-pricing theory. A related lower variance bound is that for stochastic discount factors, derived by Hansen and Jagannathan (1991). Consider again the n equations $E_t(R_{t+1}u'_{t+1}) = 0$ from the ICAPM (18.11), where R_{t+1} is the excess return vector. A more general version is $E_t(R_{t+1}D_{t+1}) = 0$, where D_{t+1} is associated with a stochastic discount factor, e.g., D_{t+1}/D_t is given by $\beta u'_{t+1}/u'_t$ in the consumption-based case and by the density or likelihood ratio (Radon-Nikodym derivative) process from sections 10.2 and 14.6 for the equivalent martingale measure in general. The question is what can be learned from the return data about D_{t+1} without making further assumptions.

The unconditional version of the pricing relation is

$$E(R_t D_t) = 0. \tag{18.32}$$

It is possible to find a stochastic discount factor $\tilde{D}_t$ with the same mean as D_t as a linear combination of excess returns,

$$\tilde{D}_t = E(D_t) + (R_t - E(R_t))'w. \tag{18.33}$$

Thus, the requirement $E(R_t\tilde{D}_t) = 0$ leads to $w = -\text{var}(R_t)^{-1}E(R_t)E(D_t)$. Then $\text{var}(\tilde{D}_t) = w'\text{var}(R_t)w = E(D_t)^2 E(R_t)'\text{var}(R_t)^{-1}E(R_t)$. This is a lower variance bound on all stochastic discount factors of mean $E(D_t)$,

$$\text{var}(D_t) \geq \text{var}(\tilde{D}_t), \tag{18.34}$$

the Hansen-Jagannathan bound. To see that it applies, note that $D_t - \tilde{D}_t$ is uncorrelated with the excess returns, i.e., $E(D_t - \tilde{D}_t) = E(D_t) - E(D_t) = 0$, so $\text{cov}(D_t - \tilde{D}_t, R_t) = E((D_t - \tilde{D}_t)R_t) = 0$. As $\tilde{D}_t$ is linear in R_t, also $\text{cov}(D_t - \tilde{D}_t, \tilde{D}_t) = 0$. Then $\text{var}(D_t) = \text{var}(D_t - \tilde{D}_t + \tilde{D}_t) = \text{var}(D_t - \tilde{D}_t) + \text{var}(\tilde{D}_t) \geq \text{var}(\tilde{D}_t)$.

The result may be restated as

$$\frac{\text{var}(D_t)}{E(D_t)^2} \geq E(R_t)' \, \text{var}(R_t)^{-1} E(R_t) \tag{18.35}$$

for all stochastic discount factors D_t. The lower bound is the Mahalonobis distance from the origin to the random vector R_t. Since the original condition was $E_t(R_{t+1}D_{t+1}) = 0$, the stochastic discount factor can without loss of generality be normalized to unit mean, so it is not necessary to use the inequality to trace out the variance bound as a function of the mean $E(D_t)$ in this case. Hansen and Jagannathan also consider the closely related case without a riskless asset, and then the same normalization cannot necessarily be made.

For a single excess return, say, on the market portfolio of risky assets, a ballpark figure for the right hand side, with an equity premium $E(R_t)$ around 6% historically in the United States and var $(R_t)^{1/2}$ around 20% comes out to about 0.09, or a ratio of the standard deviation to the mean of the stochastic discount factor, $\sigma(D_t)/E(D_t)$, of at least 0.3. Most candidate stochastic discount factors do not have such high volatility. For example, in the consumption-based case, $D_t = u'_t$, e.g., with constant relative risk aversion, $D_t = c_t^{-\gamma}$, the ratio $\sigma(D_t)/E(D_t)$ is far lower empirically unless a very high γ is used. This is the *equity premium puzzle*, that the equity premium $E(R_t)$ apparently is too high to be justified (with reasonable rates of risk aversion γ) by equity risk var(R_t). Mehra and Prescott (1985) arrived at the puzzle through slightly different means but using also the constant relative risk-aversion specification. Again, if $D_t = u'_t = y_t/c_t$ from section 18.5 is introduced, the bound is more easily satisfied, in particular with sufficiently volatile random utility shock y_t.

We have offered a full structural likelihood-based asset pricing framework in section 18.5. The distribution of asset prices is derived endogenously as depending on preference specifications and the assumed distribution of exogenous fundamentals (dividends). It is useful to contrast this approach with the alternative likelihood framework of Hansen and Singleton (1983) (chapter 16), where the joint distribution of all variables is assumed at the outset and the asset pricing theory instead is used to derive parametric restrictions on this distribution.

The specification is that of constant relative risk aversion at rate γ, so the stochastic Euler equations are

$$1 = \beta E_t \left((1 + r_{i,t+1}) \left(\frac{c_{t+1}}{c_t} \right)^{-\gamma} \right). \tag{18.36}$$

The assumption is that $y_{t+1} = (\Delta \log c_{t+1}, \log(1 + r_{1,t+1}), \dots, \log(1 + r_{n,t+1}))$ is conditionally jointly normal, given information through t. Specifically, y_{t+1} is assumed to follow a vector autoregression of order p. Thus, consumption and returns are conditionally jointly log normal. Then $(1 + r_{i,t+1})(c_{t+1}/c_t)^{-\gamma}$ is also log normal since its logarithm is linear in normals, $\log(1 + r_{i,t+1}) - \gamma \Delta \log c_{t+1}$. Let the parameterization be $\log(1 + r_{i,t+1}) \sim N(\mu_i, \sigma_i^2)$ and $\Delta \log c_{t+1} \sim N(\mu_c, \sigma_c^2)$, assuming for simplicity constant parameters and $p = 0$ (y_{t+1} is independently and identically distributed (i.i.d.); Hansen and Singleton (1983) consider also general p). In general, for any log normal variable x, if $\log x \sim N(\mu, \sigma^2)$, then $\log E(x) = \mu + \frac{1}{2}\sigma^2$. Applying this to $x = (1 + r_{i,t+1})(c_{t+1}/c_t)^{-\gamma}$ when taking logs of the Euler equations yields the parametric restrictions

$$0 = \log \beta + \mu_i - \gamma \mu_c + \frac{1}{2}(\sigma_i^2 - 2\gamma \sigma_{ic} + \gamma^2 \sigma_c^2), \qquad (18.37)$$

where $\sigma_{ic} = \mathrm{cov}(\log(1 + r_{i,t+1}), \Delta \log(c_{t+1}))$. Thus, y_{t+1} is i.i.d. $N(\mu, \Sigma)$, with $\mu = (\mu_c, \mu_1, \ldots, \mu_n)$, but $(\mu_1, \ldots, \mu_n)$ are functions of μ_c as well (through the $\sigma_i^2, \sigma_c^2, \sigma_{ic}$ parameters) and the subjective preference parameters β and γ. The assumed unrestricted model has $n + 1 + (n + 1)(n + 2)/2$ parameters in (μ, Σ). The restricted model has $n - 2$ fewer ($\mu_1, \ldots, \mu_n$ are dropped at the expense of introducing β and γ).

The model can be estimated by maximum likelihood, and the restrictions from asset pricing theory tested, e.g., in a likelihood ratio (LR) or Wald test, either of which will be asymptotically $\chi^2(n - 2)$ under the null. Thus, the likelihood function is relatively simple (this holds also in the general p case, a Gaussian vector autoregression (VAR(p)) model), and the reason the structural maximum likelihood is more complicated is that the asset price distribution is derived endogenously. We have seen that among the benefits are a more flexible stochastic discount factor in our specification.

The empirical results obtained by Hansen and Singleton (1983) using the log normal model are discussed in chapter 16. In the VAR(p) case with $p > 0$, it is μ_i and μ_c in the parametric restriction that are replaced by the conditional expectations $E_t \log(r_{i,t+1}$ and $E_t \Delta \log c_{t+1}$ depending on lagged $y_t, \ldots, y_{t-p+1}$ through the VAR(p), whereas the parameters (β, γ) still are assumed constant. The latter two are the only parameters estimated in the basic version of Hansen and Singleton's (1982) alternative GMM-approach to the ICAPM, which avoids distributional assumptions beyond the first two moments.

In the stochastic Euler equations (18.36), the common factor $(c_{t+1}/c_t)^{-\gamma}$ stems from the ratio of marginal utilities $u'(c_{t+1})/u'(c_t)$ with $u(c_t) = (c_t^{1-\gamma} - 1)/(1 - \gamma)$, in which case

$$-\frac{c_t u''(c_t)}{u'(c_t)} = \gamma; \qquad (18.38)$$

i.e., the Arrow and Pratt relative risk aversion is constant, at rate γ. One problem with the specification is that γ governs not only risk aversion, but also intertemporal substitution in consumption. To see this, consider the parametric restriction (18.37) for the case of a risk-free asset, say, a one-period T-bill,

$$0 = \log \beta + r_{f,t+1} - \gamma \mu_c + \frac{1}{2}\gamma^2 \sigma_c^2, \qquad (18.39)$$

since the risk-free rate is known at t and so the conditional variance and covariance vanish. In the general case where $\mu_c = E_t \Delta \log c_{t+1}$, this yields $E_t \Delta \log c_{t+1} = (\log \beta + r_{f,t+1} + \frac{1}{2}\gamma^2\sigma_c^2)/\gamma$ and hence

$$\frac{\partial E_t \Delta \log c_{t+1}}{\partial r_{f,t+1}} = \frac{1}{\gamma}. \tag{18.40}$$

Thus, the elasticity of intertemporal substitution, i.e., the sensitivity of expected consumption growth with respect to the interest rate, is also constant, at $1/\gamma$. The parameter γ has two different interpretations, as risk aversion and as the inverse intertemporal substitution rate, and in general there is no reason why two characteristics of the economy should be tied in this particular manner.

Another implication is that

$$\log \beta = -E(r_{f,t+1}) + \gamma\mu_c - \frac{1}{2}\gamma^2\sigma_c^2, \tag{18.41}$$

and when historical U.S. moments are substituted on the right hand side, along with the kind of large value of γ required to address the equity premium puzzle, then $\log \beta$ turns out positive, corresponding to $\beta > 1$, clearly violating the dynamic programming setup; i.e., it suggests a negative rate of time preference. This is the *risk-free rate puzzle* of Weill (1989) and is an additional aspect of the equity premium puzzle and the tight model specification.

It is possible to replace the time-separable preference structure with Kreps and Porteus (1978) recursive preferences to break the tie between risk aversion and intertemporal substitution. Both are still constant, but their product is no longer restricted to unity, in the approach along this route pursued by Epstein and Zin (1989), Weil (1989), and Campbell (1993). Recursive utility is defined by

$$V_t = \left((1-\beta)c_t^{(1-\gamma)/\theta} + \beta \left(E_t \left(V_{t+1}^{1-\gamma} \right) \right)^{1/\theta} \right)^{\theta/(1-\gamma)}, \tag{18.42}$$

with $\theta = (1-\gamma)/(1-1/\psi)$. The model is again solved by stochastic dynamic programming. In this case,

$$\frac{\partial E_t \Delta \log c_{t+1}}{\partial r_{f,t+1}} = \psi; \tag{18.43}$$

i.e., the elasticity of intertemporal substitution is still constant but now governed by the new parameter ψ and not tied to the constant rate of relative risk aversion γ as in (18.40). More general specifications would allow both to vary separately across time as functions of state variables, including consumption. In the special case $\psi = 1/\gamma$, we get $\theta = 1$, and iteration on the forward difference equation (18.42) defining recursive utility reproduces the original time-separable specification $V_t^{1-\gamma}/(1-\beta) = E_t \Sigma_{i=0}^{\infty} \beta^i c_{t+i}^{1-\gamma}$. The conditional expected excess returns or risk premia to the assets are

$$E_t(r_{i,t+1}) - r_{f,t+1} = \frac{\theta}{\psi}\sigma_{ic} + (1-\theta)\sigma_{im} - \tfrac{1}{2}\sigma_i^2, \qquad (18.44)$$

where σ_{im} is the covariance between $r_{i,t+1}$ and the return on the market portfolio $r_{m,t+1}$, the combination of assets actually selected. The term $-\tfrac{1}{2}\sigma_i^2$ is a Jensen's inequality correction arising because of the log normal framework. This general asset pricing model in principle nests both the consumption capital asset pricing model (C-CAPM) from (18.12), the case $\gamma\psi = 1$ and hence $\theta = 1$, and the ordinary CAPM from (18.13), the case $\theta = 0$, which actually corresponds to logarithmic preferences ($\gamma = 1$) and growth optimal portfolio choice, see exercise 3, chapter 1.

In the ordinary CAPM, $\theta = 0$, the covariances σ_{im} with the market explain the cross section of expected stock returns. Usually, the risk premium is represented as $\mu_m\beta_{im}$, with $\beta_{im} = \sigma_{im}/\sigma_m^2$ and μ_m the market risk premium (the price of beta risk), and this is consistent with the above for $\theta = 0$ since with $i = m$ the condition shows that the market risk premium is $\mu_m = \sigma_{mm} = \sigma_m^2$, so that the usual $\mu_m\beta_{im}$ reduces to σ_{im} (if Jensen's inequality correction is included, then $\mu_m = \tfrac{1}{2}\sigma_m^2$, see exercise 3, chapter 1).

In the consumption CAPM, $\theta = 1$, the covariances σ_{ic} with consumption explain the cross section of expected stock returns. In this case, since $\theta = 1$ and hence $1/\psi = \gamma$, the risk premia take the form $\gamma\sigma_{ic}$. This may be recast in terms of consumption betas $\beta_{ic} = \sigma_{ic}/\sigma_c^2$ as $\gamma_c\beta_{ic}$, to be compared to $\mu_m\beta_{im}$ in the standard CAPM. Thus, asset returns can be regressed on the market to estimate β_{im} and on consumption growth to estimate β_{ic}. If mean excess returns are regressed on the two set of betas separately, then the expected coefficients are the market risk premium on β_{im} and γ_c on β_{ic}, and risk aversion γ (or inverse intertemporal substitution $1/\psi$) may be estimated as γ_c/σ_c^2. In an encompassing model with both market betas and consumption betas, the coefficients on these lose the simple interpretations, but the approach can be used to assess whether consumption or market risk matters most for asset prices and whether an improvement is indeed obtained by freeing up the unit restriction on the product $\gamma\psi$.

In further analysis, Campbell (1993) uses a log linear approximation of the budget constraint in the model to get asset pricing implications from the consumption-based model that do not require the use of consumption data at all. Thus, the innovation or unexpected portion of consumption equals the innovation in market return plus an adjustment that disappears in case of unit intertemporal substitution, and otherwise is given by the revision in expectation as to discounted future market returns. Accordingly, as in Merton's (1973a) ICAPM, expected excess returns depend not only on the covariance (beta) with the market portfolio, but in addition on the covariance with a hedge portfolio tracking the expectation revision. The latter may be estimated using market returns rather than consumption data, and drops out in case of logarithmic preferences (the CAPM).

Campbell (1991) uses a similar log linear approximation, essentially substituting (10.91) into (10.90), to write the innovation in market return as the expectation revision in discounted future dividend (consumption) changes less the expectation revision in discounted future returns. Thus, current return (price) is up if there are good news about future cash flows or about (decreases in) future discount rates (returns). Campbell and Vuolteenaho (2004) use this to decompose individual stock return covariances with the market return into the sum of the covariances with cash flow and discount rate news. Dividing both covariances by market variance, CAPM beta is given as the sum of the bad cash flow beta and the good (rather, less bad) discount rate beta. Discount rate risk is less harmful to investors than cash flow risk because a price drop due to increased discount rates carries with it the expectation of increased future returns, whereas there is no such offsetting feature involved in case of a drop in expected cash flows.

There are analogies here to the complicated relations between the risk-return tradeoff, the volatility feedback effect, and the financial leverage effect. If the risk-return relation is positive, as theory would predict, then an increase in expected volatility has the dual effects of increasing discount rates, leading to a price drop and hence a negative current return (this is the volatility feedback effect of Campbell and Hentschel (1992)), and at the same time increasing expected future returns to compensate investors for the increased risk. Similarly, with Black's (1976) financial leverage effect, an initial price drop (negative return) increases the debt-equity ratio and hence expected future risk, again increasing expected future returns in case of a positive risk-return tradeoff. In both cases, negative current returns are associated with increases in expected future returns. Due to a similar offsetting feature, discount rate risk may be seen as less severe than straight cash flow risk, and should accordingly be compensated less. Thus, the cash flow beta is the bad beta, in that it should carry a higher risk price than the discount rate beta.

The *size puzzle* or small firm effect is that stocks with low market capitalization of outstanding shares tend to return more than expected according to the CAPM. The *value puzzle* is that value stocks do, too. Here, value (as opposed to growth) stocks are those with high book relative to market value (low Tobin's Q). Fama and French (1992) show that size and value factors (besides the market return) matter in an LFM of the type (10.106). The two extra factors are constructed as returns on small less returns on large stocks (the payoff to a size gamble), and returns on value stocks less returns on growth stocks. A Fama and MacBeth (1973) analysis shows that the non-CAPM factors are priced. The explanation offered by Campbell and Vuolteenaho (2004) is that (18.13) fits poorly because the separate cash flow and discount rate portions of beta carry different risk prices. This is consistent with Merton's (1973a) ICAPM, and as a two-parameter extension of the CAPM it provides an alternative to (18.44), in that it is the second covariance in the latter that is being decomposed.

The empirical results show that large and growth stocks tend to have better (in this nomenclature) betas than small and value stocks, thus justifying their lower risk prices and average returns. The exception is the extreme portfolio consisting of the smallest, most aggressive growth stocks, that continues to present a puzzle relative to this and other asset pricing theories.

Campbell and Vuolteenaho (2004) do not adjust for time-varying volatility (see chapters 10 and 14), assuming that movements in market volatility are relatively short-lived. Christensen and Nielsen (2007) use both high-frequency returns and option-implied volatilities and find that although volatility actually exhibits stochastic long memory behavior, the resulting impact on the level of the stock market is indeed relatively short-lived. Furthermore, they do confirm the positive risk-return relation and an empirically strong financial leverage effect.

18.7 EXERCISES

1. Divide through by $u'(x)$ in (18.5) and consider the right hand side as a function of p. Is this a contraction?
2. Derive the volatility bound (18.31) by invoking (17.50) in the case $Y = Z$.
3. Derive (18.44) from (18.12) in the case $\theta = 1$.

18.8 REFERENCES

Early contributions on intertemporal asset pricing are Samuelson (1969) and Hakansson (1970). We have stressed the market-wide and equilibrium aspects, including the representative investor, use of aggregate data, endogeneity of the asset pricing function, etc. The alternative focus on individual optimality, subjective preferences and behavior leads to the asset allocation approach (chapter 14). The pioneering application of GMM to intertemporal asset pricing is Hansen and Singleton (1982). Classic references on the size anomaly are Banz (1981) and Reinganum (1981), as is Rosenberg, Reid, and Lanstein (1985) on the value effect.

Chapter Nineteen

Dynamic Equilibrium: The Search Model

19.1 INTRODUCTION

Search models provide a useful framework for thinking about labor market policy in an environment with information asymmetries, turnover, and unemployment. The labor market equilibrium formulation of the search model allows consideration of firms' behavior and the potential consequences of economic policy toward firms, albeit in a rather rudimentary fashion with the current state of knowledge. This chapter considers estimation of a "pure" search model—a highly stylized model in which all heterogeneity is endogenous and due to information asymmetries.

Certainly, analysis of this pure search model must logically precede analysis of the same model augmented with external sources of dispersion. The model is fit to data on wages, duration of employment, and unemployment for a random sample representing 1% of the Danish population in the age group 16–75 years over the period 1981–1990.

In section 19.2 we describe the theoretical homogeneous search model due to Mortensen (1990) and Burdett and Mortensen (1998). The implied data distribution and likelihood function are given for several alternative parametrizations in section 19.3. In section 19.4, we consider the relevant case of partially missing data— often in real settings data on one or more of the jointly distributed variables (wages, duration, destination state after leaving employment) are missing. The likelihood requires appropriate modification. This section also considers the asymptotic information contributions of different pieces of data and develops the asymptotic distribution theory. In section 19.5, we consider some information geometry. Information on some parameter combinations is accumulated faster than that on others. We decompose the parameters into those for which learning is fast and the remaining orthogonal parameters. This gives intuition on the information content of different types of data. Labor market data from Denmark, used to illustrate the application of the model, are described in section 19.6, and results are presented and interpreted in section 19.7. The data are grouped to control nonparametrically for variations in observable characteristics (age, education, etc.). We look at the estimates for systematic variation according to characteristics.

19.2 HOMOGENEOUS EQUILIBRIUM SEARCH

In competitive models wage policy does not matter because, by definition, in
equilibrium the law of one price holds: All workers of a given type receive
the same wage. In contrast, search models generate dynamic monopsony
power for employers because of the presence of frictions such as the length
of time it takes to find a new job. A firm's wage policy is important in such
models because it directly affects the distribution of income in an economy.
Moreover, in such dynamic monopsony models, public policy experiments
such as introducing or changing a minimum wage can have employment
effects that are quite different from those expected in the standard competitive case.

Because equilibrium search models provide a natural interpretation of
interesting labor market phenomena, the estimation of such models has at-
tracted considerable attention. Although these models differ in the forces of
competition generated by firms, each predicts a disperse price equilibrium to
exist. In early models, dispersed wages are induced by exogenous dispersion
in characteristics. For example, in the Albrecht and Axell (1984) model, the
wage distribution is determined by heterogeneity in the reservation wages of
workers. In Mortensen's (1990) approach the equilibrium wage distribution
is determined by the technology that matches workers to jobs. This is a pure
search equilibrium model, in that heterogeneity in workers or firms is not
required for the existence of a dispersed equilibrium. The key insight is the
addition of the reasonable assumption that workers search while on the job
and change jobs for higher wages. We focus on this model.

The economy consists of a homogeneous population of workers and a
homogeneous population of firms. Workers conduct job searches both when
unemployed and when employed. Let λ_0 denote the offer arrival rate when
unemployed and λ_1 the corresponding rate relevant for on-the-job
searching. Unemployment income net of search costs is given by b. When
employed, workers yield productivity p in firm production and are laid
off at rate δ. Thus, the economy is described by the *structural parameter*
$\theta = (\lambda_0, \lambda_1, \delta, p, b) \in \mathfrak{R}_+^4 \times \mathfrak{R}$.

Consider first an unemployed worker receiving benefits b per period and
discounting future income at rate ρ. At times ρ may be included in θ, too,
although we shall not do so in the empirical analysis below. With $T_0 > 0$
denoting the waiting time for the first job offer x, the value of being unemployed is

$$V_0 = E\left(\int_0^{T_0} be^{-\rho t}\, dt + e^{-\rho T_0} \max\{V_0, V_1(x)\}\right), \qquad (19.1)$$

where $V_1(x)$ is the value of becoming employed at wage x per period. To assess the value of a constant flow we evaluate

$$\int_0^{T_0} e^{-\rho t}\, dt = \left[-\frac{1}{\rho} e^{-\rho t} \right]_0^{T_0} = \frac{1}{\rho}(1 - e^{-\rho T_0}). \qquad (19.2)$$

Offers arrive according to a Poisson process with intensity $\lambda_0 > 0$. Thus, $T_0 \sim \exp(\lambda_0)$; i.e., the density of the waiting time is

$$f_0(t) = \lambda_0 e^{-\lambda_0 t}, \qquad t > 0, \qquad (19.3)$$

the exponential distribution with arrival rate λ_0. Then the expected value of the random discount factor in (19.1) is

$$E e^{-\rho T_0} = \int_0^\infty e^{-\rho t} f_0(t)\, dt = \frac{\lambda_0}{\lambda_0 + \rho} \int_0^\infty (\lambda_0 + \rho) e^{-(\lambda_0 + \rho)t}\, dt = \frac{\lambda_0}{\lambda_0 + \rho}.$$
$$(19.4)$$

Combining this with (19.2) allows calculation of the expected value of the integral in (19.1) as

$$E \int_0^{T_0} b e^{-\rho t}\, dt = bE \frac{1}{\rho}(1 - e^{-\rho T_0}) = \frac{b}{\rho}\left(1 - \frac{\lambda_0}{\lambda_0 + \rho} \right) = \frac{b}{\lambda_0 + \rho}.$$
$$(19.5)$$

Offers are distributed according to F, independently of the preceding waiting times, so (19.1) is recast as

$$V_0 = \frac{b + \lambda_0 \int \max\{V_0, V_1(x)\}\, dF(x)}{\lambda_0 + \rho}. \qquad (19.6)$$

Consider next a worker employed at wage w per period. Offers now arrive at rate λ_1, with first arrival at $T_1 \sim \exp(\lambda_1)$. Layoffs occur at rate δ, so the job dissolves at $T_\delta \sim \exp(\delta)$. Thus, w is received until $T_m = \min\{T_1, T_\delta\}$. If $T_1 < T_\delta$, i.e., an offer x is received before layoff, the worker chooses between continuing with the current job at wage w or moving to the new job and receiving x per period. If $T_\delta < T_1$, the worker returns to unemployment (i.e., value V_0) at $T_m = T_\delta$. We therefore have

$$V_1(w) = E\left(\int_0^{T_m} w e^{-\rho t}\, dt \right)$$
$$+ P(T_1 < T_\delta) E(e^{-\rho T_1} | T_1 < T_\delta) E(\max\{V_1(w), V_1(x)\})$$
$$+ P(T_\delta < T_1) E(e^{-\rho T_\delta} | T_\delta < T_1) V_0. \qquad (19.7)$$

We have

$$P(T_m \le t) = 1 - P(T_m > t)$$
$$= 1 - P(T_1 > t)P(T_\delta > t)$$
$$= 1 - e^{-(\lambda_1 + \delta)t}, \tag{19.8}$$

and so $T_m \sim \exp(\lambda_1 + \delta)$. From (19.5) the first expectation in (19.7) is $w/(\lambda_1 + \delta + \rho)$. To evaluate (19.7), we need in addition

$$P(T_1 < T_\delta)E(e^{-\rho T_1}|T_1 < T_\delta) = \int_0^\infty \int_t^\infty e^{-\rho t}\lambda_1 e^{-\lambda_1 t}\delta e^{-\delta s}\,ds\,dt$$

$$= \frac{\lambda_1}{\lambda_1 + \delta + \rho}\int_0^\infty (\lambda_1 + \delta + \rho)e^{-(\lambda_1 + \delta + \rho)t}\,dt$$

$$= \frac{\lambda_1}{\lambda_1 + \delta + \rho}. \tag{19.9}$$

Treating the last term in (19.7) by symmetry produces

$$V_1(w) = \frac{w + \lambda_1 \int \max\{V_1(w), V_1(x)\}dF(x) + \delta V_0}{\lambda_1 + \delta + \rho}. \tag{19.10}$$

An unemployed worker who receives an offer x chooses between values V_0 and $V_1(x)$. Since $V_1(\cdot)$ in (19.10) is increasing, the worker becomes employed if and only if $x \ge r$, where the reservation wage r is given by $V_0 = V_1(r)$. Substituting $V_1(r)$ for V_0 in the integral in (19.6) allows writing it as

$$\int \max\{V_0, V_1(x)\}dF(x) = \int \max\{V_1(r), V_1(x)\}dF(x)$$

$$= P(x \ge r)E(V_1(x) - V_1(r)|x \ge r) + V_1(r)$$

$$= \int_r^h (V_1(x) - V_1(r))dF(x) + V_1(r), \tag{19.11}$$

where h is the upper bound of the support of F. Using (19.11) in (19.6) yields

$$V_0 = \frac{b + \lambda_0 \int_r^h (V_1(x) - V_1(r))dF(x) + \lambda_0 V_1(r)}{\lambda_0 + \rho}. \tag{19.12}$$

Writing $V_0 = V_1(r)$ on the left side of (19.12) and isolating $V_1(r)$, we get

$$V_1(r) = \frac{b}{\rho} + \frac{\lambda_0}{\rho}\int_r^h (V_1(x) - V_1(r))\,dF(x). \tag{19.13}$$

Evaluating (19.10) at $w = r$ and then invoking (19.11) produces

$$V_1(r) = \frac{r + \lambda_1 \int \max\{V_1(r), V_1(x)\} \, dF(x) + \delta V_1(r)}{\lambda_1 + \delta + \rho}$$

$$= \frac{r + \lambda_1 \int_r^h (V_1(x) - V_1(r)) dF(x) + \lambda_1 V_1(r) + \delta V_1(r)}{\lambda_1 + \delta + \rho}, \qquad (19.14)$$

which may be rearranged as

$$V_1(r) = \frac{r}{\rho} + \frac{\lambda_1}{\rho} \int_r^h (V_1(x) - V_1(r)) \, dF(x). \qquad (19.15)$$

Equating (19.13) and (19.15) yields

$$r = b + (\lambda_0 - \lambda_1) \int_r^h (V_1(x) - V_1(r)) \, dF(x). \qquad (19.16)$$

By integration by parts,

$$\int_r^h (V_1(x) - V_1(r)) \, dF(x) = [(V_1(x) - V_1(r)) F(x)]_r^h$$

$$- \int_r^h V'_1(x) F(x) \, dx$$

$$= V_1(h) - V_1(r) - \int_r^h V'_1(x) F(x) \, dx$$

$$= \int_r^h V'_1(x)(1 - F(x)) \, dx. \qquad (19.17)$$

From (19.10),

$$V'_1(w) = \frac{1 + \lambda_1 P(x \le w) V'_1(w)}{\lambda_1 + \delta + \rho} = \frac{1 + \lambda_1 F(w) V'_1(w)}{\lambda_1 + \delta + \rho}, \qquad (19.18)$$

which implies that

$$V'_1(w) = \frac{1}{\delta + \rho + \lambda_1(1 - F(w))}, \qquad (19.19)$$

thus confirming that V_1 is increasing and hence that a reservation wage policy is optimal.

Substituting (19.17) and (19.19) in (19.16) yields

$$r = b + (\lambda_0 - \lambda_1) \int_r^h \frac{1 - F(x)}{\delta + \rho + \lambda_1(1 - F(x))} \, dx. \qquad (19.20)$$

On defining $\kappa_i = \lambda_i/(\delta + \rho), i = 0, 1$, we have

$$r = b + (\kappa_0 - \kappa_1) \int_r^h \frac{1 - F(x)}{1 + \kappa_1(1 - F(x))} \, dx. \tag{19.21}$$

The case where $\rho = 0$ was considered by Mortensen and Neumann (1988) and Mortensen (1990).

Note that (19.21) returns the standard optimality condition when $\kappa_1 = 0$. When employed, any wage higher than that currently received is accepted, i.e., the on-the-job reservation wage is the current wage. It is this extension to on-the-job searching that allows an equilibrium derivation of firm behavior and, in particular, the offer distribution F. The balancing condition that equates supply and demand is that firms offer higher wages if and only if they can expect to get an additional number of workers to cover the lower per-worker profits. Higher wages attract more workers to a firm and allow firms to retain workers longer.

Let the total measure of firms be 1 and let the measure of workers be m, with $u \le m$ unemployed. Then there are $(m - u)$ employed workers, so the flow into unemployment is $\delta(m - u)$. When unemployed, workers receive offers at rate λ_0, and since in equilibrium no firm offers a wage that would never be accepted, the flow out of unemployment is simply $\lambda_0 u$. The natural rate of unemployment is determined by equating the two flows:

$$u = \frac{m}{1 + k_0}, \tag{19.22}$$

where $k_i = \lambda_i/\delta, i = 0, 1$. Note that as $\rho \to 0$, we have $\kappa_i \to k_i, i = 0, 1$.

Let G be the cumulative distribution function (CDF) of wages for employed workers, so that $H(w) = G(w)(m - u)$ workers earn less than w. Then $H(w)$ increases as unemployed workers receive and accept offers below w, the number of these events being $\lambda_0 u F(w)$. Similarly, $H(w)$ decreases as workers who already earn less than w are either laid off, at rate δ, or receive and accept offers above w, which happens at rate $\lambda_1(1 - F(w))$. In a steady-state equilibrium, $H(w)$ is constant over time for each w, and equating the increases and decreases from above produces

$$\lambda_0 u F(w) = (\delta + \lambda_1(1 - F(w)))H(w) \tag{19.23}$$

or, upon noting that $H(w) = G(w)(m - u)$,

$$G(w) = \frac{k_0 u F(w)}{(1 + k_1(1 - F(w)))(m - u)}. \tag{19.24}$$

Thus, the number of workers employed in the interval $(w - \epsilon, w)$ is

$$(G(w) - G(w - \epsilon))(m - u)$$
$$= \frac{k_0(F(w) - F(w - \epsilon))m(1 + k_1)}{(1 + k_0)(1 + k_1(1 - F(w)))(1 + k_1(1 - F(w - \epsilon)))}. \tag{19.25}$$

Similarly, $F(w) - F(w - \epsilon)$ firms offer wages in this interval, so total employment $\ell(w)$ at a given firm that offers a wage rate w is calculated as

$$\ell(w) = \lim_{\epsilon \to 0} \frac{(G(w) - G(w - \epsilon))(m - u)}{F(w) - F(w - \epsilon)} = \frac{k_0 m (1 + k_1)}{(1 + k_0)(1 + k_1(1 - F(w)))^2}.$$

$$(19.26)$$

The resulting firm profit is

$$\pi(w) = (p - w)\ell(w). \tag{19.27}$$

In particular, firms offering a wage equal to the reservation wage r earn

$$\pi(r) = (p - r)\frac{k_0 m}{(1 + k_0)(1 + k_1)}. \tag{19.28}$$

Since the firms are identical, equilibrium implies equal profits; i.e., $\pi(w) = \pi(r)$ for all w in support of F (or, equivalently, G). The more picturesque version of the condition is

$$\frac{k_0 m (1 + k_1)(p - w)}{(1 + k_0)(1 + k_1(1 - F(w)))^2} = \frac{k_0 m (p - r)}{(1 + k_0)(1 + k_1)}, \tag{19.29}$$

which implies the existence and uniqueness of a continuous steady-state equilibrium wage offer distribution; i.e., solving the above equation explicitly yields

$$F(w) = \frac{1 + k_1}{k_1}\left(1 - \left(\frac{p - w}{p - r}\right)^{1/2}\right), \qquad w \in [r, h]. \tag{19.30}$$

This is the main outcome of the equilibrium search theory. In a pure search model where the only source of heterogeneity is information asymmetry, a dispersed equilibrium characterized by the CDF of wage offers F results. Next, we turn to the empirical analysis of this model.

19.3 DATA DISTRIBUTION AND LIKELIHOOD

The assumptions underlying the theoretical model of the previous section allow endogenous derivation not only of the equilibrium CDF of wage offers F but also of the distribution of all relevant variables in realistic data sets. Thus, the model lends itself to a likelihood analysis, and this is the route we pursue here.

The structural parameters to be estimated are $\theta = (\lambda_0, \lambda_1, \delta, p, b) \in \Re_+^4 \times \Re$. Christensen and Kiefer (1997) prove that the minimal data set that permits the identification of all structural parameters consists of a panel where at least some of the individuals are observed with unemployment duration d, reemployment wage w, and subsequent job duration j, and they accordingly term the corresponding empirical model the *prototypal equilibrium search model*. In particular, the asymptotic log profile likelihood for (λ_1, δ) in the prototypal model is globally concave. The reason that it is possible to separate empirically the rates of quits and layoffs even with the postemployment destination (quit or layoff) unobserved is that the conditional hazard rate for j depends on w. It would not in the case of pure job destruction ($\lambda_1 = 0$), but with on-the-job searching, a higher reservation wage w implies a lower hazard, and the extent of this effect increases with the magnitude of λ_1.

In Nash equilibrium, firms never post wages below the reservation wage r, so unemployed workers accept the first offer received, and unemployment duration d is distributed with density

$$f_d(d) = \lambda_0 e^{-\lambda_0 d}, \qquad d > 0. \tag{19.31}$$

We now focus on the limiting case $\rho \to 0$, and so we henceforth use k_i and κ_i interchangeably, $i = 0, 1$. Hence, the wage offer density is

$$f_w(w) = \frac{1 + \kappa_1}{2\kappa_1} \frac{1}{(p - w)^{1/2}(p - r)^{1/2}}, \qquad w \in [r, h]. \tag{19.32}$$

Relationships among the quantities appearing in (19.32) and ensuring that the density integrates to 1 are given in the following. Thus, (19.32) shows that the upper bound of the support of the offer distribution is given by a certain highest wage h. Substituting (19.32) in (19.21) allows each of r and h to be written as a weighted average of the structural parameters b and p, i.e.,

$$r = \gamma b + (1 - \gamma)p \tag{19.33}$$

for the reservation wage and

$$h = \beta b + (1 - \beta)p \tag{19.34}$$

for the highest wage, and the weights are given by

$$\gamma = \frac{(1 + \kappa_1)^2}{(1 + \kappa_1)^2 + (\kappa_0 - \kappa_1)\kappa_1} \tag{19.35}$$

in (19.33) and

$$\beta = \frac{1}{(1 + \kappa_1)^2 + (\kappa_0 - \kappa_1)\kappa_1} \tag{19.36}$$

in (19.34). Thus, the derived parameters r and h and, in particular, the offer distribution (19.32), may be set as functions of the structural parameters θ. Of course, $\beta = \mu^2 \gamma$, with

$$\mu = \frac{1}{1 + \kappa_1} = \frac{\delta}{\delta + \lambda_1} < 1, \qquad (19.37)$$

so $0 < \beta < \gamma < 1$ under the maintained assumption $\lambda_1 > 0$, and since a viable equilibrium requires $r < h$ in (19.32), a comparison of (19.33) and (19.34) implies that we must impose $p > b$ on the structural parameter set (i.e., it pays to work).

On occasion, it is convenient to map the other way, expressing the structural parameters in terms of derived parameters, and we find from the above that the determinant of the system (19.33) and (19.34) is $\gamma(1 - \mu^2) \neq 0$ and that the inverse relationship is

$$\begin{aligned}
p &= \frac{\beta}{\beta - \gamma} r + \frac{\gamma}{\gamma - \beta} h, \\
b &= \frac{\beta - 1}{\beta - \gamma} r + \frac{\gamma - 1}{\gamma - \beta} h.
\end{aligned} \qquad (19.38)$$

Note that this allows us to write

$$p - r = \frac{h - r}{1 - \mu^2}, \qquad (19.39)$$

and for arbitrary w,

$$\frac{p - w}{p - r} = \frac{h - w + \mu^2(w - r)}{h - r}. \qquad (19.40)$$

Since the model may be solved completely, all other distributions of interest may be derived. Of particular importance is the conditional density of job duration j, given the accepted wage w,

$$f_j(j|w) = (\delta + \lambda_1) \frac{(p - w)^{1/2}}{(p - r)^{1/2}} \exp\left(-(\delta + \lambda_1) \frac{(p - w)^{1/2}}{(p - r)^{1/2}} j\right). \qquad (19.41)$$

The reason this depends on w is again that the current wage serves as the on-the-job reservation wage. Although it is theoretically important that the model may be solved in terms of the structural parameters $\theta = (\lambda_0, \lambda_1, \delta, p, b)$, it is useful for empirical purposes to reparametrize to $\phi = (\lambda_0, \lambda_1, \delta, r, h)$, using (19.33) and (19.34). In particular, using (19.40) and (19.32), the offer density (19.32) is rewritten as

$$f_w(w; \phi) = \frac{1 + \kappa_1}{2\kappa_1} \frac{1 - \mu^2}{(h - w + \mu^2(w - r))^{1/2}(h - r)^{1/2}}, \qquad w \in [r, h].$$
$$(19.42)$$

Similarly, using (19.42), the job duration density (19.41) becomes

$$f_j(j; \phi|w) = (\delta + \lambda_1) \frac{(h - w + \mu^2(w - r))^{1/2}}{(h - r)^{1/2}}$$

$$\times \exp\left(-(\delta + \lambda_1)\frac{(h - w + \mu^2(w - r))^{1/2}}{(h - r)^{1/2}}j\right). \qquad (19.43)$$

Combining (19.31), (19.42), and (19.43), we may form the contribution to the log likelihood from an individual who initially is unemployed for d periods, then accepts an offer w and keeps the job for j periods. For convenience, we suppress terms not depending on parameters in all of what follows. We have (since $(1 + \kappa_1)(1 - \mu^2)/\kappa_1 = (\lambda_1 + 2\delta)/(\delta + \lambda_1)$)

$$l(\phi) = \log\lambda_0 - \lambda_0 d + \log(\lambda_1 + 2\delta) - \log(h - r)$$

$$-(\delta + \lambda_1)\frac{\left(h - w + \delta^2(w - r)\big/\left[(\delta + \lambda_1)^2\right]\right)^{1/2}}{(h - r)^{1/2}}j \qquad (19.44)$$

as long as (d, w, j) belongs to the support. In particular, we require $r \leq w \leq h$. With multiple observations, the conditions are $r \leq w_{\min}$, the minimum sample wage, and $h \geq w_{\max}$, the maximum sample wage.

Kiefer and Neumann (1993) consider an extended panel where it is observed in addition how each job spell ended, whether in a layoff or a quit. The resulting requirements on r and h are the same. The estimators $\hat{r} = w_{\min}$ and $\hat{h} = w_{\max}$ are considered. Inference on the remaining parameters $(\lambda_0, \lambda_1, \delta)$ conditional on $c = (w_{\min}, w_{\max})$ is justified since although c is not exogenous (it is not a proper cut), it is in fact a *local cut* in the sense of Christensen and Kiefer (1994a, 2000). Because of the order statistic properties of $w_{\min}$ and $w_{\max}$, these converge to r and h at a rate faster than $N^{1/2}$, where N is the sample size, so the order $N^{1/2}$ distribution depends little on other parameters. This is the essential requirement in the generalized conditionality principle based on the local cut (see chapter 8).

To illustrate the usefulness of the local cut concept, differentiate (19.44) with respect to r to yield

$$l_r(\phi) = \frac{1}{h - r} - \frac{(\delta + \lambda_1)(h - w)(1 - \mu^2)j}{2(h - r)^{3/2}(h - w + \mu^2(w - r))^{1/2}}. \qquad (19.45)$$

The first term is positive and the second negative, and the sign remains ambiguous. Only if $l_r(\phi) > 0$ for $r < w$ would $\hat{r} = w_{\min}$ be guaranteed to be the maximum likelihood estimator (MLE). Still, although the estimator under the local cut is very simple and (19.45) indicates that the MLE may be complicated, the order $N^{1/2}$ asymptotic properties are the same, both for these and for the remaining parameters.

By a slight abuse of notation, we henceforth consider r and h to mean the estimated values $w_{\min}$ and $w_{\max}$. Furthermore, from (19.44), λ_0 is clearly estimated by $\bar{d}^{-1}$, where $\bar{d}$ is the average unemployment duration in the sample. The remaining parameters $\psi = (\delta, \lambda_1)$ may then be estimated based on the criterion (per observation)

$$l(\psi) = \log(\lambda_1 + 2\delta) - (\delta + \lambda_1)\frac{(h - w + \delta^2(w - r)/\left[(\delta + \lambda_1)^2\right])^{1/2}}{(h - r)^{1/2}}\, j.$$

$$\tag{19.46}$$

Treating this as a pseudo log likelihood for ψ (Barndorff-Nielsen, 1988) yields asymptotic likelihood inference. In particular, (19.46) is an *asymptotic log profile likelihood*.

Identification of all structural parameters θ follows if $\psi = (\lambda_1, \delta)$ is identified in (19.46). Intuitively, the reason that we in the present analysis can get identification is similar to that given in chapter 7. The arrival rate in the prototypal (partial equilibrium) search model is identified in pure wage data because of the parameter restriction implied by the reservation wage condition. Similarly, although wage data have already been used to estimate r and h in the present prototypal (general) equilibrium search model, the shape of the joint wage and job duration distribution still depends sufficiently on ϕ for identification.

The result presented in the following theorem is actually stronger than mere identification and implies that the criterion (19.46) is well-behaved.

THEOREM 10 *All structural parameters of the equilibrium search model are identified in the reduced panel including only unemployment duration, reemployment wage, and job duration for each worker. The asymptotic log profile likelihood is globally concave, and the observed asymptotic profile information per observation is given by*

$$i = \frac{1}{(\lambda_1 + 2\delta)^2}uu' + \frac{\delta^2(h - w)(w - r)j}{(h - r)^{1/2}(\delta + \lambda_1)^3(h - w + \mu^2(w - r))^{3/2}}vv',$$

where $u = (2, 1)'$ and $v = (-\kappa_1, 1)'$.

Proof. Write (19.46) as $l(\psi) = \tilde{l} + \overset{\approx}{l}$ with $\tilde{l} = \log(\lambda_1 + 2\delta)$ and consider this term first. We have

$$\tilde{l}_\delta = \frac{2}{\lambda_1 + 2\delta}, \tag{19.47}$$

$$\tilde{l}_{\lambda_1} = \frac{1}{\lambda_1 + 2\delta}, \tag{19.48}$$

$$\tilde{l}_{\delta\delta} = -\frac{4}{(\lambda_1 + 2\delta)^2}, \tag{19.49}$$

$$\tilde{l}_{\delta\lambda_1} = -\frac{2}{(\lambda_1 + 2\delta)^2}, \tag{19.50}$$

$$\tilde{l}_{\lambda_1\lambda_1} = -\frac{1}{(\lambda_1 + 2\delta)^2}. \tag{19.51}$$

The contribution to i corresponding to $\tilde{l}$ has entries equal to minus the second derivatives (19.49)–(19.51) and hence the term involving u in the theorem. Differentiating $\overset{\approx}{l} = -(\delta + \lambda_1)\tau^{1/2}j$, where

$$\tau = \frac{h - w + \delta^2(w - r)/\left[(\delta + \lambda_1)^2\right]}{h - r} \tag{19.52}$$

is $(p - w)/(p - r)$ from (19.46) yields

$$\overset{\approx}{l}_\delta = -\tau^{1/2}j\left(1 + \frac{\delta\lambda_1}{(\delta + \lambda_1)^2\tau}\frac{w - r}{h - r}\right), \tag{19.53}$$

$$\overset{\approx}{l}_{\lambda_1} = -\tau^{1/2}j\left(1 - \frac{\delta^2}{(\delta + \lambda_1)^2\tau}\frac{w - r}{h - r}\right), \tag{19.54}$$

$$\overset{\approx}{l}_{\delta\delta} = -\tau^{1/2}j\frac{\lambda_1^2}{(\delta + \lambda_1)^3}\frac{w - r}{h - r} + \tau^{-3/2}j\frac{\delta^2\lambda_1^2}{(\delta + \lambda_1)^5}\left(\frac{w - r}{h - r}\right)^2, \tag{19.55}$$

$$\overset{\approx}{l}_{\delta\lambda_1} = \tau^{1/2}j\frac{\delta\lambda_1}{(\delta + \lambda_1)^3}\frac{w - r}{h - r} - \tau^{-3/2}j\frac{\delta^3\lambda_1}{(\delta + \lambda_1)^5}\left(\frac{w - r}{h - r}\right)^2, \tag{19.56}$$

$$\overset{\approx}{l}_{\lambda_1\lambda_1} = -\tau^{1/2}j\frac{\delta^2}{(\delta + \lambda_1)^3}\frac{w - r}{h - r} + \tau^{-3/2}j\frac{\delta^4}{(\delta + \lambda_1)^5}\left(\frac{w - r}{h - r}\right)^2. \tag{19.57}$$

Taking out the common term

$$-\tau^{-3/2}j\frac{\delta^2}{(\delta + \lambda_1)^3}\frac{w - r}{h - r} \tag{19.58}$$

in each of (19.55)–(19.57) leaves the structure of the term involving v in the statement of theorem 10 since $\kappa_1 = \lambda_1/\delta$. Using (19.52), the remaining constant in each of the three expressions is

$$
\tau - \frac{\delta^2}{(\delta + \lambda_1)^2} \frac{w - r}{h - r} = \frac{h - w + \delta^2 (w - r) / [(\delta + \lambda_1)^2]}{h - r}
$$
$$
- \frac{\delta^2 (w - r) / [(\delta + \lambda_1)^2]}{h - r} = \frac{h - w}{h - r}.
$$
(19.59)

Multiplying (19.59) and (19.58) and using (19.52) again yields the exact form of the coefficient on vv' in the theorem.   □

Note that since $\kappa_1 > 0$, evidently u and v are linearly independent. Further, since $r < w < h$ (except for the minimum and maximum wages), the scalar multipliers on uu', and respectively vv', are positive. Consequently, i is positive definite, hence so is the Fisher information $E(i)$, and strict global concavity and parameter identification results. Of course, regularity of the Fisher information by itself ensures only local identification, but the result of theorem 10 is stronger. By strict global concavity, any maximum of the likelihood function is unique.

Global concavity implies that Newton-Raphson iteration is the method of choice for maximization of the asymptotic log profile likelihood function (19.46). In fact, the stated theorem is the strongest possible, in that any less informative data set leads to an ill-behaved likelihood function. This is why the model for data d, w, and j only is labeled the *prototypal equilibrium search model*. The problems that arise with less informative data sets are documented in the following.

19.4 PANELS WITH PARTIALLY MISSING OBSERVATIONS

In this section we consider the effect of partially missing observations on our non-linear panel model. The concavity result of the previous section applies to a panel complete with unemployment duration d, reemployment wage w, and job duration j for each observation. In many applied situations, what is actually available is a panel with partially missing observations, e.g., only one or two of d, w, and j for some people. We assess the separate information contributions of d, w, and j. Our analysis can be extended to apply to different data configurations; for example, data on unemployment income might be available, thus providing further information on the parameter b above the minimal necessary information considered here.

19.4.1 The Contribution of Unemployment Duration

The simplest case is when only d is available for a given worker. This continues to contribute a term $\log \lambda_0 - \lambda_0 d$ to the log likelihood as in (19.44), regardless of the missing (w, j). Note that d is stochastically independent of (w, j) and λ_0 is variation-independent of the remaining parameters λ_1, δ, r, and h. No matter what the sample configuration is, λ_0 is estimated by $\hat{\lambda}_0 = \overline{d}^{-1}$, the average being across all workers with observed d, and $\hat{\lambda}_0$ is stochastically independent of all other parameter estimates, even in finite samples. Censored spells can be handled without difficulty using standard methods.

By the same argument, if d is missing from some or all observations, but data on w and j are complete, this in no way changes the portion of (19.44) relevant for the remaining parameters (other than λ_0). All estimation and efficiency issues are unchanged, but λ_1, δ, r, and h remain identified. By (19.39), p is identified as well, although b is not.

Things are not as simple if either j or w is missing, and we treat these cases in turn.

19.4.2 The Contribution of Wages

A missing j does not affect inference on λ_0. At issue is inference on the remaining parameters, and this in turn is unaffected by whether d is missing or not. Thus, we focus on inference on r, h, δ, and λ_1 from wage data alone. Taking as before $\hat{r} = w_{\min}$ and $\hat{h} = w_{\max}$, the contribution to the criterion for $\psi = (\delta, \lambda_1)$ from a wage w with no accompanying job duration j is

$$
\begin{aligned}
l(\psi; w) = {} & \log(\lambda_1 + 2\delta) - \log(\delta + \lambda_1) \\
& - \frac{1}{2} \log \left(h - w + \delta^2 \frac{w - r}{(\delta + \lambda_1)^2} \right),
\end{aligned}
\tag{19.60}
$$

based on (19.46). The additional term $- \log(2) - \log(h - r)/2$ does not depend on ψ and has been suppressed. It follows by combining the first two terms as $\log(1 + \delta/(\delta + \lambda_1))$ that (19.60) depends on (δ, λ_1) through $\mu = \delta/(\delta + \lambda_1)$ from (19.37) only. Thus, if for all individuals in the sample only w (and/or d) is observed, then of course δ and λ_1 are not separately identified. Nonetheless, to assess the separate information contributions of d, w, and j for more general panels with partially missing observations, in particular where the job duration j is present for some individuals so that δ and λ_1 are separately identified, we need the contribution from (19.60) to the Hessian of the total log likelihood. Much as in the proof of theorem 10, we obtain the second derivatives as

$$l_{\delta\delta}^{w} = \frac{1}{(\delta + \lambda_1)^2} - \frac{4}{(\lambda_1 + 2\delta)^2} + \frac{\lambda_1^2 (w - r)}{(h - r)(\delta + \lambda_1)^6 \tau^2}$$

$$\times \left(2\delta^2 \frac{w - r}{h - r} - \left(1 - \frac{2}{\kappa_1} \right) (\delta + \lambda_1)^2 \tau \right), \qquad (19.61)$$

$$l_{\delta\lambda_1}^{w} = \frac{1}{(\delta + \lambda_1)^2} - \frac{2}{(\lambda_1 + 2\delta)^2} + \frac{\delta\lambda_1 (w - r)}{(h - r)(\delta + \lambda_1)^6 \tau^2}$$

$$\times \left(2\delta^2 \frac{w - r}{h - r} - \left(2 - \frac{1}{\kappa_1} \right) (\delta + \lambda_1)^2 \tau \right), \qquad (19.62)$$

$$l_{\lambda_1\lambda_1}^{w} = \frac{1}{(\delta + \lambda_1)^2} - \frac{1}{(\lambda_1 + 2\delta)^2} + \frac{\delta^2 (w - r)}{(h - r)(\delta + \lambda_1)^6 \tau^2}$$

$$\times \left(2\delta^2 \frac{w - r}{h - r} - 3 (\delta + \lambda_1)^2 \tau \right), \qquad (19.63)$$

with the subscripts indicating differentiation, the superscript w indicating that the data are wages, and τ defined in (19.52). Note that (19.61)–(19.63) imply that the second-derivative matrix is not necessarily negative definite. In terms of the local shape of the log likelihood function for an unbalanced design, this means that the contributions from observations with missing job durations may not be concave. This underscores the importance of theorem 10 from the previous section.

The easiest way to see the nonconcavity is perhaps in (19.63). When combining the two first terms of a common denominator, the numerator is $\delta(2\lambda_1 + 3\delta) > 0$, and for sufficiently small $w \geqslant r$, we have $l_{\lambda_1\lambda_1}^{w} > 0$. This shows that inference on λ_1 (and by implication on all other parameters except λ_0) from pure wage data is hazardous. Any empirical investigation is unlikely to be successful unless it relies at least to some extent on employment duration data.

Given that λ_1 indicates the on-the-job offer arrival rate and thus jointly with the layoff rate δ determines the distribution of job duration, it may not be too surprising that it is difficult to estimate λ_1 in wage data. However, in the partial equilibrium prototypal search model of chapter 7, the arrival rate is identified in pure wage data, hence the importance of establishing the negative result above for the prototypal general equilibrium model. A numerical example where (19.63) is indeed positive follows later.

In a sample where j is missing for only some observations, these may of course still be included, and the negatives of (19.61)–(19.63) give the corresponding contributions to the information on (δ, λ_1). While these can be negative, total information from complete observations is positive by theorem 10. This suggests that employment duration data add much information on these duration parameters. This is considered in the following.

19.4.3 The Contribution of Employment Duration

If w (and perhaps d) is missing from an observation (d, w, j), the above discussion suggests that considerable information on $\psi = (\delta, \lambda_1)$ can still be added by including j. Theorem 10 together with the analysis above shows that the conditional distribution of j, given w, contributes favorably to the curvature of the reduced panel likelihood for the prototypal equilibrium search model. However, if w is missing, the criterion for ψ must be based on the marginal distribution of j (recall that d is independent of (w, j) and is ancillary with respect to ψ).

Combining (19.42) and (19.43), the marginal distribution of j is

$$f_j(j) = \int_r^h f_j(j|w) f_w(w) \, dw$$

$$= \frac{\lambda_1 + 2\delta}{2(h-r)} \int_r^h \exp\left(-(\delta + \lambda_1) \frac{\left(h - w + \mu^2 (w - r)\right)^{1/2}}{(h - r)^{1/2}} j\right) dw$$

$$= \frac{\lambda_1 + 2\delta}{2(h-r)} \int_{(p-h)^{1/2}}^{(p-r)^{1/2}} 2x e^{-kx} \, dx, \tag{19.64}$$

where $x = (p - w)^{1/2}$, so that $|dw/dx| = 2x$. Dividing (19.40) by (19.39) yields an expression for x from which it readily follows that

$$k = (\delta + \lambda_1) \frac{\left(1 - \mu^2\right)^{1/2}}{(h - r)^{1/2}} j \tag{19.65}$$

in (19.64). Direct integration yields

$$f_j(j) = \frac{\lambda_1 + 2\delta}{k(h-r)} \left(\left((p - h)^{1/2} + \frac{1}{k}\right) e^{-k(p-h)^{1/2}}\right.$$

$$\left. - \left((p - r)^{1/2} + \frac{1}{k}\right) e^{-k(p-r)^{1/2}}\right). \tag{19.66}$$

From (19.39) and (19.65), $k(p-r)^{1/2} = (\delta + \lambda_1) j$, and it may be shown similarly that $k(p-h)^{1/2} = \mu(\delta + \lambda_1) j$. Substitution in (19.66) yields

$$f_j(j) = \frac{1}{\lambda_1 j^2} \left((1 + \delta j) e^{-\delta j} - (1 + (\delta + \lambda_1) j) e^{-(\delta+\lambda_1)j}\right), \tag{19.67}$$

the marginal distribution of employment duration in the equilibrium search model. Note that the distribution is parametrized by $\psi = (\delta, \lambda_1)$, the job duration parameters. The associated limited information contribution to the criterion for ψ is

$$l(\psi; j) = -\log \lambda_1 + \log \Phi, \qquad (19.68)$$

with the definition

$$\Phi = (1 + \delta j) e^{-\delta j} - (1 + (\delta + \lambda_1) j) e^{-(\delta + \lambda_1)j} > 0. \qquad (19.69)$$

Indicating the employment duration data configuration in the superscript, the second derivatives of (19.68) are

$$
\begin{aligned}
l^j_{\delta\delta} &= -\frac{j^2}{\Phi} \left((1 - \delta j) e^{\delta j} - (1 - (\delta + \lambda_1) j) e^{-(\delta + \lambda_1)j} \right) \\
&\quad - \frac{j^4}{\Phi^2} \left((\delta + \lambda_1) e^{-(\delta + \lambda_1)j} - \delta e^{-\delta j} \right)^2 \\
&= -\frac{j^2}{\Phi^2} \left(e^{-(\delta + \lambda_1)j} - e^{-\delta j} \right)^2 , \qquad (19.70)
\end{aligned}
$$

$$
\begin{aligned}
l^j_{\delta\lambda_1} &= -\frac{j^2}{\Phi} (1 - (\delta + \lambda_1) j) e^{-(\delta + \lambda_1)j} \\
&\quad - \frac{j^4}{\Phi^2} (\delta + \lambda_1) \left((\delta + \lambda_1) e^{-2(\delta + \lambda_1)j} - \delta e^{-(2\delta + \lambda_i)j} \right) \\
&= -\frac{j^2}{\Phi^2} e^{-(2\delta + \lambda_1)j} \left(1 - \lambda_1 j - e^{-\lambda_1 j} \right) , \qquad (19.71)
\end{aligned}
$$

$$
\begin{aligned}
l^j_{\lambda_1\lambda_1} &= \frac{1}{\lambda_1^2} + \frac{j^2}{\Phi} (1 - (\delta + \lambda_1) j) e^{-(\delta + \lambda_1)j} \\
&\quad - \frac{j^4}{\Phi^2} (\delta + \lambda_1) (\delta + \lambda_1)^2 e^{-(2\delta + \lambda_i)j} \\
&= \frac{1}{\lambda_1^2} + \frac{j^2}{\Phi^2} e^{-(2\delta + \lambda_1)j} \left(1 - \lambda_1 j - e^{-\lambda_1 j} - \delta (\delta + \lambda_1) j^2 \right) . \qquad (19.72)
\end{aligned}
$$

The factor $\left(j^2/\Phi^2 \right) \exp\left(-(2\delta - \lambda_1) j \right)$ common in (19.71) and (19.72) may be taken out in (19.70), too, producing

$$l^j_{\delta\delta} = -\frac{j^2}{\Phi^2} e^{-(2\delta + \lambda_1)j} 2 \left(\cosh\left(-\lambda_1 j \right) - 1 \right) ,$$

although it appears that $l^j_{\delta\lambda_1}$ and $l^j_{\lambda_1\lambda_1}$ may not be conveniently expressed in terms of hyperbolic cosine functions.

Again, the negatives of (19.70)–(19.72) are the information contributions from observations where only j (and perhaps d) is available. The contributions are different from the case where in addition w is observed, an example of which is given below.

19.4.4 A Numerical Example

The analysis above shows that observations where the job duration j is missing do contribute information on μ from (19.37) or, equivalently, on the fundamental unitless parameter κ_1, but not on both structural parameters δ and λ_1. The question is how big is this problem in practice? We begin addressing this issue by looking at some realistic data and parameter values. We consider the results obtained by Kiefer and Neumann (1993) in the National Longitudinal Survey of Youth (NLSY) 1979–1988 data on the transition from formal education to employment for young males. We focus attention on the largest homogeneous subsample, consisting of 874 white high school graduates. The estimated parameters for this subsample are $\lambda_1 = 0.0034$, $\delta = 0.0064$, $r = 30.30$ and $h = 2861.40$, implying in turn $\mu = 0.6531$ and $\kappa_1 = 0.5313$. We wish to evaluate the information contribution from a typical observation and for this purpose use $w = 186$ and $j = 72$, the subsample averages, in which case $\tau = 0.9685$ and $\Phi = 0.0792$. The resulting contributions to profile information for the various data configurations are shown in table 19.1.

The first row corresponds to the case of missing job durations and is based on (19.60). The numbers may seem large, but examples below show that the magnitude per se does not indicate exaggerated precision. The more serious problem is the negative information on λ_1, the on-the-job offer arrival rate. Indeed, the possibility of non-negative definiteness of the second-derivative matrix in (19.61)–(19.63) above is a very real one for empirically relevant data and parameter values. In particular, it is the observed information, not the Fisher (expected) information that characterizes the curvature of the log likelihood in a given data set. We conclude that applications of the equilibrium search model that rely too heavily on wage data are likely to fail—even if by coincidence they did not, the results would remain statistically unreliable.

We therefore turn to the case where job duration is included and consider first the missing wage situation. The results are given in the second row of table 19.1 and are based on (19.68). Duration data are more informative on δ, the layoff rate ($i_{\delta\delta}$ is greater in the second row than in the first row), and the information on λ_1 turns positive. Importantly, the matrix is now positive definite $\left(i_{\delta\delta}i_{\lambda_1\lambda_1} - i_{\delta\lambda_1}^2 > 0\right)$.

Next, wages are added back into the data set. The third row of table 19.1 shows the results of another kind of limited-information nonlinear panel data analysis different from the two instances of partially missing observations already considered. Here, w and j are treated as separate pieces of information, i.e., the second derivative matrix is the sum of those in (19.61)–(19.63) and (19.70)–(19.72) above. This would be appropriate if w and j

Table 19.1 Profile Information Contributions.

Data	$i_{\delta\delta}$	$i_{\delta\lambda_1}$	$i_{\lambda_1\lambda_1}$
Wages (w)	4,629	−2,801	−5,858
Employment durations (j)	15,506	7,121	4,325
w, j	20,135	4,321	1,532
Joint	15,290	7,530	3,981

were from different workers, but information is lost if they in fact are from a single observation in the panel and this is ignored in the econometric approach. Nonetheless, the information matrix remains positive definite.

The analysis suggests that the reduced panel considered above is minimal in that the identification of all structural parameters in the equilibrium search model requires that at least some of the observations contain the job duration j. Of course, if no w is observed, r and h cannot be estimated, and similarly some observations on d are needed for the estimation of λ_0. In this sense, theorem 10 of section 19.3 is the strongest possible. The global concavity is illustrated in the last row of table 19.1, where w and j are treated as stemming from a single observation and the entries are those of i from theorem 10. As predicted, i is positive definite, and it is interesting to note that the information on (δ, λ_1) from w and j jointly is not very different from the information from j in isolation, at least for the numbers we look at.

The inverse of i suggests asymptotic standard deviations of δ and λ_1 of 0.0309 and 0.0606, so if the estimated values of these parameters are close to the true values, we would expect to be able to reliably distinguish δ from zero with only about a 100 observations, whereas more than 1000 might be needed in the case of λ_1, according to this estimate.

19.5 GEOMETRIC INFORMATION DECOMPOSITION

It follows from the previous sections that the reduced panel consisting of observations of the type (d, w, j) is the minimal appropriate inference frame for the equilibrium search model. In this section, we take a closer look at the geometry of the information accumulation in this type of panel.

It was noted in section 19.3 that d is independent of (w, j), with distribution parametrized by λ_0, and that λ_0 does not enter the distribution of (w, j). Thus, separate inference on λ_0 from d and on the remaining parameters from (w, j) was indicated. Precisely, d is S-sufficient for λ_0 and S-ancillary for the remaining parameters, whereas (w, j) is S-ancillary for λ_0 and S-sufficient for the remaining parameters. In other words, d is a proper cut (see also section 19.3 on Christensen and Kiefer's (1994a) local generalization of this concept). Recall, however, that we are here referring to the remaining parameters in $\phi = (\lambda_0, \lambda_1, \delta, r, h)$, including the *derived parameters* r and h. Our ultimate interest is in inference on the structural parameters $\theta = (\lambda_0, b, p, \delta, \lambda_1)$, and the resulting model possesses no cut. In particular, by (19.42), the wage distribution certainly depends on r, which from (19.33) depends on γ, and in turn on λ_0 (by (19.35) and since $\kappa_0 = \lambda_0/\delta$).

Consider therefore $v(\theta)$, the order $N^{1/2}$ asymptotic variance matrix for the structural parameters, where N is the sample size. As the local cut $c = (w_{\min}, w_{\max})$ converges to (r, h) at a rate faster than $N^{1/2}$, these parameters may be treated as known for the purpose of constructing $v(\theta)$. The asymptotic variance matrices for λ_0 and $\psi = (\delta, \lambda_1)$ are $v(\lambda_0) = \lambda_0^2$ and $v(\psi) = i^{-1}$, respectively, interpreting i as the probability limit of the matrix in theorem 10. By the independence of d and (w, j), and hence of the estimators of λ_0 and ψ, $v(\chi)$ is block-diagonal and formed from $v(\lambda_0)$ and $v(\psi)$, where $\chi = (\lambda_0, \psi)$. It follows that

$$
\begin{aligned}
v(\theta) &= \frac{\partial \theta}{\partial \chi'} v(\chi) \frac{\partial \theta'}{\partial \chi} \\
&= \frac{\partial \theta}{\partial \lambda_0} v(\lambda_0) \frac{\partial \theta'}{\partial \lambda_0} + \frac{\partial \theta}{\partial \psi'} v(\psi) \frac{\partial \theta'}{\partial \psi} \\
&= \Lambda_0 + \Psi,
\end{aligned} \tag{19.73}
$$

with $\partial \theta / \partial \chi'$ the 5×3 Jacobian of $\chi \to \theta$, $\partial \theta' / \partial \chi = (\partial \theta / \partial \chi')'$, and similarly for other derivatives. Writing $\eta = (\lambda_0, b)$ and $\mu = (b, p, \delta, \lambda_1)$, we find

$$
\Lambda_0 = \begin{pmatrix} \lambda_0^2 \dfrac{\partial \eta}{\partial \lambda_0} \dfrac{\partial \eta'}{\partial \lambda_0} & 0 \\ 0 & 0 \end{pmatrix}, \tag{19.74}
$$

with upper left and lower right corners of dimensions 2×2 and 3×3, respectively. Furthermore,

$$
\Psi = \begin{pmatrix} 0 & 0 \\ 0 & \dfrac{\partial \mu}{\partial \psi'} i^{-1} \dfrac{\partial \mu'}{\partial \psi} \end{pmatrix}, \tag{19.75}
$$

with 1×1 and 4×4 diagonal blocks. Defining

$$
\omega = (1 + \kappa_1)^2 - r, \tag{19.76}
$$

we find that in (19.74)

$$
\frac{\partial \eta}{\partial \lambda_0} = \begin{pmatrix} 1 \\ -(h - r) \frac{\kappa_1}{\delta \omega} \end{pmatrix} \tag{19.77}
$$

since (19.33) and (19.34) may be solved to yield

$$b = r - (h - r)\frac{(\kappa_0 - \kappa_1)\,\kappa_1}{\omega}.$$
(19.78)

Similarly, in (19.79),

$$\frac{\partial \mu}{\partial \psi'} = \begin{pmatrix} \Omega \\ I_2 \end{pmatrix},$$
(19.79)

with I_2 the identity on $\mathbb{R}^2$ and

$$\Omega = \begin{pmatrix} \dfrac{\partial b}{\partial \delta} & \dfrac{\partial b}{\partial \lambda_1} \\[2mm] \dfrac{\partial p}{\partial \delta} & \dfrac{\partial p}{\partial \lambda_1} \end{pmatrix},$$
(19.80)

and we readily find

$$\frac{\partial b}{\partial \delta} = 2(h - r)\frac{(\kappa_0 - \kappa_1)\,\kappa_1}{\delta\omega^2}(1 + \kappa_1 - r),$$
(19.81)

and with $\partial b/\partial \lambda_0$ the second coordinate in (19.77),

$$\frac{\partial b}{\partial \lambda_1} = \frac{\partial b}{\partial \delta} + \left(\frac{\lambda_0}{\lambda_1} - 2\right)\frac{\partial b}{\partial \lambda_0}.$$
(19.82)

Combining (19.37) and (19.38), we get

$$\frac{\partial p}{\partial \delta} = 2(h - r)\frac{1 + \kappa_1}{\lambda_1(2 + \kappa_1)^2} > 0;$$
(19.83)

i.e., the productivity and the layoff rate are directly related, *ceteris paribus*. Finally,

$$\frac{\partial p}{\partial \lambda_1} = \frac{2(1 + \kappa_1)\,h - (2 + 3\kappa_1)\,p}{\lambda_1(2 + \kappa_1)},$$
(19.84)

and (19.81)–(19.83) may be substituted in (19.80) to complete Ω. This is used in (19.79), which along with (19.77) allows the completion of (19.74) and (19.75), and $v(\theta)$ is constructed as in (19.73).

Comparing (19.73)–(19.75), it is clear that the block-diagonality is lost in the structural parametrization once the different dimensions are accounted for. However, the equilibrium framework implies that $v(\theta)$ still has special structure. If the row and column corresponding to b, unemployment insurance benefits net of search costs, are replaced by zeroes, then block-diagonality is recovered, and we define a parameter with this property to be a *parametric pivot*.

Geometrically, as observations are accumulated, information is expanded in the direction corresponding to Λ_0 in (19.73) based on d, and in the Ψ direction based on (w, j). This means that situations with partially missing observations can still be handled: If d is missing, Ψ may still be improved, and if (w, j) is missing, Λ_0 may be improved. In both cases, information is accumulated on the parametric pivot.

The likelihood geometry of the partial equilibrium prototypal search model was used in chapter 7 to separate the directions in which economic information was accumulated slowly and rapidly. We now generalize these techniques to the present equilibrium framework and show how to separately identify slow and rapid information accumulation within each of the directions Λ_0 and Ψ. The argument turns on the new concept of a parametric pivot introduced above.

Consider first the Ψ-direction and select a unit vector σ in the orthogonal complement $\mu^\perp$ to the column space of $\partial\mu/\partial\psi' = (\Omega', I_2)'$. Form a matrix with leading column σ and expand with additional columns Σ such that $(\sigma, \Sigma) \in O(4)$, the orthogonal group acting on $\mathbb{R}^4$. With $\mu^* = (\sigma, \Sigma)'\mu$, the reparametrization from $\theta = (\lambda_0, \mu)$ to $\theta^*(\lambda_0, \mu^*)$ has several geometrically and informationally important properties. Denoting the nonvanishing submatrices of Λ_0 and Ψ in (19.74) and (19.75) by λ_0^* and Ψ^*, respectively, the leading two-dimensional component in the alternative decomposition $\theta^* = (\eta^*, \mu^{**})$ has asymptotic variance

$$v(\eta^*) = \Theta'\Lambda_0\Theta, \tag{19.85}$$

where with σ_1 the leading element in σ we have

$$\Theta = \begin{pmatrix} 1 & 0 \\ 0 & \sigma_1 \end{pmatrix};$$

i.e., there is no contribution in the Ψ-direction in (19.85). Correspondingly,

$$v(\mu^{**}) = \Sigma'\Psi^*\Sigma \tag{19.86}$$

for the second component of θ^*. The model no longer possesses a proper parametric pivot, but the transformed pivot $b^* = \sigma'\mu$ indicates the ray in the Ψ-direction in which information is accumulated rapidly because of the fast convergence of the local cut. Under this reparametrization, all order $N^{1/2}$ information on b^* is based on unemployment duration d.

In the original prototypal model, the rotation is arbitrary up to the column corresponding to σ above. In the present richer economic setting, particular rotations may be of special interest. For example, if the leading column Σ_1 of Σ is selected from $\mu^\perp$ as well, superconsistency results in the direction indicated by $p^* = \Sigma_1'\mu$.

Turning next to the information decomposition in the Λ_0-direction, the generalized approach is illustrated explicitly by letting

$$\pi = \frac{1}{\xi^{1/2}} \binom{(h-r)\kappa_1}{\delta\omega}, \tag{19.87}$$

with the definition

$$\xi = \delta^2\omega^2 + (h-r)^2\kappa_1^2. \tag{19.88}$$

In this case we consider the reparametrization from $\theta = (\eta, \varepsilon)$, with $\varepsilon = (p, \delta, \lambda_1)$, to $\theta_* = (\eta_*, \varepsilon)$, with $\eta_* = (\Pi, \pi)'\eta$, and

$$\Pi = \frac{1}{\xi^{1/2}} \binom{\delta\omega}{(r-h)\kappa_1}. \tag{19.89}$$

For the decomposition $\theta_* = (\lambda_{0*}, \mu_*)$, with $\lambda_{0*} = \pi'\eta$, the asymptotic variance

$$v(\mu_*) = \Gamma'\Psi^*\Gamma \tag{19.90}$$

results for the second component, with

$$\Gamma = \begin{pmatrix} \pi_2 & 0 \\ 0 & I_3 \end{pmatrix}, \tag{19.91}$$

π_2 denoting the second coordinate in (19.87); i.e., there is no contribution in the Λ_0-direction in (19.90). For the first component of θ_* we have

$$v(\lambda_{0*}) = \Pi'\Lambda_0^*\Pi. \tag{19.92}$$

Economic information is accumulated rapidly in the Λ_0-direction along the ray indicated by the transformed pivot $\beta_* = \pi'\eta$. In geometric terms, comparing (19.85) and (19.86) with (19.90)–(19.92) and accounting for the different dimensions, all order $N^{1/2}$ information on the transformed pivot has moved from the Λ_0-direction to the Ψ-direction (cf (19.74) and (19.75)). In the θ_* parametrization, this information is without exemption based on (w, j), wage and employment duration.

Importantly, the transforms considered thus far are norm-preserving. In addition, a parameter group such as η^* and μ^{**} or λ_{0*} and μ_* may be orthogonalized, or block diagonality of the asymptotic variance matrix may be obtained by making the parametric pivot orthogonal to either λ_0 or ε, but the consequences are less geometrically and informationally appealing, and norms change. We therefore limit ourselves to another empirically important case. Thus, it may be inferred from the numbers reported in the numerical example earlier that the correlation between δ and λ_1 implied by i is in the vicinity of negative 96.5%. Evidently, application of a transform achieving Fisher orthogonality is of interest (Cox and Reid, 1987). Writing $i = \rho u u' + \varphi v v'$ for the matrix in theorem 10, a suitable choice is

$$K = \begin{pmatrix} \rho + \varphi & 0 \\ \kappa_1 \varphi - 2\rho & 1 \end{pmatrix}; \qquad (19.93)$$

i.e., the coordinates of $K'\psi = (\delta^*, \lambda_1)$ are order $N^{1/2}$ asymptotically independent. Obviously, a companion transform achieves this property while leaving δ unchanged. The only necessary adjustment in the foregoing theory is that ΩK^{-1} replaces Ω in (19.79), and similarly for any alternative to K. In particular, operations in the Λ_0-direction, such as (19.77), (19.87), and (19.89), are completely unaffected by the orthogonalizing procedure, whereas the updating of Ω of course spills over into (19.75), the definition of σ, etc.

19.5.1 Destination State Information

We now extend the analysis and consider the additional information contained in the postemployment destination c, defining $c = 0$ for a layoff and $c = 1$ for a quit. In addition, we explicitly deal with the possibility of right-censored job durations and work with the indicator a, defining $a = 0$ for censored and $a = 1$ for uncensored spells. In this case, the distributions for unemployment duration d and wage offer w are still given by (19.31) and (19.32).

Turning to the conditional distribution of job duration j and destination c, given the wage w and the censoring indicator a, the general form from the right-censored competing risks framework is

$$f_{j,c}(j, c|w, a) = ((1 - c)h_\delta + ch_1)^a S_j, \qquad (19.94)$$

where h_δ and h_1 indicate the hazard rates associated with layoffs and quits, respectively, and S_j denotes the survivor function for j. In the present case, $S_j = \exp(-(h_\delta + h_1)j)$, and clearly $h_\delta = \delta$.

Further, a quit requires not only the arrival of an offer on the job, which occurs at rate λ_1, but in addition that the new offer exceeds the on-the-job reservation wage, namely, the current wage w. Consequently, $h_1 = \lambda_1(1 - F(w))$, and hence $S_j = \exp(-(\delta + \lambda_1(1 - F(w)))j)$. For this calculation we have

$$\delta + \lambda_1(1 - F(w)) = \delta + \lambda_1 \left(1 - \frac{\delta + \lambda_1}{\lambda_1}\left(1 - \left(\frac{p - w}{p - r}\right)^{1/2}\right)\right)$$

$$= (\delta + \lambda_1)\left(\frac{p - w}{p - r}\right)^{1/2}, \qquad (19.95)$$

so that in particular $h_1 = (\delta + \lambda_1)((p - w)/(p - r))^{1/2} - \delta$. Substituting in (19.94), we get

$$
f_{j,c}(j, c|w, a) = \left((1 - c)\delta + c \left((\delta + \lambda_1) \left(\frac{p - w}{p - r} \right)^{1/2} - \delta \right) \right)^{a}
$$

$$
\times \exp \left(-(\delta + \lambda_1) \left(\frac{p - w}{p - r} \right)^{1/2} j \right). \tag{19.96}
$$

Again, although the model may be solved in terms of the structural parameters $\theta = (\lambda_0, \lambda_1, \delta, p, b)$, we reparametrize to $\phi = (\lambda_0, \lambda_1, \delta, r, h)$.

Thus, the offer density is (19.32), and using (19.35), the job duration density becomes

$$
f_{j,c}(j, c; \phi|w, a) = \left((1 - c)\delta + c \left((\delta + \lambda_1) \frac{(h - w + \mu^2(w - r))^{1/2}}{(h - r)^{1/2}} - \delta \right) \right)^{a}
$$

$$
\times \exp \left(-(\delta + \lambda_1) \frac{(h - w + \mu^2(w - r))^{1/2} j}{(h - r)^{1/2}} \right). \tag{19.97}
$$

Instead of (19.44) from the prototypal model, we now get

$$
\ell(\phi) = \log \lambda_0 - \lambda_0 d + \log(\lambda_1 + 2\delta) - \log(\delta + \lambda_1)
$$

$$
- \frac{1}{2} \log \left(h - w + \delta^2 \frac{w - r}{(\delta + \lambda_1)^2} \right) - \frac{1}{2} \log(h - r)
$$

$$
- a \log \left((1 - c)\delta + c \left((\delta + \lambda_1) \frac{\left(h - w + \delta^2 \frac{w - r}{(\delta + \lambda_1)^2} \right)^{1/2}}{(h - r)^{1/2}} - \delta \right) \right)
$$

$$
- (\delta + \lambda_1) \frac{\left(h - w + \delta^2 \frac{w - r}{(\delta + \lambda_1)^2} \right)^{1/2}}{(h - r)^{1/2}} j \tag{19.98}
$$

when (d, w, j) belongs to the support. Apart from $d, j \geq 0$, we require $r \leq w_{\min}$, the minimum sample wage, and $h \leq w_{\max}$, the maximum sample wage. Again, inference on the remaining parameters $(\lambda_0, \lambda_1, \delta)$ conditional on $t = (w_{\min}, w_{\max})$ is justified since t is a *local cut* (Christensen and Kiefer (1994a, 2000), and chapter 8).

Thus, let r and h mean the estimated values $w_{\min}$ and $w_{\max}$. From (19.46), λ_0 is clearly estimated by $\left(\overline{d} \right)^{-1}$. The remaining parameters $\psi = (\delta, \lambda_1)$

may then be estimated based on

$$\ell(\psi) = \log(\lambda_1 + 2\delta) - \log(\delta + \lambda_1) - \frac{1}{2}\log\left(h - w + \delta^2\frac{w-r}{(\gamma + \lambda_1)^2}\right)$$

$$- a\log\left((1-c)\delta + c\left((\delta + \lambda_1)\frac{\left(h - w + \delta^2\frac{w-r}{(\delta+\lambda_1)^2}\right)}{(h-r)^{1/2}} - \delta\right)\right)$$

$$- (\delta + \lambda_1)\frac{\left(h - w + \delta^2\frac{w-r}{(\delta+\lambda_1)^2}\right)^{1/2}}{(h-r)^{1/2}}\,j. \tag{19.99}$$

The identification of all structural parameters θ follows since ψ is identified in (19.99). Interpreting $i(\psi)$ as the probability limit of the sample average of the negative second derivative with respect to ψ of (19.99), the asymptotic variance of the estimator for ψ is $v(\psi) = i(\psi)^{-1}$. In parallel with this we find $v(\lambda_0) = i(\lambda_0)^{-1} = \lambda_0^2$, and since λ_0 is the likelihood independent of the remaining parameters, the asymptotic variance matrix for $\chi = (\lambda_0, \psi)$ is given by

$$v(\chi) = \begin{pmatrix} v(\lambda_0) & 0 \\ 0 & v(\psi) \end{pmatrix}, \tag{19.100}$$

with diagonal blocks of dimension 1×1 and 2×2, respectively.

With the definition $\omega = (1 + \kappa_1)^2 - 1 > 0$, the Jacobian of the map $\chi \to (p, b)$ is given by

$$J_\chi = \frac{h-r}{\delta^2\omega}\begin{pmatrix} 0 & -2(\lambda_1 + \delta) & 2\kappa_1(\lambda_1 + \delta) \\ -\lambda_1\omega & (\lambda_0 + 2\delta)\kappa_1^2 & 2(\lambda_0 - \lambda_1)\kappa_1^2 \end{pmatrix}, \tag{19.101}$$

showing that the comparative equilibrium search dynamics imply that productivity is related directly to layoffs and inversely to on-the-job offers, *ceteris paribus*. Similarly, the value of nonmarket time increases with offers on the job and decreases with offers in unemployment. The impact of δ on b depends on the relative frequencies of offer arrivals but is positive if the rate is highest during unemployment (this is the case in our empirical findings below).

Upon estimation of ϕ as outlined, we reparametrize back to the estimator $\hat{\theta}$ of the structural parameters $\theta = (\lambda_0, \lambda_1, \delta, p, b)$. Standard errors are based on the asymptotic distribution result

$$N^{1/2}\left(\hat{\theta} - \theta\right) \overset{\sim}{\to} \mathcal{N}\left(0, Jv(\chi)J'\right), \tag{19.102}$$

where $\mathcal{N}$ indicates the normal law and

$$J = \begin{pmatrix} I_3 \\ J_\chi \end{pmatrix}, \tag{19.103}$$

with I_3 the identity on $\mathbb{R}^3$. Thus, in the equilibrium search model, we have a five-dimensional, rank 3 degenerate normal (CARRN) distribution for the structural parameters. This generalizes the rank $K - 1$ result of chapter 7 for the K-parameter simple (partial equilibrium) search model.

19.6 DATA AND SUMMARY STATISTICS

The data we consider are drawn from a random sample originating from the Danish Statistical Office and representing 1% of the Danish population in the age group 16–75 years over the period 1981–1990. This is a longitudinal data set that on a weekly basis distinguishes spells of absence from the labor force, unemployment, and employment, and in the latter case monitors changes in employer. Unemployment, may be permanent or temporary. In addition, an average hourly wage is recorded for each individual for each year. As a first approximation (which we improve upon later), we consider this wage figure to be the reemployment wage by focusing on individuals who are registered as unemployed on January 1 of any year. We record the duration of this unemployment spell, the reemployment wage, and the duration of the subsequent job, along with the destination, i.e., information on whether the job ended in a layoff (i.e., was followed by unemployment) or a quit (i.e., a change in employer) or was right-censored in the data set (because of dropping out of the labor force or the job continuing beyond the survey end). Left-censored unemployment spells are eliminated. The wage figures are deflated to 1981 levels, using the Danish consumer price index covering goods and services. Thus, we end up with a panel of observations of the type (d, w, j, c, a).

The data set furthermore contains observable individual characteristics, and we group the observations to control nonparametrically for variations in gender, age, and education. The last-mentioned is split into the categories less than high school, high school, Bachelors, and finally Masters and above. We consider the age groups 16–21, 22–30, 31–50, and 51–76, and within each education level we group on gender and age in order to maintain subsamples of at least 150 individuals. Finally, since some of the statistical procedures are sensitive to the behavior of order statistics, we omit the highest and lowest 1% of the wage observations in each subsample. A total of 9351 observations meet our selection criteria and remain in the trimmed sample.

Summary statistics are provided in table 19.2.

For the overall sample and each subsample we report the sample size (N) and the sample averages of unemployment duration (d), job duration (j), wage (w), minimum wage ($w_{\min}$), maximum wage ($w_{\max}$), the right-censoring indicator for j ($a = 1$ indicates no censoring), and the destination

Table 19.2 Summary Statistics.

Level of Education	N	d	j	w	$w_{\min}$	$w_{\max}$	a	c	$\hat{\lambda}_1$	$\hat{\delta}$
Less than high school										
Men, 16–21	294	24.39	31.87	95.40	55.10	175.91	0.94	0.26	0.016	0.021
Men, 22–30	885	30.71	34.73	110.21	55.36	267.01	0.89	0.23	0.014	0.019
Men, 31–50	1,020	33.59	43.82	118.04	60.00	397.04	0.86	0.20	0.009	0.015
Men, 51–76	419	34.44	43.75	109.47	55.36	261.38	0.84	0.12	0.006	0.017
Women, 16–21	289	31.25	42.73	92.36	50.98	286.49	0.92	0.28	0.012	0.015
Women, 22–30	863	40.93	37.68	95.22	53.35	214.47	0.90	0.20	0.010	0.019
Women, 31–50	1,181	42.16	43.58	98.18	54.13	276.78	0.83	0.15	0.006	0.016
Women, 51–76	384	47.99	36.55	101.42	58.34	328.41	0.83	0.09	0.005	0.020
High school										
Men and women, 16–21	264	26.33	48.82	91.2	51.94	191.00	0.83	0.34	0.012	0.010
Men, 22–30	745	25.79	44.23	113.84	54.74	311.20	0.86	0.32	0.014	0.012
Men, 31–50	694	32.36	44.54	124.69	63.64	388.19	0.82	0.20	0.009	0.014
Men, 51–76	256	36.81	37.95	116.06	54.51	281.49	0.83	0.14	0.007	0.018
Women, 22–30	641	36.44	46.28	95.60	53.74	272.52	0.81	0.23	0.009	0.013
Women, 31–50	492	43.56	49.29	101.68	54.02	375.32	0.80	0.18	0.007	0.014
Women, 51–76	153	51.41	32.87	98.35	52.00	362.89	0.85	0.06	0.003	0.024
Bachelors										
Men and women, 22–30	233	29.64	45.22	114.46	53.62	324.93	0.79	0.24	0.010	0.008
Men and women, 31–50	319	35.04	42.13	117.73	56.94	367.77	0.84	0.19	0.008	0.015
Masters and above										
Men and women, 22–50	219	38.79	49.79	137.98	58.95	456.43	0.79	0.17	0.001	0.012
Entire sample	9351	35.99	42.11	107.1	50.98	456.43	0.85	0.20	0.009	0.015

($c = 0$ for a layoff, $c = 1$ for a quit for a better job). Note that the difference between these two columns ($a - c$) is a count of how many individuals in a given subsample were observed to return to unemployment.

It is possible to obtain model-free (i.e., reduced-form) estimates of the transition rates λ_0, λ_1, and δ. These estimates, not depending on the structural assumptions, can be compared with the structural estimates as an informal specification check. The parameter λ_0 is likelihood-independent of the others in all our specifications: It does not depend on structural restrictions. The layoff rate δ is associated with structural restrictions. A reduced-form estimate is given by the MLE in the model $t \sim \delta \exp\{-\delta t\}$, where t is weeks employed until layoff and (heavy) censoring is accommodated. The estimator is $\hat{\delta}$ = (number of layoffs)/(total employment weeks). This estimate is reported as a summary statistic in table 19.2. The estimate of λ_1 depends on the wage distribution, even in the reduced form. We use the MLE for λ_1 in the model $t_i^* \sim \gamma_i \exp\{-\gamma_i t_i^*\}$, where t_i^* is the ith employment duration ending in a job change and $\gamma_i = \lambda_1 [1 - F(\omega_i)]$ (compare (19.43), (19.97), (15.18)). In the structural models the distribution F is endogenous. Here, we use the empirical CDF of wages accepted by the unemployed. The estimates are reported as summary statistics in table 19.2. Standard errors are not reported but were calculated and are all less than 0.002, so the reduced form is informative on these parameters.

We find that the lower the education level, the larger the subsample available, generally. Unemployment duration tends to increase with age and is higher for females than for males, and lower for high school graduates than for nongraduates, but this is not necessarily so for job duration. Wages increase with education and tend to peak in the interval 31–50 years of age, whether judged by the average or the maximum, and are highest on average for men. In addition, it is noted that it is mainly the younger age groups that manage to move on to better jobs.

In figure 19.1, we graphically depict the shape of the wage distribution in the various subsamples.

Figures 19.1a–19.1h pertain to the below-high school subsamples, figures 19.1i–19.1o to the high school cases, and figures 19.1p–19.1r to the higher levels of education, and figure 19.1s to the full sample. In each graph, the solid line represents a kernel estimate of the density function for the observed wages in the subsample. Note that both axes are different in the subsamples. The various dashed lines in the graphs correspond to the different estimated models discussed here and in chapter 20. From the kernel estimates it is clear that the observed wage densities are skewed, with a long right tail, but largely unimodal, except for the apparent bimodality in the relatively small subsample of males in the youngest age group and below the high school level.

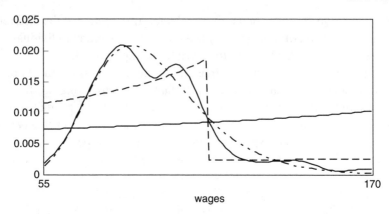

Figure 19.1.a Wage Distribution by Level of Education: Less Than High School,
            Men, Age 16–21.

Figure 19.1.b Wage Distribution by Level of Education: Less Than High School,
            Men, Age 22–30.

19.7 EMPIRICAL RESULTS

In this section we apply the pure homogeneous search empirical model to
the data described in section 19.6. The model is implemented separately in
each of the homogeneous subsamples presented in table 19.2. The results of
the estimation appear in table 19.3.

One of the structural parameters that readily allows interpretation is the
productivity p. Our results indicate that productivity rises with age, reaches
a peak between the ages 31 and 50, then declines for men but rises throughout for women. Specifically, this is so for high school graduates and those
below, which are the groups that we separate by gender. For Bachelors, too,

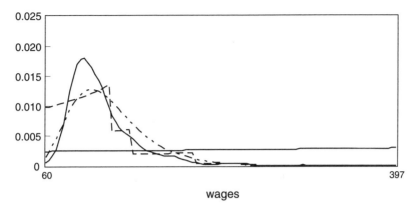

Figure 19.1.c Wage Distribution by Level of Education: Less Than High School, Men, Age 31–50.

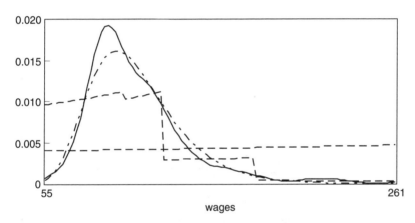

Figure 19.1.d Wage Distribution by Level of Education: Less Than High School, Men, Age 51–76.

p rises with age. Female high school graduates have higher productivity than their male counterparts and females without a high school diploma. On the other hand, high school makes no difference for males, and there is no difference by gender below high school. Bachelors are slightly more productive than those in lower groups, and Masters even more so, but the differences are not very significant. The standard errors of the estimates (reported in parentheses) are generally not large but deteriorate for higher ages, especially in women, and for higher education levels, presumably reflecting that the homogeneity approximation is of a lower quality for these groups.

Turning next to b, this comes out significantly negative in all subsamples, thus reemphasizing the need to interpret this structural parameter not as

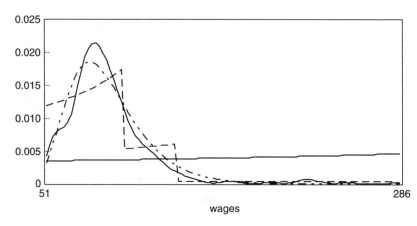

Figure 19.1.e Wage Distribution by Level of Education: Less Than High School, Women, Age 16–21.

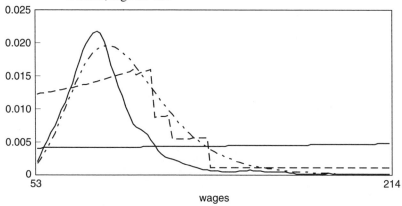

Figure 19.1.f Wage Distribution by Level of Education: Less Than High School, Women, Age 22–30.

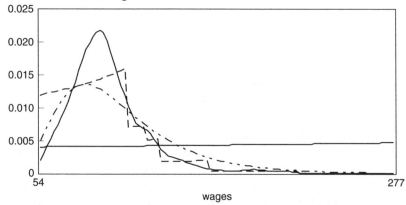

Figure 19.1.g Wage Distribution by Level of Education: Less Than High School, Women, Age 31–60.

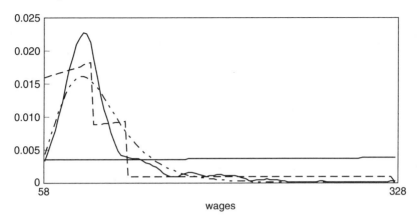

Figure 19.1.h Wage Distribution by Level of Education: Less Than High School, Women, Age 51–76.

Figure 19.1.i Wage Distribution by Level of Education: High School, Men and Women, Age 16–21.

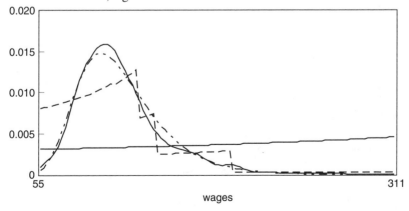

Figure 19.1.j Wage Distribution by Level of Education: High School, Men, Age 22–30.

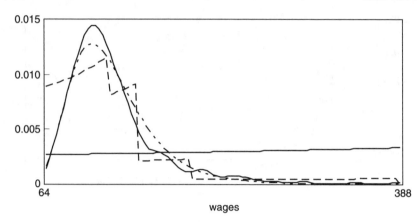

Figure 19.1.k Wage Distribution by Level of Education: High School, Men, Age 31–50.

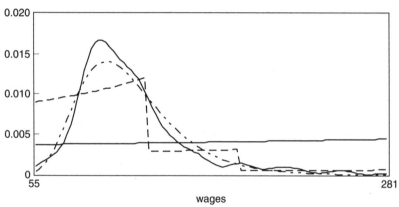

Figure 19.1.l Wage Distribution by Level of Education: High School, Men, Age 51–76.

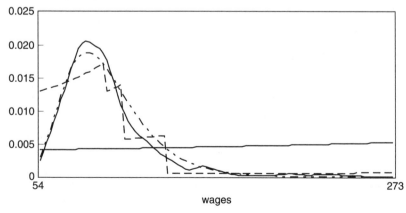

Figure 19.1.m Wage Distribution by Level of Education: High School, Women, Age 22–30.

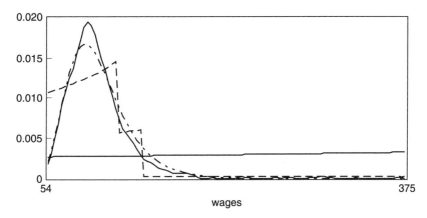

Figure 19.1.n Wage Distribution by Level of Education: High School, Women,
          Age 31–50.

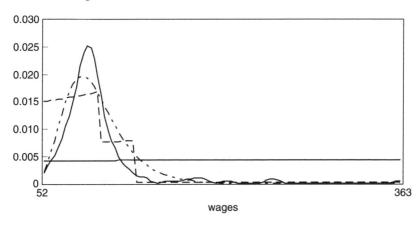

Figure 19.1.o Wage Distribution by Level of Education: High School, Women,
          Age 51–76.

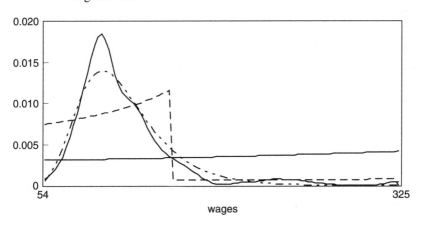

Figure 19.1.p Wage Distribution by Level of Education: Bachelors, Men and
          Women, Age 22–30.

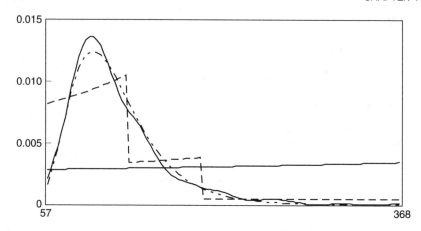

Figure 19.1.q Wage Distribution by Level of Education: Bachelors, Men and Women, Age 31–50.

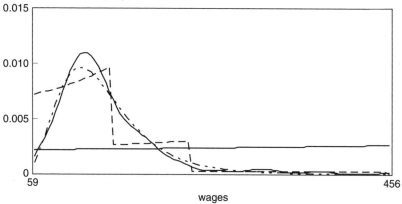

Figure 19.1.r Wage Distribution by Level of Education: Masters and above, Men and Women, Age 22–50.

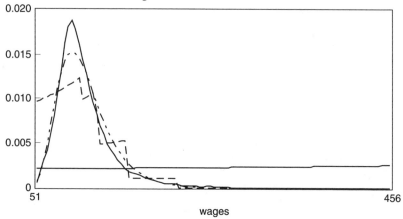

Figure 19.1.s Wage Distribution by Level of Education: Entire Sample.

Table 19.3 Pure Homogeneity Model.

Level of Education	λ_0	λ_1	δ	p	b
Less than high school					
Men, 16–21	.041	.009	.023	298	−14.9
	(.002)	(.001)	(.002)	(18)	(7.76)
Men, 22–30	.033	.007	.021	550	−60.2
	(.001)	(.0005)	(.0008)	(24.7)	(7.21)
Men, 31–50	.03	.004	.016	1069	−181
	(.0009)	(.0003)	(.0006)	(57.1)	(12.7)
Men, 51–76	.029	.003	.017	874	−91.7
	(.001)	(.0004)	(.001)	(96.2)	(11.8)
Women, 16–21	.032	.006	.017	596	−107
	(.002)	(.0006)	(.001)	(44.8)	(16.4)
Women, 22–30	0.024	0.005	0.02	493	−15.3
	(.0008)	(.0004)	(.0008)	(25.6)	(4.41)
Women, 31–50	.024	.003	.017	877	−73.4
	(.0007)	(.0002)	(.0006)	(52.6)	(6.32)
Women, 51–76	.021	.002	.021	1724	−57.6
	(.001)	(.0003)	(.001)	(259)	(9.83)
High school					
Men and women, 16–21	.038	.007	.012	285	−94.3
	(.002)	(.0007)	(.0009)	(14.6)	(16.3)
Men, 22–30	.039	.007	.014	532	−183.1
	(.001)	(.0004)	(.0006)	(19.9)	(15.5)
Men, 31–50	.031	.004	.015	955	−194.2
	(.001)	(.0003)	(.0007)	(58.3)	(16.7)
Men, 51–76	.027	.004	.019	816	−73.8
	(.001)	(.0006)	(.001)	(101)	(14)
Women, 22–30	.027	.004	.014	602	−105
	(.001)	(.0004)	(.0007)	(34.4)	(11.1)
Women, 31–50	.023	.003	.014	1082	−160.2
	(.001)	(.0003)	(.0007)	(89.8)	(16.6)
Women, 51–76	.019	.001	.024	3001	−59.6
	(.002)	(.0005)	(.002)	(926)	(14.6)
Bachelors					
Men and women, 22–30	0.034	0.005	0.014	663	−186
	(.002)	(.0007)	(.001)	(58.4)	(27.8)
Men and women, 31–50	.029	.004	0.017	983	−152
	(.002)	(.0005)	(.001)	(95.2)	(20.1)
Masters and above					
Men and women, 22–50	.026	.003	.013	1280	−247
	(.002)	(.0005)	(.001)	(159)	(35.3)
Entire sample	.028	.004	.017	1269	−212.1
	(.0003)	(.0001)	(.0002)	(22.6)	(.47)

straight benefits but rather as the value of nonmarket time, corrected for search costs and perhaps even disutility of leisure, at least for some groups. The tendency is for b to become more negative with age until the age 31–50 interval, then return back toward zero for higher ages, when leisure becomes more attractive. It is more negative for higher education levels, and more negative for males than females, save apparently for the very young.

A glance at the Poisson rates reveals that offers arrive uniformly more frequently during unemployment than during employment, corresponding to a situation where the reservation wage r exceeds b. However, it is equally uniformly the case that the on-the-job offer arrival rate remains significantly positive. This criterion, $\lambda_1 > 0$, is the key ingredient in the extension from the standard, simple search framework to the present equilibrium model. This is so even if $\lambda_1 < \delta$; i.e., jobs tend to end in unemployment rather than leading to new, higher-paying jobs, which is what we find uniformly across subsamples.

Focusing on the offer arrival rates, λ_0 and λ_1, and comparing across groups, the picture is very clear. Young people receive the most offers, and men receive more offers than women, but there is little difference by education. Comparing λ_1 with its reduced-form value from table 19.2, we note that the structural estimate is uniformly lower.

Finally, the job destruction rate δ is different. Men and women are laid off at similar rates, and individuals with less than a high school education at higher rates than others. For this group, the hazard is relatively flat in age, but for others, older workers face the highest separation rates. Comparing δ with its reduced-form value from table 19.2, we see that the structural estimates are uniformly slightly higher.

Unfortunately, the fit to the observed wage distribution is less than satisfactory. This is illustrated in figure 19.1, where the solid lines indicate the observed distributions by subsample and the monotonically increasing, but almost flat, dashed lines are predicted in the equilibrium model; i.e., they are given by (19.32), evaluated at the parameter estimates from table 19.3. The wage axis ranges from the minimum to the maximum observed wage in each subsample, and the predicted density is zero outside this interval. The increasing, convex predicted density shape is not supported by the data. Nonetheless, the analysis shows that a meaningful empirical analysis of fundamental economic parameters is possible within the pure equilibrium search model.

19.8 CONCLUSION

The equilibrium search model, with its endogenous heterogeneity in wages for homogeneous workers and its equilibrium unemployment rate, is a modern breakthrough in economic modeling. We have presented the model in some detail and explored the likelihood techniques appropriate for its empirical application in even more detail. Our analysis demonstrates the use of different types of sufficiency and likelihood reduction and the use of asymptotic analysis to understand the different information contributions of different types of data. The application shows that the model is practical and useful, giving reasonable fits to the duration parts of the data, and giving informative variation in estimates across labor market groups. The application also shows that the fit to the distribution of wages is quite poor. The model implies an upward sloping wage density since the equal profit constraint implies that firms paying high wages, and therefore making lower profit per worker since productivity is assumed to be the same, must have a larger workforce. Upward sloping wage densities are inconsistent with the data. This problem is addressed by extending the model in chapter 20.

19.9 EXERCISES

1. Show that j given w follows an exponential distribution in the prototypal equilibrium model.
2. Explain the relation between the reduced-form (section 19.6) and structural estimates of the arrival rates.
3. Does the matrix in (19.101) have full rank? How is this related to the CARRN distribution?

19.10 REFERENCES

Theoretical equilibrium search models have been introduced by Albrecht and Axell (1984), Burdett (1990), Burdett and Mortensen (1998), and Mortensen (1990). The model of Albrecht and Axell is important since it generates an equilibrium in which workers homogeneous in productivity have dispersed wages. To obtain this result, workers were assumed to have heterogeneous reservation wages, perhaps as a result of heterogeneous utilities or nonlabor incomes. Thus, the desired result, heterogeneous wages, was obtained but as a result of introducing heterogeneity elsewhere. Mortensen (1990) and Burdett and Mortensen (1998) introduced the equilibrium search specification with endogenous heterogeneity. They also provided a number of extensions that proved empirically useful (see chapter 20). Eckstein and Wolpin (1990) estimate a version of the Albrecht-Axell model. Kiefer and Neumann (1993), van den Berg and Ridder (1993, 1998) and Koning et al. (1995) estimate a version of Mortensen's model. The information analysis is from Christensen and Kiefer (1997). The empirical work reported here is from Bunzel et al. (2001).

Chapter Twenty

Dynamic Equilibrium: Search Equilibrium Extensions

20.1 INTRODUCTION

Our investigation of the effect of measurement error in state variables was initiated in chapter 4. Measurement error in wages can have an important impact in the equilibrium search model, just as in the partial equilibrium setting described in chapter 9. Here, we extend the equilibrium model to allow measurement error in the same form as in chapter 9. Thus, workers and firms see wages exactly, but the econometrician does not. The theory applies without change, though the inference procedure is different. This is the topic of section 20.2.

Exogenous heterogeneity in the productivity level of firms is introduced in section 20.3 in the form of discrete types of firms. It is not known which firms have which levels of productivity, just that different levels are present in the data. This approach allows for distinguishing empirically between heterogeneity due to pure information asymmetries and heterogeneity due to genuine productivity differences. An extension to continuous productivity types is discussed briefly in section 20.4. In this extension all wage dispersion is due to exogenous productivity dispersion.

20.2 MEASUREMENT ERROR IN WAGES

In the estimation procedure for the prototypal equilibrium search model introduced and applied in chapter 19, the theoretical minimum and maximum wages r and h are estimated by their empirical counterparts, namely, the order statistics $w_{\min}$ and $w_{\max}$, respectively. Estimators based on order statistics are potentially vulnerable to measurement error. In particular, measurement error does not wash out in order statistics the way it does, say, in a sample average. This led us in chapter 9 to allow explicitly for measurement error in wages in the estimation of the (partial equilibrium) prototypal search model. There, the Pearson type V distribution (9.16) for a proportional measurement error was empirically useful and indicated that on average about 28% of the variation in National Longitudinal Survey of Youth (NLSY) log wages may be attributed to measurement error, a finding in line with the Bound et al. (1990) results based on direct measurement.

In this chapter, we extend this approach to the prototypal equilibrium search model. We take care that the theoretical model of chapter 19 continues to describe worker and firm behavior without change, and that the change in the empirical procedure purely reflects the more complicated measurement process. Thus, assume that the wage observation x available to the econometrician when the true wage equals w is affected by proportional measurement error ϵ as in

$$x = w \cdot \epsilon, \tag{20.1}$$

but that the distribution of w is exactly as in the prototypal model of chapter 19. Based on the results of chapter 9, we may take ϵ to be stochastically independent of w, with unit mean (so that $Ex = Ew$), variance σ^2, and density,

$$f_\epsilon(\epsilon) = \frac{\left(1 + \sigma^{-2}\right)^{2+\sigma^{-2}}}{\Gamma(2 + \sigma^{-2})} \frac{1}{\epsilon^{3+\sigma^{-2}}} \exp\left(-\frac{1 + \sigma^{-2}}{\epsilon}\right). \tag{20.2}$$

In the notation from chapter 19, we now consider data of the form (d, x, j, c, a); i.e., x replaces w in the observations, where d is unemployment duration, x the observed wage, j employment duration, c a destination indicator (quit as opposed to layoff), and a indicates completion (as opposed to censoring) of j. The joint density takes the form

$$f_d(d) \int_{x/h}^{x/r} f_{j,c}\left(j, c \mid \frac{x}{\epsilon}, a\right) f_w\left(\frac{x}{\epsilon}\right) \frac{1}{\epsilon} f_\epsilon(\epsilon)\, d\epsilon; \tag{20.3}$$

i.e., the measurement error is simply integrated out, and (20.3) is the contribution to likelihood for the typical observation. The parameter vector is simply expanded by σ, the measurement error variance; i.e., $(\theta, \sigma) = (\lambda_0, \lambda_1, \delta, p, b, \sigma)$ is to be estimated. In (20.3), f_d is from (19.31) and parameterized by λ_0, which does not enter elsewhere; i.e., λ_0 is estimated by $(\overline{d})^{-1}$ as before. Next, $f_{j,c}$ is given by (19.96) and is parameterized by $(\lambda_1, \delta, r, h)$, but we no longer use order statistics for (r, h). Rather, (r, h) are estimated simultaneously with $(\lambda_1, \delta, \sigma)$ by iteratively maximizing the log likelihood based on (20.3). The expression for f_w is given in (19.32), where $\kappa_1 = \lambda_1/\delta$ and (r, h) are given in terms of the structural parameters in (19.33) and (19.34). Note that the limits of integration in (20.3) ensure that the true but unobserved wage $w = x/\epsilon$ belongs to the support $[r, h]$ of f_w. Finally, the term $1/\epsilon$ in (20.3) is the Jacobian of the transformation (20.1) between true and measured wages, conditionally on the error, and f_ϵ is given by (20.2).

The sample average of the negative inverse second derivative of the logarithm of (20.3) with respect to $\xi = (\lambda_1, \delta, r, h, \sigma)$ provides a consistent estimate of the asymptotic variance $v(\xi)$, and utilizing likelihood independence as in chapter 19, the asymptotic variance of $(\phi, \sigma) = (\lambda_0, \xi)$ is given by

$$v(\phi, \sigma) = \begin{pmatrix} v(\lambda_0) & 0 \\ 0 & v(\xi) \end{pmatrix}, \tag{20.4}$$

with diagonal blocks of dimension 1×1 and 5×5, respectively.

The Jacobian of the map $(r, h) \to (p, b)$ is given by the coefficients of the system (19.38) or, more explicitly, as

$$J_m = \frac{1}{\delta^2 \omega} \begin{pmatrix} -\delta^2 & (\delta + \lambda_1)^2 \\ \delta^2 \omega + (\lambda_0 - \lambda_1)\lambda_1 & -(\lambda_0 - \lambda_1)\lambda_1 \end{pmatrix}, \tag{20.5}$$

so the comparative equilibrium search dynamics imply that productivity is related directly to h and inversely to the reservation wage. The dependence of b on (r, h) varies with the relationship between the offer arrival rates in and out of employment, but when λ_0 dominates (which is what we find), $\partial b / \partial r > 1$ and $\partial b / \partial h < 0$. With J_χ from (19.101), J_m from (20.5), and

$$\tilde{J} = \begin{pmatrix} I_3 & 0 & 0 \\ J_\chi & J_m & 0 \\ 0 & 0 & 1 \end{pmatrix}, \tag{20.6}$$

standard errors for the structural parameters (θ, σ) may be based on the asymptotic variance matrix $\tilde{J}v(\phi, \sigma)\tilde{J}'$.

The results are given in table 20.1. When allowing for measurement error in wages, the estimates of the productivity parameter p and benefits net of search cost b are considerably different from those obtained in the previous section. The estimates of p are uniformly smaller, and those of b uniformly larger and now indeed positive, when measurement error is introduced. This is due to the fact that the measurement error model allows internal estimates of r and h; i.e., these are not bounded by $w_{\min}$ and $w_{\max}$, as may be seen by comparing the results in tables 19.3 and 20.1. Less extreme variation in p and b across subsamples is now required to explain the observations.

We still see the feature that male productivity increases initially, then turns down, and the estimates now reveal that the same phenomenon in fact occurs for females as well. Furthermore, the b parameter is now seen to follow this pattern, too, and this is true for both genders.

With measurement error, the estimates of the separation rate δ are slightly lower than without, and those of the on-the-job offer arrival rate λ_1 are somewhat higher. As expected, the possibility of measurement error induces slightly higher estimation error in λ_1, although the standard errors for δ are

Table 20.1 Measurement Error Model.

Level of Education	λ_0	λ_1	δ	p	b	σ
Less than high school						
Men, 16–21	.041	.017	.021	109	80.3	.219
	(.002)	(.002)	(.002)	(11.7)	(12)	(.013)
Men, 22–30	.033	.014	.019	126	94	.264
	(.001)	(.001)	(.0008)	(9)	(8.5)	(.008)
Men, 31–50	.03	.01	.015	125	108	.289
	(.0009)	(.0007)	(.0006)	(8)	(7.8)	(.007)
Men, 51–76	.029	.006	.017	137	90.6	.247
	(.001)	(.0008)	(.0009)	(22.4)	(14.4)	(.011)
Women, 16–21	.032	.014	.015	104	76.5	.28
	(.002)	(.002)	(.001)	(9.7)	(10.9)	(.015)
Women, 22–30	.024	.011	.019	115	80.2	.24
	(.0008)	(.0009)	(.0008)	(8.6)	(6.1)	(.008)
Women, 31–50	.024	.007	.016	109	100.7	.386
	(.0007)	(.0006)	(.0006)	(7.3)	(5.3)	(.051)
Women, 51–76	.021	.005	.02	128	98.8	.289
	(.001)	(.0009)	(.001)	(25.7)	(9.6)	(.013)
High school						
Men and women, 16–21	.038	.015	.01	92	89.9	.254
	(.002)	(.002)	(0)	(1.4)	(1.4)	(.012)
Men, 22–30	.039	.016	.012	121	100	.279
	(.001)	(.001)	(.0006)	(6.8)	(11.2)	(.009)
Men, 31–50	.031	.01	.014	142	102.7	.3
	(.001)	(.0009)	(.0007)	(11)	(12.2)	(.01)
Men, 51–76	.027	.008	.018	137	100.7	.283
	(.002)	(.001)	(.001)	(30.5)	(20.2)	(.016)
Women, 22–30	.027	.01	.013	101	87.9	0.272
	(.001)	(.0009)	(.0007)	(7.2)	(8.2)	(.009)
Women, 31–50	.023	.008	.013	105	96.7	.289
	(.001)	(.0009)	(.0007)	(10.9)	(10)	(.011)
Women, 51–76	.019	.003	.024	160	83.3	.275
	(.002)	(.001)	(.002)	(63.1)	(13)	(.02)
Bachelors						
Men and women, 22–30	.034	.012	.012	130	88.5	.291
	(.002)	(.002)	(.001)	(12.3)	(137.3)	(.017)
Men and women, 31–50	.029	.01	.015	118	115.9	.336
	(.002)	(.001)	(.001)	(2.2)	(2.2)	(.016)
Masters and above						
Men and women, 22–50	.026	.008	.012	191	81.3	.355
	(.002)	(.001)	(.001)	(27.4)	(26.1)	(.029)
Entire sample	.028	.01	.015	108	105.6	.298
	(.0003)	(.0003)	(.0002)	(.33)	(.33)	(.003)

nearly identical in the two models. The estimates are now nearly identical to the reduced-form values in table 19.2, indicating that the introduction of measurement error in the specification has improved the fit to the flow data.

Finally, the magnitude of the measurement error, as measured by σ, is highly significant throughout, indicating the relevance and empirical importance of departing from the pure homogeneity model. This is further illustrated in figure 19.1, where the smooth, unimodal dashed lines are the predicted densities of observed wages,

$$f_x(x) = \int_{x/h}^{x/r} f_w\left(\frac{x}{\epsilon}\right) \frac{1}{\epsilon} f_\epsilon(\epsilon)\, d\epsilon, \tag{20.7}$$

inserting the parameter estimates from table 20.1 for each subsample. A good fit to the observed density (the solid line) is obtained using this specification. The observed densities tend to have slightly higher peaks than the theoretical densities at the modes, but the mode points are generally close, and the right tails are nicely captured. Of course, the possibility remains that what is being captured is unobserved heterogeneity. Rather than speculating on this, we now introduce heterogeneity in the structural model and compare results.

20.3 HETEROGENEITY IN PRODUCTIVITY: THE DISCRETE CASE

In the previous section we saw that a satisfactory fit of the wage distribution may be obtained by allowing for measurement error in wages, while maintaining the same underlying economic model as in chapter 19. In this section we consider the alternative route of modifying the economic model from chapter 19 to generate a predicted wage distribution that is closer to the observed distribution. Following Mortensen (1990), this is done by introducing heterogeneity in firm productivity, and we focus on the pure case of this model, ruling out measurement error in this section so as to separate out the effects of the various alterations to the basic empirical approach of chapter 19.

Rather than modeling all firms as operating with productivity p, assume there are $q > 1$ types of firms, with productivities $p_1 < p_2 < \cdots < p_q$, respectively. All other features of the model, including offer arrival rates, the layoff rate, etc., remain unchanged. In this case, a Nash equilibrium in reservation wage and wage-setting strategies implies the existence of a family of intervals $[r_i, h_i]$, $i = 1, \ldots, q$, so that firms of type i offer wages in the ith interval. Furthermore, $r_{i+1} = h_i$, so to workers there is an offer distribution with support ranging from their reservation wage, $r = r_1$, to the highest wage ever paid, $h = h_q$.

The distribution of unemployment duration is still given by (19.31). Corresponding to the result (19.32) for the wage offer density in the simple model, we now get the density

$$f_w(w) = \frac{1 + \kappa_1(1 - \gamma_{i-1})}{2\kappa_1} \frac{1}{(p_i - w)^{1/2}(p_i - r_i)^{1/2}}, \qquad w \in [r_i, h_i],$$
(20.8)

over the ith interval. With F indicating the associated cumulative distribution function CDF, $\gamma_i = F(h_i)$ is the fraction of firms with productivity p_i or less, in particular $\gamma_q = F(h) = 1$, and we specify $\gamma_0 = 0$. The definition of γ_i implies that

$$p_i = \frac{h_i - \mu_i^2 r_i}{1 - \mu_i^2},$$
(20.9)

where $\mu_i \in (0, 1)$ replaces μ from (19.37) and is given by

$$\mu_i = \frac{1 + \kappa_1(1 - \gamma_i)}{1 + \kappa_1(1 - \gamma_{i-1})}.$$
(20.10)

In the simple model, (19.39) implies that $p = (h - \mu^2 r)/(1 - \mu^2)$, and we see that with heterogeneity, p_i is given in terms of h_i and r_i much in the same way, but now the exact relationship involves the probability γ_i. The exact form of F is

$$F(w) = \frac{1 + \kappa_1}{\kappa_1}\left(1 - \frac{1 + \kappa_1(1 - \gamma_{i-1})}{1 + \kappa_1}\left(\frac{p_i - w}{p_i - r_i}\right)^{1/2}\right), \qquad w \in [r_i, h_i],$$
(20.11)

for a wage w in the ith interval. This should be compared with (19.30).

For the distribution of the employment spells j, the right-censored competing risks framework from (19.94) still applies, namely,

$$f_{j,c}(j, c|w, a) = ((1 - c)h_\delta + ch_1)^a S_j,$$
(20.12)

and still the layoff hazard is $h_\delta = \delta$ and the quitting hazard $h_1 = \lambda_1(1 - F(w))$. The dummy variables c and a indicate a quit (as opposed to a layoff) and spell completion (as opposed to censoring), respectively. Again, $S_j = \exp(-(h_\delta + h_1)j)$, and the only difference from (19.94) is that F is taken from (20.11) above—not from (19.30).

The parameters are now $\phi = (\lambda_0, \lambda_1, \delta, r, r_2, r_3, \ldots, r_q, h, \gamma_1, \gamma_2, \ldots, \gamma_{q-1})$ since the p_i's are explicit functions of these. In the simple model ($q = 1$) we had dim $\phi = 5$, and for $q = 2$ we get dim $\phi = 7$, for $q = 3$

$\dim \phi = 9$, and in general $\dim \phi = 3+2q$. With panel data on (d, w, j, c, a) the contribution to log likelihood from a single observation is

$$\ell(\phi) = \log \lambda_0 - \lambda_0 d + \log f_w(w) + a \log((1 - c)\delta + c\lambda_1(1 - F(w)))$$
$$- (\delta + \lambda_1(1 - F(w)))j. \tag{20.13}$$

Upon estimation, we may as usual reparametrize from ϕ to θ. i.e., from $(r, r_2, \ldots, r_q, h)$ to $(b, p_1, \ldots, p_q)$ to interpret the results. Thus, the p_i's have already been given in terms of ϕ in (20.9) and (20.10), and by inserting the new expression (20.11) for F in (19.21), we find

$$b = r - \frac{\lambda_0 - \lambda_1}{\lambda_1} \sum_{i=1}^{q}(p_i - r_i)\left[1 - \mu_i^2 - 2\delta\left[\frac{1 - \mu_i}{\delta + \lambda_1(1 - \gamma_{i-1})}\right]\right].$$
$$\tag{20.14}$$

As in chapter 19, the estimates of the lowest and highest wages r and h are asymptotically equivalent at rate $N^{1/2}$ to the local cut $t = (w_{\min}, w_{\max})$, and in the present case $(r_2, \ldots, r_q)$ are local cuts, too, corresponding to kink points in the CDF (see Chernoff and Rubin (1956)). Naturally, with estimates of $(r_2, \ldots, r_q)$ in hand, the probabilities γ_i corresponding to this division of the wages are estimated by the observed frequencies. Finally, for given $(r, r_2, \ldots, r_q, h, \gamma_1, \ldots, \gamma_{q-1})$, the structural parameters $(\lambda_0, \lambda_1, \delta)$ may be estimated by quasi-Newton methods since the criterion is regular as in the Christensen and Kiefer (1997) situation. Thus, the algorithm maintains the order statistics as estimates for (r, h) and iterates between maximization with respect to the regular parameters $(\lambda_0, \lambda_1, \delta)$ and the local cuts $(r_2, \ldots, r_q, \gamma_1, \ldots, \gamma_{q-1})$.

In the empirical work, the procedure for $(r_2, \ldots, r_q, \gamma_1, \ldots, \gamma_{q-1})$, given $(r, h, \lambda_0, \lambda_1, \delta)$, follows Bowlus, Kiefer, and Neumann (1995), using simulated annealing (Kirkpatrick et al. (1983), Otten and van Ginneken (1989), Szu and Hartley (1987)), with an extension to allow for censored employment duration data. Since the model is estimated separately for homogeneous subsamples, we may allow for a different value of the number of firm types q in each. In the Mortensen (1990) model, two firms may operate with the same productivity for one kind of workers but with different productivities for another. Clearly, the likelihood function is increasing in q, but the likelihood ratio test of one value of q against another does not adhere to the usual asymptotic χ^2-distribution because of the nonstandard shape already noted—the dependence on order statistics and so forth. We expect large subsamples to contain enough information to separate out a larger number of firm types than small subsamples, where a reasonable fit might be obtained even with a small value of q. This is not to say that the smaller subsamples of workers necessarily face fewer firm types but simply that the data may not carry sufficient information to identify all the types. Given q, the sample average of the negative inverse second derivative of $\ell(\phi)$ from (20.13) with respect to $\psi = (\lambda_1, \delta)$ is used to form $v(\psi)$, and by likelihood independence we get

$$v(\chi) = \begin{pmatrix} v(\lambda_0) & 0 \\ 0 & v(\psi) \end{pmatrix}, \qquad (20.15)$$

with $\chi = (\lambda_0, \lambda_1, \delta)$ as in chapter 19. The expressions (20.9) and (20.10) for p_i and (20.14) for b are used to form the Jacobian J_h of the map $\chi \rightarrow (p_1, \ldots, p_q, b)$ (note in particular $\partial p_i / \partial \lambda_0 = 0$), and standard errors for the structural parameters $\theta = (\lambda_0, \lambda_1, \delta, p_1, \ldots, p_q, b)$ are based on $J_h v(\chi) J_h'$.

The results are displayed in tables 20.2 and 20.3. The most striking finding is that the deep parameters λ_0, λ_1, and δ take almost exactly the same values, subsample by subsample, as in the measurement error model of the previous section. Thus, the correspondence with the reduced form is again quite good. This suggests that different routes of departure from the pure homogeneity model may lead to satisfactory inference on the underlying equilibrium structure. What is important for the estimation of the Poisson rates is not whether the deviations from the wage distribution predicted by the simple model are explained by measurement error or by heterogeneity in productivity, but simply that it is allowed for in a meaningful way in the empirical approach.

Of course, unlike the model of the previous section, the heterogeneity model does permit analysis of the productivity parameters, the wage cut points, and the relative sample weights in the various intervals defined by the cut points. There is a tendency for a given productivity parameter, say p_i, to increase with age when comparing across subsamples, although the picture is complicated by the fact that, as expected, fewer parameters enter significantly (and are therefore reported) in small subsamples than in large ones. The corresponding wage cuts exhibit the by now familiar pattern of increase up to the age of 50, then decrease, for males with less than high school qualifications. The picture is less clear for the other groups, although the main tendency is an increase with age. Furthermore, the associated probabilities γ_i are very interesting: Subsamples with productivity parameters and wage cuts relatively far to the right on the wage axis, such as those in the 31–50 age group below the high school level, have relatively more individuals allocated in the low-wage range (e.g., γ_1 is high for these subsamples). Thus, firms offering high wages are not attracting the bulk of the workers.

Again, having a high school education does not compare favorably with having less than a high school education in terms of productivity, whereas workers with bachelors, and especially masters, do come in with higher estimates. Males are slightly more productive than females.

Table 20.2 Heterogeneity in Productivity.

Level of Education	λ_0	λ_1	δ	p_1	p_2	p_3	p_4	p_5	p_6
Less than high school									
Men, 16–21	.041	.017	.021	152	418				
	(.002)	(.002)	(.001)	(5)	(32)				
Men, 22–30	.033	.015	.019	177	198	305	554	1028	
	(.001)	(.001)	(.001)	(49)	(5)	(11)	(28)	(61)	
Men, 31–50	.030	.010	.015	188	278	554	2099	5443	
	(.001)	(.001)	(.001)	(5)	(10)	(27)	(141)	(390)	
Men, 51–76	.029	.007	.016	226	237	548	2625	4053	
	(.001)	(.001)	(.001)	(17)	(16)	(56)	(356)	(563)	
Women, 16–21	.032	.012	.015	145	244	1908			
	(.002)	(.001)	(.001)	(5)	(14)	(211)			
Women, 22–30	.024	.011	.018	161	165	215	284	985	
	(.001)	(.001)	(.001)	(5)	(4)	(8)	(13)	(66)	
Women, 31–50	.024	.008	.016	179	266	329	679	2401	9421
	(.001)	(.001)	(.001)	(6)	(11)	(15)	(41)	(175)	(730)
Women, 51–76	.021	.005	0.020	214	346	2506			
	(.001)	(.001)	(.001)	(20)	(39)	(395)			
High school									
Men and women, 16–21	.038	.012	.010	131	143	331			
	(.002)	(.001)	(.001)	(4)	(4)	(21)			
Men, 22–30	.039	.015	.012	166	168	204	237	1449	
	(.001)	(.001)	(.001)	(3)	(3)	(4)	(12)	(93)	

Men, 31–50	.031 (.001)	.010 (.001)	.014 (.001)	199 (6)	234 (8)	527 (30)	1806 (139)		
Men, 51–76	.027 (.002)	.009 (.001)	.018 (.001)	220 (16)	510 (56)	1797 (264)			
Women, 22–30	.027 (.001)	.009 (.001)	.012 (.001)	144 (4)	162 (5)	245 (11)	1293 (100)		
Women, 31–50	.023 (.001)	.007 (.001)	.013 (.001)	187 (9)	188 (8)	298 (19)	2850 (301)		
Women, 51–76	.019 (.002)	.004 (.001)	.024 (.002)	285 (62)	514 (130)	8266 (2674)			
Bachelors									
Men and women, 22–30	.034 (.002)	.009 (.001)	.013 (.001)	217 (11)	1239 (141)				
Men and women, 31–50	.029 (.002)	.008 (.001)	.015 (.001)	232 (14)	449 (47)	2395 (293)			
Masters and above									
Men and women, 22–50	.026 (.002)	.007 (.001)	.012 (.001)	247 (17)	526 (53)	3762 (587)			
Entire sample	.028 (0)	.010 (0)	.015 (0)	180 (2)	201 (2)	224 (2)	302 (4)	885 (17)	6956 (168)

Table 20.3 Heterogeneity in Productivity: Implications.

Level of Education	r_2	r_3	r_4	r_5	r_6	γ_1	γ_2	γ_3	γ_4	γ_5	b
Less than high school											
Men, 16–21	115					.85					22.7
Men, 22–30	115	129	156	172		.634	.781	.898	.925		19.1
Men, 31–50	122	144	203	251		.706	.835	.959	.978		5.1
Men, 51–76	102	126	179	203		.513	.795	.969	.981		−1.9
Women, 16–21	103	138				.747	.945				19.1
Women, 22–30	98	107	114	133		.608	.756	.815	.917		31.5
Women, 31–50	109	121	129	161	217	.775	.861	.903	.967	.993	20.5
Women, 51–76	96	122				.602	.828				23.0
High school											
Men and women, 16–21	84	109				.424	.773				−22.4
Men, 22–30	109	126	139	194		.506	.719	.808	.960		−16.7
Men, 31–50	120	147	198			.566	.797	.909			−12.4
Men, 51–76	127	186				.758	.754	.913			6.4
Women, 22–30	94	106	133			.593	.754	.913			8.4
Women, 31–50	91	118	140			.423	.787	.915			0.2
Women, 51–76	199	132				.693	.922				24.6
Bachelors											
Men and women, 22–30	150					.871					−42.8
Men and women, 31–50	128	193				.677	.919				−15.7
Masters and above											
Men and women, 22–50	145	234				.703	.945				−31.6
Entire sample	104	120	123	154	214	.573	.735	.754	.908	.973	1.9

In this model, the b parameter is sometimes positive and sometimes negative, and the effect of age varies—e.g., b decreases with age for males below the high school level but increases with age for males with a high school education. This parameter proves to be much harder to estimate and much more model-dependent than the Poisson rates, and its economic interpretation is probably less clear-cut, too.

In figure 19.1, the predicted density in each subsample appears as a collection of locally increasing segments connected by vertical lines at the wage cuts (namely, the local cuts, $r_2, \ldots, r_q$). Clearly, the heterogeneity model provides a much better fit to the observations (the solid curve) than the pure homogeneity model. Furthermore, it can be seen from the figures that the estimation procedure adds cut points in order to better match the detailed shape of the right tail of the wage distribution, where sometimes a curious feature (a "shoulder") occurs approximately one-third of the way between the mode and the maximum wage. Whether this reflects a real market phenomenon remains an open question, but it is certainly an aspect of the data that the heterogeneous productivity model picks up. On the other hand, the mode is not captured as well as in the measurement error model.

20.4 HETEROGENEITY IN PRODUCTIVITY: THE CONTINUOUS CASE

Adding productivity dispersion substantially increases the fit to the observed wage distribution in the equilibrium search model. With the discrete dispersion model, there is pure search dispersion, i.e., endogenous wage heterogeneity of the type the equilibrium search model was developed to explain, among firms of a given productivity. Thus, there are two sources of heterogeneity in wages for homogeneous workers, the exogenous heterogeneity in productivity and the endogenous heterogeneity generated by incomplete information and a costly searching. The empirical strategy (as developed above) is to add productivity types until the contribution to the fit is negligible. This provides a method of decomposing wage heterogeneity into the part due to productivity heterogeneity across firms and endogenous heterogeneity due to searching.

From a purely statistical point of view, we can think of our strategy as approximating the wage density with a piecewise continuous functional form. It is natural from this point of view to ask whether a continuous approximation would fit better, and in our model this leads to the approach of specifying a continuous distribution of productivity types. This approach is certainly feasible and does improve the fit to the observed wage distribution, but it has its drawbacks. In fact, it can be regarded as a polar case. On the

one hand, we have the homogeneous equilibrium search model, in which all
heterogeneity in wages is due to search and information asymmetries. On
the other hand, we have the case with a continuum of productivity types. In
this specification, all heterogeneity in wages is due to the exogenous dispersion in productivity, and there is no pure search dispersion. In between, we
have the cases with discrete productivity dispersion, in which both types of
heterogeneity arise and their relative contributions can be sorted out.

To see this result, consider adding types to the model of section 20.3. For
each productivity type, the set of wages offered by firms of that type is connected. Further, these sets are disjoint (these results are due to Mortensen,
1990). As the number of types increases, these sets become smaller (on average). In the limit these sets are singletons; i.e., the map from productivities
to wages is a function. Thus, all heterogeneity in wages for homogeneous
workers is due to heterogeneity in productivities. The wage distribution is
obtained from the exogenous productivity distribution by a change of variables. The endogenous wage dispersion due to information considerations,
the central prediction of the equilibrium search model, does not arise.

The worker's problem remains unchanged when the productivity distribution is continuous. The searching worker does not care about the source of
the wage dispersion. Thus, the equilibrium involves all the usual parameters
as well as the productivity distribution. Given parameters, there is a one-to-
one map between wages w and productivities p (Burdett and Mortensen,
1998, eq. 47),

$$w(p) = p - \int_b^p \left(\frac{1 + \kappa_1(1 - J(p))}{1 + \kappa_1(1 - J(x))} \right)^2 dx, \qquad (20.16)$$

where J is the exogenous distribution of productivities (with lower bound
b) and $\kappa_1 = \lambda_1/\delta$.

The likelihood function can thus be set up with either the wage or the
productivity distribution given in parametric form. In fact, this leads to
a complicated, though not intractable, computation. An easier approach,
advocated by Bontemps et al. (2000), is to obtain a kernel estimate of the
cross-section wage distribution, plug that into the likelihood function, and
maximize over the other parameters. This procedure is thus guaranteed to
give a good fit to observed wages (provided a reasonable kernel estimate is
obtained), while allowing estimation of the other parameters of the model. In
that sense the approach is attractive. Of course, the improved fit is bought at
the price of introducing an exogenous source of variation as the sole source
of wage heterogeneity.

20.5 CONCLUSION

We have established the feasibility of estimation and interpretation of a variety of equilibrium search models. The models are fit by maximum likelihood to a random sample of individuals in Denmark over the period 1981–1990. We have considered the basic equilibrium search model, with purely endogenous wage heterogeneity, and then practical extensions to allow for measurement error in wages and heterogeneity in firm productivity. We find that some of the deep parameters, offer arrival rates while unemployed and while on the job, and layoff rates, are fairly robust to changes in the theoretical specification. Young people receive more offers, generally. Including offer arrivals while on the job is important in modeling the labor market, empirically as well as theoretically. Productivity increases initially by the age of the cohort, then turns down. Differences based on education are mostly seen at the Bachelors' and Masters' levels; the difference between high school and less than high school is slight. The pure (homogeneous, no measurement error) equilibrium search model does not fit the wage data well, but both the model with measurement error and the one with heterogeneous productivity fit the data well.

20.6 EXERCISES

1. What is the sum of the hazards h_δ and h_1 from (20.12)? When is this estimated separately, and in which data configuration? *Hint:* See chapter 15.

2. Show that the distribution of employment duration j in (19.67) is not in the exponential family (see the appendix). Show that it may be brought into the exponential family by conditioning on the current wage. Is the exponential property lost again if type V measurement error is introduced, as in (20.1)–(20.2)?

3. What can be said about the difference between unemployment insurance benefits net of search costs for agents in categories i and $i - 1$ in (20.14)? Carefully derive this expression.

4. Given data on productivities p and wages w, interpret (20.16) in terms of the curse of degeneracy and the curse of determinacy (see chapter 2).

20.7 REFERENCES

The empirical work reported here is from Bunzel et al. (2001). Measurement error in wages was introduced in the Burdett-Mortensen equilibrium search model, in different specifications, by van den Berg and Ridder (1998) and Bunzel et al. (2001). An early approach in the context of the Albrecht and Axell (1984) model, which does not have endogenous heterogeneity but has an exogenous distribution of reservation wages, is Eckstein and Wolpin (1990). They find in that specification that most of the observed variation in wages is due to measurement error. Heterogeneity in the form of productivity variation across firms was modeled theoretically by Mortensen (1990) and Burdett and Mortensen (1998). Discrete productivity variation was modeled empirically by Bowlus et al. (1995, 2001), van den Berg and Ridder (1998), and Bunzel et al. (2001). The model with a continuous productivity distribution was developed by Mortensen (1990) and Burdett and Mortensen (1998). Empirical modeling as discussed above based on a kernel estimator of the wage distribution is advocated by Bontemps et al. (2000).

Appendix

Brief Review of Statistical Theory

A.1 INTRODUCTION

We consider parametric models for data x belonging to a sample space X. A model is specified as $M = (x, \{p(.; \theta) | \theta \in \Theta\})$ or as $p(x; \theta)$ for short. Here, $p(.; \theta)$ is a density on X and Θ is the parameter space. Thus, if θ_0 is the true value of θ, $p(.; \theta_0)$ indicates the distribution of x, whereas $p(x; .)$ is the likelihood function and $p(.; .)$ the model function. We avoid in this appendix formal statements of regularity conditions and instead emphasize heuristics. There are many sources for rigorous and detailed development. For asymptotics, see van der Vaart (1998), for exponential families, Barndorff-Nielsen (1978) and Brown (1986), and for generalized method of moments (GMM), Heyde (1997) and Davidson and MacKinnon (2004).

The axioms of expected utility theory imply (see chapter 1) that uncertainty should be quantified by probabilities and beliefs should be updated according to the rules of conditional probability theory. Thus, initial beliefs about a parameter θ are expressed in the probability distribution $p(\theta)$. This information is combined with data information in the form of the likelihood function $p(x; \theta)$ to yield a posterior distribution $p(\theta|x) \propto p(x; \theta) p(\theta)$ combining initial information with data information. The posterior distribution $p(\theta|x)$ can be used to generate point estimates for θ if desired. Common choices are the posterior mean $E\theta$ and the posterior mode (typically much easier to calculate). This formalism is rarely adopted in economics and approximate techniques are used instead. There are three reasons for this. First, the computations can be difficult (particularly the integration involved in getting the factor of proportionality). Clearly, this difficulty is rapidly becoming less important. Second, careful and consistent assessment of beliefs $p(\theta)$ is time-consuming and difficult. This assessment involves thought, not computation, and thus does not get easier as computing cycles become cheaper. Third, approximate methods that have been demonstrated to work well in many cases are available.

In particular, the method of maximum likelihood, leading to the maximum likelihood estimator (MLE), has proved useful in many cases in practice and has sound asymptotic justification. With independent observations, the likelihood function $p(x; \theta)$ takes the product form $p(x; \theta) = \Pi f(x_i|\theta)$ and thus the posterior distribution $p(\theta|x)$ can be written as

$$p(\theta|x) = c \exp \left\{ \sum \ln f(x_i|\theta) + \ln p(\theta) \right\},$$

where the term in the exponent is the sum of a term of order n and a term of order 1. The factor c depends on x but not on θ. Hence, the log likelihood and the log posterior differ by a term of relative order $1/n$, and this becomes negligible in large samples. Thus, for large samples the MLE, the posterior mean, and the posterior mode coincide. This, heuristically, is the justification for ignoring the term $p(\theta)$ in drawing inference. Clearly, if $p(\theta)$ is a mass point or has a restricted range, this justification may not apply.

A.2 EXPONENTIAL FAMILIES

The model function for the *exponential family* model M is given by

$$p(x; \theta) = \exp\{\theta \cdot t(x) - \kappa(\theta) - h(x)\},$$

where θ is the *canonical parameter* and $t(x)$ is the *canonical statistic*. Note that any exponential model has many exponential representations; for example, the statistic $s = a + Bt$ and the parameter $\gamma = c + B^{-1}\theta$ also work; further, the vectors θ and t can be "padded out" with extra elements. The smallest integer k for which the model has the exponential representation with θ and t having dimension k is the *order* of the model, and the representation (not unique) is minimal. In a minimal representation, t is a minimal sufficient statistic.

Let $\Theta = \{\theta| \int \exp\{\theta t - h(x)\}d\mu < \infty\}$, a convex subset of R^k. The *full* exponential model is the model with parameter space Θ and model function (with respect to the measure μ on X)

$$p(x; \theta) = \exp\{\theta \cdot t(x) - \kappa(\theta) - h(x)\},$$

where $\kappa(\theta) = \ln \int \exp\{\theta t - h(x)\}d\mu$.

If Θ is open, the model is *regular*. In many cases we will consider the restricted parameter space with $\theta = \theta(\omega)$, ω in Ω, a subset of R^d, with $d < k$. The model is then a (k, d) *curved exponential model*.

Note that the moment-generating function is

$$M(s) = E \exp\{t \cdot s\}$$
$$= \int \exp\{t \cdot (\theta + s) - \kappa(\theta + s) + (\kappa(\theta + s) - \kappa(\theta)) - h(x)\}d\mu$$
$$= \exp\{\kappa(\theta + s) - \kappa(\theta)\},$$

and hence the cumulant-generating function is $K(s) = \ln M(s) = \kappa(\theta + s) - \kappa(\theta)$. Thus, the mth cumulant is given by

$$\kappa_{i_1 \ldots i_m}(\theta) = \partial^m \kappa(\theta)/\partial \theta^{i_1} \ldots \partial \theta^{i_m}$$
$$= K_{s_{i_1}, \ldots, s_{i_m}}(s)|_{s=0}.$$

A useful reparametrization is given by the mean value mapping $\tau(\theta) = Et$ defined on Θ (precisely, on int Θ). Note that $\tau(\theta) = D_\theta \kappa(\theta)$. Let C be the closed convex hull of the support of t. Then $\tau(\Theta) \subset$ int C. The model is called *steep* if $|\tau(\theta)| \to \infty$ as θ goes to a boundary point of cl(Θ). Regular models are steep. A core exponential model is steep and full.

Define the Legendre transform of a real differentiable function f on $U \subset R^k$ by

$$f^*(x) = x \cdot \partial f/\partial x - f(x).$$

When f is regular on U, $f^{**} = f$. This transformation is useful for going back and forth between the canonical and mean-value parametrizations.

For a core exponential model,

1. $\tau(\Theta) = $ int C,
2. $\kappa(\theta)$ is strictly convex,
3. κ^* is strictly convex and satisfies $\kappa^*(t) = \sup_\theta \{\theta \cdot t - \kappa(\theta)\}$, the maximized value of the log likelihood function at the statistic t,
4. κ and κ^* are smooth and $\partial \kappa/\partial \theta = \tau$, $\partial \kappa^*/\partial \tau = \theta$, $\partial^2 \kappa/\partial \theta \, \partial \theta' = \Sigma$, $\partial^2 \kappa^*/\partial \tau \, \partial \tau' = \Sigma^{-1}$, where $\Sigma = \text{var}(t)$ and $\tau = \tau(\theta)$,
5. The MLE exists if and only if t is in int C.

Then $\hat{\theta}$, the MLE, is the unique solution to $Et = T$, where T is the realized value of the statistic t and E is E_θ.

Exponential families have been widely studied, and many popular models fall into this category. Any statistical model admitting a fixed-dimension sufficient statistic is an exponential model. This property is extremely useful and can be extended to the claim that models admitting "approximately sufficient" statistics are "approximately exponential." Finally, note that observed and expected information are the same in the canonical (linear) parametrization of a full family (although they are not in other parametrizations, e.g., the mean-value parametrization), and are in fact $\partial^2 \kappa/\partial \theta \, \partial \theta'$.

Example A.1 *The exponential distribution $p(x, \gamma) = \gamma \exp\{-\gamma x\}$ is an exponential family model. Write $p(x, \gamma) = \exp\{-\gamma x + \ln \gamma\}$; then $\theta = -\gamma$, $t = x$ (or Σx) and $\kappa(\theta) = -\ln(-\theta)$. Hence, the cumulant sequence is $-\theta^{-1}, \theta^{-2}, -2\theta^{-3}$, etc.*

Example A.2 *The normal distribution* $p(x, \mu, \sigma) = (2\pi\sigma^2)^{-1/2}$
$\exp\{-(x - \mu)^2/2\sigma^2\}$. *Write this as* $p(x, \mu, \sigma) = \exp\{-1/2 \ln(2\pi\sigma^2) -$
$x^2/2\sigma^2 + x\mu/\sigma^2 - \mu^2/2\sigma^2\} = \exp\{\theta \cdot t(x) - \kappa(\theta)\}$, *with* $\theta = (\mu/\sigma^2, -1/2\sigma^2)$,
$t = (x, x^2)$, *and* $\kappa(\theta) = -\theta_1^2/4\theta_2 - 1/2 \ln(-\theta_2) + \ln(\pi)/2$. *The mean-value parametrization has* $\tau_1 = -\theta_1/2\theta_2$ *and* $\tau_2 = (\theta_1^2)/4\theta_2^2 - 1/(2\theta_2)$.

A.3 MAXIMUM LIKELIHOOD

There are compelling reasons to base inference on the likelihood functions, but no reasons as compelling to choose the maximizing value as a parameter estimate in fixed samples. Asymptotically, however, the situation is clearer: The MLE is the Bayes point estimate for a variety of loss and prior information structures, and the MLE possesses an optimality property. We review here the (well-known) asymptotic properties of the MLE for the independent observation case. Here the likelihood function $p(x|\theta)$ can be written $p(x|\theta) = \Pi_i f(x_i|\theta)$, where f is the density for a single observation. Recall that we use the term "density" quite generally. In the discrete case f is a probability (still a density but using counting measure). We will not find it useful or necessary to distinguish these cases in our notation.

The theory we sketch here is a local theory, and we choose assumptions accordingly. Let $\theta_0 \in \Theta \subset \mathbb{R}^k$ be the true value of the parameter we are estimating. The log likelihood function is given by

$$l(\theta|x) = \sum_{i=1}^{N} \ln f(x_i|\theta).$$

Consistency of a point corresponding to a local maximum is straightforward. Assume the following.

ASSUMPTION 1 $f(x_i|\theta)$ *is continuous on a compact set including* θ_0 *in its interior.*

THEOREM 11 *The log likelihood function* $l(\theta|x)$ *has a local maximum at* $\hat{\theta}$ *which is consistent for* θ_0.

Proof. By Jensen's inequality,

$$E \ln f(x|\theta_0 + \delta)/f(x|\theta_0) \leq \ln Ef(x|\theta_0 + \delta)/f(x|\theta_0)$$

$$= \ln \int f(x|\theta_0 + \delta)dx = 0,$$

and similarly, $E \ln f(x|\theta_0 - \delta)/f(x|\theta_0) \leq 0$. Recalling the definition of $l(\theta|x)$ and using a law of large numbers,

$$N^{-1} [l(\theta_0 \pm \delta|x) - l(\theta_0|x)] \leq 0,$$

which implies that l has a local maximum at θ_0. $\square$

The standard results on asymptotic normality rely heavily on smoothness and Taylor expansions. Define the score function

$$s(\theta) = l_\theta(\theta|x) = \sum s_i(\theta),$$

with $s_i(\theta) = \partial \ln f(x_i|\theta)/\partial\theta$. The likelihood equation is $s(\hat{\theta}) = 0$.

ASSUMPTION 2 $s(\theta)$, $s_\theta(\theta)$, and $s_{\theta\theta}(\theta)$ exist in an interval including θ_0.

Note that there are k^3 elements in the array $s_{\theta\theta}$.

ASSUMPTION 3

$$E f_\theta/f = 0$$
$$E f_{\theta\theta}/f = 0$$
$$E f_\theta f_\theta'/f > 0.$$

This assumption restricts the way that the support of x can depend on θ. In regular problems, this assumption follows from the integral identity $\int f(x|\theta)dx = 1$ and repeated differentiation. Finally, an assumption to control the expected error in Taylor approximations is needed.

ASSUMPTION 4 $|s_{\theta\theta}| < nM(x)$, where $EM < C$ (elementwise), $|C| < \infty$, determistic.

Consistency of a solution to the likelihood equation is immediate.

COROLLARY A.3.1 *If* $\ln f$ *is differentiable, then the score equation* $s(\hat{\theta}) = 0$ *has with probability 1 a solution* $\hat{\theta}$ *that is consistent for* θ.

Proof. Follows from theorem 1 and differentiability. $\square$

Note that theorem 11 is local—it says that there is a local maximum that is consistent for θ. In fact, if there are several local maxima, it is (usually) appropriate to choose the highest to obtain the estimator. This theorem is more difficult to prove and requires more assumptions.

Assumptions 1–4 allow easy development of an asymptotic distribution theory. For simplicity of notation, let θ be a scalar parameter. First, differentiate the integral identity to obtain

$$\int f_\theta \, dx = 0 = \int (f_\theta/f)f \, dx = Es_i,$$

and again

$$\int (d^2 \ln f/d\theta^2) f \, dx + \int (d \ln f/d\theta)^2 f \, dx = 0.$$

The first term on the left-hand side is Fisher information on one observation, denoted $i(\theta)$. Hence,

$$-Es_\theta = Es^2 = ni(\theta).$$

Let $\hat\theta$ be the MLE, i.e., a solution to $s(\hat\theta) = 0$. From expansion of this first-order condition (FOC) around the true value θ_0, we obtain

$$0 = s(\theta_0) + (\hat\theta - \theta_0)s_\theta(\theta_0) + \tfrac{1}{2}(\hat\theta - \theta_0)^2 s_{\theta\theta}(\theta^*),$$

with θ^* between $\hat\theta$ and θ_0. Extracting a term in $\hat\theta - \theta$ and multiplying by $\sqrt{n}$ gives

$$\sqrt{n}(\hat\theta - \theta_0) = -\frac{1}{\sqrt{n}}s(\theta_0)\left[\frac{1}{n}\left(s_\theta + \frac{1}{2}\left(\hat\theta - \theta_0\right)^2 s_{\theta\theta}\right)\right]^{-1}.$$

Taking the probability limits of the right hand side, we see that the second factor converges to $-i(\theta)^{-1}$ since $n^{-1}s_{\theta\theta}$ is bounded in probability and $\hat\theta$ is consistent. Thus,

$$\sqrt{n}(\hat\theta - \theta_0)i(\theta_0) - \frac{1}{\sqrt{n}}s(\theta_0) \to 0$$

in probability. This is useful since it means that the two random variables $\sqrt{n}(\hat\theta - \theta_0)i(\theta_0)$ and $\frac{1}{\sqrt{n}}s(\theta_0)$ have the same asymptotic distribution. Since the latter has the form of $\sqrt{n}$ times a sample mean, we can hope to find its distribution using a central limit theorem (CLT), and the equivalence in probability implies that we will have obtained an asymptotic distribution for $\sqrt{n}(\hat\theta - \theta_0)$ and therefore an approximate distribution theory for $\hat\theta$.

Our previous results from differentiating the integral identity imply $Es_i(\theta_0) = 0$ and $Es_i^2 = V s_i = i(\theta_0)$. Applying a CLT to

$$\frac{1}{\sqrt{n}}s(\theta_0) = \sqrt{n}\left(\frac{1}{n}\sum s_i(\theta_0)\right),$$

we see that $\frac{1}{\sqrt{n}}s(\theta_0) \to N(0, i(\theta_0))$ and therefore

$$\sqrt{n}(\hat\theta - \theta_0) \to N(0, i(\theta_0)^{-1}).$$

The development for the multivariate case is identical. A multivariate CLT must be used, and $i(\theta)$ is minus the expected second-derivative matrix of the log likelihood function. Note that $i(\theta_0)^{-1}$ is consistently estimated by $i(\hat\theta)^{-1}$.

The MLE has a mild asymptotic optimality property. This is most easily developed when $E\hat\theta$ exists and is a continuous function of θ.

Then $E\hat{\theta} = \int \hat{\theta} p(x; \theta) dx$ (recall that $p(x; \theta)$ is the joint distribution of all the observations). Differentiating,

$$\frac{\partial E\hat{\theta}}{\partial \theta} = \int \hat{\theta} \frac{\partial \ln p}{\partial \theta} p \, dx$$

$$= \text{cov}(\hat{\theta}, s(\theta))$$

since $Es(\theta) = 0$. Using the Cauchy-Schwartz inequality (here $\text{cov}(x, y)^2 \le V(x)V(y)$) gives

$$(\partial E\hat{\theta}/\partial \theta)^2 \le V(\hat{\theta})V(s),$$

which implies

$$V(\hat{\theta}) \ge (\partial E\hat{\theta}/\partial \theta)^2 i(\theta)^{-1}.$$

In the unbiased case the first factor on the right hand side is 1; asymptotically we have $V(\hat{\theta}) \ge i(\theta)^{-1}$ for consistent estimators. Thus, under wide conditions asymptotically the MLE achieves minimum variance among consistent estimators. Frequently, the inverse Fisher information is referred to as the Cramer-Rao lower bound.

A.4 CLASSICAL THEORY OF TESTING

The central lesson of the theory of testing is that good tests are based on the likelihood ratio. The argument is easy in the case of simple hypotheses: $H_0 : x \sim p(x) = p(x|\theta_0)$ versus $H_1 : x \sim p(x) = p(x|\theta_1)$. The parametric specification is given explicitly, so we can discuss testing a hypothesis stated in terms of parameters. Define the decision function $d : X \to \{0, 1\}$ with $d(x) = 0$ if H_0 is chosen ("accepted") and $d(x) = 1$ if H_1 is chosen. The function d defines a partition of the sample space. Let $A \subset X$ be the region in which $d = 0$ and let A^c be the complement of A. The error probabilities are

$$\alpha = P(d = 1|H_0) = \int_{A^c} p_0(x) \, dx,$$

$$\beta = P(d = 0|H_1) = \int_{A} p_1(x) \, dx.$$

Of course, our object is to design a decision procedure, i.e., to choose the set A so that these error probabilities are as small as possible. Clearly, there is a tradeoff: α can be set to 0, its minimum, by choosing $d = 0$ always, but then $\beta = 1$. Similarly, β can be set to 0 by ignoring the data and choosing $d = 1$. These are the only ways these errors can be set to 0. Any combination of (α, β) satisfying $\alpha + \beta = 1$ can be achieved by randomizing without data. With data, things can be improved, but how much? There is a remarkable answer to this question —a characterization of the set of tests that cannot be improved (i.e., there are no tests with both α and β smaller than the tests in the set).

Let $A(T) = \{x : p_0/p_1 > T\}$ and $\alpha^* = \int_{A^c} p_0(x)\, dx$, $\beta^* = \int_A p_1(x)\, dx$. The set $A(T)$ defines a decision rule. Let $B \subset X$ be any other set with associated error probabilities (α, β). Then we have the following.

LEMMA A.4.1 (Neyman-Pearson) *If $\alpha \le \alpha^*$, then $\beta \ge \beta^*$.*

Proof. Let $A = A(T)$ and $I_A(x) = 1$ if $x \in A$, and $I_B(x) = 1$ if $x \in B$. Then $(I_A - I_B)(p_0 - T p_1) \ge 0$. To check this, note that the left hand side is zero whenever $x \in A$ and $x \in B$ or $x \notin A$ and $x \notin B$; when x is in one and not the other, the left hand side is positive from the definition of A. Multiplying, $0 \le I_A p_0 - I_A T p_1 - I_B p_0 + I_B T p_1$, and integrating (since this inequality holds for each x, it certainly holds for an average) gives $0 \le \int_A (p_0 - T p_1) dx - \int_B (p_0 - T p_1) dx$ or $0 \le T(\beta - \beta^*) + (\alpha - \alpha^*)$, recalling the definitions and rearranging. Thus, if $\beta < \beta^*$, $\alpha > \alpha^*$, and vice versa. $\square$

This result gives the family of best tests, indexed by T. Choosing T amounts to choosing which undominated pair of error probabilities is appropriate, and this depends on the losses associated with the different decisions. This simple proof is given in Cover and Thomas (1991, p. 306).

For composite hypotheses $H_0 : \theta = \theta^*$ versus $H_1 : \theta \ne \theta^*$ the situation is a little less clear. The likelihood ratio test looks at $p(x|\theta^*)/\max_\theta p(x|\theta) = p(x|\theta^*)/p(x|\hat\theta)$, where $\hat\theta$ is the MLE. Thus, $\hat\theta$ plays the role of θ_1; it is selected somewhat arbitrarily as the most likely alternative. This test has only asymptotic optimality properties. However, a convenient asymptotic distribution theory is available under the null hypothesis that $\theta^* = \theta_0$. This is useful since in general α and β can be quite difficult to calculate. Furthermore, there are asymptotically equivalent forms of the likelihood ratio that are in wide use and can be simpler to implement.

Let $w = \hat\theta - \theta_0$ be the vector of deviations and recall that $s/\sqrt{n} \sim N(0, i)$. As we have seen, $p \lim(s/\sqrt{n} - i w \sqrt{n}) = 0$ or $p \lim(\sqrt{n} w - i^{-1} s/\sqrt{n}) = 0$. The key to asymptotic testing is to note that

$$-2[l(\hat\theta) - l(\theta^*)] = n w' i w$$

asymptotically. Now, $\sqrt{n} w$ is $N(0, i^{-1})$, so $\sqrt{n} w i$ is $N(0, i)$, and the right hand side is just a quadratic form in k independent normal variables and therefore $\chi^2(k)$. The left hand side is $-2 \ln LR$, where $LR = p(x|\theta^*)/p(x|\hat\theta)$ is the likelihood ratio. Thus, we have a convenient asymptotic distribution theory for a simple transform of the likelihood ratio.

We define alternative tests, asymptotically equivalent because of the equivalence noted above. First, the Wald test,

$$W = nw'i(\hat{\theta})w \sim \chi^2(k)$$

and next the score test

$$S = n^{-1}s(\theta_0)'i^{-1}(\theta_0)s(\theta_0) \sim \chi^2(k).$$

The score test is widely known in economics as the Lagrange multiplier (LM) test since the saddle point problem

$$\max_{\theta} l(\theta) - \lambda(\theta - \theta_0),$$

where λ is a Lagrange multiplier associated with the constraint, has optimality conditions that yield $\hat{\theta} = \theta_0$ and $\lambda = s(\theta_0)$.

References

Abbring, J.H. & Heckman, J.J., 2007. Econometric Evaluation of Social Programs, Part III: Distributional Treatment Effects, Dynamic Treatment Effects, Dynamic Discrete Choice, and General Equilibrium Policy Evaluation, in: J.J. Heckman & E.E. Leamer (eds.), *Handbook of Econometrics* 6B. Amsterdam: Elsevier, 5146–5303.

Adda, J. & Cooper, R., 2000. Balladorette and Juppette: A Discrete Analysis of Scrapping Subsidies, *Journal of Political Economy* 108, 778–806.

Aguirregabiria, V., 2002. Recursive Pseudo Maximum Likelihood Estimation of Structural Models Involving Fixed-Point Problems, manuscript.

Aguirregabiria, V. & Mira, P., 2002. Swapping the Nested Fixed Point Algorithm: A Class of Estimators for Discrete Markov Decisions Models, *Econometrica* 70, 1519–1543.

Aït-Sahalia, Y., 1996. Testing Continuous-Time Models of the Spot Interest Rate, *Review of Financial Studies* 9, 385–426.

Albrecht, J.W. & Axell, B., 1984. An Equilibrium Model of Search Unemployment, *Journal of Political Economy* 92, 824–840.

Allais, M., 1953. Le Compartement de l'Homme Rationnel devant le Risk, Critique des Postulates et Axiomes de l'Ecole Americaine, *Econometrica* 21, 503–546.

Altonji, J.G. & Williams, N., 1997. Do Wages Rise With Job Seniority? A Reassessment, NBER Working Paper No. 6010, National Bureau of Economic Research, Cambridge, MA.

Altug, S., 1989. Time-to-Build and Aggregate Fluctuations: Some New Evidence, *International Economic Review* 30(4), 889–920.

Amemiya, T., 1985. *Advanced Econometrics*. Cambridge, Mass.: Harvard University Press.

An, M., Christensen, B.J. & Datta Gupta, N., 2004. Multivariate Mixed Proportional Hazard Modelling and the Joint Retirement of Married Couples, *Journal of Applied Econometrics* 19, 687–704.

Andersen, T.G., Bollerslev, T., & Diebold, F.X., 2007. Roughing It Up: Including Jump Components in the Measurement, Modeling and Forecasting of Return Volatility, *Review of Economics and Statistics* 89, 701–720.

Andersen, T.G., Bollerslev, T., Diebold, F.X. & Ebens, H., 2001a. The Distribution of Realized Stock Return Volatility, *Journal of Financial Economics* 61, 43–76.

Andersen, T.G., Bollerslev, T., Diebold, F.X. & Labys, P., 2001b. The Distribution of Exchage Rate Volatility, *Journal of the American Statistical Assocation* 96, 42–55.

Andersen, T.G., Bollerslev, T., Diebold, F.X. & Labys, P., 2003. Modelling and Forecasting Realized Volatility, *Econometrica* 71, 579–625.

Anderson, E., Hansen, L., McGratten, E. & Sargent, T.J., 1996. Mechanics for Forming and Estimating Dynamic Linear Economies, in: H. Amman, D. Kendrick & J. Rust (eds.), *Handbook of Computational Economics*. Amsterdam: Elsevier, 171–252.

Anderson, T.W., 1959. On Asymptotic Distributions of Estimates of Parameters of Stochastic Difference Equations, *Annals of Mathematical Statistics* 30, 676–687.

Andrews, D.W.K., 1998. Hypothesis Testing with a Restricted Parameter Space, *Journal of Econometrics* 84, 155–199.

Araujo, A., 1991. The Once But Not Twice Differentiability of the Policy Function, *Econometrica* 59, 1383–1393.

Araujo, A. & Scheinkman, J.A., 1984. Smoothness, Comparative Dynamics, and the Turnpike Property, *Econometrica* 45, 601–620.

Arrow, K.J., 1951. Alternative Approaches to the Theory of Choice in Risk-Taking Situations, *Econometrica* 19, 417–420.

Baba, Y., Engle, R.F., Kraft, D.F. & Kroner, K.F., 1990. Multivariate Simultaneous Generalized ARCH, Department of Economics, University of California, San Diego, mimeo.

Baillie, R.T. & Myers, R.J., 1991. Bivariate GARCH Estimation of the Optimal Commodity Futures Hedge, *Journal of Applied Econometrics* 6, 109–124.

Bakshi, G., Cao, C. & Chen, Z., 1997. Empirical Performance of Alternative Option Pricing Models, *Journal of Finance* 52, 2003–2049.

Banz, R.W., 1981. The Relation Between Return and Market Value of Common Stocks, *Journal of Financial Economics* 9, 3–18.

Barndorff-Nielsen, O.E., 1978. *Information and Exponential Families in Statistical Theory*. Chichester, U.K.: Wiley.

Barndorff-Nielsen, O.E., 1988. *Parametric Statistical Models and Likelihood*. New York: Springer-Verlag.

Barndorff-Nielsen, O.E. & Blæsild, P., 1992. A Type of Second Order Asymptotic Independence, *Journal of the Royal Statistical Society, Series B* 54, 897–901.

Barndorff-Nielsen, O.E. & Blæsild, P., 1993. Orthogeodesic Models, *Annals of Statistics* 21, 1018–1039.

Barndorff-Nielsen, O.E. & Shephard, N. 2006. Econometrics of Testing for Jumps in Financial Economics Using Bipower Variation, *Journal of Financial Econometrics* 4, 1–30.

Basawa, I.V. & Praksa Rao, B.L.S., 1980. *Statistical Inference for Stochastic Processes*. New York: Academic Press.

Basu, D., 1958. On Statistics Independent of Sufficient Statistics, *Sankhya* 20, 223–226.

Bellman, R., 1957. *Dynamic Programming*. Princeton, N.J.: Princeton University Press.

Bellman, R. & Dreyfus, S., 1962. *Applied Dynamic Programming*. Princeton, N.J.: Princeton University Press.

van den Berg, G.J. & Ridder, G., 1993. Estimating Equilibrium Search Models from Wage Data, in: H. Bunzel, P. Jensen & N.C. Westergård-Nielsen (eds.), *Panel Data and Labour Market Dynamics*. New York: North-Holland, 43–55.

van den Berg, G.J. & Ridder, G., 1998. An Empirical Equilibrium Search Model of the Labor Market, *Econometrica* 66, 1183–1221.

Benveniste, L. & Scheinkman, J., 1979. On the Differentiability of the Value Function in Dynamic Models of Economics, *Econometrica* 47, 727–732.

Berger, J.O., 1985. *Statistical Decision Theory and Bayesian Analysis*. New York: Springer.

Berger, J. & Wolpert, R., 1984. *The Likelihood Principle*. Hayward, Calif.: Institute of Mathematical Statistics.

Berkovec, J. & Stern, S., 1991. Job Exit Behavior of Older Men, *Econometrica* 59, 189–210.

Bertsekas, D., 1975. Convergence of Discretization Procedures in Dynamic Programming, *IEEE Transactions on Automatic Control* 20, 415–419.

Bertsekas, D., 1976. *Dynamic Programming and Stochastic Control*. New York: Academic Press.

Bertsekas, D. & Shreve, S.E., 1978. *Stochastic Optimal Control: The Discrete Time Case*. New York: Academic Press.

Bhattacharya, R.N. & Majumdar, M., 1989a. Controlled Semi-Markov Processes—The Discounted Case, *Journal of Statistical Planning and Inference* 21, 365–381.

Bhattacharya, R.N. & Majumdar, M., 1989b. Controlled Semi-Markov Processes—The Average Demand Criteria, *Journal of Statistical Planning and Inference* 22, 223–242.

Bhattacharya, R.N. & Majumdar, M., 2006. *Random Dynamical Systems: Theory and Applications*. New York: Cambridge University Press.

Björk, T. & Christensen, B.J., 1999. Interest Rate Dynamics and Consistent Forward Rate Curves, *Mathematical Finance* 9, 323–348.

Black, F. 1976. Studies of Stock Market Volatility Changes, *Proceedings of the American Statistical Association, Business and Economic Statistics Section*, 177–181.

Black, F., Jensen, M. & Scholes, M., 1972. The Capital Asset Pricing Model: Some Empirical Tests, in: M. Jensen (ed.): *Studies in the Theory of Capital Markets*. New York: Praeger.

Black, F. & Scholes, M., 1973. The Pricing of Options and Corporate Liabilities, *Journal of Political Economy* 81, 637–654.

Blackwell, D., 1962. Discrete Dynamic Programming, *Annals of Mathematical Statistics* 33, 719–726.

Blackwell, D., 1965. Discounted Dynamic Programming, *Annals of Mathematical Statistics* 36, 226–235.

Blume, L., Easley, D. & O'Hara, M., 1982. Characterization of Optimal Plans for Stochastic Dynamic Programs, *Journal of Economic Theory* 28, 221–234.

Bollerslev, T., 1986. Generalized Autoregressive Conditional Heteroskedasticity, *Journal of Econometrics* 31, 301–327.

Bollerslev, T., 1987. A Conditional Heteroskedastic Time Series Model for Speculative Prices and Rates of Return, *Review of Economics and Statistics* 69, 542–547.

Bollerslev, T., 1990. Modelling the Coherence in Short-Run Nominal Exchange Rates: A Multivariate Generalized ARCH Approach, *Review of Economics and Statistics* 72, 498–505.

Bollerslev, T., Engle, R.F. & Wooldridge, J., 1988. A Capital Asset Pricing Model with Time Varying Covariances, *Journal of Political Economy* 96, 116–131.

Bollerslev, T. & Wooldridge, J., 1992. Quasi-Maximum Likelihood Estimation and Inference in Dynamic Models with Time Varying Covariances, *Econometric Reviews* 11, 143–172.

Bontemps, C., Robin, J.-M. & van den Berg, G.J., 2000. Equilibrium Search with Continuous Productivity Dispersion: Theory and Nonparametric Estimation, *International Economic Review* 41, 305–358.

Bound, J., Brown, C., Duncan, G. & Rodgers, W., 1990. Measurement Error in Cross-Sectional and Longitudinal Labor Market Surveys: Results from Two Validation Studies, in: J. Hartoog, G. Ridder & J. Theeuwes (eds.), *Panel Data and Labor Market Studies*. Amsterdam: North-Holland, 1–19.

Bowlus, A.J., Kiefer, N.M. & Neumann, G.R., 1995. Estimation of Equilibrium Wage Distributions with Heterogeneity, *Journal of Applied Econometrics* 10, 119–131.

Bowlus, A.J., Kiefer, N.M. & Neumann, G.R., 2001. Equilibrium Search Models and the Transition from School to Work, *International Economic Review* 42, 317–343.

Box, G. & Pierce, D., 1970. Distribution of Residual Autocorrelations in Autoregressive-Integrated Moving Average Time Series Models, *Journal of the American Statistical Assocation* 65, 1509–1526.

Brace, A. & Musiela, M., 1994. A Multi Factor Gauss Markov Implementation of Heath, Jarrow, and Morton, *Mathematical Finance* 4, 563–576.

Brandt, M.W., 1999. Estimating Portfolio and Consumption Choice: A Conditional Euler Equations Approach, *Journal of Finance* 54, 1609–1645.

Breeden, D.T., 1979. An Intertemporal Asset Pricing Model with Stochastic Consumption and Investment Opportunities, *Journal of Financial Economics* 7, 265–296.

Broadbent, B. & Barro, R.J., 1997. Central Bank Preferences and Macroeconomic Equilibrium, *Journal of Monetary Economics* 39, 17–43.

Brock, W.A., 1976. Introduction to Stochastic Calculus: A User's Manual, manuscript, University of Chicago.

Brock, W.A. & Majumdar, M., 1978. Global Asymptotic Stability Results for Multisector Models of Optimal Growth Under Uncertainy When Future Utilities Are Discounted, *Journal of Economic Theory* 18, 225–243.

Brock, W.A. & Mirman, L.J., 1972. Optimal Economic Growth Under Uncertainty: The Discounted Case, *Journal of Economic Theory* 4, 479–513.

Brock, W.A. & Scheinkman, J.A., 1976. Global Asymptotic Stability of Optimal Control Systems with Applications to the Theory of Economic Growth, *Journal of Economic Theory* 12, 164–190.

Brown, L.D., 1986 *Fundamentals of Statistical Exponential Families with Applications in Statistical Decision Theory*. Hayward, Calif.: Institute of Mathematical Statistics.

Brown, S.J. & Dybvig, P.H., 1986. Empirical Implications of the Cox, Ingersoll, Ross Theory of the Term Structure of Interest Rates, *Journal of Finance* 41, 143–172.

Bunzel, H., Christensen, B.J., Jensen, P., Kiefer, N.M., Korsholm, L., Muus, L., Neumann, G.R. & Rosholm, M., 2001. Specification and Estimation of Equilibrium Search Models, *Review of Economic Dynamics* 4, 90–126.

Bunzel, H., Christensen, B.J., Jensen, P., Kiefer, N.M. & Mortensen, D.T., 2000. *Panel Data and Structural Labour Market Models*. Amsterdam: North-Holland.

Burdett, K., 1978. A Theory of Employee Search and Quit Rates, *American Economic Review* 68, 212–220.

Burdett, K., 1990. Search Models: A Survey. University of Essex Discussion Paper.

Burdett, K., Kiefer, N.M., Mortensen, D.T. & Neumann, G., 1984. Earnings, Unemployment, and the Allocation of Time over Time, *Review of Economic Studies* 51, 559–578.

Burdett, K. & Mortensen, D.T., 1998. Wage Differentials, Employer Size, and Unemployment, *International Economic Review* 39, 257–274.

Busch, T., Christensen, B.J. & Nielsen, M.O., 2008. The Role of Implied Volatility in Forecasting Future Realized Volatility and Jumps in Foreign Exchange, Stock and Bond Markets, *Journal of Econometries*, forthcoming.

Campbell, J., 1991. A Variance Decomposition for Stock Returns, *Economic Journal* 101, 157–179.

Campbell, J., 1993, Intertemporal Asset Pricing Without Consumption Data, *American Economic Review* 83, 487–512.

Campbell, J. & Hentschel, L., 1992. No News Is Good News: An Asymmetric Model of Changing Volatility in Stock Returns, *Journal of Financial Economics* 31, 281–318.

Campbell, J. & Shiller, R., 1987. Cointegration and Tests of Present Value Models, *Journal of Political Economy* 95, 1062–1087.

Campbell, J. & Shiller, R., 1988a. Interpreting Cointegrated Models, *Journal of Economic Dynamics and Control* 12, 505–522.

Campbell, J. & Shiller, R., 1988b. The Dividend-Price Ratio and Expectations of Future Dividends and Discount Factors, *Review of Financial Studies* 1, 195–228.

Campbell, J. & Shiller, R., 1991. Yield Spreads and Interest Rate Movements: A Bird's Eye View, *Review of Economic Studies* 58, 495–514.

Campbell, J. & Viceria, L., 2002. *Strategic Asset Allocation: Portfolio Choice and Long-Term Investors*. Oxford and New York: Oxford University Press.

Campbell, J. & Vuolteenaho, T., 2004. Bad Beta, Good Beta, *American Economic Review* 94, 1249–1275.

Cass, D. & Shell, K., 1976. The Structure and Stability of Competitive Dynamical Systems, *Journal of Economic Theory* 12, 31–70.

Chan, K., Karolyi, G., Longstaff, F. & Sanders, A., 1992. An Empirical Comparision of Alternative Models of the Short-Term Interest Rate, *Journal of Finance* 47, 1209–1227.

Chen, R. & Scott, L., 1993. Maximum Likelihood Estimation for a Multi-factor Equilibrium Model of the Term Structure of Interest Rates, *Journal of Fixed Income* 3, 14–31.

Chen, N., Roll, R. & Ross, S., 1986. Economic Forces and the Stock Market, *Journal of Business* 59, 383–403.

Chernoff, H. & Rubin, H., 1956. The Estimation of the Location of a Discontinuity in Density. *Proceedings of the Third Berkeley Symposium on Mathematical Statistics and Probability.* Berkeley: University of California Press, 1, 19–37.

Chernov, M. & Ghysels, E., 2000. A Study Towards a Unified Approach to the Joint Estimation of the Objective and Risk Neutral Measures for the Purpose of Option Valuation, *Journal of Financial Economics* 56, 407–458.

Chintagunta, P.K. & Jain, D., 1992. A Dynamic Model of Channel Member Strategies for Marketing Expenditures, *Marketing Science* 11, 168–188.

Chintagunta, P.K. & Vilcassim, N.J., 1992. An Empirical Investigation of Advertising Strategies in a Dynamic Duopoly, *Management Science* 38, 1230–1244.

Chow, C.S. & Tsitsiklis, J.N., 1989. The Complexity of Dynamic Programming, *Journal of Complexity* 5, 466–488.

Chow, G.C., 1975. *Analysis and Control of Dynamic Economic Systems.* New York: Wiley.

Chow, G.C., 1978. Evaluation of Macroeconomic Policies by Stochastic Control Techniques, *International Economic Review* 19, 311–320.

Chow, G.C., 1980. Econometric Policy Evaluation and Optimization Under Rational Expectations, *Journal of Economic Dynamics and Control* 2, 47–59.

Chow, G.C., 1981. *Econometric Analysis by Control Methods.* New York: Wiley.

Chow, Y.S., Robbins, H. & Siegmund, D., 1971. *Great Expectations: The Theory of Optimal Stopping*. Boston: Houghton Mifflin.

Christensen, B.J., 1994. Efficiency Gains in Beta-Pricing Models, *Mathematical Finance* 4, 143–154.

Christensen, B.J. & Kiefer, N.M., 1991a. The Exact Likelihood Function for an Empirical Job Search Model, *Econometric Theory* 7, 464–486.

Christensen, B.J. & Kiefer, N.M., 1991b. Statistical Analysis of an Optimal Stopping Model, Center for Analytic Economics working paper 91-02.

Christensen, B.J. & Kiefer, N.M., 1994a. Local Cuts and Separate Inference, *Scandinavian Journal of Statistics* 21, 389–407.

Christensen, B.J. & Kiefer, N.M., 1994b. Measurement Error in the Prototypal Job-Search Model, *Journal of Labor Economics* 12, 618–639.

Christensen, B.J. & Kiefer, N.M., 1997. Inference in Non-linear Panels with Partially Missing Observations: The Case of the Equilibrium Search Model, *Journal of Econometrics* 79, 201–219.

Christensen, B.J. & Kiefer, N.M., 2000. Panel Data, Local Cuts, and Ortho-geodesic Models, *Bernoulli* 6, 43–12.

Christensen, B.J., Lentz, R., Mortensen, D.T., Neumann, G.R. & Werwatz, A., 2005. On the Job Search and the Wage Distribution, *Journal of Labor Economics* 23, 31–58.

Christensen, B.J. & Nielsen, M.Ø., 2006. Asymptotic Normality of Narrow-Band Least Squares in the Stationary Fractional Cointegration Model and Volatility Forecasting, *Journal of Econometrics* 133, 343–371.

Christensen, B.J. & Nielsen, M.Ø., 2007. The Effect of Long Memory in Volatility on Stock Market Fluctuations, *Review of Economics and Statistics* 89, 684–700.

Christensen, B.J. & Poulsen, R., 2001. Monte Carlo Improvement of Estimates of the Mean-Reverting Constant Elasticity of Variance Interest Rate Diffusion, *Monte Carlo Methods and Applications* 7, 111–124.

Christensen, B.J. & Prabhala, N.R., 1998. The Relation Between Implied and Realized Volatility, *Journal of Financial Economics* 50, 125–150.

Clarida, R., Gali, J. & Gertler, M., 1999. The Science of Monetary Policy: A New Keynesian Perspective, *Journal of Economic Literature* 37, 1661–1707.

Clark, R.L., Johnson, T. & McDermed, A.A., 1980. Allocation of Time and Resources by Married Couples Approaching Retirement, *Social Security Bulletin* 43, 3–16.

Corsi, F., 2004. A Simple Long Memory Model of Realized Volatility, Working Paper, University of Lugano.

Cover, T. M. & Thomas, J.A., 1991. *Elements of Information Theory.* New York: Wiley.

Cox, D.R., 1975. Partial Likelihood, *Biometrika* 62, 269–276.

Cox, D.R. & Reid, N., 1987. Parameter orthogonality and approximate conditional inference, *Journal of the Royal Statistical Society, Series B* 49, 1–39 (with discussion).

Cox, J.C. & Ross, S.A., 1976. The Valuation of Options for Alternative Stochastic Processes, *Journal of Financial Economics* 3, 145–166.

Cox, J.C., Ingersoll, J.E. & Ross, S.A., 1981. The Relationship Between Forward Prices and Futures Prices, *Journal of Financial Economics* 9, 321–346.

Cox, J.C., Ingersoll, J.E. & Ross, S.A., 1985a. An Intertemporal General Equilibrium Model of Asset Prices, *Econometrica* 53, 363–384.

Cox, J.C., Ingersoll, J.E. & Ross, S.A., 1985b. A Theory of the Term Structure of Interest Rates, *Econometrica* 53, 385–408.

Crandall, M. & Lions, P., 1983. Viscosity Solutions of Hamilton-Jacobi Equations, *Transactions of the American Mathematical Society* 277, 1–42.

Dai, Q. & Singleton, K., 2000. Specification Analysis of Affine Term Structure Models, *Journal of Finance* 55, 1943–1978.

Das, M., 1992. A Micro-Econometric Model of Capital Utilization and Retirement: The Case of the U.S. Cement Industry, *Review of Economic Studies* 59, 277–297.

Davidson, R. & MacKinnon, J. G., 2004. *Econometric Theory and Methods.* New York: Oxford University Press.

Deaton, A., 1987. Life-cycle Models of Consumption: Is the Evidence Consistent with the Theory? in: Truman Bewley (ed.), Advances in Econometrics Fifth World Congress, *Econometric Society Monographs* (No. 14). Cambridge: Cambridge University Press, 121–148.

Debreu, G., 1959. *The Theory of Value*. New Haven: Yale University Press.

DeGroot, M., 1970. *Optimal Statistical Decisions*. New York: McGraw-Hill.

Denardo, E.V., 1967. Contraction Mappings Underlying the Theory of Dynamic Programming, *SIAM Review* 9, 165–177.

Devine, T.J., 1989. Offer Arrival Versus Acceptance: Interpreting Demographic Reemployment Patterns in the Search Framework, Pennsylvania State University, working paper.

Devine, T.J. & Kiefer, N.M., 1991. *Empirical Labor Economics: The Search Approach*. New York: Oxford University Press.

Dickey, D.A. & Fuller, W.A., 1979. Distribution of the Estimators for Autoregressive Time Series with a Unit Root, *Journal of the American Statistical Assocation*, 74, 427–431.

Dixit, A.K. & Pindyck, R.S., 1994. *Investment Under Uncertainty*. Princeton, N.J.: Princeton University Press.

Dreze, J., 1972. Econometrics and Decision Theory, *Econometrica* 40, 1–18.

Duffie, D. & Kan, R., 1996. A Yield-Factor Model of Interest Rates, *Mathematical Finance* 6, 379–406.

Dumas, B., Fleming, J. & Whaley, R., 1998. Implied Volatility Functions: Empirical Tests, *Journal of Finance* 53, 2059–2106.

Dutta, P., Majumdar, M. & Sundaram, R., 1994. Parametric Continuity in Dynamic Programming Problems, *Journal of Economic Dynamics and Control* 18, 1069–1092.

Eckstein, Z., 1989. Dynamic Labour Force Participation of Married Women and Endogenous Worker Experience, *Review of Economic Studies* 56, 375–390.

Eckstein, Z. & Wolpin, K.I., 1990. Estimating a Market Equilibrium Search Model from Panel Data on Individuals, *Econometrica* 58, 783–808.

Eichenbaum, M., 1991. Real Business-Cycle Theory: Wisdom or Whimsy? *Journal of Economic Dynamics and Control* 15, 607–626.

Eichenbaum, M., Hansen, L.P. & Singleton, K., 1988. A Time-Series Analysis of Representative Agent Models of Consumption and Leisure Choice under Uncertainty, *Quarterly Journal of Economics* 103, 51–78.

Ekeland, I. & Scheinkman, J.A., 1986. Transversality Conditions for Some Infinite Horizon Discrete Time Optimization Problems, *Mathematics of Operations Research* 11, 212–229.

Ellsberg, D., 1961. Risk, Ambiguity and the Savage Axioms, *Quarterly Journal of Economics* 75, 643–669.

Engle, R.F., 1982. Autoregressive Conditional Heteroskedasticity with Estimates of the Variance of U.K. Inflation, *Econometrica* 50, 987–1008.

Engle, R.F. & Granger, C.W.J., 1987. Co-Integration and Error Correction: Representation, Estimation, and Testing, *Econometrica* 55, 251–276.

Engle, R.F. & Kroner, K., 1995. Multivariate Simultaneous GARCH, *Econometric Theory* 11, 122–150.

Engle, R., Lilien, D. & Robins, R., 1987. Estimating Time-Varying Risk Premia in the Term Structure: The ARCH-M Model, *Econometrica* 55, 391–407.

Epstein, L. & Zin, S., 1989. Substitution, Risk Aversion, and the Temporal Behavior of Consumption and Asset Returns: A Theoretical Framework, *Econometrica* 57, 937–968.

Eraker, B., Johannes, M. & Polson, N., 2003. The Impact of Jumps in Volatility and Returns, *Journal of Finance* 58, 1269–1300.

Fama, E., 1970. Efficient Capital Markets: A Review of Theory and Empirical Work, *Journal of Finance* 25, 383–417.

Fama, E. & French, K., 1988. Dividend Yields and Expected Stock Returns, *Journal of Financial Economics* 22, 3–27.

Fama, E. & French, K., 1992. The Cross-Section of Expected Stock Returns, *Journal of Finance* 47, 427–465.

Fama, E. & MacBeth, J., 1973. Risk, Return, and Equilibrium: Empirical Tests, *Journal of Political Economy* 71, 607–636.

Fishburn, P.C., 1970. *Utility Theory for Decision Making*. New York: Wiley.

Fisher, E.O. & de Gorter, H., 1992. The International Effects of U.S. Farm Subsidies, *American Journal of Agricultural Economics* 74, 258–267.

Fisher, F.M., 1966. *The Identification Problem in Econometrics*. New York: McGraw-Hill.

Flinn, C. & Heckman, J.J., 1982. New Methods for Analyzing Structural Models of Labor Force Dynamics, *Journal of Econometrics* 18, 115–168.

Föllmer, H. & Sondermann, D., 1986. Hedging of Non-Redundant Contingent Claims, in: W. Hildenbrand & A. Mas-Colell (eds.), *Contributions to Mathematical Economics in Honor of Gerard Debreu.* Amsterdam: North-Holland.

Foley, D.K., Shell, K. & Sidrauski, M., 1969. Optimal Fiscal and Monetary Policy, and Economic Growth, *Journal of Political Economy* 77, 698–719.

Fox, B.L., 1973. Discretizing Dynamic Programming, *Journal of Optimization Theory and Applications* 11, 228–234.

French, K., Schwert, G. & Stambaugh, R., 1987. Expected Stock Returns and Volatility, *Journal of Financial Economics* 19, 3–30.

Friedman, M., 1956. *A Theory of the Consumption Function.* Princeton, N.J.: Princeton University Press.

Fuller, W.A., 1976. *Introduction to Statistical Time Series.* New York: Wiley.

Gallant, A.R. & Tauchen, G., 1996. Which Moments To Match? *Econometric Theory* 12, 657–681.

Gibbons, M., Ross, S. & Shanken, J., 1989. A Test of the Efficiency of a Given Portfolio, *Econometrica* 57, 1121–1152.

Gilboa, I. & Schmeidler, D., 1989. Maxmin Expected Utility with a Non-Unique Prior, *Journal of Mathematical Economics* 18, 141–153.

Gilleskie, D.B., 1998. A Dynamic Stochastic Model of Medical Care Use and Work Absence, *Econometrica* 66, 1–45.

Gittens, J.C. & Jones, D.M., 1974. A Dynamic Allocation Index for the Sequential Design of Experiments, in: J.M. Gani et al. (eds.), *Progress in Statistics.* Amsterdam: North-Holland, 241–266.

Goldberger, A.S., 1991. *A Course in Econometrics.* Cambridge, Mass.: Harvard University Press.

Gonul, F. & Shi, M.Z., 1998. Optimal Mailing of Catalogs: A New Methodology Using Estimable Structural Dynamic Programming Models, *Management Science* 44, 1249–1262.

Gotz, G.A. & McCall, J.J., 1984. A Dynamic Retention Model for Air Force Officers, *Report R-3028-AF.* Santa Monica, Calif.: RAND Corporation.

Granger, C.W.J., 1983. Co-Integrated Variables and Error-Correcting Models, University of California, San Diego, Discussion Paper 83–13.

Granger, C.W.J. & Newbold, P., 1974. Spurious Regressions in Econometrics, *Journal of Econometrics* 2, 111–120.

Griliches, Z., 1984. *Patents, R&D and Productivity*. Chicago: University of Chicago Press.

Grossman, S. & Shiller, R., 1981. The Determinants of the Variability of Stock Market Prices, *American Economics Review* 71, 222–227.

Gul, F., 1992. Savage's Theorem with a Finite Number of States, *Journal of Economic Theory* 57, 99–110.

Gustman, A.L. & Steinmeier, T., 1986. A Structural Retirement Model, *Econometrica* 54, 555–584.

Haigh, M.S. & Holt, M.T., 2002. Combining Time-Varying and Dynamic Multi-Period Optimal Hedging Models, *European Review of Agricultural Economics* 29, 471–500.

Hakansson, N.H., 1970. Optimal Investment and Consumption Strategies for a Class of Utility Functions, *Econometrica* 38, 587–607.

Hakansson, N.H., 1971. Capital Growth and the Mean-Variance Approach of Portfolio Selection, *Journal of Financial and Quantitative Analysis* 6, 517–557.

Hall, R., 1978. Stochastic Implications of the Life Cycle—Permanent Income Hypothesis: Theory and Evidence, *Journal of Political Economy* 86, 971–987.

Hall, R., 1988. Intertemporal Substitution in Consumption, *Journal of Political Economy* 96, 221–273.

Halpern, J.Y., 2003. *Reasoning About Uncertainty*. Cambridge, Mass.: MIT Press.

Hansen, B.E., 1992. Efficient Estimation and Testing of Cointegrating Vectors in the Presence of Deterministic Trends, *Journal of Econometrics* 53, 87–121.

Hansen, L.P., 1982. Large Sample Properties of Method of Moments Estimators, *Econometrica* 50, 1029–1054.

Hansen, L.P. & Jagannathan, R., 1991. Implications of Security Market Data for Models of Dynamic Economies, *Journal of Political Economy* 99, 225–262.

Hansen, L.P. & Sargent, T.J., 1980. Formulating and Estimating Dynamic Linear Rational Expectations Models, *Journal of Economic Dynamcis and Control* 2, 7–46.

Hansen, L.P. & Sargent, T.J., 1982. Instrumental Variables Procedures for Estimating Linear Rational Expectations Models, *Journal of Monetary Economics* 9, 263–296.

Hansen, L.P. & Sargent, T.J., 2001. Robust Control and Model Uncertainty, *American Economic Review* 91, 60–66.

Hansen, L.P. & Sargent, T.J., 2003. Robust Control of Forward Looking Models, *Journal of Monetary Economics* 50, 581–604.

Hansen, L.P. & Singleton, K., 1982. Generalized Instrumental Variables Estimation of Nonlinear Rational Expectations Models, *Econometrica* 50, 1269–1288.

Hansen, L.P. & Singleton, K., 1983. Stochastic Consumption, Risk Aversion, and the Temporal Behavior of Asset Returns, *Journal of Political Economy* 91, 249–268.

Hansen, L.P. & Singleton, K., 1984. Errata, *Econometrica* 52, 267–268.

Harris, M., 1987. *Dynamic Economic Analysis*. New York: Oxford University Press.

Harrison, M. & Kreps, D., 1979. Martingales and Arbitrage in Multiperiod Securities Markets, *Journal of Economic Theory* 20, 381–408.

Harrison, M. & Pliska, S., 1981. Martingales and Stochastic Integrals in the Theory of Continuous Trading, *Stochastic Processes and Their Applications* 11, 215–260.

Hausman, J., 1978. Specification Tests in Econometrics, *Econometrica* 46, 1251–1271.

Heath, D., Jarrow, R.A. & Morton, A., 1992. Bond Pricing and the Term Structure of Interest Rates: A New Methodology for Contingent Claims Valuation, *Econometrica* 60, 77–105.

Heckman, J.J., 1974. Life-Cycle Consumption and Labor Supply: An Explanation of the Relationship Between Income and Consumption Over the Life-Cycle, *American Economic Review* 64, 188–194.

Heckman, J.J., 1981. Statistical Models for Discrete Panel Data, in: C. Manski and D. McFadden (eds.), *Structural Analysis of Discrete Data with Econometric Applications*. Boston: Massachusetts Institute of Technology, 114–178.

Heckman, J. & MaCurdy, T., 1980. A Life Cycle Model of Female Labour Supply, *Review of Economic Studies* 47, 47–74.

Henretta, J.C. & O'Rand, A.M., 1983. Joint Retirement in the Dual Worker Family, *Social Forces* 62, 504–520.

Heston, S., 1993. A Closed-Form Solution for Options with Stochastic Volatility with Applications to Bond and Currency Options, *Review of Financial Studies* 6, 327–343.

Heyde, C. C. 1997. *Quasi-Likelihood and Its Application: A General Approach to Optimal Parameter Estimation*. New York: Springer-Verlag.

Hotz, V.J. & Miller, R.A., 1993. Conditional Choice Probabilities and the Estimation of Dynamic Programming Models, *Review of Economic Studies* 60, 497–529.

Howard, R., 1971. *Dynamic Probabilistic Systems*, vols. I and II. New York: Wiley.

Huang, X. & Tauchen, G., 2005. The Relative Contribution of Jumps to Total Price Variance, *Journal of Financial Econometrics* 3, 456–499.

Hull, J. & White, A., 1987. The Pricing of Options on Assets with Stochastic Volatilities, *Journal of Finance* 52, 281–300.

Hull, J. & White, A., 1990. Pricing Interest-Rate-Derivative Securities, *Review of Financial Studies* 3, 573–592.

Jobson, D. & Korkie, R., 1985. Some Tests of Linear Asset Pricing with Multivariate Normality, *Canadian Journal of Administrative Sciences* 2, 114–138.

Johansen, S., 1991. Estimation and Hypothesis Testing of Cointegration Vectors in Gaussian Vector Autoregressive Models, *Econometrica* 59, 1551–1580.

Johnson, N.L., Kotz, S. & Balakrishnan, N., 1994. *Continuous Univariate Distributions*, vol. 1, 2nd ed. New York: Wiley.

Judd, K., 1998. *Numerical Methods in Economics*. Cambridge, Mass.: MIT Press.

Kaldor, N., 1939. Speculation and Economic Stability, *Review of Economic Studies* 7, 1–27.

Kamihigashi, T., 2001. Necessity of Transversality Conditions for Stochastic Problems, Working Paper.

Kamihigashi, T., 2002. A Simple Proof of the Necessity of the Transversality Condition, *Economic Theory* 20, 427–433.

Karatzas, I. & Shreve, S.E., 1998. *Methods of Mathematical Finance*. New York: Springer-Verlag.

Keane, M.P. & Wolpin, K.I., 1994. The Solution and Estimation of Discrete Choice Dynamic Programming Models by Simulation and Interpolation: Monte Carlo Evidence, *Review of Economics and Statistics* 76, 648–672.

Keane, M.P. & Wolpin, K.I., 1997. The Career Decisions of Young Men, *Journal of Political Economy* 105, 473–522.

Kennan, J., 1979. The Estimation of Partial Adjustment Models with Rational Expectations, *Econometrica* 47, 1441–1456.

Kennet, D.M., 1994. A Structural Model of Aircraft Engine Maintenance, *Journal of Applied Econometrics* 9, 351–368.

Keynes, J.M., 1930. *A Treatise on Money*. London: MacMillan.

Kiefer, N.M., 1988. Economic Duration Data and Hazard Functions, *Journal of Economic Literature* 26, 646–679.

Kiefer, N.M. & Neumann, G.R., 1979. An Empirical Job Search Model with a Test of the Constant Reservation Wage Hypothesis, *Journal of Political Economy* 87, 89–107.

Kiefer, N.M. & Neumann, G.R., 1981. Individual Effects in a Nonlinear Model: Explicit Treatment of Heterogeneity in the Empirical Job-Search Model, *Econometrica* 49, 965–979.

Kiefer, N.M. & Neumann, G.R., 1993. Wage Dispersion with Homogeneity: The Empirical Equilibrium Search Model, in: H. Bunzel, P. Jensen & N.C. Westergård-Nielsen (eds.), *Panel Data and Labour Market Dynamics*. New York: North-Holland, 57–74.

Kiefer, N.M. & Nyarko, Y., 1995. Savage Bayesian Models in: Economics, in: A. Kirman and M. Salmon (eds.), *Essays in Learning and Rationality in Economics and Games*. Oxford: Basil Blackwell.

King, R.G. & Rebelo, S.T., 1999. Resuscitating Real Business Cycles, in: J.B. Taylor & M. Woodford (eds.), *Handbook of Macroeconomics*. New York: Elsevier, 927–1007.

Kirkpatrick, S., Gelatt, C.D. Jr. & Vecchi, M.P., 1983. Optimization by Simulated Annealing, *Science* 220, 671–680.

Kleidon, A., 1986. Variance Bounds Tests and Stock Price Valuation Models, *Journal of Political Economy* 94, 953–1001.

Knight, F.H., 1921. *Risk, Uncertainty and Profit*. Boston: Houghton Mifflin.

Koning, P., Ridder, G. & van den Berg, G.J., 1995. Structural and Frictional Unemployment in an Equilibrium Search Model with Heterogeneous Agents, *Journal of Applied Econometrics* 10, S133–S151.

Kreps, D.M. & Porteus, E.L., 1978. Temporal Resolution of Uncertainty and Dynamic Choice Theory, *Econometrica* 46, 185–200.

Kreps, D.M. & Porteus, E.L., 1979. Dynamic Choice Theory and Dynamic Programming, *Econometrica* 47, 91–100.

Kroner, K.F. & Sultan, J., 1993. Time Varying Distributions and Dynamic Hedging with Foreign Currency Futures, *Journal of Financial and Quantitative Analysis* 28, 535–551.

Krylov, N.V., 1980. *Controlled Diffusion Processes*. Heidelberg: Springer-Verlag.

Kushner, H.J., 1990. Numerical Methods for Stochastic Control Problems in Continuous Time, *SIAM Journal on Control and Optimization* 28, 999–1048.

Kydland, F.E. & Prescott, E.C., 1977. Rules Rather Than Discretion: The Inconsistency of Optimal Plans, *Journal of Political Economy* 85, 473–492.

Kydland, F. & Prescott, E.C., 1982. Time to Build and Aggregate Fluctuations, *Econometrica* 50, 1345–1370.

Lancaster, A., 1990. *The Econometric Analysis of Transition Data*. New York: Cambridge University Press.

Lancaster, A. & Chesher, A., 1983. An Econometric Analysis of Reservation Wages, *Econometrica* 51, 1661–1776.

Lawless, J.F., 1982. *Statistical Models and Methods for Lifetime Data*. New York: Wiley.

LeRoy, S. & Porter, R., 1981. The Present Value Relation: Tests Based on Variance Bounds, *Econometrica* 49, 555–577.

Lindley, D.V., 1961. Dynamic Programming and Decision Theory, *Applied Statistics* 10, 39–51.

Lintner, J., 1965. The Valuation of Risk Assets and the Selection of Risky Investments in Stock Portfolios and Capital Budgets, *Review of Economics and Statistics* 47, 13–37.

Lippman, S.A. & McCall, J.J., 1976a. The Economics of Job Search: A Survey: Part I, *Economic Inquiry* 14, 155–189.

Lippman, S.A. & McCall, J.J., 1976b. The Economics of Job Search: A Survey: Part II, *Economic Inquiry* 14, 347–368.

Litterman, R. & Scheinkman, J., 1991. Common Factors Affecting Bond Returns, *Journal of Fixed Income* 1, 54–61.

Ljung, G. & Box, G., 1978. On a Measure of Lack of Fit in Time Series Models, *Biometrika* 66, 67–72.

Ljungqvist, L. & Sargent, T.J., 2000. *Recursive Macroeconomic Theory.* Cambridge, Mass.: MIT Press.

Lo, A., 1988. Maximum Likelihood Estimation of Generalized Itô Processes with Discretely Sampled Data, *Econometric Theory* 4, 231–247.

Lo, A. & MacKinlay, A.C., 1988. Stock Market Prices Do Not Follow Random Walks: Evidence from a Simple Specification Test, *Review of Financial Studies* 1, 41–66.

Longstaff, F.A. & Schwartz, E.S., 2001. Valuing American Options by Simulation: A Simple Least-Squares Approach, *Review of Financial Studies* 14, 113–147.

Lucas, R.E. Jr., 1976. Econometric Policy Evaluation: A Critique, in: K. Brunner & A.K. Meltzer (eds.), *The Phillips Curve and Labor Markets, Carnegie-Rochester Conference Series on Public Policy 1.* Amsterdam: North-Holland, 19–46.

Lucas, R.E. Jr., 1978. Asset Prices in an Exchange Economy, *Econometrica* 46, 1426–1446.

Lumsdaine, R., Stock, J.H. & Wise, D.A., 1992. Three Models of Retirement: Computational Complexity Versus Predictive Ability, in Wise, D.A. (ed.), *Topics in the Economics of Aging.* Chicago: University of Chicago Press.

Machina, M., 1982. "Expected" Utility Analysis Without the Independence Axiom, *Econometrica* 50, 277–323.

Macaulay, F., 1938. *Some Theoretical Problems Suggested by the Movements of Interest Rates, Bond Yields, and Stock Prices in the United States Since 1856*. New York: National Bureau of Economic Research.

MaCurdy, T.E., 1981. An Empirical Model of Labor Supply in a Life-Cycle Setting, *Journal of Political Economy* 89, 1059–1085.

Maitra, A., 1968. Discounted Dynamic Programming in Compact Metric Spaces, *Sankhya Series A* 40, 211–216.

Markowitz, H., 1959. *Portfolio Selection: Efficient Diversification of Investments*. New York: Wiley.

McCall, J.J., 1970. Economics of Information and Job Search, *Quarterly Journal of Economics* 84, 113–126.

McCulloch, J., 1971. Measuring the Term Structure of Interest Rates, *Journal of Business* 44, 19–31.

McCulloch, J., 1975. The Tax-Adjusted Yield Curve, *Journal of Finance* 30, 811–830.

McFadden, D., 1973. Conditional Logit Analysis of Qualitative Choice Behavior, in: Zarembka, P. (ed.), *Frontiers in Econometrics*. New York: Academic Press, 105–142.

McFadden, D., 1981. Econometric Models of Probablistic Choice, in: C.F. Manski & D. McFadden (eds.), *Structural Analysis of Discrete Data with Econometric Applications*. Cambridge, Mass.: MIT Press, 198–272.

McFadden, D., 1984. Econometric Analysis of Qualitative Response Models, in: Z. Griliches & M.D. Intriligator (eds.), *Handbook of Econometrics* 2. Amsterdam: Elsevier, 1395–1457.

McKean, H., 1965. Appendix: A Free Boundary Problem for the Heat Equation Arising from a Problem of Mathematical Economics, *Industrial Management Review* 6, 32–39.

Mehra, R. & Prescott, E., 1985. The Equity Premiums: A Puzzle, *Journal of Monetary Economics* 15, 145–161.

Meiselman, D., 1962. *The Term Structure of Interest Rates*. Englewood Cliffs, N.J.: Prentice-Hall.

Merton, R.C., 1969. Lifetime Portfolio Selection under Uncertainty: The Continuous Time Case, *Review of Economics and Statistics* 51, 247–257.

Merton, R.C., 1971. Optimum Consumption and Portfolio Rules in a Continuous Time Model, *Journal of Economic Theory* 3, 373–413; Erratum 6, 1973, 213–214.

Merton, R.C., 1973a. An Intertemporal Capital Asset Pricing Model, *Econometrica* 41, 867–887.

Merton, R.C., 1973b. The Theory of Rational Option Pricing, *Bell Journal of Economics and Management Science* 4, 141–183.

Merton, R.C., 1980. On Estimating the Expected Return on the Market, *Journal of Financial Economics* 8, 33–361.

Miller, R., 1984. Job Matching and Occupational Choice, *Journal of Political Economy* 92, 1086–1120.

Mirman, L.J. & Zilcha, I., 1975. On Optimal Growth under Uncertainty, *Journal of Economic Theory* 11, 239–339.

Mortensen, D.T., 1970. Job Search, the Duration of Unemployment, and the Phillips Curve, *The American Economic Review* 60, 847–862.

Mortensen, D.T., 1986. Job Search and Labor Market Analysis: in: O. Ashenfelter & R. Layard (eds.), *Handbook of Labor Economics*. Amsterdam: North Holland, 849–919.

Mortensen, D.T., 1990. Equilibrium Wage Distributions: A Synthesis, in: J. Hartog, G. Ridder & J. Theeuwes (eds.), *Panel Data and Labor Market Studies*. New York: North-Holland, 279-296.

Mortensen, D.T. & Neumann, G.R., 1984. Choice or chance? A structural interpretation of individual labor market histories, in: G. Neumann and N. Westergaard-Nielsen (eds.), *Studies in Labor Market Dynamics*. Heidelberg: Springer-Verlag, 98–131.

Mortensen, D.T. & Neumann, G.R., 1988. Estimating Structural Models of Unemployment and Job Duration in Dynamic Econometric Modelling. *Proceedings of the Third International Symposium in Economic Theory and Econometrics*. Cambridge: Cambridge University Press, 335–356.

Myers, R.J., 1991. Estimating Time-Varying Optimal Hedge Ratios on Futures Markets, *Journal of Futures Markets* 11, 39–53.

Narendranathan, W. & Nickell, S., 1985. Modelling the Process of Job Search, *Journal of Econometrics* 28, 29–49.

Nelson, C. & Siegel, A., 1987. Parsimonious Modelling of Yield Curves, *Journal of Business* 60, 473–489.

Nerlove, M. & Arrow, K.J., 1962. Optimal Advertising Policy Under Dynamic Conditions, *Econometrica* 29, 129–142.

Newey, W. & West, K., 1987. A Simple, Positive Semi-Definite, Heteroskedasticity and Autocorrelation Consistent Covariance Matrix, *Econometrica* 55, 703–708.

Otten, R. & van Ginneken, L., 1989. *The Annealing Algorithm.* Boston: Kluwer.

Pakes, A., 1986. Patents as Options: Some Estimates of the Value of Holding European Patent Stocks, *Econometrica* 54, 755–784.

Pan, J., 2002. The Jump-Risk Premia Implicit in Options: Evidence from an Integrated Time-Series Study, *Journal of Financial Economics* 63, 3–50.

Pearson, N.D. & Sun, T., 1994. Exploiting the Conditional Density in Estimating the Term Structure: An Application to the Cox, Ingersoll, and Ross Model, *Journal of Finance* 49, 1279–1304.

Pennacchi, G., 1991. Identifying the Dynamics of Real Interest Rates and Inflation: Evidence Using Survey Data, *Review of Financial Studies* 4, 53–86.

Phillips, P.C.B., 1987. Time Series Regression with a Unit Root, *Econometrica* 55, 277–301.

Phillips, P.C.B., 1989. Partially Identified Econometric Models, *Econometric Theory* 5, 181–240.

Phillips, P.C.B. & Ouliaris, S., 1990. Asymptotic Properties of Residual Based Tests for Cointegration, *Econometrica* 58, 165–193.

Phillips, P.C.B. & Perron, P., 1988. Testing for a Unit Root in Time Series Regression, *Biometrika* 75, 335–346.

Poterba, J. & Summers, L., 1986. The Persistence of Volatility and Stock Market Fluctuations, *American Economic Review* 76, 1142–1151.

Pratt, J.W., Raiffa, H. & Schlaifer, R., 1964. The Foundations of Decision Under Uncertainty: An Elementary Exposition, *Journal of the American Statistical Association* 59, 353–375.

Protter, P., 1986. Stochastic Integration Without Tears, *Stochastics* 16, 295–325.

Protter, P., 2004. *Stochastic Integration and Differential Equations*, 2nd ed. Berlin and New York: Springer-Verlag.

Puterman, M., 1994. *Markov Decision Processes*. New York: Wiley.

Puterman, M.L. & Brumelle, S., 1979. On the Convergence of Policy Iteration in Stationary Dynamic Programming, *Mathematics of Operations Research* 4, 60–69.

Ramsey, F.P., 1928. A Mathematical Theory of Saving, *Economic Journal* 38, 543–559.

Reid, N., 1996. Likelihood and Higher Order Approximation to Tail Areas, *The Canadian Journal of Statistics* 24, 141–166.

Reinganum, M.R., 1981. Misspecification of Capital Asset Pricing: Empirical Anomalies Based on Earnings' Yields and Market Values, *Journal of Financial Economics* 9, 19–46.

Ridder, Geert, & Gorter, K., 1986. Unemployment Benefits and Search Behavior: An Empirical Investigation, manuscript, Cornell University.

Roberts, H., 1967. Statistical versus Clinical Prediction of the Stock Market, manuscript, Center for Research in Security Prices, University of Chicago.

Robinson, P.M., 1994. Semiparametric Analysis of Long-Memory Time Series, *Annals of Statistics* 22, 515–539.

Robinson, P.M. & Marinucci, D., 2003. Semiparametric Frequency Domain Analysis of Fractional Cointegration, in: P.M. Robinson (ed.), *Time Series with Long Memory*. Oxford: Oxford University Press, 334–373.

Roll, R., 1977. A Critique of the Asset Pricing Theory's Tests: Part I, *Journal of Financial Economics* 4, 129–176.

Roll, R. & Ross, S., 1980. An Empirical Investigation of the Arbitrage Pricing Theory, *Journal of Finance* 35, 1073–1103.

Rosenberg, B., Reid, K. & Lanstein, R., 1985. Persuasive Evidence of Market Inefficiency, *Journal of Portfolio Management* 11, 9–17.

Ross, S., 1976. The Arbitrage Theory of Capital Asset Pricing, *Journal of Economic Theory* 13, 341–360.

Ross, S.M., 1983. *Introduction to Stochastic Dynamic Programming*. New York: Academic Press.

Rothenberg, Thomas J., 1971. *Efficient Estimation with A Priori Information*. Cowles Foundation Monograph 23. New Haven: Yale University Press.

Rubinstein, M., 1994. Implied Binomial Trees, *Journal of Finance* 69, 771–818.

Rust, J., 1987a. Optimal Replacement of GMC Bus Engines: An Empirical Model of Harold Zurcher, *Econometrica* 55, 999–1033.

Rust, J., 1987b. A Dynamic Programming Model of Retirement Behavior, in: David Wise (ed.), *The Economics of Aging*. Chicago: University of Chicago Press, 359–398.

Rust, J., 1988. Maximum Likelihood Estimation of Discrete Control Processes, *SIAM Journal on Control and Optimization* 26, 1006–1023.

Rust, J., 1992. A Dynamic Programming Model of Retirement Behavior, in: K.R. Billengsley, H.U. Brown III & E. Derohanes (eds.), *Computer Assisted Modelling on the IBM 3090: The IBM Contest Prize Papers* vol. 2, 885–912.

Rust, J., 1994. Structural Estimation of Markov Decision Processes, chapter 51 in: D. McFadden & R. Engle (eds.), *Handbook of Econometrics* 4, Amsterdam: North-Holland, 3082–3143.

Rust, J., 1997. Using Randomization to Break the Curse of Dimensionality, *Econometrica* 65, 487–516.

Rust, J. & Rothwell, G., 1995. Optimal Response to a Shift in Regulatory Regime: The Case of the US Nuclear Power Industry, *Journal of Applied Econometrics* 10, S75–S118.

Samuelson, P.A., 1965. Rational Theory of Warrant Pricing, *Industrial Management Review* 6, 13–31.

Samuelson, P.A., 1969. Lifetime Portfolio Selection by Dynamic Stochastic Programming, *Review of Economics and Statistics* 51, 239–246.

Santos, M.S., 1991. Smoothness of the Policy Function in Discrete Time Economic Models, *Econometrica* 59, 1365–1382.

Sargent, T.J., 1978. Estimation of Dynamic Labor Demand Schedules Under Rational Expectations, *Journal of Political Economy* 86, 1009–1044.

Sargent, T.J., 1987. *Dynamic Macroeconomic Theory*. Cambridge, Mass.: Harvard University Press.

Savage, L.J., 1954. *The Foundations of Statistics*. New York: Wiley.

Schäl, M., 1994. On Quadratic Cost Criteria for Option Hedging, *Mathematics of Operations Research* 19, 121–131.

Schwartz, E., 1997. The Stochastic Behavior of Commodity Prices: Implications for Valuation and Hedging, *Journal of Finance* 52, 923–973.

Schweizer, M., 1991. Option Hedging for Semimartingales, *Stochastic Processes and Their Applications* 37, 339–363.

Schweizer, M., 1995. Variance-Optimal Hedging in Discrete-Time, *Mathematics of Operations Research* 20, 1–32.

Schwert, G., 1989. Why Does Stock Market Volatility Change Over Time? *Journal of Finance* 44, 1115–1153.

Self, Steven G. & Liang, Kung-Yee, 1987. Asymptotic Properties of Maximum Likelihood Estimators and Likelihood Ratio Tests Under Non-standard Conditions, *Journal of the American Statistical Association* 82, 605–610.

Shanken, J., 1992. On the Estimation of Beta-Pricing Models, *Review of Financial Studies* 5, 1–34.

Sharpe, W.F., 1964. Capital Asset Prices—A Theory of Market Equilibrium Under Conditions of Risk, *Journal of Finance* 19, 425–442.

Shiller, R., 1981. Do Stock Prices Move Too Much To Be Justified by Subsequent Changes in Dividends?, *American Economic Review* 71, 421–436.

Simon, H.A., 1956. Dynamic Programming Under Uncertainty with a Quadratic Criterion Function, *Econometrica* 24, 74–81.

Sims, C., 1980. Macroeconomics and Reality, *Econometrica* 48, 1–48.

Slade, M.E., 1998. Optimal Pricing with Costly Adjustment: Evidence from Retail Grocery Prices, *Review of Economic Studies* 65, 87–107.

Solow, R.M., 1956. A Contribution to the Theory of Economic Growth, *Quarterly Journal of Economics* 70, 69–94.

Stentoft, L., 2004. Convergence of the Least Squares Monte Carlo Approach to American Option Valuation, *Management Science* 50, 1193–1203.

Stern, S., 1989. Estimating a Simultaneous Search Model, *Journal of Labor Economics* 7, 348–369.

Stock, J.H., 1987. Asymptotic Properties of Least Squares Estimators of Cointegrating Vectors, *Econometrica* 55, 1035–1056.

Stock, J.H. & Watson, M.W., 1988. Testing for Common Trends, *Journal of the American Statistical Association* 83, 1097–1107.

Stock, J.H. & Wise, D.A., 1990. Pensions, the Option Value of Work, and Retirement, *Econometrica* 58, 1151–1180.

Stokey, N.L. & Lucas, Jr. R.E. (with Prescott, E.C.), 1989. *Recursive Methods in Economic Dynamics.* Cambridge, Mass.: Harvard University Press.

Strauch, R.E., 1966. Negative Dynamic Programming, *Annals of Mathematical Statistics* 37, 871–890.

Szu, H. & Hartley, R., 1987. Fast Simulated Annealing. *Physics Letters* A 12, 157–162.

Tauchen, G., 1991. Solving the Stochastic Growth Model by Using Value Function Iterations and a Quadrature-Based Grid, *Journal of Business and Economic Statistics* 8, 49–51.

Taylor, J.B., 1979. Estimation and Control of a Macroeconomic Model with Rational Expectations, *Econometrica* 47, 1267–1286.

Taylor, J.B. (ed.), 1999. *Monetary Policy Rules.* Chicago: University of Chicago Press.

Taylor, J.B. & Uhlig, H., 1990. Solving Nonlinear Stochastic Growth Models: A Comparison of Alternative Solution Methods, *Journal of Business and Economic Statistics* 8, 1–17.

Theil, H., 1958. *Economic Forecasts and Policy.* Amsterdam: North-Holland.

Theil, H., 1964. *Optimal Decision Rules for Government and Industry.* Amsterdam: North-Holland.

Theil, H., 1971. *Principles of Econometrics.* New York: Wiley.

Vasicek, O., 1977. An Equilibrium Characterization of the Term Structure, *Journal of Financial Economics* 5, 177–188.

van der Vaart, A. W., 1998. *Asymptotic Statistics.* New York: Cambridge University Press.

von Neumann, J. & Morgenstern, O., 1944. *Games and Economic Behavior.* Princeton, N.J.: Princeton University Press.

Wald, A., 1945. Sequential Tests of Statistical Hypotheses, *Annals of Mathematical Statistics* 16, 117–186.

Weil, P., 1989. The Equity Premium Puzzle and the Risk-Free Rate Puzzle, *Journal of Monetary Economics* 24, 401–421.

White, H., 1982. Maximum Likelihood Estimation of Misspecified Models, *Econometrica* 50, 1–25.

Wolpin, K., 1984. An Estimable Dynamic Stochastic Model of Fertility and Child Mortality, *Journal of Political Economy* 92, 852–874.

Wolpin, K., 1987. Estimating a Structural Search Model: The Transition from School to Work, *Econometrica* 55, 801–818.

Woodford, M., 2003. *Interest and Prices: Foundation for a Theory of Monetary Policy.* Princeton, N.J.: Princeton University Press.

Zadrozny, P., 1988. Analytic Derivatives for Estimation of Discrete-Time, Linear-Quadratic, Dynamic, Optimization Models, *Econometrica* 56, 467–472.

Zellner, A., 1962. An Efficient Method of Estimating Seemingly Unrelated Regressions and Testing for Aggregation Bias, *Journal of the American Statistical Association* 57, 348–368.

Zellner, A., 1971. *An Introduction to Bayesian Inference in Econometrics.* New York: Wiley.

Ziliak, J.P. & Kniesner, T.J., 1999. Estimating Life Cycle Labor Supply Tax Effects, *Journal of Political Economy* 107, 326–359.

Index